Law and Society

Law and Society provides a balanced and comprehensive analysis of the interplay between law and society using both Canadian and international examples. This clear and readable text is filled with interesting information, ideas, and insights. All materials and supporting statistics have been carefully updated. This edition includes an expanded discussion of the law and First Nations people, recent developments impacting LGBTIQ2S persons and persons with disabilities, and a new section on civil procedures. Each chapter is structured similarly, with an outline, learning objectives, key terms, chapter summaries, critical thinking questions, and an array of additional resources.

Steven Vago earned two Ph.D.s: one in Sociology and one in Anthropology from Washington University in St. Louis. During graduate school he was an integral part of the creation of an alcohol treatment program at Malcolm Bliss Hospital in St. Louis. He became part of the Department of Sociology at St. Louis University after finishing his graduate studies and was a full professor there by the age of 37. Thereafter, he chaired the Department of Sociology several times, teaching at St. Louis University for over 30 years. During the 1970s, he was asked by the United Nations to work for its member agency UNESCO and worked in Paris for several years in their Office of Population and Demography. At the end of his teaching career in 2001, he retired to Bellingham, Washington with his wife. He passed away in 2010, at the age of 73.

Adie Nelson received her Ph.D. from the London School of Economics and Political Science and is an Associate Professor in the Department of Sociology and Legal Studies at the University of Waterloo. Her areas of specialization are victimology, criminology, and the sociology of deviance.

Veronica Nelson received her J.D. from the University of Ottawa and is currently pursuing a LL.M. at Queen's University. Her areas of special interest are tort law, environmental law, and constitutional law.

Steven E. Barkan is Professor of Sociology at the University of Maine, where he has taught since 1979. His teaching and research interests include criminology, sociology of law, and social movements.

Nelson's text provides an indispensable bridge between critical legal perspectives and formal law, offering along the way a rich interdisciplinary foundation for the study of law and society. Readers of this updated Canadian edition will especially benefit from an expanded focus on Aboriginal peoples.

Susan Dianne Brophy, *Assistant Professor, St. Jerome's University, University of Waterloo*

Law and Society

Fifth Canadian Edition

STEVEN VAGO, ADIE NELSON,
VERONICA NELSON, AND
STEVEN E. BARKAN

Routledge
Taylor & Francis Group

NEW YORK AND LONDON

Fifth edition published 2018
by Routledge
711 Third Avenue, New York, NY 10017

and by Routledge
2 Park Square, Milton Park, Abingdon, Oxon, OX14 4RN

Routledge is an imprint of the Taylor & Francis Group, an informa business

First edition published by Prentice Hall 2002
Fourth edition published by Routledge 2011

Library of Congress Cataloging-in-Publication Data
Names: Vago, Steven, author. | Nelson, Adie, 1958– author. | Nelson,
   Veronica, author. | Barkan, Steven E., 1951– author.
Title: Law and society / Steven Vago, Adie Nelson, Veronica Nelson, and
   Steven Barkan
Description: Fifth Canadian edition. | New York, NY : Routledge, 2017. |
   Includes bibliographical references.
Identifiers: LCCN 2017016699 | ISBN 9781138215917 (hardcover : alk.
   paper) | ISBN 9781138215818 (pbk. : alk. paper) | ISBN 9781315443126
Subjects: LCSH: Sociological jurisprudence. | Law—Social aspects—Canada.
Classification: LCC K370 .V33 2017b | DDC 340/.115—dc23
LC record available at https://lccn.loc.gov/2017016699

ISBN: 978-1-138-21591-7 (hbk)
ISBN: 978-1-138-21581-8 (pbk)
ISBN: 978-1-315-44312-6 (ebk)

Typeset in Avenir, Bell and Bembo
by Apex CoVantage, LLC

Visit the eResource: www.routledge.com/9781138215818

CONTENTS

CONTENTS

DETAILED CONTENTS

PREFACE

The objective of this text is to serve as an undergraduate text in courses on law and society. Although the text was written primarily for university and college students, anyone with an interest in law and society will find it useful, informative, and provocative. The classroom-tested and -refined material has been organized and presented in a logical fashion, and each chapter builds on the previous one. Should one prefer a different organization of the contents, it would not detract from the value of the book. For example, if one desires, Chapter 9, "Researching Law in Society," can be read after Chapter 2, "Theoretical Perspectives."

In preparing the fifth Canadian edition of this text, we have built on the solid foundation established by the late Steven Vago (1937-2010). As in all editions, we have sought to create a text that is pedagogically sound and distinctive in its coverage of the subject. Wherever possible, we have emphasized clarity of language at the expense of professional jargon.

Knowledge about law and society has accumulated haphazardly. Intellectual developments in the field are influenced by a number of theoretical perspectives, resulting in a variety of strains of thought and research. Because the book has been written primarily for the undergraduate student, we opted for an eclectic approach to the often controversial subject matter without embracing or advocating a particular position, ideology, or theoretical stance. Thus, the book does not propound a single thesis or position; instead, it exposes the reader to the dominant theoretical perspectives and sociological methods used to explain the interplay between law and society in the social science literature.

In writing this new edition, we recognize that it may well be the case that more questions will be raised than answered. However, it is the abundance of unanswered questions and unexpected developments that keeps the study of law and society challenging and endlessly intriguing.

1

CHAPTER 1
INTRODUCTION

As we approach the third decade of the 21st century, law increasingly permeates all forms of social behavior. In subtle—and, at times, not-so-subtle—ways, law governs our entire existence and our every action. Law determines registration at birth and the distribution of possessions at death. It regulates prenuptial agreements, intimate relationships, pet ownership, hanging laundry outdoors to dry, and the conduct of professors and students in the classroom. It governs family and workplace relationships. Laws regulate the speed limit and the length of school attendance. Laws control what we eat and where; what we buy and when; how we use our computers; and what we can see in movie theatres, on television, or on the Internet. Laws protect ownership and define the boundaries of private and public property. Laws regulate business, raise revenue, and provide for redress when agreements are broken. Laws protect the prevailing legal and political systems by defining

Figure 1.1 Law increasingly permeates our lives.
Credit: Fotolia

power relationships, thus establishing who is superordinate and who is subordinate in any given situation. Laws maintain the status quo and provide the impetus for change. Finally, laws, in particular criminal laws, not only protect private and public interests but also preserve order. There is no end to the ways in which the law has a momentous effect upon our lives.

LEARNING OBJECTIVES

After reading this chapter, you should be able to:

1. Identify why sociologists find the study of law to be relevant to their professional interests and outline the factors that have encouraged or hampered their investigation of the law.

2. Appreciate that "law" has been defined in diverse ways by scholars.

3. Distinguish between different "types" of law.

4. Describe the dominant legal systems that exist in the world.

5. Discuss law's functions and dysfunctions.

6. Compare and contrast the "consensus" and "conflict" perspectives on law.

7. Identify the roles that are available to sociologists in their study of law and society and describe what these roles entail.

OVERVIEW

In every human society throughout history there have been mechanisms for the declaration, alteration, administration, and enforcement of the rules by which people live (Glenn, 2010). Not all societies, however, utilize a formal legal system (courts, judges, lawyers, and law enforcement agencies) to the same degree (Grillo et al., 2009). For example, throughout the developing world the formal systems of property rights taken for granted in industrial nations simply do not exist. In poor nations, most people cannot identify who owns what, addresses cannot be verified, and the rules that govern property vary from neighbourhood to neighbourhood, or even from street to street (de Soto, 2011). The notion of holding title to property is limited primarily to a handful of elites whose assets are identified in the formal documents and legal structures common in industrial nations.

Further, today's agricultural societies rely almost exclusively on custom as the source of legal rules and resolve disputes through conciliation or mediation by village elders, or by some other moral or divine authority (Pottage and Mundy, 2004). As for law, such societies need little of it. Traditional societies are more homogeneous than modern industrial ones.

Social relations are more direct and intimate, interests are shared by virtually everyone, and there are fewer things to quarrel about. Since relations are more direct and intimate, non-legal and often informal mechanisms of social control are generally more effective.

As societies become larger, more complex, and modern, homogeneity gives way to heterogeneity. Common interests decrease in relation to special interests. Face-to-face relations become progressively less important, as do kinship ties. Access to material goods becomes more indirect, with a greater likelihood of unequal allocation, and the struggle for available goods becomes intensified. As a result, the prospects for conflict and dispute within the society increase. The need for explicit regulatory and enforcement mechanisms becomes increasingly apparent. The development of trade and industry requires a system of formal and universal legal rules dealing with business organizations and commercial transactions, subjects that are not normally part of customary or religious law. Such commercial activity also requires guarantees, predictability, continuity, and a more effective method for settling disputes than that of trial by ordeal, trial by combat, or decision by a council of elders. As one legal anthropologist noted, using the male pronouns common in his time, "The paradox . . . is that the more civilized man becomes, the greater is man's need for law, and the more law he creates. Law is but a response to social needs" (Hoebel, 1954:292).

In the powerful words of Oliver Wendell Holmes, Jr. (1881/1963:5), "The law embodies the story of a nation's development through many centuries." Every legal system stands in close relationship to the ideas, aims, and purposes of society. Law reflects the intellectual, social, economic, and political climate of its time. Law is inseparable from the interests, goals, and understandings that deeply shape or comprise social and economic life (Morales, 2003; Posner, 2007; Valverde, 2012). It also reflects the particular ideas, ideals, and ideologies that are part of a distinct **legal culture**—those attributes of behaviour and attitudes that make the law of one society different from that of another (Friedman, 2002).

In sociology, the study of law embraces a number of well-established areas of inquiry (Abadinsky, 2008; Cotterrell, 2006; Friedrichs, 2010). The discipline is concerned with values, interaction patterns, and ideologies that underlie the basic structural arrangements in a society, many of which are embodied in law as substantive rules. Both sociology and law are concerned with norms—rules that prescribe the appropriate behaviour for people in a given situation. The study of conflict and conflict resolution are central in both disciplines. Both sociology and law are concerned with the nature of legitimate authority, the mechanisms of social control, issues of human rights, power arrangements, the relationship between public and private spheres, and formal contractual commitments (Griffin, 2009; Hagan and Levi, 2005). Both sociologists and lawyers are aware that the behaviour of judges, jurors, criminals, litigants, and other consumers of legal products are charged with emotion, distorted by cognitive glitches and failures of will, and constrained by altruism, etiquette, or a sense of duty.

The rapprochement of sociology (along with economics, psychology, and other social sciences) and law is not new (Canter and Zukauskiene, 2009; Donovan, 2008; Freeman and Goodenough, 2010; Posner, 2007; Zamir and Medina, 2010). North American sociologists in the early 20th century emphasized the various facets of the relationship between law and society. E. Adamson Ross (1922:106) considered law as "the most specialized and highly furnished engine of control employed by society." Lester F. Ward (1906:339), who believed in governmental control and social planning, predicted a day when legislation would endeavour to solve "questions of social improvement, the amelioration of the conditions of all the people, the removal of whatever privations may still remain, and the adoption of means to the positive increase of the social welfare, in short, the organization of human happiness."

The writings of these early sociologists greatly influenced the development of the school of **sociological jurisprudence,** or the study of law and legal philosophy and the use of law to regulate conduct (Lauderdale, 1997:132). Sociological jurisprudence is based on a comparative study of legal systems, legal doctrines, and legal institutions as social phenomena; it considers law as it actually is—the "law in action" as distinguished from the law as it appears in books (Wacks, 2009). Roscoe Pound, the principal figure in sociological jurisprudence, relied heavily on the findings of early sociologists in asserting that law should be studied as a social institution. For Pound (1941b:18), law was a specialized form of social control that exerts pressure on a person "in order to constrain him [sic] to do his [sic] part in upholding civilized society and to deter him [sic] from anti-social conduct, that is, conduct at variance with the postulates of social order."

Among sociologists, interest in law grew rapidly after World War II ended in 1945. In North America, some sociologists became interested in law almost by accident. As they investigated certain problems, such as race relations, they found law to be relevant. Others became radicalized in the mid- and late 1960s, a period of social unrest, and their work began to emphasize social conflict and the functions of stratification in society. It became imperative for sociologists of the left to dwell on the gap between promise and performance in the legal system. By the same token, those sociologists defending the establishment were anxious to show that the law dealt with social conflict in a legitimate fashion. These developments provided the necessary impetus for the field of law and society, which got its start in the mid-1960s with the formation of the American Law and Society Association and the inauguration of its official journal, the *Law & Society Review* (Abel, 1995:9).

Pue (2009) credits the formation of the Canadian Law and Society Association in the early 1980s to the participation of Canadian scholars in the American Law and Society Association and an "effervescence of intellectual energy across Canada" where "[l]aw and society teaching had been part of significant undergraduate programmes at Carleton University and York University for some time." In addition, he identifies the 1983 publication of *Law and Learning* (aka the "Arthurs Report") by the Social Sciences and Humanities Research Council of Canada as a catalyst for the establishment of both the Canadian Law and Society Association/ Association Canadienne Droit et Societé (CLSA/ACDS) and the *Canadian Journal of Law and Society*, an interdisciplinary scholarly journal that produced its first volume in 1986 and continues to promote and publish research on law and legal systems as social phenomena.

Feminist legal scholarship emerged in Canada following the release of the 1970 report of the Royal Commission on the Status of Women and gained momentum when the *Canadian Charter of Rights and Freedoms* came into effect on April 17, 1982 (Brockman and Chunn, 1993:5). The National Association of Women and the Law, a national non-profit women's organization that promotes the equal rights of women through legal education, research, and law reform advocacy, was established in 1974. In 1985, the Women's Legal Education and Action Fund, "a research and litigation organization with a mandate to initiate, and to intervene in, cases affecting women" (Mossman, 1998:193), was created and the *Canadian Journal of Women and the Law* began publication (Dawson, Quaile, and Holly, 2002:105).

There are a growing number of professional journals providing scholarly outlets for the mounting interest in law and society topics. These include *Law and Social Inquiry*, *Law and Anthropology*, *Journal of Law and Society*, *Journal of Empirical Legal Studies*, *European Law Journal*, and *International Journal of the Sociology of Law*. As the names of these journals suggest, interest in law and society is not confined to North America (Johns, 2010). A few examples: Scandinavian scholars have emphasized the social meaning of justice and the public's knowledge of the law and attitudes toward it. Russian social scientists have considered the transformation of socialist legal systems into more Western, market-oriented ones. German sociologists have studied the socio-legal implications of immigration and nationalism. International bodies such as the United Nations are also concerned with the legal issues that increasingly arise in today's global community.

Most law and society scholars would probably agree with Eugen Ehrlich's oft-quoted dictum that the "centre of gravity of legal development lies not in legislation, nor in juristic science, nor in judicial decision, but in society itself" (Ehrlich, 1975: Foreword). We share Willock's (1974:7) belief that "in so far as jurisprudence seeks to give law a location in the whole span of human affairs it is from sociology that it stands to gain most." Sociological knowledge, perspectives, theories, and methods are not only useful but also axiomatic for the understanding and possible improvement of law and the legal system in society.

But the study of law by sociologists is somewhat hampered by difficulties of interaction between sociologists and lawyers. Both nationally and internationally, language-based approaches to issues are different in the two professions (Wagner and Cacciaguidi-Fahy, 2008). As Edwin M. Schur (1968:8) noted, "In a sense . . . lawyers and sociologists 'don't talk the same language,' and this lack of communication undoubtedly breeds uncertainty in both professions concerning any involvement in the other's domain, much less any cooperative interdisciplinary endeavours." He added: "Sociologists and lawyers are engaged in quite different sorts of enterprises," and noted that "the lawyer's characteristic need to make decisions, here and now, may render him [sic] impatient with the sociologist's apparently unlimited willingness to suspend final judgment on the issue" (Schur, 1968:8). The complexity of legal terminology further impedes interaction. There is a special rhetoric of law that has its own vocabulary; terms like *subrogation* and *replivin* and *respondeat superior* and *chattel lien* abound (Garner, 2001). Although social scientists do not always write clearly, lawyers use an arcane writing style that is at times replete with multiple redundancies such as *made and entered into*, *cease and desist*, *null and void*, *in full force and effect*, and *give, devise, and bequeath*; on occasion, lawyers have sued each other over the placement of a comma (Robertson and Grosariol, 2006). Not surprisingly, "Between specialized vocabulary and arcane style, the very language of the law defies lay understanding" (Chambliss and Seidman, 1982:119) (see Box 1.1 Lay Knowledge of the Law and Legal Literacy). Problems of interaction are also brought about and reinforced by the differences in professional cultures (Strathern, 2005). Lawyers are advocates; they are concerned with the identification and resolution of the problems of their clients. Sociologists consider all evidence on a proposition and approach a problem with an open mind. Lawyers, to a great extent, are guided by precedents, and past decisions control current cases. In contrast, sociologists emphasize creativity, theoretical imagination, and research ingenuity.

The pronouncements of law are predominantly prescriptive: They tell people how they should behave and what will happen to them if they do not. In sociology, the emphasis is on description, on understanding the reasons why certain groups of people act certain ways in specific situations. The law *reacts* to problems most of the time; the issues and conflicts are brought to its attention by clients outside the legal system. In sociology, issues, concerns, and problems are generated *within* the discipline on the basis of what is considered intellectually challenging, timely, or of interest to funding agencies.

BOX 1.1 LIFE AND LAW: LAY KNOWLEDGE OF THE LAW AND LEGAL LITERACY

Although Canadians are more highly educated than ever before, the majority of us are not well informed about the law and the nature of our legal rights. For example, while the 1982 entrenchment of the *Canadian Charter of Rights and Freedoms* has been lauded as "the landmark event for Canadian law" (McLachlin, 2002), many Canadians remain unaware of the Charter's significance, content, and function. Even the most educated of laypersons in Canada may lack accurate knowledge about the law and legal institutions.

To learn what Canadian post-secondary students know about general business law in their jurisdiction, Peter Bowal and Irene Wanke (2001) gave 264 undergraduates and 12 graduate students a questionnaire that included 15 statements pertaining to business-related laws and asked them to indicate whether these statements were true or false. Student performance indicated a significant lack of knowledge of the law.

For example, students erroneously believed that discrimination against "students" is illegal. Most were unaware of the monetary limit of their jurisdiction's small claims court. Students commonly fused and confused "sexual harassment" with "sexual assault," mistakenly identifying the former as a "crime" rather than as a civil wrong against human rights and employment law. Moreover, students "strongly believed that they were legally obligated to comply with the *Charter of Rights and Freedoms*, even though that legal document only confers rights upon them and only governments are bound by it" (Bowal and Wanke, 2001:402).

The Department of Justice Canada (2009) has noted that for our system of justice to function in a way that is "accessible, efficient and fair," it is essential that all Canadians be informed about the law and its workings. A lack of knowledge of the law may be especially fateful in an era that increasingly demands our achievement of **"legal literacy"**—"the process of acquiring critical awareness about rights and law, the ability to assert rights, and the capacity to mobilize for change" (Schuler and Kadirgamar-Rajasingham,1992:2). However, while some may believe that their consumption of law-related television programs such as *Law & Order*, *CSI*, and *Judge Judy* furnishes them with much valuable knowledge, the content of such shows cannot and should not be construed as a reliable guide to Canadian law or its workings.

These differences in professional cultures are, to a great extent, due to the different methods and concepts that lawyers, sociologists, and other social scientists use in searching for "truth." Legal thinking, as Aubert (1973:50) observed decades ago, is different from scientific thinking for the following reasons:

1. Law seems to be more inclined toward the particular than toward the general (e.g., what happened in a specific case).
2. Law, unlike the physical and social sciences, does not endeavour to establish dramatic connections between means and ends (e.g., the impact the verdict has on the defendant's future conduct).
3. Truth for the law is normative and non-probabilistic—either something has happened or it has not (e.g., a person has either broken a law or they have not). A law is either valid or invalid.
4. Law is primarily past- and present-oriented and is rarely concerned with future events (e.g., what happens to the criminal in prison).
5. Legal consequences may be valid even if they do not occur; that is, their formal validity does not inevitably depend on compliance (e.g., the duty to fulfill a contract; if it is not fulfilled, it does not falsify the law in question).
6. A legal decision is an either-or, all-or-nothing process with little room for a compromise solution (e.g., litigant either wins or loses a case).

Of course, these generalizations have their limitations. They simply highlight the fact that law is an authoritative and reactive problem–solving system that is geared to specific social needs. Since the emphasis in law is on certainty (or predictability or finality), its instrumentation often requires the adoption of simplified assumptions about the world. The lawyer generally sees the law as an instrument to be wielded and is more often preoccupied with the practice and pontification of the law than with its consideration as an object of scholarly inquiry.

Sociologists who study law are sometimes asked, "What are you doing studying law?" Unlike lawyers, sociologists need to justify any research in the legal arena and may envy colleagues in law schools who can carry out such work without having to reiterate its relevance or establish their own competence. Yet this need for justification is not an unmixed evil, since it serves to remind sociologists that they are not lawyers but professionals with special interests. Like lawyers, sociologists may be concerned with the understanding, the prediction, and perhaps even the development of law. Obviously, sociologists and lawyers lack a shared experience, a common quest. At the same time, increasingly, sociologists and lawyers work together on problems of mutual interest (such as research on jury selection, conflict resolution, crime, demographic concerns, consumer problems, and so on) and are beginning to see the reciprocal benefits of such endeavours.

CONCEPTUALIZATIONS OF LAW

The question "What is law?" haunts legal thought, and probably more scholarship has gone into defining and explaining the concept of law than into any other concept still in use in sociology and jurisprudence. Indeed, there are almost as many definitions of law as there are theorists. As E. Adamson Hoebel (1954:18) wryly observed, "to seek a definition of the legal is like the quest for the Holy Grail."

Our review of some of the many definitions of law begins with those proffered by two great North American jurists, Benjamin Nathan Cardozo and Oliver Wendell Holmes, Jr. Cardozo (1924:52) defines law as "a principle or rule of conduct so established as to justify a prediction with reasonable certainty that it will be enforced by the courts if its authority is challenged." Holmes (1897:461) declares that "the prophecies of what the courts will do in fact, and nothing more pretentious, are what I mean by the law." For Holmes, judges make the law on the basis of past experience. In both of these definitions, the courts play an important role. These are pragmatic approaches to law as revealed by court-rendered decisions. Implicit in these definitions is the notion of courts being backed by the authoritative force of a political state.

From a sociological perspective, one of the most influential definitions of law is that of Max Weber. Starting with the idea of an *order* characterized by legitimacy, he suggests, "An order will be called *law* if it is externally guaranteed by the probability that coercion (physical or psychological), to bring about conformity or avenge violation, will be applied by a *staff* of people holding themselves specially ready for that purpose" (Weber, 1954:5). Weber argues that law has three basic features that, taken together, distinguish it from other normative orders, such as custom or convention. First, pressures to comply with the law must come externally in the form of actions or threats of action by others, regardless of whether a person wants to obey the law or does so out of habit. Second, these external actions or threats always involve coercion or force. Third, those who instrument the coercive threats are individuals whose official role is to enforce the law. Weber refers to "state" law when the persons who are charged to enforce the law are part of an agency of political authority.

Weber contends that customs and conventions can be distinguished from law because they do not entail one or more of these features. **Customs** are rules of conduct in defined situations that are of relatively long duration and are generally observed without deliberation and "without thinking." Customary rules of conduct are called *usages*, and there is no sense of duty or obligation to follow them. **Conventions**, by contrast, are rules for conduct and they involve a sense of duty and obligation. Pressures, which usually include expressions of disapproval, are exerted on individuals who do not conform to conventions. Weber (1954:27) points out that unlike law, a conventional order "lacks specialized personnel for the instrumentation of coercive power."

Although a number of scholars accept the essentials of Weber's definition of law, they question two important points. First, some contend that Weber places too much emphasis on coercion and ignores other considerations that may induce individuals to obey the law. For example, Philip Selznick (1969:4) argues that the authoritative nature of legal rules brings about a special kind of obligation that is not dependent on the use or threat of coercion or force. Many laws are obeyed because people feel it is their duty to obey. The second point concerns Weber's use of a special staff. Some scholars claim that Weber's definition limits the use of the term "law" in cross-cultural and historical contexts. They argue that the word "staff" implies an organized administrative apparatus that may not exist in certain illiterate societies. E. Adamson Hoebel (1954:28), for instance, proposes a less restrictive term by referring to individuals possessing "a socially recognized privilege," and Ronald L. Akers (1965:306) suggests a "socially authorized third party." Of course, in modern societies, law provides for a specific administrative apparatus. Still, these suggestions should be kept in mind while studying the historical developments of law.

From a different perspective, Donald Black (2002:118) contends that law is essentially governmental social control. In this sense, law is "the normative life of a state and its citizens, such as legislation, litigation, and adjudication." He maintains that several styles of law may be observed in a society, each corresponding to a style of social control. Four styles of social control are represented in law: penal, compensatory, therapeutic, and conciliatory. In the **penal style of social control**, the deviant is viewed as a violator of a prohibition and an offender to be subjected to condemnation and punishment (for example, a drug pusher). In the **compensatory style**, a person is considered to have a contractual obligation and, therefore, owes the victim restitution (for example, a debtor failing to pay the creditor). Both of these styles are accusatory where there is a complainant and a defendant, a winner and a loser. According to the **therapeutic style**, the deviant's conduct is defined as abnormal (for example, the person needs help, such as treatment by a psychiatrist). In the **conciliatory style**, deviant behaviour represents one side of a social conflict in need of resolution without consideration as to who is right or who is wrong (for example, marital disputes). These last two styles are remedial, designed to help people in trouble and ameliorate a bad social situation. Elements of two or more of these styles may appear in a particular instance; for example, when a drug addict is convicted of possession and is granted probation contingent upon his or her participation in some kind of therapy program.

The above-mentioned definitions illustrate some of the alternative ways of looking at law. It is the law's specificity in substance, its universality of applicability, and the formality of its enactment and enforcement that set it apart from other devices for social control. Implicit in these definitions of law is the notion that law can be analytically separated from other normative systems in societies with developed political institutions and specialized lawmaking and law-enforcement agencies. The paramount function of law is to regulate and constrain the behaviour of individuals in their relationships with one another. Ideally, law is to be employed only when other formal and informal methods of social control fail to operate or are inadequate for the job. Finally, law can be distinguished from other forms of social control primarily in that it is a formal system embodying explicit rules of conduct, the planned use of sanctions to ensure compliance with the rules, and a group of authorized officials designated to interpret the rules and apply sanctions to violators. From a sociological perspective, the rules of law are simply a guide for action. Without interpretation and enforcement, law would remain meaningless (Benda-Beckman et al., 2009). Moreover, law can be studied as a social process, instrumented by individuals during social interaction. Sociologically, law consists of the behaviours, situations, and conditions for making, interpreting, and applying legal rules that are backed by the state's legitimate coercive apparatus for enforcement.

TYPES OF LAW

The content of law may be categorized as substantive or procedural. **Substantive laws** consist of rights, duties, and prohibitions administered by courts—which behaviours are allowed and which are prohibited (such as prohibitions against murder or the sale of narcotics). **Procedural laws** are rules concerning just how substantive laws are to be administered, enforced, changed, and used by players in the legal system (such as filing charges, selecting a jury, presenting evidence in court, or drawing up a will).

At times a distinction is made between public law and private law. **Public law** is concerned with the structure of government, the duties and powers of officials, and the relationship between the individual and the state. Constitutional law, administrative law, and criminal law are all examples of public law. **Private law** is concerned with both substantive and procedural rules governing relationships between individuals (the law of torts or private injuries, contracts, property, wills, inheritance, marriage, divorce, adoption, and the like).

A more familiar distinction is between civil law and criminal law. **Civil law**, like private law, consists of a body of rules and procedures intended to govern the conduct of individuals in their relationships with others. Violations of civil statutes, called **torts**, are private wrongs for which the injured individual may seek redress in the courts for the harm he or she experienced. In most cases, some form of payment is required from the offender to compensate for the injury he or she has caused. Similarly, one company may be required to pay another a sum of money for failing to fulfill the terms of a business contract. The complainant firm is thus "compensated" for the loss it may have suffered as a result of the other company's neglect or incompetence. **Criminal law** is concerned with the definition of crime and the prosecution and penal treatment of offenders. Although a criminal act may cause harm to an individual, crimes are regarded as offenses against the state or "the people." A crime is a "public," as opposed to an "individual" or "private," wrong. It is the state, not the harmed individual, that takes action against the offender. Furthermore, the action taken by the state differs from that taken by the plaintiff in a civil case. For example, if the case involves a tort, or civil injury, compensation equivalent to the harm caused is levied. In the case of crime, some form of punishment is administered (e.g., a fine, probation, incarceration). Occasionally, a criminal action may be followed up by a civil suit, such as in a sexual assault case where the victim may seek financial compensation in addition to criminal sanctions.

A distinction can also be made between civil law and common law. In this context, **civil law** refers to legal systems whose development was greatly influenced by Roman law, a collection of codes compiled in the Corpus Juris Civilis (Code Civil). Civil-law systems are codified systems, and the basic law is found in codes. These are statutes that are enacted by national parliaments. France is an example of a civil-law system. The civil code of France, which first appeared in 1804, is called the Code Napoléon and embodies the civil law of the country. By contrast, **common law** resisted codification. Law is not based on acts of parliament but on case law, which relies on precedents set by judges to decide a case (Bennion, 2009). Thus, it is "judge-made" law as distinguished from legislation or "enacted" law. While most countries subscribe to either civil law or common law or a blend of the two, "Canada is unique from a legal perspective . . . in that part of the country utilizes the substantive and procedural law of two legal families as a basis for its legal system" (Terrill, 2009:152). The historical importance of both England and France in the founding and colonizing of this country resulted in not only two distinct cultures, but also in a dual legal culture that is most evident within the field of private law. While the private law of Quebec has its basis in the Romano-Germanic, or civil law, tradition, the private law elsewhere in Canada derives from the common law of England.

Law in Canada may be further divided into the following branches: constitutional law, case law, statutory law, administrative law, and royal prerogative. *Constitutional law* is a branch of public law. It determines the political organization of the state and its powers while also setting certain substantive and procedural limitations on the exercise of governing power. The Constitution is "the supreme law of Canada" and establishes the basic organizational framework of government and the limits on government (Statistics Canada, 1998:511). Constitutional law consists of the application of fundamental principles of law based on that document, as interpreted by the Supreme Court. Although Canada's constitution consists of more than 30 statutes, the two most important sources of constitutional law are the *Constitution Act, 1867* (formerly the *British North America Act, 1867*), which establishes the division of powers between the federal and provincial governments, and the *Constitution Act, 1982* (which includes the *Canadian Charter of Rights and Freedoms*), which imposes limits on the ability of governments to infringe upon specified rights and freedoms of Canadians.

Case law is enacted by judges in cases that are decided in the appellate courts. **Statutory law** is legislated law—legislation passed by elected officials in legislative assemblies. Finally, **administrative law** is a body of law created by administrative agencies in the form of regulations, orders, and decisions. **Royal prerogative or prerogative powers**, the residue of discretionary authority that is legally left in the hands of the Crown, are another source of law. These powers, which originate in common law, are vested constitutionally in the Crown, as represented by the governor-general and the provincial lieutenants-governor. These various categories of law will be discussed and illustrated later in the text.

MAJOR LEGAL SYSTEMS

In addition to the types of law, there is a large variety of legal systems (Clark, 2007; Gillespie, 2009; Oda, 2009; Richland and Deer, 2010; Terrill, 2015). The dominant legal systems that exist in various forms throughout the world are the Romano-Germanic (civil law), common law, socialist law, and Islamic law. The Romano-Germanic systems predominate in Europe, in most of the former colonies of France, Germany, Italy, Spain, Portugal, and Belgium and in countries that westernized their legal systems in the 19th and 20th centuries. Common-law systems are predominant in English-speaking countries. Islamic systems are found in the Middle East and some other parts of the world to which Islamic religion has spread. Socialist legal systems prevail in the People's Republic of China, Vietnam, Cuba, and North Korea. Remnants of socialist systems are still found in the former Soviet Union and Eastern European countries.

ROMANO-GERMANIC SYSTEM

The Romano-Germanic, or civil, law refers to legal science that has developed on the basis of Roman *ius civile* or civil law (Mousourakis, 2007; Plessis, 2010). The foundation of this system is the compilation of rules made in the 6th century A.D. under the Roman emperor Justinian. They are contained in the Code of Justinian and have evolved essentially as private law, as means of regulating private relationships between individuals (Mears, 2004). After the fall of the Roman Empire, the Code of Justinian competed with the customary law of the Germanic tribes that had invaded Europe. The code was reintroduced in law school curricula between A.D. 1100 and A.D. 1200 in northern Europe, then spread to other parts of the continent. Roman law thus coexisted with the local systems throughout Europe up to the 17th century. In the 19th century, the Napoleonic codes, and subsequently the code of the new German Empire of 1900 and the Swiss code of 1907, are examples of the institutionalization of this legal system.

Codified systems are basic laws that are set out in codes. A **code** is simply a body of laws (Mears, 2004). These statutes are enacted by national parliaments that arrange entire fields of law in an orderly, comprehensive, cumulative, and logical way. Today, most European countries have national codes based on a blend of customary and Roman law that makes the resulting systems members of the Romano-Germanic legal tradition. While Quebec's legal system today is best described as mixed, this system is also reflected in Quebec's Civil Code and Code of Civil Procedure, which regulates the relationships between and transactions among persons (e.g., the status of individual persons, the law of marriage and relations between married persons, the law of property and the law of contracts, and responsibility for civil wrongs) subject to Quebec law.

COMMON-LAW SYSTEM

Common law is characteristic of the English system, which developed after the Norman Conquest in 1066 (Cownie, 2010). The law of England, as well as those laws modelled on English law (such as the laws of Canada, the United States, Ireland, and India), resisted codification. Law is based on case law, which relies on precedents set by judges in deciding a case (Friedman, 2002). Thus, it is "judge-made" law as distinguished from legislation or "enacted" (statutory) law. The doctrine of "precedent" is strictly a common-law practice. The divisions of the common law, its concepts, substance, structure, legal culture, and vocabulary, and the methods of the common-law lawyers and judges, are very different, as will be demonstrated throughout this book, from those of the Romano-Germanic, or civil, law systems.

SOCIALIST LEGAL SYSTEM

The origins of the socialist legal system can be traced back to the 1917 Bolshevik Revolution, which gave birth to the Union of Soviet Socialist Republics. The objectives of classical socialist law are threefold. First, law must provide for national security. Ideally, the power of the state must be consolidated and increased to prevent attacks on the socialist state and to assure peaceful coexistence among nations. Second, law has the economic task of developing the production and distribution of goods on the basis of socialist principles so that everyone will be provided for "according to his or her needs." The third goal is that of education: to overcome selfish and antisocial tendencies that were brought about by a heritage of centuries of poor economic organization.

The source of socialist law is legislation, which is an expression of popular will as perceived by the Communist Party. The role of the court is simply to apply the law, not to create or interpret it. Even today, for example, judges in China are not required to have any legal training, and few do, and they are mostly in large urban areas. Most hold their positions because they have close connections with local governments, which are eager for quick convictions (Diamant, Lubman, and O'Brien, 2005; Muhlhahn, 2009).

Socialist law rejects the idea of separation of powers. The central notion of socialist law is the notion of ownership. Private ownership of goods has been renamed "personal ownership," which cannot be used as a means of producing income. It must be used only for the satisfaction of personal needs. Socialist law is unique with respect to "socialist" ownership, of which there are two versions: collective and state. A typical example of collective ownership is the *kolkhozi*, or collective farm, which is based on nationalized land. State ownership prevails in the industrial sector in the form of installations, equipment, buildings, raw materials, and products. Versions of this type of legal system still exist in China, Cuba, North Korea, and Vietnam.

The collapse of communism in the Soviet Union and the former Eastern-bloc countries, the dissolution of the political and economic institutions that guaranteed the conservation of communist structures, the reintroduction of a multiparty system, and the general democratization of political life had immediate implications for the socialist legal system. The former Soviet nations had to reconceptualize basic notions of property, environmental protection, authority, legitimacy, and power, and even the very idea of law (Agyeman and Ogneva-Himmelberg, 2009; Hesli, 2007; Priban, Roberts, and Young, 2003; Muravyeva, 2017).

Although the problems involved in the transition vary from country to country according to unique historical and political circumstances, all the states face common concerns, such as establishment of a new political ideology, creation of new legal rights, the imposition of sanctions on former elites, and new forms of legitimization (Feuer, 2010). Among the practical problems are the creation of new property rights; the attainment of consensus in lawmaking; the formulation and instrumentation of new laws on such matters as privatization; joint ventures; restitution for and rehabilitation of victims of the overturned regime; the revision of criminal law; the rise of nationalistic, anti-foreign, and anti-Semitic sentiments; and multi-party electoral behaviour (Oleinik, 2003; Piana, 2010). There is a whole slate of legal issues previously denied public attention by socialist law, such as prostitution, drug abuse, unemployment, and economic shortages. There are also concerns with the development of new law school curricula, selection of personnel, and replacement or resocialization of former members of the Communist Party still occupying positions of power. However, perhaps the biggest task facing the new lawmakers in the former Soviet nations is the creation of a legal climate aimed at stimulating foreign investments.

Westerners need to be assured about the safety of their investments, which requires the creation of a legal infrastructure based on democratic principles. New laws are still needed on repatriation of profits, property rights, privatization, and the movement of goods.

Another challenge that post-Communist regimes confront is crime management. In Russia and in its former satellites, the Soviet criminal code has not been significantly altered, even though it is better suited to catch political dissidents than to inspire respect for law and order. The laws were aimed at defending the totalitarian state, not the individual. Presidential decrees and legislative acts have expanded the boundaries of life—from the right to buy and sell property to the freedom to set up banks and private corporations—but the notoriously inefficient courts have no legal basis for interpreting these decrees, much less enforcing them. Consequently, the police cannot formally tackle organized criminal activity, because under present law, only individuals can be held criminally culpable. Not surprisingly, the number of organized criminal groups in Russia more than quadrupled during the last decade of the 20th century (Oleinik, 2003).

Almost every small business across Russia pays protection money to some gang. Vast fortunes in raw materials—from gold to petroleum—are smuggled out through the porous borders in the Baltics by organized groups who have bribed their way past government officials and ministries, and municipal governments peddle property and favours. Official corruption is rampant, and along with that, tax instability, licensing confusion, and disregard for intellectual property rights serve as disincentives to the kind of private Western investment Russia needs to create jobs and a functioning market economy (Eicher, 2009). Consider that when Transparency International (2017) evaluated 176 countries on a "Corruption Perception Index" (which measures the perceived level of public sector corruption on a scale from 0 ["highly corrupt"] to 100 ["very clean"]), Russia ranked as one of the most corrupt, with an assigned score of 29. For purposes of comparison, it may be noted that Canada's score on this measure was 82.

ISLAMIC LEGAL SYSTEM

Law is integral to the Islamic religion, which defines the character of the social order of the faithful who create laws in the name of God (An-Na'im and Baderin, 2010; Ende and Steinbach, 2010; Ghanim, 2010; Hallaq, 2009). "Islam" means "submission" or "surrender" and implies that individuals should submit to the will of God. Islamic religion states what Muslims must believe and includes the **Shari'a** ("the way to follow"), which specifies the rules for believers based on divine command and revelation. Unlike other systems of law based on judicial decisions, precedents, and legislation, Islamic law is derived from four principal sources (Shaham, 2010).

The first of these four sources is the *Koran*, the word of God as given to the Prophet. The second source is the *Sunna*, which are the sayings, acts, and allowances of the Prophet as recorded by reliable sources in the Tradition (*Hadith*). The third is *judicial consensus*; like precedent in common law, it is based on historical consensus of qualified legal scholars, and it limits the discretion of the individual judge. *Analogical reasoning* is the fourth primary source of Islamic law. It is used in circumstances not provided for in the Koran or other sources. For example, some judges inflict the penalty of stoning for the crime of sodomy, contending that sodomy is similar to the crime of adultery, and thus should be punished by the same penalty the Koran indicates for adultery (*Economist*, 2010:48). In the same vein, a female would get half the compensation a male would receive for being the victim of the same crime, since a male is entitled to an inheritance twice that of a female. In addition to these principal sources, various supplementary sources, such as custom, judge's preference, and the requirements of public interest, are generally followed (Nielsen and Christoffersen, 2010).

Shari'a legal precepts can be categorized into five areas: acts commanded, recommended, reprobated, forbidden, and left legally indifferent. Islamic law mandates rules of behaviour in the areas of social conduct, family relations, inheritance, and religious ritual and defines punishments for heinous crimes including adultery, false accusation of adultery, intoxication, theft, and robbery. For example, in the case of adultery, the proof of the offence requires four witnesses or confession. If a married person is found guilty, he or she is stoned to death. In the practice of stoning or "lapidation," stones are first thrown by witnesses then by the judge, followed by the rest of the community. Punishments and rules not defined by historical sources of *Shari'a* are left for contemporary government regulations and Islamic judges to decide. This practice permits an evolution of *Shari'a* law to reflect changing social, political, and economic conditions.

It is important to remember that the sanctions attached to the violation of Islamic law are religious rather than civil. Commercial dealings, for example, between Muslims and Westerners are covered by governmental rules comparable to administrative law in Canada. The fundamental principle of Islam is that of an essentially theocratic society, and Islamic law can be understood only in the context of some knowledge of Islamic religion and civilization (see, for example, Sechzer, 2004; Saeed, 2004; Ghanea, 2004; Hedley and Watson, 2018; Bano, 2018). Care should be exercised in discussing or analyzing components of Islamic law out of context and in isolation.

FUNCTIONS OF LAW

Why do we need law, and what does it do for society? More specifically, what functions does law perform? As with the definition of law, there is no agreement among scholars of law and society on the precise functions, nor is there consensus on their relative weight and importance. A variety of functions are highlighted in the literature (see, for example, Clark, 2007; Rawls, 2001), depending on the conditions under which law operates at a particular time and place. The recurrent major themes include social control, dispute settlement, and social change.

SOCIAL CONTROL

In a small, traditional, and homogeneous society, behavioural conformity is ensured by the fact that socializing experiences are very much the same for all members. Social norms tend to be consistent with each other, there is consensus about them, and they are strongly supported by tradition. Social control in such a society is primarily dependent upon self-sanctioning. Even on those occasions when external sanctions are required, they seldom involve formal punishment. Deviants are mostly subjected to informal mechanisms of social control, such as gossip, ridicule, or humiliation. Although they exist, banishment or forms of corporal punishment are rare in modern societies (Gram, 2006).

Even in a complex, heterogeneous society such as Canada, social control rests largely on the internalization of shared norms. Most individuals behave in socially acceptable ways, and, as in simpler societies, fear of disapproval from family, friends, and neighbours is usually adequate to keep potential deviants in check (Matza, 2010). Nevertheless, the great diversity of the population; the lack of direct communication between various segments; the absence of similar values, attitudes, and standards of conduct; and economic inequities, rising expectations, and the competitive struggles between groups with different interests have all led to an increasing need for formal mechanisms of social control. Formal social control is characterized by "(1) explicit rules of conduct, (2) planned use of sanctions to support the rules, and (3) designated officials to interpret and enforce the rules, and often to make them" (Davis, 1962:43).

In modern societies, there are many methods of social control, both formal and informal. Law is considered one of the forms of formal social control. Law is considered the key form of formal social control as it specifies rules for behavior and also the sanctions for misbehavior (Friedman, 1977:11). Of course, law does not have a monopoly on formal mechanisms of social control. Other types of formal mechanisms (such as firing, promotion, demotion, relocation, compensation manipulation, and so forth) are found in industry, academe, government, business, and various private groups.

DISPUTE SETTLEMENT

Legal anthropologist Karl N. Llewellyn (1960:2) famously wrote more than a half-century ago:

> What, then, is this law business about? It is about the fact that our society is honeycombed with disputes. Disputes actual and potential, disputes to be settled and disputes to be prevented; both appealing to law, both making up the business of law. . . . This doing of something about disputes, this doing of it reasonably, is the business of law.

By settling disputes through an authoritative allocation of legal rights and obligations, the law provides an alternative to other methods of dispute resolution. Increasingly, people in all walks of life let the courts settle matters that were once resolved by informal and non-legal mechanisms, such as negotiation, mediation, or forcible self-help measures. It should be noted, however, that law deals only with disagreements that have been translated into legal disputes. A legal resolution of conflict does not necessarily result in a reduction of tension or antagonism between the aggrieved parties. For example, the Canadian Labour Congress (2017) reports that "Lesbian, gay, bisexual, two-spirited, trans and queer (LGBTQ) workers often experience discrimination in the workplace. This can surface through hostility, unequal treatment, social isolation, homophobia, transphobia and violence." In a case of employment discrimination on the basis of sexual orientation and/ or gender identity, the court may focus on one incident in what is a complex and often not very clear-cut series of problems. Although this strategy results in a resolution of a specific legal dispute, it may fail to ameliorate the broader issues that produced the conflict.

SOCIAL CHANGE

Many scholars contend that a principal function of law in modern society is social engineering: purposive, planned, and directed social change initiated, guided, and supported by the law. Roscoe Pound (1959:98–99) captured the essence of this function of law in stating:

> For the purpose of understanding the law of today, I am content to think of law as a social institution to satisfy social wants—the claims and demands involved in the existence of civilized society—by giving effect to as much as we need with the least sacrifice, so far as such wants may be satisfied or such claims given effect by an ordering of human conduct through politically organized society. For present purposes I am content to see in legal history the record of a continually wider recognizing and satisfying of human wants or claims or desires through social control; a more embracing and more effective securing of social interests; a continually more complete and effective elimination of waste and precluding of friction in human enjoyment of the goods of existence—in short, a continually more efficacious social engineering.

In many instances, law is considered a "desirable and necessary, if not a highly efficient means of inducing change, and . . . wherever possible, its institutions and procedures are preferable to others of which we are aware" (Grossman and Grossman, 1971:2). Although some sociologists disagree with this contention (for example, Quinney, 2002), law is often used as a method of social change, or a way of bringing about planned social change by the government. Social change is a prominent feature of modern welfare states. For example, part of the taxes a government collects goes to the poor in the form of cash, medical and legal benefits, and housing (Friedman, 2002).

DYSFUNCTIONS OF LAW

Although law is an indispensable and ubiquitous institution of social life, it possesses—like most institutions—certain dysfunctions that may evolve into operational difficulties if they are not seriously considered (Clark, 2007; Stark, 2015). These dysfunctions stem in part from the law's conservative tendencies, the rigidity inherent in its formal structure, the restrictive aspects connected with its control functions, and the fact that certain kinds of discriminations are inherent in the law itself.

Hans Morgenthau (1993:418) suggests that "a given status quo is stabilized and perpetuated in a legal system" and that the courts, being the chief instruments of a legal system, "must act as agents of the status quo." Although this observation does not consider fully the complex interplay between stability and change in the context of law, it still contains an important ingredient of truth. By establishing a social policy of a particular time and place in constitutional and statutory precepts, or by making the precedents of the past binding, the law exhibits a tendency toward conservatism. Once a scheme of rights and duties has been created by a legal system, continuous revisions and disruptions of the system are generally avoided in the interests of predictability and continuity. Social changes often precede changes in the law. In times of crisis, the law can break down, providing an opportunity for discontinuous and sometimes cataclysmic adjustments.

The second dysfunction is related to these conservative tendencies of the law: a type of rigidity inherent in its normative framework. Since legal rules are couched in general, abstract, and universal terms, they sometimes operate as straitjackets in particular situations. A third dysfunction of the law stems from the restrictive aspects of normative control. Norms are shared convictions about the patterns of behaviour that are appropriate or inappropriate for the members of a group. Norms serve to combat and forestall *anomie* (a state of normlessness) and social disorganization. Law can overstep its bounds, and regulation can turn into overregulation, in which situation control may become transformed into repression.

Donald Black's (1989) contention that certain kinds of discrimination are inherent in law itself can also be construed as a fourth dysfunction. Rules, in principle, may apply to everyone, but legal authority falls unevenly across social place. A quotation from Anatole France's (1894) *The Red Lily* aptly illustrates this point: "The law in its majestic equality . . . forbids the rich as well as the poor from sleeping under bridges, begging in the streets, and stealing bread" (quoted in Black, 1989:72). Undoubtedly, this list of dysfunctions of law is incomplete. One may also include a variety of procedural inefficiencies, administrative delays, and archaic legal terminologies. At times, justice is denied and innocent people are convicted. One can also talk about laws being out of date, inequitable criminal sentencing, the lack of clarity of some laws resulting in loopholes and diverse interpretations, and the use of law as a tool of domination (Dickson, 2015; Newman, 2014; De Vries, 2011).

PARADIGMS OF SOCIETY

Sociological discussions of law in society often take place in the context of one of two ideal conceptions of society: the **consensus** and the **conflict** perspectives. The former describes society as a functionally integrated, relatively stable system held together by a basic consensus of values. This perspective stresses the cohesion, solidarity, integration, co-operation, and stability of society, which is seen as united by a shared culture and by agreement on its fundamental norms and values.

In contrast, the conflict perspective understands society as riddled with conflict and held together by coercion. Order is temporary and unstable because every individual and group strives to maximize its own interests in a world of limited resources and goods. In this perspective, the maintenance of power requires inducement and coercion, and law is an instrument of repression, perpetuating the interests of the powerful at the cost of alternative interests, norms, and values.

It is predictable enough that these two perspectives forward disparate conceptions of law's role in society.

THE CONSENSUS PERSPECTIVE

The consensus perspective considers law as a neutral framework for maintaining societal integration. For example, Roscoe Pound (1943:39) views society as composed of diverse groups whose interests often conflict with one another but are in basic harmony. In his words, law

> is an attempt to satisfy, to reconcile, to harmonize, to adjust these overlapping and often conflicting claims and demands, either through securing them directly and immediately, or through securing certain individual interests, or through delimitations or compromises of individual interests, so as to give effect to the greatest total of interests or to the interests that weigh most in our civilization, with the least sacrifice of the scheme of the interests as a whole.

In Pound's view, law in a heterogeneous and pluralistic society such as Canada is best understood as an effort at social compromise with an emphasis on social order and harmony. Pound argues that the historical development of law demonstrates a growing recognition and satisfaction of human wants, claims, and desires through law. Over time, law has concerned itself with an ever-wider spectrum of human interests. Law has more and more come to provide for the common good and the satisfaction of social wants (Pound, 1959:47). He considers law a form of "social change" directed toward achieving social harmony. Pound argues that the purpose of law is to maintain and to ensure those values and needs essential to social order, not by imposing one group's will on others, but by controlling, reconciling, and mediating the diverse and conflicting interests of individuals and groups within society. In brief, the purpose of law is to control interests and to maintain harmony and social integration.

Talcott Parsons (1962:58) similarly suggests that "the primary function of a legal system is integrity. It serves to mitigate potential elements of conflict and to oil the machinery of social intercourse." Proponents of the consensus perspective further maintain that law exists to maintain order and stability. Law is a body of rules enacted by representatives of the people in the interests of the people. Law is essentially a neutral agent, dispensing rewards and punishments without bias. A fundamental assumption of this perspective is that the political system is pluralistic, that society is composed of a number of interest groups of more or less equal power. The laws reflect compromise and consensus among these various interest groups and the values that are fundamental to the social order (Chambliss, 1976a:4).

THE CONFLICT PERSPECTIVE

In marked contrast to the consensus perspective, the conflict view considers law as an instrument of oppression "employed by the ruling classes for their own benefit" (Chambliss and Seidman, 1982:36). According to Richard Quinney (1970:35):

Society is characterized by diversity, conflict, coercion, and change, rather than by consensus and stability. . . .[L]aw is a *result* of the operation of interests, rather than an instrument that functions outside of particular interests. Though law may control interests, it is in the first place *created by* interests of specific persons and groups; it is seldom the product of the whole society. . . . Unlike the pluralistic conception of politics, law does not represent a compromise of the diverse interests in society, but supports some interests at the expense of others.

Proponents of the conflict perspective believe that law is a tool by which the ruling class exercises its control. Law both protects the property of those in power and serves to repress political threats to the position of the elite. Quinney (1975:285) writes that whereas the state, contrary to conventional wisdom, is the instrument of the ruling class, "law is the state's coercive weapon, which maintains the social and economic order" and supports some interests at the expense of others, even when those interests are those of the majority.

These two perspectives of society—consensus and conflict—are *ideal types* (that is, abstract concepts used to describe essential features of a phenomenon). Considering the operation of legal systems in society, there may be an element of truth in both. For example, the power of economic and commercial interests to influence legislation is illustrated by Chambliss in his study of vagrancy statutes. He notes that the development of vagrancy laws paralleled the need of landowners for cheap labour during the period in England when the system of serfdom was collapsing. The first of these statutes, which came into existence in 1349, threatened criminal punishment for those who were able-bodied and yet unemployed—a condition that existed when peasants were in the process of moving from the land into the cities. The vagrancy law served "to force labourers (whether personally free or unfree) to accept employment at a low wage in order to insure the landowner an adequate supply of labour at a price he could afford to pay" (Chambliss, 1964:69). Subsequently, vagrancy statutes were modified to protect commercial and industrial interests and to ensure safe commercial transportation. In the late 19th and early 20th centuries, vagrancy laws were used again to serve the interests of the wealthy (Chambliss and Seidman, 1982:182). This is just one illustration to show how law came to reflect the particular interests of those who have power and influence in society. This issue is addressed at greater length in Chapter 4.

OPTIONS FOR SOCIOLOGISTS

As with the approaches to the study of law and society, divergences of opinion also characterize the question of what role sociologists should play in such endeavours (van Heugten and Gibbs, 2015; Mertz, 2008). Some sociologists are concerned with the understanding of social life and social processes, and they go about their research guided by Max Weber's (1968:3) understanding of sociology as "a science which seeks to understand social action interpretively, and thereby to explain it causally in its course and its effects." Others, however, go beyond the notion of *verstehen* (to understand) and are more critical in their orientation. They believe that the task of sociology is to account for human suffering. They aim at demystifying the world; to show people what constrains them and what their routes are to freedom. Their criticisms are prompted by the twinned beliefs that the human condition and the social order have become unbearable and that they have a responsibility to not only identify the factors that have precipitated a deleterious condition but provide, through theoretical and empirical efforts, ways of rectifying or redressing the condition. Thus, they are guided by **praxis**, or the wedding of theory and action.

The second of these positions is associated with a Marxist tradition. It is based on the notion that knowledge generated from an analysis of a specific historical situation may be used as an argument for intervention, and politically engaged scholarship can contribute to the struggle for social justice. Sociologists in such situations try to demystify, clarify, and show individuals the source of their misery and the means of overcoming it. In a Marxian context, praxis means what people do, as contrasted with what they think. "Praxis is a revolutionary form of social practice (i.e., it contributes to the humanization of people by transforming reality from alienation to a hopefully better future). The concept is both a means of consciously shaping historical conditions and a standard for evaluating what occurs in any historical order. Marx maintains that a dialectical relationship exists between theory and praxis" (Reasons and Rich, 1978:431). Thus, those who adopt this perspective actively advocate changes in law and legal institutions wherever needed and work for the reformation of both the criminal system and criminal law when warranted (Munger, 2001; Nelson, 2001; Leiter, 2014; Baars, 2011).

These controversies beset the "proper" role of sociologists in the discipline. Based on one's values, ideologies, conception of sociology, and a plethora of other considerations, one may prefer to be a detached observer of social life, a critic of the social order, or an active agent of change. These roles, fortunately, are not mutually exclusive. Depending on the nature of the issue under consideration, and the degree of commitment to and involvement in that issue, one may freely select among these alternatives (Lempert, 2001). As an intellectual enterprise, sociology is flexible enough to accommodate diverse positions.

SUMMARY

- In sociology, the study of law touches on a variety of well-established areas of inquiry. It incorporates values, ideologies, social institutions, norms, power relations, and social processes.
- Since World War II, there has been a growing interest in law among sociologists both in this country and elsewhere. Some of the topics addressed in the study of law and society include the effectiveness of law, the impact of law on society, methods of dispute resolution, and research on judicial, legislative, and administrative processes. While collaboration between sociologists and lawyers is on the increase, interaction between the two groups may be complicated or forestalled by differences in each profession's terminology, perception of their roles in society, methodology, and professional culture.
- The content of law may be considered as substantive or procedural. A distinction is made also between public law and private law, as well as between civil law and criminal law. Common law generally refers to "judge-made" law or "case" law, as differentiated from statutory or enacted law.

- The principal legal systems in the world today include the Romano-Germanic (civil law), common law, socialist law with its current ramifications and problems of transition, and Islamic law.
- Sociological analyses of law and society are generally based on two ideal views of society—consensus and conflict perspectives. The former considers society as a functionally integrated, relatively stable system held together by basic consensus of values. The latter conceives of society as consisting of groups characterized by conflict and dissension on values and held together by some members who coerce others.
- There is dispute over the "proper" role sociologists should play in the study of law and society. Some sociologists maintain that their role is to try to understand, describe, and empirically analyze social phenomena in a more or less value-free context. Others argue that social scientists have a responsibility to criticize a social system's malfunctioning components and processes and seek to change deleterious social conditions by means of legal action.

CRITICAL THINKING QUESTIONS

1. Kagan (1995) has identified four factors as playing a powerful role in the rapid growth of legislation over the past few decades: the intensification of international economic competition; rapid technological change; a growing concern with the environment; and increased geographic mobility. In this context, he observes, three agendas have become dominant in socio-legal research: The first "focuses on determining the social, political and economic forces that explain law and institutional forms, the second focuses on the performance of legal institutions, and the third tries to assess the effects of legal processes on social life." While Kagan suggests that greater attention should be directed to the third, which of these research "agendas" do you find most compelling? Why?

2. Vatz (1980:160) observes that " 'the law' to most citizens comprises a massively complex, but well ordered and ultimately equitable and fair system of adjudications of disputes and alleged law breaking by which all citizens benefit. One need not belabour the metaphors of balanced scales of justice to comprehend this widespread mythology." According to Vatz, public confidence in "the law" arises not from experiencing the law but as the result of "experiencing communications about the law which convinces them that 'the law' is functioning in a way worthy of the public's considerable reverence."
   In what ways are positive impressions of the law urged upon us by opinion leaders in the socialization process (e.g., the family, the school, the peer group, and the mass media)? What are the advantages and disadvantages of this culturally inculcated mythos?

3. Various researchers have lamented the effect that television programs such as *CSI* may have on criminal jury trials by increasing the public's expectations of forensic science (the so-called "*CSI* effect"). However, the impact of such programs may be far broader. In what ways do television crime shows impact understandings of criminal law and the administration of criminal justice?

4. The chapter noted that sociologists who are interested in law and society are often asked, "What are you doing studying law?" How might law students and lawyers answer the complementary question: "What are you doing studying society?"

5. After reading this chapter, how would *you* define that elusive term "law"? Provide a justification for your preferred definition.

ADDITIONAL RESOURCES

1. Learn more about the history and activities of the Canadian Law and Society Association at www.acds-clsa.org.
2. The Carnegie Endowment for International Peace's "Democracy and Rule of Law Project" has resulted in a series of thoughtful papers on the "rule of law." Read Rachel Kleinfeld Belton's (2005) analysis of "Competing definitions and the rules of law: Implications for practitioners" at http://carnegieendowment.org/files/CP55.Belton.FINAL.pdf.
3. The Islamic Legal Studies Program at Harvard Law School hosts a webpage that provides ready access to a number of reports (in PDF format) on various aspects of Islamic law. Explore the site at http://ilsp.law.harvard.edu.
4. For information on the International Institute for the Sociology of Law, visit www.iisj.net.

2

CHAPTER 2
THEORETICAL PERSPECTIVES

This chapter examines the evolution of legal systems and reviews some of the principal classical and contemporary theories of law and society. At the outset, it should be acknowledged that there is no single, widely accepted, comprehensive theory of law and society (or of anything else in the social sciences, for that matter). While sociological theories of law abound (Abadinsky, 2008; Arrigo and Milovanovic, 2010; Banakar, 2003; Barnett, 2010; Cotterrell, 2006; Henry and Lukas, 2009; Nelken, 2009; Patterson, 2010; Ransome, 2010; Trevino, 2008), this chapter deals briefly with only a few of the important classical and contemporary theories of law and society. This approach serves certain purposes. It provides the reader with some conception of the development and content of these theories and how they relate to one another.

Although the discussion of these theories clearly shows the complex and multi-faceted nature of the relationship between law and society, it also serves as a means of differentiating, organizing, and understanding a great mass of material. Thus, although the concern is to suggest the magnitude and diversity of the field, an attempt is made to lend order to that magnitude and diversity.

A cautionary note is in order with regard to the procedures followed in this chapter for grouping various theories. It will become clear that many theories of law and society tend to overlap. For example, the reader may find that a theory that has been placed under the heading of "The European Pioneers" will contain similar elements to those embodied in "Classical Sociological Theorists." Our classification of theories should be viewed as essentially a heuristic device to facilitate discussion rather than to reflect the final status of the theories considered. We also acknowledge that, due to the tyranny of space and the introductory nature of this text, there are more theorists and theories omitted than included. Nevertheless, for those who wish to gain further knowledge about classical or modern theoretical concerns, we hope that the references cited will provide a helpful point of departure.

Figure 2.1 The law and society literature is immense.
Credit: Shutterstock

LEARNING OBJECTIVES

After reading this chapter, you should be able to:

1. Identify social conditions that encourage the emergence of formal codified law.

2. Differentiate between traditional, transitional, and modern legal systems.

3. Describe how Montesquieu, Spencer, and Maine conceptualized the relationship between legal change and social change.

4. Identify how Marx, Weber, and Durkheim explained the interrelation between legal institutions and the social order.

5. Detail the claims advanced by Dicey, Holmes, and Hoebel in arguing that law cannot be understood without regard for the realities of social life.

6. Describe why the writings of Donald Black and Roberto Mangabeira Unger on law and society can be considered to complement one another.

7. Compare and contrast the assumptions that underlie the functionalist and conflict/ Marxist approaches to law.

8. Describe how the critical legal studies movement, feminist legal theory, critical race theory and the law and literature/rhetoric movement have challenged earlier understandings of law and society.

EVOLUTION OF LEGAL SYSTEMS

Formal codified law emerges when the social structure of a given society becomes so complex that regulatory mechanisms and methods of dispute settlement can no longer be dependent on informal customs and social, religious, or moral sanctions (Zifcak, 2005). Formal and institutionalized regulatory mechanisms come into being when other control devices are no longer effective. As a society becomes larger and more complex, so too does its legal system.

Historically, legal development and industrialization, urbanization, and modernization have been closely intertwined (Grossi, 2010). In a small, homogeneous society with little division of labour and a high degree of solidarity, informal sanctions are sufficient to keep most behaviour in line with the norms. An example is the community on Tristan da Cunha, an isolated island in the middle of the South Atlantic Ocean. A few hundred people live there, growing potatoes and catching fish. When social scientists visited the island in the 1930s, they were amazed to see how "law-abiding" these people were, even though they had nothing resembling law as we know it. There was no serious crime on the island that anyone could recall; no police, courts, jails, or judges. There was no need for them. People in the community relied on informal mechanisms of social control, such as shaming and open disapproval, which can be effective and severe in their own way. Such forms of control work in small, homogeneous, face-to-face communities (Friedman, 2002).

But, in a modern, heterogeneous, and complex society, formal norms and sanctions are necessary to control behaviour so that society can continue to function in an orderly and predictable fashion. The presence of law and a legal system is essential to the maintenance of social order (Kritzer, 2002). Although modernization in a sense forces the development of law in this manner, the specifics of how this happens vary from society to society as a result of unique conditions, such as geographical location, historical events, conquest, and prevailing political and social forces.

Some have found it useful "to think of . . . stages of legal development in systems which have come to maturity" (Pound, 1959:366). Although developmental models are controversial, they have been used in almost every field of social science. Their use is justified by the attempt to make sense of history, which requires an appreciation of directionality, growth, and decay (Nonet and Selznick, 2001:19). The underlying theme in developmental models is the identification of forces that, having been set in motion at one stage, produce a characteristic outcome in another stage.

The law and society literature suggests that the more complex the society, the more differentiated the legal system (Schwartz and Miller, 1975). Underlying this proposition is the notion that legal development is conditioned by a series of integrative demands stemming from society's economic, political, educational, and religious institutions. Based on the complexity and magnitude of the interplay among these institutions and between these institutions and the law, several types of legal systems may be identified in the course of societal development. There is practically no limit to the variability of legal systems, and many scholars have developed typologies in an attempt to capture this diversity (such as Mundy, 2002; Pottage and Mundy, 2004). These typologies seldom correspond fully to the real world, but they are essential in an analytical discussion dealing with the types of legal systems. Drawing on these typologies, we discuss legal evolution with respect to three types of legal systems: traditional legal systems, transitional legal systems, and modern legal systems. Although the terms "traditional" and "primitive" are often used interchangeably in the literature on legal systems, we have elected to use the former, recognizing that the term "primitive" has negative connotations.

TRADITIONAL LEGAL SYSTEMS

Traditional legal systems are typically found in hunting-and-gathering and simple agrarian societies. The laws are not written or codified; they are permeated by customs, tradition, religious dogma, and values. In effect, the laws of traditional societies are simply their unwritten norms. The functions of law in traditional societies are essentially the same as those in more advanced societies (Rouland, 1994:153). Laws preserve important cultural elements; they coordinate interaction, settle disputes, deter or sanction deviance, and regularize social interactions.

In traditional societies, there are no well-developed political subsystems, and the polity is composed of kin leaders, councils of elders or chiefs, and various religious leaders. Legislatures as we know them do not formally exist in traditional societies. In such societies, judges and political leaders (elders and the like) are one and the same, and chiefs or elders can enact both substantive and procedural laws. Because there are no written laws, a traditional society's leader(s) can strike, rescind, or change old laws more easily than the modern legislator; if such action appears reasonable, little resistance is offered. Removing old laws from the books in modern societies is rarely that easy.

Courts, like the police force, are temporarily assembled and then dispersed as disputes arise and are settled. Although they are provisional, the courts comprise at least two clearly differentiated roles: that of judges, who hear evidence and make decisions in accordance with laws, and that of litigants, who have to abide by judges' decisions. Occasionally, a third role can be identified in such courts, that of a representative "lawyer" who pleads the case for a litigant. As the legal system develops, these roles become more clearly differentiated. In traditional societies, however, these three procedures are sufficient to maintain a high degree of societal integration and coordination.

TRANSITIONAL LEGAL SYSTEMS

Transitional legal systems are found in advanced agrarian and early industrial societies in which the economic, educational, and political subsystems are increasingly differentiated from kinship relationships. As a result of this increased complexity, the legal subsystem becomes more complex and extensive, as evidenced by a clear-cut differentiation in basic legal elements—laws, courts, enforcement agencies, and legislative structures. In the transitional stage, most of the features of the modern legal system are present, but not to the same degree. Law becomes more differentiated from tradition, customs, and religious dogma. There is a distinction between **public law** and **private law**. The former is concerned with the structure of government, the duties and powers of officials, and the relationships between the individual and the state; the latter regulates relations among non-political units. Criminal law also becomes distinguishable from torts. **Criminal law** denotes wrongs against the state, the community, and the public. **Torts** are laws pertaining to private wrongs of parties against each other rather than against the state or the public. There is, similarly, a clearer differentiation between procedural and substantive laws, and as the types of laws increase, laws become systems of rules (Friedman, 1975:291).

The increased differentiation of laws is reflected in the increased complexity of the courts. Accompanying this differentiation is the emergence of at least five distinct types of statuses: judge; representative or lawyer; litigant; court officials and administrators; and jurors. The roles of judges and lawyers become institutionalized, requiring specialized training. In transitional legal systems, written records of court proceedings become more common, contributing to the emergence of a variety of administrative roles, which, in turn, leads to the initial bureaucratization of the court.

With the development of clearly differentiated, stable, and autonomous courts, legal development accelerates for at least two reasons. First, "[l]aws enacted by the growing legislative body of the polity can be applied systematically to specific circumstances by professionals and experts" (Turner, 1972:222). Second, "[w]here political legislation of laws is absent, an established court can enact laws" that incorporate the society's prior decisions in disputes.

Initially, new courts in transitional societies are localized and characterized by local norms and values. In time, the need for a more uniform legal system leads to a more codified system of laws that apply to courts regardless of their particular location. Transitional legal systems also see the emergence of explicit police roles and also of legislative structures. This results in what political scientists call a *separation of powers*, or a clear differentiation of legislative statuses from judicial (courts) and enforcement (police) statuses. One effect of this development is that legislating new laws or abolishing old ones is no longer a matter of a simple decree from a society's leader.

In transitional legal systems, a small cluster of statuses, whether organized in a forum, a senate, or a royal council, can enact laws. Initially, these laws are dominated by a political elite and are responsive to its demands. Later on, legislative changes become more comprehensive, involving a group of laws pertaining to general problem areas. With the enactment of more comprehensive statutes and codes, a system of civil law begins to emerge to supplement common law. The development of civil codes is stimulated by an established court system and police force, a pool of educated lawyers and judges, a background of common law, and a degree of political and national unity. The functions of law in transitional legal institutions are essentially similar to those in traditional systems—perhaps a bit more complex, and, at the same time, less successful in resolving integrative problems. Structural differentiation becomes more complex. Political development increases, bringing with it inequities in power and wealth. In such situations, civil law tends to legitimize these inequalities.

MODERN LEGAL SYSTEMS

In modern legal systems, we find all the structural features of transitional systems present, but in greater and more elaborate arrangements. Turner (1972:225) notes, "Laws in modern legal systems are extensive networks of local and national statutes, private and public codes, crimes and torts, common and civil laws, and procedural and substantive rules." A distinctive feature of modern legal systems is the proliferation of public and procedural laws, referred to as **administrative law**. Another aspect is the increasing proportion of statutory law over common law. Legislation, as a result of political development, becomes a more acceptable method of adjusting law to social conditions. There are also clear hierarchies of laws, ranging from constitutional codes to regional and local codes.

Courts in modern legal systems have an important role in mediating and mitigating conflict, disputes, deviance, and problems. The roles of lawyers and judges become highly professionalized, with licensing requirements and formal sanctions. The various administrative statuses—clerks, bailiffs, and prosecutors—specialize, proliferate, and become heavily bureaucratized. The jurisdictions of courts are specified with clearly delineated appeal procedures. Cases unresolved in lower courts can be argued in higher courts that have the power to reverse lower court decisions (Dixon, Kupchik, and Savelsberg, 2007).

In modern legal systems, laws are enforced and court decisions are carried out by clearly differentiated and organized police forces. Each force possesses its own internal organization, which becomes increasingly bureaucratized at the higher levels. In addition to police forces, regulatory agencies regularly enforce and oversee compliance with laws. Administrative agencies also make and interpret laws in the context of their own mandates. Legislative bodies at various levels proliferate. There is a greater emphasis on integrative problems and on enacting comprehensive laws. Accompanying the emergence of a stable legislature, well-planned and comprehensive law enactment can become an effective mechanism of social change (Zifcak, 2005).

Inherent in modern legal systems is the notion of "modern" law. Marc Galanter's influential article on "The Modernization of Law"(1977) listed several features that characterize the legal systems of modern societies. One feature is that rules "are uniform and unvarying in their application" (p. 1047). The same rules and regulations are applicable to everyone. Modern law is also *transactional*, with rights and duties stemming from interactions between parties rather than "aggregated in unchanging clusters" that are prescribed to an individual by ascribed status. Another feature: Modern legal norms are *universalistic*; that is, their application is predictable, uniform, and impersonal. Further, the system, to be uniform and predictable, operates on the basis of written rules and has a regular chain of command. The system is *rational* in the Weberian sense, and "rules are valued for their instrumental utility in producing consciously chosen ends, rather than for their formal qualities" (p. 1048). Such a system is run by full-time professionals whose "qualifications come from mastery of the techniques of the legal system itself, not from possession of special gifts or talents or from eminence in some other area of life" (p. 1048). The legal system is also *amenable*. It can be changed and it does not have "sacred fixity." Law in modern societies is also *political*—that is, tied to the state, which has a monopoly on law. Finally, legislative, judicial, and executive functions are *separate and distinct* in modern law.

Thus far, we have identified some of the preconditions necessary for the development of modern legal systems. Let us now consider some of the theories accounting for those developments.

THEORIES OF LAW AND SOCIETY

The preceding section dealt with some general types of legal systems as they correspond to various stages of modernization and social development. The present section addresses two questions emerging from the previous discussion: Why did changes in the legal system take place? And what factors contributed to legal development from a historical perspective? In attempting to answer these questions, we can distinguish two general issues. The first is the issue of legal development in any society. The second concerns forces that produce or prevent change in the legal system.

Theorists of law and society have long been preoccupied with efforts to describe the broad historical course of legal development and to analyze the factors that influence legal systems. No attempt is made here to provide a comprehensive and systematic review of principal theories and schools. However, it is hoped that the following sample of theorists from various disciplines, historical periods, and countries will provide an understanding of the diverse issues involved in the investigation of the multi-faceted relations between law and other major institutions of society.

THE EUROPEAN PIONEERS

Early European theorists considered law as an absolute and autonomous entity, unrelated to the structure and function of the society in which it existed (Feinberg and Coleman, 2008). The idea of **natural law** forms the basis of this understanding (Donnelly, 2007). The origins of natural law can be traced back to ancient Greece. Aristotle maintained that natural law has a universal validity and is based on reason that is free from all passion (Daston and Stolleis, 2010). St. Thomas Aquinas argued that natural law is part of human nature, and, through natural law, humans participate as rational beings in the eternal laws of God.

The idea of natural law is based on the assumption that the nature of human beings can be known through reason, and that this knowledge can provide the basis for the social and legal ordering of human existence (Belliotti, 1992). Natural law is considered superior to enacted law. It is "the chief tenet of natural law that arbitrary will is not legally final"

(Selznick, 1961:100). An appeal to higher principles of justice is always permissible from the decrees of a lawmaker. When enacted law does not coincide with the principles of natural law, it is considered unjust.

From the middle of the 19th century, however, the idea of natural law was largely displaced by historical and evolutionary interpretations of law and by **legal positivism**, which considered the legal and the moral to constitute two quite separate realms. These two views sought to explain the law by reference to certain evolutionary forces that pushed the law forward along a predetermined path. Many theorists sought to discourage philosophical speculation about the nature and purposes of law and concentrated on the development and analysis of positive law laid down and enforced by the state. The most notable among these scholars include Baron de Montesquieu in France and Herbert Spencer and Sir Henry Sumner Maine in England. We shall now consider their theories in some detail.

BARON DE MONTESQUIEU (1689–1755)

Montesquieu challenged the underlying assumptions of natural law by presenting a radically different conceptualization of law and society. He considered law integral to a particular people's culture. The central thesis of his *The Spirit of the Laws* (1748) is that laws are the result of a number of factors in society, such as customs, physical environment, and antecedents, and that laws can be understood only in the context of that particular society. He further posited that laws are relative and that there are no "good" or "bad" laws in the abstract. Each law, Montesquieu maintained, must be considered in relation to its background, its antecedents, and its surroundings. If a law fits well into this framework, it is a good law; if it does not, it is bad.

But Montesquieu's fame rests above all on his political theory of the separation of powers. According to this theory, a constitution is composed of three different types of legal powers: legislative, executive, and judicial, each vested in a different body or person. The role of the legislature is to enact new laws; of the executive, to enforce and administer the laws as well as to determine policy within the framework of those laws; and of the judiciary, simply to interpret the laws established by the legislative power (Montesquieu, 1748/1989). This neat classification had considerable influence on the form of constitution subsequently adopted by the newly created United States of America after the Declaration of Independence (Bodenheimer, 1974:49) and would greatly affect constitutional thinkers in other countries throughout the late 18th and 19th centuries. Pospisil (1971:138) remarks: "With his ideas of the relativity of law in space as well as in time, and with his emphasis on specificity and empiricism, he can be regarded as the founder of the modern sociology of law in general and of the field of legal dynamics in particular."

HERBERT SPENCER (1820–1903)

Contrary to the doctrines of natural law, Spencer provided the philosophical underpinnings for the theory of unregulated competition in the economic sphere. Strongly influenced by Charles Darwin, Spencer drew a picture of the evolution of civilization and law in which natural selection and the survival of the fittest are the primary determining factors. Evolution for Spencer consists of growing differentiation, individuation, and increasing division of labour. Civilization is the progress of social life from primitive homogeneity to ultimate heterogeneity. He identified two main stages in the development of civilizations:

a primitive or military form of society, with war, compulsion, and status as regulatory mechanisms; and a higher or industrial form of society, with peace, freedom, and contract as the controlling devices.

Spencer was convinced that in the second stage, human progress is marked by a continual increase in individual liberty and a corresponding decrease in governmental activities. Government, he believed, must gradually confine its field of action to the enforcement of contracts and the protection of personal safety. He strongly opposed public education, public hospitals, public communications, and any governmental programs designed to alleviate the plight of the economically weaker groups in society. He was convinced that social legislation of this type is an unwarranted interference in the laws of natural selection (Spencer, 1899).

Spencer's ideas on law influenced a number of early North American sociologists (McCann, 2004). For example, William Graham Sumner (1940) advocated a position essentially similar to that of Spencer. He, too, saw the function of the state limited to that of an overseer who guards the safety of private property and sees to it that the peace is not breached. He favoured a regime of contract, in which social relations are regulated primarily by mutual agreements, not by government-imposed legal norms. Sumner also argued that law should promote maximum freedom of individual action. Like Spencer, he considered attempts to achieve a greater social and economic equality among all societal members to be ill-advised and unnatural:

> Let it be understood that we cannot go outside of this alternative: liberty, inequality, survival of the fittest; not liberty, equality, survival of the unfittest. The former carries society forward and favours all its best members; the latter carries society downward and favours all its worst members.
>
> (p. 25)

Reflections of the economic and social philosophies of Spencer and Sumner are still discernible in current conservative attitudes that place the rights of wealthier groups above those of the disfavoured members of society. One may also consider, in this context, resistance to legislative policies designed to equalize the bargaining power of management and labour, to protect the health and subsistence of marginal groups, or to interfere with that freedom of contract that was considered the true birthmark of an advancing civilization.

SIR HENRY SUMNER MAINE (1822–1888)

The founder and principal proponent of the English historical school of law, Maine was among the first theorists to argue that law and legal institutions must be studied historically if they are to be understood. He contended that legal history shows patterns of evolution that recur in different societies and in similar historical circumstances.

One of Maine's general laws of legal evolution is set forth in his classical treatise, *Ancient Law*:

> The movement of the progressive societies has been uniform in one respect.
> Through all its course it has been distinguished by the gradual dissolution of family

dependency and the growth of individual obligation in its place. The Individual is
steadily substituted for the Family, as the unit of which civil laws take account. . . .
Starting, as from one terminus of history, from a condition of society in which all the
relations of Persons are summed up in the relations of Family, we seem to have steadily
moved towards a phase of social order in which all these relations arise from the free
agreement of Individuals.

(Maine, 1861:170)

Thus, Maine arrived at his often-quoted dictum that "the movement of the progressive
societies has hitherto been a movement from Status to Contract" (1861:170). Status is a
fixed condition in which an individual is without will and without opportunity. Ascribed
status (based on one's position at birth) prevails and legal relations depend on birth or caste.
With the progress of civilization, this condition gradually gives way to a social system based
on contract.

Maine argued that a progressive civilization is manifested by the emergence of the
independent, free, and self-determining individual, based on achieved status, as the primary
unit of social life. He suggested that the emphasis on individual achievement and voluntary
contractual relations set the conditions for a more mature legal system that uses legislation
to bring society and law into harmony. In essence, his argument is that in modern
societies, legal relations are not conditioned by one's birth but are dependent on voluntary
agreements.

CLASSICAL SOCIOLOGICAL THEORISTS

Early sociologists recognized the essential interrelation between legal institutions and the
social order. This section explores the influential theoretical explanations of law and society
of Karl Marx, Max Weber, and Emile Durkheim.

KARL MARX (1818–1883)

Marx postulated that every society, whatever its stage of historical development, rests on an
economic foundation. He called this the "mode of production" of commodities, which has
two elements. The first is the physical or technological arrangement of economic activity.
The second is "the social relations of production," or the indispensable human attachments
that people must form with one another when engaged in economic activity. In his words:

The sum total of these relations of production constitutes the economic structure of
society—the real foundation, on which rise legal and political superstructures and to
which correspond definite forms of social consciousness.

(Marx, 1959:43)

For Marx, the determinant variable is the mode of production. Changes in this produce
changes in the way in which groups are attached to production technology. This economic
determinism is reflected in Marx's theory of law.

Marx's theory of law, which has greatly influenced social and jurisprudential thinking
throughout the world, may be summarized in three principal assumptions: (1) Law is a

product of evolving economic forces; (2) law is a tool used by a ruling class to maintain its power over the lower classes; and (3) in the communist society of the future, law as an instrument of social control will "wither away" and finally disappear.

The idea that law is a reflection of economic conditions is integral to the doctrine of **dialectical materialism**. According to this doctrine, the political, social, religious, and cultural order of any given epoch is determined by the existing system of production and forms a *superstructure* on top of this economic basis. Law, for Marx, is part of this superstructure whose forms, content, and conceptual apparatus constitute responses to economic developments. This view maintains that law is nothing more than a function of the economy but without any independent existence (Easton, 2009).

In societies with pronounced class distinctions, the ruling class owns and controls the means of production. Marx's theory of law characterizes law as a form of class rule and dominance (Collins, 1996). While addressing the bourgeoisie of his day in his *Communist Manifesto*, Marx (Marx and Engels, 1848:47) wrote, "Your jurisprudence is but the will of your class made into a law for all, a will whose essential character and direction are determined by the economic conditions of existence of your class." Marx further argued that law, as a form of class rule, is sanctioned by public authority, which has the power of enforcement through the use of armed bodies.

Finally, Marx suggested that after the revolution, when class conflict is resolved and the institution of private property is replaced by a communist regime, law and the state, hitherto the main engines of despotism and oppression, will "wither away." There will be no need for coercion, since everyone's needs will be fulfilled and universal harmony will prevail. According to this view, there will be no need for law in the future—a future that will be the final stage of humanity's evolution because stateless and lawless communism shall exist forever.

MAX WEBER (1864–1920)

Weber's typology of legal systems is based on two fundamental distinctions. First, legal procedures are rational or irrational. **Rational procedures** involve the use of logic and scientific methods to attain specific objectives (see Berg and Meadwell, 2004). **Irrational procedures** rely on ethical or mystical considerations, such as magic or faith in the supernatural. Second, legal procedures can proceed, rationally or irrationally, with respect to formal or substantive law. *Formal* law refers to making decisions on the basis of established rules, regardless of the notion of fairness. *Substantive* law takes the circumstances of individual cases into consideration along with the prevailing notion of justice. These two distinctions create four ideal types, which are seldom, if ever, attained in their pure form in specific societies:

1. *Substantive irrationality*. This exists when a case is decided on some unique religious, ethical, emotional, or political basis instead of by general rules. An example of this would be when a religious judge makes a decision without any recourse to explicit rules or legal principles.
2. *Formal irrationality*. This involves rules based on supernatural forces. It is irrational because no one tries to understand or clarify why it works and formal because strict

adherence to the procedures is required. The Ten Commandments, for example, were enacted in a formally irrational way: Moses, claiming direct revelation, presented the tablets and announced, "This is the Law." Other examples include the use of ordeals and oaths.

3. *Substantive rationality*. This is based on the application of rules from non-legal sources such as religion, ideology, and science. It is rational because rules are derived from specific and accepted sources and substantive because there is a concern for justness of outcomes in individual cases. The efforts of Ayatollah Khomeini in Iran to make decisions on the basis of the Koran would be an example of substantive rationality.

4. *Formal rationality*. This involves the use of consistent, logical rules independent of moral, religious, or other normative criteria that are applied equally to all cases. An example of this is modern Canadian or Western law.

While referring to both formal and substantive rationality, Weber identified three types of administration of justice: (1) *Kahdi* justice, (2) empirical justice, and (3) rational justice. **Kahdi justice** is dispensed by the judge of the Islamic *Shari'a* court. (See Chapter 1; see also Huff and Schlucter, 1999.) It is based on religious precepts and is so lacking in procedural rules as to seem almost completely arbitrary. The Koran contains the revealed word of God, and this bible forms the heart of the Islamic legal system in such countries as Iran and Pakistan. **Empirical justice**, the deciding of cases by referring to analogies and by relying on and interpreting precedents, is more rational than *Kahdi* justice, but notably short of complete rationality. Weber argued that modern law is rational, whereas traditional and primitive laws were irrational, or at least, less rational. Rational justice is based on bureaucratic principles. The rational legal system is basically universalistic; the irrational is particularistic. The rational legal system looks toward contract, not toward status (Parsons, 1964:339). Rationality can be further based on adherence to "eternal characteristics" (observable, concrete features) of the facts of the case. However, Weber (1954:62) perceived that Western law, with its specialized professional roles of judges and lawyers, is unique in that it is also reliant on the "logical analysis of meaning" of abstract legal concepts and rules.

Modern society differs from its past in many ways, which Max Weber summed up in a single concept: the **rational**. Modern society is in pursuit of the rational. Weber contended that the modern law of the West has become increasingly institutionalized through the bureaucratization of the state. He pointed out that the acceptance of the law as a rational science is based on certain fundamental and semi-logical postulates, such as that the law is a "gapless" system of legal principles, and that every concrete judicial decision involves the application of an abstract legal proposition to a concrete situation. There is little doubt that Weber captured, in his idea of rationality, a crucial feature of modern legal systems (Wilson, 2002). It is rather ironic that soon after Max Weber's death in 1920, rational law in Germany was in part replaced by a faith in the intuition of a charismatic leader—Adolf Hitler.

EMILE DURKHEIM (1858–1917)

Durkheim outlined his thesis on law in society in his influential work *The Division of Labour in Society* (1893/1964). While tracing the development of social order through social and economic institutions, Durkheim set forth a theory of legal development by elucidating the idea that law is a measure of the type of solidarity in a society. Durkheim maintained that there are two types of solidarity: mechanical and organic. **Mechanical solidarity** prevails in relatively simple and homogeneous societies where unity is ensured by close interpersonal ties and similarity of habits, ideas, and attitudes. **Organic solidarity** is characteristic of modern societies that are heterogeneous and differentiated by a complex division of labour. The grounds for solidarity are the interdependence of widely different persons and groups performing a variety of functions.

Corresponding to these two forms of solidarity are two types of law: repressive and restitutive. Mechanical solidarity is associated with **repressive and penal law**. In a homogeneous, undifferentiated society, a criminal act offends the *collective conscience* (i.e., the "totality of social likenesses" [Durkheim, 1964:80]) and punishment is meant to protect and preserve social solidarity. Punishment is a mechanical reaction. The wrongdoer is punished as an example to the community that deviance will not be tolerated. There is no concern with the rehabilitation of the offender.

In modern heterogeneous societies, repressive law tends to give way to **restitutive law** with an emphasis on compensation (see, for example, Alexander, 2006; Eriksson, 2009; Hayden and Gough, 2010; Ptacek, 2009; Zernova, 2008). Punishment deals with restitution and reparations for harm done to the victim. Crimes are considered acts that offend others and not the collective conscience of the community. Punishment is evaluated in terms of what is beneficial for the offender and is used for rehabilitation. This general understanding of the goals of punishment now provides the philosophical underpinning of the contemporary restorative justice approach in criminal proceedings (O'Mahoney and Doak, 2017).

Stated concisely, Durkheim's position is that penal law reflects mechanical solidarity. Modern society is bound together by organic solidarity—interdependence and division of labour flowing out of voluntary acts. Society is complex—its parts are highly specialized. People arrange their innumerable, complex relationships through contracts, which are the main concern of modern law. Contracts and contract laws are central to modern society and influence the course of societal development through the regulation of relationships.

Although Durkheim's concern was not with the elaboration of a general framework or methodology for the sociological analysis of law, his interest in law "resulted in the school that formed around him developing a considerable interest in the study of law as a social process" (Hunt, 1978:65). His ideas also contributed to our understanding of the relationship between law and social solidarity and legal evolution (McIntyre, 1994:77).

SOCIOLEGAL THEORISTS

The theorists that will be considered in this section argue that law cannot be understood without regard for the realities of social life. Since the beginning of the 20th century, scholars of jurisprudence and of related disciplines on both sides of the Atlantic have reflected the influence of the social sciences in their analysis of legal development. The more prominent scholars included in our analysis are Albert Venn Dicey, Justice Oliver Wendell Holmes, Jr., and E. Adamson Hoebel.

ALBERT VENN DICEY (1835–1922)

Dicey offered what has become a classic theory on the influence of public opinion on social change. He traced the growth of statutory lawmaking and the legal system in the context of the increasing articulateness and power of public opinion as societies modernized. He noted that the process begins with a new idea that "presents itself to some one man [sic] of originality or genius" (Dicey, 1905:23). He had in mind such individuals as Adam Smith and Charles Darwin. Next, supporters adopt the idea and "preach" it to others. As time passes, "the preachers of truth make an impression, either directly upon the general public or upon some person of eminence, say a leading statesman [sic], who stands in a position to impress ordinary people and thus to win the support of the nation" (p. 23). As a result of these efforts, public opinion begins to change. However, Dicey noted that tides of change are generally gradual and slow rather than abrupt. He also observed that the actions of judges are even more likely than those of legislators to lag behind public opinion. According to Dicey, this lag occurs because judges are guided, in part, "by professional opinions and ways of thinking which are, to a certain extent, independent of and possibly opposed to the general tone of public opinion" (p. 364). Judges, he suggested, were generally persons who were "advanced in life" and had "a conservative disposition" (p. 364).

Dicey is also known for his famous doctrine of the **rule of law**. The doctrine has three aspects: First, no one is punishable except for a distinct breach of law, and therefore the rule of law is not consistent with arbitrary or even wide discretionary authority on the part of the government. Second, the rule of law means total subjection of all classes to the law of the land, as administered by the law courts. Third, individual rights derive from court precedents rather than from constitutional codes. However, from a sociological perspective, Dicey's most crucial contribution to law and society was the recognition of the importance of public opinion in legal development.

OLIVER WENDELL HOLMES, JR. (1841–1935)

Holmes is considered one of the founders of the **legal realism** school (White, 2006). The basic contention of legal realists is that "judges make law rather than find it" (Schur, 1968:43). Judges must always exercise choice when making a decision. They decide which principle will prevail and which party will win. According to the legal realists' position, judges make decisions on the basis of their conceptions of justness before resorting to formal legal precedents. Such precedents can be found or developed to support almost any outcome. The real decisions are based on the judge's notion of justness, conditioned, in part, by values, personal background, predilections, and so forth. They are then rationalized in the written opinion.

Holmes stressed the limits that are set to the use of deductive logic in the solution of legal problems. He postulated that the life of law has been experience and not logic and maintained that only a judge or a lawyer who is acquainted with the historical, social, and economic aspects of the law will be in a position to fulfill his or her functions properly.

Holmes assigned a large role to historical and social forces in the life of law, while de-emphasizing the ethical and ideal elements. He considered law largely as a body of edicts representing the will of dominant interests in society, backed by force. Although he admitted that moral principles are influential in the initial formulation of the rules of law, he was inclined to identify morality with the taste and value preferences of shifting power groups in society. His basic philosophy was that life is essentially a Darwinian struggle for existence and that the goal of social effort is to "build a race" rather than to strive for the attainment of humanitarian ethical objectives.

In "The Path of the Law," Holmes (1897:458) outlined some of his basic propositions and stated that "a legal duty so called is nothing but a prediction that if a man [sic] does or omits certain things he [sic] will be made to suffer in this or that way by judgment of a court." A pragmatic approach to law, he declared, must view the law from the point of view of the "bad man" [sic]. Such a person does not care about the general moral pronouncements and abstract legal doctrines. What is important is simply what the courts are in fact likely to do. Holmes argued that any sense of absolute certainty about the law was bound to be illusory:

> Behind the logical forms lies a judgment as to the relative worth and importance of competing legislative grounds, often an inarticulate and unconscious judgment, it is true, and yet the very root and nerve of the whole proceeding. You can give any conclusion a logical form.
>
> (p. 465)

Lawyers and judges should be aware of this, he wrote, and should "consider the ends which the several rules seek to accomplish, the reasons why those ends are desired, what is given up to gain them, and whether they are worth the price" (p. 476).

E. ADAMSON HOEBEL (1906–1993)
Hoebel and Karl N. Llewellyn collaborated on an analysis of the "law ways" in traditional Cheyenne society. Their emphasis on the "law-jobs" having both a "pure survival" or "bare bones" aspect for the society and a "questing" or "betterment" value (Llewellyn and Hoebel, 1941, ch.3) contributed significantly to the development of a modern functional approach to the legal system. We shall return to this point in the discussion on the functionalist approach later in this chapter.

Hoebel outlined his views on the development of legal systems in *The Law of Primitive Man* (1954). In this book, he noted that "there has been no straight line of development in the growth of law" (p. 288). His description of trends in legal development is based on the assumption that cultures of contemporary traditional societies exhibit characteristics that are similar "to those that presumably prevailed in the early cultures of the infancy" of humankind (p. 290). He considered law and the legal system as properties of a specific community or subgroup of a society and asserted that "[w]ithout the sense of community there can be no law. Without law there cannot be for long a community" (p. 332).

Hoebel began his description of the trend of law with a discussion of the "lower primitive societies"—the hunters and gatherers, such as the Shoshone Indians and the Andaman Islanders. Almost all relations in such a society are face-to-face and intimate. The demands imposed by culture are relatively few. Ridicule is a potent mechanism of social control, and taboo and the fear of supernatural sanctions control a large area of behaviour. Special interests are few, for there is little accumulated wealth. Conflict arises mostly in interpersonal relations. Repetitive abuse of the customs and codes of social relations constitutes a crime, and the offender may be beaten or even killed by the members of the community. Hoebel wrote, "Here we have law in the full connotation of the word—the application, in threat or in fact, of physical coercion by a party having the socially recognized privilege-right of so acting. First the threat—and then, if need be, the act" (p. 300).

Among the more organized hunters, the pastoralists, and the rooter-gardening peoples—such as the Cheyenne, Comanche, Kiowa, and Indians of the northwest coast of North America—the size of the group and the increased complexity of the culture lead to more diverse interests among the members of society. Conflicts of interest grow, and the need arises for legal mechanisms for settlement and control of the internal clash of interests. Private law emerges and spreads, although many of the internal social control problems are handled on a non-legal basis.

In the tribes, a more formalized chieftainship develops, with a tendency toward hereditary succession (p. 309). Although homicide and adultery still represent major difficulties, the development of criminal law remains weak.

"The real elaboration of law begins," Hoebel (1954:316) wrote, "with the expansion of the gardening-based tribes," such as the Samoans and the Ashanti. The gardening activity provides an economic foundation for the support of larger populations that can no longer maintain face-to-face relationships. With the formation of more communities, "[t]he pressures to maintain peaceful equilibrium between the numerous closely interacting communities become intensified. The further growth of law and a more effective law is demanded" (p. 316). The attempt to establish the interest of the society as superior to the interests of kinship groups is the prime mover of law in this type of society. Allocation of rights, duties, privileges, powers, and immunities with regard to land becomes important, and "the law of things begins to rival the law of persons" (p. 316). "Clear-cut crimes" (p. 319) are established in the legal systems of these societies, and action for damages becomes even more frequent than on the preceding level.

For Hoebel, the "trend of law" was one of increasing growth and complexity in which the tendency is to shift the privilege-right of prosecution and imposition of legal sanctions from the individual and kinship group to clearly defined public officials representing the society. Hoebel noted: "Damages have generally replaced death as penalties in civil suits" (p. 329). He maintained that this is how law developed in human societies through the ages, but the laws of particular societies have not followed a single line of development through fixed, predetermined, and universal stages. The development of legal systems in particular societies is characterized by a trend that only in general exhibits the features described here.

CONTEMPORARY LAW AND SOCIETY THEORISTS

Our intention in this section is to describe influential (and possibly controversial) theoretical developments that have taken place since the 1970s. There is, of course, no shortage of other theorists who could have been discussed and will be discussed in various places within this text.

DONALD BLACK

In *The Behaviour of Law*, *Sociological Justice*, and *The Social Structure of Right and Wrong*, Black (1976, 1989, 1998) sets forth a theory of law that aims to explain variations in law from a cross-national perspective, as well as among individuals within societies. As noted in Chapter 1, he considers law as governmental social control, which makes use of legislation, litigation, and adjudication. He distinguishes between behaviour that is controlled by these means and behaviour that is subject to other forms of social control, such as etiquette, custom, and bureaucracy.

Black contends that law is a quantitative variable that can be measured by the frequency by which, in a given social setting, statutes are enacted, regulations are issued, complaints are made, offences are prosecuted, damages are awarded, and punishment is meted out. Consequently, the quantity of law varies from society to society and from one historical period to another in a given society. Different organizations may have more or less law both for themselves and in regards to other groups and organizations.

The direction of law (that is, the differential frequency and success of its application by persons in different social settings) also varies. So does the style of law that, as we mentioned earlier, may be accusatory (with penal or compensatory consequences) or remedial (with therapeutic or conciliatory consequences).

Next, Black develops a number of propositions that explain the quantity, direction, and style of law in regards to five measurable variables of social life: stratification, morphology, culture, organization, and social control. **Stratification** (inequality of wealth) can be measured in such ways as differences in wealth and rates of social mobility. **Morphology** refers to those aspects of social life that can be measured by social differentiation or the degree of interdependence (for example, the extent of division of labour). **Culture** can be measured by the volume, complexity, and diversity of ideas and by the degree of conformity to the mainstream of culture. **Organization** can be measured by the degree to which the administration of collective action in political and economic spheres is centralized. Finally, the amount of non-legal **social control** to which people are subjected is a measure of their respectability, and differences between people indicate normative distance from each other.

On the basis of sociological, historical, and ethnographic data, Black arrives at a number of conclusions. He points out that the quantity of law varies directly with stratification rank, integration, culture, organization, and respectability and inversely with other forms of social control. Thus, stratified societies have more law than simple ones, wealthy people have more law among themselves than poor people, and the amount of law increases with the growth of governmental centralization.

The relationships between the quantity of law and the variables of differentiation, relational distance, and cultural distance are curvilinear. Law is minimal at either extreme of these variables and accumulates in their middle ranges. For example, law relating to contractual economic transaction is limited in simple societies, where everyone engages in the same productive activity, and in the business world, where manufacturers operate in a symbiotic exchange network.

The style of law varies with its direction: In relation to stratification, law has a penal style in its downward direction, a compensatory or a therapeutic style in its upward direction, and a conciliatory style among people of equal rank. In regard to morphology, law tends to be accusatory among strangers and therapeutic or conciliatory among intimates. Less organized people are more vulnerable to penal law and more organized people can count on compensatory law.

These patterns of stylistic variation explain, for example, why an offence is more likely to be punished if the rank of the victim is higher than that of the offender, but is more likely to be dealt with by compensation if their ranks are reversed; why accusatory law replaces remedial law in societies undergoing modernization; why members of subcultures are more vulnerable to law enforcement than conventional citizens; and why organizations usually escape punishment for illegal practices against individuals.

Over the years, Black's theory of law has generated considerable critical debate and analysis (see, for example, Cooney, 2003; Cooney and Phillips, 2002; Wong, 1998). Although empirical testing has yielded scant support for some of its propositions (see, for example, Borg and Parker, 2001; Geiger-Oneto and Phillips, 2003), Black's theory of law has been influential and will likely inspire further testing, criticism, revision, and reformulation.

ROBERTO MANGABEIRA UNGER

In *Law in Modern Society* (1976), Unger revived the sweeping scope of Weber's theorizing on law by placing the development of rational legal systems within a broad historical and comparative framework. Unger located the study of law within the major questions of social theory in general: the conflicts between individual and social interests, between legitimacy and coercion, and between the state and society. His main thesis is that the development of the rule of law, law that is committed to general and autonomous legal norms, could take place only when competing groups struggle for control of the legal system and when there are universal standards that can justify the law of the state.

Unger's analysis emphasizes the historical perspective, and his goal is an understanding of modern law and society. He examines the nature of society and compares rival systems (for example, the Chinese) with the Western tradition and with the range of special types of law—customary or interactional law, regulatory law, and autonomous legal order. Customary or interactional law is "simply any recurring mode of interaction among individuals and groups, together with the more or less explicit acknowledgment by these groups and individuals that such patterns of interaction produce reciprocal expectations of conduct that ought to be satisfied" (Unger, 1976:49). Bureaucratic or regulatory law for Unger "consists of explicit rules established and enforced by an identifiable government" (p. 50). This type of law is not a universal characteristic of social life: "It is limited to situations in which the division between state and society has been established and some standards of conduct have assumed the form of explicit prescriptions, prohibitions, or permissions, addressed to more or less general categories of persons and acts" (p. 51).

Unger calls the third type of law the legal order or legal system, which is both general and autonomous as well as public and positive (p. 52). From an evolutionary perspective, these different types of law turn out to be stages, for they build upon one another—regulatory law upon customary law, the autonomous legal order upon regulatory law.

For Unger, law is indicative of the normative structure of social life. He contends that there are two competing forms of normative integration: consensual and instrumental: "Consensual law expresses the shared values of a group or community and manifests the stable structure in recurring interactions. Regulatory law is instrumental social control by political institutions through positive and public rules" (Eder, 1977:142). Unger considers autonomous law as both instrumental and consensual.

Unger accounts for these different types of law in an evolutionary context. The change of customary law into bureaucratic law is characterized by an extension of instrumental rules that have normative quality (state law, governmental sanctions). This extension of the instrumental rule is dependent upon the recognition of the consensual basis of law. Unger argues that sacred and natural law can provide the cultural context within which instrumental norms can be legitimized. The development of an autonomous legal order brings about a further extension of instrumental rules to everybody. Everyone can pursue his or her personal objectives as long as they do not infringe upon those of others. Laws set these limits. He notes, however, that this situation requires a further legitimization of the principles of law, and consensus must be generated by social contract and by agreement upon the criteria of substantive justice.

Unger (1998, 2004, 2009; 2015; Unger and West, 1998; Lothian and Unger, 2012) is a prolific writer and provides a fresh and unified, albeit somewhat controversial, solution to a number of problems in social theory—the problem of social scientific method, the problem of social order, and the problem of modernity. His theory of law has influenced recent sociolegal theorizing and scholarship and promises to do so for the foreseeable future

CURRENT INTELLECTUAL MOVEMENTS IN LAW

As noted in Chapter 1, sociological discussions of the role of law in society generally take place in the context of two ideal conceptions of society: the consensus and conflict perspectives. The **consensus perspective** is grounded in the functionalist approach, and the **conflict perspective** in the conflict and Marxist approaches to the study of law in society. These are the two prevailing approaches in the sociological literature. Most sociologists opt either for a version of the functionalist approach or for the conflict and Marxist approach to law and the legal system.

Functional analysis examines social phenomena with respect to their consequences for the broader society. Proponents of this approach ask specific questions, such as: What does a kinship system do for society? What does law do for society? What are the "functions" of government, of social classes, or of any social phenomenon? (Turner, 2003:11). In the context of the analysis of law, functionalists are concerned with identifying the characteristics of legal phenomena, as well as with indicating how legal institutions fit into the workings of the overall structure. Theorists embracing conflict and Marxist approaches emphasize the structuring of economic relations that provide, for them, the foundation for various specific studies of legal trends. We shall now consider these two approaches in some detail.

THE FUNCTIONALIST APPROACH

Functionalism derives from the work of early sociologists, most notably Durkheim, and was the most influential sociological theory before the 1960s. Functionalism views society in the same way that biology views the human body. Just as the body consists of limbs, organs, and other bodily parts, so society consists of social institutions and other components. Just as the body's many parts each contribute to the health of the body, so do society's components each contribute to the health of society.

The basic tenets of functionalism are summarized in the following key assumptions (van den Berghe, 1967:294):

1. Societies must be analyzed "holistically as systems of interrelated parts."
2. Cause-and-effect relations are "multiple and reciprocal."
3. Social systems are in a state of "dynamic equilibrium," such that adjustment to forces affecting the system is made with minimal change within the system.
4. Perfect integration is never attained, so that every social system has strains and deviations, but the latter tend to be neutralized through institutionalization.
5. Change is a fundamentally slow adaptive process, rather than a revolutionary shift.
6. Change is the consequence of the adjustment of changes outside the system, growth by differentiation, and internal innovations.
7. The system is integrated through shared values.

In a classic application of functionalism to a legal issue, Emile Durkheim (1895/1962) emphasized that deviance could serve certain social functions in a society. Durkheim insisted that a society needed deviance to continually reaffirm its boundaries of propriety. He pointed out, for example, that without the existence of sinners, a church could not exist. Their very existence provides the opportunity for believers to reaffirm the faith that has been offended by the sinner. Thus, the worst thing that could happen to a church is to completely eliminate sin from the world and completely propagate the faith to society.

Functionalism is also present in legal anthropology. For example, in *The Cheyenne Way*, Llewellyn and Hoebel (1941) outline their law–job theory about society as a whole. For societies to survive, certain basic needs must be met. It is within this context that the wants and desires of individuals, their "divisive urges," assert themselves. The conflicts produced are unavoidable but, at the same time, essential to group survival: "The law–jobs entail such arrangement and adjustment of people's behaviour that the society (or the group) remains a society (or a group) and gets enough energy unleashed and coordinated to keep on functioning as a society (or as a group)" (p. 291). They consider the law–jobs as universal, applicable, and necessary to all groups and to all societies.

Functionalism is also evident in other legal writings. For example, in Jerome Frank's (1930) *Law and the Modern Mind*, the entire discussion of the "basic legal myth" and the associated "legal magic" is grounded in an examination of their functional consequences for the legal system. Similarly, Thurman Arnold's (1935) concern with the role of symbolism within legal institutions is consciously functionalist. Felix Cohen (1959) also resorts to functional analysis in his elaboration of "functional jurisprudence." The writings of Lon Fuller (1969) on law morality, Julius Stone's *Law and the Social Sciences in the Second Half Century* (1966), Philippe Nonet's (1976) ideas on jurisprudential sociology, and Andras Sajo's (2003) study of the functions of governmental corruption in post-Communist transitions all illustrate the functionalist approach to the study of law and society (see also Nuijten and Anders, 2009).

Almost from the beginning, however, the functionalist approach has been challenged. Criticisms of this approach include complaints that the whole notion of function is oversimplified. Questions such as "Functional for whom?" are raised, as the interests and needs of different groups in a society are often in conflict. What may be functional for one group may be dysfunctional for another. Others argue that functional analysis is a static, anti-historical mode of analysis with a bias toward conservatism. Some sociologists even suggest that there is an implicit teleology in functional analysis, in that this mode of analysis inappropriately attributes purposes to social institutions as if they were conscious beings. Scholars continue to advance or refute such charges (see, for example, Turner and Maryanski, 1995; Habermas, 2015; Haas, 2008; Garzone, 2000; Weinrib, 2012).

CONFLICT AND MARXIST APPROACHES

Conflict and Marxist approaches are based on the assumption that social behaviour can best be understood in terms of tension and conflict between groups and individuals (Appelrouth and Edles, 2016; du Bois-Pedain, Ulväng, and Asp, 2017). Proponents of these approaches suggest that society is an arena in which struggles over scarce commodities take place. Closely intertwined with the idea of conflict in society is the Marxian notion of **economic determinism**. Economic organization, especially the ownership of property, determines the organization of the rest of society. The class structure and institutional arrangements, as well as cultural values, beliefs, and religious dogmas, are, ultimately, a reflection of the economic organization of a society.

According to Marx, law and the legal system are designed to regulate and preserve capitalist relations. For the Marxists, law is a method of domination and social control used by the ruling classes. Law protects the interests of those in power and serves to maintain distinctions between the dominated and domineering classes. Consequently, law is seen as a set of rules that arise as a result of the struggle between the ruling class and those who are ruled. The state, which is the organized reflection of the interests of the ruling class, passes laws that serve the interests of this domineering class.

This breakdown of society into two classes—a ruling class that owns the means of production and a subservient class that works for wages—*inevitably* leads to conflict. Once conflict becomes manifest in the form of riots or rebellions, the state, acting in the interest of the ruling class, will develop laws aimed at controlling acts that threaten the interests of the status quo. As capitalism develops and conflict between social classes becomes more frequent, more acts will be defined as criminal.

A notable proponent of this general view, Richard Quinney (1974), maintains that law in capitalist society gives political recognition to powerful social and economic interests. The legal system, he asserts, serves the needs of the ruling class and is a mechanism for the forceful control of the majority in society. In *Critique of the Legal Order*, Quinney (2002:16) argued that as a capitalist society is further threatened, criminal law is increasingly used in the attempt to maintain domestic order. The underclass will continue to be the object of criminal law as the dominant class seeks to perpetuate itself. To remove the oppression, to eliminate the need for further reward, would necessarily mean the end of that class and its capitalist economy.

William Chambliss and Robert Seidman (1982) adopt a similar approach in their analysis of law. While emphasizing conflicting interests in society, they argue that "the state becomes a weapon of a particular class. Law emanates from the state. Law in a society of classes must therefore represent and advance the interests of one class or the other" (1982:72). For them, law is an instrument sought after and employed by powerful interest groups in society. Chambliss (1978:149) further reinforces the notion of law as an instrument of the powerful in society by specifically pointing out that "acts are defined as criminal because it is in the interests of the ruling class to so define them." Austin Turk (1978) also sees law as "a weapon in social conflict," an instrument of social order that serves those who are in power. The control of legal order represents the ability to use the state's coercive authority to protect one's interests. The control of the legal process further means the control of the organization of governmental decisions and the workings of the law, which diverts attention from more deeply rooted problems of power distribution and interest maintenance.

In a classic historical application of the conflict approach, Jerome Hall (1952) traced the growth of property and theft laws to the emergence of commerce and industrialization. With the advent of commerce and trade, a new economic class of traders and industrialists emerged, and the need to protect their business interests grew. As a result, new laws were established to protect the interests and economic well-being of the emergent class. These laws included the creation of embezzlement laws and laws governing stolen property and obtaining goods under false pretense. Hall's analysis supports the views of conflict theorists. According to these theorists, notions of crime have their origins less in general ideas about right or wrong than in perceived threats to groups with the power to protect their interests through law.

Critics have not been kind to this type of argumentation, holding that it involves enormous simplification, reification, and absence of sensitivity to the complexity of social interaction (Downes and Rock, 2003:249). Some concede the validity of conflict and interest-group arguments but, at the same time, contend that bold assertions about the "ruling class" conceal more than they reveal. Surely, lawmaking phenomena are more complex than implied in these statements that hint at a monolithic ruling class that determines legislative behaviour and the creation of rules. Nevertheless, conflict and Marxist views will undoubtedly continue to influence scholarly thinking on law and society.

THE CRITICAL LEGAL STUDIES MOVEMENT

Critical legal studies (CLS, but also referred to as CRITS) is a controversial addition to the ongoing jurisprudential debate on law, legal education, and the role of lawyers in society (Bauman, 2002; Kennedy, 2007; Tushnet, 2008; Unger, 2004, 2015). It is widely considered, by critics and followers alike, to comprise some of the most exciting socio-legal scholarship around.

The movement began with a group of junior faculty members and law students at Yale in the late 1960s. However, the movement has been greatly influenced by Marxist-inspired European theorists, such as Karl Marx, Friedrich Engels, Max Weber, Max Horkheimer, Herbert Marcuse, Antonio Gramsci, Michel Foucault, and Jacques Derrida, and its roots can be traced back to American legal realism (Tomasic, 1985:18). Legal realists in the 1920s and 1930s argued against the 19th-century belief that the rule of law was supreme. They contended that because a good lawyer could argue either side of a given case convincingly, there was actually nothing about the law that made any judicial decision inevitable. Rather, they pointed out, the outcome of a case depended largely, if not entirely, on the predilections of the judge who happened to be deciding it. Thus, far from being a science, the realists argued, law was virtually inseparable from politics, economics, and culture. They rejected the idea that law is above politics and economics.

Proponents of the movement reject the idea that there is anything distinctly legal about legal reasoning. As with any other kind of analysis, legal reasoning, they maintain, cannot operate independent of the personal biases of lawyers or judges, or of the social context in which they are acting (Bankowski and MacLean, 2007). Furthermore, law is so contradictory that it allows the context of a case to determine the outcome. That attribute of law—its inability to cover all situations—is called **indeterminacy** (Tushnet, 2005). Because law consists of a variety of contradictions and inconsistencies, judicial decisions cannot be the self-contained models of reasoning that some scholars claim them to be. Decisions rest on grounds that are outside of formal legal doctrine and are inevitably political.

Critical legal scholars also reject law as being value-free and above political, economic, and social considerations. Laws only *seem* neutral and independent, even those that reflect the dominant values in society. Moreover, laws legitimize those values that predominate in society. Therefore, laws legitimate the status quo. These scholars maintain that law is part of the system of power in society rather than a protection against it.

CLS arguments generated a great deal of criticism, with the movement called Marxist, utopian, hostile to rules, and incoherent. Critical legal scholars have been accused of favouring violence over bargaining, advancing a nihilistic understanding of law, advocating for the inculcation of leftist values in legal education, and teaching cynicism to their students. Nevertheless, CLS views remind us that law may not be as purely logical and unbiased as traditional legal scholarship assumes.

FEMINIST LEGAL THEORY

Feminist legal theory is another intellectual movement of considerable significance and impact. It is concerned with issues that are central to a broader intellectual and political feminist movement: equality in the workplace, reproductive rights, domestic violence, sexual harassment, and sexual assault, to mention just a few (Chamallas, 2012; Levit and Verchick, 2016). It draws from the experiences of women and from critical perspectives developed in other disciplines in analyzing the relationship between law and gender (Greenberg et al., 2008; Heinzelman, 2010). Unlike critical legal studies, which started in elite law schools and were inspired predominantly by notions of contemporary Marxism, feminist legal theories emerged against the backdrop of mass political movements organized around such issues as equality rights, abortion, sexual subordination and exploitation in the profession of law, and the general prevalence of sexism in most walks of life (Chesney-Lind and Pasko, 2004a, 2004b; Leiper, 2006; Sheehy, 2012; Koshan, 2017).

A dominant tendency in feminist legal theories is to regard patriarchy as the source of women's problems (Lorber, 2009; Wing, 2003). Society is viewed as basically patriarchal, organized and dominated by men, and, as a result, not very hospitable to women. Not surprisingly, proponents of the theory consider it one of the most crucial challenges to contemporary law and legal institutions.

There are at least three predominant, although by no means mutually exclusive, themes in feminist legal literature (Moran, 2006). The first deals with women's struggle for equality in a male–dominated legal profession and in broader society. Feminists challenge legal claims of fairness and the impartiality of law in dealing with women (Grana, 2009). The argument is that men directly or indirectly have endeavoured to maintain their own power and to keep women "in their place." For example, in pointing to law's respect for precedent, they have noted how existing precedents tend to support and reinforce a status quo that may be more favourable to male than to female interests. An example of this concern is suggested in Box 2.1: Paid Work and the Costs of Parenting.

The second broad theme of feminist legal scholarship is that the law is androcentric and that this androcentricity is pervasive. The law, according to this theme, is a reflection of a typical male culture, a masculine way of doing things. Law, therefore, is corrupted for women by its inherent masculinity. The task that feminists face is to come up with a completely new law for women. Such law should be devoid of norms and characteristics that reinforce male prerogatives and female powerlessness about gender roles and private intentions. For example, it is argued that the male legal culture dismisses or trivializes many problems that women face, such as sexual harassment and date rape (Horvath and Brown, 2009).

BOX 2.1 LIFE AND LAW: PAID WORK
AND THE COSTS OF PARENTING

In the early 20th century, first-wave feminists seeking to establish women's rights to participation in the public sphere confronted an entrenched "separate spheres" ideology that maintained that woman's role within the family disqualified her from the world of paid work. Much has changed since that time; however, insofar as mothers usually fill the role of primary child-care provider, women who seek to combine paid employment with those responsibilities are compelled to grapple with the tension between parenting and work in a way that men are not.

Consider in this context that until 1983, under the old *Unemployment Insurance Act*, most women were denied the right to claim pregnancy benefits; furthermore, it was only in 1989 that the Supreme Court of Canada ruled that employment discrimination against pregnant women was an instance of discrimination on the basis of sex and, as such, a violation of human-rights protections under Canadian law.

Despite dramatic increases in the employment of women with children in the past few decades, Canada's tax laws have yet to catch up with the changing composition of the Canadian workforce. In 1993, the Supreme Court ruled the cost of childcare did not qualify as a legitimate "business deduction" (i.e., expenditures incurred for the purpose of gaining or producing income from business) as defined under section 18 of the *Income Tax Act of Canada*.

This ruling stemmed from a court challenge by Elizabeth Symes, a self-employed Toronto lawyer, who had hired a nanny to provide in-home care for her two young children on weekdays while she and her spouse purposed their respective careers. The Minister of National Revenue disallowed Symes childcare deductions, maintaining that the nanny's salary was a living or personal expense rather than a business expense. Symes appealed this decision, arguing that the Minister's interpretation of section 18 constituted discrimination on the basis of sex, contrary to the equality guarantee in section 15 of the Charter. The Supreme Court gave short shrift to her argument and ruled against her, with both women members dissenting. The dissenting opinion, delivered by Madam Justice L'Heureux-Dubé, recommended that the tax laws be modified, emphasizing that women's ability to pursue employment often rests on their ability to secure childcare. Macklin (1992:514) concurs, noting that "the courts have . . . permitted men to deduct club fees because men like to conduct business with each other over golf" and to deduct the costs of driving a Rolls Royce "[b]ecause some men believe expensive cars enhance their professional image." As she wryly observes, "[A]s long as business has been the exclusive domain of men, the commercial needs of business have been dictated by what men [think they] need to spend in order to produce income. . . . [O]ne might reasonably demand a reconceptualization of 'business expense' that reflects the changing composition of the business class" (p. 515).

The third dominant theme challenges the very concepts law invokes to support its contention that it is a just and fair institution. Contrary to professed notions, law is not value-neutral, objective, rational, dispassionate, and consistent. This is because law defines those concepts in a typically masculine way, ignoring or devaluing the qualities associated with the experiences of women. Essentially, the problem is that law is claimed to be neutral in relation to the sexes (and other social categories); yet the very way this neutrality is argued is gender-biased. The particular style of maleness can best be illustrated by the concept of "rational person," a mythical legal subject who is coherent, rational, acts on *his* free will, and in ordinary circumstances can be held fully accountable for *his* actions (Bender, 2003; Lahey, 2003; Shaffer, 2003).

Many feminists are pragmatists and rely on feminist legal methods (Jarviluoma et al., 2003; Kleinman, 2007; Ramazanoglu and Holland, 2002) to advance their cause. These methods seek to reveal features of a legal concern that more traditional approaches tend to ignore or suppress. There are three such basic methods (Bartlett, 1991:370).

One method asks the **woman question**, which is designed to probe into the gender implications of a social practice or rule (Lamarche, 2000; Scott, 2003). Asking the woman question compensates for law's failure to take into account experiences and values that are more typical of women than of men. Feminists ask the woman question in many areas of the law. In the case of sexual assault, they have challenged the 1983 legislation that enshrined the defence of "honest but mistaken belief" and asked why this defence dealt with the perspective of the defendant and what he "reasonably" thought the woman wanted, rather than the point of view of the woman and what she "reasonably" thought she conveyed to the defendant (Bonnycastle, 2000). Pursuing the woman question entails continuing to ask why conflict between family and work responsibilities is still often considered a private matter for women to resolve rather than a public concern involving the restructuring of the workplace (Condon, 2000; Johnson, 2000). Essentially, the woman question shows how the predicament of women reflects the organization of society rather than the inherent characteristics of women.

Another method, **feminist practical reasoning**, deals with features not usually reflected in legal doctrine. The underlying assumption is that women approach the reasoning process differently than men, that women are more sensitive to situation and context, and that they tend to resist universal generalizations and principles. Feminist practical reasoning challenges the legitimacy of the norms of those who claim to speak on behalf of the community and seeks to identify perspectives not represented in the dominant monolithic male culture.

A third method, **consciousness-raising**, provides an opportunity to test the validity of legal principles through the personal experiences of those who have been affected by those principles. The idea is to explore common experiences and patterns that come about from shared recollection of life events. It enables feminists to draw insights from their own experiences and those of other women and to use these newly formed insights to challenge dominant versions of social reality. In consciousness-raising sessions, women share their experiences publicly as victims of marital rape, pornography, sexual harassment on the job, or other forms of oppression or exclusion based on sex (Lloyd et al., 2010; Williams, 2004) in an attempt to alter public perception of the meaning to women of practices that the dominant male culture considers acceptable or innocuous.

Critics of feminist legal theory point out that not all men benefit equally from legal sexism: low-income men, Indigenous men, men of colour, and gay and bisexual men have historically not enjoyed the same legal rights and benefits of white middle- and upper-class men (Cante, 2010). It is also noted that while some feminist legal theorists maintain that equality is best realized by treating men and women the same (with accommodation made only for such sex-irreducible differences as pregnancy, lactation, and childbirth), others insist that equality necessitates that the sexes be treated differently (Glasbeek, 2010). Despite such criticisms, however, feminist legal theory is an important intellectual movement that continues to challenge traditional legal doctrine in Canada and elsewhere (Chamallas, 2012; Levit and Verchick, 2016; Gavigan, 2000; Richardson and Seidman, 2002). It has also contributed to the emergence of Indigenous feminist legal theory (Snyder, 2014; see also Dyck and Lux, 2016), queer legal theory (Fineman, Jackson, and Romero, 2009; Valdes, 2016; Marinucci, 2016), and "outsider" legal scholarship (Matamanadzo, Valdes, and Velez-Martinez 2016a, 2016b).

CRITICAL RACE THEORY

Critical race theory (CRT) is another highly significant movement in law with hundreds of law review articles and dozens of books directly or indirectly devoted to it (Browne-Marshall, 2013; Delgado and Stefancic, 2012).

Like feminist legal theory, CRT is concerned with questions of discrimination, oppression, difference, equality, and the lack of diversity in the legal profession. Although its intellectual origins go back much further, the inception and formal organization of the movement can be traced to a 1989 workshop on CRT in Madison, Wisconsin (Delgado and Stefancic, 2012). Many of the proponents have been previously involved with critical legal studies or feminist jurisprudence, and the 1989 conference effectively ratified critical race theory as an important component of legal theory. The CRT movement attempts to rectify the wrongs of racism while acknowledging that racism is an inherent part of modern society. Racism is embedded in the legal and political systems, and proponents recognize that its elimination is impossible. However, they insist that an ongoing struggle to countervail racism must be carried out.

In a way, the word *critical* in "critical race theory" reflects continuity between critical legal studies (CLS) and critical race studies. Both seek to explore the ways in which law and legal education and the practices of legal institutions work to support and maintain a system of oppressive and inequitable relations. But much more than CLS, CRT highlights the urgency of racial problems and an uncompromising search for real solutions to these problems. The basic premise is that Indigenous peoples and racialized minorities are oppressed and that oppression creates fundamental disadvantages for those who are so treated. Because of oppression, racialized minorities perceive the world differently than those who have not had such experience. CRT scholars bring to legal analyses perspectives that were previously excluded. Through narratives and "story telling," some scholars share their experiences or the experiences of other racialized minorities to make their presence felt in legal scholarship. For example, Crenshaw (1998) has argued that the experiences of visible minority women cannot be presumed to be interchangeable with the experiences of visible minority males or non-visible minority females. The term "**intersectionalism**" is employed to "capture some of the unique dimensions and circumstances of being both a woman and a person of colour" (Friedrichs, 2006:108).

Critical race theorists extend traditional civil rights scholarship to locate problems beyond the surface of doctrine to the deep structure of law and culture (Fleury-Steiner and Nielsen, 2006). CRT views racism not only as a matter of individual prejudice and everyday practice, but also as a phenomenon that is deeply embedded in language and perception. Racism is a ubiquitous and inescapable feature of modern society, and despite official rhetoric to the contrary, race is always present, even in the most neutral and innocent terms. Concepts such as "justice," "truth," and "reason" are open to questions that reveal their complicity with power. This extraordinary pervasiveness of unconscious racism is often ignored by the legal system.

As with all other intellectual developments, CRT has its detractors. Its critics emphasize that as a matter of formal law, persons of colour are no longer barred from professional jobs and insist that evolving laws and social norms have opened the door for employment and other social and economic opportunities. How wide this door has opened is, of course, the subject of debate. Another criticism is that CRT articulates its conception of race as a social construction at the macro level, focusing primarily on legal and socio-political processes, and has neglected the micro, interpersonal ways in which racial oppression is produced. Yet another criticism is that CRT is essentially a reformist project, not really new and distinguishable from traditional civil rights scholarship on the law. These criticisms notwithstanding, CRT has had a highly significant impact on the field of law and understandings of law and society.

LAW AND LITERATURE/RHETORIC

In recent decades, "law and literature" has emerged as both "a significant movement in American jurisprudence" and a "growing part of the law school curriculum" (Scallen, 1995:705). By the early 1990s, 84 of North America's 199 law schools offered some variation of a law and literature course (Luyster, 1997). The law and literature/rhetoric movement has continued to flourish in the new millennium, inspiring communities of scholars not only in Canada and the United States but also in Italy, France, the U.K., Scandinavia, Germany, Turkey, the Netherlands, Australia, and China (Weisberg, 2005; Richards, 2016; Simonsen and Tamm, 2017; Gürbilek, 2015).

However, the "law and literature" label is, in itself, at least somewhat misleading, for it seems to invite the assumption that scholars within this field are engaged upon a singular quest. Instead, perhaps the most notable features of this movement are its rich intellectual diversity and its avowedly interdisciplinary nature, attracting scholars not only in the field of law but also in literary criticism and poetics, in linguistics and communication studies, in sociolinguistic and cultural history, in critical theory, and in cultural, race, and gender studies (Ost, 2006; Peters, 2005; Cormack, Nussbaum, and Strier, 2013; Sharp and Leiboff, 2016; Carpi and Leiboff, 2016).

Scallen (1995:705) identifies three "schools" within law and literature studies:

(1) the "law in literature school," which emphasizes legal themes and characters within works of fiction and employs these fictionalized accounts as prisms to scrutinize legal

proceedings; (2) the "legal literary/rhetorical criticism school," which employs the methods and theories of literary and rhetorical criticism to study various types of actual legal discourse (e.g., constitutional provisions, judicial opinions); and (3) a hybrid of these two schools, the "legal storytelling school," which makes "extensive use of personal narratives as evidence in legal scholarship."

The **law in literature school** is the oldest of these three, with legal scholars exploring the implications of law as it is depicted in literary classics. This endeavour, which is often traced back to Dean John Wigmore's (1913) compilation of lists of fictional works featuring lawyers or law-related themes, was revitalized by the publication of White's (1973) *The Legal Imagination*, which commends the use of great works of literature as a source of insight into the nature of crime and judging; the paradoxes of equity; and the relationship between customs, norms, law, power, and the political order. It has been argued that the critical analysis of literary works allows lawyers to "liberate themselves from the narrow-mindedness that comes from specializing in law . . . sensitize themselves to the timeless moral and ethical issues that stories of law and justice raise . . . [and] gain a critical perspective on what it means to be a lawyer or a nonlawyer engaged with the law" (Scallen, 1995:706; see also Posner, 2005).

The more recently developed **legal literary/rhetorical criticism school** derives, in part, from the same claims and concerns that spawned the critical legal studies movement (which, as earlier noted, argues that legal doctrine and arguments often attempt to shore up existent and unjust power structures). Scallen (1995:707) observes that if the CLS critique "seems to say that law has no inherent logic, that its meanings are limited only by the skill or audacity of its interpreters," some scholars have found it appealing to turn toward literary and rhetorical theory and to the interpretive strategies of critical social theory (e.g., post-structuralism, deconstructionism, intentionalism, neopragmatism, and cultural studies) "in an attempt to find some limits to the process of interpretation and some justification for the study of it." This agenda has broadened the field of inquiry as legal scholars have "begun to accept the idea that law could be viewed as the cultural and literary discourse of a group of people who have adopted a particular form of communication for doing what they do when they 'do law'" (Minda, 1997:246; see also Milovanovic, 2003; Mundy, 2002).

The most recent of the three schools, **legal storytelling**, employs narratives as an essential part of a scholarly argument; these personal stories are not viewed as digressions or as illustrations of a point but, instead, as evidence for the argument that is being advanced.

Like each of the movements discussed earlier, the law and literature movement has its critics. A fundamental criticism is that this movement lacks a clear definition of its subject matter, its constituency, and its goals. Rather than a unified body of knowledge and an agreed-upon set of procedures for resolving analytic difficulties, the law and literature enterprise seems to have only a tenuous unity. Scallen (1995:713) notes that a further criticism of the movement is that "its proponents are unclear as to the scope of their project—to what degree are they attempting to be theoretical, to state 'overarching inductive generalities?' [Morawetz, 1993:501]." Domnarski (2003:109) charges that "critical theorists seem invariably to have taken up ideologically-based (pluralist, feminist, radical) approaches that use literature to set the real world straight by reforming, deconstructing, or excoriating the texts which they associate with hegemony. . . . Much of this ideological critique may turn out to be of little relevance to students as they take up the practice of law."

Proponents of the law and literature movement within law schools have also been charged with ignoring the works of minority writers. As Resnick (1990:221) observed, "The question is that of the canon: what (and who) is given voice; who privileged, repeated, and invoked; who silenced, ignored, submerged, and marginalized. Law and literature have shared traditions—of silencing, of pushing certain stories to the margin and of privileging others" (see also Desai, Smith, and Nair, 2003).

Finally, it should be emphasized that the use of narratives and storytelling as evidence is not confined to scholars of one specific "class" in one delimited "school" within the law and literature movement. As noted, both critical race theory and feminist legal theory champion analyses that raise the "voices" of previously ignored (or "silenced") groups of women and men.

SUMMARY

- In a historical context, legal development, industrialization, urbanization, and modernization are closely intertwined. Legal development is conditioned by a series of integrative demands, stemming from society's economic, political, educational, and religious institutions.
- What distinguishes the traditional, transitional, and modern legal systems from each other is the comparative degree of differentiation between basic legal elements. Accompanying the emergence of laws, court systems, police forces, and legislation is a trend toward increasing size, complexity, differentiation, and bureaucratization.
- Efforts at explaining the interplay between law and society should be seen in the context of the intellectual, political, and social climates of the particular theorists. In each historical epoch, every interpretation of social reality posits certain questions and provides certain answers.
- Sociologists embracing the functionalist approach attempt to account for law in society within the overall framework of the theory that society consists of interrelated parts that work together for the purpose of maintaining internal balance. Sociologists advocating conflict and Marxist approaches to the study of law in society consider conflict inevitable and ubiquitous in societies as a result of inescapable competition for scarce resources.
- Proponents of the critical legal studies movement maintain that law is riddled with contradiction and prejudice and that it is heavily in favour of the wealthy and powerful. Feminist legal theorists challenge the impartiality of law in dealing with women and argue that law is androcentric and reflective of male culture. Critical race theorists argue that the root causes of racial inequality still persist in our society, embedded in law, language, perception, and structural conditions. The law and literature movement positions the language of law and its narratives as focal concerns.

CRITICAL THINKING QUESTIONS

1. The legal definition of "homicide" varies across time and space. Examine the forms of culpable homicide contained in the Canadian Criminal Code. What is included? What is excluded? In what ways does the Code's definition of criminal homicide reflect a general consensus of the Canadian population? In what ways may it suggest elitist control over the relatively powerless?
2. Reflect upon a literary work that you have read with a law-related theme (e.g., George Orwell's *1984* or *Animal Farm*; Fyodor Dostoyevsky's *The Brothers Karamazov*; Margaret Atwood's *The Handmaid's Tale*; Toni Morrison's *The Bluest Eye*, *Beloved*, or *Tar Baby*). How did it present the relationship between law, norms, and power? Did reading this work encourage you to challenge customs, norms, and/or laws that you had previously accepted in an uncritical way?
3. Since the 1970s, legal reforms have sought to make family law gender neutral, with the assumption that equality is best assured by treating women and men the same. What are the strengths and weaknesses of adopting a gender-neutral approach?
4. Compare and contrast how those who subscribe to the functionalist approach and conflict/Marxist approaches would account for the passage of Canada's *Charter of Rights and Freedoms* in 1982.
5. Can increasing Canadians' awareness and knowledge of Indigenous laws assist in the creation of a more harmonious society?

ADDITIONAL RESOURCES

1. The Canadian Women's Information Centre at http://womencan.ca furnishes ready access to an array of invaluable information on a wide variety of topics.
2. The Canadian Research Institute for the Advancement of Women (CRIAW) is a research organization that offers assistance to groups seeking to advance the goals of social justice and equality. Visit its website at http://criaw-icref.ca.
3. The website http://divisiononcriticalcriminology.com is hosted by the American Society of Criminology, Division of Critical Criminology. A variety of links on the site provide easy access to a host of articles on critical legal theory and its role in legal education.
4. Listen to civil rights advocate and pioneering critical race theorist Kimberlé Crenshaw discuss intersectionality and its import at www.ted.com/talks/kimberle_crenshaw_the_urgency_of_intersectionality/transcript?language=en.

3

CHAPTER 3
THE ORGANIZATION OF LAW

Nowadays, in one way or another, law touches all of us. The contact may be pleasant or unpleasant, tangible or intangible, direct or indirect, but it is nonetheless a constant force in our lives. For a sociological understanding of law in society, we need to know about the social organization of law, the types of social arrangements and relations involved in the legal process, and the social characteristics of people who interpret and administer the law. This chapter examines the social organization of legal systems in the context of the judicial, legislative, administrative, and enforcement agencies that carry out the official (and at times unofficial) business of law.

Figure 3.1 The Supreme Court of Canada is our country's highest court of law.
Credit: Shutterstock

LEARNING OBJECTIVES

After reading this chapter, you should be able to:

1. Distinguish between "private," "public-initiated," and "public defendant" disputes.

2. Describe the structure of Canada's court system.

3. Identify four groups of participants in court processes and discuss their roles.

4. Describe the flow of litigation in civil and criminal cases

5. Discuss the conflict management and integrative functions of legislatures.

6. Appreciate the unique status of Aboriginal peoples within Canadian law.

7. Explain the roles of legislators and lobbyists in the legislative process.

8. Describe the organization of law enforcement agencies, identify three styles of police work, and discuss why police discretion can be problematic.

COURTS

One of the most important functions of courts is to process disputes (see, for example, Mays and Gregware, 2009). By definition, a **dispute** is a conflict of claims or rights—an assertion of right, claim, or demand on one side met by contrary claims on the other. When courts hear disputes, they attempt to decide (adjudicate) between or among those who have some disagreement, misunderstanding, or competing claims. Such disputes may arise between individuals, between organizations (private or governmental), or between an individual and an organization. When a judge renders the official judgment of the trial court in a civil or a criminal case, the process is called **adjudication**.

Unlike legislative and administrative bodies, courts do not place issues on their own agendas (Abadinsky, 2008; Dixon, Kupchik, and Savelsberg, 2007). Judges generally do not decide proactively to make rulings about what constitutes adultery in same-sex marriages or on the extent of freedom of expression on the Internet or on any other issue. Rather, courts are passive; they must wait until matters are brought to them for resolution. The passivity of courts places the burden on citizens or organizations to recognize and define their own needs and problems and to determine which require legal judgments. As Black (1973:138) notes, this method of acquiring cases "assumes that each individual will voluntarily and rationally pursue his [sic] own interests." The courts are indifferent to those issues or disputes that individuals or organizations fail to notice or wish to ignore. This reactive nature of courts ensures that they consider disputes only after the injuries have taken place or the problems have developed.

In theory, courts differ from other kinds of dispute-regulation methods in that they are available to all members of society. In principle, everyone who has a dispute for which there is legal redress ought to be able to use the courts (Connolly, 2010). Unlike dispute-settlement methods that are available only to specific groups in society (for example, university grievance committees or religious tribunals), courts are truly public. As judges make their decisions, they are expected to be impartial, with their decisions governed by legal principles not by personal preferences or by political pragmatism.

DISPUTE CATEGORIES

To understand what courts do, it is necessary to examine the kinds of disputes they process. Goldman and Sarat (1989:4) outline three categories of disputes that provide the courts' bulk of work.

The first is called the **private dispute**. This kind of dispute is characterized by the absence of any initial participation by public authorities. For example, when spouses quarrel or two business people debate the terms of a contract, these events are likely to give rise to private disputes. Although they may occur in public places and may involve competing interpretations of law, they remain private as long as the government is not a party. Since these disputes arise more or less spontaneously in the course of normal social life, they are usually processed and managed without government intervention. For example, spouses may seek marriage counselling and business people may arrive at a compromise through negotiation. At times, however, non-legal intervention is insufficient for the disputing parties. The courts may be asked to settle disputes in a large variety of civil cases where parties seek legal redress in private interests, such as for breach of contract.

The second category of disputes is called the **public-initiated dispute**. It occurs when the government seeks to enforce norms of conduct or to punish individuals who breach such norms. An illustration of a public-initiated dispute is the ordinary criminal case in which the state, or some official acting on its behalf, seeks to use the courts to determine whether a particular breach of law has occurred and whether sanctions should be applied. Public-initiated dispute is unique because it always involves and is governed by the law of the entire community. In the case of a criminal law violation, dispute processing occurs in a public forum, for no society could allow the development of private mechanisms for the enforcement of breaches of public norms, since that could easily lead to anarchy. It should be noted, however, that not all public-initiated disputes are resolved or processed by means of judicial action. A variety of informal mechanisms—ranging from the warnings that a police officer may give to a traffic violator, to the prosecutor's choice not to go ahead with a criminal case, to the practice of plea bargaining—may be used to deal with breaches of public norms (Fisher, 2003; Forester, 2009). Furthermore, disputes involving the breach of public norms are, at times, not called to the attention of public authorities. For instance, the husband who beats his wife has committed a violation of public norms, but until a complaint is lodged with law enforcement agencies, their dispute remains private.

The third kind of dispute is the **public defendant dispute**. In this type, the government participates as a defendant. Such disputes involve challenges to the authority of some government agency or questions about the propriety of some government action that may be initiated by an individual or by an organization. In such cases, the courts are called upon to review the action of other branches of government. These disputes involve claims that the government has not abided by its own rules or followed procedures that it has prescribed. In illustration, one may look to two landmark cases that advanced the rights of the differently-abled in Canada. In *Eldridge v. British Columbia (Attorney General)* (1997), the Supreme Court ruled that the British Columbia government's refusal to provide sign language interpreters for medical patients who were hearing-impaired violated Charter guarantees of equality of treatment. In *Moore v. British Columbia (Education)* (2012), the Supreme Court ruled that "adequate special education . . . is not a dispensable luxury" and that the purpose of British Columbia's *School Act* "is to ensure that 'all learners . . . develop their individual potential and . . . acquire the knowledge, skills and attitudes needed to contribute to a healthy, democratic and pluralistic society and a prosperous and sustainable economy'" (at 5).

These three types of dispute—private, public-initiated, and public defendant—represent, for the most part, the workload of Canadian courts. It should be noted that, contrary to widespread beliefs, courts, in general, process rather than solve disputes. A court decision is seldom the last word in a dispute. Let us now consider the structure of courts where decisions are rendered.

THE ORGANIZATION OF COURTS

Since Canada is a federal state, legislative powers are divided between two levels of government: federal and provincial. Under the *Constitution Act, 1867*, the provinces were granted the power to create and maintain provincial courts that would deal with matters that fell within their jurisdiction. In addition, the Act gave federal Parliament the authority to establish "a general court of appeal for Canada" as well as "any additional courts for the better administration of the laws of Canada." As a result, Canada's court system is complex; it is composed of a range of courts that have varying jurisdictions, and "questions of jurisdiction can be difficult to sort out, especially since courts that share the same functions may go by different names" (Department of Justice, 2011:1).

Canada's courts can be distinguished into four basic levels. In ascending order, these levels are: (1) provincial/territorial courts; (2) provincial/territorial superior courts and the Federal Court; (3) provincial/territorial courts of appeal and the Federal Court of Appeal; and (4) the Supreme Court of Canada, which is the highest court in Canada and the final court of appeal from all other Canadian courts.

PROVINCIAL/TERRITORIAL COURTS

Provincial/Territorial Courts only hear provincial matters, i.e., those matters defined and outlined in s.92 of the *Constitution Act, 1867* that the provinces are given authority to regulate. Every Canadian province and territory, with the notable exception of Nunavut, has a provincial/territorial court; in Nunavut, cases that would ordinarily be heard in a provincial/territorial court are heard by the Nunavut Court of Justice, a court that "combines the power of the superior trial court and the territorial court so that the same judge can hear all cases that arise in the territory" (Department of Justice, 2011:7).

The role of provincial/territorial courts is the same across the country, even though the names and divisions of these courts may vary:

> Provincial/territorial courts deal with most criminal offences, family law matters (except divorce), young persons in conflict with the law (from 12 to 17 years old), traffic violations,

provincial/territorial regulatory offences, and claims involving money, up to a certain amount (set by the jurisdiction in question). Private disputes involving limited sums of money may also be dealt with at this level in Small Courts. In addition, all preliminary enquiries—hearings to determine whether there is enough evidence to justify a full trial in serious criminal cases—take place before the provincial/territorial courts.

(Department of Justice, 2011:2–3)

A number of courts at the provincial/territorial level are devoted entirely to particular types of offences or offenders. For example, the **Drug Treatment Court** (DTC) program attempts to address the needs of non-violent individuals who are charged with criminal offences that were motivated by their addictions (see Chapter 5). In some provinces and territories (e.g., Manitoba, Alberta, Ontario, the Yukon), **Domestic Violence Courts** have been established in an attempt to "improve the response of the justice system to incidents of spousal abuse by decreasing court processing time; increasing conviction rates; providing a focal point for programs and services for victims and offenders; and, in some cases, allowing for the specialization of police, Crown prosecutors, and the judiciary in domestic violence matters" (Department of Justice, 2011:3). **Youth Courts** address cases in which young persons, aged 12 to 17, are charged with offences under federal youth justice laws. In some jurisdictions, there are also specialized courts for those accused/offenders who identify as Aboriginal. These courts are known by various names including **First Nations Courts (FNC)**; Aboriginal Courts; Gladue Courts; Healing Courts, and Peacekeeping Courts. Their name may also refer to a specific Nation (e.g., the Tsuu T'ina Peacemakers Court in Alberta; the Cree Court in Saskatchewan; the Cknúcwentn First Nations Court in Kamloops, B.C; the Teslin Tlingit Council Peacemaker Court in the Yukon). Unlike other provincial courts, the focus of these courts is upon healing. Towards this end they draw upon "diverse Indigenous problem solving and therapeutic jurisprudence approaches, including Elders and spirituality, to focus attention on Indigenous healing plans for individuals, families, communities, and nations" (Johnson, 2014:11).

PROVINCIAL/TERRITORIAL SUPERIOR COURTS

Every Canadian province and territory has a superior court. The superior court is a court of original jurisdiction; this means that cases are heard by this court first before they are heard by any other court. In other words, the superior court is a court of first instance. The superior court is called by different names in different provinces. In Ontario, the superior court is called the Superior Court of Justice. In other provinces, the superior court may be known as the Court of Queen's Bench, the High Court of Justice, or the Supreme Court Trial Division. This list of names is not exhaustive. The superior courts have inherent jurisdiction, i.e., the jurisdiction to hear all civil and criminal cases and any matter before it (unless a statute specifically says otherwise). The superior court can hear matters listed in either s.91 or s.92 of the *Constitution Act, 1867*; its power to hear these matters is only limited by statute. In most provinces and territories, the superior court has special divisions (e.g., the family division). While superior courts are administered by the provinces and territories, superior court judges are appointed and paid by the federal government.

APPELLATE COURTS

Appellate courts are provincial institutions that hear appeals of a decision of the provincial superior court and are variously referred to as the Court of Appeal, the Supreme Court Appeal Division, or the Appellate Division. "The justices in a provincial court of appeal . . . do not in most instances rehear witnesses, testimonies or accept evidence" (Yates, Yates, and Bain, 2000:99). Rather, they examine the written transcripts of a trial and listen to legal arguments that are presented by lawyers representing the parties involved in the dispute. In addition, courts of appeal also hear constitutional questions "that may be raised in appeals involving individuals, governments, or governmental agencies" (Department of Justice, 2011:4).

THE FEDERAL COURTS

The Federal Court of Canada consists of a trial division and a court of appeal. "The Federal Court and Federal Court of Appeal are essentially superior courts with civil jurisdiction. However, since the Courts were created by an Act of Parliament, they can only deal with matters specified in federal statutes (laws)" (Department of Justice, 2011:4). The jurisdiction of these Courts includes interprovincial and federal-provincial disputes, intellectual property proceedings (e.g., patents, trademarks, copyright), *Competition Act* cases, citizenship appeals, and cases involving Crown corporations or departments of the Government of Canada. Only Federal Courts "have jurisdiction to review decisions, orders and other administrative actions of federal boards, commissions, and tribunals; these bodies may refer any question of law, jurisdiction or practice to one of the Courts at any stage of a proceeding" (Department of Justice, 2011:5).

SPECIALIZED FEDERAL COURTS

In an attempt to deal more effectively with certain areas of law, the federal government has created specialized courts. These include the Tax Court of Canada and courts that serve the Military Justice System. In 1983, the Tax Court of Canada was created to address disputes arising from the assessment of federal taxes. This court, which is independent of the Canada Revenue Agency and all other government departments, hears disputes between taxpayers and the federal government after a taxpayer has exhausted all of the other options for appeal under the *Income Tax Act*. Canada's *National Defence Act* provides for the establishment of military courts to hear cases involving the Code of Service Discipline—"a system of disciplinary offences designed to further the good order and proper functioning of the Canadian Forces"—and "applies to all members of the Canadian Forces as well as civilians who accompany the Canadian Forces on active service" (Department of Justice, 2011:6). The role of the Court Martial Appeal Court is to hear appeals from military courts. The function of this court is similar to that of a provincial/territorial appeal court and its powers are the same as those of a superior court.

THE SUPREME COURT OF CANADA

Created by federal statute in 1875, the Supreme Court of Canada is the country's highest court of law. Originally, decisions of the Supreme Court could be appealed to the Judicial Committee of the Privy Council in the British House of Lords. However, these types of appeals were abolished in 1933 for criminal cases and in 1949 for civil cases. As a result, the Supreme Court of Canada now acts as the court of last resort. "It is the final authority on the interpretation of the entire body of Canadian law, whatever its source" (Hogg, 1997:217). It has jurisdiction over disputes in all areas of the law (e.g., constitutional law, administrative law, criminal law, civil law) and is the final court of appeal from all other Canadian courts. However, "[b]efore a case can reach the Supreme Court of Canada, it must have used up all available appeals at other levels of court. Even then, the Court must grant permission or 'leave' to appeal before it will hear the case" (Department of Justice, 2011:7). "Leave to appeal" is not routinely granted; rather, it occurs only when a case "involves a question of public importance; if it raises an important issue of law or mixed law and fact; or if the matter is, for any other reason, significant enough to be considered by the country's Supreme Court" (Department of Justice, 2011:7). "Most applications for leave are rejected" (McCormick, 2006:2). Of the roughly 500 applications submitted annually between 2005–2015, merely 10–13 percent were successful in any of these years (Supreme Court of Canada, 2016; see also Moghtaderi and Du Vent, 2013). In some cases, however, the right to appeal to the Supreme Court is automatic. For example, a person who has been acquitted at trial but found guilty by a court of appeal automatically has the right to appeal to the Supreme Court. Moreover, "no leave is required in criminal cases where a judge on the panel of a court of appeal has dissented on how the law should be interpreted" (Department of Justice, 2011:7).

The Supreme Court of Canada is additionally empowered to rule on the legality of bills submitted by the government and to declare the law on questions referred to it by the federal cabinet: "The government may ask the Court to consider questions on any important matter of law or fact, especially concerning interpretation of the Constitution. It may also be asked questions on the interpretation of federal or provincial/territorial legislation or the powers of Parliament or the legislatures" (Department of Justice, 2011:7). Between 1892 and 2005, there were 76 federal references. For example, in the *Constitutional Patriation Reference* (1981), the Supreme Court ruled that the federal government could patriate the constitution without the consent of the provinces even though it would violate a political tradition if it did so without securing "a substantial degree" of provincial consent. In the *Quebec Secession Reference* (1998), the Supreme Court unanimously ruled that while a unilateral declaration of independence by a province (i.e., Quebec) would be illegal according to the Canadian Constitution and international law, Quebec had the right in principle to negotiate a separation agreement and that a constitutional amendment would make secession possible. The court also said that if a clear majority of Quebeckers voted for secession in a referendum, the rest of Canada would be obliged to negotiate the terms of independence and that these negotiations would have to respect democracy, federalism, the rule of law, and the protection of minorities. In *Reference re Same-Sex Marriage* (2004) the Supreme Court held that passage of the *Civil Marriage Act* was within the legislative purview of Parliament and that the meaning of "marriage" was not frozen to what the term meant in 1867 but could evolve in step with Canada's pluralistic society (McKay-Panos,2014). In *Reference re Senate Reform* (2014) the Supreme Court of Canada considered the constitutional validity of proposals to change the Senate. It held that changes in relation to term limits and consultative elections could not be accomplished by the Federal Government alone through Parliament; rather, they required the consent of seven provinces representing more than 50% of the population." It also ruled that the abolishment of the Senate requires the unanimous consent of the Senate, House of Commons and legislative assemblies of all ten provinces. In *Reference re Supreme Court Act, ss. 5 and 6*, (2014) the Supreme Court of Canada examined the constitutional status of the Supreme Court as well as the eligibility of members of the Quebec courts and the Quebec Bar to be appointed to the seats on the Supreme Court that are reserved for Quebec. It concluded that the Court has been constitutionally entrenched by the *Constitution Act*,

1982, and that changes to its composition require the unanimous consent of Parliament and the provincial legislatures. It also held that only current members of Quebec's superior courts or the Bar of Quebec who possess a minimum of ten years' standing can be appointed to the three Quebec seats on the Supreme Court.

The role of the Supreme Court in particular and the role of Canadian courts in general have been expanded by the *Constitution Act, 1982* and its *Canadian Charter of Rights and Freedoms*. Although Canadian courts have long possessed the power to declare laws or actions of government to be invalid, this power was fairly narrow prior to 1982. The only basis for striking down legislation was if the government that introduced it had exceeded its legislative authority under the *Constitution Act, 1867* (the *BNA Act, 1867*). That is, the federal government was not allowed to legislate on matters that fell under provincial jurisdiction (e.g., property and civil rights, administration of justice, education, health and welfare, municipal institutions, and matters of a local or private nature), and the provincial governments were not permitted to legislate on matters that fell under federal jurisdiction (e.g., criminal law, employment insurance, postal service, regulation of trade, external relations, money and banking, transportation, citizenship, Indian affairs, and defence). However, provided that the legislation was not *ultra vires* (Latin for "beyond, or in excess of, the power" [that passed it]) and did not encroach on the legislative authority of the other, it was valid.

The powers of the courts expanded when the *Constitution Act* became law in 1982. The requirement that federal Parliament and the provincial legislatures must now comply with constitutional provisions, including the *Canadian Charter of Rights and Freedoms*, made the Supreme Court, and the judges who compose it, the supreme guardians of our constitutionally defined rights. As Sauvageau, Schneiderman, and Taras (2006:8) pointedly remark, "The adoption of the *Charter of Rights and Freedoms* in 1982 transformed Canadian political life. It placed the Supreme Court at the nexus of societal power and change. Judges had to give life to the Charter, and in doing so it can be argued that they redefined and reordered much of the Canadian social contract." Legislation or government actions that infringe or deny any of the fundamental rights and freedoms recognized by the *Canadian Charter of Rights and Freedoms* may be struck down by the courts, and the Supreme Court has the final say on the matter.

The Supreme Court, which is composed of eight puisne justices and one Chief Justice, hears cases in panels of three, five, or seven members or as an entire body. It is a "lawyers' court: lawyers typically appear before it to argue points of law, but the parties to a dispute do not appear" (Boyd, 1998:141). Although a decision of the Supreme Court of Canada "is binding on all courts within Canada at every level. . . [when it] hears a case requiring its interpretation of a provincial statute, its decision will only be applicable to those provinces having similar statutory provisions in place" (Yates, Yates, and Bain, 2000:28). In addition, a ruling of the Supreme Court that concerns the application of the civil law in Quebec will not apply outside of that province.

Sauvageau, Schneiderman, and Taras (2006:16) observe that the Supreme Court "has dominated the Canadian political landscape" in terms of both credibility and prestige.

Nevertheless, they note that surveys have found that approval for the Court's performance has fallen since the onset of the new millennium. Moreover, they acknowledge that the Supreme Court has been the target of significant criticism. For example, they observe that "[g]overnments and nationalists within Quebec have traditionally viewed the court as a leaning Tower of Pisa that always leans in the same direction, a centralist one"; for western populists, the Supreme Court has long been thought to symbolize "the entrenched power of the East" (2006:24). Nevertheless, "most Canadians have, until recently at least, seen the Supreme Court as an essential and welcome part of our governance system, keeping the legislative branch in check and reigning in the extraordinarily powerful executive branch" (Slayton, 2015:16).

PARTICIPANTS IN COURT PROCESSES

Courts, as dispute-processing institutions, are composed of four distinct groups of participants: litigants, lawyers, judges, and juries. These participants bring to the judicial process diverse interests, values, and perspectives that influence the ways in which disputes are processed.

LITIGANTS

Since the principal function of courts is to process disputes, the most obvious participants must be the disputants. This group includes individuals, organizations, and government officials who are trying to settle disagreements and to regulate their own behaviour and the behaviour of others. Clearly, not all individuals, groups, or organizations can or are willing to resort to courts in their attempts to settle disputes. Questions of cost, efficiency, availability, the fulfillment of the legal requirements of a suit, and the nature of the dispute affect differently the potential users of courts. Consequently, two distinct types of litigants emerge.

Galanter (1974) designates the two types of litigants as "one-shotters" and "repeat players." These two types are distinguished by the relative frequency with which they resort to court services. As will be discussed further in Chapter 6, those who use the courts only occasionally are called **one-shotters**. Examples of one-shotters include an author suing her or his publisher for breach of contract, and a professor filing charges against a university for racial discrimination in promotion. **Repeat players** engage in many similar litigations over a period of time. Whereas one-shotters are usually individuals, repeat players are organizations, such as finance companies, moving companies, or insurance companies. Their investment and interest in a particular case is moderately small. Because of their high frequency of participation in litigation, repeat players are more concerned with the ways a decision may affect the disposition of similar cases in the future than with the outcome of a single case (Ross, 1980). Repeat players can also invest greater resources in litigation than one-shotters, and their frequent appearances in court enable them to develop expertise. Such expertise is reflected in the way in which they select cases for litigation and in the manner in which they carry on disputes that have been transformed into lawsuits. By contrast, participants who have only a one-time interest in litigation are generally more concerned with the substantive result of their case than the way in which the outcome may affect other cases.

Research suggests that repeat performers (generally organizations) using the courts for the routine processing of clients have the highest success rates and do better as both plaintiffs and defendants than one-shotters (generally individuals) (Relis, 2002). Refining these categories and applying them to the courts of appeal, McCormick's "party capability" theory suggests that senior levels of government (federal and provincial) fare better than their municipal counterparts, "and that the Crown will do better still because it acts against isolated individuals in a clearly defined legal background that maximizes returns to experience and organization" (McCormick, 1994:156). Moreover, he suggests that compared to "small" businesses, "big business" (e.g., banks, insurance companies, and major corporations such as CPR, Hydro-Québec, or the Irving business empire in the Maritimes) enjoys greater success and that individuals are least successful.

In his research, which considered the performance of various categories of litigants on the basis of a sample of provincial appeal court decisions (including all reported decisions for the second and seventh year of every decade since 1920), McCormick found confirmation of his hypothesis:

> The government category was the most successful as both appellant and respondent; appeals by governments succeeded well over 50 percent of the time. The rank ordering within the government category (Crown, federal/provincial, municipal) was also as expected. Business as a whole was slightly less successful, with a combined success rate of just over 50 percent. However, the spread between "big business" and "other business" is surprisingly large, so much so that big business litigants rank above the federal/provincial government category and second only to the Crown. Unions and individuals bring up the rear, with combined success rates well below 50 percent.
>
> (1994:158)

With regard to the surprisingly poor performance of trade unions, McCormick suggests that while these large organizations are "repeat players" that have "considerable resources and access to first-rate legal advice," they are most effective when they appear as respondents (successfully defending the trial court decisions more than half of the time) rather than as appellants. McCormick also notes that the courts are more likely to take the side of capital in its clashes with labour (1994:159).

In addition, McCormick analyzed the 3,993 decisions of the Supreme Court of Canada that were reported in either the *Supreme Court Reports* or the *Dominion Law Reports*. Here, too, the general category of government was most successful as both appellant and respondent, and unions and individuals had success rates well below 50 percent. He concludes: "The general message remains the same, during as before the age of the Charter" (1994:165) (see also McCormick, 2006).

LAWYERS

Law is a technical game and the players are highly trained in its complex rules and elusive categories (Hutchinson, 2005). Without the assistance of lawyers, most individuals would be unable to activate the courts on their own behalf. Disputants generally need to retain the services of lawyers to receive advice about legal rules and how those rules apply to specific issues in dispute. By being familiar with both court operations and legal rules, lawyers are instrumental in determining whether a particular dispute warrants judicial intervention. Lawyers, in effect, play the role of gatekeepers for the judiciary (Hughes, 1995:109).

Lawyers are repeat players in the adjudication process. Casper (1972) distinguished among types of trial lawyers by the manner in which they perceive their clientele. He argued that a small number of lawyers view themselves principally as representatives of public interests. These lawyers are concerned, for example, with consumer interests or with the protection of the environment. For them, individual cases are simply vehicles for achieving broad public objectives that generally necessitate major changes in the law. They prefer to take only cases they believe involve significant issues. The second type of lawyer represents particular interests or organizations. For example, some companies have in-house lawyers whose principal role is to represent members of the organization.

The third type of lawyer, typically criminal defence lawyers, is most often involved in actual court work. These lawyers are legal specialists who most closely approximate the public's preconception of lawyers. Although the role of defence lawyers is most often couched in the general term of "defending a client," they perform a number of specific roles. These include the roles of advocate, intermediary, and counsellor (Cohn, 1976:261). In the primary role of *advocate*, defence lawyers take all possible steps within legal and ethical bounds to achieve a victory for the client while protecting the rights of the client at each step of the criminal justice process. Often, this can best be accomplished by acting as an *intermediary* between the client and the law, working through negotiation and compromise to secure the best possible benefits from the system. The third role is that of *counsellor*. It is the responsibility of defence lawyers to give advice to the client as to what to expect and what appears to be in the client's best interest.

The fourth type of trial lawyer perceives a lawyer's role primarily as serving individuals who retain him or her. These lawyers are often referred to as "hired guns" (Blumberg, 1979:238). They are interested only in the case in which they are involved, and they will do everything within legal and ethical limits to ensure favourable outcomes for their clients. In their view, they serve a case, not a cause.

JUDGES

Although a variety of officials work around courtrooms, none has the prestige of the judge, who is responsible for the administration of the court and its reputation for honesty and impartiality. The courtroom is designed so that attention is focused on the judge, who sits on a pedestal above everyone else. Any visitor to a courtroom will notice that the level of the visitors' gallery never rises above that of the judge, and that those who work in the courtroom are not allowed to sit or stand at the judge's level. When the judge enters the courtroom, everyone rises, and all attention is directed at the judge, who is addressed as "Your Honour." The judge alone interprets the rules that govern the proceeding, although this power may be shared with a jury of laypersons, and the judges see themselves as autonomous decision makers whom nobody bosses around (Jacob, 1997; Spohn, 2009). Moreover, while one may speak disparagingly of our Prime Minister or criticize our elected representatives with relative impunity, showing disrespect toward a judge (or engaging in any act "which is calculated to embarrass, hinder or obstruct a court in the administration of justice, or which is calculated to lessen its authority or its dignity" [Judicial System Glossary, 2012]) may result in an individual being charged with "contempt of court." These offences, which are punishable summarily, are also referred to as "criminal contempts" (Neufeld, 2013; Duhaime, 2012).

While Canadian judges enjoy high occupational prestige, salaries (see Chapter 8), and job security, their freedom is limited by virtue of their role. Specifically:

> A judge must avoid anything that creates a conflict of interest. He or she must give up directorships or other management positions in corporations and business ventures. A judge must also be very careful when speaking on public matters that he or she may later be required to adjudicate. If charged with traffic or other minor offences, a judge is expected not to contest the charge, in order to avoid embarrassing colleagues by having to appear before them.
>
> (Yates, Yates, and Bain, 2000:113)

Nevertheless, while in theory judges may be removed from office if they breach the requirements of good behaviour, in practice they would appear to be relatively immune from sanctioning. Under the *Judges Act*, the process to assess alleged breaches of conduct by federally appointed judges falls to the Canadian Judicial Council (CJC), established in 1971 by an Act of Parliament. One of the four responsibilities of the CJC is to investigate complaints about the conduct of federally appointed judges (the others include making recommendations, generally in conjunction with the Canadian Superior Courts Judges Association, on judicial salaries and benefits, continuing education of judges, and developing consensus among Council members on issues involving the administration of justice). On receipt of a complaint that a judge has breached the requirements of good behaviour, the CJC must decide whether the judge has become "incapacitated or disabled from the due execution of the office of judge" by reason of "age or infirmity; having been guilty of misconduct; having failed in the due execution of office, or having been placed, by conduct or otherwise, in a position incompatible with the due execution of that office" (Canadian Judicial Council, 2002:11). However, since the Council's creation, it has referred only eleven complaints to an Inquiry committee for formal investigation (Canadian Judicial Council, 2017).

Judges come from the middle or upper classes and have a history of party identification, if not activism (Carp, Stidham, and Manning, 2013; McCormick and Greene, 1990:66). As we note in Chapter 8, while virtually all judges in Canada are lawyers, only a small fraction of lawyers are, or ever become, judges (Friedman, 2002). Other than their experience as barristers and solicitors, Canadian judges "are not required to have any formal training on how to be a judge before they are appointed" (Department of Justice, 2012:11). Nevertheless, once appointed, Canadian judges

> have access to a range of programs at both the provincial/territorial and federal levels on all aspects of judging, as well as areas of the law. The National Judicial Institute, in particular, coordinates and delivers educational programs for all federal, provincial, and territorial judges . . . and regularly offers courses for new judges.
>
> (Department of Justice, 2011:12)

In contrast, in civil-law countries such as France and Italy, judges are civil servants and have different training and experience from practising lawyers. Those who aspire to become judges take a competitive examination after law school. The ones who pass will become judges with careers of their own. Previous practice of law is not required. It is also unlikely that they will ever practise law. Their roles and functions are also different from their Canadian counterparts of the adversarial system. Unlike in common-law countries, judges in civil-law countries rely on the inquisitorial method, which has its roots in ecclesiastical courts (Parisi, 2004). In France, for example, the main figures at a trial are the investigating magistrate and the presiding judge. The magistrate is responsible for the investigation and sends investigative materials to the trial's presiding judge, who interrogates the defendant and the witnesses. This interrogation resembles a conversation more than a cross-examination (Loh, 1984:497). In general, judges in civil law countries are much more active than in Canada. They play a greater role in building and deciding a case, they put the evidence together, and they go far beyond the "refereeing" role characteristic of common-law judges.

JURIES

An ancient Welsh king, Morgan of Glamorgan, established trial by jury in A.D. 725, and the origins of the Canadian jury system can be traced back to civil and criminal inquiries conducted under old Anglo-Saxon law in England (Brooks, 2009; Jonakait, 2003; Kleining and Levine, 2005). The original concept of the jury was most likely imported to England after the Norman Conquest. The Normans started the practice of placing a group of local people under oath to tell the truth. Early jurors acted as sources of information on local affairs, and they gradually came to be used as adjudicators in both civil and criminal cases.

Before the 12th century, criminal and civil disputes were resolved by various types of ordeals, For example, in ordeal by water, the accused person was bound by rope and dropped into a body of water. If the person floated, it was a sign of guilt; if he or she sank, it was a sign of innocence. There was also ordeal by fire, in which the accused carried heated stones or iron—if the subsequent burn did not get infected in three days, the accused was declared innocent—and ordeal of the morsel that did or did not choke the accused. Civil disputes were often resolved by oaths on the assumption that a false oath would expose someone to the judgment of God.

Juries are used predominantly in common-law countries (Hans, 2006). However, while the British invented the jury system, they have been steadily dismantling it for decades (Gunnell, 2000). There are no juries in British civil cases, except those involving libel or police misconduct (Beggs and Davies, 2009). Around 93 percent of criminal cases are heard before panels of three lay magistrates. There is no *voir dire* (a trial within a trial to decide upon the admissibility of evidence), and cross-examination of juries and criminal cases do not require unanimous verdicts. In the United States, where the Constitution provides the right to a jury trial for both criminal and civil cases (Hemmens et al., 2017), juries are essential to the operation of American courts. According to Richard Posner (1995), the American commitment to the jury system reflects the legacy of American distrust of officials, which has its roots in colonial times, and to a lesser extent to the political power of trial lawyers. It is estimated that 80 percent of all jury trials worldwide take place in the United States (Barkan and Bryjak, 2011; Terrill, 2015).

The jury system came to Canadian shores with the British settlers in the mid-1700s and, in current times, juries are used in criminal trials and, less frequently, in civil trials. According to the *Canadian Charter of Rights and Freedoms*, a person accused of criminal activity "has the right, except in the case of an offence under military law tried before a military tribunal, to the benefit of trial by jury where the maximum punishment for the offence is imprisonment for five years or a more severe punishment." In consequence, criminal cases involving summary and minor indictable offences are tried without a jury. Although cases involving such serious offences as murder, treason, hijacking, intimidating Parliament or a legislature, or bribery by the holder of a judicial office require trial by jury in a superior court, this statutory requirement may be waived with the consent of the accused and the attorney general. An accused may also opt for a jury trial in cases involving many less serious indictable offences. In relation to civil proceedings that are governed by provincial statutes, cases such as libel, slander, malicious arrest or prosecution, and false imprisonment require a jury unless both sides agree to dispense with the services of a jury. In other cases, especially those that are highly complicated and very technical, the use of juries is very rare. For example, while civil jury trials are more common in Ontario than some of the other English-speaking provinces (Vidmar and Schuller, 2001:129), the right to a jury trial in that province is a "substantial" but not absolute right. Ontario prohibits the use of juries in certain types of claims (e.g., claims for injunctive relief; the partition of real property; foreclosure of a mortgage; specific performance; declaratory judgment; claims against municipalities) and "even when the claims at issue are permitted to be tried to a jury, courts have broad discretion to strike the jury and proceed with a bench trial" (McMillan, 2011b:8). In deciding whether or not to strike the jury, the court will generally consider "whether 'justice will be better served' by proceeding with or without a jury" and, provided its decision is neither arbitrary nor capricious, it will not be second-guessed by an appellate court (McMillan, 2011b:8). In Quebec, the right to a jury trial has been abolished in civil matters, with the reasoning that a jury may fail to properly review and weigh the evidence before making a determination.

The selection and constitution of juries falls under provincial jurisdiction in Canada and, in consequence, qualifications vary somewhat. Until the 1950s, most provinces did not permit women to be jurors. Since 1972, however, the Criminal Code has stated that "no person may be disqualified, exempted or excused from serving as a . . . juror in criminal proceedings on the grounds of his or her sex." In addition, all provinces now allow women to serve as jurors for civil trials. In general, all Canadian citizens who are between 18 and 65 (or 69) years of age, who have not been convicted of an indictable offence (or have received a pardon for an indictable offence) and who are free from any mental or physical disability that might impede their performance as a juror, are considered qualified to serve on a jury. Certain occupational groups are exempted from serving as jurors. These groups include members of the Privy Council, provincial cabinets, the Senate, the House of Commons, and provincial legislatures, as well as lawyers, law students, judges, law enforcement officers and officers of a court of justice, doctors, coroners, dentists, veterinarians, armed forces personnel, superintendents and wardens of correctional facilities, and some essential service providers (e.g., firefighters, nurses, persons required in the running of transportation or communication services). Lists of jurors are prepared each year from various sources such as voter registration lists and provincial lists of Medicare beneficiaries. The selection of names, often done by computer, must be random.

In criminal cases the jury is composed of 12 persons. The verdict of the jury in criminal cases in Canada must be unanimous. If the jury seems unable to reach agreement after a reasonable amount of time, the judge may set the case for retrial or call for a new jury to replace a "deadlocked" or "hung jury." In civil cases, fewer jurors are required and unanimity is not required. In general, agreement by five of the typically six jurors who compose the jury in a civil case will suffice.

Dispute processing in trial courts involves two basic types of issues: issues of law and issues of fact. **Issues of law** emerge as participants in the dispute seek to identify and interpret norms that will legitimize their behaviour. In a sense, a trial is a contest of interpretation and legal reasoning (Bankowski and MacLean, 2007). The judge has the authority to determine which interpretations of law are proper and acceptable, but a trial is more than a question of legal reasoning. It also provides the opportunity for a reconstruction, description, and interpretation of events (that is, **issues of fact**). The purpose of a trial is to answer the question of who did what to whom and whether such conduct is legal. Juries are called "triers of fact," and the function of the jury is to listen to and decide among competing and conflicting interpretations of events. The jury acts as a referee in an adversary contest dealing with the presentation of differing versions of the same event. By a crude division of labour, the jury is the authority on facts; the judge is the authority on law. But judges can also control the jury in some ways. For instance, judges can exclude prejudicial evidence from a jury's consideration. They can also instruct the jury in the law and discharge a juror who cannot continue to serve due to illness or another reason (Umphrey, 2009). In addition, criminal juries in Canada do not participate in the sentencing of those who have been judged guilty; sentencing is strictly the duty of the judge.

JURY SELECTION
In the United States, jury selection has become one of the most important functions of a trial lawyer (Hemmens et al., 2017). Indeed, some American lawyers now contend that by the time the jury has been chosen, the case has been decided (Davies and Emshwiller, 2006). During the process of jury selection called the *voir dire* (literally, "to see, to tell"), prospective jurors in the United States are questioned first by the judge then by the lawyers representing the defence and the prosecution. This questioning has a threefold purpose. First, it is used to obtain information to assist in the selection of jurors and to ferret out any juror bias. Second, it enables the lawyers to develop rapport with potential jury members. Finally, there is an attempt by both sides to try to change the attitudes, values, and perspectives of jurors (Klein, 1984:154). If a juror admits to a racial, religious, political, or other bias that would influence his or her decision, the lawyers whose client would be harmed can ask the judge to excuse the juror for cause.

The hypothesis that the composition of the jury is crucial for a trial's outcome is reflected in the process of jury selection. Lawyers may employ various strategies that they perceive will maximize their side's chances for success (Hoffman, 2004). In the past, these strategies were informed by a combination of folklore and intuition. However, since the 1970s, American lawyers have increasingly drawn on the expertise of social scientists a and relied on "scientific jury selection" (Lieberman and Krauss, 2010a, 2010b). **Scientific jury selection** consists of three steps. First, a random sample is drawn from the population, and the demographic profile of this sample is compared with that of the prospective jurors. If the jurors were randomly selected, the profiles should match. If there is substantial over- or underrepresentation of particular characteristics (ethnic groups, age, occupation, and so forth), the jury pool can be challenged. Second, after it is established that the prospective jurors represent the population at large, the demographic, personal, and attitudinal characteristics considered to be favourable to one's own side are then assessed to determine the ideal juror for one's side. Third, after establishing the psychological and demographic profile of this ideal juror, the social scientist can make recommendations for selection of individual jurors.

There are serious reservations about the appropriateness of the use of scientific jury selection. Noting that it is clearly designed to achieve juror partiality, critics contend that it undermines the purpose of having an adversarial system of justice (Lieberman and Krauss, 2010a, 2010b). Moreover, because scientific jury selection is very expensive, it is an advantage only to rich defendants in criminal cases and the richer side in civil suits. The ability of the adversary system to guarantee a fair and impartial jury and trial is obviously tested when the adversaries possess unequal resources (Vidmar and Hans, 2007).

In stark contrast to the selection process in the United States, intensive questioning that places the juror on trial is contrary to both Canadian law and tradition. Only limited questioning of prospective jurors is allowed for in Canada, and, in the vast majority of cases, jurors are selected without any questioning whatsoever (Vandor, 2001:16). However, although the only information readily available to Canadian lawyers about a potential juror is the juror's name, address, occupation, and whatever their physical appearance and general demeanour are thought to convey, three types of challenges can be used to eliminate prospective jurors. First, the jury list can be challenged if it can be shown that the list was fraudulent or partial or that there was wilful misconduct in selecting prospective jurors. For example, in *R. v. Nepoose* (1991) the jury was successfully challenged because it had too few women. In *R. v. Born with A Tooth* (1993), the Crown successfully challenged the jury panel selection procedure after a list of 200 persons who were selected at random from the city of Calgary was supplemented with the names of 52 Aboriginal persons living on three nearby reserves who were not randomly selected.

The second type of challenge, a **challenge for cause,** can be made on the grounds that, for example, a prospective juror fails to meet the requirements of the provincial statute that governs juries (e.g., the person's occupation places him or her within an exempted category). On occasion, the challenge for cause procedure is used to screen potential jurors whose impartiality has been tainted by mass media coverage of a case or exposed to the rumours and gossip that may circulate in a small community about a crime. A challenge for cause may lead to a potential juror being asked, for example, if he or she has heard about the case or has any preconceived notions about the proper outcome of the case and so on. So long as a judge rules that a challenge for cause is valid, there are no limits placed on how many of these challenges can be made.

The third type of challenge, a **peremptory challenge**, allows either the defence or the Crown prosecutor to eliminate a prospective juror without giving a specific reason. The number of such challenges is limited by the nature of the offence. For example, for charges of high treason or first degree murder, a maximum of 20 challenges are allotted to each side; in cases where the maximum sentence upon conviction would be less than five years, a maximum of four peremptory challenges are allowed. In using these challenges, lawyers rely on their private judgments about which jurors are likely to be unsympathetic to their side and eliminate those who worry them most. Decisions to exclude or include a juror may be based on a variety of considerations: gut reactions to the juror's looks and manner, advice passed down by other lawyers, and various maxims or rules of thumb (Wrightsman et al., 1998:371).

Various concerns have been expressed in relation to the involvement of jurors in dispute processing in courts (Prentice and Koehler, 2003; Leigh-Bell, 2016). The first is whether the presumption that juries are capable of assessing the facts presented to them in an impartial way is, indeed, valid. In *R. v. Sherratt* (1991), the Supreme Court of Canada observed that the "perceived importance of the jury and the Charter right to jury trial is meaningless without some guarantee that it will perform its duties impartially and represent, as far as possible and appropriate in the circumstances, the larger community." In *R. v. Williams* (1998), the Supreme Court explicitly acknowledged that four types of bias could potentially have an impact upon jurors:

> **Interest prejudice** arises when jurors may have a direct stake in the trial due to their relationship to the defendant, the victim, witnesses or outcome. **Specific prejudice** involves attitudes and beliefs about the particular case that may render the juror incapable of deciding guilt or innocence with an impartial mind. These attitudes and beliefs may arise from personal knowledge of the case, publicity through mass media, or public discussion and rumour in the community. **Generic prejudice** . . . . arises from stereotypical attitudes about the defendant, victims, witnesses or the nature of the crime itself. Bias against a racial or ethnic group or against persons charged with sex abuse are examples of generic prejudice. Finally, **conformity prejudice** arises when the case is of significant interest to the community causing a juror to perceive that there is strong community feeling about a case coupled with an expectation as to the outcome (at 10)

An additional concern about juries was addressed in the 2013 Report of the Independent Review conducted by The Honourable Frank Iacobucci: the years-long under-representation of First Nations peoples on juries (Iacobucci, 2013). "[T]he fact is," he wrote, "many First Nations people are plainly reluctant to participate in the jury system." This reticence, he observed, was due to many factors, but included:

> (1) "the conflict that exists between First Nations' cultural values, laws, and ideologies regarding traditional approaches to conflict resolution, and the values and laws that underpin the Canadian justice system";

> (2) the "systemic discrimination that First Nations people have experienced within the justice system in relation to criminal justice or child welfare" and the "negative perspectives and . . . inter-generational mistrust of the criminal justice system" that these experiences have fostered;

> (3) a "lack of knowledge and awareness" among First Nations peoples of the justice system in general and the jury system in particular;

(4) a desire by First Nations leaders "to assume more control of community justice matters as an element of what they strongly believe is their inherent right to self-government";

(5) negative perceptions of the criminal justice system the "limited and under-resourced" local police services;

(6) a "concern for the protection of the privacy rights of their citizens with respect to the unauthorized disclosure of personal information for the purposes of compiling the jury roll";

(7) the content of the jury questionnaire, which (i) threatens that failure to respond within a five day period will result in the imposition of a fine or imprisonment (a threat which is viewed as coercive), (ii) demands that one declare oneself a Canadian citizen (and does not provide the individual with the option of declaring First Nations citizenship or membership), (iii) requires the use of English or French; and

(8) practical barriers (e.g., prohibitive transportation costs; inadequate allowances for accommodation and meals; the exclusion of child and elder care as eligible costs; a lack of income supplements).

Moreover, Iacobucci observed that "the existence of criminal records and lack of knowledge and access to pardon procedures serves to exclude many potential First Nations jurors."

Concerns have also been expressed about the ability of jurors to comprehend the judge's instructions, so that they do not make up their mind about the results of the case before the evidence is presented (Burnett and Badzinski, 2000; Somer, Horowitz and Bourgeois, 2001). In addition, some query the competence of jurors in civil cases. For example, some observers argue that many disputes are so complex that an average person is incapable of understanding either the nature of the dispute or the complicated issues involved (see, for example, Zeni, 2016). However, research finds that juries generally do grasp the facts and that actual incompetence is a rare phenomenon (Greene and Johns, 2001; Horowitz and Bordens, 2002). Moreover, in *Cyr v. Anderson* (2014), the Nova Scotia Court of Appeal concluded that it was patronizing to presume that juries are less competent than judges. "While justice may require some cases to be heard by a judge rather than a jury," Justice David Farrar wrote, "there is a paternalistic aspect to some cases that suggest that juries are less capable than judges" (at 92). In addressing the thorny question of when a case is too complex for a jury, Justice Farrar reached ten conclusions. Among these were that "factual complexity" on its own will "rarely be sufficient to strike a jury" and that "cases calling for medical, scientific or other specialized knowledge on the factual issues with conflicting and contradictory opinions from experts should not, save in the rarest of cases, be taken from a jury." He also concluded that "[t]he fact that judicial instruction on the law may be difficult is not itself a ground for striking a jury" (at 96).

Despite their shortcomings, juries play an essential and symbolically significant role within our system of law:

> The jury . . . serves as the conscience of the community because it is drawn precisely from the community in which the crime was committed. In addition, because the jurors can apply their own sense of fairness in reaching a verdict, never having to justify that decision, it can serve as a guardian against oppressive or rigid laws.
>
> (Vidmar and Schuller, 2001:130)

On occasion, the decision of a jury may transmit a powerful message from the community to the government. For example, after four separate jury trials in the 1970s and 1980s failed to convict Dr. Henry Morgentaler for providing abortions in a non-accredited or approved hospital—even though his actions were in clear violation of the Criminal Code—the government was moved to amend the laws governing access to abortion (Schuller and Yarmey, 2001:159).

THE FLOW OF LITIGATION

Several characteristics of the flow of litigation are significant. The processes by which cases are decided differ widely according to the type of dispute, the participants involved, and the stage of the judicial process at which the dispute is settled. In many instances, civil and criminal cases are quite different, and we shall review them separately.

CRIMINAL CASES

A high degree of discretion is characteristic of every phase of criminal procedure. For example, to issue a search warrant to investigating officers, a justice of the peace must be satisfied that the officers have reasonable and probable grounds to search for evidence. A police officer also uses discretion in deciding whether or not to arrest a suspected lawbreaker. Once an arrest is made, a justice of the peace or judge must decide whether to release the accused prior to trial and whether conditions such as a surety (i.e., the deposit of money) should be imposed on the accused in addition to his or her promise to appear for trial. With hybrid offences, the Crown counsel decides whether to treat the offence as a summary conviction offence or to proceed by indictment. At a preliminary inquiry, a judge must decide whether there is sufficient evidence to proceed to trial or if the accused should be discharged. At trial, the judge or jury must decide whether the Crown has proven its case "beyond a reasonable doubt." At sentencing, a judge may request that a probation officer prepare a pre-sentence report or receive a statement about the impact of the crime on the victim(s). The judge must also consider the goals of sentencing, bearing in mind that the Criminal Code requires that "all available sanctions other than imprisonment that are reasonable in the circumstances should be considered for all offenders." At each stage in the criminal justice process, it is possible that the "wheels of justice" may turn in unexpected directions because of the use of discretion by agents of the criminal justice system.

Despite the impression fostered by film and television representations of the criminal justice process, not all criminal defendants wind up exercising their right to a fair public hearing in court. "In fact, the vast majority of cases never go to trial; rather they are resolved by way of a guilty plea to the charges laid or a guilty plea to a lesser offence" following "resolution discussions" or plea negotiations between Crown and defence counsel (Public Prosecution Service of Canada, 2014: 2). **Plea bargaining,** a form of negotiation that can be traced back to the earliest days of common law (Nasheri, 1998), "involves an agreement between the accused and the prosecutor, wherein the accused pleads guilty in exchange for the prosecutor agreeing to take a particular course of action" (Maxwell, 2015). Subtypes of plea-bargaining include: "(1) *Charge bargaining*, which involves promises concerning the nature of the charges to be laid; (2) *Sentence bargaining*, which involves promises relating to the ultimate sentence that may be meted out by the court; and (3) *Fact bargaining*, which involves promises concerning the facts that the Crown may bring to the attention of the trial judge" (Verdun-Jones and Tijerino, 2002:3). However, plea-bargaining is subject to limitations. For example, while joint submissions on sentence "help to resolve the vast majority of criminal cases in Canada" and "contribute to a fair and efficient criminal justice system" (*R. v. Nixon*, 2011 at 47), they are not sacrosanct and trial judges may depart from their contents. In addition, various appellate courts have ruled that the Crown is divisible. In other words, an agreement made by a prosecutor in a lower court does not bar the Crown from changing its position on appeal as long as it can demonstrate that it has a good reason for doing so.

Prior to trial, a defendant's lawyer may ask his or her client if the client wishes to plea bargain. In doing so, the lawyer may believe that the evidence against the client is very compelling and suggest that the client would be better off pleading guilty to a lesser charge with the expectation of receiving a lighter sentence. If the client agrees, the accused person, through his or her counsel, enters into negotiation with a Crown prosecutor. In *R. v. Burlingham* (1994), the Supreme Court of Canada ruled that the Crown or police could not enter into a plea bargain without the participation of a defence counsel, unless the accused specifically waived that right. This decision extended and reinforced the right, guaranteed in the *Canadian Charter of Rights and Freedoms*, of an accused to retain and instruct counsel without delay.

Although plea bargaining generally takes place before the actual trial, it may also take place during the trial if unanticipated evidence is introduced that significantly increases the perception of the Crown prosecutor that s/he will not secure a conviction or causes the defence counsel to feel that the client's chances of acquittal are slim. Simply put, plea bargaining functions to increase certainty. Both the Crown and the defence are aware that the Criminal Code provides judges, for most crimes, with wide discretion in sentencing a convicted offender. In consequence, the Crown may perceive that a plea bargain simplifies the process of obtaining a conviction against the accused and guarantees that the person will be penalized in some way—albeit to a lesser degree than if the person were convicted at trial for a more serious charge. A negotiated guilty plea also saves the court time and costs, especially in lengthy and complicated proceedings (Piccinato, 2009). Thus, in describing plea agreements as "vitally important to the well-being of our criminal justice system," the Supreme Court noted in *R. v. Anthony—Cook* (2016) that without these negotiated agreements "our justice system would be brought to its knees, and eventually collapse under its own weight" (at 25 and 40). Plea bargains also spare victims and witnesses "the emotional cost of a trial" and may provide victims with some comfort inasmuch as a guilty plea "indicates an accused's acknowledgement of responsibility and may amount to an expression of remorse" (*R. v. Edgar*, 2010 at 111).

Nevertheless, there are many objections to plea-bargaining. Among the most common: that criminals are allowed to obtain "cheap" convictions (i.e., ones in which they do not pay for the real crimes they committed); that plea bargaining moves criminal justice into an administrative process rather than an adversarial one; and that this process generates cynicism about criminal justice among the accused, the system's participants, and the public at large. As noted by the Auditor General's 2002 report on the criminal justice system, the practice of plea bargaining has "the potential to undermine the integrity of the criminal justice system, in part because disclosure of the basis for agreements and accountability for the decisions have been inadequate" (Auditor General, 2002:5).

There is also a concern that the process of plea-bargaining may increase the likelihood of wrongful convictions. Thus, Michael Spratt (2017) maintains that due to the "massive power imbalance between the state and the accused," an innocent accused who is indigent may succumb to the "perverse incentives that many prosecutors can unwittingly leverage to extract guilty pleas." While admissions of guilt must be fully voluntary and "no arm twisting" is allowed, Spratt insists that "all actors in the justice system turn a blind eye to all the subtle arm twisting that takes place" and make "many" guilty pleas other than "truly voluntary." In illustration, he conjures a situation in which a homeless individual is charged with shoplifting and, while warehoused in jail and unable to make bail, confronts two options: Plead guilty (despite his innocence) and "walk out of jail today" or, alternatively, plead not guilty and remain incarcerated for three months while awaiting trial. Moreover, he emphasizes that those who face far more serious charges than shoplifting may confront equally vexatious choices. He reminds his readers of *R. v. Brant* (2011), a case in which the court heard why a nineteen-year-old man, Richard Brant, plead guilty to aggravated assault following the death of his nine-week-old son. Although the infant's death had originally been attributed to pneumonia and respiratory failure, this finding was countered by a "world-renowned expert" on child forensic pathology (the now-disgraced pathologist, Dr. Charles Smith) who concluded the child had likely died from shaken baby syndrome. As a result, Brant was charged with manslaughter and the Crown informed him that it would seek a lengthy penitentiary sentence if he was found guilty at trial. However, it also offered up an alternative: plead guilty to a reduced charge (aggravated assault) and receive a six-month jail sentence. "With Brant's word against Smith's, facing a lengthy prison term if convicted of manslaughter and having just found out his girlfriend was pregnant, Brant pleaded guilty in 1995 to the lesser charge and served six months in jail" (CBC, 2011). Fifteen years later, the Ontario Court of Appeal would order Brant's acquittal, set aside his conviction, and the Crown would concede that the case had been a miscarriage of justice.

The final step in most criminal proceedings is sentencing the defendants who have been found guilty. Although sentencing decisions are made within a specific legal framework,

Canadian judges, along with their counterparts in other common law countries, are afforded a considerable degree of discretion in terms of the sentences they impose (Roberts, 2001:194).

In 1996, Parliament passed Bill C–41 and enacted a law codifying a set of sentencing principles that are to act as a guide for judges and reduce disparities in sentencing. According to the statement of purpose and principle contained in section 718 of the Code, "A sentence must be proportionate to the gravity of the offence and the degree of responsibility of the offender." This section identifies various objectives that are to be considered by a judge in sentencing:

(A) **Denunciation**: the attempt to censure an individual for culpable criminal conduct. The court imposes a sentence to denounce the crime of which the offender has been convicted.
(B) **Specific deterrence**: the attempt to prevent crime by arousing fear of punishment in the individual being sentenced. Individual offenders are inhibited from further offending by fear of what will happen to them if they are re-convicted.
(C) **General deterrence**: the attempt to prevent crime by creating fear of punishment among the general public. Potential offenders are said to be deterred by being made aware of the punishments imposed on criminal offenders.
(D) **Incapacitation**: the prevention of crime by the incapacitation of the individual offender for a specific period of time. This usually means incarceration.
(E) **Rehabilitation**: the attempt to change an individual by promoting law-abiding behaviour. This usually involves sentencing the offender to some alternative to custody, such as probation with conditions.
(F) **Reparation**: the court may order the offender to make reparations to individual victims or the community.
(G) Promote a sense of responsibility in offenders. (Roberts, 2001:190)

The options available to Canadian judges in sentencing include imprisonment, which may be continuous, intermittent (e.g., served on weekends), or indeterminate (e.g., as is the case for those identified as Dangerous Offenders); suspended sentence with probation; probation; the imposition of a fine; conditional and absolute discharge; restitutions; and various specific prohibitions (such as prohibiting the individual from being in possession of a handgun). In an attempt to reduce the use of incarceration as a sanction, the 1996 sentencing reforms created a variety of elements including a disposition called a "conditional sentence," which allows an offender to serve his or her sentence in the community provided that the individual complies with the conditions imposed. If the individual fails to abide by the conditions, he or she may be sent to prison. Not all individuals are eligible for this type of sentence. In applying this sentence the court must feel confident that "serving the sentence in the community would not endanger the safety of the community," and the sentence originally imposed must be for a period of incarceration that is less than two years (CBC News, 2009). In addition, as noted in Box 3.1 Canadian judges are encouraged to consider alternatives to imprisonment, especially in relation to Aboriginal peoples.

BOX 3.1 LIFE AND LAW: REDRESSING THE OVERREPRESENTATION OF ABORIGINAL PEOPLES IN CANADA'S PRISONS

For more than half a century, various law reform commissions and task forces have commented upon the jarring overrepresentation of Aboriginal peoples within Canada's prisons (e.g., Canadian Corrections Association, 1967; Correctional Service of Canada, 2009; Manitoba Public Inquiry into the Administration of Justice and Aboriginal People, 1991; Task Force on the Criminal Justice System and Its Impact on the Indian and Metis People of Alberta, 1991; Task Force on Aboriginal Peoples in Federal Corrections, 1989). This situation endures. As the Correctional Investigator of Canada observed in 2016, " 'In federal corrections, 25.4 per cent of the incarcerated population are now of aboriginal ancestry.' Of 14,624 inmates across the country, 3,723 are aboriginal people. In the Prairie provinces, 48 per cent of federal inmates are aboriginal people. For aboriginal women, the numbers are even higher. According to the most recent statistics, more than 36 per cent of women in prison are of aboriginal descent" (CBC, 2016).

Section 718.2(e) of the Criminal Code attempts, in part, to redress this situation. It specifies that "all available sanctions other than imprisonment that are reasonable in the circumstances should be considered for all offenders, *with particular attention to the circumstances of Aboriginal offenders*" (emphasis added). While being Aboriginal does not automatically result in a person receiving a lesser sentence, in *R. v. Gladue* (1999) the Supreme Court of Canada directed judges who were sentencing an Aboriginal offender to look at alternative sentencing options and consider the broad systemic and background factors that affect Aboriginal people in general and the offender in particular. In *R. v. Ipeelee* (2012), the Supreme Court reiterated that "judicial notice" must be taken of factors that "provide the necessary context for understanding and evaluating the case-specific information; these factors include 'the history of colonialism, displacement and residential schools and how that history continues to translate into lower educational attainment, lower incomes, higher unemployment, higher rates of substance abuse and suicide, and of course higher levels of incarceration' " (at 60). It additionally confirmed that "sentencing judges have a duty to apply s. 718.2(e) in every case involving an Aboriginal offender and that a judge's failure to do so was an error that should be corrected by an appeals judge." The written decision of Justice LeBel also sadly noted that in the years that have passed since *Gladue*, "statistics indicate that the overrepresentation and alienation of Aboriginal peoples in the criminal justice system has only worsened" (at 62). However, as Comack and Balfour (2004:107) observe, if the over-incarceration of Aboriginal peoples stems from the "deep-rooted problem of social and economic oppression," addressing this problem at time of sentencing "does not really attend to the reasons that the case came to court in the first place."

Sentencing circles (or **circle sentencing**) represent a relatively recent attempt
to implement more culturally appropriate forms of justice for Aboriginal peoples:
"Sentencing circles operate within the Canadian criminal justice system, and therefore
within parameters set out by the *Canadian Criminal Code* and case law/appeals, often taking
the place of criminal court sentencing hearings, once guilt has been established" (Spiteri,
2002:2). Although circle sentencing has historic roots in the "healing circles" used by
Aboriginal communities to address community wrong-doings (Brown, 2002), the term
and its practice were first introduced by judges in the early 1990s in the Yukon Territorial
Courts. In *R. v. Morin* (1995), the judge noted that while punishment and retribution are
focal concerns within the Canadian justice system, "healing circles," as their name implies,
emphasize rehabilitation, the healing of wounds, the restoration of balance, and community
harmony.

Although there are no specific provisions for sentencing circles in Canada's *Criminal Code*,
a judge has the discretion to order a sentencing circle, having regard to various factors
including: the agreement of an accused to be referred to a sentencing circle; the existence
of deep ties between an offender and the community in which the circle is to be held and
in which the accused has deep roots; the willing participation of elders or respected non-
political leaders of that community; and the prior resolution of disputed facts (*R. v. Morin*,
at 8). A judge must also be satisfied that the community in which the sentencing circle will
be held is reasonably well-defined and distinguishable from other communities (e.g., on
the basis of its racial, religious or cultural composition); recognizes the offender as someone
who has the type of relationship with the community that fosters feelings of accountability
to that community; supports the offender in his/her endeavour to heal their relationship
with the victim(s) and community; and possesses sufficient resources to help the accused
and others impacted by the wrongdoing (*R. v. Muson*, 2003).

In circle sentencing, the court typically invites "interested members of the community
to join the judge, prosecutor, defence counsel, police, social service providers, community
elders, along with the offender, the victim and their families and supporters" (Spiteri,
2002:2) to meet and, within a circle, discuss the crime, factors that may have been
impacted upon its commission, sentencing options, and strategies through which the
offender may be reintegrated into the community. Sentencing circles seldom hear
cases that carry a minimum punishment of over two years imprisonment: "Often only
offenders who are eligible for a suspended or intermittent sentence, or a short jail
term with probation, make it before a sentencing circle. Although some communities
allow sexual assault cases to be heard by a circle, circles almost never hear offences such
as murder" (Spiteri, 2002:2). It is common that the circle will forward a restorative
community sentence that involves some type of restitution to the victim, community
service, and/or treatment or counselling services; only on rare occasions, it seems, do
sentencing circles recommend a term of imprisonment. It should be noted, however, that
judges are not bound to accept the recommendations of sentencing circles
(Department of Justice, 2011:9).

The use of sentencing circles has not been without criticism. Critics have charged that the
victim's inclusion within sentencing circles may be traumatic or the reluctant aftermath

of family or community pressure (Razack, 1998; Gaudreault, 2009; Stobbs and Mackenzie, 2009). On occasion, sentences arrived at by sentencing circles have been decried as excessively lenient (CBC News, 2000, 2004b; Libin, 2009; Tibbetts, 2008a). In addition, some have queried whether the use of sentencing circles within Aboriginal communities is truly empowering for those communities, observing that "[e]ven if communities have been able to retain and implement traditional justice practices, these practices are ruled over by the Canadian justice system in today's day and age" (Spiteri, 2002:2).

It is evident that judges do have some choice between sentencing options for most crimes, and they tend to exercise it. Factors that might influence a judge's decision include the race, sex, age, and socioeconomic and criminal background of the defendant, and the skill of the defence lawyer involved. The decision to plea bargain is also a factor. Yet, "judicial discretion in sentencing has never meant an unfettered entitlement to impose any sentence deemed appropriate by the particular judge" and, since the passage of Canada's first *Criminal Code* in the 1890s, mandatory sentencing tools have delimited judicial discretion in the sentencing of some offenders (Caylor and Beaulne, 2014:2, 8). For example, the first Criminal Code (enacted in 1892) specified a minimum term of imprisonment for six offences: "engaging in a prize fight (three months), frauds upon the government (one month), stealing post letter bags (three years), stealing post letters (three years), stopping the mail with intent to rob (five years), and corruption in municipal affairs (one month)" (Crutcher, 2001:273). In recent decades, these Parliamentary restrictions on judicial discretion in sentencing have increased notably. Indeed, "[m]andatory minimum penalties appear to be the punishment of choice for many Members of Parliament" (Crutcher, 2001:280).

The Liberal government of Jean Chrétien launched one of the largest enactments of mandatory minimum sentences in the history of the Code with Bill C-68, *An Act Respecting Firearms and Other Weapons*, which added 18 mandatory minimums to the *Code* (Caylor and Beaulne, 2014:9). However, while 29 offences carried mandatory minimum sentences at the cusp of the new millennium, this number rose under the Conservative government of Stephen Harper (February 6, 2006 to November 4, 2015) with 51 code offences amended to either increase existing mandatory penalties or introduce a new one. For example, Bill C-2, the *Tackling Violent Crime Act* (2008), increased the length of the mandatory minimums sentences for firearms and impaired driving offences; Bill C-10, *The Safe Streets and Communities Act (2012)*, included mandatory minimum sentences for certain sexual offences and mandatory minimum penalties for certain drug offences. Both of these omnibus bills reduced judicial discretion and gave Parliament a greater say in the sentencing of offenders. In like spirit, Bill C-25, *The Truth in Sentencing Act* (2010), eliminated the court's discretion to give more than one day credit for each day spent in pretrial custody.

By the end of the Harper government's decade in power, there were 64 mandatory minimum penalties in the *Criminal Code* and nine mandatory minimums in the *Controlled Drugs and Substances Act*. However, while such measures were touted by their champions as essential in holding "violent hard-core" criminals to account, they also catalyzed a "litigation-fuelled backlash," and 100 constitutional challenges to mandatory minimum penalties (Bronskill, 2016). Moreover, a series of recent decisions by the Supreme Court of

Canada have invigorated debates on both the wisdom and utility of legislated mandatory minimum.

For example, in *R. v. Nur* (2015), the Supreme Court quashed mandatory minimums for firearm possession offences, ruling 6–3 that they constituted "cruel and unusual punishment" in violation of section 12 of the *Charter*. In the majority decision, Chief Justice Beverley McLachlin wrote that "[m]andatory minimum sentences, by their very nature, have the potential to depart from the principle of proportionality in sentencing . . . They function as a blunt instrument that may deprive courts of the ability to tailor proportionate sentences at the lower end of a sentencing range" (at 44). In *R. v. Lloyd* (2016), the Supreme Court of Canada struck down a second federal law when it ruled 6-3 that a mandatory, one year minimum sentence for a drug crime when the offender has a similar charge on their record was unconstitutional. Chief Justice McLachlin noted that the mandatory minimum sentence provisions not only catch "the serious drug trafficking that is its proper aim, but conduct that is much less blameworthy" (at 27). "If Parliament hopes to maintain mandatory minimum sentences for offences that cast a wide net," she wrote on behalf of the majority, "it should consider narrowing their reach so that they only catch offenders that merit that mandatory minimum sentence" or, alternatively, "build a safety value that would allow judges to exempt outliers for whom the mandatory minimum will constitute cruel and unusual punishment" (at 35-36). The unanimous decision of the Supreme Court of Canada in *R. v. Safarzadeh-Markhali* (2016) ended limits on credit for pre-trial detention in certain circumstances where bail is denied and allowed trial judges greater discretion in how they deal with offenders. Although provisions passed in 2009 had "prohibited a trial judge from giving more than one-for-one credit for pre-trial detention if a justice of the peace had denied bail to the person because of a previous conviction," the Supreme Court found this law to be "overly broad and would capture offenders who, for instance, might have been convicted for failing to appear in court" (CTV, 2016).

In November of 2016, Justice Minister Jody Wilson-Raybould announced that the Trudeau government intended to cut the widespread use of mandatory minimum sentences and restore the ability of judges to exercise "appropriate discretion" in the sentencing of offenders and impose sentences that are based "on the actual circumstances of the case before them" (in Fine, 2016). This plan would be supported by research on the impact of mandatory sentencing laws elsewhere. For example, studies in the United States and Australia have generally concluded that while this type of law-and-order initiative dramatically increases the numbers of persons incarcerated, mandatory sentencing provisions do not act as general deterrence and have little, if any, measurable impact on crime rates (Walker, 2015; Morgan, 2000; Merritt, Fain, and Turner, 2006; Cano and Spohn, 2012; Ulmer, Kurlychek, and Kramer, 2007; Auerhahn, 2008; Webster, Doob, and Zimring, 2006; Sevigny, 2009). Moreover, as a review of the research on mandatory sentencing laws concludes, "Mandatory penalties often result in injustice to individual offenders. They undermine the legitimacy of the courts and the prosecution process by fostering circumventions that are willful and subterranean. They undermine . . . equality before the law when they cause comparably culpable offenders to be treated radically differently" (Tonry, 2009:100).

CIVIL CASES

Civil cases involve three stages: pleadings, discovery, and trial. A dispute reaches the court when a plaintiff files a pleading that details his/her complaint against the defendant and remedy s/he is seeking. "A court officer then issues the claim by affixing the seal of the court and signing the pleading on behalf of the court. Copies are then delivered to, or **served on**, the defendant" (Department of Justice, 2016b). If the defendant does not provide the court with a **statement of defence**, the court will assume that the allegations that the plaintiff has raised against are true. Prior to trial, both parties are entitled to an **examination for discovery**; the dual purposes of this stage are to clarify the plaintiff's claim against the defendant and to permit each side to examine the evidence that the other side intends to introduce in court. If the case proceeds to trial, the plaintiff "must prove that it is more probable than not that the defendant is legally responsible, or **liable**, because a civil case is decided on a **balance of probabilities**. This is the standard of proof for a civil case, just as the standard of proof for a criminal case is proof beyond a reasonable doubt" (Department of Justice, 2016b). However, just as plea bargaining is common in criminal cases, bargaining often leads to negotiated settlements in civil cases.

For example, in relation to family law issues, the Honourable Frederick L. Myers began his written decision in *Nikolaev v. Fakhredinov* (2015) by stating that "[t]here are few litigation policies more strongly advocated than the policy favouring settlement out of court in family law cases" (at 1). Similarly, negotiated settlements may be reached in other cases that are the subject matter of civil law, such as "disputes about contracts, estates, property, commercial ventures, law applied by administrative tribunals, and torts (a wrongful act, like causing a car accident)" (British Columbia Court of Appeal, 2017). Indeed, it is estimated that in Canada's current "litigation landscape," between "95% to 97% of all civil cases are settled without a trial" through negotiations that involve "a back-and-forth dialogue between counsel" (McAllister, 2016). In *Sable Offshore Energy v. Ameron International Corp.* (2013), the Supreme Court observed that negotiated settlements are concordant with the justice system's "constant quest for ameliorative strategies that reduce litigation's stubbornly endemic delays, expense and stress" (at 1). "In this evolving mission to confront barriers to access to justice," Justice Abella wrote, "some strategies for resolving disputes have proven to be more enduringly successful than others. Of these, few can claim the tradition of success rightfully attributed to settlements. Settlements allow parties to reach a mutually acceptable resolution to their dispute without prolonging the personal and public expense and time involved in litigation." *Pre-trial conferences* may provide a venue for negotiation in the civil litigation process by encouraging settlement (Osborne, 2007). In Ontario, for example, parties (and their lawyers, if any) in a civil action in the Superior Court of Justice "must attend a pre-trial conference before a judge or court officer to attempt to settle the case or narrow the issues" (Government of Ontario, 2016). A number of matters can be discussed at this pre-trial conference including: "settlement, whether the issues can be simplified, and how long the hearing is expected to last. A judge who conducts a pre-trial conference will not preside at the trial unless all parties consent in writing" (Government of Ontario, 2016).

If a civil action proceeds to trial and the defendant is found liable, a judge must consider the facts, the remedy that the plaintiff requested in his/her pleadings, and other possible ways of resolving the case. The three types of remedies available are declaratory remedies, injunctions, and monetary remedies. "**Declaratory remedies** simply state the rights of the parties. For example, when a court interprets a will or decides who owns personal property or land, its decision is declaratory" (Department of Justice, 2017a). **Injunctions** are restraining orders that announce what someone can or cannot do. However, the most common of the three types of available remedies in civil courts are monetary awards (damages). In *Ratych v. Bloomer* (1990), a tort action, the Supreme Court stated that "[t]he general principles underlying our system of damages suggest that a plaintiff should receive full and fair compensation, calculated to place him or her in the same position as he or she would have been in had the tort not been committed, insofar as this can be achieved by a monetary award. This principle suggests that in calculating damages under the pecuniary heads, the measure of the damages should be the plaintiff's actual loss" (at 71). In contract actions, compensatory damages are intended to place the wronged party in the position that s/he would have been in had the contract been performed. Damages that are intended to cover what the wronged party expected to receive in a breach of contract case are referred to as *expectation damages*. *Consequential damages*, a second subtype of compensatory damages for pecuniary loss, may be awarded for indirect damage that is caused by the defendant's wrongful action. A defendant may also be ordered to pay *general damages* (aka *non-pecuniary damages*). This type of award in a personal injury action, for example, is intended to provide compensation for the plaintiff's losses and sufferings in the past, present, and future. "In determining fair compensation in the particular circumstances of a case, courts look at such factors as the plaintiff's age, the nature of the injury, the severity and duration of the pain, the level of the disability and the loss of lifestyle or impairment of life" (Hosseini, 2013). Judges may also award *pecuniary* (or *special*) *damages* to compensate losses that are more easily quantified (e.g., medical bills, lost wages).

While the damages discussed thus far are primarily intended to be remedial, other types of damages are punitive. For example, *exemplary damages* are intended to punish an offender for misconduct that represents "a marked departure from ordinary standards of decent behaviour" and dissuade them from repeating this behavior in the future (*Whiten v. Pilot Insurance Co.*, 2002 at 36). As Justice Cory wrote in delivering the ruling of the majority of the Supreme Court in *Hill v. Church of Scientology of Toronto* (1995), "Punitive damages may be awarded in situations where the defendant's misconduct is so malicious, oppressive and high-handed that it offends the court's sense of decency" (at 196). The aim of punitive damages, he wrote, "is not to compensate the plaintiff, but rather to punish the defendant. It is the means by which the jury or judge expresses its outrage at the egregious conduct of the defendant" (at 196).

Aggravated damages are "for aggravation of the injury by the defendant's misbehavior" and "will frequently cover conduct that could also be the subject of punitive damages" (Hosseini, 2013). A judge may also award *nominal* or *token* damages to acknowledge a violation of a legal right and affirm the import of that legal right. In such cases, the award may be of greater symbolic than monetary value.

LEGISLATURES

A legislature is defined as a "group of people having the duty and power to make laws for a country, province or state. This group may be elected (as are members of Parliament and provincial legislature) or appointed (as are members of the Senate)" (Statistics Canada, 1998:474). The functions of the legislature, at both the federal and the provincial levels, are numerous. Of course, the hallmark of legislative bodies is their lawmaking function. Following the title, the initial words one reads in a Canadian statute or law are: "Her Majesty, by and with the advice and consent of the Senate and House of Commons of Canada, enacts as follows. . . " Yet lawmaking takes up only a portion of the legislature's time. Legislative bodies are also engaged in conflict and integrative functions.

CONFLICT-MANAGEMENT FUNCTIONS

Although conflict management is part of both the administrative and the judicial subsystems, the legislature may be distinguished by the extent to which compromise, as a mode of conflict management, is institutionalized in the system. The emphasis is on conflict management rather than on conflict resolution since, in a sense, few political decisions are final.

The conflict-management functions of legislative bodies can be seen in the context of their deliberative, decisional, and adjudicative activities. Frequently, legislative bodies deliberate without arriving at a decision or taking action. However, the deliberation process itself and the rules under which it occurs contribute to the reconciliation of divergent interests. In addition to formal debates, deliberation is carried on in the hearing rooms, in the offices of legislators, or in lobbies and other meeting places. At times, these informal deliberations are more important, for they provide an opportunity to incorporate a variety of viewpoints and interests. Some adjudicative activities are routinely undertaken by legislative bodies, and the principles of dispute resolution currently being applied in the judicial system also benefit the legislators (Melling, 1994). For example, the work of some legislative committees has been adjudicative, as when hearings before investigating committees have been, in effect, trials during the course of which sanctions have been applied.

INTEGRATIVE FUNCTIONS

Legislative bodies contribute to the integration of the polity by providing support for the judicial and executive systems. They provide this support through authorization, legitimization, and representation (Jewell and Patterson, 1986:10). In Canada, for example, the Prime Minister's authority comes from the office, not from custom or the individual's personal attributes. As an elected Member of Parliament, as well as the national leader of the political party that holds the majority of seats in the House of Commons, the Prime Minister has a mandate to speak on behalf of Canada and to govern the country in a way that will, one hopes, benefit all Canadians.

In 1848, the provinces of Canada and Nova Scotia were granted "**responsible government**." This meant that Cabinet members had to be drawn from sitting members of the legislature and that the Cabinet could direct the administration of government only so long as it enjoyed majority support in the legislature. Without this support, it lost its mandate to govern. By the time of Confederation in 1867, responsible government—with the executive branch accountable to the legislature—had been achieved in all of the colonies. The executive could no longer tax and spend on its own authority or on the authority of the Crown. Rather, the legislature controlled the purse strings.

Continuing today, the Cabinet is responsible to the House of Commons, and if it fails to enjoy the support of the majority in the House of Commons it must, by convention, call an election or make way for a new government to be formed. In turn, the House of Commons is responsible to the people through the electoral process. In stark contrast, in the United States, a president may remain in office even if one or both houses of Congress consistently block the bills he or she puts forward. In addition, while both Canada and the United States are democracies and federal states, "the two systems of government grew out of opposite approaches to federalism: Canada's Fathers of Confederation envisioned a strong central government whereas the American version—as the name 'United States' implies—has always been highly decentralized" (Statistics Canada, 1998:479). Ironically, perhaps, Canada is becoming more decentralized due, in large measure, to the forces of globalization, while the United States is becoming less decentralized (Bricker and Greenspon, 2001:307).

Legislative bodies also authorize the courts to establish jurisdiction, to create their organizational machinery, and to qualify their members. Moreover, legislatures oversee bureaucratic activities and attempt to balance them against prevailing special interests in a community. The integrative functions are also promoted through legitimization of activities. Most people consider legislative actions legitimate.

A characteristic of any constitution is the specific delegation of authority to different components of government. In Canada, the *Constitution Act, 1867*, remains the basis of our written constitution. It identifies which level of government has jurisdiction over which powers. The federal government's 29 areas of jurisdiction are set out in section 91, while the 16 areas of provincial jurisdiction are outlined in section 92. Although the *Constitution Act* established only two levels of government, the provinces have delegated some of their power to the third level of government—local municipalities (e.g., cities, towns, townships) that operate and pass bylaws to regulate their activities.

Debating political jurisdiction has sometimes been termed a "national pastime" of Canadians, and, admittedly, the division of powers can sometimes appear to be inordinately complex. For example, "[a]s a result of legal interpretation, labour legislation (except that pertaining to certain industries) and social security (except employment insurance and shared power over pensions) come under provincial law" (Statistics Canada, 1998:480). In some areas (e.g., agriculture, immigration, and certain aspects of natural resources), responsibility is shared. However, when laws conflict, the national laws hold sway (the **doctrine of paramountcy**).

ABORIGINAL PEOPLES

One of the most contested powers given to the federal government under section 91 of the *Constitution Act, 1867* was the power to pass legislation with respect to Aboriginal peoples and the lands reserved for their use. This was accomplished without the involvement or consent of the Native peoples (who had previously made their treaty arrangements with England)—a fact that has become increasingly important as Natives continue their struggle to enforce the terms of original treaties (Yates, Yates, and Bain, 2000:57; 7). A second point of controversy is that even though Aboriginal rights are constitutionally protected, these rights are not absolute in Canadian law (Borrows, 2002; Coulthard, 2007; Foster, Raven, and Webber, 2011).

Traditional First Nations forms of social organization have undergone significant changes as a consequence of contact with European cultures (Henderson and Wakeham, 2009; Kuokkanen, 2015; Lavallee and Poole, 2010; Long and Brown, 2016). Even prior to Confederation, assimilationist policies promoted the "civilization" and "Christianization" of Aboriginal peoples (Woolford, 2009; Blackstock, 2011). The introduction of European law, which supported patrilineality and patrilocality, forcibly changed the descent rules and residence patterns of many First Nations cultures. Ever since the 1850 *Act for the Better Protection of the Lands and Property of Indians in Lower Canada* defined an "Indian," foreign criteria have been imposed on "Indian" status, the determination of band membership, and access to rights tied to status and membership. The *Gradual Civilization Act* of 1857 explicitly declared as its goal the assimilation of Aboriginal peoples. In 1868, following Confederation, the federal Parliament passed an *Act for the Gradual Civilization of Indian Peoples*, designed with the express intent of assimilating Aboriginal people through the use of three primary tools: "The first was the creation of reservations, which in most cases did not correspond to the traditional territories the tribes had occupied. Secondly, band councils with limited powers were appointed to replace tribal governments. The Act also defined who could be classified as Indian and to which band they belonged" (Yates, Yates, and Bain, 2000:57).

The goal of assimilation would be further reinforced in the post-Confederation period by the *Enfranchisement Act* of 1869 and, most notably, by the *Indian Act* of 1876. This Act, although presented as a "temporary measure" for controlling "Indians" on reserves, clearly reflected the federal government's agenda: "to act as guardians over Aboriginal Peoples, giving them 'protection' but with the ultimate goal of assimilation and absorption into [the] general population" (Canadian Labour Congress, 2005:2.40). It defined who was an "Indian" under the law and what "Indians" could and could not do. For example, "Status Indians" (persons who were registered as "Indians" for the purpose of special entitlements) were not eligible to vote; it was not until 1960 that First Nations members were extended the right to vote in federal elections (their right to vote in provincial/territorial elections was acquired in various years, with Quebec the last province to grant this right in 1969). An early (1880) amendment also provided for the automatic "enfranchisement" (loss of status) of those who earned a university degree and of any Indian woman who married a non-Indian or a non-registered Indian. As a report by the Canadian Labour Congress (2005:2.11) observes, "The word 'enfranchisement' was used by the government to describe the process by which to deny one's right to register for Status under the *Indian Act*. However, the dictionary meaning of the term is 'certification.' In this case, therefore, it was actually a system which was used to 'de-enfranchise' (de-certification or loss of Status) the Aboriginal Peoples." In a 1920 House of Commons discussion of changes to the *Indian Act*, Deputy Superintendent General Duncan Campbell Scott clearly announced the intended purpose of the Act: "Our object is to continue until there is not a single

Indian in Canada that has not been absorbed into the body politic and there's no Indian question, and no Indian department, that is the whole object of the Bill" (in Legacy of Hope Foundation, 2012; see also Turner, 2006; Bohaker and Iacovetta, 2009). It may be noted that the *Indian Act* is now widely regarded as having provided a framework for South Africa's apartheid system (abolished in 1994); it also currently holds the dubious distinction of being one of the few—if not the only—piece of legislation in the world that is aimed at a specific "racial group" (Orkin, 2003; Bednasek, 2009; Langer and Brown, 2016).

Although the Royal Proclamation of 1763 by King George III had recognized that Aboriginals lived as nations, acknowledged that they possessed traditional territories until they were "ceded to or purchased by" the Crown, established an Indian territory in which whites could not settle or buy land, and "clearly stated that land cessations could only be made by Aboriginal Peoples through treaties with the Crown" (Canadian Labour Congress, 2005:2.3), the federal government allowed a persistent encroachment onto Aboriginal land following Confederation (Miller et al., 2012; Steckley, 2016). Moreover, in 1927 the federal government passed an amendment to the *Indian Act* that made it illegal to "receive, obtain, solicit or request from any Indian any payment for the purpose of raising a fund or providing money for the pursuing of any claim" without "the written consent of the Superintendent of Indian Affairs." In 1969, a federal government White Paper candidly rejected the notion of any "special status" for Aboriginal peoples and proposed the repeal of the *Indian Act* and the abolition of all treaties (Canadian Labour Congress, 2005:2.13). In response, Aboriginal leaders presented their own Red Paper, tellingly entitled "Citizen Plus"; the term, in itself, directs attention to the status of Aboriginal peoples as the original occupants and founding members of Canada whose rights have never been extinguished by treaty or conquest and, explicitly, suggests that this status demands the extension of rights beyond those enjoyed by all Canadians (Cairns, 2011; Blackburn, 2009; Hoehn, 2012, Ray, 2016).

In January 1973, the Supreme Court of Canada rendered its historic *Calder* decision— recognizing land rights based on Aboriginal title (i.e., based on an Aboriginal group's traditional use and occupancy of that land) and that "Aboriginal peoples who had never signed treaties still hold some claim and title to the lands they traditionally used and occupied" (Canadian Labour Congress, 2005:2.28). Until this decision, the policy of the federal government in relation to Aboriginal title to land where a treaty had not been signed was simple: The government denied its existence. The impact of the Supreme Court's ruling in Calder was momentous; "[b]ecause the majority of Native people north of the 60th parallel had never signed treaties, it meant that Inuit, Dene and Yukon Indians still potentially retained a legal right to lands covering one-third of Canada" (Canadian Labour Congress, 2005:2.28). In addition, it effectively forced the federal government to tend to Aboriginal land claims with a degree of seriousness and urgency that had been formerly lacking. In the aftermath of this decision, the federal government established an office to deal with Aboriginal land claims and recognized two broad classes of these claims: (1) *comprehensive* (based on ancestral rights to lands and natural resources that were not formerly dealt with by treaty and other legal means) and (2) *specific* (which address specific grievances that First Nations peoples may have in relation to the government's administration of Indian land and other assets and that allege non-fulfillment of treaties).

Along with the resolution of land claims, there was also increased discussion of Aboriginal self-government: "A significant result of this was the recognition and affirmation in the *Constitution Act, 1982* of 'existing Aboriginal and treaty rights' for all Aboriginal peoples of Canada, Indian, Métis and Inuit" (Canadian Labour Congress, 2005:2.4).

Aboriginal rights, such as treaty rights, are recognized and affirmed by section 35 of the *Constitution Act, 1982*. The Supreme Court of Canada has also ruled that this section provides for the protection of a wide range of rights that may be asserted by Aboriginal people in respect of certain lands or activities (e.g., the legal recognition of customary practices in relation to marriage and adoption). These provisions are not subject to the "reasonable limits" of our rights and freedoms found in section 1 of the Charter. In addition, section 25 provides that Charter rights cannot infringe on rights (including those rights and freedoms recognized by the Royal Proclamation of 1763 as well as those existing or acquired through land-claims agreements) pertaining to Aboriginal peoples. Stated somewhat differently, this section attempts to ensure that the Charter does not function as a way of abrogating or derogating the rights of Aboriginal peoples.

In *Grassy Narrows First Nation v. Ontario (Natural Resources)* (2014) the Supreme Court reiterated that "When a government—be it the federal or a provincial government—exercises Crown power, the exercise of that power is burdened by the Crown obligations toward the Aboriginal people in question. . . . It must exercise its powers in conformity with the honour of the Crown, and is subject to the fiduciary duties that lie on the Crown in dealing with Aboriginal interests" (at 50). For example, the Crown has a legal and constitutional duty to consult Aboriginal peoples "when the Crown has knowledge, real or constructive, of the potential existence of the Aboriginal right or title and contemplates conduct that might adversely affect it" (*Haida Nation v. British Columbia (Minister of Forests)* [2004] at 35). In *Delgamuukw v. British Columbia* (1997), the Supreme Court described this duty as being part of the process for achieving "the reconciliation of the pre-existence of aboriginal societies with the sovereignty of the Crown" (at 186). More recently, in *Haida Nation v. British Columbia (Minister of Forests)* (2004), the Supreme Court confirmed that the duty to consult was "an essential corollary to the honourable process of reconciliation that s. 35 [of the *Constitution Act, 1982*] demands" (at 38). Although Aboriginal and treaty rights are collective in nature (*R. v. Sparrow*, 1990 at 1112), the Supreme Court noted in *Behn v. Moulton Contracting Ltd.* (2013) that "certain rights, despite being held by the Aboriginal community, are nonetheless exercised by individual members or assigned to them. These rights may therefore have both collective and individual aspects" (at 33).

"In 1995, the Government of Canada recognized the inherent right of self-government as an existing right within Section 35 of the *Constitution Act, 1982*" (Government of Canada, 2014a). The articulation of its "Approach to Implementation of the Inherent Right and the Negotiation of Aboriginal Self-Government," (Government of Canada, 2010a) also recognized that this right:

> may find expression in treaties, and in the context of the Crown's relationship with treaty First Nations. Recognition of the inherent right is based on the view that the Aboriginal peoples of Canada have the right to govern themselves in relation

to matters that are internal to their communities, integral to their unique cultures, identities, traditions, languages and institutions, and with respect to their special relationship to their land and their resources.

(Government of Canada, 2010a)

While acknowledging that this inherent right "may be enforceable through the courts," it opined that such litigation is likely to be "lengthy, costly and. . . . to foster conflict." It declared itself "convinced that litigation should be a last resort," with "[n]egotiations among governments and Aboriginal peoples . . . clearly preferable as the most practical and effective way to implement the inherent right of self-government" (Government of Canada, 2010a:1). It additionally asserted that the lack of uniformity in the circumstances of Aboriginal peoples throughout Canada precluded a "'one-size-fits-all' form" of Aboriginal self-government.

In delineating the scope of negotiations with First Nations people, the federal government acknowledged that "to give practical effect to the inherent right of self-government," "Aboriginal governments and institutions will require the jurisdiction or authority to act in a number of areas," with these areas "likely extending to matters that are internal to the group, integral to its distinct Aboriginal culture, and essential to its operation as a government or institution" (Government of Canada, 2010a). To wit:

- establishment of governing structures, internal constitutions, elections, leadership selection processes
- membership
- marriage
- adoption and child welfare
- Aboriginal language, culture and religion
- education
- health
- social services
- administration/enforcement of Aboriginal laws, including the establishment of Aboriginal courts or tribunals and the creation of offences of the type normally created by local or regional governments for contravention of their laws
- policing
- property rights, including succession and estates
- land management, including: zoning; service fees; land tenure and access; and expropriation of Aboriginal land by Aboriginal governments for their own public purposes
- natural resources management
- agriculture
- hunting, fishing, and trapping on Aboriginal lands
- taxation in respect of direct taxes and property taxes of members
- transfer and management of monies and group assets
- management of public works and infrastructure
- housing
- local transportation
- licensing, regulation, and operation of businesses located on Aboriginal lands

This document also announced the government's readiness to negotiate "some measure of Aboriginal jurisdiction or authority" over other areas but specified that when Aboriginal laws conflicted with the laws and regulations of the federal (or provincial) governments, "primary law-making authority would remain with the federal, or provincial governments, as the case may be" (Government of Canada, 2010a). These areas include administration of justice issues (e.g., "matters related to the administration and enforcement of laws of other jurisdictions, which might include certain criminal laws"; penitentiaries and parole; environmental protection, assessment and pollution prevention; fisheries co-management; migratory birds co-management; gaming; emergency preparedness). In addition, it identified another category of matters for which there was "no compelling reasons for Aboriginal governments or institutions to exercise law-making authority" and for which it was "essential that the federal government retain its law-making authority." These matters were grouped into two broad areas: (i) "powers related to Canadian sovereignty, defence, and external relations" (e.g., international/diplomatic relations and foreign policy; national defence and security; security of national borders; international treaty-making; immigration, naturalization and aliens; international trade, including tariffs and import/export controls); and (ii) "other national interest powers" (e.g., management and regulation of the national economy; maintenance of national law and order and substantive criminal law; protection of the health and safety of all Canadians; federal undertakings and other powers [e.g., broadcasting and telecommunications; aeronautics; navigation and shipping; maintenance of national transportation systems; postal service; census and statistics]).

By April, 2015, Canada, "[i]n collaboration with its negotiation partners, . . . [had] signed 22 self-government agreements recognizing a wide range of Aboriginal jurisdictions that involve 36 Aboriginal communities across Canada" (Government of Canada, 2015a); of those, 18 were part of a comprehensive land claim agreement (modern treaty). Other forms of governance or self-government have also been implemented, such as *Nunavut Land Claims Agreement* (1993). This Agreement, the result of more than two decades of negotiation between the Tunngavik Federation of Nunavut (now Nunavut Tunngavik Incorporated) and the governments of Canada and the Northwest Territories, is structured as an exchange, with the Inuit exchanging Aboriginal title (i.e., ceding, releasing, and surrendering to the Crown their Aboriginal claims, rights, title, and interests) to their traditional lands and waters for certain constitutionally protected rights and benefits. These included: "ownership of about 18 per cent of the land in Nunavut, including mineral rights to two per cent of these lands; [a] cash settlement of $1.173 billion, and [the] [c]reation of the territory of Nunavut, with an elected government to serve the interests of all Nunavummiut" (Nunavut Tunngavik Incorporated, 2004: 5). With the enactment of the *Nunavut Act* (1993), Canada's political map would be altered and, on April 1, 1999, a separate territory called Nunavut was created with a territorial government controlled, effectively, by the Inuit of northern Canada.

Another landmark event occurred with the ratification of *Nisga'a Final Agreement* (1998), a treaty negotiated between the Nisga'a Nation and the governments of Canada and British Columbia, that was "the first modern treaty settlement in British Columbia since 1859" (Fleras, 2017b: 195). These negotiations addressed issues that had arisen more than a century earlier when "much of Nisga'a traditional territory was declared Crown land and the Nisga'a people began petitioning government to recognise their connection to this territory" (Government of Canada, 2010b). On April 13, 2000, 1,930 square kilometres of land in the Nass River Valley in Northwest British Columbia were returned to the Nisga'a people. The self-government provisions in this treaty also endowed the Nisga'a people with "the legal authority to conduct their own affairs" (Government of Canada, 2010b) and the powers of a "super-municipality," empowering them to "pass laws on any matter other than defence, currency and foreign affairs" and providing them with "control over citizenship, land and assets, policing; education, community and health care services, harvesting rights, and direct taxation" (Fleras, 2017b: 196). On May 10, 2000 the *Indian Act* ceased to apply to the Nisga'a people (except for the purpose of Indian registration), and, on the following day, Nisga'a Lisims Government came into effect, constituted itself, and passed its first laws. Thus, "[t]he body responsible for considering and passing laws, the *Wilp S'ayuukhl Nisga'a*, elected its first speaker and deputy speaker. . . [and] moved quickly to pass 18 pieces of legislation regarding lands, forest resources, fisheries, wildlife, and financial administration" as well as the *Nisga'a Administrative Review Board Act*, which "established a board which is responsible for reviewing decisions made by the Nisga'a government" (Government of Canada, 2010b).

The 2003 signing of the *Tlicho Agreement* marked "the first combined land claim and self-government agreement of its kind in the Northwest Territories," creating the "largest single block of First Nation owned land in Canada" and providing new systems of self-government for the Tlicho First Nations (formerly known as the Dogrib) (CRIC, 2006:11). The Supreme Court's unanimous decision in *Tsilhqot'in Nation v. British Columbia* (2014) was also groundbreaking for it marked "the first time in Canadian history that a court had declared Aboriginal title to lands outside of a reserve." Moreover, rather than restricting Aboriginal title to "small intensively used sites," the Court held that "Aboriginal title extends to all the territory that a First Nation regularly and exclusively used when the Crown asserted sovereignty." The Court confirmed that Aboriginal title: gave the Tsilhqot'in the right to control the land and that these lands can be managed according to Tsilhqot'in laws and governance; means that the Tsilhqot'in possess the right to the economic benefits of the land and its resource; and is the "right to choose" how these lands will be used, with the only limit being that Aboriginal title lands cannot be used in a way that would deprive future generations of the control and benefit of the land. In addition, the Court confirmed that while both the province of British Columbia and Canada possess some element of jurisdiction in exceptional circumstances, "the government must first seek the consent of the Tsilhqot'in people before interfering with Tsilhqot'in Aboriginal title lands" and, without this consent, it cannot interfere with Tsilhqot'in Aboriginal title unless it can well justify this infringement (Tsilhqot'in National Government, 2014). "To justify overriding the Aboriginal title-holding group's wishes on the basis of the broader public good, the government must show: (1) that it discharged its procedural duty to consult and accommodate; (2) that its actions were backed by a compelling and substantial objective; and (3) that the governmental action is consistent with the Crown's fiduciary obligation to the group" (at 77).

For reasons of space, it is impossible to detail the complex relationships that exist between Canada and its indigenous peoples (Farget, 2014; Goulet, 2010; Hamilton, 2008; Holden,

2014; Miller et al., 2012; Morgan and Castleden, 2014); "[o]wing to Canada's complex social and constitutional history, the special legal rights of Canada's First peoples vary from one part of the country to another and in their application to different groups" (Henderson, 2016). However, some bands have rejected the idea that their exercise of self-government must derive from negotiations with their federal government and have acted unilaterally. For example, in January 2014, when the Nipissing First Nation passed the first Ontario Aboriginal constitution (with a vote of 319 to 56), Chief Marianna Couchie declared this development "a major step towards self-government" and announced that the Nipissing constitution "would replace the *Indian Act* as the supreme law which regulates the governance of the First Nation" (CBC, 2014). On October 2 2016, the Akwesasne band council (Mohawk) announced its creation of the "first court in Canada for and by Indigenous people" and, in doing so, introduced what is arguably "the first Indigenous legal system in Canada outside a federal framework" (Valiante, 2016). "While First Nations band councils have been passing and enforcing legislation on reserves across the country for decades, those bylaws are either tied to the *Indian Act* or within a self-governance agreement with the federal government" (Valiante, 2016). In contrast, the Akewsasne Mohawk Court is "the first institution of its kind established under the inherent Aboriginal right to self-government, recognized and affirmed by section 35 of the *Constitution Act, 1982*" (Philpott, 2016).

The *Akwesasne Tekaia'rorehthà:ke Kaianerénhsera* (Akwesasne Court Law), which came into force on August 12, 2016, outlines the principles, power, and authorities of the Akwesasne Mohawk Court. Its authority is derived, from the Akwesasne community itself, and is an assertion of both the Mohawk's cultural identity and its "existing and inherent right of self-determination, which includes the inherent jurisdiction over their lands, peoples and territory." It identifies its principles as being *Sken:nen* (peace); *Kasatstensera* (strength); and *Kanikonri:io* (a good mind). It also records that "the three pillars of justice" in Akwesasne are: "respect for life; respect for the person/being; and respect for property" (Mohawk Council of Akwesasne, 2016). In articulating the values that will guide the *Akwesasne Tekaia'torehthà:ke* (Akwesasne Court), *Ratiianerenhserakweniénhstha* (Justice) and *Teshatiia'torètha* (Appeal Justice), it identifies that these institutions will consider:

a) that actions of individuals have an impact on the community as a whole and on the collective rights of the Mohawks of Akwesasne;
b) the protection of the collective inherent rights and the interests of the Mohawks of Akwesasne;
c) the importance of individuals to take responsibility for their actions;
d) the goal of applying sanctions for improper acts is to:

   i. restore balance in the community;
   ii. maintain cultural values of the community; and
   iii. in so far as reasonably possible to move away from confrontation and adversarial approaches in resolution of disputes or consideration of violations of Akwesasne Law;

d) that every person is unique and possesses unique gifts and skills;
e) the necessity to be impartial and independent;

f) the need for individuals to be aware of charges against them in a timely manner, except in the case of emergency orders; and

g) the support and encouragement of dispute resolution processes. (s.3.3)

It additionally directs that "in considering sanctions and remedies and seeking to restore balance to the community, the *Ratiianerenhserakweniénhstha* (Justice) shall consider the talents of the individual before them and may make an Order that effectively and efficiently remedies the situation by having the individual participate in activities in the community that engage the individual, and reinforce their gifts and skills" (s. 3.4). Section 4.1 of Akwesasne Court Law declares the official languages of the Akwesasne Tekaia'torehthà:ke (Akwesasne Court) to be Mohawk and English.

While criminal matters that occur in Akwesasne continue to be settled outside of this community in Canada's federal or provincial courts, prosecutors and justices in Akewsasne are tasked with the enforcement of 32 laws which address civil matters (e.g., tobacco regulations, sanitation, elections, property, and wildlife conservation) (Valiante, 2016). Akin to Canada's adversarial justice system, plaintiffs and defendants in Akwesasne plead their cases before a justice, and the court proceedings are in accordance with fundamental principles of Canadian justice. However, unlike the Canadian system, the Akwesasne Court is based on restorative justice principles and the restoration of community relationships and harmony; its sanctions do not include jail terms. There are also other differences. Among them: although a *Raontiwennakará:tats* (Prosecutor) or *Tsionkwéta Teshakowennákhwa* (Duty Counsel) must be at least 25 years of age (s.4.16a) and possess "related post-secondary education or work experience in the field of advocacy" (4.16c), they are not required to have a law degree. Similarly, a law degree is not required of a *Ratiianerenhserakweniénhstha* (Justice) or *Teshatiia'toréhtha* (Appeal Justice), although those who aspire to these positions must be enrolled as a member of a First Nation or of the Haudenosaunee Confederacy (s. 6.1[a]) and fulfill a series of requirements, which include being of "good character, credibility and reputation in their community" (s. 6.1[c]); possessing "an adequate combination of education, work and life experience"; having "an interest in the settling of disputes" (s. 6.1[d]) and "knowledge of Mohawk culture and traditions" (s. 6.1[f]). Moreover, while women have historically been marginalized in the operation of the Canadian justice system, it is noteworthy that the director, public prosecutor, and the territory's two justices are all women (Valiante, 2016).

PARTICIPANTS IN THE LEGISLATIVE PROCESS

The legislative process encompasses a variety of participants. In this section, we have chosen to give attention to participants who are particularly relevant to legislative activity: legislators and lobbyists.

LEGISLATORS

Contrary to popular belief, legislators are not representative of the population at large, and obviously not all citizens have an equal chance to be elected to legislative office. As a group, legislators have a much higher educational attainment than the general population. In part, this high educational level can be accounted for by their relatively high social origins. Moreover, recruitment of legislators is also very selective by occupational status. By and large, those in the professional and business occupations dominate the legislative halls in Canada at both the federal and the provincial levels.

Protestant Anglo-Saxon males are also substantially overrepresented among legislators. Nevertheless, Canada certainly has come a long way since 1921, the year of the first federal election in which women were allowed to vote and run for office. In the 2015 federal election, women accounted for one third of the 1,427 candidates running for the five main parties and Canadians elected 88 women to the House of Commons—a record high, raising female representation in the House of Commons to 26 percent. Other notable "firsts" have occurred in recent decades. In 1989, the election of Audrey MacLaughlin as leader of the New Democratic Party marked the first time that a woman had been elected leader of a national Canadian political party. On June 13, 1993, Kim Campbell was elected leader of the Progressive Conservative Party, and on June 25, she was sworn in as Canada's first female prime minister. On September 8, 1999, when the Right Honourable Adrienne Clarkson was appointed Governor-General of Canada, she became the second woman and the first member of a visible minority to hold this (largely symbolic) role as the resident representative of the Crown. In 2001, the Liberal government appointed the first woman— Marlene Cattarall—to the post of chief government "whip" in the House of Commons. (Canadian MPs are expected to conform to their party's position, and each party selects one MP to act as the party whip—a person who is expected to figuratively whip the other MPs into line on policy issues and to corral MPs into attendance when their votes are needed.) In 2015, Jody Wilson-Raybould, a member of the We Wai Kai Nation and descendant of the Musgamagw Tsawataineuk and Laich-Kwil-Tach peoples, became Minister of Justice of Canada and the first Indigenous person to be named to that prestigious position. Nevertheless, it remains true that women, Aboriginal peoples, visible minorities, and foreign-born Canadians are underrepresented in our legislatures.

LOBBYISTS

Organizations and groups that attempt to influence political decisions that affect their members or their goals are called *interest groups* (Baumgartner et al., 2009; Holyoke, 2014). At the most general level, the interest group system has a distinct bias favouring and promoting upper-class and predominantly business interests. Interest groups are usually regarded as self-serving—with some justification (Rozell and Wilcox, 2006). The very word "interest" suggests that the ends sought will primarily benefit only a segment of society. Although industry associations, trade groups, and unions may engage in lobbying, not all the groups that attempt to influence legislative bodies profit directly: lobbyists may also advocate for charities, for the environment, the differently-abled, the homeless, children and consumers. Among many other causes, they may work to promote the rights of people with "diverse gender identities and experiences of attraction (sexual orientation)," such as those who self-identify as lesbian, gay, bisexual, trans, intersex, queer or questioning or Two-Spirited (LGBTIQ2S) (Egale, 2016:2).

The lobbyist plays a variety of roles in the legislative process. As a contact person, the lobbyist's time and energies are devoted to walking the legislative halls, visiting legislators, establishing relationships with administrative assistants and others of the legislator's staff, cultivating key legislators on a friendship basis, and developing contacts on the staffs of critical legislative committees. As a campaign organizer, the lobbyist gathers popular support for his or her organization's legislative program. As an informant, the lobbyist conveys information to legislators without necessarily advocating a particular position. Finally, as a watchdog, the lobbyist scrutinizes the legislative calendars and watches legislative activity carefully. This way, the lobbyist can be alert to developments that might affect client groups (Levine, 2009).

Forcese and Freeman (2005:460) observe that although lobbying as a formal industry in Canada is relatively recent, originating with the 1968 formation of Executive Consultants Ltd. (ECL) by two former executive assistants to Liberal Cabinet ministers, Bill Lee and Bill Neville, "the process of lobbying predates this, of course. In fact, law firms often billed themselves as 'Parliamentary Agents,' although this more often referred to the use of lawyers for certain statutory applications such as divorce or corporate charters than to the performance of lobbying roles per se." They note that, prior to the emergence of ECL, lobbyists were typically "party-connected lawyers and 'bagmen' who could fix a client's problems with a call to a minister." However, they argue, the lobbying industry changed dramatically in the 1980s when Prime Minister Mulroney opted to place a lesser degree of reliance than had his predecessors on the expertise of public servants and, instead, positioned his ministers "at the centre of policy-making." This change, they suggest, prompted the lobbying industry to focus "increased attention on these ministers in their campaigns, and those with personal contacts with these ministers often sold their services for a premium" (Forcese and Freeman, 2005:461).

In an attempt to rein in the power of professional lobbyists and to curb the excesses of the lobbying industry, the *Lobbying Registration Act* (LRA) was passed in 1988 and came into force on September 30, 1989. The LRA focused attention on those who are paid to lobby and was intended to reveal who wields political influence and to make lobbying more transparent; the expectation was that "sunshine" would "be the best disinfectant" and deter "suspect lobbying practices" (Forcese and Freeman, 2005:478). Amendments introduced by Bill-43 (*An Act to Amend the Lobbyists Registration Act and to Make Related Amendments to Other Acts*), which came into force in 1996, included the mandated development of a code of conduct for lobbyists and, in 1997, the *Lobbyists' Code of Conduct* came into effect. Following a 2001 parliamentary review by the House of Commons Standing Committee on Industry, Science, and Technology, further amendments to the LRA were passed in 2003 as Bill C-15 (*An Act to Amend the Lobbyists Registration Act*). Additional changes were ushered in, in 2004, by the government's introduction of Bill C-4 and, in 2005, the *Regulations Amending the Lobbyists Registration Act* and the *Act to Amend the Lobbyists Registration Act* came into force. The amended Act acknowledged that lobbying "is a legitimate part of our democratic system" and that "[p]eople, organizations and businesses have the right to communicate, to decision makers, information and views on issues that are important to them" (Office of the Registrar of Lobbyists, 2005). While earlier versions of this Act had defined lobbying loosely as "attempting to influence a public office holder," a clearer definition was provided: "any oral or written communication made to a public office holder." The revised Act required all categories of lobbyists to file a disclosure every six months and obliged former public office holders who become paid lobbyists to disclose the positions they previously held with the federal government. In addition, the Act's enforcement provisions were strengthened, with notification of the appropriate police authorities required when the Registrar of Lobbyists, "in conducting an investigation into an alleged breach of the Lobbyists Code of Conduct, has reasonable grounds to believe that an offence has been committed" (Government of Canada, 2005).

Further changes to the Lobbyists Registration Act occurred as the result of Bill C-2, the *Federal Accountability Act,* which received Royal Assent in December 2006 and was intended to ensure that lobbying is done in an "ethical and transparent way." To reflect its broader scope, the name of the Act was changed to the *Lobbying Act.* The *Lobbying Act* and its associated regulations, which came into force on July 2, 2008, are based on four principles: "[f]ree and open access to government is an important matter of public interest; [l]obbying public office holders is a legitimate activity; [i]t is desirable that public office holders and the general public be able to know who is engaged in lobbying activities; [and] [t]he system of registration of paid lobbyist should not impede free and open access to government" (Office of the Commissioner of Lobbying of Canada, 2012). It focused upon two types of lobbyists: *consultant lobbyists* (persons hired to communicate on behalf of a client with a public office holder, or to set up meetings between the client and public office holders) and *in-house lobbyists* (who either work for compensation in a for-profit entity [corporation] or non-profit organization). It also defined "lobbying" as "communicating with public office holders, for payment with regard to: the making, developing or amending of federal legislative proposals, bills or resolutions, regulations, policies or programs; the awarding of federal grants, contributions or other financial benefits; and the awarding of a federal government contract (for consultant lobbyists only)" (Office of the Commissioner of Lobbying of Canada, 2014).

The 2008 changes established a new Commissioner of Lobbying as an independent Agent of Parliament and provided the Commissioner with enhanced investigative powers and a mandate to enforce compliance with the proposed *Lobbying Act.* These changes also prohibited "designated public officer holders" (DPOH) (e.g., ministers, ministerial staff, and senior public servants) from registering and lobbying the Government of Canada for five years after leaving office; required lobbyists to disclose certain details of their "oral and arranged" communications with DPOHs; banned any payment or other benefit contingent on the outcome of a consultant lobbyist's activity; and required all government contracts and agreements to state that contingency fees will not be paid. Other changes extended the time period for the investigation/prosecution of possible infractions or violations of the *Lobbying Act* and the Lobbyists' Code of Conduct from two to ten years; increased the maximum penalties that may be imposed on lobbyists who are convicted of breaching the *Lobbying Act*'s requirements (to $200,000 and/or two years incarceration); and endowed the Commissioner with the authority to prohibit those who have been convicted of offences under the Act from engaging in lobbying for up to two years.

In 2010, the positions or classes of positions that fall under the DPOH regulations were increased from 11 to 14. As a result, this definition now includes "all members of Parliament and all Senators, as well as any staff working in the offices of the Leaders of the Opposition in the House of Commons and the Senate" (Office of the Commissioner of Lobbying of Canada, 2012). Following public consultation, the Commissioner of Lobbying amended the Lobbyists' Code, and the second version of this professional code came into force in December 2015. Its mandatory standard of conduct for lobbyists identify the principles of "Respect for Democratic Institutions," "Integrity and Honesty," and "Openness and Professionalism" as important goals. However, unlike violators of the *Lobbying Act*, those who depart from the Code are not subject to criminal penalties; breaches of the Code "only require that the breach be made public in a report by the commissioner to Parliament" [Pross and Parrott, 2017].)

All of these measures attempt to curtail corruption and political patronage. Yet those who work as "unpaid or 'volunteer' lobbyists and private individuals are exempt from registration" (Parkin, 2016). In consequence, "wealthy and connected volunteers may . . . contact and influence public office holders without scrutiny" (Pross and Parrott, 2017). Moreover, the co-founder of Democracy Watch (Conacher, 2016) charges that the "very weak enforcement records of the Commissioner of Lobbying and the Ethics Commissioner" and their failure to conduct random audits makes it likely that "only five percent of rule violators have been caught." He estimates that "since 2007 likely more than 1,500 public office holders have violated ethics rules, and likely more than 1,500 lobbyists have violated lobbying rules, without getting caught."

ADMINISTRATIVE AGENCIES

One of the most striking developments in Canadian law over the course of the past century was the growth in administrative law, the multiplication of administrative agencies, and the extension of their power and activities (Mullan, 2001). Federal and provincial legislatures have delegated legal authority to various administrative tribunals or boards to decide a range of issues. These include quasi-judicial determinations, such as whether an individual will receive social assistance benefits or a broadcasting licence, and broad policy rulings, such as whether to permit increases in prescription drug prices or local competition in the delivery of telephone or cable services. Examples of administrative tribunals include liquor control boards, the Canadian Radio-television and Telecommunications Commission (CRTC), the Canada Council, and the Employment Insurance Commission. However, provincial law alone has established almost 1800 administrative boards. Two-thirds of these are lawmaking boards dealing with matters "related to human rights, labour and employment standards, land assessment and expropriation, public utilities, transportation, financial institutions and securities, immigration, employment insurance, police and parole, consumer protection, parks, entertainment and athletics" (Statistics Canada, 1998:519); the rest of administrative boards are simply advisory bodies.

THE ORGANIZATION OF ADMINISTRATIVE AGENCIES

Administrative agencies are authorities of the government created for the purpose of administering particular legislation. They can be called commissions, bureaus, boards, authorities, offices, departments, administrations, or divisions. The powers and functions of an agency are generally contained in the legislation that created it (Breyer and Stewart, 2006:9–15) and that serves as the source of its authority. For example, in deciding whether to deny workers' compensation benefits, a decision maker is not free to act capriciously or arbitrarily. The decision maker's power derives from legislative authority and regulations passed under that authority.

As social life in general and economic activity in particular became more complex, legislative bodies were unable or unwilling to prescribe detailed guidelines for regulation. In consequence, agencies were established and given considerable discretion in determining the applicability of often vaguely written legislation to specific situations, such as mass transport and communication. These agencies were expected to provide certain advantages over the courts in the instrumentation of public policy. These advantages included speed, informality, flexibility, expertise in technical areas, and continuous surveillance of an industry or an economic problem.

Yates, Yates, and Bain (2000:120) acknowledge that "because there are as many different forms of tribunals as there are government bureaucracies, it is difficult to describe their structure and procedures." Nevertheless, they point out that, in general, certain basic rules of procedure that are sometimes referred to as "due process" or the "rules of natural justice" must be followed whenever government administrators assume a judicial or quasi-judicial function and make decisions affecting the rights of others (e.g., deciding whether a union should be certified or if an individual qualifies for parental benefits):

> Rules of natural justice are basically the rules of fair play, and primarily embodied in the idea of having a fair hearing. In fact, what constitutes a fair hearing may vary with the nature of the matter discussed. It may involve no more than allowing the interested party to write a letter describing his or her position. In other situations, it may require having the opportunity to appear before the decision-maker or to cross-examine a witness.
>
> (Yates, Yates, and Bain, 2000:122)

While natural justice requires that a respondent be given the opportunity to make his or her case heard and to receive a decision that is made by an impartial decision maker, the specific procedures adopted by the administrative tribunal can vary. Moreover, administrative tribunals are not bound by the stringent rules of procedure that govern the courts. For example, they need not follow strict rules of evidence (i.e., rules that govern the types of evidence that can be introduced and how that evidence must be obtained). "As long as the decision is made within the parameters of the rule of law and the rules of natural justice and the policies set out in the legislation, the decision-maker is free to make a decision and the agency to implement it" (Yates, Yates, and Bain, 2000:124).

Nevertheless, there are certain curbs placed on administrative tribunals and "[w]e expect our administrative tribunals to be bound by the law, to render decisions in an equal and predictive manner and to act in accordance with law and social values" (McLachlin, 1992: 168). For example, administrative tribunals are bound to follow the terms of the *Charter of Rights and Freedoms* and cannot violate Charter rights by denying the liberty or security of a person or violate the principles of fundamental justice that are set out in section 7 of the Charter. Tribunals are also required to act in a reasonable way. If an individual who appears before an administrative tribunal believes that his or her Charter rights have been violated, that due process has not been followed, or that a decision made by a tribunal is unreasonable, that person may apply for a judicial review, usually after they have exhausted all internal appeal mechanisms.

In general, the role of the court is to provide a counterbalance to the discretionary power wielded by government-appointed members of administrative tribunals. While members of tribunals are generally appointed because of their expertise and familiarity with a particular area of legislation, the court plays a supervisory role. The court may consider whether the tribunal was operating within its territorial jurisdiction and whether it was acting under appropriately passed legislation within that jurisdiction, respected the rights set out within the *Charter of Rights and Freedoms*, and followed the rules of natural justice. If the court finds that the tribunal failed to satisfy any of these conditions, it may review the decision and apply remedies.

For example, an order of *certiorari* may be issued, quashing the decision or declaring it to be of no effect. An order of *prohibition* may be issued when administrators have made a decision that exceeds their jurisdiction. The court may make a *declaratory judgment* that announces the law that will apply in a situation. However, if "court[s] have always been protective of their supervisory right over other adjudicative bodies . . . legislators have been just as keen to stop courts from interfering" (Yates, Yates, and Bain, 2000:125). Statutes empowering tribunals may contain *privative clauses* stating that a decision made by a board (e.g., the Workers' Compensation Board) is not reviewable by a court of law or that an order of *certiorari*, prohibition, etc., cannot be applied to any decision made by the board. However, these clauses are less ironclad than they may appear, and the courts "have always treated such privative causes with a certain amount of resistance" (p. 125).

THE ADMINISTRATIVE PROCESS

Administrative agencies affect the rights of individuals and businesses by exercising powers of investigation, rulemaking, enforcement, and adjudication. The creator of an agency, which is generally the legislature, retains the power to destroy it or alter the rules governing it. The judiciary retains the power of final review of the determinations of administrative agencies, but this right is, as a practical matter, rather limited. The principal administrative processes include investigation, rulemaking, and adjudication. We shall consider these separately.

INVESTIGATION
The authority to investigate is given to practically all administrative agencies. Without information, administrative agencies could not regulate industry, protect the environment, collect taxes, or issue grants. Most administrative actions in both formal and informal proceedings are conditioned by the information obtained through the agency's prior investigation. As regulation has expanded and intensified, agencies' quests for facts have gained momentum. Some agencies are created primarily to perform the investigative function. This authority is one of the functions that distinguishes agencies from courts and is usually exercised to properly perform another primary function, that of rulemaking.

Statutes usually grant an agency the authority to use several methods to carry out its information-gathering function, including requiring reports from regulated businesses and conducting inspections. Necessary information is often available from the staff, from the agencies' accumulated records, and from private sources. If these resources prove inadequate, the agency may seek further information by calling in witnesses or documents for examination or by conducting searches. The authority of an agency to investigate is intertwined with the objectives of administrative investigation. The purposes of investigations vary, ranging over the entire spectrum of agency activity. For example, if an agency is responsible for enforcing a statute, its investigations may set the groundwork for detecting violations and punishing wrongdoers (e.g., inspecting employers' payroll records when checking for compliance with minimum wage laws).

RULEMAKING

Rulemaking is the most important function performed by government agencies (Kerwin, 2003). It defines the mission of the agency and essentially involves the formulation of a policy or an interpretation that the agency will apply to all persons engaged in the regulated activity. As quasi-legislative bodies, administrative agencies issue three types of rules: procedural, interpretive, and legislative. *Procedural rules* identify an agency's organization, describe its methods of operation, and list the requirements of its practice for rulemaking and adjudicative hearings. *Interpretive rules* are issued to guide both the agency's staff and regulated parties as to how the agency will interpret its statutory mandate. These rules range from informally developed policy statements announced through press releases to authoritative rulings binding upon the agency and usually issued after a notice and hearing. *Legislative rules* are, in effect, administrative statutes. In issuing a legislative rule, the agency exercises lawmaking power delegated to it by the legislature.

ADJUDICATION

Administrative agencies of all kinds and at all levels must settle disputes or mediate among conflicting claims. Adjudication is the administrative equivalent of a judicial trial. It applies policy to a set of past actions and results in an order against (or in favour of) the named party.

Much of this adjudication is handled informally through the voluntary settlement of cases at lower levels in an agency. At these levels, agencies dispose of disputes relatively quickly and inexpensively, and they take an immense burden off the courts (Feldman, 2016). But this practice is not without criticism. Many individuals—in particular, lawyers pleading cases before the agencies—have expressed concern over the extent of judicial power vested in agencies. They complain that administrators violate due process of law by holding private and informal sessions, by failing to give interested parties an adequate hearing, and by basing their decisions on insufficient evidence.

These complaints stem, in part, from the institutional differences between agency and court trials. Agency hearings, unlike court hearings, tend to produce evidence of general conditions, as distinguished from the facts relating specifically to the respondent. This distinction is due to one of the original justifications for administrative agencies—the development of policy. Another difference is that in an administrative hearing, a case is tried by a trial examiner and never by a jury. As a result, the rules of evidence applied in jury trials, presided over by a judge, are frequently inapplicable in an administrative trial. The trial examiner decides both the facts and the law to be applied. Finally, the courts accept whatever cases the disputants present. As a result, their familiarity with the subject matter is accidental. By contrast, agencies usually select and prosecute their cases. Trial examiners and agency chiefs either are experts or at least have a substantial familiarity with the subject matter, since their jurisdictions tend to be restricted. As we have noted, however, the courts do have the power to overturn the agencies' judgments on points of law, as in cases where an agency has exceeded its authority, misinterpreted the law, or simply been unfair. Judicial review of agency activities also deals with procedural safeguards, such as more formalized hearings and proper notice of action (Box, 2005). But the role of the courts is essentially limited to procedural matters—advising agencies, sometimes repeatedly, to go about their business in a fairer manner and to pay serious attention to all affected interests. In technical, complex disputes, courts cannot decide major issues. They will not set tariffs, allocate airline routes, or control the development of satellite communications (Breyer and Stewart, 2006).

LAW ENFORCEMENT AGENCIES

The principal functions of the police are law enforcement, maintenance of order, and community service (Dempsey and Forst, 2016). Like other components of our legal system, the origins of the Canadian police can be traced to early English history. In the 9th century, Alfred the Great started paying private citizens for arresting offenders. The population was broken down into units of 10 families or "tithings," and each person was responsible for watching over the others. Subsequently, the unit was expanded to the "hundred," and one person, designated as the constable, was in charge of maintaining order. In time, the hundred was increased to include the countrywide "shire" under the control of an appointed "shire-reeve," who later on became known as the "sheriff." The first city-wide police force was created by Sir Robert Peel in London in 1829; and in 2004, one in every 115 employed Londoners was a police officer (*Economist*, 2004). Police officers were uniformed, organized along military lines, and called "Bobbies" after their founder. While Canadian municipal policing was initially modelled primarily on the example provided by the London Metropolitan Police, the more militaristic example provided by the Royal Irish Constabulary provided the model for the Northwest Mounted Police (the precursor of the Royal Canadian Mounted Police).

There are three levels of policing in Canada: federal, provincial, and municipal. The Royal Canadian Mounted Police (RCMP) is our national or federal police force. The Ontario Provincial Police (OPP) and the Sûreté du Québec (SQ) are the provincial police forces in Ontario and Quebec, respectively; in other provinces, the RCMP also serves as the provincial police force. At the third level are municipal police forces and services, such as the Edmonton Police Service and the Vancouver Police Department. In large metropolitan areas, municipal forces have been established under provincial laws. In small municipalities that do not have their own police forces, the RCMP, the OPP in Ontario, and the SQ in Quebec carry out this role under contract with the provinces. Regardless of whether they are federal, provincial, or municipal police officers, all are responsible for protecting the safety, health, and morals of the public and enforcing the law. As of May 15, 2016, there were 68,773 police officers in Canada (Statistics Canada, 2017).

In addition, governments in Canada authorize other forms of police with powers that may be limited to specific areas or specific groups (military police, harbour police, etc.). Prior to July 1984, the RCMP Security Service was the principal authority in domestic intelligence work. However, since that time, the Canadian Security Intelligence Service (CSIS), an agency of the Department of the Solicitor General, has been charged with conducting security investigations within Canada that are related to suspected subversion, terrorism, and foreign espionage and sabotage. Although its members are not police officers, the agency can obtain judicial warrants to conduct searches and electronic surveillance.

THE ORGANIZATION OF LAW ENFORCEMENT AGENCIES

Police organizations have evolved in response to changes in technology, social organization, and political governance at all levels of society (Carter, 2002; Thurman and Jamieson, 2005). They are structured along the lines of complex bureaucratic organizations. In addition to their bureaucratic characteristics, law enforcement agencies are structured like quasi-military institutions, which give these agencies their special character:

> Both institutions are instruments of force and for both institutions the occasions for using force are unpredictably distributed. Thus, the personnel in each must be kept in a highly disciplined state of alert preparedness. The formalism that characterizes military organization, the insistence on rules and regulations, on spit and polish, on obedience to superiors, and so on, constitute a permanent rehearsal for "the real thing."
>
> (Bittner, 1970:53)

This system of law enforcement is built on a subordinating chain of command (Dempsey and Forst, 2016). Although all units of a particular department may be related to a central command, the overall chain of command is divided into units so that different divisions are immediately responsible to a localized authority. The functional divisions of police departments follow the kinds of activities they handle, such as traffic patrol, investigative work, sex crimes, homicide, undercover work (for example, in vice and narcotics), juveniles, and uniformed patrol. Employment requirements of Canadian police forces generally require a high school diploma and give preference to those with post-secondary education. Although similar curricula exist in major regional recruit training centres, there is no "standard training" for Canadian police officers, and the duration of basic recruit training varies from 12 weeks in some municipal police forces to 26 weeks for RCMP officers at the Regina depot. Police training is pragmatic and brief and usually takes place in an individual police department. This training is generally followed by some type of mentoring or supervised in-service training for up to the first half-year on the job.

Compared with other occupational groups, there is a high degree of cohesion and solidarity among police officers. They are, by virtue of occupational expectations, suspicious and tend to be skeptical toward outsiders, and much of their outlook and conduct has an authoritarian character (Bartol and Bartol, 2011; Terrill, Paoline, and Manning, 2003; Twersky-Glasner; 2005; Embrick, 2015; Willis and Mastrofski, 2017). Their subculture includes a code of silence, and fellow officers rarely incriminate each other

(Wright, 2010; Rothwell and Baldwin, 2007; Miller, 2010; Meine and Dunn, 2012; Crank, 2015). Contrary to popular image, police officers, with the exception of detectives, spend about 20 percent of their time in criminal investigations. Their primary activities consist of routine patrol and maintaining order—such duties as attending to domestic disturbances, handling drunks, assisting motorists, controlling traffic, escorting dignitaries and funeral processions, and processing juveniles (Lyman, 2010; Thurman and Jamieson, 2005; Nickels and Verma, 2008).

In a now-classic study, Wilson (1968b) identified three styles of police work: the watchman style, the legalistic style, and the service style. Although elements of all three can be found in any law enforcement agency, different agencies tend to emphasize one style more than the others and, as a result, practice different law enforcement policies.

The **watchman style** emphasizes the responsibility for maintaining public order, as contrasted with traditional law enforcement. The police officer in such an agency is viewed as a peace officer, ignoring or handling informally many violations of the law and paying much greater attention to local variations in the demand for law enforcement and maintenance of order. The role of peace officer is characterized by a great amount of discretion, since peacekeeping is poorly structured by law or by agency regulation. Underenforcement, corruption, and low arrest rates characterize watchman–style departments.

The **legalistic style** is the opposite of the watchman style. Agencies characterized by this style tend to treat all situations, even commonplace problems of maintaining order, as if they were serious infractions of the law. Members of such agencies issue a high rate of traffic tickets, arrest a high proportion of young offenders, and crack down on illicit enterprises. The police typically act as if there were a single standard of conduct rather than different standards for different groups. As a result, some groups, especially youths, visible minorities, and Aboriginal peoples, are more likely to be affected by law enforcement than others considered "respectable" by the police. Although this style of law enforcement is characterized by technical efficiency and high arrest rates, it also results in inequality in law enforcement, with complaints of harassment and police brutality by groups who are disproportionately subjected to police scrutiny.

The **service style** combines law enforcement and maintenance of order. An emphasis is placed on community relations, the police on patrol work out of specialized units, and command is decentralized. This style differs from the watchman style in that the police respond to all groups and apply informal sanctions in the case of minor offences. It differs from the legalistic style in that fewer arrests are made for minor infractions, and the police are more responsive to public sentiments and desires. In this sense, the service style is less arbitrary than the watchman style and more attuned to the practical considerations of public service than the legalistic style. There is little corruption, and complaints against police in service-style departments tend to be low. The emphasis is on problem-solving policing, with attention focused on the problems that lie behind incidents, rather than on the incidents only. The service style aims at reducing alienation and distrust between police and people of colour and between police and the poor.

POLICE DISCRETION

A significant feature of law enforcement—indeed of the entire judicial process and the criminal justice system—is the discretionary power officials can exercise in specific situations. The exercise of discretion is integral to the daily routine of police officers in a large variety of activities, ranging from routine traffic stops to responding to domestic violence calls (Bala, Carrington, and Roberts, 2009; Fitzgerald and Carrington, 2011; Robertson, 2012). Police discretion is highly institutionalized in our system of criminal justice, and questions about police discretion increasingly appear in lawsuits against the police (Pratt and Thompson, 2008; Choudhry and Roach, 2003; Patry, 2008; Freund, 2007).

In large part, police discretion and disparity stem from the general organization of modern police work (Reiss and Bordua, 1967; Boivin and Cordeau, 2011). As a largely reactive force, primarily dependent on citizen mobilization, the police officer functions in criminal law much as a private lawyer functions in civil law—determining when the victim's complaint warrants formal action and encouraging private settlement of disputes whenever possible. Many decisions by police officers do not lend themselves to either command or review. As a result, police exercise a considerable amount of discretionary power, as reflected in disparities in the volume of arrests, parking tickets, and pedestrian stops (see, for example, Geiger-Oneto and Phillips, 2003; Sylvestre, 2010; Dauvergne, 2009).

Because of their discretionary power, "the police are among our most important policymaking administrative agencies. One may wonder whether any other agencies . . . make so much policy that so directly and vitally affects so many people" (Davis, 1975b:263; see also Rice and White, 2010; Wortley and Owusu-Bempah, 2011; Millar and Owusu-Bempah, 2011). The police exercise discretion in both reactive and proactive policing. *Reactive* police work is a response to citizen mobilization via a 911 call or other means. *Proactive* police work is undertaken on the initiative of police themselves without citizen mobilization.

There is a thin line between discretion and discrimination in discretionary law enforcement (Skolnick, 1994). If the likelihood that an individual will be considered a criminal is dependent on the discretionary power of the police to respond to or to ignore a citizen's complaint, to arrest or to release a suspect, and the like, then the probability that any one person will be labelled a criminal increases or decreases depending on that person's correspondence to police conceptions of the criminal (Bernard and Kurlychek, 2010; Karmen, 2013). Research suggests that the young, the poor, and racialized minorities are more likely to be stopped by the police, to experience one or another form of police brutality, and to be arrested (Tanovich, 2006; Meng, Giwa, and Anucha, 2015; Melchers, 2003; Wortley and Tanner, 2005; Oriola, Neverson, and Adeyanju, 2012).

Police discretion not to enforce the law is attributed to a number of conditions. These include the police beliefs that (1) the legislative body does not desire enforcement; (2) the community wants non-enforcement or lax enforcement; (3) other immediate duties are more urgent; (4) the offenders promise not to commit the act again; (5) there is a shortage of police officers; (6) there is sympathy with the violator; (7) a particular criminal act is common within a subculture; (8) the victim is likely to get restitution without arrest; (9) non-enforcement can be traded for information; (10) the probable penalty is likely to be too severe; and (11) the arrest would unduly harm the offender's status (Beggs and Davies, 2009).

However, if police discretion cannot be entirely eliminated, it can be guided by clear policy directives and subject to administrative scrutiny by overseeing agencies. These measures attempt to bridle the use of discretion and ensure that selective enforcement does not deteriorate into abusive and discriminatory conduct.

SUMMARY

This chapter has been concerned with the organization of law in society in the context of judicial, legislative, administrative, and enforcement agencies.

- Courts, as dispute-processing institutions, are composed of four distinct groups of participants—litigants, lawyers, judges, and juries.
- Although the flow of litigation is different in criminal and civil cases, a high degree of discretion at every level is characteristic of both.
- Although the principal function of legislative bodies is lawmaking, they also engage in conflict-management and integrative functions.
- Administrative agencies reach into virtually every corner of modern life and are created for the purpose of administering particular legislations. Administrative agencies have powers of investigation, rulemaking, and adjudication.
- An important characteristic of law enforcement is the strongly bureaucratic and militaristic organization of the police. The effectiveness of law enforcement agencies depends on the way in which departments are organized.

CRITICAL THINKING QUESTIONS

1. The Royal Commission on Aboriginal Peoples included recommendations for separate legal structures of self-government (e.g., an eventual separate Aboriginal parliament), as well as enhanced Aboriginal self-sufficiency and self-control in such areas as health, education, and housing. However, David Elliott (2005:191) has rhetorically asked, "How much self-control can individual groups exercise within a large polity without threatening its viability or effective operation?" How would you answer Elliott's question? Explain your reasoning.
2. Why do women, Aboriginal peoples, visible minorities, and foreign-born Canadians remain underrepresented in our legislatures?
3. Should any one of the sentencing principles that are contained in section 718 of the Criminal Code be accorded primacy over the others? Investigate how others have answered this question.
4. What obstacles may hamper the work of civil bodies that attempt to "police the police"? How might they be redressed?

ADDITIONAL RESOURCES

1. For information on the work of the Canadian Judicial Council, visit http://www.cjc-ccm. gc.ca.
2. A rich variety of information on Aboriginal peoples in Canada can be found at the Government of Canada's "Aboriginal Canada Portal" at https://aboriginalcanada.ca/en/.
3. The website of the Canadian Civil Liberties Association, at http://ccla.org/talkrights/ learn/police-accountability/ furnishes ready access to a wide range of materials on the issue of police accountability
4. Canada Court Watch, a program of the National Association for Public and Private Accountability, provides a web-based forum at http://www.canadacourtwatch.com for those who feel ill-served by the Canadian court system, most especially in relation to the administration of family law.

4

CHAPTER 4
LAWMAKING

Routinely and seemingly mechanically at the local, provincial, and federal levels, legislative, administrative, and judicial bodies grind out thousands of new laws each year. Each has its own distinct set of precipitating factors, special history, and raison d'être. Still, some generalizations are possible about how laws are formed, the sociological factors that play a role in lawmaking, and the social forces that provide an impetus for making or altering laws. This chapter focuses on the more important sociological theories of lawmaking; the ways in which legislatures, administrative agencies, and courts make laws; the roles of vested interests, public opinion, and social science in the decision-making process; and the sources of impetus for laws.

Figure 4.1 Legislative, administrative, and judicial bodies produce thousands of new laws each year.
Credit: Shutterstock

LEARNING OBJECTIVES

After reading this chapter, you should be able to:

1. Compare and contrast four perspectives on lawmaking: the rationalistic model, the functional view, conflict theory, and the "moral entrepreneur" thesis.

2. Describe legislative and judicial lawmaking.

3. Outline the six "pre-lawmaking" stages of activity.

4. Describe how lawmaking occurs in the context of administrative rulemaking and adjudication.

5. Discuss judicial lawmaking in the wake of the *Charter of Rights and Freedoms*.

6. Outline lawmaking by precedents and by interpretation of statutes.

7. Describe how vested interests, public opinion, and the social sciences influence lawmaking.

8. Identify six sources that may provide impetus for law creation.

PERSPECTIVES ON LAWMAKING

The creation and instrumentation of laws are routine, and ongoing processes and theoretical perspectives dealing with the many facets of lawmaking abound in the sociological literature (see, for example, Lange, 2009; Monahan and Walker, 2010; Parisi, 2008). We will consider briefly four such theories to illustrate the diversity of perspectives—the rationalistic model, the functionalistic model, conflict theory, and a "moral entrepreneur" thesis.

The **rationalistic model** proposes that laws (in particular, criminal laws) are created as rational means of protecting the members of society from social harm. In this perspective, crimes are considered socially injurious. This is a popular theory of lawmaking, but also one that is lacking (Goode, 2016). One of the principal difficulties with this perspective is that it is the lawmakers and powerful interest groups who define what activities may be harmful to the public welfare. Value judgments, preferences, and other considerations obviously enter into the process of definition.

The **functionalistic model** of lawmaking, as formulated by Paul Bohannan (1973), is concerned mainly with how laws emerge. Bohannan argues that laws are a special kind of "re-institutionalized custom." Customs are norms or rules about the ways in which people must behave if social institutions are to perform their functions and society is to endure.

Lawmaking is the restatement of some customs (for example, those dealing with economic transactions and contractual relations, property rights in marriage, or deviant behaviour) so that legal institutions can enforce them.

This view suggests that failure in other institutional norms encourages the re-institutionalization of the norms by the legal institution. It also implies a consensual model of lawmaking in a society. From the functionalist perspective, laws are passed because they represent the voice of the people. Laws are essentially a crystallization of custom, of the existing normative order. Although there are conflicts in society, they are relatively marginal, and they do not involve basic values. In this view, conflict and competition between groups in a society actually serve to contribute to its cohesion and solidarity.

The **conflict perspective** cites value diversity, unequal access to economic goods, and the resulting structural cleavages of a society as the basic determinant of laws. Specifically, the origin of law is traced to the emergence of an elite class whose members, it is suggested, use social control mechanisms, such as laws, to perpetuate their own advantageous positions in society. In the event of conflict over the prescription of a norm, conflict theorists would argue that the interest group(s) more closely tied to the interests of the elite group would probably win the conflict. To define who the elites or the powerful groups of the society are, conflict theorists often employ structural indices of power. For example, Perelman's (2003:29) analysis of the development of intellectual property rights since the early 19th century suggests the important role played by elite groups. He reports that while capitalist entrepreneurs were initially suspicious of the concept of intellectual property, "economic depressions during the mid-19th century and following WWII prompted corporate leaders to advocate stronger intellectual property rights in order to increase revenues." In addition, he argues that companies that were able to secure intellectual property rights effectively limited potential sources of competition and that this promoted the growth of monopolies within certain industries (see also Mai and Stoyanov, 2014).

The **moral entrepreneur theory** attributes the precipitation of key events to the "presence of an enterprising individual or group. Their activities can properly be called *moral enterprise*, for what they are enterprising about is the creation of a new fragment of the moral constitution of society, its code of right and wrong" (Becker, 1963:146). The role of moral entrepreneurs in lawmaking is illustrated in Dua's (1999) research on the historical discouragement of interracial marriage in Canada. She argues that laws prohibiting mixed-race marriages emerged in Canada—as well as in other British, white-settler colonies such as the United States, South Africa, Australia, and New Zealand—as part of "the project of creating a white settler colony with political power in the hands of white settlers" (p. 244). "As eugenicists linked miscegenation [interracial marriage] to the deterioration of the race and nation," Dua (1999:253) reports, "sexual purity became a controlling metaphor for racial, economic and political power."

While the United States enacted a series of laws specifically prohibiting marriage between white settlers and those of African descent (Haney-Lopez, 1997; Sollors, 2000), "[i]n Canada the regulation of interracial sexuality took place through other legal mechanisms" such as the *1876 Indian Act*, which was "employed to govern marriage and sexual relations between white settlers and First Nations people" (Dua, 1999:256). For example, until 1985 when the *Indian Act* was modified, an Indian woman who married a non-Indian man lost her Indian status, and both she and her descendants lost those benefits to which Status Indians were entitled (Kallen, 2003:135).

In addition, Das Gupta (1999:159) observes that in the early part of the 20th century, single male Chinese workers were seen as posing "a threat of miscegenation" and vilified in newspapers as sexual predators who lusted after white women. Such inflammatory, racist stereotypes were consequential and galvanized Protestant moral reformers, middle-class white women's groups, the owners of small businesses, and trade unionists to jointly campaign for legislation that prohibited Asian employers from hiring white women as employees (Backhouse, 1999a:5). Toward the end of "protecting" white womanhood and keeping the "races" pure, a Saskatchewan statute colloquially referred to as the "white women's labour law" was enacted in 1912. It specified, "No person shall employ in any capacity any white woman or girl or permit any white woman or girl to reside or lodge in or work in or, save as a bona fide customer in a public apartment thereof only, to frequent any restaurant, laundry or other place of business or amusement owned, kept or managed by any Japanese, Chinaman or other Oriental person" (as quoted by Sir Charles Fitzpatrick, C.J. in *Quong-Wing v. R.* (Supreme Court of Canada) [1913–1914]). Similar statutes were also passed in 1913 in the province of Manitoba (where indications are that it was never actually proclaimed), in 1914 in Ontario, and in 1919 in British Columbia, and remained in force for many years. Manitoba was the first province to repeal its statute (in 1940); Ontario followed in 1947 and British Columbia in 1968. The Saskatchewan statute, "veiled in racially neutral language, was not repealed until 1969" (Backhouse, 1999b:15).

In addition to seeking real gains through lawmaking, moral entrepreneurs also seek symbolic victories. This symbolic victory has two dimensions. First, the passing of a law may symbolize the supremacy of the groups that support it. Second, the creation of a law is a statement that certain behaviours are disreputable. Where groups differ significantly in prestige and status, or where two groups are competing for status, each sees the law as a stamp of legitimacy. They will seek to use it to affirm the respectability of their own way of life. According to Gusfield (1967:178):

> The fact of affirmation, through acts of law and government, expresses the public worth of one set of norms, or one subculture vis-à-vis those of others. It demonstrates which cultures have legitimacy and public domination, and which do not. Accordingly it enhances the social status of groups carrying the affirmed culture and degrades groups carrying that which is condemned as deviant.

Scholars continue to debate the relative merits of the four theories of lawmaking just outlined. Yet none of these theories can account for the creation of all laws. Because a large number of laws are made by the legislative, administrative, and judicial bodies each day, it is always possible to select a few examples that illustrate almost any conceivable theoretical position. At best, the theories we have discussed explain, in part, how laws are made. Probably all of these theories are at least partially correct, but it is doubtful that any single theory fully explains the creation of law, although one or another may account for the formation of any particular law or kind of law. With these considerations in mind, let us now turn to an examination of the processes of legislative, administrative, and judicial lawmaking.

LEGISLATION

The foremost legal task of legislative bodies is to make law (Loewenberg et al., 2002). The term *legislation* describes the deliberate creation of legal precepts by a body of government that gives articulate expression to such legal precepts in a formalized legal document. In Canada, "[t]he ultimate source and maker of law . . . is the legislative body having jurisdiction in the area. Because Canada is a confederation with 11 legislative bodies, each must be considered supreme in its own right, and therefore they are the ultimate makers of law" (Yates et al., 2000:35). However, since the 1982 introduction of the *Charter of Rights and Freedoms* into the Constitution of Canada, Canada has adopted a limited judicial check on the supremacy of Parliament in that any parliamentary enactment that violates the Charter can be struck down by the courts.

Legislation, as such, must be distinguished from normative pronouncements made by the courts. The verbal expression of a legal rule or principle by a judge does not have the same degree of finality as the authoritative formulation of a legal proposition by a legislative body. Consider that while "[h]istorically, changes to the law, which were made by judges in the common law system, occurred slowly and minutely, almost imperceptibly. . . [a] new statute . . . can make drastic changes with the stroke of a pen" (Yates et al., 2000:38). Furthermore, although both adjudication and legislation involve the deliberate creation of laws by a body of government, the judiciary is not a body set up primarily for the purpose of lawmaking. As Chapter 2 explained, the judiciary's main function is to decide disputes under a pre-existing law, and the law-creating function of the judges should be considered incidental to their primary function of adjudication.

There are several other differences between legislative and judicial lawmaking that should be kept in mind. Judge-made law stems from decisions on actual controversies. It provides no rules in advance for the decision of cases but waits for disputes to be brought before the court for decision. Although legislators are chronically playing catch-up and most commonly act in response to the rise of a social problem, they may also formulate rules in anticipation of cases. A judicial decision is based on a justification for applying a particular rule, whereas a statute usually does not contain an argumentative or justificatory statement. It simply states: This is forbidden, this is required, this is authorized.

In general, legislators have much more freedom to make significant changes and innovations in the law than do the courts. Legislators are also more responsive to public and private pressures than judges. Whereas judges deal with particular cases, legislators consider general problem areas with whole classes of related situations. At times, the attention of legislative bodies is drawn to a problem by a particular incident, but the law it eventually passes is designed for general applicability. For example, when the Canadian government passed the *Anti-Terrorism Act* (Bill C-36) in 2001, the terrorist attacks in the

United States of September 11 were fresh in legislators' minds, although the law that was enacted was designed to deal with a whole class of such possible occurrences.

Legislative lawmaking, at times, represents a response to some kind of problem, one acute enough to intrude on the well-being of a large number of individuals and their organizations or on the well-being of the government itself—one conspicuous enough to attract the attention of at least some legislators. Consider here that within a year of the September 11 attacks, governments in no fewer than 50 nations worldwide enacted or proposed laws (e.g., the 2001 *USA Patriot Act*; Britain's *Anti-Terrorism Crime and Security Act 2001*) that shifted the balance between security and liberty away from a privacy-protective stance and toward a stance that emphasizes the preservation of security. According to the human rights group Privacy International and the Electronic Privacy Information Centre (EPIC), four trends were discernible in the legislation created in the immediate aftermath of the September 11 attack: "[t]he swift erosion of pro-privacy laws; greater data sharing among corporations, police and spy agencies; greater eavesdropping; and sharply increased interest in people-tracking technologies, such as face recognition systems and national ID cards" (McCullagh, 2002). However, legislation can also be generated (among other ways) by social unrest, conflict, and environmental deterioration (Lazarus, 2004). In addition, legislation can be prompted by technological innovation—with nations electing to respond in quite different ways (see Box 4.1).

However, neither legislators' perception that a socially problematic condition exists nor their agreement with a group's particular claims for action is certain to lead to legislation. The probability of some form of legislative response increases when (1) powerful interest groups mobilize their members to seek legislative action; (2) the unorganized public becomes intensely concerned with an issue or, conversely, is indifferent to the particular measures advocated by an interest group; and (3) there is no pressure to maintain the status quo or opposition to the proposed legislation.

BOX 4.1 LIFE AND LAW: LEGAL RESPONSES TO THE NEW
REPRODUCTIVE TECHNOLOGIES

New reproductive technologies (e.g., artificial insemination, ovum donation, and in-vitro fertilization) provide many with expanded opportunities to have children. However, nations vary in their responses to these developments. To illustrate, consider the disparate legal landscapes of Israel and Canada. Kahn (2000:2) notes that Israel has not only been a "global leader" in the research and development of the new reproductive technologies, but that its lawyers "have actively fought for legislation guaranteeing broad-based access to reproductive technology, whether by challenging existing regulations that limit access to these technologies or by drafting innovative legislation regarding their use." She observes that in Israel, the issue of reproduction has "deep political and historical roots." Some Israelis, she reports, perceive that a high birth rate is essential in order to offset "a demographic threat represented by Palestinian and Arab birthrates," to "produce soldiers to defend the fledgling state," or to "'replace' the six million Jews killed in the

Holocaust." In addition to Judaism's encouragement of fertility and child-centred family traditions, she observes that Israelis possess a heightened sensitivity to "practices designed to limit Jewish births, given that such policies were often employed in various diaspora contexts as part of other anti-Semitic measures" (p. 3). In consequence, it is perhaps not surprising that Israel's laws and social policies encourage and facilitate the use of new reproductive technologies. For example, when Israeli legislators passed the *Embryo-Carrying Agreements Law* in 1996, it became the first country in the world to legalize surrogate mother agreements. In addition, there are more fertility clinics per capita in Israel than in any other country in the world and "every Israeli, regardless of religion or status, is eligible for unlimited rounds of in-vitro fertilization treatment free of charge, up to the birth of two live children"—a commitment that "theoretically obligates the state to subsidize hundreds of thousands of dollars of infertility treatment . . . as a standard part of the basic basket of health services" (pp. 3–4).

Research on the prevalence of infertility in Canada suggests that between 11.5 to 15.7 percent of all heterosexual couples aged 18 to 44 experience infertility (Bushnik et al., 2012); these couples may benefit from the new reproductive technologies along with those who seek to conceive in same-sex unions or as lone parents. Yet, in contrast to Israel, Canada's response to these technologies has been notably more cautious. Indeed, it seems telling that the 1993 report of the Royal Commission on New Reproductive Technologies was entitled *Proceed with Care*. It recommended that the government ban surrogate motherhood; the sale of eggs, sperm, embryos, and fetal tissue; and the sale of eggs in exchange for in-vitro services. It also proposed that Canada close clinics that provide sex selection services and control in-vitro fertilization. After four failed attempts to create a law to govern reproductive technologies, the *Assisted Human Reproduction Act* (AHRA) (Bill C-6) received Royal Assent in 2004 and came fully into force in 2007. It prohibited "human cloning, commercial (but not volunteer) surrogacy contracts, the sale of human sperm and eggs, sex selection [if used for purposes other than the prevention, diagnosis and treatment of a sex-linked disorder or defect], genetic alteration, creation of artificial wombs and retrieval of eggs from fetuses and cadavers" (Dranoff, 2011:25). In *Reference re Assisted Human Reproduction Act* (2010), the Supreme Court of Canada found that various parts of this federal law were unconstitutional for they encroached upon provincial/territorial jurisdictional authority over the delivery of health care. However, "most provinces have not taken up the issue" and, as a result, "many fertility services remain largely unregulated" (Weeks, 2015). On October 1, 2016, Health Canada issued a notice of its intent to develop regulations under the AHRA that would "strengthen and clarify the regulatory framework governing assisted human reproduction in Canada" (Government of Canada, 2016). It also acknowledged that "scientific and technological advances have introduced procedures and techniques not previously envisioned, and the attitudes of Canadians towards assisted human reproduction may have shifted" (*Canada Gazette*, 2016).

Typically, a series of pre-lawmaking stages precedes the introduction of a legislative plan. The first stage is the *instigation and publicizing* of a particular problem (such as nuclear waste disposal). Typical instigators include the mass media (such as special TV programs or a series of articles or editorials in major newspapers or news magazines) or an author (as we shall see later in this chapter) who documents and dramatizes a social problem. The second stage is *information-gathering*. This stage entails collecting data on the nature, magnitude, and consequences of a problem; alternative schemes for solving the problem and their costs, benefits, and inherent difficulties; the likely political impact of each scheme; and the feasibility of various compromises. The third stage is *formulation*, or devising and advocating a specific legislative remedy for the problem. The fourth stage is *interests-aggregation*, or obtaining support for the proposed measure from other lawmakers through trade-offs and compromises, the championing of one interest group over others, or mediating among conflicting groups. The fifth stage is *mobilization*, the exertion of pressures, persuasion, or control on behalf of a measure by one who is able, often by virtue of his or her institutional position, to take effective and relatively direct action to secure enactment. Whether an issue goes beyond the first three stages usually depends on the support it receives from individuals, groups, or governmental units that possess authority and legitimacy in the policy area and on the support that the proponents of a proposal are able to muster from key figures in the legislature. The last stage is *modification*, the marginal alteration of a proposal—sometimes strengthening it and sometimes granting certain concessions to its opponents to facilitate its introduction (Price, 1972:4).

These six stages, although they show a certain sequential character and complementarity, do not simply represent the components that the legislative process must *necessarily* include. They also illustrate the norms that govern the legislative process (for example, the airing of an issue and the attempt to accommodate diverse interests) and the thoroughly political character of the legislative lawmaking process.

ADMINISTRATIVE LAWMAKING

Administrative agencies engage in lawmaking through rulemaking and through the adjudication of cases and controversies arising under their jurisdiction. Administrative agencies pursue both civil remedies and criminal sanctions to promote compliance with regulatory and administrative laws (Warren, 2010; Feldman, 2016).

ADMINISTRATIVE RULEMAKING

Administrative rulemaking refers to the establishment of prospective rules (Beerman, 2006; Kerwin and Furlong, 2010). A *rule* is a law made by an administrative agency. Through rulemaking, a particular administrative agency legislates policy:

> For example, a workers' compensation board is created by provincial legislation called the *Workers' Compensation Act*, and the chairman [sic] of its board (or the minister responsible) is given the power under that act to make the regulations necessary

to fulfill the goals of the legislation. The board's authority would include the power to specify under what circumstances a person will receive compensation, and how much. As long as the regulations are within the limits of the authority granted by the legislation, they have the force of law.

(Yates et al., 2000:37)

As the example above suggests, administrative powers are principally created by statutes ("enabling legislation"). It is frequently the case that these statutes establish an entity (e.g., agency, board, commission, tribunal) that is to exercise these powers. For example, human rights legislation established human rights commissions and endowed these newly created administrative decision makers (ADM) with certain powers. Although either the federal or provincial government may create an ADM, "the authority given the ADM cannot be contrary to the division of powers in sections 91 and 92 of the Constitution Act, 1867; thus, the federal government cannot create an ADM to decide matters that fall within the provincial sphere, and vice versa" (Nova Scotia Barristers' Society, 2016:2).

The flexibility of agencies in rule-making procedures is much greater than in administrative adjudication. Formal hearings are not held unless required by statute or some rule created by the ADM. Insofar as legislation permits, administrators can be free to consult informally with interested parties; administrative hearings are not bound to follow the same rigid rules that dictate procedure in civil courts. As a result, the number of parties that may participate is also potentially far greater than in court proceedings.

Much of the immense code of federal regulations is composed of the substantive rules of administrative agencies. Consider that the rules and regulations of the *Income Tax Act* are amended so often that they are republished annually in book form, with the version current to January 1, 2017 no less than 3,167 pages! In addition, administrative agencies issue a variety of pronouncements that are less formal and binding than their legislative regulations, which are designed to clarify the laws they are administering (see, for example, Beerman, 2006). Some of these pronouncements represent *interpretative regulations*. In response to inquiries, agencies may issue advisory rulings that interpret the law with reference to particular types of situations. Some agencies also publish instructions, guides, pamphlets, and other explanatory materials.

Regulatory agencies state many of their regulatory policies through rulemaking. Rate-setting proceedings (for example, limits on the fees brokerage houses may charge for a certain class of service) of regulatory bodies are also considered to be rulemaking. Outside of the regulatory realm, various government departments are constantly stating their general policies through the issuance of rules ranging from banking practices to dress codes in the military (McCartney, 2010).

ADMINISTRATIVE ADJUDICATION

The second way agencies create rules is through their adjudicative powers. **Administrative adjudication** is the process by which an administrative agency issues an order.

Administrative orders have retroactive effect, as contrasted with the prospective effect of rulemaking. In rulemaking, the agency is apprising in advance those under its jurisdiction of what the law is. When an agency opens proceedings with the intention of issuing an order, it must eventually interpret existing policy or define new policy to apply to the case at hand. The parties involved do not know how the policy is going to be applied until after the order is issued, giving the agency decision retroactive effect. Adjudicative lawmaking tends to produce inconsistencies because cases are decided on an individual basis. The rule of *stare decisis* (requiring precedent to be followed, which will be discussed in the context of judicial lawmaking) need not prevail (Feldman, 2016), and the high turnover of top-level administrators often results in a lack of continuity.

When an agency believes that the time has come to formulate a policy decision in an official text, it can draft and issue a regulation. But when an agency prefers to wait until the contours of a problem become clearer, it can continue to deal with the problem on a case-by-case basis, formulating a series of decisional rules couched in terms that ensure continuing flexibility. Furthermore, an agency, unlike a court, does not have to wait passively for cases to be brought before it. Its enforcement officials can go out looking for cases that will raise the issues its adjudicating officials want to rule on. An appeal of a decision made by an ADM is not always possible for "[a] right to appeal a decision made by an ADM, whether to another administrative body or to a court, exists only if such a right is explicitly created in the enabling legislation" (Nova Scotia Barristers Society, 2016:3).

JUDICIAL LAWMAKING

The role of the judiciary in the administrative state has been complex. In reviewing the historical record, Arthurs (1980:225) charges that "the courts utterly failed to deal with the most significant legal repercussions of the Industrial Revolution in the nineteenth century and with the revolution of rising expectations in the twentieth." Bogart (1994:111) concurs that, historically, in areas such as workers' compensation, labour relations, and human rights, the courts almost invariably responded with a "distressing rigidity":

> In administrative issues our judges have mostly been the keepers of pure liberal ideology: the state assigned minimalist policing functions, and the market was the best distributor of goods and services. Whether it was in such matters as occupational health and safety, the development of human rights, or the advent of unions and collective bargaining, the courts' activities wove a pattern of indifference, even hostility towards state activities. . . . [U]nder the guise of principles that seemed to treat everyone equally, the health and safety of workers were ignored with abandon, poisons were dumped into the environment, and the most insidious acts of prejudice were taken as a hallmark of self-regarding behaviour.

Within these areas, Bogart (p. 116) observes, a common pattern emerged: (1) the courts' initial proposal of rules that extolled "strict liberal notions of individual responsibility, autonomy, and freedom centred on economic entitlement"; (2) the adoption of a more communitarian perspective by legislatures that "inquired into the actual results, and recognized other values (such as the need for compensation, legitimacy of collective action, and claims to equal treatment)"; (3) the creation of an administrative body; and, finally, (4) the removal of these issues from the courts, "at least in terms of initial decision-making and the creation of some administrative agency to decide such questions."

Although the record of the courts is not exemplary, in the postwar period, a number of countries have attempted to "harness litigation and the courts to effect social and political change" (Bogart, 2002:144). The most notable example is the United States, where, as early as the mid-19th century, de Tocqueville (1835:270) observed that there was "hardly a political question . . . which does not sooner or later turn into a judicial one." In the United States, there has been a steady increase in judicial lawmaking over the years (McCloskey, 2016), with legislators and administrators showing considerable willingness to let judges take the heat for controversial actions, such as allowing or disallowing abortion or ordering busing to desegregate schools. As a result, the judiciary in the United States has assumed an increasingly powerful role. However, the question of whether courts *should* assume an enhanced role in society is of obvious interest to Canadians since the 1982 adoption of the *Charter of Rights and Freedoms*.

While the Charter, unlike the U.S. Bill of Rights, explicitly provides that any rights are subject to "reasonable limits prescribed by law as can be demonstrably justified in a free and democratic society," it additionally empowers judges to strike down legislation and/or nullify actions of public officials that contravene the rights enumerated within it. And, after displaying a certain initial timidity, Canadian courts have now tackled "questions relating to abortion, mercy killing, assisted suicide, language rights, and a broad array of issues relating to the administration of criminal justice" (Bogart, 2002:151). Indeed, Sauvageau, Schneiderman, and Taras (2006:21) point out that there is a notable congruence between de Tocqueville's mid-19th century comments about the judiciary in America and an observation by Chief Justice Beverley McLachlin: "More and more, courts are being called upon to decide questions of central importance to great numbers of people in our society."

As Kelly (2005:124) observes, "Since the entrenchment of the *Charter of Rights and Freedoms* in the Constitution, there are some who take the view that [Canadian] judges have, to a certain extent, usurped or taken over the role of the legislature in the making of law." However, a number of questions remain unanswered: "Does equipping courts with the power to nullify the enactments of elected officials change the political process, making the forging of policy through popular politics more difficult? Do rights anchored in courts mean less agreement regarding the common good?" (p. 150). As well, given concern with maintaining a national identity in the shadow of the most powerful nation of the world, one might also ask if the entrenchment of rights and the enhanced role of the judiciary might lead to our country becoming progressively more indistinguishable from the United States.

In the United States, judicial activism has also evoked criticism. Thus, some charge that judicial activism has created an "Imperial Judiciary" (Glazer, 1975) that is not accountable to the American people (Graglia, 1994; Dow, 2009, Lindquist and Cross, 2009). For example, Glazer (1975) contends that too much power has moved from the elected, representative branches of government to the judiciary, and that the courts "are now seen as forces of nature, difficult to predict and impossible to control" (p. 110). (For an opposing view see Kozlowski, 2003.) In like spirit, Bogart (2002:145) has argued that no matter how "wrong-headed" Canadian politicians may seem to be, they "can point to the power of the ballot as the source of legitimacy of their actions: the force they wield rests on the base of the democratic process. . . . Life, for courts," he notes, "is more complicated. Since the power they exercise can, by definition, be anti-majoritarian, proponents of an ambitious judicial role have to offer a rationale that does not depend on popular will or authority" (for a fuller discussion of this issue see Lewans, 2016; Leishman, 2006; Roach, 2005; Songer, 2008).

LAWMAKING BY PRECEDENTS

In common-law countries, the doctrine of *stare decisis* ("stand by what has been decided") is a deeply rooted common-law tradition, with judicial decisions typically building on the precedents established by past decisions. By contrast, civil-law countries, such as France and Germany, have a codified legal system where the basic law is stated in *codes*. These are statutes enacted by the national parliament, which arranges whole fields of law (family law, housing law, and so forth) in an orderly, logical, and comprehensive way. The judges follow the basic principles of law found in acts of parliament. In common-law countries, judges base their decisions on **case law**, a body of opinion developed by judges over time in the course of deciding particular cases. The doctrine of precedent, the notion that the judge is bound by what has already been decided, is a strictly common-law doctrine (Friedman, 2002).

In the common-law system, following precedents is often much easier and less time-consuming than reformulating solutions to problems that have already been faced. Precedent enables the judge to take advantage of the accumulated wisdom of earlier generations and helps to minimize arbitrariness in judicial decision-making. It conforms to the belief that like wrongs deserve like remedies and to the desire for equal justice under the law. More important, the practice of following precedents enables individuals (with the assistance of lawyers) to plan their conduct in the expectation that past decisions will be honoured in the future. Although certainty, predictability, and continuity are not the only objectives of law, they are certainly important ones. Many disputes are avoided, and others are settled without litigation, simply because individuals are familiar with how the courts will respond to certain types of behaviour (van Geel, 2009).

Despite the importance of precedent, judges do make decisions that overturn prior decisions. A judge may also be confronted with a case for which there is simply no precedents. To make a decision, judges must search through cases for any analogies that seem applicable. Through the selection of appropriate and desirable analogies (which is, indeed, a value judgment), judges make law in instances when precedents do not guide them.

THE INTERPRETATION OF STATUTES

In interpreting statutes, judges determine the effects of legislative decisions. In the vast majority of cases involving the application of statutes, the courts have no trouble determining how to apply the statute. Most cases fall squarely inside or outside of the law's provisions.

In some cases, however, the intent of a legislature is ambiguous. Some statutes contain unintentional errors and ambiguities because of bad drafting of the law. Other statutes are unclear because those who pushed them through the legislature sought to avoid opposition by being vague or silent on potentially controversial matters. An important reason for the lack of clarity in many instances is that the proponents have not been able to foresee and provide for all possible future situations. This provides the courts with a potential opportunity to engage in lawmaking.

In order to forestall misinterpretation, a statute is generally crafted to begin with a section that defines terms used within it. There are also federal and provincial interpretations that outline certain rules of interpretation that apply to all statutes. Beyond these legislative interpretation rules, the courts have developed three main rules of statutory interpretation: the literal rule, the golden rule, and the mischief rule. The foremost principle of interpretation, the **literal rule** (sometimes called the "plain meaning rule") sets out that the statute should be applied literally, regardless of whether the judge approves or disapproves of its result. As Olivo (2004:71) remarks of this rule, "If Parliament is supreme, then it may be unfair or absurd if it chooses to be, subject to limits on legislative action imposed by the *Charter of Rights and Freedoms*." The golden rule and mischief rule address ambiguous legislation. The **golden rule** specifies that in cases where the literal interpretation of a statute would lead to a "logical absurdity, an inconsistency or a repugnancy," the court can move from the literal interpretation—but "only so far as is necessary to remove the conflicting construction" (Olivo, 2004:71). The **mischief rule** states that when confronted by ambiguous statutes, "attention should be given to the problem the statute was created to solve" or "what mischief . . . the statute [was] designed to suppress, or what remedy is being advanced by it" (Yates et al., 2000:39).

In addition, judges may use a variety of external aids to assist their interpretation of statutes, including scholarly and interpretive writings, interpretation statutes (which exist at both the federal and provincial levels), and the legislative history of statutes. Olivo (p. 73) notes that although "[i]n the search for legislative intent, it has long been traditional in Canada and Britain to ignore Hansard (the official record of debates in a legislature), committee reports, royal commission reports, ministers' speeches, press releases, and other such documents" with the assumption that "one need go no further than the words of the statute" to find its meaning; there is "some indication that legislative history may have a legitimate interpretive role" in *Charter of Rights* cases. He reports a "growing use of the technique in constitutional cases as a way of gaining insight into the meaning of legislation under the constitutional challenge."

INFLUENCES ON THE LAWMAKING PROCESSES

Lawmaking is a response to many social forces. The forces that influence lawmaking cannot always be precisely determined, measured, or evaluated. At times, a multitude of forces operate simultaneously. In this section we consider a limited number of influences on lawmaking: interest groups, public opinion, and the social sciences.

INTEREST GROUPS

The **interest group thesis** contends that laws are created because of the special interests of certain groups in the population (Mahood, 2000). Examples of interest group influence in lawmaking abound (see, for example, Di Gioacchino et al., 2004; Hastie and Kothari, 2009; Rozell et al., 2006; Smith, 2009). Laws governing the use of alcohol, regulations concerning sexual conduct, abortion bills, pure food and drug legislation, antitrust laws, and automobile safety standards are all documented instances of interest group activity.

The nature of the interaction between interest groups and lawmakers varies to an extent based on the branch of government. Judges, although they are not immune to interest group pressures, are generally not lobbied in the same way as legislators or administrators. To reach the courts, a lawyer must be hired, formal proceedings must be followed, and grievances must be expressed in legal terminology. To influence legislators, a group must be economically powerful or able to mobilize a large number of voters. Minorities and the poor may find the courts more attractive because they are more readily available: If a group has enough money to hire a lawyer, it can seek court action to further its interests. Interest groups may also turn to courts because they assume that the judiciary may be more sympathetic to their objectives than legislators (Carp et al., 2017). However, the importance of wealth in accessing the courts or mobilizing an effective interest group should be apparent.

The techniques used by interest groups to influence courts are different from those used to influence legislative or administrative bodies. As political scientist Herbert Jacob observed: "The principal techniques are: to bring conflicts to a court's attention by initiating test cases, to bring added information to the courts through *amicus curiae* (friend of the court) briefs, and to communicate with judges indirectly by placing information favourable to the group's cause in legal and general periodicals" (1984:151). By instituting test cases, interest groups provide judges with opportunities to make social policy. Often, such briefs communicate relevant social science research findings to a particular case). By providing information through *amicus curiae* briefs, interest groups expand the confines of the judicial process and build coalitions with other groups (Anderson, 2014; Kearne and Merrill, 2000; McGuire, 1994). The final technique is to publish decisions in legal periodicals. Judges generally read these journals to keep abreast of legal scholarship and sometimes even cite them as authority for their rulings. Publication in these journals gets one's views before the courts and before their attentive public.

Interactions between interest groups and legislative and administrative lawmakers are more overtly political in nature. Many interest groups maintain offices staffed with people who keep track of developments in the legislative and administrative branches and attempt to influence their activities. Some groups pay for the services of law firms in dealing with legislators or administrators. These firms provide expertise in such areas as antitrust and tax regulations and use their personal contacts with important lawmakers on behalf of their clients.

Several specific conditions enhance the potential influence of interest groups on lawmakers (Ripley, 1988). In many instances, there may not be two competing groups on an issue. When only one point of view is presented, the group is likely to get much of what it wants. Similarly, if the groups on one side of a controversy are unified and coordinated on the principal issues they want to advance (or if they can minimize their disagreements), their chances of success are increased. If certain key members of legislative bodies believe in the interest group's position, the probability of success also rises. The visibility of an issue is another consideration in influencing lawmakers. When the issue is not too visible, or when interest groups seek single distinct amendments to bills (such as to alter soybean export quotas in addition to others proposed by farming interests), as contrasted with large legislative packages, the chances for success increase. Conversely, as the visibility of issues increases and public attention grows (such as with wage-price controls), the influence of interest groups tends to diminish. Interest groups are likely to have greater influence on issues that coincide with the interests of the groups they purport to represent. For example, unions such as the United Steel Workers Canada or CAW Canada may be very influential in matters concerning working conditions, but they are likely to receive less attention from lawmakers when they advocate higher tariffs for imported goods or when they make attempts to guide foreign policy. Finally, interest groups are likely to have greater influence on amendments than on entire pieces of legislation. This is because amendments are generally technical and less understood by the public.

In general, the effectiveness of interest groups in influencing lawmakers is related to such considerations as their financial and information resources, their offensive or defensive positions, and the status of the group in the eyes of lawmakers. Financial resources determine the ability of an interest group to support court suits, lobbying, public relations, and other activities (Abramson, 1998; Marlin, 2016). Interest groups that support the status quo have an advantage over groups trying to bring change, because whereas the latter must overcome several obstacles in the lawmaking process, the former may frustrate change at any of several points in the process. But the influence of an interest group depends mainly on its status as perceived by lawmakers. An interest group is particularly influential in situations where a lawmaker shares the same group affiliation (for example, when farm groups talk to legislators who are farmers), where the group is considered important to the legislator's constituency, and where the group is recognized as a legitimate and reliable source of information. In addition, a group's competence to influence lawmaking is enhanced by its ability to bring about social or economic disruptions. Threats of disorder, disruption, and violence have been, at times, effective bargaining weapons of relatively powerless groups (Shaw et al., 2010). Similarly, the threat of a decline in the supply of such necessities as food, medical services, and energy has been used to influence lawmakers. There is little doubt that the ability of an interest group to create a crisis (whether a social disorder, an economic slowdown, or the reduction of supply of a needed product or service) gives it considerable clout in the lawmaking process.

PUBLIC OPINION

Although certain legal issues capture public attention, Canadians are unlikely to be aware of the plethora of laws that impact their lives. As a result of such limited awareness, there is a fair amount of selectivity involved in the expression of opinions toward the law. Some questions, therefore, arise in the discussion of the influence of public opinion on lawmaking. One concerns the timing of the relationship between the two. At what point does the accumulation of practice and belief make the reflection of those practices and beliefs in law inevitable? For example, how many marijuana violations cause the law relating to marijuana to be changed?

A related question concerns the identification of those individuals whose opinion is expressed in lawmaking and the means of translating those opinions into legal outcomes. The *people* may mean a numerical majority, an influential elite, women, the poor, the middle class, the young, the aged, students, professors, and so forth. Popular views may be similar throughout all segments of the population, but on many important issues opinions will differ (Norrander and Wilcox, 2009).

A more meaningful way of looking at the influence of public opinion on lawmaking would be to consider the diverse opinions of many "publics" (that is, segments of society) bearing on specific concerns such as sentencing offenders for particular crimes (Davies et al., 2007:12–14). These opinions are expressed through a multitude of channels, such as the media, political parties, and the various types of interest groups. Care should be exercised, however, not to overestimate the catalytic part played by public opinion in lawmaking. As Friedman states:

> The "public opinion" that affects the law is like the economic power which makes the market. This is so in two essential regards: Some people, but only some, take enough interest in any particular commodity to make their weight felt; second, there are some people who have more power and wealth than others. At one end of the spectrum stand such figures as the president of . . . General Motors; at the other . . . babies, and prisoners.
>
> (1975:163)

The differential influence of public opinion on lawmaking processes is a well-known phenomenon and is recognized by lawmakers. Lawmakers are aware that some people are more equal than others because of money, talent, or choice. Notes Friedman:

> They know that 100 wealthy, powerful constituents . . . outweigh thousands of poor, weak constituents . . . Most people do not shout, threaten, or write letters. They remain quiet and obscure, unless a head count reveals they are there. This is the "silent majority"; paradoxically, this group matters only when it breaks its silence—when it mobilizes or is mobilized by others.
>
> (p. 164)

Lawmakers also know that most people have no clear opinions on most issues with which judicial, administrative, and legislative bodies must deal. This means that they have a wide latitude within which to operate. Thus, for example, when legislators claim to be representing the opinion of their ridings, they are, on most issues, representing the opinion of only a minority of their constituents, most of whom do not know or care about the issue at hand and do not communicate their views on it.

In spite of these considerations, public opinion does exert an influence on the lawmaking process (Carp et al., 2017). Dennis S. Ippolito and his colleagues (1976) identified three types of influences that press lawmakers into formulating certain decisions: direct, group, and indirect influences.

Direct influence refers to constituent pressures that offer rewards or sanctions to lawmakers. Rewards for compliance and sanctions for noncompliance may be votes in an election or re-election campaign, financial assistance, and other forms of pressure that could possibly range from the representative's standing in lawmaking bodies to prestige in his or her own particular community. This kind of influence is not confined to legislators. Members of the judiciary are also pressured by partisan publications to make certain decisions consistent with opinions and interests that run throughout the jurisdiction of a particular court.

Group influence is exerted by organized interest groups representing a special constituency. Political parties, interest groups, and citizen action groups are continually influencing the lawmaking process. The motivation behind joining such groups is the perceived need for expressing a point of view in a manner that will influence lawmakers. In this context, public opinion becomes organized around a specific issue or an immediate objective (for example, the pros and cons of euthanasia). Through the process of organizing, interests are made specific, and public opinion backing is sought in the attempt to gain an advantage in pressing for change or redress through the legal machinery.

Indirect influence occurs when legislators act in accordance with constituent preferences because they either share such preferences or believe such preferences should prevail over their own judgment. This type of influence is indicative of the importance attached to public opinion polls.

Public opinion polls seek to determine the aggregate view people in a community hold on current important issues. Generally, the use of polls in lawmaking is encouraged. Decades ago, Irving Crespi (1979) recognized their benefit and argued forcefully that lawmakers could be more effective if they learned to draw upon the full fruits of survey research. Direct evidence—unfiltered by the interpretations of special interests or lobby groups—of the wants, needs, aspirations, and concerns of the general public needs to be accounted for in lawmaking activities. In lawmaking processes, Irving Crespi advised that first there should be an attempt to determine the views of both the general public and that segment of the public that would be directly affected by a particular law. Then that public opinion should be made part of the formative stages of the lawmaking process, and not simply a force to be coped with after the fact: "The difference between treating public attitudes and opinions as a relatively minor variable instead of an influence that should be authoritative is ultimately the difference between technocratic and democratic government" (p. 18). Yet, the issue may be more complex than Crespi's commentary suggests. For example, one might rhetorically ask: If a democratic government enacts rights–enhancing legislation in a country whose population has been polled and revealed to oppose such legislation (or to be blatantly racist, misogynistic, or homophobic), would that indicate bad government?

LAWMAKING AND SOCIAL SCIENCE

Lawmakers have long been aware of the contribution that social scientists can make to the lawmaking process (Costanzo, Krauss, and Pezdek, 2007). Experts abound in a variety of fields, and there is a growing reliance on social scientists and the research data they generate in diverse areas ranging from consumer surveys in trademark suits to the impact of mandatory arrest policies for abusers in cases of domestic violence.

Efforts to bring social science to bear on lawmaking processes involve the use of both qualitative and quantitative social science data and reliance on the social scientist as an expert witness in specific legal cases. Social science data may be collected and analyzed for academic purposes and later utilized by one or more sides of a dispute (see, for example, Gold, 2005). Social science research may also be reactive in the sense that parties initially request it in a dispute. In such instances, the materials may address facts in the case or initiate an intervention in the lawmaking process. Social science research may also be undertaken in a proactive fashion. In such a situation, a social scientist may undertake an investigation with the anticipation of subsequent use of the results by lawmakers. For example, 40 researchers from Canada, the United States, the United Kingdom, Australia, Ireland, Thailand, Malaysia, South Korea, and China joined together in the International Tobacco Control Policy Evaluation Project; the project's aim was to investigate and evaluate national-level tobacco control policies that were scheduled for introduction in more than 100 countries. Their research, the first to evaluate the policies introduced by the first-ever international health treaty—The Framework Convention on Tobacco Control—sought to establish an evidence base for FCTC policies by evaluating the effectiveness of such strategies as warning labels, advertising and promotion bans, higher taxes, and protections against second-hand smoke (University of Waterloo, 2006).

At times, social scientists are asked to directly assist either the court or the legislator in the preparation of background documents pertinent to a particular issue or to serve on commissions intended for policy recommendations. However, there are controversies surrounding the role of social scientists in lawmaking. Moynihan (1979) proposes two general reasons why social scientists have been criticized for their involvement in lawmaking processes. First, he points out that social science is basically concerned with the prediction of future events, whereas the purpose of the law is to order them. Notes Moynihan: "But where social science seeks to establish a fixity of *relationships* such that the consequences of behaviour can be known in advance—or, rather, narrowed to a manageable range of possibilities—law seeks to dictate future performance on the basis of past *agreements*" (p. 16). For example, it is the function of the law to order alimony payments; it is the function of social science to attempt to estimate the likelihood of their being paid, of their effect on work behaviour and remarriage in male and female parties, or similar probabilities. The second reason he suggests is that "social science is rarely dispassionate, and social scientists are frequently caught up in the politics which their work necessarily involves" (p. 19). Social scientists are, to a great extent, involved with problem solving, and the identification of a "problem" usually entails a political statement that implies a solution. According to Moynihan (1979:19), "Social scientists are never more revealing of themselves than when challenging the objectivity of one another's work. In some fields almost *any* study is assumed to have a more-or-less-discoverable political purpose."

SOURCES OF IMPETUS FOR LAW

An **impetus** is a fundamental prerequisite for setting the mechanism of lawmaking in motion. Demands for new laws or changes in existing ones come from a variety of sources. These sources, which are not mutually exclusive, include detached scholarly diagnosis, a voice in the wilderness, protest activities, social movements, public interest groups, and the mass media.

DETACHED SCHOLARLY DIAGNOSIS

The impetus for law may come from a detached scholarly undertaking. From time to time, academicians may consider a given practice or condition as detrimental in the context of existing values and norms. They may communicate their diagnoses to their colleagues or to the general public through either scholarly or popular forums. In some cases, they may even carry the perceived injustice to the legislature in search of legal redress.

There have been a number of attempts by academics in a variety of disciplines to provide an impetus for lawmaking as an outgrowth of their investigations. Notable early efforts include David Caplovitz's *The Poor Pay More* (1963) and *Consumers in Trouble: A Study of Debtors in Default* (1974), which argued for reform of consumer credit laws, and Amitai Etzioni's *Genetic Fix* (1973), which examined the implications of "human engineering." Research by feminist scholars on sexual and domestic violence led to new understandings of these crimes and a series of reforms which have altered the legal system's response to their victims and offenders (Sheehy, 2012; McOrmond-Plummer et al.; Johnson and Dawson, 2011; Ursel et al, 2008). The source of impetus, however, is not limited to ivory towers. It can have other origins, as the following sections will demonstrate.

A VOICE IN THE WILDERNESS

Through their writings, many people outside of academe succeed or even excel in calling public attention to a particular problem or social condition. For example, in the domain of environmental protection laws, it would be difficult not to consider the book *Silent Spring* by Rachel Carson (1962). It was the first time that the environmental threat posed by pesticides was announced to a wide audience. There is a long list of those whose literary efforts stimulated changes in the law. For our purposes, it will suffice to call attention to simply two.

Ralph Nader was an unknown young lawyer at the time he published *Unsafe at Any Speed* (1965), which alerted the public to the automobile industry's unconcern for safety in the design and construction of American cars. This book is a model of the kind of journalism that, at times, initiates the rise of public concern over a given issue. As a result of his book, and General Motors's reaction to it, Nader became front-page news, and his charges took on new weight. Perhaps more than anyone else, he has contributed to and provided the impetus for the passing of a substantial number of auto safety provisions (Buckhorn, 1972:226). Isabel LeBourdais was a Canadian journalist who, in 1966, published *The Trial of Steven Truscott*. At the age of 14, Truscott was found guilty of the rape and murder of 12-year-old schoolgirl Lynn Harper and sentenced to hang. In her book, LeBourdais ravaged both the police investigation into Harper's killing and the conduct of Truscott's trial; simultaneously, she called into question a justice system that many people at the time believed to be infallible and beyond reproach. "Her argument that the court had erred and sentenced an innocent teen to death made front-page headlines and sparked public demonstration. The resulting uproar in Parliament led Lester Pearson's Liberal government to order a Supreme Court review" (CBC News, 2004a). Even though the Supreme Court ruled against Truscott being granted a new trial, Truscott became "the poster boy against capital punishment" (Halperin, 2004). His sentence was eventually commuted to life imprisonment and, after spending ten years in prison, Truscott was paroled. In August 2007, Truscott was formally acquitted of the crime by the Ontario Court of Appeal, and the Attorney General of Ontario, Michael Bryant, issued a formal apology to Truscott on behalf of the government for the "miscarriage of justice" that he had been subjected to (City News, 2007). In July 2008, Truscott was awarded $6.5 million in compensation by the government of Ontario (Ontario Ministry of the Attorney General, 2008). Many experts believe that the controversy over the Truscott case, which had been prompted by LeBourdais's scathing analysis, led to Canada's abolishment of the death penalty in 1976 (CBC News, 2004a).

There are other ways of transforming "private troubles into public issues" (Spector and Kitsuse, 1973:148). While some engage in a war of words to advance their concerns, others adopt more overtly confrontational tactics.

PROTEST ACTIVITY

Protest activity involves demonstrations, sit-ins, strikes, boycotts, and, more recently, various forms of electronic civil disobedience or "hacktivism" (Whyte, 2011) that dramatically emphasize a group's grievances or objectives (Staggenborg, 2016). Consider, in this context, that when in June 1990, Elijah Harper, "clasping an eagle feather in his hand, used procedural delays to block ratification of the Meech Lake Accord, which he felt did not adequately address the concerns of First Nations Canadians," he became a hero to at least some Canadians, with Indian leaders dubbing him "our Wayne Gretzky" (Morton and Weinfeld, 1998:320). In the same year, "members of the Kanesetake and Kahnawake reserves blockaded roads and a bridge to protest expansion of a golf course onto land at Oka that had been subject to Aboriginal claims since the 18th century" (Elliott, 2005:8). This protest activity, which was to escalate into violent confrontation between Aboriginals and members of the armed forces and police, "was followed by a series of Aboriginal occupations and blockages in support of claims and grievances throughout most of the rest of the 1990s" (Elliott, 2005:8).

Often, protest strategies have been considered tools of those who are unable or unwilling to engage in more conventional lawmaking or who regard it as useless (Lipschutz, 2006; Malleson and Wachsmuth, 2011). It should be noted at the outset that

> the relationship among law, protest, and social change is neither unidirectional nor symmetrical—nor always predictable. One major function of protest may be to secure changes in the law as a means of inducing change in social conditions. Another may be to bring about change directly without the intervention of the law. Still a third may be to bring about legal change which ratifies or legitimizes social change accomplished by other means. These functions are not mutually exclusive.
>
> (Grossman and Grossman, 1971:357)

But the impact of protest activities on law creation is clearly evident, for "the law in general, and the Court in particular, lacks a self-starter or capacity for initiating change on its own" (Grossman and Grossman, 1971:358).

Racial and sexual orientation minorities, poverty organizations, antiwar groups, and opponents of nuclear power have been among those who have employed protest techniques in recent years in attempts to create laws in favour of their objectives (see e.g., Hedican, 2012; Herman, 1994; Ramos, 2006; Warner, 2002; Yalden, 2009). Much of this activity is designed to generate favourable media coverage and, through this, the support of organizations and persons important in the eyes of lawmakers. But the young, the poor, and minority groups have not been the only ones to use protest techniques such as strikes and boycotts. Strike action has long been a central tactic of organized labour, including the unions of public employees, in pursuing political and economic goals. Consumers have used boycotts to protest high prices.

SOCIAL MOVEMENTS

Over the years, there have been many social movements that have culminated in proposals for, or the actual creation of, new laws and social policies (Johnston, 2010; Lipschutz, 2006; Tilly and Tarrow, 2007). By definition, a **social movement** is a type of collective behaviour whereby a group of individuals organize to promote certain changes or alterations in certain types of behaviour or procedures. Invariably, the movement has specified stated objectives, a hierarchical organizational structure, and a well-conceptualized and precise change-oriented ideology. The movement consciously and purposefully articulates the changes it desires through political, educational, or legal channels (see, for example, McAdam and Snow, 2010; Vanhala, 2011; Woods et al., 2012).

A good example is the movement to legalize abortion (Bennett, 2004). People had for some time regarded illegal abortion as dangerous, but efforts to prevent it (and thus end the death or serious injury of women) were unsuccessful. Then, the combined efforts of women's rights activists and trailblazing physician Dr. Henry Morgentaler led to an organized campaign for the repeal of abortion laws. Women's group leaders argued that a woman has an unassailable right over her own body and ought to be able to choose whether or not to terminate pregnancy.

On occasion, tragic events have caused the claims advanced by a social movement to resonate forcefully. For example, on December 6, 1989, the largest mass shooting in Canadian history occurred when a 25-year-old man, armed with a Sturm Ruger Mini-14 semiautomatic rifle, knives, and bandoliers of ammunition, entered the École Polytechnic in Montreal, killed 14 female students, and wounded 13 other students (nine women and four men). His rampage, which deliberately targeted women, ended with his suicide. The "Montreal Massacre," as it has come to be known, prompted the Canadian government to proclaim December 6 the National Day of Remembrance and Action on Violence Against Women and to create a Panel on Violence Against Women, which delivered its final report in 1993. In addition, it provided a catalytic environment for the inauguration of new legislation aimed at gun control and resulted in Bill C-68 receiving Royal Assent in December 1995. This legislation, which had as its centerpiece a licensing and registration system, was part of a wider framework of weapons control and sought to deter the use of firearms in criminal offences.

Of course, there are many other social movements, including ecology, civil rights, "crime without victims," and "law and order movements." However, it should be pointed out that not all social movements are successful in bringing about changes through laws. As a matter of fact, at any given moment, hundreds of groups with hundreds of messages are trying to get public attention; most will fail.

PUBLIC-INTEREST GROUPS

Lawmakers are very aware that private interests are much better represented than public interests (Farrand, 2015; Smit and Valiante, 2015; Van Wagner, 2016; Scully, 2012). There are literally hundreds of organizations and individuals who represent one or more private interests on a full- or part-time basis (Mahood, 2000). They range from extremely well financed organizations, involved in worldwide affairs and supported by lawyers and public relations experts, to small, single-issue groups. While there are over 20,000 entries in the 37th (2016) edition of *Associations Canada*, most represent specific private interests; the number of groups that claim to represent public interests (e.g., the Canadian Environmental Law Association; Public Interest Research Groups [PIRGs]) is comparatively small. Nevertheless, the latter have been instrumental in the initiation of a series of changes in the law designed to benefit and protect the public. For example, spurred by the belief that the world faces an ultimate ecocatastrophe unless immediate and successful efforts are made to halt the abuse and deterioration of the environment, the Sierra Club and like-minded organizations have provided the impetus for a series of laws dealing with the protection of the environment. While PIRGs were originally launched in the United States in the 1970s by activist Ralph Nader as a means of harnessing the energy and talent of students in solving social problems, there are now over 100 PIRG chapters in the United States and 21 in Canada, funded through voluntary student fees. The goals of PIRGs are to motivate civic participation and responsibility by encouraging individuals to become informed, concerned, and active in their communities; to recognize and pursue integrative analyses of societal and environmental issues; to respect and encourage local and global ecosystem integrity; to encourage diversity and social equality for all people by opposing all forms of oppression; to work in a cooperative way, employing a consensual decision-making process; and to work in solidarity with other like-minded environmental and social justice movements. PIRGs in Canada have produced a variety of issue-oriented publications and audio-visual materials on such topics as the food industry, acid rain, nuclear power, tenant rights, Ontario Hydro, freedom of information, and the management of toxic waste.

Impetus for law may also come from the various quasi-public specialized interest groups. They may represent certain economic interests, such as consumer groups or organized labour. Or they may represent certain occupational interests, such as the Canadian Medical Association, which not only exercises considerable control over the practice of medicine in this country, but also takes stands, raises money, and lobbies in favour of specific positions on such issues as euthanasia, drugs, and alcohol. The same can be said for the Canadian Association of University Teachers (though not on the same issues). Still others include groups representing what may be called moral interests and bringing together those with similar views on, for example, drug use, pornography, or suicide-assistance. The important point to remember is that all these organizations can agitate for changes in the law and can provide the needed impetus for it.

For a group to effectively promote its interests and to provide an impetus for lawmaking, it naturally must have access to lawmakers. But access to lawmakers depends, at least in part, on the socioeconomic status of the group. Groups with the most financial resources, the most prestigious membership, and the best organization are likely to have the greatest access to legislators. Moreover, lawmakers, on the local as well as the higher levels, may be more sympathetic to groups that represent interests of the middle and upper classes than to groups representing poor people, welfare recipients, and the like. Generally, groups with "mainstream" views, seeking only small changes in the status quo, may be given a more sympathetic hearing than those advocating large-scale radical changes.

THE MASS MEDIA

The mass media (newspapers, magazines, and radio and television stations) function in part as an interest group. Each component of the mass media is a business, and like other businesses, it has a direct interest in various areas of public policy. For example, the media have had a general objective of securing legislation, such as freedom of information laws that facilitate their access to the news, and legislation or court decisions that affect the confidentiality of news sources (see, for example, Klosek, 2010).

The mass media also function as conduits, although not altogether impartial ones, for others who would shape policy. Wealthier groups, for example, purchase media time or space in an effort to align public opinion with their causes. Through the media, these groups may reach the ears of legislators and administrators by publicly exposing problems and proposals about which they might not otherwise hear or, in some instances, about which they might not want to hear.

The mass media, especially the news media, are able to generate widespread awareness and concern about events and conditions—to bring matters before the public so that they become problematic issues. One might consider in this context that in addition to being a father of Confederation, George Brown, the founder of the Toronto *Globe*, "is perhaps best known as one of Canada's most prominent opponents of American slavery . . . [and he] expressed his views on this subject in issue after issue" of this newspaper (Morton and Weinfeld, 1998:29). Much more recently, the Canadian media helped to expose the egregious treatment of Canadian Maher Arar by both Canadian and American officials and the horrors he experienced following his deportation, as a suspected "terrorist," to his homeland of Syria. In the aftermath of a commission of inquiry headed by Justice O'Connor, and widespread media coverage of "allegations of corruption and dereliction on the part of various government and police officials, in January 2007 Prime Minister Harper extended an official apology to Arar along with $10.5 million (plus legal fees) in compensation" (Hogeveen and Woolford, 2012:397). The media additionally alerted Canadians to the ravages caused by cyberbullying and revenge porn. The media's attentiveness to the bullycides of young Canadians such as Amanda Todd and Rehtaeh Parsons helped fuel the passage of Bill C-13, the *Protecting Canadians from Online Crime Act* (SC 2014, c. 31) which received royal assent in December 2014, as well as provincial efforts such as Manitoba's Bill 38, *The Intimate Image Protection Act*, which came into effect in that province in January 2016.

Since public opinion is an important precursor of change, the mass media can set the stage by making undesirable conditions visible to a sizable segment of the public with unparalleled rapidity. Through the exposure of perceived injustices, the mass media play a crucial role in the formation of public opinion. Ralph Turner and Lewis M. Killian (1987) discuss six processes considered essential in understanding how the mass media can influence public opinion. First, the mass media *authenticate* the factual nature of events, which is decisive in the formation of public opinion. Second, the mass media *validate* opinions, sentiments, and preferences: It is reassuring to hear one's views confirmed by a well-known commentator. A third effect of the mass media is to *legitimize* certain behaviours and viewpoints considered to be taboo. Issues that were discussed only in private can now be expressed publicly, since they have already been discussed on television. Fourth, the mass media often *symbolize* the diffuse anxieties, preferences, discontents, and prejudices that individuals experience. By giving an acceptable identification for these perplexing feelings, the mass media often aid their translation into specific opinions and actions. Fifth, the mass media *focus* the preferences, discontents, and prejudices into lines of action. Finally, the mass media *classify into hierarchies* persons, objects, activities, and issues. As a result of the amount of consideration, preferential programming, and placement of items, they indicate relative importance and prestige.

In addition to providing investigative reporting and shaping public opinion, the mass media can pressure or challenge lawmakers into taking action on an issue or into changing their stand on a question. Influential newspapers such as the *Globe and Mail* and the *National Post* can make or break legislators through the use of the editorial pages (Sauvageau, Schneiderman, and Taras, 2006). Endorsement by a major newspaper can greatly facilitate a candidate's chances for being elected. Conversely, opposition to a candidate on the editorial pages can influence the outcome of an election. Legislators are quite aware of the power of the press, and as a result, editorial recommendations are given serious consideration. Similarly, articles in various influential weekly or monthly publications and the diverse specialized professional and legal journals can agitate for change.

An indirect way by which the mass media can furnish an impetus for lawmaking is through the provision of a forum for citizens' concerns. The "letters to the editor" page in newspapers is a traditional outlet for publicizing undesirable conditions. Such letters can accomplish several objectives. First, a letter can alert the community that an issue is before a lawmaking body; second, it can persuade the reader to take a position; third, it can make clear that there are responsible and articulate people in the community who are concerned with the issue; and fourth, it can enlist the active support of others. Similarly, many radio and television stations have local talk shows and public affairs programs that can be used to air grievances and to seek redress. However, media coverage can also serve to protect the interests of the powerful and preserve the status quo. For example, Kellar (2011:73–74) reports that prior to the G20 summit in Toronto in June 2010, "the national newspapers in Canada used their front pages to demonize protest organizers; after the G20 they became sounding boards for state operations to criminalize dissent (by publishing 'most wanted' pictures of alleged vandals, for example. [. . .] The fifteen thousand people who came out to show their opposition to G20 policies," he reports, "were largely ignored" with "the mainstream press . . . only interested in showing images and telling stories of property destruction and protestor 'violence'" that were sandwiched between a "repetitive chorus of words from representatives" and "pro-authoritarian pundits" (see also Poell and Borra, 2012). Analyses of the Canadian mainstream mass media also make clear that in their coverage of protest activity of Indigenous peoples, the "colonial imaginary has thrived, even dominated, and continues to do so" in the Canadian mainstream English-language media (Anderson and Robertson, 2011:3; see also Gardam and Giles, 2016; Harding, 2005. 2006; Lambertus, 2004; Henry and Tator, 2002).

SUMMARY

- Although various theories attempt to account for lawmaking, including the rationalistic model, the functionalistic model, conflict theory, and the "moral entrepreneur" thesis, none of these theories can account for the creation of all laws. At best, they explain in part how laws are made.

- Three general types of lawmaking process—legislative, administrative, and judicial— were analyzed. Legislative lawmaking basically consists of finding major and minor compromises regarding ideas advanced for legislation by administrative agencies, interest groups, and various party agencies and spokespersons. Administrative lawmaking consists of rulemaking and adjudication. Rulemaking is essentially legislation by administrative agencies. Adjudication differs from rulemaking in that it applies only to a specific, limited number of parties involved in an individual case and controversy before the agency. Judicial lawmaking is generally directed at government agencies rather than at private individuals.
- Interest groups, public opinion, and social science all exert an influence on the lawmaking process.
- Demands for lawmaking come from a multitude of sources, including scholarly investigations and novels; institutionalized forces, such as lobbying activities and public-interest groups; and organized protest activities or social movements. The mass media can also set the stage for lawmaking by calling attention to issues.

CRITICAL THINKING QUESTIONS

1. Identify laws that illustrate the contentions of the rationalistic model of lawmaking, the functionalistic model, conflict theory, and the "moral entrepreneur" thesis. For each of the four laws, explain why you believe that it is best understood with reference to the theory that you linked it with rather than the others.
2. How has the role of the judiciary changed in Canada with the entrenchment of the *Charter of Rights and Freedoms* in the Constitution?
3. The term "bullycide" directs attention to suicides that are prompted by bullying behaviours. While this term alerts us to the potentially lethal effects of bullying, some urge lawmakers to proceed cautiously in responding to this issue. Should bullying on- and/or offline be the subject of Canadian law? In contemplating this question, investigate the contents and short history of Nova Scotia's *Cyber-Safety Act*. What events prompted this law and what did it prohibit? Why was it struck down by the Supreme Court of Nova Scotia?
4. While the media heightens our awareness of social conditions at home and abroad, their reports are seldom limited to "just the facts"; rather, they impose frames upon these events. Examine your local paper's coverage of a group's protest activity (e.g., a demonstration, a strike, a sit-in). What images are evoked by the paper's description of the activity and the actors involved? Is the group's behaviour represented as legitimate? Illegitimate? How may the media's descriptions impact public understanding of the group's grievances or objectives and support for or opposition to their cause?

ADDITIONAL RESOURCES

1. The website of Angus Reid Public Opinion at http://angusreid.org provides access to the results of national and international polls on a wide range of issues.

2. To learn more about PIRGs or to join in their activities, visit PIRG.ca at http://pirg.ca.
3. The Council of Canadians is the country's largest citizens' organization, with chapters nationwide. The Council works to "protect Canadian independence by promoting progressive policies on fair trade, clean water, energy security, public health care, and other issues of social and economic concern to Canadians." Learn more about this group and its activities at http://canadians.org.
4. Learn more about the Canadian Environmental Law Association (CELA) by visiting http://www.cela.ca.

5

CHAPTER 5
LAW AND SOCIAL CONTROL

Social control refers to the methods used by members of a society to maintain order and promote predictability of behaviour (Chriss, 2013; Moore and Recker, 2016). There are many different forms of social control, and law is only one of them. The emphasis in this chapter is on social control through laws that are activated when other control mechanisms are ineffective or unavailable. This chapter examines the processes of informal and formal social control, the use of criminal sanctions, the effectiveness of the death penalty, and civil commitment to regulate behaviour. Part of the chapter is concerned with crimes without victims (drug addiction, prostitution, and gambling), white-collar crime, and the control of dissent. The chapter concludes with a consideration of administrative law as a means of control in the context of licensing, inspection, and the threat of publicity.

There are two basic processes of social control: the internalization of group norms and control through external pressures (Clinard and Meier, 2016). In the first instance, social control is the consequence of

Figure 5.1 Criminal sanctions represent one type of formal social control.
Credit: Shutterstock

socialization, the process of learning the rules of behaviour for a given social group. Individuals develop self-control by being taught early what is appropriate, expected, or desirable in specific situations. People acquire a motivation to conform to the norms, regardless of external pressures.

People conform to norms because individuals have been socialized since childhood to believe that they should conform, regardless of and independent of any anticipated reactions of other persons.

LEARNING OBJECTIVES

After reading this chapter, you should be able to:

1. Explain the differences between informal and formal social control.

2. Identity the goals of punishment.

3. Summarize the arguments for and against the death penalty.

4. Discuss the use of civil commitment as a mechanism of legal control.

5. Define "victimless crimes" and discuss arguments for and against the criminalization of prostitution, gambling, and drug use.

6. Define "white-collar crime" and discuss mechanisms for its control.

7. Describe, with the use of examples, how governments may employ law to suppress dissent.

8. Identify how administrative law provides for social control through licensing, inspection, and the use of publicity.

Mechanisms of social control through external pressures include both negative and positive sanctions. *Negative sanctions* are penalties imposed on those who violate norms. *Positive sanctions*, such as a promotion, a bonus, or encouragement, are intended to reward conformity. Some types of social control are formal or official in character, and others are informal or unofficial. Typical reactions to deviance and rule breaking may generate both informal and formal sanctions. Although there is a considerable amount of overlap between informal and formal mechanisms of social control, for analytical purposes they will be discussed separately in the chapter.

INFORMAL SOCIAL CONTROLS

Methods of informal social controls are best exemplified by **folkways** (established norms of common practices such as those that specify modes of dress, etiquette, and language use) and **mores** (societal norms associated with intense feelings of right or wrong and definite rules of conduct that are simply not to be violated—for example, incest). These informal controls consist of techniques whereby individuals who know each other on a personal basis accord praise to those who comply with their expectations and show displeasure to those who do not (Shibutani, 1961:426). These techniques may be observed in specific behaviours such as ridicule, gossip, praise, reprimands, criticisms, ostracism, and verbal rationalizations and expressions of opinion. One might consider, in this context, the potency of "click to judge" internet ranking sites, which "now assemble tens of millions of reviews of everything from restaurants to university lecturers," and how these sites, and the anonymous reviews they contain, contribute to the making and unmaking of reputations (Slee, 2012:13) (see Box 5.1: "Preserving Reputation in the Internet Era"). Unlike formal social controls, informal controls are not exercised through official group mechanisms, and there are no specially designated persons in charge of enforcement.

Informal mechanisms of social control tend to be more effective in groups and societies where relations are face-to-face and intimate and where the division of labour is relatively simple. For example, Durkheim argued that in simple societies, such as tribal villages or small towns, legal norms more closely accord with social norms than in larger and more complex societies. In simple societies, laws are often unwritten, necessitating the direct teaching of social norms to children. Socialization in such simple societies does not present children with contradictory norms that create confusion or inner conflict. Intense face-to-face interaction in such societies produces a moral consensus that is well known to all members; it also brings deviant acts to everyone's attention quickly.

There is substantial evidence in the sociological literature to support the contention that informal social control is stronger in smaller, traditional, more homogeneous communities than in larger, more modern heterogeneous communities (Hanawalt, 1998). In a classic study of deviance in the 17th-century Massachusetts Bay Colony, Erikson found that the small size and the cultural homogeneity of the community helped control behaviour, since everyone in the community pressured potential deviants to conform to dominant norms. There was a substantial amount of surveillance by neighbours watching for acts of deviance, and moral censure immediately followed any observed act (Erikson, 1966:169).

BOX 5.1 LIFE AND LAW: PRESERVING REPUTATION
IN THE INTERNET ERA

Canadian law recognizes the fatefulness of words and seeks to protect
the reputations of individuals as well as certain identifiable groups (e.g.,

corporations, labour unions, non-profit organizations) from harmful falsehoods under the law of defamation. The statutes that govern the laws vary somewhat in their contents between jurisdictions (most notably in relation to Quebec and the common-law jurisdictions) but are generally identifiable by the title *Defamation Act* or *Libel and Slander Act*.

A "classic definition of a libel" is "any statement which tends to discredit or lower an individual 'in the estimation of right-thinking members of society generally.' It also applies to statements that may cause others to shun or avoid a person, or tend to expose them to 'hatred, ridicule, or contempt' " (Canadian Judicial Council, 2007:7). If a defamatory statement is spoken, it is slander; if written, it is libel.

For a statement to be considered defamatory, it must be untrue and potentially damage or reduce its target's reputation in the community. For example, false allegations of criminal behaviour, of acts of sexual impropriety, of mental incompetency, or of infection with a sexually transmitted communicable disease may all result in successful civil actions if they demonstrably mar a person's reputation in the community.

The defence of "absolute privilege" may be used if the statement is made "in Parliament; as evidence at a trial or in court documents, in a criminal or civil case; [or] to a quasi-judicial body, such as a regulatory professional association. . . . that is investigating a complaint"; the defence of "qualified privilege" may be used "where remarks that may otherwise be defamatory were conveyed to a third party non-maliciously and for an honest and well-motivated reason" (Canadian Bar Association, 2016). However, while "[f]air comments that are made in good faith on subjects of public interest are protected from legal action," "the law affords no such protection to statements motivated by malice" and an individual may be sued successfully for making or repeating a slanderous statement to another party (Dranoff, 2011:342). Our Charter right to freedom of speech does not allow us to defame others with impunity (Manson and Turk, 2007; Reid, 2013; Drucker, 2013; Roach and Schneiderman, 2013). Yet protecting one's good name can be a challenging endeavour, especially in an era in which reputations are increasingly shaped by the contents of what appears online.

More than a decade ago, the Ontario Court of Appeal acknowledged the potency of the Internet to damage reputations in *Barrick v. Lopehandia* (2004), observing that a defamatory statement that is made online may cause its target immense damage due to "its absolute and immediate worldwide ubiquity and accessibility." Unfortunately, defamatory statements that appear online are neither easily policed nor expunged after the fact (Slee, 2012).

The greater effectiveness of informal social control mechanisms in small communities is demonstrated by Boggs's study of formal and informal social controls in central cities, suburbs, and small towns. When asked what it was that made their neighbourhood safe,

83 percent of study respondents in rural areas and small towns said that it was informal controls; 70 percent in suburbs and 68 percent of those in the cities attributed safety to informal controls. When they said that their neighbourhood was kept safe by informal social controls, people meant that they felt secure because of the character of the community and its residents—"good, decent, law-abiding, middle-class citizens" (Boggs, 1971:323). Safety in a neighbourhood was also attributed to the social network in the community that might lead to bystander intervention in a crime. Respondents who lived in suburbs and large cities were more likely than those who lived in rural areas and small towns to attribute safety to such formal control agents as the police (p. 234). Boggs concluded that people in cities were most inclined to expect crime but least likely to feel that they could rely on their neighbours rather than the police to protect their community. As a result, they were more likely to take precautions, such as purchasing weapons or a watchdog, than their counterparts who lived in suburbs, small towns, and rural areas.

Similar conclusions about the role of informal social-control mechanisms can be drawn from studies dealing with developing nations. For example, in comparing a low-crime-rate community and a high-crime-rate community in Kampala, Uganda, Clinard and Abbott found that the areas with less crime showed greater social solidarity, more social interaction among neighbours, more participation in local organizations, less geographical mobility, and more stability in family relationships. There was also greater cultural homogeneity and more emphasis on tribal and kinship ties in the low-crime community, helping to counteract the anonymity of recent migrants to the city. The stronger primary-group ties among residents of the low-crime area made it more difficult for strangers in the community to escape public notice. To prevent theft, residents of an area must feel that it is wrong, must share some responsibility for protecting their neighbours' property, must be able to identify strangers in the area, and must be willing to take action if they observe a theft (Clinard and Abbott, 1973:149).

These and other studies show that legal or formal controls may be unnecessary if there is intense social interaction on an intimate face-to-face basis, normative consensus, and surveillance of the behaviour of community members. As an example, one may consider the "old lady" network that China established in the 1950s as a means of grass-roots social control (Diamant, Lubman, and O'Brien, 2005). In the mid-2000s, there were an estimated 1 million neighbourhood committees in cities and villages around the country, employing 6.4 million retirees, virtually all women. The primary task of these committees is to seek out and resolve squabbles among neighbours. They report everything they see to higher-ups, investigate disturbances, routinely stop strangers, and pry into couples' plans for having children. This technique of community-based surveillance is modelled after the one introduced in the former Soviet Union in the 1920s, which was based on the principle of denouncement. People were encouraged to report (and rewarded for doing so) on friends and relatives who were suspected of engaging in activities contrary to the interests of the government. Various versions of this technique were subsequently used in Nazi Germany and other totalitarian regimes. However, community-based surveillance techniques are not exclusive to communist or totalitarian regimes or to times past. For example, they are discernible in the United States' post-9/11 war on terror. As simply one example, the Los Angeles iWATCH program counsels citizens, "If you see something, say something"; it urges the public to tend to "suspicious behaviours" and report those who engage in them to police (Sullivan, 2009).

FORMAL SOCIAL CONTROLS

Although there is no clear-cut dividing line, formal social controls are usually characteristic of more complex societies with a greater division of labour, heterogeneity of population, and subgroups with competing values and different sets of mores and ideologies. Formal controls arise when informal controls alone are insufficient to maintain conformity to certain norms. Formal controls are characterized by systems of specialized agencies, standard techniques, and general predictability of universal sanctions. The two main types are those instituted by the state and authorized to use force and those imposed by agencies other than the state, such as churches, business and labour groups, and universities.

Formal social controls are incorporated in the institutions in society and are characterized by the explicit establishment of procedures and the delegation of specific bodies to enforce them (laws, decrees, regulations, codes). Since they are incorporated in the institutions of society, they are administered by individuals who occupy positions in those institutions. Generally, anyone who attempts to manipulate the behaviour of others through the use of formal sanctions may be considered an agent of social control (Clinard and Meier, 2016).

Social institutions are organized for securing conformity to established modes of behaviour and consist of established procedures for satisfying human needs. These procedures carry a certain degree of compulsion. They involve mechanisms of imposing conformity. Non-political institutions may resort to a variety of penalties and rewards to ensure compliance (see, for example, Vaughan, 1998). For example, an organization may fire an employee, or a league owner may fine or suspend a professional athlete for infractions of rules. These same organizations may also use formal rewards to ensure conformity. To illustrate, through bonuses and promotions, an organization often rewards those who make outstanding contributions. Dedicated employees may be commended for exemplary service, and professional athletes are often enticed by financial rewards.

It should be noted at the outset that control through law is seldom exercised by the use of positive sanctions or rewards. A person who, throughout his or her life, obeys the law and meets its requirements seldom receives rewards or commendations. State control is exercised primarily, but not exclusively, through the use or threat of punishment to regulate the behaviour of citizens.

CRIMINAL SANCTIONS

The social control of criminal and delinquent behaviour exemplifies the most highly structured formal system used by society—the criminal justice system (Bosworth, 2010; Husak, 2010; Simon, 2009). At the start of the new millennium, no fewer than 2,600,994 men and 681,199 women in Canada had a criminal record (including young offenders); the total population of Canada in that year was 30,750,087 (15,232,909 men and 15,517,178 women). Stated somewhat differently, in 2000, about 1 in 10 persons living in Canada (17 percent of men and 4 percent of women) had a criminal record. Moreover, although Canada's incarceration rate of 114 people per 100,000 population in 2014 was far lower than that of the United States (693 per 100,000 population), it was much higher than the rates found in many industrialized countries, including Germany (78), Denmark (59), Sweden (53), and Japan (47) (World Prison Brief, 2016).

The laws, enacted by legislators and modified by court decisions, define criminal behaviour and specify the sanctions imposed for violations (Husak, 2010). Over time, there has been an increasing reliance on law to regulate the activities and, thus, the lives of people. As the law has proliferated to incorporate more types of behaviour, many changes in penalties for certain crimes have also occurred. These increases inevitably result in more social control and in further changes in the control methods. As more behaviours are defined as criminal, more acts become the interest of the police, the courts, and the prison system.

The term **legalization** is used to describe the process by which norms are moved from the social to the legal level. Not all social norms become laws; in fact, only certain norms are translated into legal norms. Why is it that the violation of certain norms, but not others, is chosen to be incorporated into the criminal code? Turk (1972) suggests that there are certain social forces involved in legalization and the creation of legal norms: moral indignation, a high value on order, response to threat, and political tactics.

As discussed in Chapter 4, laws may be created by the actions of "moral entrepreneurs" who become outraged over some practice they regard as reprehensible. Others prefer order and insist on provisions to regulate life and to make society as orderly as possible. They promulgate laws to ensure order and uniformity, as in the case of traffic regulation. Some people react to real or imaginary threats and advocate legal–control measures. For instance, some people may assume that the availability of pornographic material is not only morally wrong but also directly contributes to the increase of sex crimes (although acts of sexual violence undoubtedly predate pornographic magazines and websites). In this instance, it would appear certain that these people would attempt to legally prohibit the sale of pornographic material (Trebilcock, 2006). The final source of legalization of norms is political, where criminal laws are created in the interest of powerful groups in society. This source is identified with the **conflict perspective** that we considered in the preceding chapters.

The process of legalization of social norms also entails the incorporation of specific punishments for specific kinds of criminal law violators. Rusche and Kurchheimer (2003:5) note: "Every system of production tends to discover punishments which correspond to its productive relationships." Foucault (1977) tells us that before the Industrial Revolution, life was considered cheap, and individuals had neither the utility nor the commercial value that is conferred on them in an industrial economy. Under those circumstances, punishment was severe and often unrelated to the nature of the crime (for example, death for stealing a chicken). When more and more factories appeared, the value of individual lives, even criminal ones, began to be stressed. Beginning in the last years of the 18th century and in the early years of the 19th century, efforts were made to connect the nature of a given punishment to the nature of the crime.

Fitting the punishment to the crime is a difficult and at times controversial and politically sensitive task (Brooks, 2010; Tonry, 2010). The definition of crime and the penalty for it, and the components of the culture of control (Cusac, 2009; Garland, 2001), vary over time and from one society to another. For example, according to *World Report 2017* (Human Rights Watch, 2017), while North Korea has "ratified four key international human rights treaties and its constitution includes rights protections," it is one of "the most repressive authoritarian states in the world." In this country, which has been "ruled for seven decades by the Kim family and the Workers' Party of Korea," "the government curtails all basic human rights, including freedom of expression, assembly, and association, and freedom to practice religion. It prohibits any organized political opposition, independent media, free trade unions, and independent civil society organizations" (Human Rights Watch, 2017). By contrast, in a democracy the power to define crime and punishment rests with the citizenry. This power is largely delegated to elected representatives. Their statutes are often broad and subject to various interpretations. As Chapter 3 demonstrated, legislative enactments allow judges, prosecutors, and juries considerable flexibility and discretion in assessing guilt and imposing punishment.

But what does it mean to punish an individual who violates a criminal law? Sutherland and Cressey (1974:298) provide the following definition of the ingredients of punishment as a form of social control: "Two essential ideas are contained in the concept of punishment as an instrument of public justice. (a) It is inflicted by the group in its corporate capacity upon one who is regarded as a member of the same group. . . . (b) Punishment involves pain or suffering produced by design and justified by some value that the suffering is assumed to have."

The punishment of lawbreakers has several purposes. One is the goal of **retribution** or social retaliation against the offender (Zaibert, 2006). This means punishment of the offender for the crime that has been committed and, to an extent, punishment that (in principle) matches the impact of the crime upon its victim (for instance, a person or an organization). The state is expected to be the agent of vengeance on behalf of the victim. Punishment also involves **incapacitation** (for example, a prison term), which prevents a violator from misbehaving during the time he or she is being punished. Judicially created public humiliations are also being introduced in courtrooms as alternatives to incarceration and to satisfy a "retributive impulse" (Karp, 1998:277). They are considered as "shaming penalties"—after punishments such as the stocks favoured by 17th-century Puritans—and they take a *mea culpa* message to the community. Shaming and embarrassment are potent forces in social control and, as noted earlier, various techniques are used to accomplish this end in current times (Allyn, 2004; van Kleef, 2016).

Further, punishment is supposed to have a *deterrent effect*, both on the lawbreaker and on potential deviants. **Individual** or **specific deterrence** may be achieved by intimidation of the person, frightening him or her against further deviance, or it may be affected through reformation, in that the lawbreaker changes his or her deviant behaviour. **General deterrence** results from the warning offered to potential criminals by the example of punishment directed at a specific wrongdoer. It aims to discourage others from criminal behaviour by making an example of the offender being punished.

The theory of **deterrence** is predicated on the assumption that individuals weigh the costs and rewards associated with alternative actions, and select behaviours that maximize gains and minimize costs. Thus, deterrence theorists argue that crime takes place when law breaking is perceived as either more profitable (rewarding) or less costly (painful) than conventional activities. Moreover, the effectiveness of these threats is believed to be conditioned by the operation of three variables: (1) the severity of the punishment for an offence, (2) the certainty that it will be applied, and (3) the speed with which it is applied. Research generally supports the view that certainty of punishment is more important than severity for achieving deterrence, but there is little research data as yet on the impact of the swiftness of punishment (Nagin, Solow and Lum, 2015).

Sociologists also recognize that punishment may deter only some crimes and some offenders. For example, Chambliss (1975) makes a useful distinction between crimes that are instrumental acts and those that are expressive. **Instrumental offences** include burglary, tax evasion, embezzlement, motor vehicle theft, identity theft, and other illegal activities directed toward some material end. **Expressive offences** include murder, assault, and sex offences, where the behaviour is an end in itself. Chambliss hypothesized that the deterrent impact of severe and certain punishment may be greater on instrumental crimes because they generally involve some planning and weighing of risks. Expressive crimes, by contrast, are often impulsive and emotional acts. Perpetrators of such crimes are unlikely to be concerned with the future consequences of their actions.

Chambliss further contends that an important distinction can be made between individuals who have a relatively high commitment to crime as a way of life and those with a relatively low commitment. The former would include individuals who engage in crime on a professional or regular basis. They often receive group support for their activities, and crime for them is an important aspect of their way of life (such as participants in organized crime). For them, the likelihood of punishment is a constant feature of their life, something they have learned to live with, and the threat of punishment may be offset by the supportive role played by their peers. In contrast, a tax evader, an embezzler, or an occasional shoplifter does not view this behaviour as criminal and receives little, if any, group support for these acts. Fear of punishment may well be a deterrent for such low-commitment persons, particularly if they have already experienced punishment (for example, a tax evader who has been audited and then subjected to legal sanctions).

On the basis of these two distinctions—instrumental and expressive acts, and high- and low-commitment offenders—Chambliss argues that the greatest deterrent effect of punishment would be in situations that involve low-commitment individuals who engage in instrumental crimes. Deterrence is least likely in cases involving high-commitment persons who engage in expressive crimes. The role of deterrence remains questionable in situations that involve low-commitment individuals who commit expressive crimes (such as murder), which can be illustrated by the arguments used for or against the death penalty.

DISCORD OVER THE DEATH PENALTY

As the most severe form of punishment, the death penalty is the most obvious, controversial, and emotional issue in the concept of deterrence (see, for example, Bedau and Cassell, 2004; Christianson, 2010; Yorke, 2009). Historically, property offences, rather than violent crimes, accounted for the majority of executions (Ferguson, 2010). In the 18th century, the death penalty was imposed in England for more than 200 offences, including poaching and smuggling. Executions were performed in public and were a popular spectacle. Although the colonies inherited many of the capital punishments from England, by the middle of the 19th century most of them were repealed and the death sentence was imposed primarily for murder and, to a lesser extent, rape.

While the precise number of people hanged in early Canada remains unknown, inasmuch as accurate records date only from 1867, the first person executed for a crime is reputed to have been a young girl who was hanged in the early 1600s at the age of 16 for the crime of petty theft. In 1976, capital punishment was formally abolished in this country and, in 2001, the Supreme Court of Canada demonstrated its opposition to the use of capital punishment when it unanimously ruled, in *United States v. Burns*, that "[i]n the absence of exceptional circumstances" Canada is constitutionally required, prior to extraditing any fugitive—Canadian or otherwise—to another country, to seek assurances that the death penalty will not be imposed (Religious Tolerance.org, 2001). However, in November 2007, the Canadian government announced that it would no longer seek clemency from "democratic countries that adhered to the rule of law" (Amnesty International, 2008).

As of December 2015, 140 countries had abolished the death penalty in law or in practice (Amnesty International, 2016a); the United States, India, and Japan are the only democracies that retain capital punishment. In 2015, a minimum of 1,998 people worldwide were sentenced to death; 1,634 were executed, and, at year's end, 20,292 prisoners were on death row. According to Amnesty International (2016b), "of all executions recorded in 2015, 89% were carried out in just three countries: Iran, Pakistan and Saudi Arabia." However, not all countries are willing to report their use of the death penalty. For example, data on the use of the death penalty is classified as a state secret in Belarus, China, and Vietnam (Amnesty International, 2016b: 2).

According to Amnesty International, the death penalty was imposed and/or implemented in 2015 to punish drug-related offences (e.g., China, Indonesia, Iran, Kuwait, Laos, Malaysia, Saudi Arabia, Singapore, Sri Lanka, Thailand, United Arab Emirates, and Vietnam), adultery and sodomy (Saudi Arabia, Maldives), religious offences such as apostasy (Saudi Arabia) and "insulting the prophet of Islam" (Iran), economic crimes (China, North Korea, and Vietnam), rape (Afghanistan, Jordan, Pakistan), and armed robbery (Saudi Arabia). Various forms of "'treason,' 'acts against national security,' 'collaboration' with a foreign entity, 'espionage,' 'questioning the leader's policies,' participation in 'insurrectional movement and terrorism' and other 'crimes against the state,' whether or not they led to a loss of life, were punished with death sentences in China, Iran, Lebanon, North Korea, Pakistan, Palestine (State of) (in the West Bank and in Gaza), Qatar and Saudi Arabia" (Amnesty International, 2016b:9).

In the United States, capital punishment was declared unconstitutional by the U.S. Supreme Court in the case of *Furman v. Georgia* (1972). The Court held that the discretionary application of the death penalty to only a small fraction of those eligible to be executed was capricious and arbitrary and hence unconstitutional. However, a number of states responded to the ruling by legislating modifications in state laws that make the death penalty mandatory for certain offences, such as multiple killings; killing in connection with a robbery, rape, kidnapping, or hostage situation; murder for hire; killing a police officer or prison guard; and treason. Some of these revised statutes were held to be constitutional by the Supreme Court in 1976 when it voted seven to two in *Gregg v. Georgia* to reinstate the death penalty. Since 1976, 1,426 men and 16 women have been judicially executed in the United States. While the number of death sentences per year has dropped dramatically in the United States since 1999, on July 1, 2016 there were 2,849 men and 56 women on death row in American prisons (Death Penalty Information Center, 2016).

Empirical studies of the use of the death penalty in the United States find that the race and gender of victims are associated with the severity of legal responses in homicide cases even after controlling for legally relevant factors. For example, Holcomb, Williams, and Demuth (2004) report that defendants convicted of killing white females were significantly more likely to receive death sentences than killers of victims with other race-gender characteristics. Other things being equal, those who kill white people in the United States are more likely to receive death sentences than those who kill blacks (Bohm, 2015). An analysis of the race of victims in American death penalty cases since 1976 concludes that "[o]ver 75 percent of the murder victims resulting in an execution were white, even though nationally only 50 percent of murder victims generally are white" (Death Penalty Information Center, 2016). In the United States, the death penalty is also more likely to affect poor and minority group members than affluent whites (Berlow, 2001; Ogletree and Sarat, 2006). In part, this reflects the quality of legal help available to murder defendants. Those with court-appointed lawyers are more likely to be sentenced to death than those represented by private lawyers. A study conducted in Texas found that people represented by court-appointed lawyers were 28 percent more likely to be convicted than those who hired their own lawyers and, if convicted, 44 percent more likely to be sentenced to death (*New York Times*, 2001).

Proponents of the death penalty contend that it constitutes retribution; removes the possibility of recidivism; acts as a deterrent to others; and protects society in general and, in particular, police officers and prison guards (Peppers and Anderson, 2009). However, little empirical evidence supports the use of the death penalty as a deterrent (Kirchgässner, 2011; Durlauf, Fu, and Navarro, 2013; Chalfin, Haviland, and Raphael, 2013; Dezhbakhsh and Rubin, 2011). Aside from ethical and moral considerations, there are many arguments against the death penalty. For serial killers, and particularly for female serial killers, capital punishment is not a deterrent (Fisher, 1997; Kelleher and Kelleher, 1998). Moreover, while more than 80 percent of American executions to date have been carried out in the South, this region of the United States has consistently had the highest murder rate (6.7 per 100,000 in 2014). The Northeast United States, which accounts for less than 1 percent of all executions, had the lowest murder rate (4.2 per 100,000) (Death Penalty Information Center, 2016). This suggests a possible "**brutalization effect**"—with executions increasing violent crime rather than serving as a deterrent. A survey of research findings on the relationship between the death penalty and homicide rates concluded that "it is not prudent to accept the hypothesis that capital punishment deters murder to a marginally greater extent than does the threat and application of the supposedly lesser punishment of life imprisonment" (cited in Hood, 2002:230).

Studies in Canada, England, and other abolitionist countries have found nothing to suggest that the death penalty is a more effective deterrent than long prison sentences. For example, in Canada, while the homicide rate per 100,000 population was 3.09 in 1975 (the year before the abolition of the death penalty for murder), by 1980 it had fallen to 2.4, and in 2014 was 1.45, its lowest level since 1966 (Statistics Canada, 2015). As a United Nations survey pointedly noted, "The fact that the statistics continue to point in the same direction is persuasive evidence that countries need not fear sudden and serious changes in the curve of crime if they reduce their reliance upon the death penalty" (cited in Hood, 2002:214). While a cause-and-effect relationship cannot be inferred between capital punishment and murder rates, Friedman (1998:214) speculates that while capital punishment may work efficiently in some societies "which use it quickly, mercilessly, and frequently," in democratic countries that have elaborate due-process safeguards, its use will inevitably be "rare, slow, and controversial." It is also costly. Trials of capital cases are vastly more costly and time-consuming than other trials and the costs of maintaining inmates on death row are higher than for their housing elsewhere (Fagan, 2016; Death Penalty Information Center, 2016).

In addition, there is always the possibility that an innocent person will be executed (Kanefeld, 2014). The most common reasons for wrongful convictions are: mistaken eyewitness testimony; the false testimony of informants and "incentivized witnesses"; incompetent lawyers; defective or fraudulent scientific evidence; prosecutorial and police misconduct; and false confessions (Garrett and Neufeld, 2009; Huff and Killias, 2010; Westervelt and Cook, 2010).

Moreover, noting that the homicide rate in the United States is three times higher than that of Canada, four times higher than western Europe's, six times higher than Great Britain's, and seven times higher than Japan's, some researchers have argued that America's high homicide rate may reflect the ready availability of firearms in that country. Thus, observing that the United States has the world's highest rate of gun ownership (90 weapons per 100 civilians [followed by Yemen at 61 weapons per 100 civilians, Finland at 56, and Iraq at 39]), it has been suggested that gun control measures might be more effective at reducing the homicide rate than capital punishment (*Focus on Law Studies*, 2003; Warden, 2009; Henderson, 2005). However, some bristle at this suggestion (Lott, 2003, 2006, 2010) and gun control, in the United States and elsewhere, continues to be a topic of heated debate among social scientists and policymakers (see, for example, Acker and Bellandi, 2012; Burbick, 2006; Cukier and Sidel, 2006; Melzer, 2009; Holmes and Holmes, 2010; Warden, 2009; Marcus and Waye, 2010; Sarver Jr., 2014).

CIVIL COMMITMENT

The formal control of deviant behaviour is not limited to criminal sanctions (Arrigo, 2002; Diesfeld and Freckelton, 2003; Boyd-Caine, 2009). There is another form of social control through laws that operates via the medicalization of deviance (Conrad, 1996:69). **Medicalization** refers to the process of defining behaviour as a medical problem or illness and mandating the medical profession to provide treatment for it (Conrad, 1996:69). For example, Mugford and Weekes (2006) observe that "[o]ver the course of the 20th century in Canada, civil commitment or custody for treatment were used to varying degrees depending on the changing perceptions of the political and medical communities with respect to the necessity to incarcerate or confine 'habitual users' and serious 'addicts' to deal appropriately with their behaviour." They note that under British Columbia's 1978 *Heroin Treatment Act*, "one of Canada's first mandatory treatment initiatives . . . heroin-addicted individuals who were unwilling to enter treatment were forced to take part in an intensive government-funded heroin treatment program." Although repealed, this Act was later upheld on appeal to the Supreme Court of Canada in the 1982 case of *Schneider v. British Columbia*.

Procedurally, civil commitment is different from criminal commitment. Douglas and Koch (2001:355) note that "in comparison to criminal procedures, there are fewer safeguards protecting the rights of persons confined under civil commitment legislation." In civil commitment, certain procedural safeguards are not available, such as a right to trial by jury, which involves confronting witnesses against the defendant, and the right to avoid testifying against oneself. Moreover, the formal moral condemnation of the community is not an issue in involuntary commitment. Forst (1978:3) notes, "This situation may arise if the behaviour is intentional but not morally blameworthy, as in a civil suit for damages, or if the behaviour would have been morally blameworthy, but because of mental impairment, criminal culpability is either mitigated or negated. In the latter instance, the . . . issue is not the person's behaviour but his [sic] status." In this view, a heroin addict, a mentally incompetent person, or a sex offender is not held morally responsible for his or her actions. The general consensus is that the individual deserves treatment, not punishment, even though the treatment may entail the loss of liberty in a mental institution without due process.

Civil commitments can be controversial (Baughman, 2015; Levine, 2009). For example, in 1996, a Winnipeg judge attempted to protect the fetus of a pregnant, glue-sniffing 22-year-old Aboriginal woman by ordering the woman into the custody of the Director of Child and Family Services and permitting the Director to have the woman committed under mental health legislation if she failed to take treatment during her pregnancy for her addiction. In this case, the judge based his ruling on the *parens patriae* jurisdiction of judges "to act beyond the scope of the statute or interpretive law to protect the weak, vulnerable, and mentally incompetent" (Dranoff, 2011:12). He emphasized the risk the woman's conduct posed to herself and her unborn child, and noted that the woman's glue sniffing had already resulted in damage to three other children (all of whom had become Crown wards). Nevertheless, the judge's decision was reversed by the Manitoba Court of Appeal on the grounds that (i) a fetus is not a "legal person" under Canadian law with all the rights and privileges that legal personhood confers; (ii) the courts should not be placed in the position of choosing between the rights of a mother and her fetus; and (iii) the lower court had no jurisdiction to force the woman into treatment since psychiatric testimony had established that the woman was not mentally ill as defined by law. Therefore, as a mentally competent person, the woman was entitled to consent to or refuse treatment as she saw fit. In *Winnipeg Child and Family Services (Northwest Area) v. G. (D.F.)* (1997), the Supreme Court of Canada affirmed the decision of the Manitoba Court of Appeal, with J. McLachlin noting that "[t]he *parens patriae* jurisdiction has never been used to permit a court to make such decisions for competent women, whether pregnant or not. Such a change . . . would seriously intrude on the rights of women. If anything is to be done, the legislature is in a much better position to weigh the competing interests and arrive at a solution that is principled and minimally intrusive to pregnant women" (at 56).

In contrast, however, one may consider three provincial Acts that were enacted and/ or came into effect in 2006. Alberta's *Protection of Children Abusing Drugs Act* (Alberta Regulation 138/2006) enables a guardian to apply to the Court for an order to protect a child who is abusing drugs and "requires persons under 18 with an apparent alcohol or other drug problem to participate, with or without their agreement, in an assessment and subsequent outpatient treatment program or in a program within a 'protective safe house'" for up to ten days (Alberta Health Services, 2017). Saskatchewan's *Youth Drug Detoxification and Stabilization Act* allows for "the apprehension and detainment against their will of persons under 18 for assessment, detoxification, and stabilization of substance abuse problems" (Mugford and Weekes, 2006). Manitoba's *Youth Drug Stabilization (Support for Parents) Act* "provides a way to access involuntary detention and short-term stabilization for young Manitobans under 16 years of age" and "is intended as a last resort, when other measures have been unsuccessful and where a youth is causing serious self-harm through severe, persistent substance abuse" (Government of Manitoba, 2017). In addition, in the aftermath of amendments made to Ontario's mental health law in 2000, it is now easier in that province to force psychiatric patients to undergo unwanted treatment. Its mental health law also allows for the use of "community treatment orders," which are "in essence, a kind of parole for psychiatric patients after they are discharged from the hospital" (Dranoff, 2011:551).

In the legal arena, the causes of criminal behaviour and the responsibility for such behaviour lie within the individual. But in a legal system that posits individual causation, complications arise in attempts to control individuals who are threatening yet have broken no law (see, for example, Peay, 2005; Horowitz, 2002; Friedman, 2016). One way to control such individuals is to define their conduct as a mental disorder. As Greenaway and Brickey (1978:139) observe, "This definition has the combined effect of imputing irrationality to the behaviour and providing for the control of the individual through ostensibly benign, but coercive psychiatric intervention."

CRIMES WITHOUT VICTIMS

Canada invests enormous resources in controlling victimless crimes where harm occurs primarily to the participating individuals. In 2015, about 1.9 million criminal incidents (excluding traffic offences) were reported to Canadian police agencies. Many of these incidents involved crimes without victims. For example, of the approximately 96,000 offences under the *Controlled Drugs and Substances Act* that were reported to Canadian police services in 2015, "half (51%) were incidents of cannabis possession and another 9% were related to the trafficking, production or distribution of cannabis" (Allen, 2016).

The criminalization of some acts that have no victims stems from the fact that society regards those acts as morally repugnant or vexatious and wishes to restrain individuals from engaging in them. These acts are crimes *mala prohibita*—behaviours made criminal by statute—but there is no consensus as to whether these acts are criminal in themselves. They are acts against public interest or morality and appear in criminal codes as crimes against public decency, order, or justice. Crimes like sexual assault and homicide are *mala in se* (that is, evils in themselves, with public agreement on the dangers they pose).

Victimless crimes are differentiated from other crimes by three additional factors; (1) the element of consensual transaction or exchange; (2) the lack of apparent direct harm to others; and (3) the difficulty in enforcing the laws against them as a result of low visibility and the absence of complainants. In other words, they are plaintiffless crimes— those involved are willing participants who, as a rule, do not complain to the police that a crime has been committed. Although many people do not consider these activities "criminal," the police and the courts continue to apply laws against such groups as drug users, gamblers, and pornography distributors—laws that large sections of the community do not recognize as legitimate and simply refuse to obey. The formal controls exerted on these types of behaviour are expensive and generally ineffective. Still, they serve certain functions. Rich (1978:28) notes that persons who are labelled criminals serve as an example to community members. When the laws are enforced against lower-class and minority- group members, it allows those who occupy relatively more powerful positions (i.e., middle- and upper-class people) to feel that the law is serving a useful purpose because it preserves and reinforces the myth that low-status individuals account for most of the deviance in society. Finally, the control of victimless crimes, in the form of arrests and convictions, strengthens the notion in the community that the police and the criminal justice system are doing a good job of protecting community moral standards. Let us now consider law as a means of social control for certain victimless crimes, such as drug addiction, prostitution, and gambling.

DRUG USE

Before 1908, there were only sporadic attempts to regulate the use of drugs in Canada. Moreover, "[w]hile there were instances of prior restrictive and regulative legislation deriving from medical concern about the free availability of 'poisons' and consumer protection interest in product purity, it appears that no Western nation used the criminal law to prohibit the distribution of narcotics for recreational purposes until Canada's pioneering effort of 1908" (Green, 1986:24). In 1908, Canada's first criminal narcotics legislation, *An Act to Prohibit the Importation, Manufacture and Sale of Opium for Other than Medicinal Purposes*, a simple two-paragraph statute, was passed (without discussion in the House of Commons and with an absence of effective opposition in the Senate) within a period of three weeks. Although some maintain that the real statutory beginning of narcotic control in Canada occurred with the 1911 passage of the *Opium and Drug Act* (Giffen, Endicott, and Lambert, 1991:13), there is little doubt that racism directed against the Chinese played a critical role in the history of Canadian narcotics legislation (Backhouse, 1999a:142).

Hostility to the use of opium emerged in part because of a labour surplus that followed the completion of railway construction and the diminished intensity of the Gold Rush. Green (1986:25) notes that before this time, in the midst of a labour shortage, "the Chinese were

regarded as industrious, sober, economical and law-abiding individuals." As jobs became
scarce and the Chinese were viewed as competitors for the positions that existed, "the
earlier friendly feelings toward the Chinese changed." Simultaneously, opium use, which
had been previously viewed, at worst, as "an individual medical misfortune or personal
vice, free of severe moral opprobrium," became defined as a significant social "evil."
Morgan (1978:59) observes, "The first opium laws . . . were not the result of a moral
crusade against the drug itself. Instead, it represented a coercive action directed against
a vice that was merely an appendage of the real menace—the Chinese—and not the
Chinese per se, but the labouring 'Chinamen' who threatened the economic security of the
white working class." The criminalization of other drugs, including cocaine, heroin, and
marijuana, followed similar patterns of social control of the powerless, political opponents,
and minorities (see, for example, Carstairs, 2002). As Hackler (2003:213) emphasized, "the
societal demand to punish, stigmatize, and exclude users of certain substances is not based
on pharmacological evidence" and evidence of such damage "plays a secondary role in
drug policy."

Since 1987, Canada's Drug Strategy has emphasized the need for a "balanced" approach that
combines prevention and education with law enforcement. Its stated objectives include:

> reducing the demand for drugs; reducing drug-related mortality and morbidity by
> reducing high-risk behaviours, such as spreading HIV/AIDS through needle sharing;
> improving the effectiveness of and accessibility to substance abuse information and
> interventions; restricting the supply of illicit drugs; reducing the profitability of illicit
> trafficking; and reducing the costs of substance abuse to Canadian society.
>
> (Auditor General, 2001)

Consistent with this emphasis, Canada's National Anti-Drug Strategy (NADS), which was
launched in 2007, employs a three-pronged approach: (1) the Prevention Action Plan seeks
to prevent "illicit drug use and prescription drug abuse among young people" by providing
reliable information "to those most affected by drug use, including parents, young people,
educators, law enforcement authorities, and communities"; (2) the Treatment Action Plan:
strives to enhance "treatment systems, programs and services" for those who are dependent
upon illicit and prescription drugs; and (3) The Enforcement Action Plan attempts to
increase "law enforcement's capacity to proactively target organized crime involvement
in illicit drug production and distribution operations" and "the capacity of the criminal
justice system to investigate, interdict and prosecute offenders" (Government of Canada,
2014b).

In May 1997, the *Controlled Drugs and Substances Act* (CDSA) became law in Canada,
consolidating most of the earlier illicit drug legislation and outlining the six federal
criminal offences of possession, trafficking, possession for the purpose of trafficking,
production, importing or exporting, and "prescription shopping." While the penalties
for possession it specified varied depending on the type of drug, the maximum penalties
for the majority of offences were severe. For example, for "Schedule 1" drugs (i.e.,
cocaine, heroin, opium, phencyclidine), the specified maximum penalty for trafficking,
possession for the purpose of trafficking, producing, and importing and exporting was life

imprisonment. With the passage of the *Safe Streets & Communities Act*, an omnibus crime bill (C-10) in March 2012, the CDSA was amended and the penalties it imposed made additionally harsh, with mandatory minimum penalties for serious drug offences (e.g., production, trafficking, possession for the purpose of trafficking, importing and exporting, possession for the purpose of exporting) when these offences are carried out for organized crime purposes, target youth, or constitute a potential hazard to security, health, or safety.

Although the overarching thrust of these changes was punitive, section 10(5) of the CDSA did permit a court to suspend a sentence while an addicted offender participated in a drug treatment program and allowed the court to impose a suspended or reduced sentence if the offender successfully completed that program (Department of Justice, 2012). Nevertheless, in *R. v. Lloyd* (2016), the Supreme Court of Canada ruled 6 to 3 that mandatory minimum sentences for repeat drug traffickers violate the constitutional guarantee against cruel and unusual punishment and that the exception afforded by section 10(5) of the CDSA was "too narrow to cure" this "constitutional infirmity" (at 34). In *R. v. Dickey* (2016), the B.C. Court of Appeal overturned compulsory two-year minimum sentences for drug trafficking convictions that involve someone under the age of 18 or that occur in a public place frequented by youth. In this unanimous decision, the court declared the laws to be unconstitutional and held that, in some circumstances, a minimum two-year prison sentence would be "grossly disportionate to an appropriate sentencing disposition" and therefore constitute cruel and unusual punishment (at 11).

The majority of the federal government's changes to legislation in relation to illicit drugs over the past few decades have targeted the issue of supply rather than demand. These efforts have included the amendment of the Canadian Criminal Code to include organized crime offences and the creation of the Financial Transactions and Reports Analysis Centre of Canada. The latter attempts to detect money laundering by monitoring financial transactions. The federal Integrated Proceeds of Crime initiative, whose mandate involves investigating organized crime groups and seizing assets gained through criminal activities, is acknowledged as largely a drug-related initiative, with an estimated 90 percent of seizures related to drugs. Between 2000 and 2012, the Proceeds of Crime branch of the RCMP seized criminal assets in excess of more than $243 million (RCMP, 2012). The "accumulation of money through the sale of illegal drugs" has been described as an "archetypal" example of conduct that is targeted by civil forfeiture legislation (Krane, 2011:160). Civil forfeiture legislation, such as the *Proceeds of Crime (Money Laundering) and Terrorist Financing Act* (2000), is generally cast by governments as either a crime-control or crime-prevention measure and provides for "a public form of restitution whereby the state can exact profits, proceeds, and future interests in property based on an underlying unlawful act" (Krane, 2011:16; see also Young, 2009).

While Canadian federal agencies spend approximately $500 million each year to fight drugs, some maintain that "[t]he use of the criminal law—the 'war on drugs' or 'prohibitionist' approach—is too often the wrong means to reduce the harms associated with the production, sale and possession of currently available drugs" (Oscapella, 2012:3; see also Werb et al., 2012; Ogrodnik et al., 2015). The lack of a complainant, the sheer volume of available drugs, and the extreme profitability of the illicit drug trade make enforcement efforts difficult (see, for example, Beare, 2002; Lindsey and Nicholson, 2016). Moreover, critics of current drug policies pointedly note that "drug use hasn't decreased since the $1-trillion US 'war on drugs' in North America was declared and aggressive drug law enforcement began" (CBC, 2012). Instead, prohibitionist efforts have had a paradoxical effect and created a highly lucrative illegal market with "[i]llicit drug production . . . the most significant source of money for gangs and organized crime in Canada" (Department of Justice, 2010). In order to support their drug habits, users may engage in various criminal activities (Buxton et al., 2009; Public Safety Canada, 2011, 2015; Braitstein, Li, and Tyndall, 2003; Erickson, Butters, and McGillicuddy, 2000). In addition, "[t]he inflated price of drugs on the illegal market may lead those who use them to more dangerous forms of use, such as injecting, to get the best 'bang for the buck'" (Oscapella, 2012:11).

Drug laws have also contributed to a situation in which politicians and police may ignore drug traffic because of payoffs. A federal government report on organized crime concluded that "with drugs as its primary source of revenue, organized crime has intimidated police officers, judges, juries, and correctional officers" (Auditor General, 2001). Efforts at enforcement may encourage the police to resort to entrapment and illegal search and seizure tactics. Furthermore, there is obvious potential for conflict and recrimination in the control of the flow of illegal drugs. For example, some charge that "Canada's support for using the criminal law as the principal instrument for dealing with certain drugs has fostered staggering levels of violence, corruption and dysfunction around the world— primarily in countries that produce drugs or ship them across their territories" (Oscapella, 2012:3).The principal consumer countries are affluent and industrialized; the principal drug-producing countries are poor and basically agricultural. Consuming and producing countries vehemently accuse and blame each other and, depending on which side they are on, advocate either demand-side or supply-side solutions—controlling the demand of users as opposed to controlling the supply of drugs.

In short, there is little prospect of effective control of drugs through criminal law (Scherrer, 2010; Nadelmann, 2017). Some even argue that the so-called "war on drugs" has corrupted government institutions and that no law enforcement agency has escaped the effects of the profit and racism that drive the drug trade and its criminalization (Marez, 2004). Many would concur that the various punitive approaches—attacking drug production abroad, interdiction (seizing drugs in transit), and domestic law enforcement (arresting and incarcerating sellers and buyers)—have failed and that the "war on drugs" should be abandoned.

There are two controversial alternatives. The first is a consideration of drug addiction and drug use as more a medical than a legal problem, with an emphasis on comprehensive treatment. The European Monitoring Centre for Drugs and Drug Addiction (2008) noted in its 2008 Annual Report that, over the past decade, the majority of European countries have "moved towards an approach that distinguishes between the drug trafficker, who is viewed as a criminal, and the drug user, who is seen more as a sick person in need of treatment." The understanding of drug addiction as an illness is implicit in the 2003 opening of Insite, North America's first supervised drug-injection clinic, by the Vancouver Coastal Health Authority, in partnership with PHS Community Services

Society. "Recognising the limitations of abstinence-based approaches in dealing with a street-entrenched open drug scene, Insite was part of a larger strategy to minimise the negative consequences of drug use for communities and individuals by facilitating contact between healthworkers and people who inject drugs, thereby providing means to reduce those individuals' risk of injecting drug use-related health complications and death and assisting them to access other health and social service" (Chu, 2012). This facility, modelled on 27 similar injection sites in Europe and Australia, furnishes a safe place for up to 800 drug addicts a day (*Economist*, 2003; see also Green, Hankins, and Palmer, 2003) and has operated under an exemption from the prohibition of illicit drugs in the CDSA. More specifically, s. 56 of the CDSA permits the federal Minister of Health to issue exemptions from the application of all or any of its provisions if an exemption "is necessary for a medical or scientific purpose or is otherwise in the public interest." As such, Insite's clients were allowed to inject drugs under medical supervision within the facility without the fear of arrest and prosecution. When the federal Minister of Health refused to extend Insite's exemption in 2008, this decision became the focus of scrutiny in *Canada (AG) v PHS Community Services Society* (2011).

In this case, the Supreme Court noted that Canada had conceded at trial "that addiction is an illness" (at 101) and lingered upon the dual purposes of the CDSA: the protection of both public safety and public health. It described the Minister of Health's powers to grant exemptions as an important "safety valve" and stressed that these discretionary powers had to be used in ways that conformed to the Charter. The Court held that the Minister's decision to withhold an exemption to Insite did not accord with the principles of fundamental justice and infringed upon the s. 7 rights of Insite's staff and clients. "Since exempting Insite from the application of the prohibition on drug possession furthered the objectives of public health and safety, the government action qualified as arbitrary. Furthermore, the effect of denying the services of Insite to the population it served was grossly disproportionate to any benefit that Canada might derive from presenting a uniform stance on the possession of narcotics, since the facility had been proven to save lives with no discernible negative impact on Canada's public safety and health objectives" (Chu, 2012). Accordingly, it ruled that the federal Minister of Health had to grant Insite an "extended exemption" from the application of federal criminal laws in the CDSA. Following this decision, the Quebec government announced that it would allow safe injection sites to open in Quebec City and Montreal.

The understanding of drug addiction as a medical problem also underlies Canada's Drug Treatment Court Funding Program. Justice Canada spends $3.6 million annually for this diversionary system, which is intended "to stop the 'revolving door' of addiction and crime" (Beeby, 2015). Beginning with the 1998 creation of a DTC in Toronto as a pilot program (Evans, 2001), these federally run courts impose court-supervised treatment, rehabilitation (including group and individual counselling), random drug testing, and job training rather than jail time for non-violent drug addicts who have committed a crime to support their addiction. Offenders are given one year to graduate from the program, with those who fail or are expelled returning to the regular court system. Early evaluations suggested that DTCs offered an innovative and cost-effective way to combine two systems—justice and health—in responding to the problem of drug-related crime. For example, it was noted that "[i]n Toronto, only 11.6 percent of offenders who graduated from the program ended up getting into trouble with the law again, compared to 63.4 percent who were expelled" (Rabson, 2005) and that the program's costs were relatively low, with " an average of $8,000 a year for each offender, compared to $50,000 a year to keep them in jail" (*Edmonton Journal*, 2005). Buoyed by such reports, DTCs were introduced in Vancouver (2001), Edmonton (2005), Winnipeg (2006), Ottawa (2006), and Regina (2006). An evaluation of the DTC program (Department of Justice, 2015b) found it to be generally effective in reducing drug use and criminal recidivism, and far more economical than imprisonment, "with net savings of up to 88 percent" (Beeby, 2015). However, it acknowledged that white males over the age of 30 account for the majority of the program's participants and that it has achieved only limited success in attracting and retaining women, Aboriginal people, visible minorities and youth (Beeby, 2015).

The second alternative is the legalization or decriminalization of drugs. Proponents of this approach emphasize that while drugs are dangerous, so is the illegality that surrounds them (Sullum, 2003; Bean, 2010). When drugs are illegal, governments cannot insist on minimum quality standards for cocaine, for example, or demand that distributors take responsibility for the way their products are sold. With alcohol and tobacco, such restrictions are possible; with illicit drugs, they are not. The legalization of drugs, it is argued, would allow governments to control product purity and restrict sales to licensed dealers in specific locations.

Those who champion decriminalization often point to the lost taxes and the immense amounts that Canada spends in charging, prosecuting, and incarcerating drug users and sellers (Werb et al., 2012; Ogrodnik et al., 2015). They also stress the significant human costs of criminalization. These include the social stigma of a criminal record, along with its negative impact upon employment opportunities and the ability to travel freely across borders (Leyton, 2016:75). There is also evidence that the enforcement of Canada's drug laws has had a disproportionate impact on various racialized groups. For example, Akwatu Khenti (2014:190) contends that Canada's war on drugs has been a racialized war, with Black Canadians men vilified as "the main enemy" and drug control efforts functioning "to diminish the health, well-being, and self-image of Black men via discriminatory and inequitable treatment before the law."

In October 2015, Canadians elected a federal government that pledged to legalize marijuana for recreational use. On April 20, 2016, the Liberal government announced that it would introduce new legislation on cannabis in the spring of 2017; three months later, it launched a nine-member task force, chaired by the Honourable Anne McLellan, that would consult with provincial, territorial and municipal governments, Indigenous peoples and youth, as well as addiction/health experts and whose findings would guide the government on this plan (Tunney, 2016). On November 30, 2016, the final report of the *Task Force on Cannabis Legalization and Regulation* (McLellan, 2016) was released. Included among its more than 80 recommendations: the displacement of the illegal market by a system of well-regulated production, manufacturing, and distribution; safeguards for the testing, packaging, and labeling of products; the establishment of a minimum age of access; restrictions on advertising and promotion; and public education on the health and safety risks of cannabis use. A recent report estimates that "legalizing recreational use of the drug could ignite a $22.6-billion industry in Canada" (with that figure including sales of marijuana products as well as ancillaries such as security, transportation, and testing labs) (Pozadski, 2016). However, at the time of writing, the production and possession of marijuana remain illegal in Canada, unless it is for medical purposes (e.g., to relieve symptoms associated with such conditions as HIV, cancer, and multiple sclerosis).

In *R. v. Parker* (2000), the Ontario Court of Appeal declared that the blanket prohibition on possession of marijuana without medical exemption was unconstitutional for it violated s. 7 of the Charter as it did not contain any exemption for medical use. This landmark ruling led to the 2001 implementation of the *Marijuana Medical Access Regulations* (MMAR), which contained three main components: (1) authorizations to possess dried marijuana; (2) licences to produce marijuana (which include *personal-use production licences* and *designated person production licences*); and (3) access to supply of marijuana seeds or dried marijuana (Health Canada, 2012). These regulations allowed persons whose use of medical marijuana was authorized by their health care provider to access dried marijuana through Health Canada. Although the 2013 introduction of the *Marijuana for Medical Purposes Regulations* (MMPR) fertilized the ground for a commercial industry that would produce and distribute quality-controlled dried medical marijuana, the Supreme Court ruled in *R. v. Smith* (2015) that restricting medical access to cannabis in only its dried form was arbitrary and inconsistent with the Canadian Charter of Rights and Freedoms. This restriction, it held, "subjects the person to the risk of cancer and bronchial infections associated with smoking dry marijuana, . . . precludes the possibility of choosing a more effective treatment" and forced individuals who required medical marijuana "to choose between a legal but inadequate treatment and an illegal but more effective choice" (at 18). In response, exemptions under section 56 of the *Controlled Drugs and Substances Act* after July 2015 allowed for the production and sale of different forms of cannabis by licensed producers and their possession by authorized users.

The Federal Court of Canada's decision in *Allard et al. v. Canada* (2015) would lead to further changes in Canada's medical marijuana regime. It ruled that requiring individuals to purchase cannabis only from licensed producers violated the liberty and security rights that are protected by section 7 of the Canadian Charter of Rights and Freedoms. The Court found this requirement to be unconstitutional for it denied "reasonable access" to medical marijuana by those who needed it. In response to this decision, the MMPR was replaced by the *Access to Cannabis for Medical Purposes Regulations* (ACMPR) on August 24, 2016. Akin to the MMPR, the ACMPR establishes a framework for the commercial production of cannabis in various forms by licensed producers who are responsible for the production and secure distribution of quality-controlled products. Its provisions also delineate the requirements that are placed upon those who are allowed to produce, for their own medical use, a limited amount of cannabisis or to have it produced for them by a designate. Nevertheless, "[b]roadly speaking, the role for law enforcement has not changed. Law enforcement officials have a central role in enforcing the CDSA, including whether individuals who possess, produce, sell or provide and transport, deliver or ship cannabis are operating outside of the ACMPR framework" (Department of Justice, 2016a).

PROSTITUTION

If there is one area in the criminal law that arouses the most anxiety concerning public morals, it is sexual conduct (Scoular and Sanders, 2010). The range of sexual conduct that has historically been covered by the law is so extensive that these laws, if re-enacted, would undoubtedly make criminals of most Canadians. One of the justifications for such a complete control of sexual behaviour has been to protect the family system (Horvath and Brown, 2009). Criminal laws prohibiting adultery, for example, were designed to protect the family by preventing sexual relations outside of marriage (Quinney, 1975:83). In addition, a complex set of laws have historically surrounded the advertising, sale, distribution, and availability of contraceptives; the performance of abortion; voluntary sterilization; and artificial insemination (Childbirth by Choice Trust, 2000). However, due to the need for brevity, this section will be limited to a discussion of the legal controls of prostitution.

It is now recognized that laws throughout the world against prostitution discriminate against women (see, for example, Abrol, 2014; Brock, 2009; Butler, 2016; Dala et al., 2011a, 2011b; Ditmore, 2011). Although a definitional amendment in 1983 provided that the term *prostitute* in Canada referred to "a person of either sex engaging in prostitution" and extended liability for engaging in prostitution to men, both as prostitutes and as purchasers, the enforcement of laws on prostitution remained gendered, with women "charged more often than men" (Shaver, 1993:154). Compared to their male counterparts, women were also more likely to be found guilty of prostitution and to receive a prison sentence (Kong and AuCoin, 2008:11). Many prostitutes' rights groups and some feminists' groups here and abroad (e.g., Sex Professionals of Canada; the Toronto Sex Workers Action Project) maintain that adults should have the right to engage in sexual relations for pay if they so desire (McKee, 2011; Rabinovitch and Strega, 2004).

Although prostitution has never been a crime in Canada, the prohibition of acts surrounding prostitution (e.g., laws that criminalize procuring or living on the avails of prostitution; owning, operating, or occupying a bawdy house; public communication for the purpose of prostitution) have made it practically impossible to engage legally in prostitution. Three sex trade workers challenged this situation and, in *Canada (AG) v Bedford* (2013) the Supreme Court of Canada ruled in a 9–0 decision that three sections of the Criminal Code—s.213(1)(c), which prohibited communicating in public for the purposes of prostitution; s. 212(1)(j), that criminalized living on the avails of prostitution; and s. 210, which made it a criminal offense to operate or be in a "bawdy house" for purposes of prostitution—did not pass *Charter* muster. "As an entrenched bill of rights, the Charter empowers judges to declare any piece of legislation to be invalid—and of no force or effect—if the latter infringes on an individual's Charter Rights" (such as . . . the right not to be deprived of the right to life, liberty, and security of the person except in accordance with the principles of fundamental justice [section 7])" (Verdun-Jones, 2016:61). Observing that these laws sought primarily to redress the "public nuisance" aspect of prostitution, rather than to deter prostitution more generally, the Court found the bawdy house and communicating offences to be grossly disproportionate in their impact upon the safety of prostitutes relative to their objective. Moreover, they ruled that the living on the avails offence was overly broad in its scope and failed to distinguish between those who exploited prostitutes (pimps) and those who could provide them with legitimate services that enhanced their safety and security (e.g., bodyguards, drivers, accountants). As Chief Justice Beverley McLachlin wrote, "Parliament has the power to regulate against nuisances, but not at the cost of the health, safety and lives of prostitutes" (at 136).

The Government's legislative response to this ruling was Bill C-36, the *Protection of Communities and Exploited Persons Act*, which received Royal Assent on November 6, 2014. This legislation "reflects a paradigm shift away from the treatment of prostitution as nuisance" and towards its treatment as "a form of sexual exploitation that disproportionately and negatively impacts . . . women and girls" (Department of Justice, 2017b). Its "purchasing offence," which criminalizes the purchase of sexual services and communication for that purpose, is novel for it targets buyers rather than sellers and marks "the first time that purchasing sexual services has been made illegal in Canada" (Canadian Civil Liberties Association, 2015). The maximum penalty for this offence is five years imprisonment when prosecuted by indictment and it is doubled to ten years when the purchase of sexual services is from a person under the age of 18. The "advertising offense," which prohibits the advertising of sexual services, is also a first in Canadian criminal law. Although it exempts those who advertise their provision of sexual services, it "criminalizes knowingly advertising an offer to provide sexual services for consideration" and "targets those who place advertisements in print media or post advertisements on websites" (e.g., publishers, website administrators) (Department of Justice, 2017b).

The "material benefit offense" is an updated variant of the "living on the avails of prostitution" offense that was struck down by the Supreme Court as unconstitutional in *Bedford*. It makes it a criminal offence to knowingly receive a material benefit from the furnishing of sexual services and carries a maximum penalty of ten years imprisonment when the provider of these services is an adult; when the provider is a child, this offence has a mandatory minimum penalty of two years and a maximum of 14 years imprisonment.

In comparison to the "living on the avails" offence, the materials benefits offence is narrower in scope and does not apply when a financial or material benefit occurs in the context of a legitimate living arrangement with the prostitute (e.g., a benefit derived by a spouse, child, or roommate); or as the result of the prostitute's legal or moral obligation or payment for the purchase of a good or service that is offered on the same terms and conditions to the general public (Department of Justice, 2017b). However, these exceptions to the material benefit offense will not apply where the individual who derived a financial or material benefit used or threatened violence or employed intimidation or coercion; exploited a position of trust, power, or authority in relation to the individual who provided the benefit; provided the benefit-provider with intoxicating substances; or received the benefit in the context of a commercial enterprise that offers sexual services for money (Canadian Civil Liberties Association, 2015). The "procuring offense" "criminalizes procuring a person to offer or provide sexual services for consideration or recruiting, holding, concealing or harbouring a person who offers or provides sexual services for consideration, or exercising control, direction or influence over the movements of that person, for the purpose of facilitating the purchasing offence" (Department of Justice, 2017b). The maximum penalty for this offence is 14 years incarceration, with a mandatory minimum penalty of five years imprisonment when the person procured is a child.

For some, the current situation is less than ideal. For example, critics note that the "purchasing offence" makes it criminal to communicate publically with any person in a place that is next to a school ground, playground or daycare centre for the purposes of offering or providing sexual services. This prohibition is assuredly more delimited than the total ban on communication that existed pre-*Bedford*. However, it may imperil the security of prostitutes by encouraging them to communicate with prospective buyers in secluded spaces and/or for abbreviated periods of time that preclude "bargaining for conditions that would materially reduce their risk, such as condom use and the use of safe houses" (*(AG) v. Bedford*, at 156). The advertising offence may also violate section 2(b) of the Charter, which protects freedom of expression, for it curtails the ability of prostitutes to advertise the services they provide. The material benefits offence has also attracted criticism. Thus, in noting that those who receive benefits in the context of a commercial enterprise are not exempted from this offence, it is argued that this omission makes it difficult for prostitutes "to arrange the provision of their services in an organized manner" (Canadian Civil Liberties Association, 2015; see also Benoit et al., 2017).

Laws against adult prostitution represent an attempt to control private moral behaviour through punitive social control measures. Some maintain that such efforts are futile; as the influential Wolfenden Report noted decades ago, as long as there is a demand for the services of prostitutes and there remain those individuals who choose this form of livelihood, "no amount of legislation directed towards its abolition will abolish it" (Committee on Homosexual Offenses and Prostitution, 1963:132). However, others insist that adult prostitution is immoral and/or criminogenic. Its legalization may also be perceived as imperiling the safety and well-being of women. For example, the Coalition Against Trafficking in Women International (CATW) declares the legalization/ decriminalization of prostitution "a gift to pimps, traffickers and the sex industry," which promotes sex trafficking; expands the sex industry; increases street prostitution and child prostitution; does not protect sex workers; increases the demand for prostitution; and neither promotes women's health nor enhances their choices (Raymond, 2003). As Holly Johnson and Karen Rodgers (1993:101) somberly remark, "Prostitution thrives in a society which values women more for their sexuality than for their skilled labour, and which puts women in a class of commodity to be bought and sold."

GAMBLING

Since its enactment in 1892, Canada's Criminal Code has always allowed gambling under certain conditions. A 1910 amendment permitted "pari-mutuel" betting (gambling on horse races with a cut of the bet going to the track, to the horsemen, and to the state), certain games at agricultural fairs, and occasional games of chance that profited charitable or religious organizations. Similarly, while section 189 of the Criminal Code specifies that it is an indictable offence to conduct any of a variety of activities related to "any proposal, scheme or plan for advancing, lending, giving, selling or in any way disposing of any property, by lots, cards, tickets, or any mode of chance whatever," a 1969 amendment (rewritten in 1985) allowed exceptions.

In 1970, amendments to the *Criminal Code* provided provinces with the right to license and regulate gambling—a situation that has made legal gambling a multibillion-dollar industry in Canada. All of Canada's provinces and territories are now involved in conducting and managing lotteries. Lotteries are managed and conducted in Alberta, Saskatchewan, and Manitoba by the Western Canada Lottery Corporation; in New Brunswick, Newfoundland, Nova Scotia, and Prince Edward Island by the Atlantic Lottery Corporation; in British Columbia by the British Columbia Lottery Corporation; and in Quebec by the *Société des loteries et courses du Québec* ("Loto-Québec").

Canada's provincial governments are shareholders within the Interprovincial Lottery Corporation, which conducts several national lottery schemes. In 1989, Canada's first commercial casino opened in Winnipeg and commercial casinos exist everywhere in Canada, except in Newfoundland and Labrador where casino-style gaming in illegal. By 2013–14, there were approximately 34,955 gaming venues in Canada, with Québec and Ontario having the highest number (10,448 and 9,992, respectively) and Prince Edward Island the lowest (214) (Canadian Partnership for Responsible Gambling, 2015:2).

The question of whether the right to control gambling on Indian reserves is an Aboriginal right similar to the rights to hunt and fish was raised in the case of *R. v. Pamajewon* (1996). In this case, the First Nations of Shawanaga and Eagle Lake asserted the right to authorize and regulate games of bingo involving high stakes on their respective reserves. However, the Supreme Court of Canada ruled that such gaming was not protected as an Aboriginal right. Assuming that the right to self-government was included in section 35(1) of the *Constitution Act, 1982*—an issue that the court did not address—Chief Justice Lamer held that gaming for high stakes was not a distinctive and defining feature of the culture and traditions of Aboriginal societies prior to their contact with Europeans. Noting that the evidence presented before the court did not demonstrate that part of their territory had ever been used for that purpose, the court rejected the claim that the right to self-government included the right to control gambling on Indian reserves (Beaudoin, 1999). As a result, First Nations gambling operates under permission of provincial governments.

By 1999, First Nations in Canada had negotiated the right to operate on-reserve video lottery terminal gambling in Manitoba and Nova Scotia, casinos in Saskatchewan and British Columbia, and to share in profits from Ontario's on-reserve casino, Casino Rama (*Casino Gambling*, 1999; *Gaming Magazine*, 2001); by 2008, 17 First Nations casinos were operating in Canada (Belanger, 2010:13). In the years that have followed, "gaming has emerged as one of the most important engines driving the economies of aboriginal communities across the country"; it has provided "hundreds of millions of dollars" to these communities, funding "countless community projects and services, from hospitals to schools" and brought "a new spirit of dignity and economic self sufficiency to Canada's aboriginal peoples" (Hall and Lazarus, 2016). For example, under the Ontario formula for distributing gaming revenues to First Nations bands, First Nations receive "1.7% of the global gaming revenue generated from all gaming activities in Ontario" and "may use the net casino revenues for economic development, community development, health, education, and cultural development" (Hall and Lazarus, 2016).

In Quebec, where, the province "does not contribute any funds to First Nations from its global gaming revenues," the *Regie des Alcohols des Course et des Jeux* ("La Régie") mediates arrangements between the provincial government and Aboriginal groups and, in relation to reserve-based gaming, provides licenses which allow for bingos and VLTs in liquor-licensed establishments. However, while only the provincial government is authorized to hand out gaming licences under Canada's *Criminal Code*, the Kahnawake Mohawk reserve has consistently asserted sovereignty and jurisdiction over their own territory, maintaining that the Mohawk Nation "never relinquished its independence (sovereignty) nor its jurisdiction over territory or peoples" and that "[t]heir status as sovereign, both collective and inherent, has never been usurped by treaty or declaration or declaration between Iroquois and Europeans" (Fleras, 2017b: 193). Consistent with their self-identity as a sovereign people, the Mohawk Council of Kahnawake (KCK) established the Kahnawake Gaming Commission (KGC) in 1996, pursuant to its enactment of the *Kahnawake Gaming Law* (Kahnawake Gaming Commission, 2017). In *Horne v. Kahnawake Gaming Commission (KGC) and Mohawk Council of Kahnawake (KCK)* (2007), the respondents argued that the KGC's authority to license and regulate gaming is a facet of its sovereign rights and protected by s. 35(1) of the *Constitution Act*, 1982, since gaming has formed an integral part of Mohawk culture for centuries. This argument was "favourably considered" in the decision of the Superior Court of Quebec (Kahnawake Gaming Commission, 2017).

The KGC currently licenses and regulates terrestrial poker rooms and raffles conducted within the Mohawk territory of Kahnawake as well as interactive online gaming. "Online gaming operators that are licensed by the Commission must be hosted at Mohawak Internet Technologies, a data center located within the Mohawak Territory at Kahnawake and managed by Continent 8 Technologies" (Kahnawake Gaming Commission, 2017). Its e-gaming enterprise has been extremely successful and is "internationally recognized as one of the pre-eminent e-gaming jurisdictions in the world" (Hall and Lazarus, 2016). As of May 2016, the KGC had licensed almost a hundred international gambling sites and operated "one of the world's most popular sports gambling sites, Sports Interaction" (Strashan, 2016a).

Excluding gambling revenue generated by and for charities and on Indian reserves, legal gambling revenue in Canada increased from $2.7 billion in 1992 to $10.7 billion in 2001. During this same period, gambling profit (the net income of provincial governments from total gambling revenue, less operating and other expenses) rose from approximately $1.7 billion to $5.6 billion (Statistics Canada, 2002:2). Since that time, the profits have only increased: "For 2003–04, the gross profit from government-run gambling activity in Canada was $12.742 billion" (Azmier, 2005) and in 2010, $13.74 billion (Marshall, 2011). Once again, these figures include only those activities "in which governments directly participate as gambling providers" (Azmier, 2005:2) and exclude gambling activities run by charities, First Nations, and horse races. However, the liberalization of legal gambling in Canada since 1970 does not appear to have had any effect on illegal gambling (Sheppard and Smith, 2013). Currently, legal and illegal gambling exist practically side by side, with participants often crossing the line.

In the victimless-crime literature, illegal gambling, just like drug use and prostitution, is considered a consensual transaction and a plaintiffless crime (see Beare, 1996; Cozic and Winters, 1995; Wolfe and Owens, 2009). The parties involved in gambling do not complain about it, and a typical gambling transaction is probably more easily, rapidly, and privately consummated than is any other kind of illegal consensual transaction. Moreover, public opinion does not consider gambling as particularly wrong, a sentiment both affected by and reflected in the lenience with which gambling offenders are treated.

Justifications for controlling gambling activities include fighting organized crime with some emphasizing that illegal gambling supplies organized crime with a steady source of income (Banks, 2017; Harmon, 2016; Savona, Calderoni, and Remmerswaal, 2011; Wolfe and Owens, 2009). The objective of controlling organized crime is reflected both in the intent of some gambling searches by police and in the view that illegal gambling is related to organized crime. For example, the mandate of the Combined Forces Special Enforcement Unit (CFSEU) (a multi-jurisdictional operation that involves the RCMP, the Ontario Provincial Police [OPP], York Regional Police, the Toronto Police Service, and Peel Regional Police Service) is "to expose, investigate, prosecute and dismantle organized criminal enterprises" (RCMP, 2016). As part of "Project Oeider," an illegal video gaming machine investigation, members of the CFSEU, along with the OPP's Illegal Gaming Unit and the Toronto Police Services, executed warrants on eleven social clubs and cafes and one residence in Toronto and York Region in 2016, seizing seventy-four illegal gambling machines and making 15 arrests. In the aftermath of these events, the RCMP issued a press release that declared that "[o]ver recent years there has been a marked increase in serious acts of violence, including targeted murders" at social clubs and cafes and that "[c]riminal violence, sometimes unreported in any formal complaint to police, also flows from the illicit gaming occurring within." It also identified illegal gaming machines as "a major source of revenue for organized crime groups," with this revenue facilitating "criminal activities that pose a pervasive threat to Canadian communities" (RCMP, 2016). Yet, various commentators have expressed fears that enforcement efforts may result in the corruption of those involved. While few police officers are willing to accept bribes from murderers or other criminals whose acts are blatantly harmful and have identifiable victims, more may feel that gambling is not particularly serious and that, in any case, it is impossible to eradicate (see Klockars, Ivkovic, and Haberfeld, 2004; Krauss, 2004).

One response to the difficulty and wastefulness of trying to enforce laws against gambling is to completely remove the criminal label. The Knapp Commission recommended: "The criminal law against gambling should be repealed. To the extent that the legislature deems that some control over gambling is appropriate, such regulation should be by civil rather than criminal process. The police should in any event be relieved from any responsibility for the enforcement of gambling laws or regulations" (Wynn and Goldman, 1974:67). Although a number of similar suggestions have been made, the question of the decriminalization of gambling still remains a hotly debated and controversial issue (see, for example, Belanger, 2010; Wolfe and Owens, 2009). Among the concerns fuelling this controversy is recognition that gambling can become "problem gambling" that involves some type of harmful consequence (Tepperman and Wanner, 2009; Bridges and Williamson, 2004; National Council on Problem Gambling, 2017; Arthur, Williams, and Belanger, 2014). It is estimated that about 5 percent of Canadian adults "experience problems as a result of their gambling," with the adolescent problem gambling rate three times higher" (Sheppard and Smith, 2013).

Research suggests that only a minority of Canada's problem gamblers finance their gambling through criminal activity (Williams, Rehm, and Stevens, 2011; Williams, Royston, and Hagen, 2005). Nevertheless, a recent study that examined the prevalence of moderate and severe problem gambling in a sample of 254 incarcerated Canadian male federal offenders discerned a troubling "cycle of gambling, debt and crime" (Turner et al., 2009:153; see also Turner et al., 2016; May-Chahal et al., 2017; Pinde, 2016).

WHITE-COLLAR CRIME

White-collar crimes are essentially crimes of privilege (Benson and Simpson, 2015; Payne, 2017; Friedrichs, 2010), being of the suite rather than of the street. The term "white-collar crime" was coined by Sutherland (1949:9) and first used in an address to the American Sociological Association in 1939. He criticized proponents of social disorganization and social pathology theories of crime and introduced class and power dimensions. "White-collar crime," he proposed, "may be defined approximately as a crime committed by a person of respectability and high status in the course of his [sic] occupation." He documented the existence of this form of crime with a study of the careers of 70 large, reputable corporations that together had amassed 980 violations of the criminal law, or an average of 14 convictions apiece. Behind the offences of false advertising, unfair labour practices, restraint of trade, price-fixing agreements, stock manipulation, copyright infringement, and outright swindles were perfectly respectable middle- and upper-middle-class executives.

Geis (1978:279; 1994) argues that "white-collar crimes constitute a more serious threat to the well-being and integrity of our society than more traditional kinds of crime" and that workplace injuries, unnecessary surgeries, and illegal pollution consign far more people to the cemeteries than the offences of traditional criminals. According to Moore and Mills (1990:414), the effects of white-collar crime include "(a) diminished faith in a free economy and in business leaders, (b) loss of confidence in political institutions, processes and leaders, and (c) erosion of public morality." Society's response to white-collar crime also raises questions about the equity of law and provides justification for other types of law violations.

The full extent of white-collar crime is difficult to assess. Many illegal corporate activities go undetected, and many wealthy individuals are able to evade taxes for years without being found out. White-collar crimes, often dubbed "crimes of the middle class" (Green, 2006), are generally considered less serious than the crimes of the lower class, and there is often strong pressure on the police and the courts not to prosecute white-collar crime at all—to take into account the offenders' "standing in the community" and to settle the matter out of court. For example, a bank that finds its safe burglarized at night will immediately summon the police, but it may be more circumspect if it finds that one of its executives has embezzled a large sum of money. To avoid unwelcome publicity, the bank may simply allow the offender to resign after making an arrangement for him or her to pay back whatever possible.

The concept of white-collar crime generally incorporates both occupational and corporate crimes (Salinger, 2005; Simpson and Gibbs, 2007). Individuals commit **occupational**

crime for personal gain in connection with their occupations. For example, the Canadian Health Care Anti-Fraud Association insists that "it would be entirely erroneous for Canadians to smugly assume that every doctor is squeaky clean or that the problem of health care fraud is non-existent"; it estimates that the costs of medical fraud in Canada is "upwards of $20 billion per year." Among the various forms of health care fraud it identifies are "the performance of medically unnecessary services, misrepresentation of services as being medically necessary, unbundling of services for separate billing, theft or misrepresentation of identity, exaggeration of identity, exaggeration of illness or injury, shopping for medications from multiple physicians, and misrepresenting eligible dependents" (Miller, 2013:E31).

Lawyers may also engage in various illegalities with an analysis of "every discipline case of lawyers sanctioned by the Law Society of Upper Canada between 2003 and 2013 finding no fewer than 236 cases in which the offence merited a criminal investigation" (Wallace, Mendleson and Brazao, 2017). However, while these lawyers had misused client funds "by stealing, defrauding, failing to account, overdrawing, and improperly dispersing, among other law society classifications, to the tune of $61,457,642," less than one in five of the lawyers who were disciplined by the law society were prosecuted criminally and of the 41 who were, only twelve received a jail sentence (Wallace, Mendleson, and Brazao, 2017). Similarly, a CBC analysis of lawyer discipline records from 2010 to end of 2015 found that while Canadian lawyers were disciplined by law societies for misappropriating a total of $160 million, simply 19 of these lawyers faced criminal charges during that time period (Nicholson, Kubinec, and Pedersen, 2017).

Corporate crimes are illegal activities that are committed in the furtherance of business operations but are not the central purpose of business. A convenient distinction between occupational and corporate crimes may be in the context of immediate and direct benefit to the perpetrator. In occupational crimes, generally the benefit is for the individual who commits a particular illegal activity. In corporate crime, the benefit is usually for the organization.

Corporate crime is distinguished from ordinary crime in two respects: the nature of the violation and the fact that administrative and civil law are more likely to be used as punishment than criminal law. Despite the perception that corporate crime is less serious than street crime, "corporate crimes cause far more financial harm, and many more personal injuries (some leading to death) than do traditional crimes such as theft, robbery and assault" (Snider, 1999:2504). Indeed, some have argued that the term "corporate murder" (Swartz, 1978) is an appropriate label for deaths resulting from such circumstances.

In Canada, corporate crime did not exist until the 19th century because there were no laws against dangerous or unethical corporate practices. Corporations were free to sell unsafe products, keep workers in unsafe conditions, pollute the atmosphere, engage in monopolistic practices, overcharge customers, and make outrageously false advertising claims for their products. By the end of the 19th century and the beginning of the 20th, however, laws were passed that attempted to regulate some of the more flagrant business practices. Early efforts included the *Customs Tariffs Act* (1897) and the *Patent and Propriety Medicines Act* (1908). Since that time, a vast array of federal, provincial, and municipal laws have been passed to regulate potentially harmful corporate activities, including the *Food and Drugs Act*, the *Weights and Measures Act*, and various environmental protection laws.

Canada's *Competition Act*, first enacted in 1889, is the oldest antitrust statute in the Western world. Its introduction represents an attempt by Parliament "to encourage competition, promote greater economic efficiency and enhance Canada's position in world markets" (Bériault and Borgers, 2004:76). This federal statute, which applies to all businesses in Canada, regulates anti-competitive conduct through an amalgam of criminal offences, civil reviewable practices, and private rights of actions. It prohibits certain mergers and monopolies that are believed to be contrary to the public interest and price fixing that would eliminate normal competition among businesses in the marketplace (e.g., bid-rigging). The **Competition Bureau,** an independent law enforcement agency headed by the Commissioner of Competition, is responsible for the Act's administration and enforcement (Government of Canada, 2015d).

The *Competition Act* adopts a two-pronged approach in its regulation of anti-competitive behavior. First, it criminalizes certain conduct—conspiracy and big-rigging—that is believed to be highly egregious to competition. *Conspiracy* occurs when competitors agree to "fix, maintain, increase or control prices (including discounts, rebates, allowances, concessions or other advantages); allocate sales, territories, customers or markets, fix or control the production or supply of a product"; *bid-rigging* occurs when "two or more persons agree that one or more of them will not submit a bid/tender, or will submit and then withdraw a bid/tender in response to bind/tenders; bid/tenders are submitted that are arrived at by agreement between two or more bidders" (MacDonald, 2016). Both conspiracy and bid-rigging are *per se illegal* (meaning that the courts will simply assume the adverse economic effects of anticompetitive conduct). When the Commissioner believes that criminal anti-competitive conduct has occurred or is about to be committed, she or he will commence a formal inquiry and will collaborate with the Public Prosecution Service of Canada (PPSC). Those who are convicted under the *Competition Act's* criminal-offences provisions confront potentially onerous sanctions. In 2009, the maximum fine for an offence committed under the Act's conspiracy provisions was increased from $10 million to $25 million and the maximum term of imprisonment nearly tripled, rising from five to 14 years (Government of Canada, 2015d). The penalties for bid-rigging are also harsh, with the Act now providing for "an unlimited fine, imprisonment of up to 14 years or both" (Naudie and Rodal, 2017:4).

Second, the Act regulates potentially anti-competitive behavior through its "reviewable-practices" provisions. These provisions address conduct that is presumptively lawful and can only be prohibited if the Competition Tribunal finds, on a balance of probabilities, that the conduct has significant anti-competition effects. The Competition Tribunal, a specialized administrative body, consists of up to six judicial members who are appointed from among the judges of the Federal Court and a maximum of eight lay experts. This strictly adjudicative body, which operates independently of any government department, hears cases that deal with such matters as "business mergers; abuse of dominant position; agreements between competitors; refusal to comply; price maintenance; other restrictive trade practices; deceptive marketing practices; specialization agreements; delivered pricing;

foreign judgments, law and directives that adversely affect economic activity in Canada; and refusals to supply by foreign suppliers" (Competition Tribunal, 2017). "For all but one of the reviewable practices, the only remedy available is a prohibition order"; "[a]buse of dominance is the exception" (MacDonald, 2016). Abuse of dominant position occurs when a dominant firm or group of dominant firms engage in anti-competitive acts that are thought "likely to prevent or lessen competition substantially in a market" (Naudie and Rodal, 2017:9). If the Tribunal finds abuse of dominance, it may issue an order that prohibits the act(s) in question. It may also order the dominant firm(s) to take action that is intended to overcome the anti-competitive conduct's impact; this may include the divestiture of assets or shares (Addy, Cornwall, and Kearney, 2005:3). The Tribunal may also impose a significant *administrative monetary penalty* (AMP): up to $10 million for a first abuse of dominant position occurrence and up to $15 million for subsequent occurrences.

Under the *Competition Act*, misleading advertising constitutes both a criminal offence and a civil reviewable matter. When treated as an administrative law matter, the maximum AMP is substantial: $ 1 million for individuals and, for businesses, $15 million. In the past, the Act's criminal provisions against deceptive marketing practices (e.g., bait-and-switch selling; pyramid selling; double ticketing) "tended to be enforced rigorously and were widely recognized as among the Act's most frequently invoked provisions"; however, with the limited resources available to it in recent times, the Competition Bureau has generally focused its attention on cases with national implications (Naudie & Rodal, 2017:5). Since 2009, the Criminal Matters Branch of the Competition Bureau has focused on anti-competitive behaviours in the auto parts industry: "investigating allegations of bid-rigging in respect of the pricing of a number of automotive components, including safety systems such as seat belts, airbags, steering wheels and anti-lock brake systems, and critical parts such as anti-vibration rubber, instrument panel clusters, starter motors and wire harnesses"(Naudie and Rodal, 2017:6).

Between 2000 and 2014, the efforts of the Criminal Matters Branch of the Competition Bureau resulted in more than 80 convictions for cartel offences with fines totaling over $300 million (Naudie, Lally, and Ritchie, 2015:2); in 2015, it secured $2.9 million in fines for cartel and bid-rigging offences and this figure rose to $13.4 million in 2016 (Naudie and Rodal, 2017). In Canada, the second-largest fine ever secured by the Commissioner of Competition occurred in April 2016, when Showa Corporation, a Japanese auto parts company plead guilty to a single count of bid-rigging for participating in an international conspiracy and was fined $13 million by the Ontario Superior Court of Justice (Government of Canada, 2016b). Although domestic enforcement activities in 2016 led to five guilty pleas in criminal cases and resulted in $378,000 in fines, "it remains rare for an individual to serve significant prison time for a criminal conspiracy or bid-rigging offence in Canada" (Naudie and Rodal, 2017:7). Since 2009, the majority of sentences reached in plea agreements between individuals and the Commissioner of Competition have resulted in "the imposition of a fine, often coupled with a prohibition order and/or community service order"; similarly, "in cases involving more serious sanctions, the Commissioner and the PPSC have continued to agree to pleas involving conditional sentences. Even in cases where the PPSC has sought prison time, the courts have imposed prison sentences that are measured in months, rather than years" (Naudie and Rodel, 2017:10). As Hagan and

Linden (2016:486–487) conclude grimly, "There is no evidence that Canadian courts have become more punitive toward corporate criminals and the police and securities regulators have not made much effort to clean up the business world."

In Canada and elsewhere, corporate crime is controlled by a variety of regulatory agencies. The control of corporate activities may be *prospective*, as in licensing, when control is exercised before deviant acts occur; *processual*, as in inspection where control is continuous; and *retrospective*, as when a lawsuit is brought for damages after deviance has occurred.

In addition, if a business concern defies the law, the government may institute, under civil law, an injunction to "cease and desist" from further violations. If further violations occur, contempt-of-court proceedings may be instituted. Fines and various forms of assessments are also used in attempts to control deleterious corporate activities, as, for example, in cases of levying fines on water and air polluters. At times, the government can also exercise control through its buying power by rewarding firms that comply and withdrawing from or not granting governmental contracts to those that do not (Nagel, 1975:341). However, as Christopher Stone (1978:244) pointed out decades ago, "Whether we are threatening the corporation with private civil actions, criminal prosecutions, or the new hybrid 'civil penalties,' we aim to control the corporation through threats to its profits."

Corporate offenders are rarely criminally prosecuted and even more rarely imprisoned. A large proportion of these offenders are handled through administrative and civil sanctions, and the penalty is monetary. In a sense, the penalty imposed for violating the law amounts to little more than a reasonable licensing fee for engaging in illegal activity. As such, controlling corporations through the law often becomes a "misplaced faith on negative reinforcement" (Stone, 1978:250). Although there are now sophisticated detection and record-keeping technologies, forensic accountants, and other legal specialists (O'Brien, 2017), the law constitutes only one of the threats that the corporation faces in dealing with the outside world. Often, paying a fine is considered part of doing business. For a businessperson, reducing the profits by a lawsuit does not involve the same loss of face as losses attributable to other causes. In financial reports, losses through lawsuits are generally explained in footnotes as non-recurring losses.

ABUSE OF SOCIAL CONTROL OF DISSENT

A universal governmental activity is the control of dissent (Hier and Greenberg, 2010; Lovell, 2009; Sarat, 2005). Political trials, surveillance, and suppression of information and free speech are rampant in most countries (see, for example, Sunstein, 2003). In Islamic countries the press is state controlled, and dissidents, at best, are jailed. In some African and Asian countries, journalistic fealty to the ruling dictatorship is demanded; the abuse of psychiatry to intimidate and torture dissidents in the former Soviet Union is well documented.

In China, the democracy movement continues to be suppressed in the aftermath of the 1989 Tiananmen crackdown (Diamant, Lubman, and O'Brien, 2005; Luo, 2000), and the abuse of psychiatry as a form of social control for dissents once again appears to be increasing. For example, the government has forcibly imprisoned members of Falun Gong in psychiatric hospitals. Falun Gong, a popular movement that advocates channeling energy through deep breathing and exercises, has been identified by the Chinese Communist Party as a "heretical cult" and made the target of government crackdowns, with abuses reminiscent of the Cultural Revolution decades earlier (Fu, 2003; Keith and Lin, 2003; Kurlantzick, 2003; Thornton, 2002). Since 1999, over 4,000 practitioners "have been killed by torture, while hundreds of thousands are still held in some form of detention" (with 961 practitioners arrested and prosecuted by the Chinese regime in the first ten months of 2016) and Chinese human rights lawyers typically facing "detention and torture just for defending Falun Gong" (Ong, 2016). Falun Gong members have been taken to psychiatric institutions and drugged, physically restrained, isolated, or given electric shocks (Chan, 2004; *Economist*, 2002a). An investigative report by Canada's former Secretary of State, David Kilgour, and Canadian human rights lawyer David Matas (2008) reported that, in China, there is an ongoing practice of harvesting organs from Falun Gong practitioners and selling their organs to "transplant tourists." An updated (June 2016) investigation by Kilgour and Matas, working with human investigator Ethan Gutmann, reports that China performed between 60,000 and 100,000 transplants each year from 2000 to 2015, using organs derived from prisoners of conscience, the majority of whom were Falun Gong. According to their report, "the large-scale organ harvesting from Falun Gong practitioners was directly ordered by the Standing Committee of the Party and implemented by both military and civilian institutions" (Kilgour, Matas, and Gutmann, 2016:424). There is also the development of a network of new police psychiatric hospitals—called *Ankangs*, which means "peace and happiness"—built in recent years. Chinese law includes "political harm to society" as legally dangerous mentally ill behaviour. Law enforcement agents are instructed to take into psychiatric custody "political maniacs," defined as people who make anti-government speeches, write reactionary letters, or otherwise express opinions in public on important domestic and international affairs contrary to the official government position.

Democratic countries such as Canada and the United States, which welcome dissent in the abstract, may nevertheless punish it in the concrete (Millman, 2016). Hatch (1995) notes that while Canadian governments have long shown remarkable tolerance of right-wing extremism and anti-Semitism, they have evidenced considerably less sympathy for those on the left. It was the fear of a communist conspiracy, she argues, that lay behind the violent government reaction to the Winnipeg General Strike in 1919, which resulted in 30 casualties and one death. In its aftermath, she points out, "the federal government passed section 98 of the *Criminal Code*, prohibiting 'unlawful associations,' and amended the *Immigration Act* to permit the deportation of British-born immigrants, a move clearly aimed at the leaders of the General Strike" (p. 264). From the time that the Communist Party of Canada was founded in 1921, the RCMP used section 98 of the Code to harass its members, break up its meetings, raid its offices, and confiscate its literature (Reilly, 1999). Until 1937, when section 98 was declared illegal, "hundreds were deported as suspected communists, without recourse to due process protections" (p. 264). Similarly, while the *Trade Union Act*, assented to in June 1872, implicitly recognized the right of workers to strike, picketing remained a criminal offence in Canada until the *Criminal Code* was amended in 1934 to allow information picketing. In addition, in 1937, a Quebec statute known as the "Padlock Act" (or, more formally: *An Act to Protect the Province Against Communistic Propaganda*) allowed the Attorney General to close, for a period of one year, any building used for propagating "communism or bolshevism" and to confiscate or destroy any printed matter that propagated such ideas. Those who were convicted of printing, publishing, or distributing such materials could be incarcerated for up to a year without the possibility of appeal. It was only in 1957 in *Switzman v. Elbing* that this law was struck down by the Supreme Court of Canada as *ultra vires* ("beyond the powers")—an unconstitutional invasion of the provincial government into the federal field of criminal law.

In addition, from the 1950s to the late 1990s, Canadian state agents spied on, harassed, and interrogated gays and lesbians; persons who deviated from the heterosexual norm were cast as "threats to society" and "enemies of the state" (Kinsman and Gentile, 2010). Malleson and Wachsmuth (2011) direct attention to more recent events with the title of their book *Whose Streets? The Toronto G20 and the Challenges of Summit Protest.* According to these scholars, what occurred in Toronto during the G20 summit in June 2010 is best understood as an "assault on democratic rights" and an attempt to "wipe out or at least weaken some of the country's most effective and militant anti-poverty, Indigenous solidarity, and migrant rights groups" (Klein, in Malleson and Wachsmuth, 2011:xiii–xiv).

Others focus upon Canada's *Anti-Terrorism Act* (Bill C-36). Drafted in the wake of the September 11, 2001 terrorist attacks on the Pentagon and World Trade Center, Bill C-36 was passed in the Senate with a vote of 45 to 21 and became law in December 2001. Although "key parts of the legislation expired in 2007 under a 'sunshine clause' . . . which provided that the law, if not renewed after a review, would be repealed" (Dranoff, 2011:11), the Act's provisions were troubling to many. For Whitaker (2012:20), "September 11" "re-created the conditions of the Cold War. . . [with] Islamist terrorists replacing communists." Canada's response to 9/11 suggested to Whitaker (2012:20) that our country had failed to learn two lessons that the Cold War should have taught us. First, that (1) "the darkness of the deeds of the other side . . . did not magically cleanse our side of moral responsibility for the means we employed to defend ourselves" and (2) "confronting antagonists abroad by hunting down an alleged fifth column of traitors within is deeply divisive and destructive of the very fabric of liberal democracy" (see also Whitaker, Kealey, and Parnaby, 2012; Duffy, 2017; Geist, 2015). Many have noted the Act's broad definition of terrorism and protested its limited measures for oversight and review (Barkun, 2002; Borovoy, 2002; Tremblay, 2002). For some, it signaled "the recriminalization of dissent" inasmuch as it provided law enforcement with "intrusive new powers, and the wherewithal to detain a person as a criminal solely on the basis of ideology" (Clarke, 2002:49; see also Turk, 2004; Cohen 2005; Jurgenson, 2004).

Other bills that were passed in the shadow of 9/11 have also evoked controversy, including Bill C-11, the *Immigration and Refugee Protection Act*; Bill C-42: the *Public Safety Act*; and Bill C-18, the *Citizenship of Canada Act.* More recently, Bill C-24 the *Strengthening Canadian Citizenship Act* (SCCA) (2014) and Bill S-7, the *Zero Tolerance For Barbaric Cultural Practices Act* (2015) have prompted criticism and concern that the government has erred in its calibration of security interests and fundamental rights (Starr, 2016; Canadian Bar

Association, 2014). Thus, in launching a constitutional challenge to Bill C-24 in federal court, two legal advocacy groups decried it as "anti-immigrant, anti-Canadian, anti-democratic, and unconstitutional" and charged that it created a discriminatory "two-tier citizenship regime" (Black, 2015). Moreover, while the campaign promises of now-Prime Minister Justin Trudeau included a pledge to repeal Bill C-24, his Liberal government did not do so; instead, it introduced Bill C-6, *An Act to Amend the Citizenship Act.* Some charge that as a result of these amendments, some Canadian citizens may have their citizenship revoked in a process that lacks procedural fairness (see e.g., Ling, 2017).

The law supports the government as the legitimate holder of power in society (Cram, 2006). The government in turn is legitimately involved in the control of its citizens. The principal objectives of the government are to provide for the welfare of its citizens, to protect their lives and property, and to maintain order within society. To maintain order, the government is mandated to apprehend and punish criminals. However, in a democratic society, there are questions about the legitimacy of a government that stifles dissent in the interest of preserving order. In principle, in a democratic society, tradition and values affirm that dissent is appropriate. At the same time, for social order to prevail, a society needs to ensure that existing power relationships are maintained over time. Furthermore, those in positions of power who benefit from the existing power arrangement use their influence to encourage the repression of challenges to the government. Consequently, governments generally opt for the control and repression of dissent.

One way of controlling dissent is through the selection processes used to place individuals into desirable social positions (Oberschall, 1973:249). In most political systems, the leaders have ways of controlling the selection and mobility of people through patronage systems, the extension of the government bureaucracy, and co-optation in its many forms. Loyalty and conformity are generally the primary criteria for advancement. Another form of control in this context is the dismissal of individuals who do not comply with the stated expectations and voice "unpopular" opinions. In some instances, the leaders can directly control the supply and demand of certain services and skills.

Control can also be achieved through the manipulation of the structure of material benefits. For example, Piven and Cloward (1993) contend that welfare programs serve as a social-control mechanism in periods of mass unemployment by diffusing social unrest and thus reducing dissent. They argue that public assistance programs are used to regulate the political and economic activity of the poor. In periods of severe economic depression, the legitimacy of the political system is likely to be questioned by the poor. The possibility of upsetting the status quo of power and property relationships in society increases, and demands grow for changing the existing social and economic arrangements. Under this threat, public assistance programs are initiated or expanded by the government. Piven and Cloward cite case after case, from 16th-century Europe to mid-20th-century North America, to document their thesis that social welfare has, throughout the ages, been used as a mechanism of social control and a strategy of the government to diffuse unrest through direct intervention. They note, however, that when economic conditions improve, the relief rolls are cut back in response to pressures from those who employ the poor so as to ensure an adequate supply of low-wage labour.

Another option for the government to use in the control of dissent is its coercive social-control apparatus to deal with crime, enforce the law, and keep social interaction peaceful and orderly. As compared with other mechanisms, "a coercive response to social disturbances is the cheapest and most immediately available means of control to the authorities" (Oberschall, 1973:252). The government is expected by the citizens, and is required by law, to protect life and property and to arrest the perpetrators of illegal activities. In addition to these coercive responses to dissent, the government has in its arsenal a variety of less overt, though equally effective, control mechanisms. For example, the federal Royal Commission of Inquiry into Certain Activities of the RCMP revealed RCMP surveillance of radicals on university campuses, breaches of the confidentiality of the files of the National Revenue Department and Unemployment Insurance Commission, and the use of illegal activities designed to discredit, impede, deter, or undermine political radicals in an effort known as "Operation Checkmate" (Brannigan, 1984:65). In *Whose National Security? Canadian State Surveillance and the Creation of Enemies*, Kinsman (2001) suggests that by collecting, concealing, suppressing, and manipulating information, the government has shown a strong tendency to closely watch the activities of people who threaten it (see also Monaghan and Walby, 2012a, 2012b).

Obviously, the government has to exert some control over its citizens, but there is a thin line between governmental control of dissent and the creation of a police state (Peters and Ley, 2016). The growing power of technology to help government to invade privacy is also a new disturbance to the delicate balance between the privacy rights of citizens and the need for government control (Bloss, 2010; Cox, 2006; Cole, Fabbrini, and Schulhofer, 2017; Goold and Neyland, 2009; Rule, 2009). And this is further exacerbated by the relentless information gathering on the market that is transforming shoppers into "glass consumers" (Lace, 2005). We are all "glass consumers"—organizations know so much about us that they can almost see through us. Governments and businesses collect and process our personal information on a massive scale. Everything we do, and everywhere we go, leaves a trail (Nissenbaum, 2009).

This control technology is ubiquitous in the modern state. Perhaps it is time to start thinking about some effective controls and checks to be devised and imposed upon the users of this technology, so that they do not overstep the boundaries (Geist, 2015; Helfer and Austin, 2011; Taylor, 2015). If not, privacy may just become extinct, civil rights may be sacrificed for security (Welsh and Farrington, 2009), and there will be additional breakdowns of traditional boundaries between public and private space, resulting in substantial reductions of autonomy and privacy (Suk, 2009).

ADMINISTRATIVE LAW AND SOCIAL CONTROL

A broadly and popularly held misconception about the law is that it consists almost entirely of criminal law, with its apparatus of crime, police, prosecutors, judges, juries, sentences, and prisons. Another misconception is that all law can be divided into criminal law and civil law. But the resources of legal systems are far richer and more extensive than either of these views implies. This section discusses how distinctive legal ways can be used to control what

Summers and Howard (1972:199) call "private primary activity." They use this concept to describe various pursuits, such as production and marketing of electricity and natural gas; provision and operation of rail, air, and other transport facilities; food processing and distribution; construction of buildings, bridges, and other public facilities; and radio and television broadcasting. But these activities are not confined to large-scale affairs such as electrical production and provision of air transport. The list can be expanded to include provision of medical services by physicians, ownership and operation of motor vehicles by ordinary citizens, construction of residences by local carpenters, and the sale and purchase of stocks and bonds by private individuals. Private primary activities not only are positively desirable in themselves, but also are essential for the functioning of modern societies. These activities generate legal needs that are met through administrative control mechanisms (Beermann, 2006; Blake, 2017; Régimbald, 2016; Warren, 2010).

Today, all kinds of services are needed, such as those provided by physicians, transport facilities, and electric companies. But an incompetent physician might kill rather than cure a patient. An unqualified airline pilot might crash a plane, killing everyone on board. A food processing plant might poison half a community. In addition to incompetence or carelessness, deliberate abuses are also possible. An individual may lose his or her entire savings through fraudulent stock operations. A utility company might abuse its monopoly position and charge exorbitant rates. An owner of a nuclear waste disposal facility may want to cut corners, thus exposing the public to harmful radiation.

Private primary activities, Summers and Howard (1972:199) note, can cause avoidable harm. At the same time, such activities can have great potential for good. Airplanes can be made safer and stock frauds by fly-by-night operators can be reduced. Legal control of these activities is then justified on two grounds: the prevention of harm and the promotion of good. Control is exerted on private primary activity through administrative laws, primarily in the context of licensing, inspection, and the threat of publicity.

LICENSING

The power of administrative law goes beyond the setting of standards and the punishing of those who fail to comply. Horack notes, "The belief that law enforcement is better achieved by prevention than by prosecution has contributed to the emergence of administrative regulation as a primary means of government control" (cited in Summers and Howard, 1972:202). In Canada, three types of regulatory agencies can be distinguished: self-governing bodies that regulate the conduct of their own members (e.g., professions such as law, medicine, accounting, and engineering), independent regulatory agencies (e.g., the Canadian Radio-television and Telecommunications Commission), and departmental regulatory agencies (e.g., an occupational safety branch of a provincial Ministry of Labour that enforces employment safety standards) (Janisch, 1999).

Requiring and granting licences to perform certain activities is a classic control device. Licensing is pervasive, and by one estimate, at least 5,000 different licenses have been granted to more than 5,000 occupations (Simon, Sales, and Sechrest, 1992:542). With so many groups being licensed, licensing as a form of social control affects a substantial portion of the labour force. Nowadays, a licence may be required to engage in an occupation, to operate a business, to serve specific customers or areas, or to manufacture certain products (Tashbrook, 2004). Physicians and lawyers must obtain specific training and then demonstrate some competence before they can qualify for licences to practise. Here, licensing is used to enforce basic qualifying standards. Airplane companies just cannot fly any route they wish, and broadcasters are not free to pick a frequency at will. Underlying all regulatory licensing is a denial of a right to engage in the contemplated activity except with a licence.

The control of professions and certain activities through licensing is justified as protection for the public against inferior, fraudulent, or dangerous services and products. But, under this rubric, control has been extended to occupations that, at the most, only minimally affect public health and safety, such as licences for cosmetologists, strippers, auctioneers, weather-control practitioners, taxidermists, junkyard operators, and weather-vane installers. In addition to the requirement of obtaining a licence to practise these occupations, control is exerted through the revocation or suspension of the licence.

For example, under administrative law, the state may withdraw the right to practise from a lawyer, a physician, or a beautician, and it may suspend a bar or restaurant owner from doing business for a few days, a year, or even permanently. Administrative laws generally specify the conditions under which a license is required, the requirements that must be met by applicants, the duties imposed upon the licensees, the agency authorized to issue such licenses, the procedures in revoking licenses and the grounds that constitute cause for revocation, and the penalties for violations.

INSPECTION

Administrative law grants broad investigatory and inspection powers to regulatory agencies (Pagnattaro et al., 2016; Reed, 2010). Periodic inspection is a way of monitoring ongoing activities under the jurisdiction of a particular agency. Such inspections determine whether cars and trains can move, planes fly, agricultural products meet quality standards, and so forth. Similar procedures are used to prevent the distribution of unsafe foods and drugs, to prohibit the entry of diseased plants and animals into the country, or to suspend the licence of a pilot pending a disciplinary hearing.

Inspections constitute a primary tool of administrative supervision and control. A housing official may inspect buildings to determine compliance with building codes. In some such instances, inspection takes place occasionally; in others, inspection is continuous, as in food inspection. Both forms of inspection, sporadic and continuous, exert pressure for self-regulation and contribute to the maintenance of internal controls specified by the law. At times, inspections may also lead to proposals for corrective legislation governing regulatory standards.

THREAT OF PUBLICITY

In small communities where people tend to know each other, adversely publicizing wrongdoers can have a significant effect on changing their behaviour. Such a system of social control normally would not work in an urban industrial society for individual deviance. However, large companies selling widely known brand-name products might be greatly influenced by the threat of well-circulated publicity. For example, the publicity surrounding the Ford Motor Company's internal documents on defective and recalled Pintos, which showed that structural fuel tank improvements at a cost of about $11 per car could have prevented 180 fiery deaths a year, resulted in a significant drop in market share for the company (Fisse and Braithwaite, 1993). The public was aghast to realize that Ford had pragmatically calculated that it was preferable to lose $49.5 million in death and injury claims for exploding Pintos rather than retool the assembly line to make the car safer, at a cost of $137 million (Brannigan, 1984:119). More recently, Volkswagen sales dropped precipitously after it became known in 2015 that the auto company had cheated on diesel emissions testing (Noskova, 2016).

Publicity can serve a highly useful, if not indispensable, control function. Indeed, perhaps the most potent tool in any administrator's hands is the power to publicize (Gellhorn and Levin, 1997). A publicity release detailing the character of a suspected offence and the offender involved can inflict immediate damage. Furthermore, in the enforcement of legislation protecting consumers against the manufacture and sale of impure food and drugs, the ability of administrative agencies to inform the public that a product may contain harmful ingredients can play an important role in preventing consumption of the product under investigation until the accuracy of this suspicion can be determined.

In some cases, however, firms that have a monopoly on their products, such as local gas and electric companies, are not likely to be hurt by adverse publicity. Agencies are, at times, also reluctant to stigmatize firms because adverse publicity is considered a form of informal adjudication, although it is often used and justified by the notion that people have a right to know. Moreover, it would be naïve to suppose that the threat of adverse publicity is always sufficient to prevent corporate wrongdoing. Consider that, in 1999, GM was ordered to pay US$4.9 billion to six people who were severely burned when their cars exploded in flames after rear-end collisions. In court, lawyers for the plaintiffs produced an internal GM study that acknowledged that the gas tanks in the Chevrolet Malibu and El Camino, the Pontiac Grand Am, and Oldsmobile Cutlass were mounted in unsafe positions—27 centimetres from the rear bumper. However, the GM study also noted that it would be cheaper to settle lawsuits that might arise from accidents in which victims were fatally burned (calculated to be $2.40 per car produced) than to change where the tanks were placed (calculated to be $8.59 per car produced). Here, like in the case involving the Ford Pintos, a profit-motivated decision was made and the placement of the gas tanks in these cars remained unaltered from 1979 to 1983. Moreover, it should be noted that while the amount awarded in this case was both the largest product-liability award and the largest personal injury verdict in U.S. history, legal experts predicted early on that the enormous punitive award was unlikely to stand on appeal and that "[e]ven with awards in the tens of millions, it is rare for a plaintiff to actually get anything close to the jury's verdict" (White, 1999). They were correct—on appeal, a Los Angeles judge "pruned the jury's $4.8-billion punitive judgment against the world's largest car company to $1.09 billion" (Hong, 1999).

SUMMARY

- Laws are one type of formal social control. Other types of formal social control rely on both penalties and rewards, whereas control through the law is exercised primarily, but not exclusively, by the use of punishment to regulate behaviour.
- The goals of punishment include retribution or social retaliation, incapacitation, and both specific and general deterrence.
- Formal control of deviant behaviour is not limited to criminal sanctions. The use of civil commitment as a mechanism of legal control is also widespread.
- Canada invests enormous resources in controlling victimless crimes. These are crimes *mala prohibita* and are differentiated from other crimes by the element of consensual transaction or exchange. The legal control of victimless crimes, such as drug addiction, prostitution, and gambling, tends to be expensive and ineffective and may lead to the corruption of law enforcement agents.
- White-collar crimes constitute a greater threat to the welfare of society than more traditional kinds of crime. The notion of white-collar crime incorporates both occupational and corporate crimes.
- Control through administrative law is exercised in the context of licensing and inspection and the use of publicity as a threat.

CRITICAL THINKING QUESTIONS

1. Although evidence for a causal link between exposure to and use of pornography and sexual violence remains inconclusive, the movement to ban pornography has recently intensified in reaction to cyberporn, the spread of child pornography on the internet, and the advent of internet rape sites in which "the pain caused to the victim is a primary selling point" (Gossett and Byrne, 2002:689). Investigate why internet-based porn sites are considered to be problematic and how they are currently policed.
2. Imagine: you "Google" yourself and discover that you are described online in ways that are highly unlikely to endear you to potential employers, landlords, or in-laws (e.g., your morality is maligned, your honesty impugned). How would you respond? What difficulties might you face in your attempts to restore your reputation through informal or formal mechanisms?
3. Dowbiggin (2012) fumes that "our society is becoming saturated with therapism, the notion that life is impossible without the assistance of the psychological sciences." Investigate this charge with reference to the crime of infanticide or, in the context of family law, parental alienation syndrome. In what ways may such medicalized constructs function as powerful mechanisms of social control?

ADDITIONAL RESOURCES

1. For down-to-earth information on the impact of criminalization, visit the websites of the John Howard Society of Canada (http://johnhoward.ca) and the Canadian Association of Elizabeth Fry Societies (http://www.elizabethfry.ca).
2. The mandate of the *Canadian Journal of Women and the Law* is "to provide an outlet for those wishing to explore the impact of law on women's social, economic and legal

status, and on the general conditions of their lives." Visit the website of this journal at http://www.utpjournals.com/Canadian-Journal-of-Women-and-the-Law.html.

3. The *Canadian Journal of Criminology and Criminal Justice* (at http://www.ccja-acjp. ca/pub/en/criminology-journal/) is a quarterly journal that publishes scholarly articles based on research and experimentation.

4. Visit the website of the International Criminal Court (http://www.icc-cpi.int) to learn how this "court of last resort" operates and attempts to hold governments accountable for their actions.

6

CHAPTER 6
LAW AND DISPUTE RESOLUTION

One of the major functions of law is the orderly resolution of disputes. The purpose of this chapter is to examine the questions of why, how, and under what circumstances laws are used in disagreements between individuals, between individuals and organizations, and between organizations.

Figure 6.1 One of the major functions of law is the orderly resolution of disputes.
Credit: Shutterstock

LEARNING OBJECTIVES

After reading this chapter, you should be able to:

1. Outline the three phases or stages of the disputing process.

2. Describe the two principal forms of resolving legal disputes throughout the world.

3. Distinguish between negotiation, mediation, and adjudication.

4. Provide three examples of "hybrid resolution processes."

5. Identify characteristics that distinguish the major primary and hybrid dispute-resolution processes.

6. Identify three generic factors that may explain litigation.

7. Define "justiciability" and "standing" and explain how each impacts the use of courts in dispute resolution.

8. Employ Galanter's taxonomy of litigants to describe and discuss disputes between individuals, between organizations and individuals, and among organizations.

A NOTE ON TERMINOLOGY

A number of different terms are used in the sociological and legal literature to describe the role of law in controversies. Terms such as "conflict resolution," "conflict regulation," "conflict management," "dispute processing," "dispute settlement," "dispute resolution," or simply "disputing" are often used more or less interchangeably (Binder et al., 2011; Chase, 2007; Coltri, 2010; Goldberg et al., 2012; Kriesberg, 2007; Macfarlane et al., 2011).

Some scholars contend that disputes are processed in society rather than settled, and conflicts are managed or regulated rather than resolved (Menkel-Meadow, 2003; Palmer and Roberts, 1998). In this view, third-party intervention, whether through legal or non-legal means, represents only the settlement of the public component of the dispute or conflict, rather than the alleviation of the underlying forces or tensions that created it. Thus, Abel (1973:228) chided anthropologists and sociologists who "have tended to write as though 'settlement' must be the ultimate outcome of disputes, 'resolution' the inevitable fate of conflicts"; according to Abel, "the outcome of most conflicts and disputes are other conflicts and disputes, with at most a temporary respite between them."

Other authors point out that the disputing process consists of several phases (e.g., Felstiner, Abel, and Sara, 1980). For example, Nader and Todd (1978:14) contend that there are three distinct phases or stages in this process: (1) the **grievance** or **preconflict stage**, (2) the **conflict stage**, and (3) the **dispute stage**. The grievance or preconflict stage refers to situations that an individual or group perceives to be unjust and considers grounds for resentment or complaint. The situation may be real or imaginary, depending on the aggrieved parties' perception. This condition may erupt into conflict or it may wane. If it is not resolved, it enters into the conflict stage, in which the aggrieved party confronts the offending party and communicates his or her resentment or feelings of injustice to the person or group. The conflict phase is dyadic; that is, it involves only two parties. If it is not de-escalated or resolved at this stage, it enters into the final, dispute stage when the conflict is made public. The dispute stage is characterized by the involvement of a third party in the disagreement. Gulliver (1969:14) suggests that "no dispute exists unless and until the right-claimant, or someone on his [sic] behalf, actively raises the initial disagreement from the level of dyadic argument into the public arena, with the express intention of doing something about the denied claim." Ideally, then, a grievance is *monadic*, involving one person or a group; a conflict is *dyadic*; and a dispute is *triadic*, since it involves the participation of a third party who is called upon as an agent of settlement.

The legal approach to dispute resolution entails the transition from a dyad of the conflicting parties to the triad, "where an intermediary who stands outside the original conflict has been added to the dyad" (Aubert, 1963:26). However, the stages discussed by Nader and Todd are not always clear-cut or sequential. A person may file a lawsuit without ever confronting the offender, or one party may quit or concede at any stage in the disagreement.

When disagreements formally enter the legal arena (that is, at trial), from the perspective of the law, disputes are authoritatively settled rather than processed through the intervention of third parties (that is, judges), and conflicts are resolved rather than simply managed or regulated. The use of the terms "conflict resolution" and "dispute settlement" is thus, in this sense, justified.

In this chapter, we shall use these concepts interchangeably, and at the same time, we will repeatedly emphasize, in different contexts, that the law resolves or settles only the legal components of conflicts and disputes, rather than ameliorating the underlying causes. A legal resolution of conflict does not necessarily lead to a reduction of tension or antagonism between the aggrieved parties. In illustration, sociolegal research on divorce as a legal resolution of marital conflict shows clearly that divorce does not necessarily reduce the spousal tensions that lead to divorce and that ongoing acrimony between former spouses can culminate in lethal violence (Brennan and Boyce, 2013; Burczycka, 2016; Sinha, 2013). Moreover, while Macfarlane et al. (2011:xxxi) acknowledge that lawyers are "more often seen as conflict 'warriors' than as 'resolvers,'" they emphasize that the "growth of alternatives to trial, in both the public sphere of the courts and in the private sector is having a huge impact on the legal profession" (see also Macfarlane, 2008; Susskind, 2008).

METHODS OF DISPUTE RESOLUTION

Disputes are ubiquitous in every society, and a wide variety of methods are used to manage these disputes (Chase, 2007; Coltri, 2010). Most societies use fairly similar methods; the differences among them consist in the preference given to one method over others. Cultural factors and the availability of institutions for settling disputes will usually determine such preferences.

Two main forms of resolving legal disputes are used throughout the world: "*Either* the parties to a conflict determine the outcome themselves by negotiations, which does not preclude that a third party acting as a mediator might assist them in their negotiations. *Or*, the conflict is adjudicated, which means that a third, and ideally impartial, party decides which of the disputants has the superior claim" (Ehrmann, 1976:82).

In some societies, direct interpersonal violence constitutes an approved method of dispute settlement (Roberts, 1979). This violence may be in retaliation for violence suffered or in response to some other form of perceived injustice (Adinkrah, 2005). In earlier eras, physical violence was sometimes channeled into a restricted and conventionalized form, such as *duelling*. Another historic form of physical violence in response to grievances has been **feuding** (Gulliver, 1979). Feuding is a state of recurring hostilities between families or groups, instigated by a desire to avenge an offence (insult, injury, death, or deprivation of some sort) against a member of the other group. The unique feature of a feud is that responsibility to avenge is carried by all members of the group. The killing of any member of the offender's group is viewed as appropriate revenge, since the group as a whole is considered responsible. At times, the feud can turn into a full-scale battle when, in addition to families, communities are drawn into a dispute (Alther, 2012).

Disagreements are sometimes channeled into rituals (Rosati, 2009; Stewart and Strathern, 2010). For example, the parties to the dispute may confront each other before the assembled community and voice their contentions through songs and dances improvised for the occasion. In the form of a song, the accuser states all the abuse he or she can think of; the accused then responds in kind. A number of such exchanges may follow until the contestants are exhausted, and a winner emerges through public acclaim for the greater poetic or vituperative skill.

In some societies, **shaming** is used as a form of public reprimand in the disapproval of disputing behaviour. Ridicule directed at those guilty of anti-social conduct is also used to reduce conflict. At times, the singing of rude and deflating songs to, or about, a troublesome individual is also reported as a means of achieving a similar end. Ridicule, reproach, or public exposure may also take the form of a "public harangue," in which a person's wrongdoings are embarrassingly exposed by being shouted out to the community at large (Roberts, 1979:62). Another form of shaming, however, does not employ it as a form of humiliation, but rather as a method of resolving disputes through the "healing" of wounds. For example, the report of the Aboriginal Justice Inquiry of Manitoba (1991:27) noted that, within traditional Aboriginal societies, the underlying philosophy stressed atonement and the restoration of harmony—not punishment (see also Ross, 1992). In "**reintegrative shaming**," disapproval is expressed toward the rule-violating act, but the essential value of the offender, him or herself, is reaffirmed along with the prospect of reacceptance (McAlinden, 2005). According to Siegel (1998:121), "A critical element of re-integrative shaming occurs when the offenders begin to understand and recognize their wrongdoing and shame themselves. To be re-integrative, shaming must be brief and controlled and then followed by 'ceremonies' of forgiveness, apology, and repentance."

In attempts to resolve disputes, parties may also choose to resort to supernatural agencies (Chase, 2007). In the traditional societies studied by anthropologists, the notion that supernatural beings may intervene to punish wrongdoers is rather widespread. This notion is often accompanied by the belief that harm may be inflicted by witches or through the practice of sorcery. In some societies, witchcraft and sorcery are seen as a possible cause of death and of almost any form of illness or material misfortune. Collier (1973:113), for example, identifies a variety of witchcraft beliefs among the Zinacantecos in Mexico. They include witches who send sickness, ask that sickness be sent, perform specific actions (such as causing the victim to rot away), control weather, talk to saints, or cause sickness by an evil eye. Consequently, in such societies the procedures for identifying witches or sorcerers responsible for particular incidences or misfortunes assume great importance in the handling of conflict.

Of course, not all disputes are handled by violence, rituals, shaming, ostracism, or resorting to supernatural agencies (Chase, 2007). Most societies have access to a number of alternative methods of dispute resolution. These alternatives differ in several ways, including whether participation is voluntary, the presence or absence of a third party, the criteria used for third-party intervention, the type of outcome and how it may be enforced, and whether the procedures employed are formal or informal. Before considering them, let us look at two other popular ways of coping with disputes: "lumping it" and avoidance.

"Lumping it" refers simply to inaction, to not making a claim or a complaint. "This is done all the time by 'claimants' who lack information or access or who knowingly decide gain is too low, cost too high (including psychic cost of litigating where such activity is repugnant)" (Galanter, 1974:124). Mullis's (1995) investigation of doctor–patient conflict found that "lumping it" was an especially common response among poor patients, with these patients less likely to file a malpractice suit against their physician than their higher-income counterparts. In "lumping it," the issue or the difficulty that gave rise to the disagreement is simply ignored and the relationship with the offending party continues. Greenhouse (1989) earlier described a different form of "lumping it" in her study of Baptists in a southern American town. Greenhouse found that the Baptists she studied considered disputing a profoundly unchristian act because the Bible states that Jesus is the judge of all people. The implication was that to partake in a dispute is to stand as judge over another person, representing lack of faith and a preemption of Jesus's power. For these reasons, the Baptists she studied tended to shy away from disputes.

Avoidance refers to limiting the relationship with other disputants sufficiently so that the dispute no longer remains salient (Felstiner, 1974:70). Hirschman (1970) calls this kind of behaviour "exit," which entails withdrawing from a situation or terminating or curtailing a relationship. For example, a consumer may go to a different store rather than complain about a rude salesperson or high prices. Avoidance entails a limitation or a break in the relationship between disputants, whereas "lumping it" refers to the lack of resolution of a conflict, grievance, or dispute for the reason that one of the parties prefers to ignore the issue in dispute. Decisions to practice lumping behavior or avoidance arise from feelings of relative powerlessness or from concern over the possible social, economic, or psychological costs involved in seeking a solution. Avoidance is not always an alternative, especially in situations when the relationship must continue—for example, with certain companies that have monopolies, such as gas or electric companies, or with the Canada Revenue Agency.

PRIMARY RESOLUTION PROCESSES

The primary dispute resolution mechanisms can be depicted on a continuum ranging from negotiation to adjudication. In *negotiation*, participation is voluntary and disputants arrange settlements for themselves (Manwaring, 2011). Next on the continuum is *mediation*, in which a third party facilitates a resolution and otherwise assists the parties in reaching a voluntary agreement (Bush and Folger, 2005; Smyth, 2011). At the other end of the continuum is *adjudication* (both judicial and administrative), in which parties are compelled to participate, the case is decided by a judge, the parties are represented by counsel, the procedures are formal, and the outcomes are enforceable by law (Hausegger, Hennigar, and Riddell, 2009). Close to adjudication is *arbitration*, which is more informal and in which the decision may or may not be binding. Negotiation, mediation, and arbitration are the principal components of what is referred to as alternative dispute resolution (ADR) (Barrett and Barrett, 2004; Partridge, 2009). This movement is spreading to other parts of the world. In France, for example, ADR is regularly promoted by French authorities and legal scholars alike as a means of relieving the burden of the courts; of rendering dispute resolutions that are faster, simpler, and cheaper and of "de-dramatizing" disputes to render their resolutions more satisfactory to the parties (Gaillard, 2000).

Let us now consider these processes and some of their variants in some detail.

Negotiations in disputes take place when disputants seek to resolve their disagreements without the help of neutral third parties. Negotiation is a two-party arrangement in which disputants try to persuade one another, establish a common ground for discussion, and feel their way, by a process of give-and-take, toward a settlement. It involves the use of debate and bargaining (Lewicki, Barry, and Saunders, 2011). A basic requirement for successful negotiation is the desire of both parties to settle a dispute without escalation and without resort to neutral third parties. Aubert (1969a:284) states: "The advantage of negotiated solutions is that they need not leave any marks on the normative order of society. Since the solution does not become a precedent for later solutions to similar conflicts, the adversaries need not fear the general consequences of the settlement." When interests are contradictory to the extent that gains and losses must cancel each other out, negotiations are inadequate for resolving the conflict, and, in such situations, parties may bring the case to court for legal settlement. Types of negotiation include *dispute negotiations* between parties over an incident in the past (e.g., a breach of a contract) or in anticipation of a future event (e.g., the management of an estate); *distributive bargaining*, with each party seeking individual gain in the division of limited resources; *zero-sum bargaining*, with one party seeking to acquire a benefit for themselves at the expense of the other party (e.g., acquiring a property for less than the seller's asking price); *transactional negotiations*, with parties planning cooperatively for a future event (e.g., the registration of a trademark); *positional bargaining*, with one party arguing consistently for an often-extreme position and hoping to make few (if any) concessions; and *integrative negotiations*, with parties in a non-antagonistic relationship seeking mutual gain (Davies, 2008). In industrialized countries, such as Canada, lumping behaviour, avoidance, and negotiation are the most frequent responses to dispute situations.

Mediation is a common dispute resolution method that interposes a disinterested and non-coercive third party, the *mediator*, between the disputants (Georgakopoulos, 2017; McCorkle and

Reese, 2010; Smyth, 2011). Unlike litigation, in which the judge imposes the ultimate decision, the mediator does not make the final decision. Rather, the terms of settlement are worked out solely by and between the disputants. It can be an effective way of resolving a variety of disputes if both parties are interested in a reasonable settlement of their disagreement (Haynes, Haynes, and Fong, 2004). Mediation begins with an agreement to undertake mediation; it is non-adversarial, and the basic tenet is co-operation rather than competition.

The role of the mediator in the dispute is that of a guide, a facilitator, and a catalyst. The disputants may choose a mediator, or someone in authority may appoint a mediator. Depending on the society and situation, a mediator may be selected because the person has status, position, respect, power, money, or the alleged power to invoke sanctions on behalf of a deity or some other superhuman force. A mediator may have none of these attributes and simply be a designated agent of an organization set up to handle specific disputes. Bringing disputes to a mediator may be the choice of both parties or of one but not the other party to a conflict, or it may be the result of private norms or expectations of a group that "require" that disputes be settled as much as possible within the group.

Mediation essentially consists of influencing the parties to come to an agreement by appealing to their own interests. Both parties should have confidence in the mediator, be willing to co-operate, listen to his or her advice, and consider the mediator as impartial. In general, "[t]he conditions for mediation are best in cases where both parties are interested in having the conflict resolved. The stronger the common interest is, the greater reason they have for bringing the conflict before a third party, and the more motivated they will be for cooperating actively with. . . [the mediator] in finding a solution, and for adjusting their demands in such a way that a solution can be reached" (Eckhoff, 1978:36).

Two broad types of mediation approaches may be distinguished: facilitative or "interest-based" mediation and rights-based mediation. **Facilitative** or **interest-based mediation** is characterized as process-oriented, client centered, and communication focused (Smyth, 2011:265–266). As its name implies, the mediator acts as a facilitator and does not direct the parties towards a particular settlement. Rather, s/he encourages the parties to identify their needs and expectations to the other and arrive at a win–win solution. Facilitative mediators "focus on the integrative (rather than the distributive) dimension of the conflict—that is, on how to identify options that will increase the degree to which all parties can obtain their goals" (Smyth, 2011:266). **Rights-based mediation,** sometimes referred to as "early neutral evaluation" or "evaluative mediation," involves a mediator's evaluation of the case in the context of formal rules (e.g., the law or accepted principles of accounting) and ensures that the agreement mediated reflects both statutory rights and legal entitlements. For example, labour mediation, which has been widespread across Canada for decades, is generally rights-based (Bumstead, 2001:513). Among the advantages of mediation are the process is generally less time-consuming, complicated, and expensive than either litigation or arbitration; the costs involved are typically shared; the focus may look beyond the legal issues and examine the circumstances which caused the conflict; and it endows parties with greater autonomy inasmuch they control the process. However, while one of mediation's principal attractions derives from its potential to furnish an alternative to "what law and legal institutions offer and represent: complexity, expense, delay, inaccessibility, formality, alienation, and elitism," its practice increasingly witnesses the legal profession's "power and influence" (Picard and Saunders, 2002:232). Noting that courses in ADR are now routine offerings at law schools and that lawyers' ads may include boasts of expertise in this area, Picard and Saunders warn that "[t]he imposition of the values and direction of a profession that continues to reflect the advantaged and elite . . . threatens to leave mediation trapped within the narrow confines of a rights-based, cost-effective, and settlement-focused framework."

Related to mediation is the **ombudsman/ombudsperson process**, which combines mediatory and investigatory functions in dispute resolution. In the classic Scandinavian model, the ombudsman is a public official designated to hear citizen complaints and carry out independent fact-finding investigations in order to correct abuses of public administration. In a traditional sense, ombudsmen are independent agents of the legislature, and they can criticize, publicize, and make recommendations, but they cannot reverse administrative actions (Rosenbloom and Kravchuck, 2005). In like fashion, Canadian ombudspersons "have no judicial or legislative authority to make binding decisions" (Davies, 2008) and can act only "within the authority established by Parliament or a provincial legislature, to which she or he is responsible" (Dranoff, 2011: 239).

In general, there are three types of mandates under which Canadian ombudspersons operate. To wit:

Ombudsman/person established by provincial, territorial or federal legislation with strong powers of investigation and structural independence. [Example: provincial and territorial ombudsman/person, some federal ombudsman/person offices].

Ombudsman/person established by policy or terms of reference by both private and public sector organizations. They primarily use various forms of early resolution methods but may also have the power to investigate and the authority to publish annual and special reports. [Example: ombudsman/ombudspersons in universities and colleges, banks, utilities].

Ombudsman/person established by corporate or organizational policy or terms of reference, which generally use only facilitative methods for assisting with the resolution of complaints. [Example: employee ombudsman for banks and some federal agencies.
(Forum of Canadian Ombudsman, 2011)

In their role, ombudspersons may use tools such as mediation and negotiation for the informal resolutions of complaints. An ombudsperson may furnish advice, make referrals and alert complainants to the options available to them. S/he may also conduct "[i]nquiries and structured investigations to determine whether a complaint is founded along with the ability to make recommendations to correct unfair situations, both in individual cases and to address systemic issues" (e.g., "looking for trends and patterns in complaints to identify and make recommendations to address potential systemic issues and seek system-wide improvements to influence positive changes") (Forum of Canadian Ombudsman, 2011). In these fact-finding investigations, the ombudsman does not act as an advocate, as a lawyer does, but as a neutral party. Nevertheless, a major criticism against the ombudsman process is that the person acting as mediator often represents the vested interest of a particular agency, which suggests bias in favour of his or her employer.

Arbitration is another way of involving a third party in a dispute. Unlike mediation, in which a third party assists the disputants in reaching their own solution, arbitration requires that a decision be made for the disputants by a third party; this decision may or may not always be binding. Disputants will agree beforehand to both the intervention of a neutral third party arbitrator and whether his or her decision will be final and binding on the parties to the dispute. In general, the rules of evidence and procedure are more relaxed than in the court process. Arbitration is a rights–based, adversarial process and, in this way, resembles a civil trial. However, the proceedings in arbitration, unlike in courts, can remain private. Arbitration and other nonjudicial methods tend to reduce the cost of dispute resolution, especially when lawyers are not hired, because of the lack of opportunity to appeal the arbitrator's decision. It is also faster than adjudication because participants can proceed as soon as they are ready, rather than waiting for a trial date to be set.

Nowadays, almost all collective bargaining contracts contain a provision for final and binding arbitration (Warskett, 2002). For example, "[p]ublic sector employee arbitration (e.g., police, teachers) allows negotiation of terms contained in collective bargaining agreements where strikes are prohibited by statute during labour negotiations" (Davies, 2009). Similarly, "under the Canadian Labour Code, which applies to about 10 percent of Canadian workers who are within the regulatory sphere of the federal Parliament, a worker claiming to have been dismissed without just cause can have the claim adjudicated by a neutral arbitrator appointed by the government" (Mac Neil, 2002:184). Arbitration clauses are also showing up more often in business contracts and even in executive employment letters. Many private organizations, professional groups, and trade associations have their own formal arbitration machinery for the settlement of disputes among members. In general, willingness to submit disputes to private but formal arbitration is characteristic of parties that have a commitment to long–term relationships (Sarat, 1989). Although "arbitration awards are not usually subject to judicial review after the decision has been rendered," exceptions occur and this general statement would not hold true, for instance, in situations "involving misrepresentation or fraud, partiality or corruption of the arbitrator, misconduct on behalf of the arbitrator, or proof that the arbitrator exceeded the powers of the position" (Davies, 2009).

Arbitration is increasingly considered as an alternative to judicial and administrative processes. Compulsory arbitration, especially for small claims, can free courts for more substantial disputes, and, depending upon the issues involved, it may reduce the cost to litigants and be a more effective way of solving problems. However, as Box 6.1 describes, the use of arbitration can be controversial.

BOX 6.1 LIFE AND LAW: FAITH-BASED ARBITRATION

A primary intent behind the passage of the *Arbitration Act* in Ontario in 1991 was to reduce the backlog within the court system by allowing individuals to settle their disputes outside of that system. To this end, the *Arbitration Act* allowed for both mediation and arbitration, including faith-based arbitration.

Only civil matters could be arbitrated and the rulings arrived at through arbitration were subject to Canadian law (Walter, 2012).

As a result of this Act, from 1991 to 2005 Jews, Catholics, and members of other faiths in Ontario were afforded the right to use the guiding principles of their religions to settle divorce, custody, inheritance, and other civil disputes outside of the court system. Following its passage, it was possible for Catholics, for example, to annul religious marriage according to Canon Law (although it took a secular court to legally dissolve a civil marriage). Similarly, although the Orthodox Jewish community in Ontario had, since 1889, been using a "millennia-old rabbinical court system—called *Beit Din* (House of Law)—to settle marriage, custody and business disputes," the 1991 Act made its rulings, as well as those of other private arbitrations, "legally enforceable in a secular court, provided the parties consented beforehand" (Csillag, 2006; CTV, 2005). In 2003, the Toronto-based Canadian Society for Muslims proposed the creation of a formalized tribunal: the Islamic Institute of Civil Justice. "There, Muslim arbitrators would be allowed to make legally-binding decisions for Ontario Muslims when it comes to family and personal law" (CTV, 2005). Although the process already existed informally, the announcement generated heated opposition. Opponents charged that such tribunals would disadvantage women by forcing them to participate in a male-dominated process. In the months that followed, Amnesty International, along with dozens of other international groups and some 80 national organizations, voiced concern that these tribunals would discriminate against women and fail to fully comply with international human rights standards, and demonstrations were held in various Canadian and European cities (McIlroy, 2005). It was claimed that Sharia law "runs counter to the *Charter of Rights and Freedoms*"; that under "most interpretations of Islamic law, women's rights to divorce are strictly limited and they only receive half the inheritance of men"; and that this system of law "allows for polygamy and often permits marriage of girls at a younger age than does secular law" (Duff-Brown, 2005:541).

In June 2004, the Ontario government announced that a review of the entire *Arbitration Act* would be conducted. The report, conducted by former Ontario Attorney-General Marion Boyd, ultimately recommended that the province's existing arbitration system be strengthened and concluded that Muslims should enjoy the same rights as other religions to use faith-based arbitration to settle family disputes. To many, it appeared that Ontario was well on its way to becoming the first Western jurisdiction to allow Sharia tribunals to settle marital and other family disputes according to the tenets of Islamic law. However, in September 2005, Ontario premier Dalton McGuinty announced, "There will be no Sharia law in Ontario. . . . There will be no religious arbitration in Ontario. There will be one law for all Canadians" (cited in McIlroy, 2005). McGuinty maintained that religious arbitrations "threatened our common good" and pledged to move quickly to introduce legislation that would outlaw all religious arbitrations. "Ontarians will always have the right to seek advice from anyone in matters of family law, including religious advice," he commented, "But no longer will religious arbitration be deciding matters of family law" (cited in Duff-Brown, 2005). In the summer of 2006, the Ontario government passed Bill 27, the *Family Statute Amendment Act*. This provincial law prohibits all forms of binding arbitration in family matters (e.g., divorce, child custody, and division of property) and states that resolutions "based on other laws and principles— including religious principles—will have no legal effect and will not be enforced by the courts." In addition, it specifies that family arbitrators must be trained and hold membership within a professional arbitration organization (Chotalia, 2006). However, this stance has also proven controversial (Berger, 2014; Berger and Moon, 2016. As Natasha Bakht (2007:119) points out, while feminist organizations focused their lobbying efforts "on proscribing religious arbitration as the only acceptable means of protecting vulnerable women," a "strategy of secularism as the obvious solution to gender inequality" must be recognized as troubling for at least two reasons: "First, it shows no consideration for religious women who might want to live a faith-based life. Second, the feminist endorsement of an exclusively state-run apparatus fails to understand the legitimate resistance to government policies post 9/11 that have perpetuated punitive and stigmatizing measures against people of colour."

Adjudication is a public and formal method of conflict resolution and is best exemplified by courts. Courts have the authority to intervene in disputes whether or not the parties desire it and to render a decision and enforce compliance with that decision. In adjudication, the emphasis is on the legal rights and duties of disputants, rather than on compromises or on the mutual satisfaction of the parties. Adjudication is also more oriented toward zero–sum decisions than the other mechanisms we have noted. Courts require disputants to narrow their definitions of issues in the identification of the nature of their problems. Felstiner states: "Adjudication as a consequence tends to focus on 'what facts' and 'which norms' rather than on any need for normative shifts" (1974:70). In other words, courts deal with issues and facts. Consequently, they can deal only with disagreements, grievances, or conflicts that have been transformed into legal disputes. For example, in a divorce case, the court may focus on one incident in what is a complex and often not very clear-cut series of problems. This results in the resolution of a legal dispute but not necessarily of the broader issues that have produced that conflict.

Although courts occasionally seek compromise and flexibility, generally the verdict of the court has an either–or character: The decision is based upon a single definite conception of what has actually taken place and upon a single interpretation of legal norms. When a conflict culminates in litigation, one of the parties must be prepared for a total loss. Aubert says: "One aspect of legal decisions that is closely linked to their either–or character is the marked orientation toward the past" (1969a:287). The structure of legal thinking is also oriented toward comparisons between actions and sanctions rather than toward utility and effectiveness. Because of this orientation, and because of the use of precedents, there is a fair amount of predictability in how similar cases will be settled by courts. But since the courts are dealing only with the legal issues, they do not take into consideration the possibility that the applicable legal facts and norms may have been influenced by different social conditions and that, in many instances, courts are treating only the symptoms rather than the underlying causes of a problem.

HYBRID RESOLUTION PROCESSES

In both the public and private sectors, the intervention of a third party—a person, a government agency, or another institution—can often facilitate dispute resolution among conflicting parties (Ross and Conlon, 2000), and there are currently several "hybrid" dispute-resolution processes in use. The term *hybrid* is employed because these processes incorporate features of the primary processes discussed in the preceding section. The main ones include rent-a-judge, med-arb, and mini-trial (Goldberg et al., 2012)

The **rent-a-judge** process is basically a form of arbitration. In this process, the disputants, in an attempt to avoid the use of a regular court, select a retired judge to hear and decide a pending case as an arbitrator would. The same procedure is used as in court, and the decision of the judge is legally binding. Unlike in arbitration, the "referee's" decision can be appealed for errors of law or on the ground that the judgment was against evidence, though such appeals are rare.

Another hybrid process is **med-arb**, in which the issues that were not solved by mediation are submitted to arbitration; sometimes, the same person serves first as mediator, then as arbitrator. Med-arb has been used often in contract negotiation disputes between public employers and their unionized employees. A third process is the **mini-trial**, which has been utilized repeatedly in a number of big intercorporate disputes. In this method, lawyers for each disputant are given a short time (not more than a day) in which to present the basic elements of their case to senior executives of both parties. After the presentation, the senior executives try to negotiate a settlement of the case, usually with the aid of a neutral adviser. If there is no settlement, the adviser gives the parties his or her opinion of the likely outcome if the dispute were litigated. At times, this dose of reality helps to break the deadlock.

Obviously, no single procedure is applicable to every kind of problem. A number of considerations appear relevant in the selection of a particular method. One is the relationship between the disputants; that is, is there an ongoing relationship between the disputants, such as business partners, or is the dispute the result of a single encounter, such as an automobile accident? When an ongoing relationship is involved, is it more productive for the parties to work out their difficulties through negotiation or mediation, if necessary? An advantage of mediation is that it encourages the restructuring of the underlying relationship so as to eliminate the source of conflict rather than dealing only with the manifestation of conflict. Another consideration is the nature of the dispute. If a precedent is required, as in civil rights cases, litigation in the form of class action may be appropriate. The amount at stake in a dispute also plays a role in deciding on the type of dispute-resolution procedure. Small, simple cases might end up in small claims courts, whereas more complex issues might require court-ordered arbitration, such as in contract negotiation disputes between public employers and unions. Speed and cost are other relevant factors. For example, arbitration may be speedier and less costly than a court trial.

Finally, consideration must be given also to the power relationship between the parties. When one party in a dispute has much less bargaining strength than the other, as in the case of a pollution victim faced by a powerful corporation, an adjudicatory forum in which principle, not power, will determine the outcome may be desirable. In the remainder of this chapter, we shall consider why some disputants turn to legal mechanisms of conflict resolution, under what circumstances they choose the law rather than some other procedures, and the limitations of the law in resolving conflicts.

DEMANDS FOR COURT SERVICES IN DISPUTE RESOLUTION

Bogart (2002:5) observes that "[a] survey of the last five decades of Western industrialized society would highlight, as a defining element, the insinuation of law into all manner of human endeavour." He acknowledges that the United States, "more than any other industrialized nation, is the land of law," "the society of detailed legal rules, deterrence-oriented enforcement practices, intensely adversarial procedures, and frequent judicial review of administrative orders and legislative enactments. It is the country of rights, most obviously in the courts, but also in the legislatures, in the media, and on the streets." Yet he points out that in some areas—most notably in relation to health care, education, and social assistance—other nations, including Canada, actually surpass the United States in the level of regulations they impose through law. The "lure of law," he maintains, is strong and is attested to in Canada by the increased number of lawyers, statutes, regulations, law reports, administrative tribunals and agencies, and litigation (p. 24). Bogart additionally notes that "turning to litigation in Canada has been accelerated by the advent of the *Charter of Rights and Freedoms* (the approximate Canadian equivalent to the U.S. Bill of Rights)" and maintains that, with the incorporation of the *Charter of Rights and Freedoms* into the Canadian Constitution, it is possible that Canadian society may increasingly come to "mimic America's approach to law" (pp. 33, 37).

Bogart (2002:77) emphasizes that one of the more important uses of the administrative state in Canada has been as a "direct alternative to tort litigation" in areas such as human rights discrimination, collective organizing and bargaining, compensation for victims of crime, and workplace injuries.

Bogart (1994:169) describes Canada's "three-level system of compensation" in the following way:

> At the base are social welfare schemes that provide hospital and medical care and some income replacement for injury or illness. At the second level are several schemes that provide fuller compensation on a no-fault basis for special groups in society, such as workers or victims of crime and, in some jurisdictions, auto accidents. At the third level is tort litigation, which provides the fullest compensation for those who are willing to sue and who can establish that their injury is the fault of the person they seek to hold responsible.

However, Bogart (2002:152) acknowledges that with the entrenchment of the Charter, there is some evidence that Canada is moving in the same direction as the United States—

specifically, toward an enhanced role for the judiciary, dominance by the courts, and, perhaps, the development of a political and legal culture that is more individualistic and less amenable "to collective solutions to problems agreed to through legislative processes and implemented through governmental programs."

Whether or not Bogart's prediction comes to fruition, there can be little doubt that our lives are increasingly bound up in laws and legalisms (Rosen, 2001). Indeed, Galanter (1992) observes that in Canada, the United States, and Great Britain there is now "law abounding" within areas that, in the past, were not viewed as in need of legal structuring.

One indicator of this in industrialized countries worldwide is the growth of the legal profession (Wood, 2016). This is most notable in the United States, which has about 5 percent of the world's population but more than two-thirds of its lawyers. In 2009–10, there were 391 lawyers for every 100,000 people in the United States (compared to 292 in Canada, 277 in England and Wales, 259 in Australia, and simply 23 in Japan) (Ramseyer and Rasmusen, 2010:20). Nevertheless, the profession in Canada has also experienced significant growth, with a ten-fold increase in the numbers of lawyers between 1951 (~9,000) and 2002 (~86,000) (Canadian Bar Association, 2005:9, 13). Moreover, while in 2009, Canada had about 95,000 lawyers plus 3,500 notaries in Quebec, these numbers had increased by 2017 to 117,000 and 4,500, respectively (Federation of Law Societies of Canada, 2017).

Not surprisingly, perhaps, this growth in the number of lawyers has been accompanied by growing dependence on lawyers and the services they provide (Nelson, 2010). In the United States, for example, the estimated cost of the tort system in 2010 was US$264.6 billion (Towers Perrin, 2011:3), and American tort costs exceed those of other countries "by a sizeable margin, when measured as a ratio to economic output measured by GDP" (Towers Perrin, 2006a). In part, this difference may be explained by the lack of a national health care system in the United States. Simply put: "Injured parties in countries with national health care may have less of a need to sue to recover the medical costs of injuries" (Towers Perrin, 2006b:1). For example, a study that used data from 21 countries over 12 years to investigate the relationship between the size of government programs and the size of private tort liability found a "strong negative relationship between government social program expenditures and national liability costs" (Kerr, Ma, and Schmit, 2006:4). It also suggested that "in nations where government programs are far more readily available to pay for health care and lost income [than they are in the United States], the compensation objective [of the tort liability system] has far less purpose." However, while most researchers seem to agree that, in relation to civil litigation, a large divide exists between the U.S. and other Western democracies, the specific reasons they advance vary.

Some emphasize the growth in the American legal profession since the 1960s and insist that the increased competition among lawyers has resulted in lower costs for consumers and made litigation a more affordable option (Nelson, 2009). It has also been argued that Americans view the possibility of being sued as the price of freedom and, when compared to people in other nations, they are fascinated rather than cowed by the prospect of litigation. Indeed, pointing to the availability of American board games such as So Sue Me! (marketed with the tagline: "Sue your friends. Take their stuff!") and the popularity of programs such as Judge Judy and the People's Court, it has been suggested that Americans may view litigation as a form of entertainment (Rapping, 2004; Young, 2005). Others insist that both the professional culture and legal ethics of American lawyers encourage litigation. For example, F.H. Buckley (2013) maintains that "[i]n America, more than elsewhere, lawyers are encouraged to advance their client's interests without regard to the interests of justice in the particular case or broader social concerns." He also discerns that American lawyers' professional culture is "unique in permitting and implicitly encouraging them to assert novel theories of recovery, coach witnesses, and wear down their opponents through burdensome pretrial discovery." Moreover, while the legal systems of both Canada and the U.S. evolved from British traditions and institutions, the civil procedures that have emerged in these countries are not equally encouraging of litigation.

In contrast to Canada, for example, where "the discovery process in civil litigation is tightly restricted," "generous U.S. discovery rules, which often impose on defendants millions of dollars in expenses, permit opportunistic plaintiffs to hold up defendants with settlement offers that are less than the costs the defendant would incur on discovery alone" (Buckley, 2013). Moreover, while in the U.S. each side in a civil action pays his or her own way, win or lose, Canada abides by the so-called "English rule" (Polinsky and Rubinfeld, 1998) and makes the loser in a civil action pay for a portion of the winner's costs. As Buckley (2013) laconically remarks, "Subsidize something and you get more of it; penalize it and you get less of it." In America, substantive tort law provides potential plaintiffs with additional inducements inasmuch as courts in that country impose strict liability on manufacturers for product defects. In contrast, Canadian courts require a finding of negligence and are far more parsimonious in their assessment of damages. In 1978, rulings by the Supreme Court of Canada on a trilogy of cases limited the maximum amount of non-pecuniary damages a plaintiff could receive in a civil action to $100,000 (*Andrews v. Grand & Toy Alberta Ltd.*, 1978; *Thornton v. School District No. 57 (Prince George) et al.*, 1978; *Arnold v. Teno*, 1978). While the Supreme Court later agreed that the upper limit would be adjusted for inflation (*Lindal v. Lindal*, 1981; see also *Clost v. Relkie*, 2012) with the 2014 cap approximately $360,000 (Bau, 2014), Canadian courts have signalled their resolve to abide by such limits and have only departed from them in clearly exceptional circumstances (e.g., *Hill v. Church of Scientology*, 1995; *Whiten v. Pilot Insurance Co.*, 2002; *Young v. Bella*, 2006). Since American courts have struck down caps when they have been enacted by state legislatures, it is predictable enough that awards for punitive damages in that country are many times larger than in Canada (Buckley, 2013).

Although Canada "has but a quarter of the litigation in the U.S." (Ramseyer and Rasmusen, 2010: 9), increases in litigation in both countries can be explained with reference to the increase in the range and variety of legally actionable or resolvable problems. Thus, as Goldman and Sarat observe:

> As the scope of law expands, as more legal rights and remedies are created, the amount of litigation increases as a result of the new opportunities for court action. As new rights are created, litigation may be necessary to clarify the way in which those rights will be defined and understood by the courts. Furthermore, the creation of new rights may direct the attention of organized interest groups to the judiciary. Interest

groups may come to perceive litigation as a viable strategy for stimulating group mobilization to achieve the group's political goals.

(Goldman and Sarat, 1978:41)

Goldman and Sarat (1978:41) additionally identify three generic factors that may explain litigation. The first they call *social development*. Variation in the frequency of litigation is a function of changes in the level of complexity, differentiation, and skill of the society in which courts operate. Social development and changes in the structure of society bring about increased reliance on courts to process disputes. In less developed societies, which feature stable and enduring contacts among individuals, disputes are easier to resolve informally. Consequently, courts play a less important role in disputes. In more complex societies, relationships are typically more transitory and disputes often take place between strangers. Furthermore, in developed societies, there is no longer a single dominant ethos or a set of customs. As such, some interpret increases in litigation as evidence of a breakdown in the forms of community that traditionally held a society together and warn that, at best, law is only capable of creating a tenuous and fractious social bond. As one commentator has cynically observed, "The better the society, the less law there will be. . . . The worse the society, the more law there will be. In Hell there will be nothing but law, and due process will be meticulously observed" (Gilmore, 1977:111).

The second generic factor that explains why disputes are translated into demands for court services is subjective cost–benefit calculations on the part of disputants. For some disputants, the decision to use courts is a relatively objective, well-thought-out decision, since they must calculate a "risk" factor and weigh what they may lose against the possible benefits of doing nothing or of using different methods of conflict resolution. For others, however, resorting to courts may be an act "that has value because of its cathartic effect, even though it may not produce tangible, material benefits" (Goldman and Sarat, 1978:42). In such a situation, vindictiveness, spite, or the desire for a "moral" victory outweigh the lack of material rewards from litigation. Moreover, the disputants' decision to use the court decreases the pressure on them to resolve disputes by using non-legal resources that they can mobilize. Informal and private settlements seem less likely where the parties have the option for legal recourse (Turk, 1978:224).

The third generic factor in litigation is the creation of more legally actionable rights and remedies by legislatures and courts. Goldman and Sarat state: "The greater the reach and scope of the legal system, the higher its litigation rate will be" (1989:42). To some extent, the expanded use of courts is attributable to the expansion of rights. As William Bogart observes, "the 'rights revolution,' especially in America, focused on giving recognition to interests, individuals, and groups mainly through litigation. It was primarily courts, not politicians, that would confer entitlements, often constitutionalized. There were many ambitions for this revolution, but a primary one was to gain recognition legally that had not been obtained politically" (2002:43).

The growing scope of law increases litigation implicitly or explicitly by expanding the jurisdiction of the courts. The creation of new rights is likely to stimulate litigation designed to vindicate or protect those rights. Thus, with the creation of new norms, courts actually (although unintentionally) promote disputing, since these new norms may lead to claims that otherwise would not have been asserted. Moreover, in clarifying certain norms, courts may make other normative conflicts salient and thus more likely to be disputed. For example, in 1988 the Supreme Court ruled in *R. v. Morgentaler* that the law on abortion was unconstitutional because it restricted a woman's right to control her own reproductive life and, as such, violated her constitutionally protected guarantees to security of the person, liberty, and freedom of conscience. This ruling invalidated the consent requirements in the Criminal Code, decriminalized abortion, and also led to a series of disputes concerning such issues as access and whether the provinces would pay for abortions and whether abortions would be permitted in clinics outside of hospitals. In addition, the *R. v. Morgentaler* decision has led to disputes over whether parents must consent to a minor's abortion and whether the prospective father of the fetus can veto the woman's decision to terminate a pregnancy (the answer, delivered in the 1989 Supreme Court's decision in the case of *Tremblay v. Daigle*, is no. In this case, the Supreme Court held that the woman's right to control her own body overrode the man's interest in the fetus and declared that a fetus had no rights until it was born alive).

Rights, protections, and entitlements for whole groups of people can generate potentially conflict-laden situations conducive to further litigation. For example, the entrenchment of the *Canadian Charter of Rights and Freedoms* has impacted litigation, with Canadian courts, "after some hesitation," involving themselves in myriad questions relating to "abortion, mercy killing, assisted suicide, language rights, and an array of issues relating to the administration of criminal justice, to name but a few" (p. 151). In addition, the Court Challenges Program of Canada (CCP), a national non-profit organization, made funding available to launch certain Charter challenges that focused on equality issues (Court Challenges Program, 2006). The stated objective of the CCP was the clarification of certain constitutional provisions related to equality and language rights.

Although questions are increasingly being raised by critics and others about the "rights industry" and its impact on major institutions, it has also been argued that lawsuits are good for a nation and can usher in much-needed and progressive reforms (Bogus, 2001; Howard, 2002). For instance, product liability litigation has undoubtedly saved countless lives, brought critical information to light (along with labels that warn us about most everything that could be potentially harmful), forced manufacturers to make products safer, and driven unreasonably dangerous products off the market when regulatory agencies lacked the political will to do so (Koenig and Rustad, 2004). Class action suits in Canada have resulted in compensation for such disparate groups as those who have contracted hepatitis C from tainted blood, received faulty cardiac pacemakers or leaky breast implants, suffered in train and subway crashes, experienced sexual abuse as children at the hands of authority figures within such settings as church-run orphanages and residential schools, or lost their jobs as a result of large-scale corporate restructuring.

VARIATIONS IN LITIGATION RATES

There are two general ways of measuring judicial involvement in dispute settlement (Galanter, 1988). It can be measured by the percentage of disputes that courts play some part in resolving and by the percentage of the adult population who take disputes to courts.

With both measures, there are some difficulties. As Richard Lempert (1978:99) points out, there are several ways in which courts contribute to dispute settlement:

1. Courts establish norms that influence or control the private settlement of disputes. For example, norms established in an appellate opinion resolving one dispute can lead other disputants to resolve their conflict without legal intervention.
2. Courts ratify private settlements and provide guarantees of compliance. For example, in divorce cases where the parties have already reached an agreement, courts ratify that agreement, which carries with it the probability of sanctions should it be breached.
3. Courts can escalate the cost of disputing, thereby increasing the likelihood of private settlement.
4. Courts provide opportunities to disputants to learn about each other's cases, thus increasing the probability of private settlement by decreasing mutual uncertainty.
5. Court staff act as mediators to encourage consensual private settlement.
6. Courts resolve certain issues in the case, leading disputants to agree on others.
7. Courts authoritatively resolve disputes.

At times, it is difficult to determine the extent to which courts contribute to dispute settlement. The clearest case is when disputes are adjudicated and a settlement is imposed after a full trial. But many cases do not end up at trials. A settlement may be reached during a pretrial conference or through informal negotiations where the judge is a participant. Judges also exert informal pressure, even after litigation has commenced, and lawyers usually listen to the recommended solutions. Settlement may also be encouraged by the mounting financial costs. Defendants may calculate that it is cheaper and less time-consuming to settle than to try a case. Thus, attempts to explore the dispute-settlement functions of courts over time must consider the different roles courts play and the influences they exert.

Some charge that in modern societies, the use of courts as a forum for conflict resolution is on the increase as a result of societal developments toward increased complexity, heterogeneity, and prevalence of impersonal and contractual relations. For example, it has been argued that increasing levels of urbanization, which result in greater social distance between community members, leads to higher litigation rates. Simply put, "[s]uing a friend is considered far more costly than suing a stranger" (Kerr, Ma, and Schmit, 2006:6). It is also evident that urbanization may result in greater availability of and access to legal services. Gerson (1994) suggests that computers have made a major contribution to increases in litigation by making it feasible to engage in protracted and occasionally frivolous litigation. Although data are available to support both of these contentions, others observe that social, economic, and technological developments do *not* necessarily lead to higher rates of litigation.

Noting a substantial amount of differentiation in the use of courts in disputes among nations, Ehrmann (1976:83) early argued that *litigiousness*, the propensity to settle disputes through the judicial process, is a cultural factor of some importance. For example, in his oft-quoted article, "Dispute Resolution in Japan," Kawashima (1969) discussed specific social attitudes toward disputes that are reflected in the Japanese judicial process. Traditionally, the Japanese prefer to resolve disputes informally rather than take them to court. This aversion to litigation exists for two reasons. First, the Japanese culture emphasizes harmonious relationships, and litigation can disrupt relationships. When disputes do arise, the Japanese culture leads many people either to apologize for a perceived wrongdoing or to forgive someone for doing something wrong. Second, the Japanese culture also emphasizes authority and hierarchy. Subordinate persons and groups are supposed to defer to more dominant persons and groups. This means that subordinate parties simply "lump it" (to recall our earlier term) when they feel they are wronged. As a result, Kawashima contends, the Japanese not only hesitate to resort to lawsuits but are also quite ready to settle disputes through informal means, such as mediation and conciliation. However, while Kawashima suggests that Japan's low rate of litigation reflects a cultural preference for informal methods of dispute resolution, others maintain that his analysis failed to give sufficient weight to institutional factors, such as the scarcity of lawyers and judges and the weakness of legal remedies, as important barriers to litigation.

For example, Reutter (2005) charges that "the picture of a Japan as a culturally harmonious country whose inhabitants value peace and consensus over the clash of lawsuits and lawyers" is simply a "cliché that has outlasted its value." Over the past two decades, he reports, Japan has experienced a "burst of litigation," which certainly challenges the notion that the country has "pioneered a system of 'capitalism without lawyers.'" Ginsburg and Hoetker's (2005) empirical analysis of lawsuits filed in Japan's 47 prefectures between 1986 and 2001 found that the rate of civil litigation in Japan increased by 29 percent during this time period. They suggest that the increase is best attributed to an increase in the number of judges and lawyers in Japan coupled with the economic downturn that it experienced after 1990. "Taken together, civil procedure reform and the expansion of the bar and judiciary account for over 20,000 additional cases per year, an almost 20 percent increase over the number of cases that would otherwise have been predicted" (p. 20).

Litigation, they argue, moves inversely with the economy: During economic downturns, litigation increases "as bad times mean more broken contracts and a willingness to break relationships" (p. 21). Observing that Japan has experienced a "10-fold rise in medical malpractice rates in the last four decades, as well as an increase in monetary awards," Feld (2006:1949) points to the possible significance of institutional changes that made civil procedures more "user-friendly" for plaintiffs—specifically, the 1996 amendment of the Japanese Code of Civil Procedure that ushered in a "less restrictive approach to discovery, changes regarding expert witness, introduction of a small claims procedure, and modification to the procedure to appeal to the Supreme Court." In the past, he suggests, it was "the cost and difficulty of pursuing litigation, especially given the limitations of trial capacity and legal remedies. . . [that] helped tip the balance toward settlement."; "Even in a country where cultural norms are reportedly non-confrontational," Feld (2006:1949) argues, "problems with settlement and structural changes to the legal system that make lawsuits easier may tip the balance between settlement and suit." Findings from Ramseyer and Rasmusen's (2010:5, 9) examination of civil litigation in six countries (the U.S., Canada, Japan, Germany, France, and Australia) also counters the claim that Japan is singularly adverse to litigation; they noted that Canada—with 1,450 civil cases per 100,000 population—has less litigation than the famously "non-litigious" Japanese (1,768 per 100,000)!

PREREQUISITES FOR THE USE OF COURTS IN DISPUTE RESOLUTION

Courts provide a forum for the settlement of a variety of private and public disputes. The courts are considered a neutral and impartial place for dispute processing. Other than criminal cases, legal disputes are processed in civil courts. Individuals and organizations that want to use the courts for dispute processing must meet certain legal requirements. At the minimum, plaintiffs must be able to demonstrate justiciability and standing (Hessick, 2015).

Justiciability means that the conflict is viable to trial and courts. The court must be mandated to provide a remedy. Essentially, justiciability refers to real and substantial controversy that is appropriate for judicial determination, as differentiated from disputes or differences of a hypothetical or an abstract character. Furthermore, in some instances, the courts may not be authorized to intervene in certain types of disputes.

Until relatively recently, **standing** has posed a more severe limitation to litigation than justiciability. The traditional view of standing was that individuals should be able to bring lawsuits only if their personal legal rights have been violated. For example, a mother-in-law cannot sue for a divorce—such proceedings must be initiated by the husband or wife. It should be noted, though, that there are a number of examples where standing rules have been liberalized by legislation. For example, since 1975, the issue of standing has been examined by the Supreme Court of Canada five times and, on four of these occasions, the court "relaxed the requirement that the ability to sue must be based on a traditional legal interest, i.e., a pecuniary, proprietary, or economic claim or one to personal liberty" (Bogart, 1994:80). In doing so, the court established the vague requirement that a plaintiff must simply have a "'genuine interest,' meaning that a traditional legal interest is no longer the boundary between those who are and those who are not entitled to litigate" (p. 80). Moreover, Brisbin (2004:540) points out that

> standing to appeal some government actions is often more difficult to achieve in Canada than in the U.S. For example, there are rules restricting appeals to the judiciary of aspects of the determinations of uniquely Canadian adjudicatory institutions such as the Ontario Municipal Board, Manitoba Municipal Board, and Nova Scotia Utility and Review Board. These bodies possess broad powers to define property rights, evaluate challenges to local and provincial environmental initiatives, and even—in Nova Scotia—establish the age-group rating of movies.

However, justiciability and standing are not the only limitations to the use of courts in disputes. There is also the old legal axiom *de minimus non curat lex*—The law will not concern itself with trifles. Trivial matters may not be litigated. For example, a court may refuse to hear a suit to recover a $10 overcharge even if the cause appears just (Lempert and

Sanders, 1986:137). There are also statutes that limit the period of time in which lawsuits for various causes of action must be commenced in every Canadian province and territory. Depending upon the manner in which the injury arose and the identity of the defendant (e.g., a case alleging malpractice versus actions against government bodies), there may be different limitation periods in the area of tort law. In addition, untold numbers of disputes arise over which courts have clear jurisdiction and whether someone has standing to sue. But using the court is dependent on a number of other factors.

Economic resources for both plaintiffs and defendants are important in their decision to pursue a suit through trial and appeal. With the exception of magistrate courts and individuals who qualify for legal aid services, plaintiffs are unlikely to use the courts unless they have sufficient funds to hire a lawyer and bear the costs of litigation. Disputants must also be able to afford the costs of delay, which occur when disputes are submitted to the courts. Often the cost of waiting must be calculated against the benefits of a quick settlement for only part of the claim. Obviously, for many people, economic resources play an important role in the use of court services and may be decisive in out-of-court settlements.

Before initiating a lawsuit, individuals must recognize the relevance of court services to their problems. Posner (1996) reports a positive relationship between litigation rates and education levels, suggesting that those with greater levels of education may have greater knowledge of the law and/or more skill in obtaining legal assistance. Socioeconomic status is also related to the use of the judiciary in disputes. Those who cannot afford a lawyer and the necessary court fees are less likely to litigate than those who have sufficient funds. Moreover, social status is related to the kind of court services that are used. In general, the poor are more likely to be defendants and recipients of court-ordered sanctions. Middle-class litigants are less likely to be subjected to court sanctions and more likely to benefit from the use of court services in their own behalf from the legitimization of their private agreements or from out-of-court negotiations. However, as Kerr, Ma, and Schmit (2006:6) observe, "income . . . also can represent time costs, with higher income suggesting that undertaking litigation itself is costly." They note that some research has reported a negative relationship between income and litigation and suggest that the liability system may act "as a lottery with great potential payoff at low probabilities. Low-income individuals often have little to lose in this lottery, and perhaps value their time at lower levels, leading to the negative relationship."

A TYPOLOGY OF LITIGANTS

As noted in Chapter 3, Galanter (1974) advanced a highly influential typology of litigants by the frequency of the utilization of courts. Those who have only occasional recourse to the courts are called **one-shotters**, and those who are engaged in many similar litigations over time are designated as **repeat players**. Based on this typology, Galanter proposes a taxonomy of litigation by the configuration of parties. He comes up with four types of litigation—one-shotter versus one-shotter, repeat player versus one-shotter, one-shotter versus repeat player, and repeat player versus repeat player.

Divorces are common illustrations of cases involving one-shotters. Disputes between one-shotters are "often between parties who have some intimate tie with one another, fighting over some unsharable good, often with overtones of 'spite' and 'irrationality'" (Galanter, 1974:108). The second type of scenario, involving repeat players versus one-shotters, is exemplified by suits initiated by finance companies against debtors and landlords against tenants.

For repeat players, the use of law is a regular business activity. When they win their case, as usually happens, they in effect are borrowing the government's power for their private purposes. Repeat players may use that power to achieve many objectives, such as to collect debts, oust tenants, or prohibit some harmful activity. The third combination of litigants involves one-shotters versus repeat players. Illustrations of this include tenant versus landlord, injury victim versus insurance company, student versus university, defamed person versus publisher, and client versus welfare agency. Outside of the personal injury area, litigation in this combination is not routine. It usually represents the attempt of some one-shotters to invoke outside help to create leverage on an organization with which the individual has a dispute.

The fourth type of litigation is repeat players versus repeat players. Examples of this include litigation between union and management, purchaser and supplier, and regulatory agency and firms of regulated industry, as well as church—state litigations focusing on value differences (who is right) rather than interest conflicts (who gets what). With these types of litigation in the background, let us now turn to certain types of conflicts between individuals, between individuals and organizations, and between organizations where one of the disputants resorts to the judiciary in an attempt to resolve the conflict.

DISPUTES BETWEEN INDIVIDUALS

Even though most controversies between individuals never come to the attention of courts, the handling of interpersonal differences is a traditional function of courts. Most individual disputes involve one-shotters. For those individuals whose disagreements come before a court, the manner in which the dispute is handled is likely to have a marked effect on their attitudes toward the government.

Individual disputes often deal with the distribution of economic resources and a variety of non-economic problems. Economic disputes include various claims associated with contests over wills, trusts and estates, landlord—tenant controversies, and disputes over property, titles, and sales. Non-economic conflicts include allegations of slander and libel, custody cases, divorce proceedings, involuntary commitments, and malpractice suits.

Courts often make an effort to encourage disputants to settle their differences by agreement, since this is a less costly way to re-establish an equilibrium, which any conflict is likely to disturb. Settlements may even be encouraged after the disputants have brought their complaint to a court. The judge may initiate such efforts in pretrial hearings or in open court. The success of such efforts, to a great extent, depends on the skills of the judge and on the nature of the disputes. When the parties are unable or unwilling to resolve their disputes by agreement, and when they have decided against letting matters rest, formal adjudication must take over and will normally end in a decision that claims to be binding on the parties.

In the adjudication of individual disputes, one party wins and the other loses. Seidman (1978:213) points out that in situations in which parties want to, or must, co-operate after the dispute, both must leave the settlement procedures without too great a sense of grievance. If, however, there are opportunities for avoidance (that is, parties need not live or work together), then the disputants may continue their antagonism. Compromises tend to resolve the disputes in the sense that they reduce any continuing antagonism. As noted earlier, the win-or-lose outcomes typical of litigation threaten enduring relations between the parties. Therefore, disputants who wish to maintain an ongoing relationship will generally engage in compromise settlements. The structure of social relationships thus plays a role in the decision as to whether to take a dispute to court. When continuing relations are important to the individuals involved in the dispute, they are generally more predisposed to resolve their differences through non-legal means. In a classic paper, Macaulay (1969:200) described the avoidance of the law as a way of building and maintaining good business relations. Business people prefer not to use contracts in their dealings with other business people: "Disputes are frequently settled without reference to the contract or potential or actual legal sanctions. There is a hesitancy to speak of legal rights or to threaten to sue in these negotiations."

Although a desire for continuing relationships may deter many disputants from litigating, litigation may nonetheless result if the stakes are high and if hostility between the parties builds. Nader and Todd point out: "[i]t is not enough to state that because litigants wish to continue their relation they will seek negotiated or mediated settlement with compromise outcomes" (1978:17). For example, a family may be torn by disputes over inheritance, leading one or more siblings to sue the others for what they consider to be their fair share.

When any dispute ends up in court, a judge takes control of the case (Soeharno, 2016). Judges are supposed to decide disputes by reference to the facts of who did what to whom, and by identifying, interpreting, and applying appropriate legal norms. As they do so, they are required to remain objective and impartial. Impartiality is displayed when both parties in a dispute are given the same opportunities and are shown the same considerations. It requires that the judge not be influenced by an interest in the outcome or by attitudes toward the disputants and the situations in which they are involved. However, even if courts appear impartial in their procedures, they may still produce biased results if the laws that they apply favour one type of litigant.

The type of lawyer that disputants are able to retain may also influence the outcomes of court decisions. Availability of resources to disputants directly affects the quality of legal talent they can hire. Access to a skillful lawyer increases the likelihood of a favourable court decision, since courts assume that in individual disputes both parties can marshal the resources and legal skills needed to present a case effectively.

DISPUTES BETWEEN INDIVIDUALS AND ORGANIZATIONS

Disputes between individuals and organizations may take place over a variety of issues, many of which may be included in four general categories: (1) disputes over property and money (economic disputes); (2) claims for damages and restitution; (3) issues of civil rights; and (4) disputes concerning organizational actions, procedures, and policy. These broad categories of disputes are, of course, not mutually exclusive.

Usually, organizations are plaintiffs in the first category of disputes and defendants in the other three. In general, organizations are more successful as both plaintiffs and defendants than are individuals (Galanter, 1975; Relis, 2002). They enjoy greater success against individual antagonists than against other organizations. Individuals fare less well contending against organizations than against other individuals. Consider, for example, that while "Wal-Mart is sued two to five times every business day somewhere in the United States in federal court alone," in the vast majority of cases (no exact numbers are available), Wal-Mart wins by aggressively fighting cases even when it would be cheaper for the company to settle (Wal-Mart Litigation Project, 2017). As this example suggests, when individuals bring lawsuits against organizations, the latter have a considerable advantage due to their wealth and legal resources. Despite the supposed impartiality of the courts, David normally has little chance of defeating Goliath in a courtroom.

Although organizations have a greater chance of winning and a higher frequency of initiating lawsuits, it does not mean that individuals do not sue organizations (see, for example, Hellman, 2004). On the contrary, individuals are increasingly taking their disputes with organizations to court. For example, when Toronto-Dominion Bank introduced a mandatory drug-testing policy for both newly hired and returning employees in 1990, the screening of employees for drug use was presented as an attempt to "maintain a safe, healthy and productive workforce, to safeguard bank and customer funds and information and to protect the bank's policy" (Schmidt, 2001:A1). Nevertheless, a complaint was filed with the Canadian Human Rights Tribunal that alleged that the policy constituted discrimination on the basis of disability (defined as "any previous or existing mental or physical disability and includes disfigurement and previous or existing dependence on alcohol or a drug"). Although a Canadian Human Rights tribunal initially issued a finding of non-discrimination, a federal Court of Appeal later ruled that the policy *did* constitute "adverse-effect discrimination" (Canada [Human Rights Comm.] v. Toronto Dominion Bank [1996]). As defined by the Supreme Court of Canada in *Ont. Human Rights Comm. v. Simpsons-Sears* (1985, at 18), *adverse-effect discrimination* refers to "a rule that is neutral on its face but has an adverse discriminatory effect on certain members of the group to whom it applies." In consequence, the policy was found to be in violation of the Canadian Human Rights Act because it could discriminate against certain employees and because it was not sufficiently related to job performance.

A similar decision was reached in relation to Imperial Oil's drug and alcohol testing policy for "safety-sensitive" positions within that company. In 1992, four employees of Imperial Oil filed complaints of discrimination with the Ontario Human Rights Commission.

One of the complainants maintained that, despite giving up alcohol eight years earlier and participating in a company-sponsored substance-abuse program, he had been demoted as a result of the policy. The Ontario Human Rights Commission later ruled that, under the Ontario Human Rights Code, alcoholism is a handicap protected from discrimination and that the employer has the duty to accommodate the employee. The Commission ordered Imperial Oil to reinstate the employee in his "safety-sensitive" position and awarded the complainant $21,241 in damages. When Imperial Oil appealed this decision, the Ontario Court of Appeal ruled in July 2000 that Imperial Oil's use of both a pre-employment drug testing screening test and random drug testing for employees was discriminatory and in violation of the province's human rights code. The court held that a breathalyzer is permissible for people in high-risk jobs, such as oil refinery workers, pilots, and train engineers, because it determines whether someone is impaired at the moment the test is administered. Since drug testing only measures past use, not present impairment or future impairment on the job, the court ruled that Imperial Oil could not justify pre-employment testing or random drug testing for employees (*Entrop v. Imperial Oil Ltd.*, [2000]).

After losing its court case, Imperial Oil introduced random saliva testing in 2003 and unionized workers, in turn, challenged this practice. In *Imperial Oil Limited v. Communications, Energy & Paperworkers Union of Canada, Local 900* (2009), the Ontario Court of Appeal ruled that Imperial Oil's random drug-testing measures infringed a collective agreement provision which required that they treat their employees with "respect and dignity" and breached the company's obligation "to respect an employee's expectation of privacy absent consent to or reasonable cause for a random drug test" (at 72). According to this judgement, "companies cannot, without reasonable cause, require random saliva mouth-swab drug tests from their unionized workers who perform safety-sensitive jobs" (Dranoff, 2011:64).

More recently, in *Communications, Energy and Paperworkers Union of Canada, Local 30 v. Irving Pulp & Paper Ltd.* (2013), the Supreme Court of Canada ruled that an employer's implementation of random drug and alcohol testing is not automatically justified even in inherently dangerous work environments. It found that the employer had exceeded the scope of its rights by unilaterally imposing random testing without evidence that alcohol or drug use was a problem in the workplace. The Court ruled that "even in a non-unionized workplace, an employer must justify the intrusion on privacy resulting from random testing by reference to the particular risks in a particular workplace" (at 20). The Court also provided guidance on the standard that employers must meet in order to subject their employees to these types of tests. In *Re Mechanical Contractors Association Sarnia v. UA Local 663 (2014)*, these principles were extended to pre-employment testing, with the arbitrator emphasizing that a positive test prior to hiring is not a valid predictor of future workplace impairment and rejecting the employer's attempt to establish the need for drug-testing by "broad-based statistical inferential reasoning" (e.g., extrapolations from regional drug/alcohol use; correlations between pre-employment testing and a reduction in post-incident tests). In *Suncor Energy Inc. v. Unifor Local 707A* (2016), the Alberta Court of Queen's Bench addressed the evidentiary burden that an employer must meet to justify the implementation of a universal random drug and alcohol testing policy. It ruled that an employer must demonstrate both that the setting is a dangerous workplace and that a general problem with drug and/or alcohol abuse exists in that workplace.

For the remainder of this section, we shall consider disputes initiated by individuals and organizations separately. For the former, we shall illustrate the use of law as a method of dispute resolution in academe, and, for the latter, we shall discuss the use of courts as collection agencies in the field of consumer credit.

LAW AS A METHOD OF DISPUTE RESOLUTION IN ACADEME

As we move further into the 21st century, law remains a potent force in institutions of higher learning (Alexander and Alexander, 2017; Gerstein and Gerstein, 2007; Oppenheimer, 2006) and is becoming more pronounced at all other levels of education (Bissonette, 2009; Essex, 2009). More and more, disputes that develop in school settings are resolved elsewhere, as students, educators, and institutions become litigants in steadily growing numbers (Gajda, 2010).

We will briefly consider law as a method of dispute resolution in academe in the context of faculty–administration, student–faculty, and student–administration relations.

The *faculty–administration* relationship in post-secondary institutions is defined by an increasingly complex web of legal principles and authorities. The essence of this relationship is contract law, but "that core is encircled by expanding layers of labour relations law, employment law, human rights law and, in public institutions, constitutional law and public employment statutes and regulations" (Kaplin and Lee, 2006:159). The growth in the number and variety of laws and regulations governing faculty–administration relations provides a fertile ground for grievances and coincides with an increase in the number of lawsuits stemming from that relationship (Brake, 2010; Hunter, 2006; Nelson, 2010; Sataline, 2007).

Many legal disputes centre on the meaning and interpretation of the faculty–institution contract. Depending on the institution, a contract may vary from a basic notice of appointment to a complex collective bargaining agreement negotiated under labour laws. In some instances, the formal document does not encompass all the terms of the contract, and other terms are included through "incorporation by reference"—that is, by referring to other documents, such as the faculty handbook, or even to past custom and usage at an institution. In the context of contract interpretation, legal disputes arise most often in the context of contract termination and due notice for such termination.

A number of suits instituted by faculty members to redress their grievances against university administrations have focused on faculty personnel decisions, such as appointment, retention, promotion, and tenure policies; pecuniary matters affecting women and minority groups; and sex discrimination. Termination procedures must also follow specific guidelines and deadlines, and in recent years faculty members have increasingly resorted to lawsuits on the grounds of procedural matters.

Other potentially conflict-laden situations in academe arise from *student–faculty* relations. Students are increasingly considering themselves consumers of education, treating education like other consumer items; concomitantly, there is a growing emphasis on the proper return for their educational dollars (see, for example, Usman, 2016). Well over a generation ago, Ladd and Lipset (1973:93) observed: "students are the 'consumers,' the buyers, the patrons of a product sold by the faculty through a middle-man, the university system. In economic class terms, the relationship of student to teacher is that of buyer to seller, or of client to professional. In this context, the buyer or client seeks to get the most for his [sic] money at the lowest possible price." Moreover, the Supreme Court of Canada has recognized that the relationship between a student and a university does have "a contractual foundation that gives rise to duties that sound in both contract and tort" and confirmed that a university owes a duty of care to its students (*Bella v. Young* [2006 at 31]). University calendars, internal admission, withdrawal and appeal procedures, and academic policies establish the terms of the contract between an educational institution and its students (*Yen v. Alberta [Ministry of Advanced Education and Technology]* [2010]), and an institution that fails to meet its expressed or implied obligations may be liable to a student for either breach of contract or the tort of negligence (*Gauthier c. Saint-Germain* [2010] at 48–49; *Jaffer v. York University*, [2010] at 30).

"Canadian courts have traditionally been reluctant to wade into disputes between schools and their students, deferring academic matters to internal school procedures" (Thompson and Slade, 2011). The Quebec Court of Appeal articulated the reasoning behind this stance in *Blasser v. Royal Institution for the Advancement of Learning* (1985):

> In any university . . . there are certain internal matters and disputes that are best decided within the academic community rather than by the Courts. This is so, not only because the Courts are not as well equipped as the universities to decide matters such as academic qualifications, grades, the conferring of degrees and so on, but also because these matters ought to be able to be more quickly, more economically and at least as accurately by those who are specialized in educational questions of that kind. In addition, of course, there is very good reason not to risk compromising the essential independence of universities by undue interference in their academic affairs.
>
> (at 40)

Moreover, as Justice Rouleau pointed out in *Gauthier c. Saint-Germain* (2010), "when a student enrolls in a university, it is understood that the student will be subject to the discretion of that institution when it comes to resolving academic issues, whether in the evaluation of the quality of the student's work, the structure and implementation of university programs, or the identification of the skills required to serve as a professor or thesis supervisor. This discretion is very broad" (at 47). In consequence, a student grumble that a grade was too low or is best attributed to the incompetence of a professor will generally not, on its own, serve as sufficient grounds on which to base a cause of action for breach of contract or tort. As Justice Rouleau advised, "In order to establish a cause of action for breach of contract, the student must demonstrate that the university failed to fulfill an express or tacit obligation to which this institution had committed by accepting the student's registration" (at 47).

In *Gauthier c. Saint-Germain* (2010), the Ontario Court of Appeal confirmed that a court "will have jurisdiction when the cause of action is framed in tort or breach of contract even if the dispute arises out of the scholastic or academic activities of the University" and that the Superior Court's jurisdiction "can only be limited by clear and express legislative or contractual provisions" (Thompson and Slade, 2011). Courts have intervened when institutions have engaged in acts of fraud, malice, or bad faith or flagrantly violated the rules of natural justice intervened (*Ahmed v. Dalhousie University*, 2014 NSSC 330 at 27). At the same time, Canadian courts have not hesitated to "strike claims against universities where those claims are, at their heart, attempts to re-litigate the factual underpinnings of previously unsuccessful challenges to academic decisions that have already been subject to the university's internal appeal processes" or where a "plaintiff attempts to dress up the previous academic dispute by adding claims for relief—such as a monetary claim for wrongful conduct—that are unavailable through the internal academic review process" (*Fernandes v. Carleton University* [2016] at 38). Moreover, when the pleadings do not provide the necessary information to demonstrate that the university or its employees have surpassed their broad discretion, the court may strike out the cause of action.

Student–administration relations provide a third area for potential conflict in academe. Although institutions of higher learning have the right to dismiss, suspend, or otherwise sanction students for misconduct or academic deficiency, this right is determined by a body of procedural requirements that must be observed in such actions. Under the due process clause, students are entitled to a hearing and notice before disciplinary action is taken. In general, there is a trend toward increased protection of student rights, in both public and private institutions cases (Gerstein and Gerstein, 2007; Kaplin and Lee, 2006:379–404).

For example, *Pridgen v. University of Calgary* (2012) involved twin brothers at the University of Calgary who were students in the undergraduate course *Law and Society*. Along with eight other students in this course, they had joined a Facebook group called "I no longer fear Hell, I took a course with Aruna Mitra"; students had posted comments on this Facebook wall that were highly critical of the course instructor's qualifications and teaching skills (Fullick, 2012). Their instructor complained to the university's administration about these public accusations of incompetence and the ten students who had joined the Facebook page (including those who had not posted any comments) were sanctioned; the university adjudged their actions to be in breach of the University of Calgary's "Code of Conduct" and to constitute "non-academic misconduct." As defined by that university's calendar: "non-academic misconduct" comprised "(a) conduct which causes injury to a person and/or damage to University property and/or the property of any member of the University community; (b) unauthorized removal and/or unauthorized possession of University property; (c) conduct which seriously disrupts the lawful educational and related activities of other students and/or University staff." Among the disciplinary sanctions imposed upon the students, one of the Pridgen brothers was placed on a two-year period of probation and both were required, under threat of expulsion, to write their instructor a letter of apology and "refrain from posting or circulating defamatory material regarding any faculty members of the University of Calgary" (McKay-Panos, 2015).

Some of the students appealed their sanctioning to the university's General Faculties Council Review Committee; they were unsuccessful. The Pridgens also appealed to the University's Board of Governors, arguing, in part, that the university's decision violated

Section 2(b) of the *Charter of Rights and Rights and Freedoms*. Although unsuccessful at this level, the brothers' application for judicial review on both Charter and administrative law grounds was granted by the Alberta Court of Queen's Bench. It ruled that the students' freedom of speech was protected under section 2(b) of Charter and that universities are not "Charter-free zones." This decision was later upheld by the Alberta Court of Appeal, with the court rejecting the university's argument that the application of the *Charter* in these circumstances would undermine or threaten the University's "academic freedom or institutional autonomy." Thus, Justice Paperny noted that "academic freedom and freedom of expression are not conceptually competing values" but "inextricably linked" and "handmaidens to the same goals; the meaningful exchange of ideas, the promotion of learning, and the pursuit of knowledge. There is no apparent reason why they cannot comfortably co-exist" (at 114–115, 117). Moreover, she wrote that even though some of the posted comments "had not been particularly gracious," they nevertheless "had utility in encouraging discussion and providing feedback to current and future students" (at 125). The decision of the court in this case alerts educational institutions of the need to be "mindful of Charter considerations before considering disciplinary action against a student" (Lauks, 2012). It should simultaneously remind Canadian students that freedom of expression (on social networking sites or elsewhere) is not an unqualified right. Although the critical remarks that the students in this case made about their professor fell within the ambit of section 2(b) of the Charter, postings that are threatening or defamatory would not (Lauks, 2012).

Other cases in recent times have addressed whether Canadian universities are subject to the *Charter* and if so, under what circumstances (McKay-Panos, 2016). For example, in *R v Whatcott* (2012), the University of Calgary enforced trespass legislation in banishing from campus a non-student who was distributing anti-gay leaflets. In this case, both the trial judge and the Court of Appeal found that the university's action had restricted the anti-gay activist's freedom of expression and that this restriction could not be justified under Charter section 1 (the "reasonable limits clause"). Although expressive activities may propagate views that some find objectionable, their relation to "learning, the exchange of ideas and the advancement of knowledge (or other legislated activities of the university), could provide the 'governmental' nexus required to invoke the application of the Charter to the University" (McKay-Panos, 2016). However, courts have been inconsistent in their categorization of expressive activities, with similar acts sometimes described as related to learning and, on other occasions, perceived to be purely non-curricular pursuits.

For example, in *B.C. Civil Liberties Association and Cam Côté v. University of Victoria* (2016), a pro-life student group "Youth Protecting Youth" (YPY) at the University of Victoria held a peaceful demonstration on campus and distributed printed materials; although the university had originally granted the group a permit for this purpose, it had revoked the permit when made aware that YPY had been sanctioned previously by the university's student union. After the YPY held its demonstration, the university stripped the group of some of its privileges and threatened its members that future violations could result in sanctions for non-academic misconduct. In response, the group's president, along with the British Columbia Civil Liberties Association, petitioned the BC Supreme Court for relief. They argued that a university is "not a purely private entity" but a "complex corporate body that can be subject to the Charter for some purposes." They sought a declaration that (1) the university's policy on the booking of outdoor space by students violated section 2(b)(c) and (d) of the Charter and was not saved by section 1, and (2) that the university's policies in relation to the use of its common areas for expressive purposes must be consistent with the Charter. Alternatively, they sought a declaration that the university's decision in relation to YPY had failed to appropriately weigh the infringement of section 2(b), (c), and (d) of the Charter against the justifications for such infringement and was therefore unreasonable and should be quashed. However, the chambers judge dismissed their petition and ruled that the *Canadian Charter of Rights and Freedoms* does not apply to public universities, and that the University's impugned decision fell within its "autonomous operational decision-making." In 2016, the BC Court of Appeal dismissed an appeal of this decision and found "no basis upon which it can be said on the evidence that when (UVic) regulated the use of space on the campus it was implementing a government policy or program (that would be subject to the Charter)" (at 33).

As this case suggests, disputes between student groups and administrations may arise when post secondary institutions revoke or withhold recognition of a group and seek to regulate the organization's use of campus facilities (Kotecha, 2016). When a mutually acceptable and satisfactory balance between the organization's rights and the institution's authority cannot be attained, the organizing students may turn to the courts to settle their dispute with the administration and, in doing so, forward Charter-based arguments. A recent report by the Justice Centre for Constitutional Freedoms (2016) suggests that these types of disputes will continue into the future. Since 2011, this Centre has assessed "the free speech climate" at Canadian universities using a "Campus Freedom Index" and "grading" each university and its associated student union on both their policies and practices. Of the 240 grades it assigned to 60 Canadian campuses in 2016, "A" grades were uncommon and awarded to simply six universities and student unions; "[c]onversely, 'F' grades were earned 32 times: seven times by universities, and 25 times by student unions."

THE COURTS AS COLLECTION AGENCIES

Disputes between individuals and organizations, where organizations are the plaintiffs, are most often triggered by disagreements over property and money. Such disputes are most prevalent in the creditor–debtor relationship, where the creditor is usually an organization such as a finance and loan company, car dealership, or department store. In such situations, there is a gross power disparity between the debtor and the organization (Goldberg et al., 2012). To use earlier-introduced terms, the organization is typically a repeat player when it comes to the law, while the debtor is a one-shotter. This means that the organization has much more legal knowledge and resources than the debtor and can use these advantages to win any legal action it brings against a debtor.

Kagan (1984:324) comments: "If the extension of credit is the lifeblood of a dynamic commercial society, the forcible collection of unpaid debts is its backbone." When debtors default on their contractual obligation to make payments, the standard legal remedy is for the creditor to sue in civil court. The purpose is to establish the legality of the debt and its amount. Of course, creditors "hope to collect the debt by invoking the power of the court, but even if they do not collect, a judgment against the debtor is still of value for income tax purposes" as a deduction (Caplovitz, 1974:191).

A creditor who is successful in court obtains a judgment against the debtor. Once obtained, there are a variety of legal remedies available for collecting the judgment, including garnishment, liens, and the forced sale of the debtor's property. A **garnishment** is a court order directing someone who owes or possesses money due to the debtor (such as an employer) to pay all or some of that money to the court, which then turns it over to the creditor (Bryant, 2004). A **lien** can establish a creditor's claim on property (such as a house or a car). A **writ of seizure and sale** results in a forced sale involving the seizure and sale at an auction of the debtor's property. The proceeds are then turned over to the creditor to satisfy the judgment.

Before going to court, a creditor may resort to a number of social pressures and sanctions of varying severity, ranging from impersonal routine "reminders" and dunning letters to telephone appeals to get the debtor "in" to make some kind of "arrangement" and to remind or threaten him or her, to personal visits to the debtor's home from a "skip tracer" (investigator) in an attempt to elicit payments or, at least, promises (Hobbs, 2011). At times, creditors have resorted to unusual extrajudicial methods of collection. For example, a London firm used a rather unconventional method of extracting money from debtors—smell: "Smelly Tramps, Ltd. is just what it sounds: a motley crew of ragged, foul-smelling tramps, who specialize in dunning particularly evasive debtors. The tramps are really otherwise respectable chaps, dressed in disgusting clothes and treated with a special stomach churning chemical" (*Economist*, 1979:104). Their technique was simply to sit around the victim's office or home until s/he signed a cheque. Not to be outdone, a debt-collecting firm in Bombay, India employed six eunuchs who threatened to remove their saris if the defaulters did not pay up. Fearing to be embarrassed in front of their colleagues or neighbours, the debtors generally paid their debts (*Vancouver Sun*, 1999:E3). In Spain, debt collectors use shame to recoup money. Since the Middle Ages, public shaming has been used as a tool of coercion across Europe. One illustration of the famous *El Cobrador del Frac* (The Debt Collector in Top Hat and Tails) will suffice. This agency had a case that involved a couple who did not pay their $83,000 wedding bill. The agency obtained a guest list and started to phone their guests, asking them if they had the lobster or chicken and then asking them where to send the bill. The embarrassed bride and groom promptly paid up (Harman, 2010). Finally, a high-tech version of debt collection is the automobile starter-interrupt device: A cigarette-pack-sized contraption can be mounted under the car dashboard and flashes green when a car payment is made. When a payment is late, the device will not let the car start (Yao, 2006).

When such dunning efforts fail and creditors have exhausted non-litigation alternatives, they are likely to sue. A characteristic of most civil suits for debt is that the plaintiff usually wins by default. Most defendants are not represented by counsel. In fact, many of them are not present when their cases are heard. Their absence is treated as an admission of the validity of the claim, and a default judgment is entered against them. Such judgments are rendered in the vast majority of consumer cases.

There are a number of reasons why defendants fail to respond to summonses and to appear in court. Some recognize the validity of the creditor's claim and see no point in attempting to contest it or cannot afford a lawyer to do so (Hobbs, 2011). Others may simply find it impossible to leave work (with consequent loss of pay), travel to court, and spend most of the day waiting for their cases to be called. At times, the wording of a summons is so complicated and abstruse that many debtors cannot grasp what is at stake, or that they must appear if they are to avoid a default judgment. Others simply do not know that they are being sued. These individuals learn the hard way about suits against them—when a garnishment or eviction notice is served.

Although we have focused on suits for debts, there are a number of other important types of actions initiated by organizations against individuals. Real estate companies regularly initiate legal action in the form of evictions against unknown numbers of tenants. The Canada Revenue Agency continuously files suits against individuals (and at times organizations) for back taxes or for tax evasion. Radio and television stations regularly use the courts to settle disputes with former announcers or disc jockeys that have decided to join competing stations, contrary to the desires of their former employers. In the final section, we shall consider disputes between organizations.

DISPUTES BETWEEN ORGANIZATIONS

Disputes between organizations cover a wide spectrum of participants and controversies (Axelrod, Vandeveer, and Downie, 2010). Examples of *interorganizational* conflict include disputes between a university and the community over such matters as zoning and land use; disputes between a corporation and the federal government concerning compliance with federal regulations, such as occupational safety, pollution, and human rights; or disputes between two corporations over such matters as copyright infringement or possible theft of business secrets. **Social-policy disputes** develop when the government pursues broad national objectives that may involve or impinge upon many interests and groups, such as equality and economic opportunity, environmental protection, income security, and public health and safety. In fact, large-scale social welfare programs have often generated complex public-policy disputes (Mink and Solinger, 2004). While social-policy disputes raise difficult political and value questions, **regulatory disputes** frequently involve difficult technical questions (Morriss, Yandle, and Dorchak, 2009). In both types of dispute, information about important variables is often incomplete or inaccurate, effects of alternative choices are hard to ascertain, and often there are no easy answers to cost–benefit questions or to questions of trade-offs among various interests. The various regulatory agencies discussed in Chapter 3 also process large numbers of routine disputes.

In many instances, the formal quasi-adjudicative procedures used by regulatory agencies are ill suited to resolving large and complex disputes. Delays in settling disputes are frequent, and the situation is further compounded by the fact that some agencies traditionally engaged in economic regulations are now being asked to consider environmental claims as well. The regulatory process, in a sense, encourages conflict, rather than acting to reconcile opposing interests.

PUBLIC-INTEREST LAW FIRMS IN ENVIRONMENTAL DISPUTES

Since the mid-1960s, there has been a proliferation of the types of activities associated with Ralph Nader and his consumer organizations (Reske, 1994), with the Sierra Club and its environmental programs, and with a new institutional form embodied in law firms that characterize their activities as partly or wholly "public interest" law and "cause lawyering" (Sarat and Scheingold, 1998).

Public-interest law is the term frequently used to describe the activities of law firms that represent environmentalists, consumers, and like groups, as well as test-case litigation in civil rights and poverty controversies. It is generally oriented toward causes and interests of groups, classes, or organizations, rather than individuals. Although public-interest law firms engage in activities such as lobbying, reporting, public relations, and counselling, litigation is by far their most important activity.

Private groups may use the courts to pursue better environmental quality. For example, in various countries, environmental lawyers are exploring novel legal strategies to adopt, such as **toxic torts**—a subtype of personal injury lawsuits "in which the plaintiff claims that exposure to a chemical caused injury or disease" (Venton and Mitchell, 2015; see also McLeod-Kilmurray, 2014). Others have challenged dams and other water resource projects, raised questions about nuclear power plants and bio-engineered food, attacked the use of dangerous pesticides, and recommended various changes to regulatory systems (Bodansky, 2010; Stone, 2010; Weibust, 2010). For example, since its creation in 1970, the Canadian Environmental Law Association (CELA), a non-profit, public interest organization, has both advocated for environmental law reforms and used extant laws to protect the environment. Its objectives are to: "provide equitable access to justice to those otherwise unable to afford representation for their environmental problems; . . . advocate for comprehensive laws, standards and policies that will protect and enhance public health and environmental quality in Ontario and throughout Canada; . . . increase public participation in environmental decision-making; work with the public and public interest groups to foster long-term sustainable solutions to environmental concerns and resource use; [and] . . . prevent harm to human and ecosystem health through application of precautionary measures" (CELA, 2017). In like spirit, Ecojustice, "Canada's largest environmental law charity," pursues "innovative cases that have the potential to set precedents nation-wide and deliver solutions to our most urgent environmental problems" and marshals "the power of law to defend nature, slow climate change, and stand up for their health of our communities" (Ecojustice, 2017).

Environmental disputes typically fall into two broad categories—enforcement and permitting cases. *Enforcement disputes* come about when a public-interest group raises questions about a party's compliance with a law or laws setting specific environmental standards, such as air or water quality. *Permitting cases* involve disputes over the planned construction of new facilities, such as a dam or an airport. Environmental disputes are also different from more traditional disputes in several ways: Irreversible ecological damages may be involved; at least one party to the dispute may claim to represent broader public interest—including the interests of inanimate objects, wildlife, and unborn generations;

and the instrumentation of a court decision may pose special problems (such as what will happen to the community if the major employer is forced to close a factory responsible for water pollution) (Goldberg et al., 2012).

Over the years, there has been a steady growth in the number of environmental disputes in all advanced industrialized countries (Baier, 2016). This growth reflects the significant increase in public awareness that our civilization causes substantial and possibly irreparable damage to the natural environment. Consequently, the recognition of the costs society pays for environmental damage and the failure of companies to internalize environmental costs has led to a proliferation of regulatory laws designed to protect the natural environment. Many environmental controversies are about the extent to which the government should regulate private-sector decisions that are considered contributive factors in environmental degradation. At the same time, the government itself is also a potential cause of environmental damages. Public programs of many types, from flood control to mineral leasing, have a potential for environmental damage.

Environmental disputes are further complicated by the establishment of a number of mission-oriented government agencies that are set up to carry out programs (e.g., to build dams, construct highways, or develop nuclear power). Such activities may cause environmental harm, but if an agency recognizes this harm, it will be forced to curtail its own activities and thus undermine, at least in part, the justification for its existence. At the same time, since these activities are perfectly lawful, they tend to magnify the advantages of those organized groups that favour development and to increase the obstacles facing environmental groups that set out to challenge agency decisions. Much environmental advocacy occurs in complex policy disputes. In many such disputes, the resources available to environmental advocates may be insufficient to ensure that their concerns receive the degree of attention from decision makers that they would if the full extent of their demands were reflected in their representational resources.

SUMMARY

- Disagreements are ubiquitous in social relationships. Non-legal methods of dispute resolution include violence, rituals, shaming and ostracism, supernatural agencies, "lumping it," avoidance, negotiation, mediation, and arbitration.
- As a result of social developments, the increased availability of legal mechanisms for conflict resolution, and the creation of legally actionable rights and remedies, there is a growing demand for court services in dispute resolution.
- Courts provide a forum for the settlement of a variety of private and public disputes. To qualify for the use of court services, plaintiffs must be able to demonstrate justiciability and standing, at the minimum. Those who have only occasional recourse to the courts are called one-shotters, and those who are engaged in many similar litigations over time are termed repeat players.
- Disputes between individuals and organizations may take place over economic issues, claims for damages and restitution, issues of rights, and issues concerning organizational actions, procedures, and policy. In general, more organizations are plaintiffs and more individuals are defendants, and organizations tend to be uniformly more successful than individuals in the courts.

- Disputes between organizations cover a wide spectrum of participants and controversies. In general, the party that is better organized with greater resources and greater capacity to generate data will have a higher probability of influencing the outcome of the dispute.

CRITICAL THINKING QUESTIONS

1. Is faith-based arbitration more likely to privilege men and disadvantage women than other forms of ADR?
2. The grievance policies of Canadian universities and colleges provide a mechanism for students to challenge a decision of a university/college authority or the action of a university/college member that they believe has been unreasonable, unjust, or unfair. However, it is evident that not all students who perceive that they have been unfairly treated will initiate a grievance or appeal. What factors might limit the effectiveness of these policies and make them more rhetorically appealing than practically potent?
3. What advantages or disadvantages does alternative dispute resolution offer over adjudication?
4. Should Canadian universities be bastions of free speech? If not, what types of speech and speakers should be censored?

ADDITIONAL RESOURCES

1. To learn more about Ecojustice's ongoing efforts to protect the environment, visit http://www.ecojustice.ca/.
2. For information on the mandate of Canada's federal ombudsman for victims of crime, visit http://www.victimsfirst.gc.ca.
3. ADR Institute of Canada Inc. is a national, non-profit organization that "provides national leadership in the development and promotion of dispute resolution services in Canada and internationally." For information on this organization and the services it provides, explore its website at www.amic.org.
4. The Centre for Restorative Justice, an initiative of Simon Fraser University's School of Criminology, facilitates ready access to a wealth of information. Explore its website at http://www.sfu.ca/crj/index.html.

7

CHAPTER 7
LAW AND SOCIAL CHANGE

The initial step in understanding the relationship between law and social change is conceptual. What is social change? In its most concrete sense, social change means that large numbers of people are engaging in group activities and relationships that are different from those in which they or their parents engaged in previously. Society is a complex network of patterns of relationships in which all the members participate in varying degrees. These relationships change, and behaviour changes at the same time. Individuals are faced with new situations to which they must respond. These situations reflect such factors as new technologies, new ways of making a living, changes in place of residence, innovations, new ideas, and new social values. Thus, **social change** means modifications in the way people work, rear a family, educate their children, govern themselves, and seek ultimate meaning in life. It also refers to a restructuring of the basic ways people in a society relate to each other with regard to government, economics, education, religion, family life, recreation, language, and other activities (McCarthy, 2005; Vago, 2004).

Social change is a product of a multitude of factors and, in many cases, the interrelationships among them. In addition to law and legal cultures, there are many other mechanisms of change, such as technology, ideology, competition, conflict, political and economic factors, and structural strains (Anleu, 2009; Jimenez, 2010; McMichael, 2017). All the mechanisms are related in many ways. One should be very careful not to assign undue weight to any one of these "causes" in isolation. Admittedly, it is always tempting and convenient to single out one "prime mover"—one factor, one cause, one explanation—and use it for a number of situations. This is also the case with legal change: It is extremely difficult, perhaps impossible, to set forth a simple cause-and-effect relationship in the creation of new laws, administrative rulings, or judicial decisions. Although there are exceptions, one should be somewhat skeptical and cautious concerning one-factor causal explanations in general and about such explanations for large-scale social changes in particular.

Figure 7.1 Laws can both prompt and reflect social change.
Credit: Shutterstock

LEARNING OBJECTIVES

After reading this chapter, you should be able to:

1. Describe the complex relationship that exists between law and social change.

2. Discuss social changes as causes of legal changes.

3. Provide examples of how law has been used to accomplish social change.

4. Identify seven advantages of employing law as an instrument of social change.

5. Describe how social stratification impacts the efficacy of the law as an instrument of social change.

6. Describe five social factors that limit the effectiveness of law as an instrument of social change.

7. Identify five psychological factors that impact law's effectiveness as a vehicle of social change.

8. Discuss how cultural and economic factors may limit law's capacity to create social change.

RECIPROCITY BETWEEN LAW AND SOCIAL CHANGE

The question of whether law can and should lead, or whether it should never do more than cautiously follow changes in society, has been and remains controversial. The conflicting approaches of Bentham and Savigny provided the contrasting classical paradigms for this long-standing debate. At the beginning of industrialization and urbanization in Europe, Bentham expected legal reforms to respond quickly to new social needs and to restructure society. He freely gave advice to the leaders of the French Revolution, since he believed that countries at a similar stage of economic development needed similar remedies for their common problems. In fact, it was Bentham's philosophy, and that of his disciples, that turned the British Parliament—and similar institutions in other countries—into active legislative instruments. Writing at about the same period, Savigny condemned the sweeping legal reforms brought about by the French Revolution that were threatening to invade Western Europe. He believed that only fully developed popular customs could form the basis of legal change. Since customs grow out of the habits and beliefs of specific people, rather than expressing those of an abstract humanity, legal changes are codifications of customs, and they can only be national, never universal.

Well over two centuries later, the relationship between law and social change remains controversial. As Aubert (1969b:69) observed, in the first view "law is determined by the sense of justice and the moral sentiments of the population, and legislation can only achieve results by staying relatively close to prevailing social norms. According to the other view, law, and especially legislation, is a vehicle through which a programmed social evolution can be brought about."

At one extreme, then, is the view that law is a dependent variable, determined and shaped by current mores and opinions of society. According to this position, legal changes would be impossible unless preceded by social change; law reform could do nothing except codify custom. This is clearly not so, and ignores the fact that throughout history, legal institutions have been found to "have a definite role, rather poorly understood, as instruments that set off, monitor, or otherwise regulate the fact or pace of social change" (Friedman, 1969:29). The other extreme is exemplified by jurists in the former Soviet Union, who saw the law as an instrument for social engineering. As Gureyev and Sedugin (1977:12) observe:

> during the period of the transition from capitalism to socialism, the Soviet state made extensive use of legislation to guide society, establish and develop social economic forms, abolish each and every form of exploitation, and regulate the measure of labour and the measure of the consumption of the products of social labour. It used legislation to create and improve the institutions of socialist democracy, to establish firm law and order, safeguard the social system and state security, and build socialism.

These views represent the two extremes of a continuum that characterizes the relationship between law and social change. The problem of the interplay between law and social change is obviously not a simple one. As Olivo (2001a:10) emphasizes, in some cases the law leads; in others, the law may been seen to follow social change. However, he acknowledges that "[i]n many cases it is hard to say whether the law is bringing about social change or social change is transforming the law. The process of lawmaking is a dynamic process."

Essentially, the question is not "Does law change society?" or "Does social change alter law?" Both contentions are likely to be correct. Instead, it is more appropriate to ask under what specific circumstances law can bring about social change, at what level, and to what extent. Similarly, the conditions under which social change alters law need to be specified. To this end, in the next section we will examine the conditions under which social change induces legal change; then, in the following section, we will discuss law as an instrument of social change

SOCIAL CHANGES AS CAUSES OF LEGAL CHANGES

In a broad historical context, social change has been slow enough to make custom the principal source of law. Law could respond to social change over decades or even centuries (Edgeworth, 2003). Even during the early stages of the Industrial Revolution, changes induced by the invention of the steam engine or the advent of electricity were gradual enough to make legal responses valid for a generation. As time went by, however, social change became more rapid, forcing the law to respond more quickly. In a sense, people in modern society are caught in a maelstrom of social change, living through a series of contrary and interacting revolutions in demography, urbanization, bureaucratization, industrialization, science, transportation, agriculture, communication, bio-medical research, education, and civil rights. Each of these revolutions has brought spectacular changes in a string of tumultuous consequences and transformed people's values, attitudes, behaviour, and institutions.

Many sociologists and legal scholars assert that technology is one of the great moving forces for change in law (Cox, 2006; Tiersma, 2010; Volti, 2010). According to Stover, law is influenced by technology in at least three ways:

> The most obvious . . . is technology's contribution to the refinement of legal technique by providing instruments to be used in applying law (e.g., fingerprinting or the use of a lie detector). A second, no less significant, is technology's effect on the process of formulating and applying law as a result of the changes technology fosters in the social and intellectual climate in which the legal process is executed (e.g., televised hearings). Finally, technology affects the substance of law by presenting new problems and new conditions with which law must deal.
>
> (quoted in Miller, 1979:14)

Illustrations of technological changes leading to legal changes abound. The advents of the automobile and air travel brought along new regulations. The automobile, for example, has been responsible for an immense amount of law: traffic rules, rules about drunk driving, rules about auto safety, drivers' licence laws, rules about pollution control, registration, and so on. The computer and easy access to cyberspace, especially the Internet, have also inspired legislation to safeguard privacy, to protect against abuse of credit information and computer crime (Jewkes and Yar, 2009; Zimmerman, 2006; Carr, 2009; Downes, 2009). Another impact of technological changes on law concerns various developments in crime detection over the years, including fingerprinting, DNA use, and electronic surveillance. These developments prompted many changes in the law, such as the kinds of evidence admissible in court (Carr, 2009; Grabosky, 2016).

Change in law may also be induced by shifts in community values and attitudes. People may come to think that poverty is bad and laws should be created to reduce it in some way. People may come to condemn the use of laws to further racially discriminatory practices in voting, housing, employment, education, and the like, and may support changes that forbid the use of laws for these purposes. People may come to think that business people should not be free to put just any kind of foodstuff on the market without proper governmental inspection, fly any plane without having to meet governmental safety standards, or show anything on television that they wish. So laws may be enacted as appropriate, and regulatory bodies may be brought into being as necessary. And people may come to think that the practice of abortion is not evil, that the practice of contraception is desirable, or that divorce and remarriage are not immoral. Hence, laws governing these practices may undergo repeal or revision.

Alterations in social conditions, technology, knowledge, values, and attitudes, then, may induce legal change. In such instances, the law is reactive and follows social change. It should be noted, however, that changing the law is one of many types of response to social change. But the legal response in some respects is important, since it represents the authority of the state and its sanctioning power. A new law in response to a new social or technological problem may aggravate that problem—or alleviate and help to solve it. Often, the legal response to social change, which inevitably comes after a time lag, induces new social changes. For example, laws created in response to air and water pollution brought about by technological changes may result in unemployment in some areas, where polluting firms are unwilling or unable to install the required pollution–abatement controls. Thus, law can be considered as both reactive and proactive in social change. In the next section, the proactive aspect of law as an initiator of social change will be considered.

LAW AS AN INSTRUMENT OF SOCIAL CHANGE

There are numerous historical and cross-cultural examples of law's use to induce broad social changes in society (Jimenez, 2010; Nisbet, 2000). Since Roman times, great ages of social change and mobility almost always involved great use of law and of litigation. There are several illustrations of the idea that law, far from being simply a reflection of social reality, is a powerful means of *accomplishing* reality—that is, of fashioning it or making it. Although Marx, Engels, and Lenin maintained that law is an epiphenomenon of bourgeois class society, doomed to vanish with the advent of the Revolution, the former Soviet Union did, notably, succeed in making enormous changes in society by the use of laws (Dror, 1968). In Spain during the 1930s, law was used to reform agrarian labour and employment relations (Collier, 1989:201). More recently, the attempts by Eastern European countries to make wholesale social changes through the use of laws—such as the nationalization of industry, land reform and the introduction of collective farms, provision of free education and health care, and the elimination of social inequities—illustrate the effectiveness of law to induce change (Eorsi and Harmathy, 1971). Another example is provided by China. China managed to moderate through law its population growth and, as a result, devote more of its resources to economic development and modernization (Diamant, Lubman, and O'Brien, 2005; Muhlhahn, 2009).

Recognition of the role of law as an instrument of social change is becoming more pronounced in contemporary society. Says Friedmann: "The law—through legislative or administrative responses to new social conditions and ideas, as well as through judicial reinterpretations of constitutions, statutes or precedents—increasingly not only articulates but sets the course for major social changes" (1972:513). Thus, "attempted social change, through law, is a basic trait of the modern world" (Friedman, 1975:277). Recognizing this fact, many sociolegal scholars consider law as a desirable, necessary, and often effective means of inducing social change.

In present-day societies, the role of law in social change is of more than theoretical interest. In many areas of social life, such as education, race relations, housing, transportation, energy utilization, the protection of the environment, and crime prevention, the law and litigation are important instruments of change (Milkman, Bloom, and Narro, 2010; Prosterman, Mitchell, and Handstad, 2010). In Canada, the law has been used as the principal mechanism for improving the political and social position of minorities, for dismantling a discriminatory system embedded in the law and in practice for generations, and for entrenching the concept of **human rights**. In contrast to **civil liberties**, which, in general, refer to a narrower class of fundamental freedoms such as freedom of religion, expression, assembly, and association, human rights also include such rights as the right to education, accommodation, and employment.

In the past, the law functioned as an instrument of discrimination, depriving minority groups of civil, political, and economic rights (Hall, 2000). For example, prior to the *British Emancipation Act* of 1833, slavery was legal in the colonies. Discriminatory laws were also passed to discourage or entirely prohibit the immigration of non-whites (Knowles, 2016). Canada's 1910 *Immigration Act* gave the government the formal power "to prohibit for a stated period of time, or permanently, the landing in Canada . . . of immigrants belonging to any race unsuited to the climate or requirements of Canada" (Sher, 1983:33).

Canada's *Chinese Immigration Act* of 1923 completely barred the Chinese from entering Canada, and Chinese persons already in Canada were not allowed to sponsor family or relatives. From 1952 to 1977, immigration laws also prohibited homosexuals from entering Canada and subjected those who were homosexual to the threat of deportation if their sexual orientation became known (Kinsman, 1996). Moreover, from Confederation until 1969, homosexual acts were punishable by up to 14 years in prison under Canadian criminal law. From 1946 to 1977, a practising homosexual faced the possibility of life in prison if decreed a "criminal sexual psychopath" (Kinsman, 1996); it was not until 1969 that homosexual acts, taking place in private between two consenting adults over the age of

21 (later reduced to 18) were decriminalized in this country. Although Quebec included sexual orientation in its Human Rights Code in 1977 and, in doing so, made it illegal to discriminate against gays in housing, public accommodation, and employment (Gudgeon, 2003:198), until 1983 Quebec was the only jurisdiction in Canada in which "sexual orientation" was a prohibited ground of discrimination under statute law (Yogis, Duplak, and Trainor, 1996:1).

Consider as well that, in 1868, when the first federal general election was held, only men who owned a specified amount of property were allowed to vote; in 1885, the *Electoral Franchise Act* defined a "person" who was eligible to vote as a male who was of other than Mongolian or Chinese origin. While the *1917 Wartime Election Act* granted wives, sisters, and mothers of servicemen the right to vote, it was not until 1918 that all Canadian women won the right to vote in federal elections (Frank, 1994). Women over the age of 21 were granted the right to vote in provincial elections in 1916 in Manitoba, Saskatchewan, and Alberta; in 1917 in British Columbia and Ontario; in 1918 in Nova Scotia; in 1919 in New Brunswick; in 1922 in Prince Edward Island; in 1925 in Newfoundland (where initially this right was limited to women over the age of 25); and in 1940 in Quebec (Whitla, 1995:320). These rights were first granted to white women; women from certain other ethnic groups did not receive the franchise until later years (Mossman, 1998).

Laws also imposed **segregation**—the separation of groups in residence, workplace, and social functions. Sher (1983:33) observes that, in British Columbia, "where anti-Asian sentiment was endemic from the 1850s to the 1950s, Chinese, Japanese and South Asians could not vote, practise law or pharmacy, be elected to public office, serve on juries, or work in public works, education or the civil service." Nelson and Fleras (1995:246) report that, during the 1920s and 1930s, Jews were automatically excluded from employment in major institutions such as banks, universities set limits on Jewish enrollment, and "signs warning. . . 'Jews and dogs not allowed' were posted along Lake Ontario beachfronts in Toronto." They note that African-Canadians were treated as inferior in this country from the time they began to settle here and were "routinely excluded from restaurants and other public venues by laws as discriminatory as those in the southern United States. Segregated schools, for example, were not taken off the books in Ontario or Nova Scotia until the early 1960s." While the last segregated school in southwestern Ontario closed in 1956, it was not until 1975 that Windsor desegregated its public facilities (Borovoy, 1999:35).

Beginning with the introduction of Ontario's 1944 *Racial Discrimination Act* and Saskatchewan's 1947 *Bill of Rights*, the first acts dealing with human rights in this country, a variety of legislation has attempted to counter the problem of discrimination in Canada. In 1960, Parliament adopted the *Canadian Bill of Rights,* and currently every Canadian province and territory, as well as the federal government, has adopted anti-discrimination legislation and established human rights commissions. Since 1982, the Constitution has contained an entrenched *Canadian Charter of Rights and Freedoms*, which applies to federal and provincial jurisdiction.

Another example of law as an instrument of social change is provided in the former Eastern-bloc countries, where the law was a principal instrument in transforming society after the Second World War from a bourgeois to a socialist one. Legal enactments initiated and legitimized rearrangements in property and power relations, transformed basic social institutions such as education and health care, and opened up new avenues of social mobility for large segments of the population. Legislation guided the reorganization of agricultural production from private ownership to collective farms, the creation of new towns, and the development of a socialist mode of economic production, distribution, and consumption. These changes, in turn, affected values, beliefs, socialization patterns, and the structure of social relationships.

There are several ways of considering the role of law in social change. In an influential article, "Law and Social Change," Dror (1968) distinguished between the *indirect* and *direct* aspects of law in social change. Dror argued that "law plays an important indirect role in social change by shaping various social institutions, which in turn have a direct impact on society" (p. 673). He used the illustration of the compulsory education system, which performed an important indirect role in regard to change. Mandatory school attendance upgraded the quality of the labour force, which, in turn, played a direct role in social change by contributing to an increased rate of industrialization and modernization. Dror argues that law exerts an indirect influence on social change in general by influencing the possibilities of change in various social institutions. For example, the existence of a patent law protecting the rights of inventors encourages inventions and furthers change in the technological institutions, which, in turn, may bring about other types of social change.

Dror (1968:674) also emphasized that law interacts in many cases directly with basic social institutions, constituting a direct relationship between law and social change. He warned, however, that "the distinction is not an absolute but a relative one: in some cases the emphasis is more on the direct and less on the indirect impact of social change, while in other cases the opposite is true" (p. 674). For all modern societies, Dror (1968:674) insisted, every collection of statutes and delegated legislation is "full of illustrations of the direct use of law as a device for directed social change." A good example of social change directly induced by law was the enactment of Prohibition in both Canada and the United States to shape social behaviour. (It was also a conspicuous failure in both countries, showing that there are limits to the efficacy of law to bring about social change, as we will discuss later.)

Another way of considering the role of law in social change is in the context of Mayhew's (1971:195) notion of the possibility of either redefining the normative order or creating new procedural opportunities within the legal apparatus. The former, which he designates as an *extension of formal rights*, can be illustrated by the unanimous decision of the Supreme Court of Canada in *New Brunswick (Minister of Health and Community Services) v. G. (J.)* (1999). Although there is "no overarching constitutional right to legal aid" in Canada, the SCC's ruling "recognized that, in some cases, there may be a right to legal aid based on section 7 of the *Charter*" (Heinrich, 2013). In this case, the government of New Brunswick had sought to extend a temporary custody order for the three children of an indigent mother in child protection proceedings. When the mother applied for legal aid, she learned that the province's legal aid plan did not cover temporary custody cases; as a result, she was unable to hire representation. The SCC found that, based on the specific circumstances of the case, the woman had a constitutional right to be provided with government-funded counsel and that her section 7 Charter rights to security of the person had been violated. "[W]ithout the benefit of counsel," Justice Lamer wrote on behalf of the Court, "the appellant would not have been able to participate effectively at the hearing, creating an unacceptable risk of error in determining the children's best interests and thereby threatening to violate both the appellant's and her children's Section 7 right to security of the person" (at 81).

The creation of new procedural opportunities, which Mayhew termed the *extension of formal facilities*, is exemplified in Canada by the development of small-claims courts, which were established in a number of provinces in the 1970s in an attempt to make justice accessible to citizens, as well as in the creation of publicly funded legal aid, with services provided by either salaried or fee-for-service lawyers. The extension of formal rights and of formal facilities has definite implications for the criminal justice system in the form of greater protection of individual rights.

A rather different perspective on law in social change is presented by Friedman. He describes two types of change through law: "planning" and "disruption." *Planning* "refers to architectural construction of new forms of social order and social interaction. *Disruption* refers to the blocking or amelioration of existing social forms and relations" (Friedman, 1973a:25). Planning through law is an omnipresent feature of the modern world. Although it is most pronounced in socialist countries (for example, five-year plans of social and economic development), all nations are committed to planning to a greater or lesser extent. Both planning and disruption operate within the existing legal system and can bring about "positive" or "negative" social change, depending on one's perspective. Although revolution is the most distinct and obvious form of disruption, Friedman (1975:277) notes that "[m]ilder forms are everywhere and include legal disruptions that are occasioned through the use of litigation, injunctions and judicial review." Whether the change produced by such action is considered destructive or constructive, the fact remains that law can be a highly effective device for producing social change.

Although Friedman considers social change through litigation an American phenomenon, he raises the question: Will this spread to other countries? His own response is that creative disruption of the judicial type presupposes a number of conditions that include an activist legal profession, financial resources, activist judges, a genuine social movement, and what he describes as "the strongest condition": that "elites—the power holders—must accept the results of disruptive litigation, like it or not" (p. 278). Clearly, the legal structures of socialist or authoritarian countries are not designed to accommodate these patterns.

THE EFFICACY OF LAW AS AN INSTRUMENT OF SOCIAL CHANGE

As an instrument of social change, law entails two interrelated processes: the **institutionalization** and the **internalization** of patterns of behaviour. Institutionalization of a pattern of behaviour refers to the establishment of a norm with provisions for its enforcement (such as nondiscrimination in employment), and internalization of a pattern of behaviour means the incorporation of the value or values implicit in a law (for example, discrimination is "wrong"). Evan (1965:287) notes: "Law . . . can affect behaviour directly only through the process of institutionalization; if, however, the institutionalization process is successful, it, in turn, facilitates the internalization of attitudes or beliefs."

Law is often an effective mechanism in the promotion or reinforcement of social change. However, the extent to which law can provide an effective impetus for social change varies according to the conditions present in a particular situation. Evan (p. 288) suggests that a law is likely to be successful to induce change if it meets the following seven conditions: (1) The law must emanate from an authoritative and prestigious source; (2) the law must introduce its rationale in terms that are understandable and compatible with existing values; (3) the advocates of the change should make reference to other communities or countries with which the population identifies and where the law is already in effect; (4) the enforcement of the law must be aimed at making the change in a relatively short time; (5) those enforcing the law must themselves be very much committed to the change intended by the law; (6) the instrumentation of the law should include positive as well as negative sanctions; and (7) the enforcement of the law should be reasonable, not only in the sanctions used but also in the protection of the rights of those who stand to lose by violation of the law.

The efficacy of law as a mechanism of social change is conditioned by a number of factors. One is the amount of information available about a given piece of legislation, decision, or ruling. When there is insufficient transmission of information about these matters, the law will not produce its intended effect. Ignorance of the law is not considered an excuse for disobedience, but ignorance obviously limits the law's effectiveness. In the same vein, law is limited to the extent that rules are not stated precisely, and not only because people are uncertain about what the rules mean. Vague rules permit multiple perceptions and interpretations. What do phrases such as "willfully promote" or "unreasonable delay" mean? As one can appreciate, there is an obvious need for the language of the law to be free of ambiguity, with care exercised to prevent multiple interpretations and loopholes (Carter and Burke, 2005).

Legal regulations and the required behaviour of people to whom the law is addressed must be clearly known, and the sanctions for noncompliance need to be enunciated precisely. The effectiveness of the law is directly related to the extent and nature of perception of officially and clearly stated and sanctioned rules. Perceptions of rules, in turn, vary with their sources. Rules are more likely to be accepted if they reflect a notion of fairness and justice that is prevalent in society and their source is considered legitimate (Jacob, 1995). It should be noted, however, that the contrast between legitimacy and legality can remain, at times, confusing. As Friedrich (1958:202) observes: "Law must not be seen as operating only in one dimension of the state, but in the many dimensions of the community if we are to comprehend legitimacy as an objective pattern. Legitimacy is related to right and justice; without a clarification of what is to be understood by the rightness and justice of law, legitimacy cannot be comprehended either. Hitler's rule was legal but it was not legitimate. It had a basis in law but not in right and justice."

The responsiveness of enforcement agencies to a law also has an impact on its effectiveness (Kerley, 2005). Law enforcement agents not only communicate rules, but also show that the rules are to be taken seriously and that punishment for their violation is likely. But for a law to be enforceable, the behaviour to be changed must be observable. For example, it is more difficult to enforce a law against incest than a law against being drunk and disorderly in a public place. Moreover, law enforcement agents need to be fully committed to enforcing a new law. One reason for the failure of Prohibition, for example, was the unwillingness of law enforcement agents to instrument the law. Selective enforcement of a law also hinders its effectiveness. The more high-status individuals are arrested and punished, the greater will be the likelihood that a particular law will achieve its intended objective (Zimring and Hawkins, 1975:337). Laws regularly and uniformly enforced across class and group lines tend to be perceived as more binding than they would be if they were seldom and selectively enforced, because enforcement establishes behavioural norms, and in time, as Hoebel (1954:15) put it: "The *norm* takes on the quality of the *normative*. What the most do, others should do."

As a strategy of social change, law has certain unique advantages and limitations as compared with other agents of change. Although these advantages and limitations go hand in hand and represent opposite sides of the same coin, for analytical purposes we will examine them separately.

ADVANTAGES OF LAW IN CREATING SOCIAL CHANGE

Social change is a complex, multi-faceted phenomenon brought about by a host of social forces. At times, change is slow and uneven and can be brought about by different factors to differing degrees. Change in society may be initiated by a number of means. Of these, the most drastic is revolution, aimed at fundamental changes in the power relation of classes within society. Others include rebellions, riots, *coup d'états*, violent protest movements, sit-ins, boycotts, strikes, demonstrations, social movements, education, mass media, technological innovations, ideology, and planned but non-legal social-change efforts dealing with various behaviours and practices at different levels in society.

Compared with this incomplete list of change-inducing forces, the law has certain advantages. Change efforts through law tend to be more focused and specific. Change through law is a deliberate, rational, and conscious effort to alter a specific behaviour or practice. The intentions of legal norms are clearly stated, with a concomitant outline of the means of instrumentation and enforcement and sanction provisions. Essentially, change through law aims at improving or controlling behaviours and practices in precisely defined social situations—as identified by the proponents of a particular change. The advantages of law as an instrument of social change are attributed to the fact that law in society is seen as legitimate, more or less rational, authoritative, institutionalized, generally not disruptive, and backed by mechanisms of enforcement and sanctions.

LEGITIMATE AUTHORITY

A principal advantage of law as an instrument of social change is the general feeling in society that legal commands or prohibitions ought to be observed even by those critical of the law in question. To a great extent, this feeling of obligation depends on respect for legitimate authority (Ewick and Silbey, 2003).

The classic treatment of legitimate authority is that of Weber (1947). Weber defines *imperative coordination* as the probability that specific commands from a given source will be obeyed by given groups of persons. Obedience to commands can rest on a variety of considerations, from simple habituation to a purely rational calculation of advantage. But there is always a minimum of voluntary submission based on an interest in obedience. In extreme cases, this interest in obedience can be seen in the tendency for people to commit illegal acts when so ordered by authority (and for others to excuse such acts as not subject to ordinary morality).

Obedience to authority can be based on custom, affectual ties, or a purely material complex of interests—what Weber calls "ideal motives." These purely material interests result in a relatively unstable situation and must therefore be supplemented by other elements, both affectual and ideal. But even this complex of motives does not form a sufficiently reliable basis for a system of imperative co-operation, so that another important element must be added: the belief in legitimacy.

Following Weber, there are three types of legitimate authority—traditional, charismatic, and rational-legal. **Traditional authority** bases its claims to legitimacy on an established belief in the sanctity of traditions and the legitimacy of the status of those exercising authority. The obligation of obedience is not a matter of acceptance of the legality of an impersonal order but, rather, a matter of personal loyalty. The "rule of elders" is an example of traditional authority. **Charismatic authority** bases its claim to legitimacy on devotion to the specific and unusual sanctity, heroism, or exemplary character of an individual and the normative patterns that are revealed or ordained. The charismatic leader is obeyed by virtue of personal trust in his or her revelations, or in his or her exemplary qualities. Individuals exemplifying charismatic authority include Moses, Christ, Mohammed, and Gandhi.

Rational-legal authority bases its claims to legitimacy on a belief in the legality of normative rules and in the right of those elevated to authority to issue commands under such rules. In such authority, obedience is owed to a legally established impersonal order. The individuals who exercise authority of office are shown obedience only by virtue of the formal legality of their commands and only within the scope of authority of their office. Legal authority is not entirely conceptually distinct from traditional authority, although the distinction is nonetheless worth having. In modern society, "legality" suggests a component of rationality that traditional authority seems to lack (see Berg and Meadwell, 2004; Lassman, 2006). Indeed, during the transition to modernity, especially in the 16th and 17th centuries, authority tends more and more to be rationalized in distinctively legalistic and voluntaristic terms. "Rational" people "voluntarily" make a "contract," which generates the impersonal legal order.

Legitimate authority can wield considerable influence over both actions and attitudes. It can be the result of both the coercive processes involved and the individual's internalized values regarding legitimate authority. There is a tendency on the part of individuals to assume that the law has the right to regulate behaviour and then to justify conformity to the law (Cohen, 2001). To an extent, obedience to the law stems from respect for the underlying process:

> People obey the law "because it is the law." This means they have general respect for procedures and for the system. They feel, for some reason, that they should obey [if a law is passed by parliament] . . ., if a judge makes a decision, if the city council passes an ordinance. If they were forced to explain why, they might refer to some concept of democracy, or the rule of law, or some other popular theory sustaining the political system.
>
> (Friedman, 1975:114)

Acceptance of legitimate authority can also minimize the possibility of cognitive dissonance (discrepancies between action and cognition) in that individuals interpret or construe legally prohibited actions as "wrong" or morally bad. The law, consequently, not only represents accepted modes of behaviour but also enforces and reinforces those accepted modes of behaviour. Further, it defines the "correct" way of behaving in our daily lives. This effect is ingrained and institutionalized and is present even without the sanctions that are part of the enforcement machinery. In fact, most people in most situations tend to comply with the law without consciously assessing the possibility of legal sanctions or punishment. The legal definitions of proper conduct become to a large extent subsumed in individual attitudes toward everyday life and become part of internalized values.

THE BINDING FORCE OF LAW

There are many reasons that law is binding. They range from the assertion that laws are ordained by nature to the belief that law results from the consensus of a constituency's subjects to be bound. The simplest and most immediate answer is that law is binding because most people in society consider it to be. The awareness and consciousness of law by most people serve as the foundation for its existence. People generally submit their behaviour to its regulations, although they may have many different reasons for doing so. Some may believe that in obeying the law, they obey the higher authority of the law: God, nature, or the will of the people (Negley, 1965; Darwall, 2013; Dorsey, 2016).

Others consider the content of the law to command obedience, which in turn is seen as a compelling obligation. The law achieves its claim to obedience, and at least part of its morally obligatory force, from a recognition that it receives from those, or from most of those, to whom it is supposed to apply. In addition to agencies that encourage obedience through the application of law, other ingredients are normally present and essential. They include an inner desire of people to obey, reinforced by a belief that a particular law is fair and just because it is applied equally; a feeling of trust in the effectiveness and legitimacy of the government; and a sense of civic-mindedness. They also include self-interest and the knowledge that most people obey the law and recognize it as having a certain morally rightful claim upon their behaviour, or at the very least, that they behave as though they felt that way. Even when laws go against accepted morality, they are often obeyed. The deliberate extermination of more than 6 million Jews by Nazi Germany, clearly the most extreme instance of abhorrent immoral acts, was carried out by thousands of people in the name of obedience to the law. Milgram (1975:xii) contends that the essence of obedience is that individuals come to see themselves as instruments for carrying out someone else's wishes, and they therefore no longer view themselves as responsible for their actions. In many instances, the acceptance of authority results in obedience. An additional reason for the binding force of the law may be that people prefer order over disorder and favour predictability of behaviour. Individuals are creatures of habit because the habitual way of life requires less personal effort than any other and caters well to a sense of security. Obedience to the law guarantees that way. It also pays to follow the law—it saves effort and risk, a motivation sufficient to produce obedience. Obedience to the law is also related to the socialization process. People in general are brought up to obey the law. The legal way of life becomes the habitual way of life.

SANCTIONS

Sanctions for disobedience to the law are surely among the primary reasons that laws have binding force (Evan, 1990:72). As Hoebel eloquently states: "The law has teeth, teeth that can bite if need be, although they need not necessarily be bared" (1954:26). **Sanctions** are related to legal efficacy and are provided to guarantee the observance and execution of legal mandates—to enforce behaviour. The sanctions recognized and used by legal systems are usually of a diversified character. For example, in developed legal systems, the administration of sanctions is, as a general rule, entrusted to the organs of political government. Among the means of coercive law enforcement are punishment by fine or imprisonment; the imposition of damage awards; the ordering by a court of specific acts or forbearances at the threat of a penalty; and the impeachment or removal of a public officer for dereliction of duty. As Kelsen (1967:35) notes, the sanctions characteristic of modern legal systems go beyond the exercise of merely psychological pressure and authorize the performance of disadvantageous coercive acts—namely, "the forceable deprivation of life, freedom, economics and other values as a consequence of certain conditions."

Seidman (1978:100) points out that "laws more or less consistent with the existing social order need not rely upon the threat of legal sanction to induce behaviour." However, not all laws are consistent with the existing social order, and an advantage of the law as an agent of social change is that potential violation of the law is often deterred by actual or perceived risk and by the severity of sanctions attached to noncompliance. Even the threat of sanctions can deter people from disobedience. Perhaps sanctions also play a part by inducing a moralistic attitude toward compliance (Penalver and Katyal, 2010).

The types of sanctions used obviously vary with the purposes and goals of a law or legal policy. An essential distinction is whether the main purpose of a law is to prevent individuals from doing things that others in society oppose as being harmful or immoral, or whether its purpose is to create new types of relationships between groups or individuals—essentially the difference between proscriptive and positive policy (Grossman and Grossman, 1971:70). **Positive policymaking** often involves negative sanctions as well as positive rewards, although **proscriptive policymaking** usually involves only negative sanctions (Friedland, 1989). The distinction is not always perfect. For example, within federal systems, transfer payments may be used by the central government as rewards or incentives to promote public policy in areas where it lacks constitutional jurisdiction. A notable illustration of this within Canada exists in relation to the Canadian system of universal health insurance. This system has been achieved "through a federal statute that commits the central government to funding a large portion of the health-care system [despite a sharply curtailed, constitutional competence over health care] *so long as these governments maintain systems that adhere to a set of requirements designed to achieve universal access*" (Bogart, 2002:65, emphasis added). Rewards are also frequently part of regulatory statutes attempting to change established patterns of economic behaviour. Those who violate such laws not only lose prospective rewards but also may be liable for fines or criminal penalties. As Grossman and Grossman point out: "Laws or statutes which seek positive societal changes of major proportion must rely as much on education and persuasion as on negative sanctions. For the carrot and stick approach to be successful, the latter must be visible and occasionally used" (1971:70).

The circumstances are different where the changes sought through the law are the reduction or elimination of deviant behaviour. In such instances, the law does not provide rewards or incentives to dissuade individuals from committing such acts—only the possibility, if not the certainty, of detection and punishment. In such instances, the emphasis is on deterrence, punishment, and vengeance, and the objective is the elimination or reduction of a particular type of behaviour considered harmful.

There are, of course, additional discernible advantages of the law in creating social change. For example, the law as an instrument of change can effectively be involved in the context of Mill's notion of the law:

> (i) to achieve common purposes which cannot be left to the forces of supply and demand—such as education; (ii) to protect the immature and helpless; (iii) to control the power of associations, managed not only by the persons directly interested but by delegated agencies; (iv) to protect individuals acting in concert in cases where such action cannot be effective without legal sanctions; (v) to achieve objects of importance to society, present and future, which are beyond the powers of individuals or voluntary associations or which, if within their powers, would not normally be undertaken by them.
> (Ginsberg, 1965:230)

The list of conceivable advantages of the law as an instrument of social change is indeed incomplete. What has been said so far is intended simply to demonstrate that the law has a peculiar and unparalleled position among agents of social change. At the same time, it has certain limitations. Knowledge and an awareness of the limitations will help us to understand more fully the role of the law in social change, and they need to be taken into account for the use of the law in change efforts.

LIMITATIONS OF LAW IN CREATING SOCIAL CHANGE

In a period when many people distrust government and there is disagreement on myriad social and moral issues, it seems naïve to suggest that the law expresses the will of the people. For the great majority of individuals, the law originates externally to them and is imposed upon them in a manner that can be considered coercive. In reality, very few individuals actually participate in the formation of new laws and legislation. Consequently, one of the limitations of the law as an instrument of social change is that elites tend to determine which laws are promulgated and which alternatives are rejected. Other limitations bearing on the efficacy of the law as an instrument of social change include the divergence of views on the law as a tool of directed social change and the prevailing morality and values.

In every society, access to scarce resources and highly cherished objects is limited. In the struggle to achieve them, some individuals and groups win; others lose. Several decades ago, Weber recognized, as did Marx before him, that many laws are created to serve special economic interests. Individuals with the control of ownership of material goods are generally favoured by laws since "economic interests are among the strongest factors influencing the creation of law" (Weber, 1968:334). Weber further recognized that other special interests, in addition to economic ones, influence the formation of law. Says Weber: "Law guarantees by no means only economic interest, but rather the most diverse interests ranging from the most elementary ones of protection of personal security to such purely ideal goods as personal honour or the honour of the divine powers. Above all, it guarantees political, ecclesiastical, familial, and other positions of authority as well as positions of social pre-eminence of any kind" (p. 333).

Weber's points contain two important insights. The first is that conflict of interest provides the framework in which laws are framed and change is brought about. Consequently, social stratification in a society will determine to a large extent the part that laws will play in bringing about changes, based on the selectiveness and preferences exercised by those who promulgate those changes. The second point concerns the significance of the use of power to back up those changes. Studies of the legislative, judicial, and administrative processes in a society could lead very quickly to a discovery of not only who wields the power in society but also what interests are significant and influential in that group. Thus, the law as an instrument of a change can be viewed in the context of the organization of power and the processes by which interests are established in everyday social life; the resulting changes might very well be evaluated in those terms.

In a sense it is understandable that the powerful make and administer the laws in society. If anything gets done, it is because somebody had the power to do it. At the same time, those who are powerful and influential tend to use the law to protect their advantageous position in society, and for them "the law in effect structures the power (superordinate-subordinate) relationships in a society; it maintains the status quo and protects the various strata against each other" (Hertzler, 1961:421).

Many legislative enactments, administrative rulings, and judicial decisions reflect the *power* configurations in society. Some groups and associations are more powerful than others, and, by virtue of being at the centre of power, they are better able to reinforce their interests than those at the periphery. Even members of the legal profession are considered "professional go-betweens" for the principal political, corporate, and other interest groups, and hence serve to "unify the power elite" (Mills, 1957:289; Porter, 1965). Yet there are also numerous instances of racial, ethnic, and sexual minorities, women, and workers organizing to challenge the status quo (see, for example, Cowan, 2005; Scholes, 2002).

For example, labour was instrumental in the enactment of a series of laws dealing with occupational safety and health, flex-time work schedules, collective bargaining, and unemployment compensation (Laycock and Erickson, 2015; Morton, 2007). Activists in the first and second waves of the women's movement in Canada have seen their efforts result in such changes as the right to vote, the entrance of women into higher education, reforms in the direction of greater equality between spouses within family law, equal pay legislation, the striking down of Canada's abortion law, and legislation providing redress for victims of discrimination, domestic violence, and sexual harassment (Backhouse, 2004, 2008; Chunn, Boyd, and Lessard, 2007; Kilty, 2014; Sheehy, 2012). Activists in the LGBTIQ2S (lesbian, gay, bisexual, trans, intersex, queer or questioning, two-spirited) community have also lobbied aggressively for more equitable laws and have achieved considerable success in recent decades (Egale, 2017).

In 1996, for example, the federal *Human Rights Act* was amended to prohibit discrimination on the basis of sexual orientation and all provincial and territorial human rights acts now include sexual orientation as a prohibited basis for discrimination (with Alberta forced to do so by the Supreme Court of Canada's decision in *Vriend v. Alberta* [1998]) (Filax, 2004). In addition, throughout the 1990s and, with growing momentum in the new millennium, many of the rights and obligations that were once exclusively associated with marriage (e.g., the right to spousal support; the right to benefit from a partner's job benefits plan) were extended to couples living in marriage-like relationships. However, perhaps the most noteworthy legal change has occurred in relation to the definition of marriage itself. In July 2002, three Ontario Superior Court judges made Canadian legal history when they ruled that the opposite-sex limitation in common law (which restricted marriage to the union of one man and one woman) was unconstitutional; this decision was echoed in 2003 by courts in British Columbia, Quebec, the Yukon, and, in 2004, Manitoba, Nova Scotia, Saskatchewan, Quebec, Newfoundland, and Labrador. In fall 2004, the federal government of Canada presented a "Reference re Same-Sex Marriage" to the Supreme Court, requesting that the Court clarify whether the opposite-sex requirement for marriage was consistent with Charter guarantees of equality. In response, the Supreme Court stated that the federal government had the power to change the definition of marriage to include same-sex couples and that its doing so would be constitutional. The Supreme Court likened our systems of laws to a "living tree which by way of progressive interpretation, accommodates and addresses the realities of modern life," noting that the definition of marriage in Canada's constitution "does not exclude same-sex marriage." The Court also observed that clergy could, as an expression of freedom of religion, refuse to conduct marriage ceremonies involving same-sex couples. With the passage of Bill C-38, Parliament changed the definition of marriage to comply with the Charter and, on July 20, 2005, the *Civil Marriage Act* received Royal Assent (Larocque et al., 2016).

Among other legal milestones: In 2002, the Northwest territories identified "gender identity" as a prohibited ground of discrimination in its Human Rights Act with Manitoba and Saskatchewan following its lead in 2012 and 2014, respectively. Other Canadian provinces and territories have amended their human rights legislation to prohibit discrimination on the basis of both gender identity and gender expression, with this occurring in Ontario and Nova Scotia (2012), Prince Edward Island, Newfoundland, and Labrador (2013), Alberta (2015), Quebec (2016), and Nunavut [2017]; the Government of Yukon has also declared its commitment to eliminating discrimination based on a person's gender identity or gender expression and proposed amendments to its *Human Rights Act* that will prohibit discrimination on these grounds (Yukon Government, 2017). In May 2016, Bill C-16, *An Act to Amend the Canadian Human Rights Act and the Criminal Code*, was introduced in the House of Commons by Canada's Minister of Justice. Bill C-16 seeks to protect trans people from discrimination within the sphere of federal jurisdiction by adding "gender identity or expression" to the prohibited grounds of discrimination within the *Canadian Human Rights Act*. It also proposes to amend two sections of the Criminal Code by adding "gender identity and gender expression" to s. 318 of the Code, which addresses hate propaganda, and to s. 718.2, which makes evidence that a criminal offence was motivated by bias, prejudice, or hate an aggravating factor that a court must take into consideration when it imposes a sentence (Mas, 2016; McElroy, 2016; Wherry, 2016). Although like-spirited proposals had been put forward in earlier years in private member's bills, Bill C-16 was the first time that a governing party had introduced such legislation in the House of Commons. At the time of writing (March 2017), Bill C-16 had been passed by House of Commons (by a margin of 248 to 40) but delayed in the Senate, with experts slated to testify on the bill in April 2017.

BOX 7.1 LIFE AND LAW: CHANGING LAWS, CHANGING LIVES: FIRST NATIONS AND NOTABLE LEGAL EVENTS

1970: *R. v. Drybones*: The Supreme Court affirmed the rights of Aboriginal peoples in the Constitution and stated that these rights must be interpreted broadly. It held that section 94(b) of the Indian Act (which prohibited "Indians" from being intoxicated off of a reserve) impermissibly violated section 1(b) of the *Canadian Bill of Rights* (i.e., "the right of the individual to equality before the law and the protection of the law"), and struck down the offending part of the *Indian Act*.

1973: *Calder et al. v. B.C. Attorney General*: A split Supreme Court of Canada decision which paved the path for ongoing land claims negotiations between the government and First Nations by acknowledging that Aboriginal title to land existed prior to colonization and the *Royal Proclamation of 1763*.

1983: *Lovelace v. Canada*: The United Nations Human Rights Committee found that the *Indian Act* discriminated on the basis of sex and contained provisions that were contrary to the Universal Declaration of Human Rights. In response, the Canadian federal government passed Bill C-31, *An Act to Amend the Indian Act*, which brought the *Indian Act* into line with Charter provisions.

1984: *Guerin v. The Queen*: The Supreme Court clarified the legal nature and origins of Aboriginal title: It was not a "privilege" granted to First Nations by the Royal Proclamation of 1763 but a true legal right based on Aboriginal occupancy of lands prior to the arrival of Europeans. It also established that the Canadian government's fiduciary duty to First Nations stems from a unique relationship (*sui generis*).

1985: *Simon v. The Queen*: Supreme Court rules that the principles of international treaty law relating to treaty termination are not determinative because an Indian treaty is "unique; it is an agreement *sui generis* which is neither created nor terminated according to the rules of international law."

1990: *R. v. Sparrow*: Results in the first Supreme Court test of the scope of Section 35(1) of the *Constitution Act, 1982*. In its decision, the court for the first time set out criteria for determining whether a right can be considered to be an "existing" right and whether the government is justified in curtailing such a right. Establishes that existing Aboriginal rights cannot be infringed upon unless the government has a "compelling and substantial rationale" (e.g., conservation, public safety) and only if it upholds its fiduciary duty to take Aboriginal rights into account.

1996: *R. v. Gladstone*: A Supreme Court decision that affirms the Aboriginal right to fish commercially.

1996: *R v Van der Peet*: The Supreme Court examined the broad purpose of section 35 of *Constitution Act, 1982* and concluded that "the Aboriginal rights recognized and affirmed by section 35(1) must be directed towards the reconciliation of the pre-existence of Aboriginal societies with the sovereignty of the Crown." It urged lower courts that were assessing Aboriginal rights claims to recognize that the knowledge system of Aboriginal peoples was traditionally oral rather than in written. For the purposes of determining an aboriginal right under s. 35, the Court also crafted a ten-part "Integral to a Distinctive Culture Test" that required the following things to be established: that the right involved an activity that was a central and significant part of the society's distinctive culture; that the activity existed prior to contact with European settlers; and that the activity, even if evolved into a modern form, was one that continued to exist after the passage of the *Constitution Act*.

1997: *Delgamuukw v. British Columbia*: The Supreme Court of Canada confirmed that Aboriginal title entails rights to the land itself and not merely the right to extract resources from the land. The court additionally ruled that the government has a duty to consult with First Nations on issues concerning Crown land (with the level/intensity of consultation commensurate with the level/intensity of the infringement) and that, in some cases, the government may have to compensate Aboriginal peoples for infringing upon their rights to the land.

1999: *R. v. Marshall*: The Supreme Court ruled on the case of Donald Marshall Jr., a Mi'kmaq Aboriginal charged with various offences contrary to fishery regulation and who claimed, in response, that as a Mi'kmaq he had a right to fish based on the 1760–61 LaHave treaties. The Marshall case "was the first case in which the court analyzed treaty rights using section 35 of the Constitution Act, 1982" and also "the first time the court found that a treaty afforded a limited commercial right to fish" (Sauvageau, Schneiderman, and Taras, 2006:140).

1999: *Corbiere v. Canada:* John Corbiere and other members of the Batchewana challenged s. 77(1) of the *Indian Act*, which denied band members who lived off reserve the right to vote in band elections. They argued that this part of the Act violated the equality provision of the Charter of Rights and Freedoms and the Supreme Court agreed. The *Indian Act* was subsequently changed and its definition of an elector was altered to a person who is at least 18 years of age and a registered member of a band.

2001: *Osoyoos Indian Band v. Oliver (Town):* Entrenched the fiduciary obligations of the Crown in relation to the taking of reserve lands.

2004: *Haida Nation v. British Columbia (Minister of Forests)* and *Taku River Tlingit First Nation v. British Columbia:* The Supreme Court ruled that "[w]here the government has knowledge of an asserted aboriginal right or title, it must consult with Aboriginal people on how exploitation of the land should proceed." Thus, before allowing logging, mining, and other invasive activities to occur on disputed land, governments have a moral and legal duty to negotiate with Aboriginal groups who have asserted, but not yet established, Aboriginal title. The written decision of Chief Justice Beverley McLachlin also established a general framework for the Crown's duty to consult (and possibly accommodate) Aboriginal people, with the "Honour of the Crown" demanding a fair and honourable consultative process. The Court affirmed that treaty making was not intended to replace or extinguish Aboriginal rights but, instead, to reconcile these rights with other rights and interests and achieve "just settlements" and "honourable agreements."

2005: *R. v. Marshall; R. v. Bernard:* The Supreme Court of Canada placed limits on aboriginal title, established strict proof of aboriginal title, and emphasized the need for continuity between a pre-sovereignty group of Aboriginal peoples and those asserting the modern right. It outlined that claims to Aboriginal title are dependent on the specific facts of the group, the group's historic relationship to the land, and evidence of exclusive and regular use of the land in question (e.g., for hunting, fishing). Although nomadic or semi-nomadic peoples were not precluded from acquiring Aboriginal title, it noted that seasonal hunting/fishing in a particular location amounts to hunting or fishing rights rather than aboriginal title.

2006: *R. v. Sappier; R. v. Gray:* Established the Aboriginal right to harvest timber on Crown land.

2009: *McIvor v. Canada:* A BC Court of Appeal decision that forced the federal government to amend the *Indian Act* to eliminate discrimination against the wives and children of non-status Indians. Prior to 1985, Aboriginal women lost Indian status upon marriage to a non-Aboriginal, but an

Aboriginal man who married a non-Aboriginal retained his Aboriginal status and this status was conferred upon his wife and the couple's children. Although this disparity was eliminated by a 1985 amendment to the *Indian Act*, another discriminatory provision remained within it, which conferred status to those whose Indian grandparent was a man but not to those whose Indian grandparent was a woman. The Court of Appeal gave the government a year to amend this discriminatory provision.

2014: *Tsilhqot'in Nation v. British Columbia*: The first declaration of Aboriginal Title in Canadian history. The Supreme Court recognized that Aboriginal title can exist over large tracts of land and found that holders of Aboriginal title have rights similar to those of private property owners (i.e., the right to decide how the land will be used; enjoyment and occupancy of the land; possession of the land; the economic benefits of the land; and the use and management of the land). Although Aboriginal title is a collective right, and Aboriginal titleholders cannot use the land in ways that would prevent future generations from its use and enjoyment; uses of the land are not restricted to traditional practices.

2016: *Daniels v. Canada (Indian Affairs and Northern Development)*: The Supreme Court of Canada ruled unanimously that the Métis and non-status Indians are "Indians" under s. 91(24) of the *Constitution Act, 1867*. The ruling noted that, in the absence of this definition's clarity, these indigenous communities had existed in a "jurisdictional wasteland with significant and obvious disadvantaging consequences."

Aboriginal peoples have also notably engaged with the law, seeking recognition of their sovereign status as the ancestral occupants of Canada. As Fleras (2005:314, 320) observes, "Aboriginal peoples increasingly claim to be relatively autonomous political communities with an inherent right to self-determining autonomy" and seek "to construct Aboriginal models of self-determining autonomy over jurisdiction, identity and political voice." Indigenous peoples have laboured to reclaim their historic land and contractual rights from the government and sought the right to make and interpret laws in relation to their own people; Box 7.1 records simply some of the notable legal decisions that have occurred during this odyssey. Aboriginal efforts were also responsible for three provisions within the *Constitution Act, 1982*, specifically: (1) section 25 of the Charter, which provides that guarantees of rights and freedoms do not detract "from any Aboriginal, treaty or other rights or freedoms" that Aboriginal people possess as the result of the Royal Proclamation, 1763, or any then-existent or future land-claims agreements; (2) section 35 (in Part II) of the act, which recognizes and affirms "the existing Aboriginal and treaty rights of Aboriginal peoples"—a significant phrase that acknowledges Aboriginal rights as inherent rather than delegated rights; and (3) section 37, which guarantees the convening of a constitutional conference that would include "an item respecting constitutional matters that directly affect the Aboriginal peoples of Canada, including the identification and definition of the rights of those peoples to be included in the Constitution of Canada" within one year of the act coming into force (Carson, 1999).

Do these types of developments not mean that minorities can also become a part of the power structure? And if they are, does this not mean that the distribution of power in society is more widespread and complicated than is suggested by writers who speak of a simple division of society into "the powerful" and "the powerless" or who suggest, for example, that Aboriginal peoples are destined to remain in "helpless bondage to fundamental principles firmly established in the common law" (Bell and Asch, 1997:45)?

Large-scale participation of the citizenry in legal change, even in a democratic society, is seldom feasible. But lack of participation does not necessarily mean lack of representation. In Canada, the United States, and most parts of Europe, people do have access (albeit of varying degrees) to lawmakers and to the legal apparatus, and their aspirations for change through the law have, at least on occasion, been realized (Anleu, 2009; Diamant, Lubman, and O'Brien, 2005; Jimenez, 2010; Engel and Engel, 2011; McMichael, 2017; Nussbaum, 2010; Rosenberg, 2008).

LAW AS A POLICY INSTRUMENT

A different school of thought on the limits of the law as an instrument of social change is epitomized by Dror. He contends that "law by itself is only one component of a large set of policy instruments and usually cannot and is not used by itself. Therefore, focusing exclusive attention on law as a tool of directed social change is a case of tunnel vision, which lacks the minimum perspective necessary for making sense from the observed phenomena" (Dror, 1970:554). He suggests that it is necessary to redefine the subject of "law as a tool of directed social change" and to consider it as part of other social policy instruments, since the law is but one of many policy instruments that must be used in combination. In the context of social problems such as race relations, public safety, drug abuse, and pollution, "the necessity to use law as a policy instrument should be quite convincing" (p. 555). This view certainly has merits. At times, change through the law can and should be construed as an ingredient of a larger policy. However, the law is often used as an instrument of change outside of the context of a broad policymaking framework. This is typically the situation in reform-oriented litigation, where the object is to alter a particular institutionalized practice. For example, the 1988 Supreme Court decision to strike down the abortion sections of the Criminal Code as unconstitutional was not carried out within specific policy considerations, and yet it obviously had a tremendous impact on women seeking to terminate pregnancy legally. Although judicial decisions are generally not considered a policy instrument, because of the adversarial nature of litigation, legislative and administrative reforms dealing with larger social issues should take place in a broader social policymaking framework, such as environmental and natural resource management activities (Dean, 2012; Hill, 2006; Jordan, 2007). Such an approach would greatly enhance the efficacy of the law as an instrument of change. To this end, Dror advocates the establishment of interdisciplinary teams of lawyers, social scientists, and policy analysts to engage in relevant studies and prepare policy recommendations.

Increasingly, this seemingly common-sense advice is being translated into practical applications, and policy preparatory and advisory teams are becoming interdisciplinary.

MORALITY AND VALUES

The sociological literature recognizes that the ability of the law to produce social change depends on many factors. Some of these factors are related to the prevailing morality and values in society (Sterba, 2004). Devlin (1965) argues that a society owes its existence less to its institutions than to the shared morality that binds it together. Although his thesis is only partly true, morality and values affect the efficacy of the law in social change. Obviously, society could not exist without accepting certain basic values, principles, and standards. On certain issues, such as violence, truth, individual liberty, and human dignity, a shared morality is essential. This does not mean, however, that all the values in our shared morality are basic and essential, or that decline in one value spells decline in all the rest. Moreover, not all our values are essential. Rules about property, for example, are not. Some principles about property are essential, but no society needs to have those very property principles that are characteristic of, for example, Canada—the principle of private ownership. A society could own all property in common without ceasing to count as a society. Indeed, for Canada's Aboriginal peoples, the notion that one "owns" the land one inhabits is ludicrous and analogous to imagining that one "owns" one's mother.

In general, when the law is used as an instrument of social change, it needs the support of society. Says Schur: "A good illustration of the systematic ineffectiveness of unsupported law is provided by the utter failure of legislation designed to enforce private morality" (1968:132). Thus, an obvious limitation of the law in social change appears when it tries to deal with what may be called moral issues in society. The well-known failure of the prohibition of alcohol through legislation to produce a truly "dry" society, or to keep most people from drinking, is a potent example of the limitation of the law to bring about social change in public "morals" (McGirr, 2016; Raz, 2009). A comparable situation exists with regard to the prohibition of several kinds of drugs, especially marijuana. Interestingly, the marijuana laws have been called the "new prohibition" to underline the similarity to alcohol prohibition and the futility of legal control over the consumption of those substances (Nadelmann, 2006).

The link between law and morality in the making and unmaking of law raises two questions: (1) What needs to be done in considering a change in the law when moral opinion is divided? Are there criteria other than individual likes and dislikes to which appeal can be made?; (2) How can the line be drawn between that part of morality or immorality that needs legal enforcement and that which the law ought to leave alone (Ginsberg, 1965:232)? In response to these questions, Ginsberg suggests that the law ought to deal only with what can be ascertained on reliable evidence and with acts that can be precisely defined, and primarily with overt or external observable acts; and the law must, as far as possible, respect privacy. He contends that these are "principles of demarcation arising from the limitations inherent in the machinery of the law" (p. 238).

Thus, laws are more likely to bring about changes in what may be called external behaviour. However, changes in external behaviour are after a while usually followed by changes in values, morals, and attitudes. As Berger (1952:172) emphasizes:

> While it is true that the province of law is "external" behaviour, it is also true that in an urban, secular society an increasing number of relations fall within this province. Thus

the range of behaviour that can be called "external" is enlarged. At the same time, law can influence "external" acts which affect or constitute the conditions for the exercise of the private inclinations and tastes that are said to be beyond the realm of law.

The fact that a change in attitude is only partial at first does not make it any less of a change. If the law can change morality and values only under some conditions, those conditions need to be specified. As Seidman (1978:156) notes, "The literature contains little more than speculations," and there is a great lack of empirical studies. In general, the law will more readily change morality and values where it first changes behaviour. Such a change is usually followed by a justification of the new activity. To a great extent, however, the efficacy of the law depends much upon its adaptation to morality and values if it is intended to induce change (Peach, 2002).

There is still much to be learned about when and under what conditions the law cannot "only *codify* existing customs, morals, or mores, but also. . . *modify* the behaviour and values presently existing in a particular society" (Evan, 1965:286). In efforts to effect change through the law, the prevalence and intensity of moral feelings and values need to be taken into account in both preserving and altering the status quo.

RESISTANCE TO CHANGE

In addition to the limitations of law as an instrument of social change discussed in the preceding section, the efficacy of the law (as well as other mechanisms of change) is further hindered by a variety of forces. In the modern world, situations of resistance to change are much more numerous than situations of acceptance. Members of a society can always find justification, in some more or less practical and rational terms, for active resistance to change. Often change is resisted because it conflicts with traditional values and beliefs and/ or prevailing customs (Banks, 1998); a particular change may simply cost too much money; and sometimes people resist change because it interferes with their habits or makes them feel frightened or threatened. Although the law has certain advantages over other agents of change, for a greater appreciation of the role of law in change it is helpful to identify some general conditions of resistance that have a bearing on the law. The awareness of these conditions is a major, but often overlooked or underutilized, prerequisite for a more efficient use of law as a method of social engineering.

For the sake of clarity, we shall consider resistance to change through law in the context of social, psychological, cultural, and economic factors. The categories are only illustrative, and this distinction is made only for analytical purposes, for many of these factors operate in various combinations and intensities, depending on the magnitude and scope of a particular change effort.

SOCIAL FACTORS

There are several factors that may be construed as potential barriers to change. They include vested interests, social class, ideological resistance, and organized opposition.

VESTED INTERESTS

Change may be resisted by individuals or groups who fear a loss of power, prestige, or wealth should a new proposal gain acceptance. There are many different types of vested interests for which the status quo is profitable or preferable. For example, residents in a community often develop vested interests in their neighbourhood. They often organize to resist zoning changes or the construction of correctional facilities nearby. However, the acceptance of almost any change through law will adversely affect the status of some individuals or groups in society, and to the degree that those whose status is threatened consciously recognize the danger, they will oppose the change.

SOCIAL CLASS

Rigid class and caste patterns generally tend to hinder the acceptance of change. In highly stratified societies, people are expected to obey and take orders from those in superior positions of authority or power. The prerogatives of the upper strata are jealously guarded, and attempts to infringe upon them by members of lower socioeconomic groups are often resented and repulsed. In most cases, there is a tendency for the upper classes to cherish the old ways of doing things and to adhere to the status quo (Beeghley, 2007).

In Canada, those who identify themselves as working-class people tend to agree more readily that legal intervention is necessary to rectify deleterious social conditions and that the government should intervene in the economy. However, while the working class is more liberal on economic issues (i.e., favours government spending), it is more conservative on social issues (e.g., the teaching of religion in schools) (Lambert and Curtis, 1993; Graves 2014, 2017).

IDEOLOGICAL RESISTANCE

Resistance to change through law on ideological grounds is quite prevalent. An example of ideological resistance to change through law was on display in the reaction of religious fundamentalists and other conservative groups in Canada to legislation that equalized the rights of same-sex and opposite-sex couples. This legislation, which challenged heterosexual hegemony over the meanings of marriage and the family, made clear that law reform may be part of ideological battles (Morton, 2002: 394; see also Farney, 2012).

A second illustration of ideological resistance (which goes hand in hand with vested interests) was the fierce opposition of the medical profession to the launching of medical-services insurance in Saskatchewan in 1962 and later toward "medicare." It was feared that medicare would result in "state medicine" and that both the role and the status of physicians would be reduced to those of civil servants. In general, the basic intellectual and religious assumptions and interpretations concerning existing power, morality, welfare, and security tend to be rather consistent and adversely disposed to change (Vago, 2004:232).

ORGANIZED OPPOSITION

Occasionally, widespread individual resistance to change may become mobilized into organized opposition, which can assume formal organizational structures or be channelled through a social movement, political action committees, or lobbyists. In modern societies, with their multiplicity of informal and formal organizations often in conflict with each other, a variety of new organizations have developed to combat specific threats to the status quo. Much organized resistance to change results from efforts of groups that oppose extending rights and liberties to historically subordinate groups. For example, members of REAL Women of Canada decry a whole range of social changes from liberalized divorce laws to the acceptance and legal protection of homosexuals. Other Canadian groups protest against Canada's anti-discrimination laws as well as its immigration policies and identify with "white nationalism." While Canada's right-wing extremist movement has been described as "a motley crew of white supremacists, anti-government 'sovereignists' and pro-militia crusaders" who are "prone to booze-fuelled in-fighting" (Quan, 2016), a recent study (Perry and Scrivens, 2015) warned that such groups remained a public threat and have carried out acts of violence and targeted attacks on various minority groups, including Muslims, Jews, people of colour, Aboriginal people, and LGBT people. At other times, however, when organized opposition to change through law has *not* been forthcoming, the consequences have been disastrous. For instance, more than 6 million Jews were slaughtered in concentration camps during the Second World War in part because there was no well-organized and effective resistance to the heinous activities that began in the early 1930s in Nazi Germany and were buttressed by legal measures, such as the now-infamous Nuremberg Laws (Vago, 2004:259).

PSYCHOLOGICAL FACTORS

Several psychological factors may impede change generally and, therefore, weaken the ability of law to produce social change. These factors include habit, motivation, ignorance, selective perception, and moral development.

HABIT

From a psychological perspective, habit is a barrier to change. Once a habit is established, its operation often becomes satisfying to the individual. Nimkoff (1957:62) suggests that the customs of a society are *collective habits*; for this reason, custom is slow to change when challenged by new ideas and practices. When the law is used as an instrument of social change to alter established customs, it is more likely that the achievement of acceptable rates of compliance will require an active reorientation of the values and behaviours of a significant part of the target population (Zimring and Hawkins, 1975:331).

MOTIVATION

The acceptance of change through law is also conditioned by motivational forces (Ginsberg and Fiene, 2004). Some motivations are culture-bound, in the sense that their presence or absence is characteristic of a particular culture. For instance, in some cultures religious beliefs offer motivations to certain kinds of change, whereas in other cultures these motivations centre on the preservation of the status quo. Other kinds of motivations tend to be universal, or nearly universal, in that they cut across societies and cultures, Examples of these motivations include the desire for prestige or for economic gain, and the wish to comply with friendship obligations.

IGNORANCE

Ignorance is another psychological factor generally associated with resistance to change. At times, ignorance goes hand in hand with fear of the new. Ignorance can also be a factor in noncompliance with laws designed to reduce discriminatory practices. Ignorance is obviously an important factor in prejudice when a pre-existing attitude is so strong and inflexible that it seriously distorts perception and judgment (Beeghley, 2007).

SELECTIVE PERCEPTION

Law, by design and intent, tends to be universal. The perception of the intent of the law, however, is selective and varies with socioeconomic, cultural, and demographic variables. The unique pattern of people's needs, attitudes, habits, and values derived through socialization determines what they will selectively attend to, what they will selectively interpret, and what they will selectively act upon (Engel and Engel, 2011). For example, a few weeks after the Supreme Court of Canada upheld the constitutionality of the Criminal Code section on obscenity, "the obscenity provisions were invoked, not against material designed to arouse men, but against material designed to interest lesbians. . . . In short, the law that was supposed to protect women was being used against women and against the constituency of women that has long been a 'repressed voice'" (Borovoy, 1999:8). People in general will be more receptive to new ideas if they are related to their interests, consistent with their attitudes, congruent with their beliefs, and supportive of their values (Baker, 2005).

MORAL DEVELOPMENT

To a great extent, obedience to the law stems from a sense of moral obligation, which is the product of socialization. Only relatively recently, however, has there been some awareness of moral codes that are not necessarily linked to conventional external standards of right and wrong behaviour, but represent internally consistent principles by which people govern their lives.

Perhaps the most extensive work on moral development was carried out by Kohlberg (1964, 1967, but see also Gibbs, 2010). Kohlberg defined six stages in moral development. The first stage is described as an *obedience and punishment orientation*. This stage involves "deference to superior power or prestige" and an orientation toward avoiding trouble. The second stage, *instrumental relativism*, is characterized by naïve notions of reciprocity. With this orientation, people will attempt to satisfy their own needs by simple negotiation with others or by a primitive form of equalitarianism. Kohlberg called these two stages "premoral." The third stage, *personal concordance*, is an orientation based on approval and pleasing others. It is characterized by conformity to perceived majority beliefs, whereby people adhere to what they consider to be prevailing norms. Stage four is the *law and order stage*. People with such orientations are committed to "doing their duty" and being respectful to those in authority. Stages three and four combine to form a *conventional moral orientation*.

Stages five and six indicate the *internalized-principle orientation*. Kohlberg called stage five the *social contract stage*; it involves a legalistic orientation. Commitments are viewed in contractual terms, and people at this stage will avoid efforts to break implicit or explicit agreements. The final and highest stage of moral development is *individual principles*. This emphasizes conscience, mutual trust, and respect as the guiding principles of behaviour.

If the development theory proposed by Kohlberg is correct, the law is more or less limited, depending on the stage of moral development of members of a society. In this context, Danelski (1974:14) suggests that both qualitative and quantitative considerations are important. We would need to know the modal stage of the moral development of elites, of "average" citizens, and of deprived groups. If most members of a society were at the first and second stages, institutional enforcement would be essential to maintain order and security. Law would be least limited in a society in which most people were at the third and fourth stages of development. Law at the last two stages is probably more limited than at stages three and four, "but it might be otherwise if it is perceived as democratically agreed upon and consistent with individual principles of conscience. If it is not, it is likely to be more limited" (p. 15). The limits of law, in other words, appear to be curvilinear with respect to moral development.

CULTURAL FACTORS

When long-established practices or behaviours are threatened, resistance to change is usually strong, often on the basis of traditional beliefs and values. The status quo is protected and change resisted. Other cultural factors that may discourage change include fatalism, ethnocentrism, notions of incompatibility, and superstition.

FATALISM
Fatalism refers to feelings of resignation or powerlessness. People who are fatalistic perceive themselves as lacking control over their lives and, for example, believe that everything that happens to them is caused by God or evil spirits. Such a fatalistic outlook undoubtedly results in resistance to change, for change is seen as human-initiated rather than having a divine origin.

ETHNOCENTRISM
Ethnocentrism often constitutes a bulwark against change in that it encourages groups to consider themselves "superior" to others. Feelings of superiority about one's group are likely to make people unreceptive to the ideas and methods used in other groups (Asante, 2003). As a result, ethnocentrism often constitutes a bulwark against change.

INCOMPATIBILITY
Resistance to change is often due to the presence in the target group of material and systems that are, or are considered to be, incompatible with the new proposal. For example, the minimum age that Canada sets for marriage may impose a rule of behavior that is incompatible with the customs and habits of immigrants from other countries, where marriage is usually contracted at a younger age. When such incompatibility exists in a culture, change comes about with difficulty.

SUPERSTITION
Superstition is defined as an uncritical acceptance of a belief that is not substantiated by facts (Ambrose, 1998). Nevertheless, people may act on the basis of these beliefs. For example, a 2006 news report noted that "[w]hen the upper teeth of a 17-month-old girl in eastern India appeared before her lower teeth, her family, members of the Santhal tribe, took it as a bad omen. To remove the 'evil eye' that had fallen upon her, the girl married a stray dog to confuse and thwart evil spirits. Her father . . . led three days of ceremonies to mark the girl's marriage to the dog" (Maclean's, 2006:11). Similarly, while one may suppose the burning of "witches" to be a thing of the past, "superstitious belief in witchcraft continues to plague parts of India" and can have deadly consequences; "[a]ccording to the Times of India, a National Crime Records Bureau report revealed that

more than 1,700 women were murdered for witchcraft between 1991 and 2010" (Schaffer, 2014). In simply one Indian state—Jharkhand—there were 127 cases of "murder for witchcraft" committed between 2012 and 2014 (Times of India, 2016). In response, some Indian states have passed laws that are intended to prevent the heinous treatment that those who are alleged to be witches may confront. For example, in 2001, Jharkhand, a state in eastern India, passed the *Dayan Pratha* (*Prevention of Witch Practices*) *Act*; in 2005, a state in central India, Chhattisgarh, passed the *Witchcraft Atrocities Prevention Act*; in 2011, Rajasthan, the largest state in India, passed the *Rajasthan Women* (*Prevention and Protection from Atrocities Bill*); and, in 2015, "the Assam state assembly unanimously passed *Assam Witch Hunting* (*Prohibition, Prevention and Protection*) *Bill*, in a bid to eliminate rising cases of superstition leading to the murder of so-called 'witches'" (Bhonde, 2016). However, where superstitious beliefs prevail, change efforts through law will predictably have less than optimal results.

ECONOMIC FACTORS

Even in affluent societies, limited economic resources constitute a barrier to changes that might otherwise be readily adopted. For instance, in Canada, many people would probably accept the desirability of more effective controls on pollution, enhanced systems of public transportation, and improvements in our systems of welfare, health care and education if all these changes were costless. The fact that changes in these areas come very slowly is thus a matter of not only psychological and cultural factors but also of financial cost. A society's limited economic resources, in effect, provide a source of resistance to change.

It is a truism that change through law can be expensive. In most instances, the instrumentation of legislation, administrative ruling, or court decision carries a price tag. In addition to the direct cost of a particular change effort, the way costs and benefits are distributed also affects resistance. For example, when costs and benefits are widely distributed (as in social security), there is minimal resistance to programs. The cost to each taxpayer is relatively small, and the benefits are so widely distributed "that they are almost like collective goods; beneficiaries will enjoy the benefits, but only make small contributions to their retention or growth" (Handler, 1978:15). Resistance will be forthcoming in situations where benefits are distributed while costs are concentrated. For example, automakers still resist (although not too successfully) legal attempts to impose more sophisticated pollution-control measures on cars.

Although a particular change through the law may be desirable, limited economic resources often act as barriers to such change efforts. Of the four sources of resistance to change, the economic factors are perhaps the most decisive. Regardless of the desirability of a proposed change, its compatibility with the values and beliefs of the recipients, and many other considerations, it will be resisted if the economic sacrifice is too great. Simply stated, regardless of how much people in a society want something, if they cannot afford it, chances are they will not be able to get it. As Foster (1973:78) suggests: "Cultural, social and psychological barriers and stimulants to change exist in an economic setting. . . [and] economic factors . . . seem to set the absolute limits to change."

SUMMARY

- Law is both a dependent and an independent variable in social change.
- Increasingly, law is being considered an instrument of social change. In many areas of social life, such as education, race relations, housing, transportation, energy utilization, and the protection of the environment, the law has been relied on as an important instrument of change.
- The advantages of law as an agent of change are attributed to the perception that the law in society is legitimate, more or less rational, authoritative, institutionalized, generally not disruptive, and backed by mechanisms of enforcement and sanctions.
- The law has certain limitations in creating social change: It is not always able to resolve conflicting interests, and generally the powerful in society fare better than the less privileged and the unorganized. The law is further limited by the divergences in values and moral codes, the difficulty in enforcing some laws, the occasional lack of clarity of law, and the questionable diligence in enforcing certain laws.
- A variety of social, psychological, cultural, and economic forces may provide direct or indirect resistance to change efforts. The social factors include vested interests, social class, moral sentiments, and organized opposition. Psychological resistance may be triggered by habit, motivation, ignorance, selective perception, and the complexities inherent in moral development. Cultural barriers to change include fatalism, ethnocentrism, notions of incompatibility, and superstition. Cost and limited economic resources effectively set a limit to change.

CRITICAL THINKING QUESTIONS

1. Some recommend the expansion of Canada's hate laws to criminalize speech that exposes "identifiable groups" to ridicule, mockery, or contempt and urge the establishment of a new media code of conduct that would prevent the media from publishing words or images that may give offence to such groups. Others, however, decry these suggestions as mindless capitulation to the dictates of "political correctness." Which of these positions would you favour? Why?
2. What limits (if any) do you believe should be placed on your right to freedom of expression?
3. Examine the editorials in local and campus newspapers and within news magazines. What changes to law are proposed? What arguments and types of evidence are used to support the writer's arguments that such changes are necessary? If the editorial suggests that Canada will be ill-served by proposed or pending legislation, what justifications are offered in defence of the status quo?
4. Does Canada's embrace of multiculturalism necessitate cultural accommodation for the practices of minority groups? Consider in this context that while polygamy is legal in 58 sovereign states (the majority of which are Muslim-majority countries in Africa and Asia), polygamy in Canada is a criminal offence. What changes to Canadian law, if any, are demanded by our commitment to multiculturalism?

ADDITIONAL RESOURCES

1. Egale Canada is a national Canadian human rights organization that promotes the equality of LGBTQ2S peoples. Visit its website at http://egale.ca.
2. Find out more about the Canadian Women's Legal Action and Education Fund (LEAF) by visiting its website at http://www.leaf.ca.
3. The Canadian Abilities Foundation envisions "an inclusive, universally accessible society, where all people belong and are valued" and its website (http:// www.abilities. ca) provides a wealth of information on organizations that are concerned with the rights of peoples with disabilities and campaign for their meaningful inclusion in all aspects of social life.
4. Information about the Canadian Department of Justice's Legal Education for Aboriginal Peoples program can be obtained at http://www.justice.gc.ca/eng/fund-fina/acf-fca/lsap-aeda.html.

CHAPTER 8
THE LEGAL PROFESSION

This chapter analyzes the character of the legal profession and the social forces shaping it. It begins with a historical background of law, with an emphasis on the professionalization of lawyers and the evolution of the legal profession in Canada. Next, the chapter focuses on the legal profession today: What lawyers do and where, their income, and how they compete for business. The emphasis is then placed on the accessibility of legal services to the poor and the not-so-poor, followed by a discussion of law schools and the training and socialization of lawyers into the profession. The section concludes with some comments on bar admission, bar associations as interest groups, and professional discipline.

Figure 8.1 Canada's legal profession is increasingly diverse.
Credit: Fotolia

After reading this chapter, you should be able to:

1. Identify the attributes of a profession and the five stages that are involved in the professionalization of an occupation.

2. Describe the evolution of the Canadian legal profession.

3. Discuss the composition of the Canadian legal profession in the past and present.

4. Describe the four principal subgroups in the legal profession.

5. Discuss the options available for those who require legal counsel but are unable to pay full legal fees.

6. Summarize the general requirements of Canadian law schools and why these requirements have attracted criticism.

7. Outline how law schools socialize their students into "thinking like lawyers."

8. Describe how Canadian law associations police their members.

BACKGROUND

The development of the legal profession has been intimately connected with the rise and development of legal systems. The origins of the legal profession can be traced back to Rome (Brundage, 2010). Initially, Roman law allowed individuals to argue cases on behalf of others; however, those persons were trained not in law but in rhetoric. They were called orators and were not allowed to take fees. Later on, by Cicero's time (106–43 B.C.), there were jurists as well—individuals who were knowledgeable about the law and to whom people went for legal opinions. They were called *juris prudentes*, but these men learned in the law did not yet constitute a profession. Only during the Imperial Period (approximately 44 B.C. to 410 A.D.) did lawyers begin to practise law for a living and schools of law emerge. By this time, the law had become exceedingly complex in Rome. The occupation of lawyers arose together with a sophisticated legal system, and the complexity of that system made the Roman lawyer indispensable (Brundage, 2010).

Jeffery (1962:314) points out that by the Middle Ages, the lawyer had three functions—agent, advocate, and jurisconsult. The word *attorney* originally meant "an agent, a person who acts or appears on behalf of someone else." In this role of agent, the lawyer appeared in court to handle legal matters in place of his client. In ancient Athens and Rome, an agent was allowed to appear in the place of another person. In France, however, a person had to appear in court him- or herself and in England, needed special permission from the king to be represented in court by an agent. In France, by 1356, there were 105 *legistes* (men of law) representing clients in court (Jacoby, 1973:14).

The distinction between an agent and an advocate appeared when the lawyer went to court with a client to assist the client in presenting a case. In addition to law, the advocate was trained in the art of oratory and persuasion. In England, the function of the agent was taken over by solicitors and attorneys; the advocate became the barrister (trial lawyer). The function of a lawyer as a jurisconsult was to provide both legal advice and to act as a writer and teacher. Although contemporary lawyers perform essentially the same functions, the modern legal profession is fundamentally different. Friedman notes: "It is organized. It is lucrative. It is closed except to those who have undergone training or apprenticeship. It holds a monopoly of courtroom work and the giving of 'legal' advice" (1977:21).

THE PROFESSIONALIZATION OF LAWYERS

Law is considered one of the three archetypical "learned" professions—the clergy and medicine are the other two (Kritzer, 1990:5). But what is a profession, and what does the process of professionalization entail? In the sociological literature, **professionalization** implies the transformation of some nonprofessional occupation into a vocation with the attributes of a profession, and the specification of these could be discussed in great detail (see, for example, Macdonald, 1995). Foote (1953:371) captures the essential ingredients: "As a modicum, the possession (1) of a specialized technique supported by a body of theory, (2) of a career supported by an association of colleagues, and (3) of a status supported by community recognition may be mentioned as constituting an occupation as a profession." Also usually included in the discussion of professions are the ideas of a client–practitioner relationship and a high degree of autonomy in the execution of one's work tasks. Wilensky (1964:143) has studied those occupations that are now viewed as professions, such as law, medicine, and the church, and notes that they have passed through the following general stages in their professionalization:

1. Became full-time occupations
2. a. Training schools established   b. University affiliation of training schools
3. a. Local professional associations started   b. National professional associations evolved
4. State licensing laws
5. Formal codes of ethics established

Larson (1977) provides additional insights into professionalization as the process by which producers of special services seek to constitute and to *control* a market for their expertise. Because marketable expertise is an important element in the structure of inequality, professionalization also appears as a collective assertion of special social status and as a collective process of upward mobility. She considers professionalization an attempt to translate one type of scarce resources—special knowledge and skills—into another—social and economic rewards. The attempt by professions to maintain scarcity implies a tendency toward monopoly: monopoly of expertise in the market and monopoly of status in a system of stratification. She contends: "Viewed in the larger perspective of the occupational and class structures, it would appear that the model of professional passes from a predominantly economic function—organizing the linkage between education and the marketplace—to a predominantly ideological one—justifying inequality of status and closure of access in the occupational order" (p. xviii). For Larson, the following elements in the professionalization process are inseparably related: differentiation and standardization of professional services; formalization of the conditions for entry; persuasion of the public that they need services only professionals can provide; and state protection (in the form of licensing) of the professional market against those who lack formal qualifications and against competing occupations. She argues that educational institutions and professional associations play a central role in attaining each of these goals.

A crucial element in the professionalization process is *market control*—the successful assertion of unchallenged authority over some area of knowledge and its professional instrumentation (Abel, 2003). Until the body of legal knowledge, including procedure, became too much for the ordinary person to handle, there was no need for a legal profession. Before the 13th century, it was possible for a litigant to appoint someone to do his or her technical pleading. This person was not a member of a separate profession, for apparently anyone could act in that capacity. The person who did the technical pleading eventually developed into, or was superseded by, the attorney who was appointed in court and had the power to bind his employer to a plea.

"The profession of advocate," writes Tigar (2000:157), "in the sense of a regulated group of (law) practitioners with some formal training, emerged in the late 1200s." Both the English and the French sovereigns legislated with respect to the profession, limiting the practice of law to those who had been approved by judicial officers. These full-time specialists in the law and in legal procedures appeared initially as officers of the king's court. The first professional lawyers were judges who trained their successors by apprenticeship. The apprentices took on functions in the courtroom and gradually came to monopolize pleading before the royal judges. In England, training moved out of the courtroom and into the Inns of Court, which were the residences of the judges and practising attorneys. The attorneys, after several reorganizations of their own ranks, finally became a group known as barristers. Members of the Inns became organized and came to monopolize training in the law as well as control of official access to the government. Signs of the professionalization of lawyers began to appear.

In England, the complexity of court procedures required technical pleading with the aid of an attorney, and oral argument eventually required special skills. By the time of Henry III (1216–72), judges had become professionals, and the courts started to create a body of substantive legal knowledge as well as technical procedure. The king needed individuals to represent his interests in the courts. In the early 14th century, he appointed sergeants of the king to take care of his legal business. When not engaged in the king's business, these fabled sergeants-at-law of the Common Pleas Court could serve individuals in the capacity of lawyers.

A crucial event in the beginning of the legal profession was an edict issued in 1292 by Edward I. During this period, legal business had increased enormously; yet there were no schools of common law, and the universities considered law too vulgar a subject for scholarly investigation. The universities were, at that time, agencies of the church, and the civil law taught there was essentially codified Roman law, the instrument of bureaucratic centralization. Edward's order, which directed Common Pleas to choose certain "attorneys and learners" who alone would be allowed to follow the court and to take part in court business, created a monopoly of the legal profession.

The effect of placing the education of lawyers into the hands of the court cannot be overestimated. It resulted in the relative isolation of English lawyers from Continental, Roman, and ecclesiastical influences. Lawyer taught lawyer, and each learned from the processes of the courts, so that the law had to grow by drawing on its own resources and not by borrowing from others. The court itself was no place for the training of these attorneys and learners. It did, however, provide aid in the form of an observation post, called "the crib," in which students could sit and take notes and from which occasionally they might ask questions during the course of a trial.

The Inns of Court provided training for lawyers. A small self-selecting group of barristers gave informal training and monopolized practice before the government courts of London, as well as judgeships in those courts. Barristers evolved into court lawyers (that is, lawyers who acted as the mouthpiece of their clients in court proceedings). Originally they were called "story-tellers" (Latin *narrators*); they told their client's story in courts, and this is their essential function to this day. The barristers' monopoly of court activities helped create a second group within the legal profession, named the "solicitors" (or "fixers"), who advised clients, prepared cases for trial, and handled matters outside the courtroom (Simpson, 1988:148). This group arose to meet the needs of clients, because barristers were too involved as officers of the court to be very responsible to outsiders. The barristers outranked solicitors, both by virtue of their monopoly of access to the court and through their control of training. Originally, solicitors were drawn from the ranks of those who attended the Inns of Court, and later they came to be trained almost entirely by apprenticeships or through schools of their own. At first, in the Inns of Court, lawyers lived together during the terms of court, and for them the Inns represented a law school, a professional organization, and a tightly knit social club, all in one.

Initially, universities such as Oxford and Cambridge saw little reason to include training such as it was practised in the Inns in their teaching programs. (Until fairly recently, law was not regarded highly as a university subject. The number of law professors was small, and their prestige was rather low, since "law school was treated as the appropriate home for rowing men of limited intellect" [Simpson, 1988:158].) Only subjects such as legal history, jurisprudence, and Roman and ecclesiastical law were considered part of a liberal education to be provided by the universities (Kearney, 1970). "Gentlemen" sought a university education, whereas legal training at the Inns of Court became the cheapest and the easiest route of social mobility for those who aspired to become gentlemen. Many sons of prosperous yeomen and merchants chose legal apprenticeship in an attempt to adopt a lifestyle associated with a gentleman. The appointment in 1758 of Sir William Blackstone to the Vinerian chair of jurisprudence at Cambridge marked the first effort to make English law a university subject. Blackstone thought it would help both would-be lawyers and educated people generally to have a "system of legal education" (as he called it), which would be far broader than the practical legal training offered in the Inns of Court. Blackstone may thus be considered the founder of the modern English system of university education in law (Berman, Greiner, and Saliba, 2004; see also Carrese, 2003).

By the end of the 18th century, law in England had become a full-fledged profession. Members of the profession considered the law a full-time occupation, training schools were established, universities began to offer degrees in law, and a professional association evolved in the form of a lawyers' guild. The practice of law required licensing, and formal codes of ethics were established. Knowledge of law and skills of legal procedures became a marketable commodity, and lawyers had a monopoly on them. The practice of law in royal courts was limited to members of the lawyers' guild, which in turn enhanced their political power, their monopoly of expertise in the market, and their monopoly of status in a system of stratification (Frank, 2010). Access to the profession became controlled, and social mobility for those admitted assured.

By the end of the 18th century, the name "attorney" had been dropped in favour of the term "solicitor," with the formation of the Society of Gentlemen Practicers in the Courts of Law and Equity, which was their professional society until 1903, when the Law Society came into being. In the following section, we shall examine the rise of the legal profession in Canada.

THE EVOLUTION OF THE CANADIAN LEGAL PROFESSION

The Canadian legal profession, like Canada more generally, reflects the influence of the "charter groups"—the English and French. Guillaume Audouart, who began practice as a "notaire public" in 1649, was the first legal professional to settle in New France. By 1663, there were 26 meagrely trained notaires practising in New France. During this early time period, *avocats* (barristers) were not allowed, for Louis XIV desired to maintain tight control over the legal and political affairs of the colony and "[t]he authorities feared that 'avocats' would not only slow down the judicial process with lengthy arguments, but that their presence would also promote additional disputes and litigation" (Thompson, 1979:18). In 1733, Louis-Guillaume Verrier, an expatriate Parisian, launched Canada's earliest structured program of legal education. This led, in 1744, to the development of a system whereby those who had obtained Verrier's certificate were licensed as "assessors" before the Sovereign Council and the lower courts of New France. The notaires enjoyed a monopoly of legal practice until after the British conquest.

Following the British conquest and the Treaty of Paris in 1763, the French judicial institutions were replaced by the English courts of King's Bench and Common Pleas. A hybrid legal system developed, with certain concessions made to traditional French practices. For example, while would-be lawyers in "proudly Protestant Britain" during this time period were required to declare, under oath, that they rejected the Catholic doctrine of transubstantiation, British governors granted Roman Catholics the right to practise law (Moore, 1997:18). As the need for trained courtroom lawyers became increasingly evident, *avocats* were authorized to appear before the Court of Common Pleas in 1765 and, in the following year, to practise in all the province's civil courts. However, it would not be until 1835 that *avocats* were permitted to represent accused persons in criminal courts.

Following the reintroduction of French civil law by the *Quebec Act* of 1774, Lieutenant Governor Henry Hamilton proclaimed the earliest operative regulation on the training of Canadian lawyers—the 1785 "Ordinance Concerning Advocates, Attorneys, Solicitors and Notaries." Until that year, a lawyer of the British colony was any person that the governor declared as such. While the granting of licence remained exclusively within the governor's discretion, the 1785 ordinance affirmed the right of any qualified English or colonial to practise in the province's courts and stipulated that those who wished to practise law in old Quebec were required to serve a minimum five years' apprenticeship (*la clericature*) and successfully pass a bar admission examination. The Ordinance additionally prohibited the double commissioning of advocates and notaries, forbidding one person to simultaneously occupy both roles. Although this forced separation of the profession led to protests to both the colonial government and to the king of England, neither were moved, "thinking perhaps that by having a single individual act in both capacities it would be easier to bring an action in court, and would encourage litigation" (Thompson, 1979:18). The Ordinance was to survive the 1791 division of old Quebec into the provinces of Upper and Lower Canada and continue to govern the profession well into the 19th century.

In 1847, the Chambre des Notaires du Québec was established to control entry into the profession of a *notaire*. Two years later, the *Communauté des Avocats*, a voluntary association of *avocats*, was transformed by a legislative enactment that created the Barreau du Québec. The 1849 *Act for the Incorporation of the Barreau of Lower Canada* granted the province-wide corporation the power to regulate admission to practise. Canada's first university faculties of law were established in 1853 at McGill and, in 1854, at Laval. Additional law schools were later established at what are now the Université de Montréal and the Université de Sherbrooke.

In Quebec, the division of the profession into two mutually exclusive branches has endured with the passage of time: "Like branches on a tree, both have a common trunk, source or base. . . . But after the basic education in the law they go their separate directions" (Thompson, 1979:18). In that province, the principal function of the *notaire* is to draft or receive acts and contracts (e.g., marriage covenants, mortgages on immoveables, trust deeds, and deeds of sale involving mortgages) that parties wish to have authenticated. *Notaires* specialize in non-litigious matters and have exclusive rights "where there is no question between the parties as to the law or the facts" (p. 19). In consequence, they often act for parties on both sides of a transaction. While both *notaires* and *avocats* may deal with a variety of non-litigious matters such as "tax, intellectual property and trade marks, and all areas of non-litigious commercial and business law" (Gill, 1988:7), the role of the *avocat*, like that of the barrister in England, focuses upon areas of contention. In Quebec, *avocats* have the exclusive right to plead cases in court that involve a conflict between the parties. Every practising *avocat* in Quebec must be a member of the Barreau.

Those pursuing a degree in law in Quebec must declare their intention to become *notaires* by December 1 in the last year of their three-year program. After graduation, those who wish to become *notaires* are required to spend an additional year in *notarial* practice at a civil law school and to pass a *notarial* examination. Those who intend to work as *avocats* must complete an eight-month *formation professionelle*, roughly similar to a bar admission course, followed by a six-month *stagiarie,* or skills-training course, and pass a bar examination.

In Upper Canada, the introduction of the 1797 *Law Society Act* appears to have stemmed from dual motives: "to provide a means for the existing bar to organize and improve itself, but also to shelter its members from being superseded by better-qualified newcomers who might find the incumbents' credentials inadequate" (Moore, 1997:31). The Act established the Law Society of Upper Canada as a self-governing body with exclusive authority over the admission of barristers and solicitors and the control of their education. Under the Act, immigrant lawyers were allowed to practise—provided that they joined the Society and agreed to conform to its rules. The Law Society was additionally empowered to assume a wide range of functions, including the establishment and maintenance of professional standards and the dispensing of discipline when those standards were breached.

As in the two other Loyalist-populated provinces, Nova Scotia and New Brunswick, the bar in Upper Canada was grounded in the English model, with a "rigid, functional division between solicitor and barrister . . . with different periods of clerkship, or articles, specified for each. Carrying over the traditional labels from the Inns of Court, the law society was to be composed of elected 'benchers' and the governing body was to be called 'convocation.'" However, because there were relatively few practitioners of the law during this early period (a few dozen at most), the English-style, divided distinction between barrister and solicitor was always a "legal fiction" and, by 1822, it had "effectively disappeared" (Buckingham et al., 1996:2).

To obtain a licence to practise law from the Law Society required five years' study as a legal apprentice. However, beginning in 1854, the apprenticeship period was shortened for those who earned the University of Toronto's Bachelor of Civil Law degree. The Law Society would later create, in 1862, its own law school, Osgoode Hall, named after the first chief justice of Upper Canada, William Osgoode (1754–1824).

In Upper Canada, legal education would remain "exclusively or principally the prerogative of the Law Society of Upper Canada for almost two centuries" (Baker, 1983:49). In 1889, the Law Society adopted a recommendation that reaffirmed its control over education and asserted that this function would not be shared with the province's universities. It was not until 1957 that the Law Society of Upper Canada would relinquish its statutory monopoly over legal education and grant recognition to other Ontario schools.

In the first half-century of its existence, the Law Society of Upper Canada declared itself open to applicants of little wealth and little or no social prominence. During this early period, the parents of entrants included blacksmiths, farmers, stonemasons, and labourers, along with lawyers and other professionals. In consequence, "the construction of Upper Canada's legal elite was neither an exclusively English, metropolitan, nor family enterprise" (Baker, 1983:56). As long as applicants could pass the entrance exams, exist for several years on a fairly meagre income, and find a lawyer who was willing to accept them as an articling student, they could aspire to the gentlemanly status that the profession offered. However, legal education for most law students remained anchored in apprenticeship, and finding articles often made it difficult, if not impossible, for cultural and racial minorities to gain entrance into the profession. While the Act of 1797 had authorized each legal practitioner to have one student, the vast majority of Ontario's 19th-century lawyers were

English, Scottish, Irish, and Protestant, and "they tended to take in students of their own class and kind" (Moore, 1997:176). While the first black Ontarian, Robert Sutherland, was called to the bar in 1855, the second black lawyer to practise in Ontario, Delos Rogest Davis, was forced to petition the Ontario legislature declaring that, as a result of prejudice and bigotry, he had been unable to locate a single lawyer, over a period of 11 years, who was willing to accept him as an articling student. As the result of his petition, Davis was allowed to sign the solicitors' roll—without serving articles in the usual fashion—after passing the Law Society's exams in 1885 and paying his fees. (Davis's son, who articled with his father and later entered into partnership with him, became Ontario's third black lawyer when he was called to the bar in 1900. It would not be until 1926, however, that another black Ontarian would become a lawyer.)

Over time, entrance into the legal profession in Ontario became progressively more exclusionary: "As it began to promulgate rules for entry, the Law Society wanted to identify gentlemen far more than to test for any specific legal skill or aptitude" (Moore, 1997:43). As Archdeacon John Strachan emphasized in an 1826 letter written to Lieutenant-Governor Sir Peregrine Maitland, "Lawyers must, from the very nature of our political institutions—from there being no great landed proprietors—no privileged orders—become the most powerful profession, and must in time possess more influence and authority than any other. They are emphatically our men of business, and will gradually engross all the colonial offices of profit and honour" (cited in Baker, 1983:55).

Toward this end, the practice of admitting talented but impoverished students was increasingly criticized as misguided. Admission standards were raised and, increasingly, an unlevel playing field was created. The benchers had demanded "proofs of a liberal" education and begun to test would-be students for their competence in Latin and English as early as 1820; the test was stiffened in 1825 and, "by the 1830s, the entrance exam covered Latin and English composition, history, geography, and the elements of Euclid. . . [M]astery of such a curriculum indicated that one had a disciplined mind, a certain breath of culture, and *the time and means for thought and study*" (Moore, 1997:89, emphasis added). Intermarriage among families already ensconced in the legal elite became more common during the second half of the 19th century and successful applicants to Ontario's legal fraternity were increasingly likely to bear the surnames of earlier Society members: "[T]he caste was beginning to close ranks and . . . the occupational status of lawyers was becoming hereditary" (Baker, 1983:56). Porter (1965) emphasized the linkages between legal professionals, elite economic interests, and the Canadian political system in his now-classic analysis of the structure of the Canadian economic elite.

Eastern Canada was influenced by the American example: "In the maritime provinces of Nova Scotia and New Brunswick, the bar, such as it was at the end of the 18th century, tended to follow the professional practices of the lawyers in American states, from whose ranks these Loyalist lawyers came" (Buckingham et al., 1996:3). Gaining admission to the bar entailed articling for a period of three to five years and then convincing a Superior Court justice of one's competence. Professional organizations such as the Nova Scotia Law Society and the Law Society of New Brunswick, both incorporated in 1825, "were loosely structured gentlemen's clubs brought together for mutually advantageous projects, such as accumulating a library for the use of the local bench and bar" (Buckingham et al., 1996:3). However, in contrast to the experience in Upper Canada, the task of educating lawyers in the Maritime provinces was quickly transferred to the universities. Dalhousie University founded its law school and a full-time, three-year course in 1883 and became the first law school to teach common law in the British Empire. The Saint John Law School (which was to become the University of New Brunswick Faculty of Law) later followed.

From its inception, Dalhousie Law School had links to Harvard Law School. It is therefore not surprising that the teaching method adopted reflected the "case method" model developed by Harvard Law Dean Christopher Columbus Langdell. Instead of using the older system of text reading and lectures, the instructor carried on a discussion of assigned cases designed to bring out their general principles. Langdell believed that law was a general science and that its principles could be experimentally induced from the examination of case materials. He rejected the use of textbooks and instead used casebooks as teaching materials; these were collections of reports of actual cases, carefully selected and arranged to illustrate the meaning and development of principles of law. The teacher became a Socratic guide, leading the student to an understanding of concepts and principles hidden as essences among the cases. While common-law schools in Canada typically adopted teaching methods based on the case method model, this method of teaching has been increasingly challenged (Olivo, 2004:147; Bryden, 2014; Pue and Sugarman, 2003; Pue, 2016).

Beginning in the colony of New Caledonia (renamed British Columbia in 1858), practising lawyers (primarily English-trained) in western colonies approaching provincial status began to lobby for formal recognition of their professional status and for the creation of standards regulating training and admission to the profession. The *Legal Professions Act* of 1863 gave formal recognition to the professions of barrister and solicitor and "gave the Supreme Court the power to examine and admit new members, and administer discipline to existing members" (Buckingham et al., 1996:3). Following the 1866 union of Victoria and British Columbia and the granting of provincial status upon that territory, the expanding bar demanded and was granted increasing professional autonomy: "In 1874 the Law Society of British Columbia was incorporated under the *Legal Professions Act* and benchers were ceded full authority over legal training, admission, and discipline. The self-governing status of the law society was made permanent in 1895, by which time the society had put into place a course of mandatory lectures in its Vancouver Law School" (p. 3). It was not until the 1930s that the responsibility for education would be transferred to provincial universities.

In 1877, the Law Society of Manitoba was incorporated by provincial law and, over time, achieved the power to control entry into the profession, specify education, and dispense discipline. By the time Alberta and Saskatchewan attained provincial status in 1905, there were substantial numbers of legal practitioners living in the major centres of these provinces, and legislation that created law societies was quickly passed. Fledging law schools in these provinces represented the joint efforts of the bar and the universities.

The increased emphasis on professionalization and monopoly of the practice of law brought about concerted efforts to improve the quality of legal education, to raise admission standards, and to intensify the power of bar associations. By the 1920s and 1930s, the legal profession in Canada, when compared to its counterpart in the United States, revealed four distinctive features:

> First, admission to the profession was far more difficult, demanding, time-consuming and expensive in Canada. In the United States a considerably more casual, laissez-faire approach obtained; the only entrance requirement for the Indiana bar, for example, was "good moral character," and only a few states had mandatory exams or prescribed periods of study of clerkship. . . .

> Second, admission to the bar in Canada was controlled (except, anomalously, in Manitoba) exclusively by the law society of the province. This was the practice in Great Britain as well, but the common practice in the United States put control of admission fully into the hands of the bench. . . .

> [Third], the law societies in Canada acquired piecemeal, or simply assumed, far more powers of self-governance and control over the profession than equivalent associations in the United States. . .

> [Fourth], [t]he autonomy of the Canadian legal profession created a smaller, more highly trained, more cohesive, and, as a result, more elitist profession than that in the United States.
>
> (Buckingham et al., 1996:2–4)

However, some similarities between the two systems can be noted. For example, in both countries, white males have historically dominated the profession. Women, particularly married women, were not considered suitable for the practice of law. They were seen as delicate creatures, equated with children and lunatics, and lacked full legal rights. It was argued that allowing women to practise law would derail the traditional order of the family. In the notorious opinion of a justice of the U.S. Supreme Court in 1873, "the natural and proper timidity and delicacy which belongs to the female sex evidently unfits it for many of the occupations of civil life. . . . The paramount destiny and mission of women are to fulfill the noble and benign offices of wife and mother. This is the law of the Creator" (Stevens, 1983:82). When Mabel Penery French petitioned to be admitted to the legal profession in New Brunswick in 1905 after completing all the necessary training, the Canadian judge approvingly quoted from the decision in this earlier case and ruled that it was not possible for women to be lawyers. Echoing this viewpoint, when Anne Macdonald Langstaff applied to become a lawyer in Quebec in 1915 after graduating from McGill University, Judge Saint-Pierre ruled that "to admit a woman and more particularly a married woman as a barrister, that is to say, as a person who pleads cases at the bar before judges or juries in open court, and in the presence of the public, would be nothing short of a direct infringement upon public order and a manifest violation of the law of good morals and public decency" (in cited in Mossman, 1994:214). Assuredly, this situation was not unique to Canada and the United States. In exploring the struggles European women faced in attempting to gain access to the legal profession, Albisetti (2000:825) argues that access to law "universally trailed access to medicine not because of issues related to the study or practice of law, but because the arguments put forward to justify admission to the bar appeared to many opponents to lead directly to women's suffrage and equality in other areas."

When Clara Brett Martin was admitted to practise law by the Law Society of Upper Canada in 1897, she became the first woman lawyer in the British Empire. A trailblazer, Martin confronted hostility at each step of her professional path. In 1891, when she had first applied to the Law Society of Upper Canada for admission as a student, she had been refused; it was only with the support of such influential persons as Premier Sir Oliver Mowat and Dr. Emily Stowe and the passage of a provincial act that admitted women as solicitors that she was finally admitted in 1893 (Backhouse, 1991). Between 1898 and 1923, the overwhelming majority of European countries also allowed women to become lawyers. However, it was not until 1941 that Quebec granted women the right to be admitted to the practice of law, with access delayed even longer to women of racialized minorities. In 1946, Greta Wong Grant became Canada's first Chinese-Canadian lawyer. In 1979, Delia Opekokew became the first Native woman to be admitted to the bar in Saskatchewan and also, four years later, the first Native woman to be admitted to the bar in Ontario. In 1984, when Marva Jemmott was appointed as a Queen's Counsel, she became the first black woman in Canada to receive this honour. The first woman president of the Canadian Bar Association (CBA), Paule Gauthier, was appointed in 1997 (Dawson and Quaile, 1998:119). As late as 1971, women accounted for only a very small proportion of the legal profession (5 percent). However, the proportion of women who are law students at Canadian universities has grown rapidly in recent decades, from 6 percent in 1965 to 11 percent in 1969, 20 percent in 1973, 30 percent in 1976, and about 42 percent in 1986 (Mazer, 1989). By the early 1990s, women accounted for approximately half of Canada's law school students (Canadian Bar Association, 1993:9), with this development continuing in the new millennium (Law Society of Upper Canada, 2006; Hatfield, 2014). Thus, women and men are entering and graduating from Canadian law schools at roughly equal rates, with the Law Society of Upper Canada reporting that women accounted for over half of law school graduates during the 2000s. In addition, Macaulay (2014a) reports that in many areas of the country, women account for at least half of Canada's newest lawyers (i.e., those who had practiced for five years or less) (e.g., Manitoba [52.4%], Saskatchewan [50.4%], Ontario [52.3%], British Columbia [51.2%]).

The profession in both Canada and the United States also historically discriminated against ethnic and racial minorities. This was particularly overt in the United States, where the legal profession explicitly discriminated against blacks and where blacks were excluded from the American Bar Association and many law schools until the 1950s (Abel, 1986; Smith, 2000). As recently as 1965, African-Americans made up 11 percent of the U.S. population but less than 2 percent of lawyers and only 1.3 percent of law students, half of them in all-black law schools. Even in 1977, only 5 percent of the country's law students were African American (Friedman, 2002). Although in 2013–14, African Americans comprised about 9.3% of law school students, this figure is still lower than their percentage of the U.S. population (approximately 13 percent) (American Bar Association, 2017).

During recent decades, Canadian lawyers have become a more diverse group; the proportion of lawyers born in Canada has decreased slightly while "the proportion of different ethnicities, genders, nationalities, and religious affiliations has changed significantly" (Hutchinson, 1999:36). For example, while about 55 percent of lawyers were of British ethnicity in 1961, this decreased to just over 50 percent in 1971 and to about

44 percent in 1981. Nevertheless, in the early 1990s, fewer than 3 percent of lawyers were members of a visible minority and fewer than 1 percent were Native Canadians (Henry et al, 2000:150).

In 1994, the Canadian Bar Association adopted a recommendation to conduct a full inquiry into racial equality in the legal profession. The results of this inquiry into the position of racialized groups within the Canadian legal community were reported in 1999 and resulted in Resolution 99–04-A-Revised, *Racial Equality in the Legal Profession.* Among its recommendations, it encouraged law schools to review their admission criteria for possible systemic barriers; create an internal results-based monitoring process to ensure that Aboriginal students and students from racialized communities were fairly treated in admission decisions; diversify perspectives of admission committees by including third-year students from equality-seeking communities; ensure student exposure to human rights principles and ethics, critical race theory, and Aboriginal law; develop a strategic hiring plan to diversify the faculty at all levels; and develop bursaries and scholarships to increase and encourage representation of students from racialized communities at the undergraduate and graduate levels. It additionally urged the federal Department of Justice to conduct a feasibility study to design and establish an Aboriginal law school (Canadian Bar Association, 1999).

Although the 2005 Report of the Canadian Bar Association's Futures Committee (Canadian Bar Association, 2005:16) observed that "[r]ace data for the Canadian legal profession are sketchy and even misleading, particularly since most depend on self-identification," it acknowledged that visible minorities were under-represented, relative to their proportion of the population, in the legal profession. While the 2001 Census found that 13.4 percent of the Canadian population were members of a visible minority, only 6.8 percent of Canadian lawyers identified themselves as such—a situation that compared unfavourably with many other professions. For example, in 2001, more than one-fifth (21.3 percent) of Canadian dentists and 17.5 percent of specialized physicians self-identified as members of a visible minority group. It is also evident that, despite "important inroads across various fields of law and across different practice settings, including law firms of all sizes, . . . people of racialized communities are under-represented relative to their numbers in the Canadian population" (Kay, Masuch, and Curry, 2004).

In 2006, the Ornstein Report on the "Racialization and Gender of Lawyers in Ontario" reported that visible minorities accounted for 23 percent of Ontario's population but merely 11.5 percent of its lawyers. Within that province, "the progress of visible minority lawyers can be seen in the dramatic increase in the percentage of lawyers between the ages of 25 and 34 who are members of a visible minority: 2 percent in 1981, 3 percent in 1986, 6 percent in 1991, 11 percent in 1996, 17 percent in 2001 and 2006" (Orenstein, 2010:i) and 27.5 percent in 2013 (Law Society of Upper Canada, 2013). However, a statistical snapshot of lawyers in Ontario taken by the Law Society of Upper Canada (2013) revealed that while, in general, the "proportion of racialized lawyers has increased, this has not been true of Black and Aboriginal lawyers." Rather, "the similarity in the proportion of Aboriginal lawyers in the 25–34, 35–44 and 45–54 age groups, and of Black lawyers under 35, and in the 35–44 and 45–54 age groups suggests that their proportion entering the profession is not increasing." Moreover, it noted that Aboriginal peoples (First Nations, Inuk, and Metis) accounted for a scant 1.2 percent of those called to the bar in Ontario in 2013.

In the past, law firms in both Canada and the United States were about as exclusionary as law schools. Many excluded Jews, Catholics, visible minorities, Aboriginal peoples, and women. Through the 1950s, most firms were solidly and resolutely WASP (White Anglo-Saxon Protestant) (Stevens, 1983:100). Since then, discriminatory practices have decreased but, unfortunately, have not fully disappeared (Babcock, 2016; Hirshman, 2016; Smith, 2008; Madon, 2016; Law Society of British Columbia, 2012; Dinovitzer, 2015). For example, Hutchinson (1999:35) observes that "[w]hile the profession has diversified, the typical lawyer remains male, white, English-speaking, early middle-aged, and Christian; lawyers who deviate from this norm are greater in number, but still less powerful in prestige and influence." An update of the Ornstein Report (Ornstein, 2010:35) found that "racialized lawyers tend to occupy less favourable niches in the profession"; when "[c]ompared to Whites, racialized lawyers are more likely to be law firm associates and employees, to work for government or outside of law offices and governments, and to be self-employed without paid help. They are *less* likely to be partners in a law firm or sole practitioners with paid help" (emphasis in original). It also found that "[w]omen and especially visible minority lawyers earn less than their White male counterparts" and "strong evidence that racialized lawyers have lower earnings than White lawyers the same age and this difference is much larger than the gender difference. The difference in the median earnings of racialized and White lawyers, just $4,000 per year for lawyers between 25 and 29, grows to more than $40,000 by ages 40 to 44. The difference in mean earnings is even larger" (Orenstein, 2010: ii).

The 2013 report of the Law Society of Upper Canada echoed these findings: "Aboriginal and racialized lawyers, compared to White lawyers, are more likely to be in sole practice or in a legal clinic and less likely to be law firm partners"; it additionally reported that in comparison to White lawyers, Aboriginal lawyers are more likely to work in government. In relation to the location of their employment within Ontario, it detailed that Aboriginal lawyers are less likely to work in Toronto and much more likely to work in the Central North, Northern Ontario, Eastern Ontario, and Ottawa. In Ontario, "[r]acialized lawyers are concentrated in Toronto, except for the high representation of Arab lawyers in Ottawa and South Asian lawyers in the combination of Durham, Halton, Peel and York" (Law Society of Upper Canada, 2013). According to this report, LGBTQ lawyers are also "less likely to be sole practitioners and law firm partners" and "about three times more likely to be in education, to work in a legal clinic and to work for government"; they are also largely concentrated in Toronto and Ottawa.

A study conducted by the Canadian Centre for Diversity and Inclusion in partnership with the Canadian Bar Association (CDI 2016a) reported that women are under-represented in equity partner and senior leader roles and over-represented as associates and articling or summer students; racialized lawyers are under-represented in equity partner, income partner, and senior leader roles and over-represented as associates and articling or summer students. Its examination of the intersectional experience of gender and race together also concluded that race "is more strongly associated with becoming an equity partner than gender" and that, regardless of gender, Caucasian lawyers enjoy a higher likelihood of being an equity partner than racialized lawyers. According to this research, a Caucasian male lawyer is seven times more likely than a racialized female lawyer to be an equity partner (CDI, 2016a:10; see also Hagan and Kay, 2007; Cooper, Brockman, and Hoffart, 2004; Canadian Bar Association, 2005). In addition, there are complaints about alleged disparate treatment of male and female lawyers in court in demeanour and language (Oliver, 2015). Minority female lawyers report that they lack support by white female and minority male lawyers, face both race and sex discrimination, and have difficulties establishing networks (Jackson, 2016; Raiswell, 2014; Garcia-Lopez, 2008; Quade, 1995; Segura and Zavella, 2008). Various studies have concluded that the current business structure of Canadian law firms creates a culture that adversely impacts women and racialized lawyers (Smith, 2008; Madon, 2016; Law Society of British Columbia, 2009, 2012). According to the Canadian Centre for Diversity and Inclusion (2016b:14–15), for example, a diverse and inclusive workplace environment is forestalled by "[t]he process of billable hours, the emphasis placed on client relationships, and the hierarchal 'old boys club' network in law firms." In addition, it reports that "[w]omen lawyers find it difficult to balance work with family life, particularly if they choose to take maternity leave or take on a financial penalty when it is not offered" (p. 16; see also Correll, Benard, and Paik, 2007). A study by the Criminal Lawyers Association (Madon, 2016) examined why Canadian women lawyers are quitting the practice of criminal law at a "significantly higher rate" than their male counterparts and found that the reasons included "low pay, lack of financial support for maternity leave and being treated differently than male peers by judges and court staff" (Broshnahan, 2016).

THE PROFESSION TODAY

As noted in Chapter 3, law has become one of the fastest-growing of all professions in Canada. However, while lawyers are often presumed to be richly rewarded for their work and to enjoy enviable work conditions, these assumptions may be more apparent than real. The Canadian Bar Association (2006:17) reports that "[m]any first- and second-year lawyers are frustrated with being 'out of the loop' for stimulating work, instead finding themselves relegated to a form of 'hazing' (long hours, high volumes of routine work, relatively low pay)." Key stressors identified included excessive demands on their time, heavy workloads, and diminished opportunities for a personal life. These feelings of dissatisfaction were also common among more experienced lawyers: "even among lawyers with seven to eight years of practice, almost 70 percent are still thinking of leaving the profession."

Writing at the cusp of the new millennium, Hutchinson (1999:35) observed that the legal profession in Canada "is differentiated into megafirms, smaller partnerships, and single practitioners, not to mention government lawyers and the like; there is little shared experience, little interaction among them, and each operates in line with different cultures and norms." Nevertheless, for the sake of analytic simplicity, we can identify four principal subgroups within the legal profession: lawyers in private practice, lawyers in government service, lawyers in private employment, and the judiciary.

WHERE THE LAWYERS ARE

Each year, growing numbers of young adults graduate from law school, pass the bar, and enter an increasingly competitive marketplace. Some go into private practice; some find jobs in government, private industry, and the teaching professions; and others decide not to stay in law.

According to the 2014 Statistical Report of the Federation of Law Societies of Canada, the majority of lawyers in every Canadian province and territory were either sole practitioners or practised in small firms composed of ten lawyers or fewer (Federation of Law Societies of Canada, 2015). For example, almost half (47.2 percent) of British Columbia's lawyers were solo practitioners (35.9 percent) or worked in firms with two to ten lawyers (11.2 percent). Although almost 70 percent of lawyers (69.98 percent) in Ontario were solo practitioners, the identification of a lawyer as a "sole practitioner" in that province "is determined solely by a lawyer's status and does not take into account the size of the law firm at which s/he works" (Federation of Law Societies of Canada, 2015). In Nova Scotia, 29.7 percent of lawyers were solo practitioners, while 12.8 percent worked in firms with two to ten lawyers (37.2 percent of female lawyers and 39.0 percent of male lawyers). The percentage of lawyers who worked in very large firms in that year were relatively small (approximately 15 percent), with firms that were composed of 51 or more lawyers most common in Ontario (with 37 firms of this size in 2014), followed by British Columbia (15), Alberta (15), and Manitoba (6) (Federation of Law Societies of Canada, 2015).

PRIVATE PRACTICE

The majority of lawyers in Canada are in private practice. Contrary to the popular image that is reinforced by television (Rapping, 2004), only a small proportion of lawyers engage in litigation. In private practice, lawyers perform a number of significant roles. One is *counselling*. Lawyers spend about one-third of their time advising their clients about the proper course of action in anticipation of the reactions of courts, agencies, or third parties. Another is *negotiating*, both in criminal and in civil cases. Plea bargaining is an example of negotiation and is widely used in criminal cases (Palermo et al., 1998). Pretrial hearings and conferences in the attempt to reach a settlement and avoid a costly trial are illustrative of the negotiating role of lawyers in civil cases. *Drafting*, the writing and revision of legal documents such as contracts, wills, deeds, and leases, is the "most legal" of a lawyer's roles, although the availability of standardized forms for many kinds of legal problems often limits the lawyer to filling in the blanks. *Litigating* is a specialty, and relatively few lawyers engage in actual trial work. Much of the litigation in Canada is generally uncontested in cases such as debt, divorce, civil commitment, and criminal charges. Some lawyers also engage in *investigating*. In a criminal case, for example, the defence lawyer may search for the facts and gather background information in support of the client's plea. Finally, lawyers take part in *researching*—searching, for example, for precedents, adapting legal doctrine to specific cases, and anticipating court or agency rulings in particular situations. Much of this research activity is carried out by lawyers in large firms and appellate specialists. Experienced lawyers working in their specialty (or those working for a small fee) usually do little research.

Solo practitioners and big law firms represent the two extremes in private practice. In between, there are partnerships and small law firms of relatively modest size. Solo practitioners are generalists, and they operate in small offices (Jacob, 1995). Many of these lawyers engage in marginal areas of law, such as collections, personal injury cases, rent cases, and evictions. They face competition from other professionals, such as accountants and real estate brokers, who are increasingly handling the tax and real estate work traditionally carried out by the solo practitioner. Carlin's (1962:209) classic work emphasized how the pressures to make a living could force individual practitioners to submit to pressures to violate legal ethics; a later study (Gunning et al., 2009) suggests that this, indeed, is the case. Lawyers in solo practice often act, he found, as intermediaries between clients and other lawyers to receive referral fees. In such an instance, the individual practitioner could become a businessperson rather than a lawyer, often defeating his or her original purpose in becoming a professional. Carlin (p. 206) observed that the individual lawyer was "rarely called upon to exercise a high level of professional skill" due, in large measure, "to the character of the demands placed upon him [sic] by the kinds of work and clients he [sic] is likely to encounter."

Carlin notes that these lawyers attempt to justify their low status in the profession by emphasizing their independence and pointing out that they are general practitioners and thus knowledgeable about all facets of the law. This notion of autonomy, however, does not compensate for their feeling of insignificance in the overall legal structure and their frustration over not realizing their initial high ambitions, although they are professionals. Carlin (p. 206) suggests that these individual practitioners, like their counterparts in general practice in medicine, are "most likely to be found at the margin of (their) profession, enjoying little freedom in choice of clients, type of work, or conditions of practice."

There are also differences between individual and firm practitioners in acceptance of and compliance with ethical norms. Carlin (1966) found that the individual practitioner was the most likely to violate ethical norms (for example, soliciting kickbacks), with the nature of the client and the type of case being important contributing factors in the violations. Since solo practitioners often represent individuals, as contrasted with corporations that are represented by larger firms, the quality of the lawyers involved adversely affects the legal representation that many individuals receive. Because these lawyers are often from minority groups, minority clients are the ones who are adversely affected. Moreover, many of the larger, more prestigious, and more ethical firms will not accept the kinds of cases the individual practitioner confronts, and in fact refer those cases to him or her, so that the organization of the bar is such that ethical violations and ineffective practice are almost built into certain situations (see also Carle, 2005; Gumming, Holm, and Kenway, 2009; Rhode and Luban, 2005).

Practising in large law firms is very different from solo practice. These firms employ legions of supporting staff, including paralegals, business-trained administrators, librarians, and technicians (*Lawyer's Almanac*, 2017). As noted earlier, many of these large firms are becoming national and international in scope. These firms shy away from less profitable business—individual legal problems such as wills and divorces—in favour of corporate clients who often have a global presence (Peel, 2006). Unlike solo practitioners, firms maintain long-term relationships with their clients, and many firms are on retainers by large corporations. Large firms offer a variety of specialized services, with departments specializing in a number of fields such as tax law, mergers, antitrust suits, and certain types of government regulations. These firms deal generally with repeat players and provide the best possible information and legal remedies to their clients, along with creative and innovative solutions for their clients' problems (Jacob, 1995).

Large firms have a pronounced hierarchical organization structure (Hagan, Huxter, and Parker, 1988). Young lawyers are hired as associates. Beginning associates are seen as having limited skills, in spite of their elite education, and are assigned the task of preparing briefs and engaging in legal research under the supervision of a partner or a senior associate. In seven or eight years, they either become junior partners or leave the firm. For a new associate who has a strong desire to move into a partnership position, the competition with cohorts is very strong.

Associates are on a fixed salary, whereas partners' incomes are based on profits. In most firms, law partners earn profits largely on hourly billings of associates: the more associates per partner, the higher the profits. How profits are divided among partners is usually decided by a small committee that looks at such factors as work brought in, hours billed, and seniority. The traditional rule is that associates should produce billings of about three times that of their salaries—a third goes to the associate, a third to overhead, and a third to the firm's profit. At most firms, lawyers' time is billed in 6-minute or 15-minute units, with each nonbusiness conversation, personal phone call, and vacation day cutting into billable hours. No wonder many associates are labelled "workaholics" and spend evenings and weekends in their offices.

Heinz and Laumann (1994) note that much of the "differentiation within the legal profession is secondary to one fundamental distinction—the distinction between lawyers who represent large organizations (corporations, labour unions, or government) and those who represent individuals. The two kinds of law practice are the two hemispheres of the profession." Most lawyers, they add, "reside exclusively in one hemisphere or the other and seldom, if ever, cross the equator" (p. 319). The two sectors of the profession are separated by the social origins of lawyers, the schools where they were trained, the types of clients they serve, office environment, frequency and type of litigation, values, and different circles of acquaintance; the two sectors "rest their claims to professionalism on different sorts of social power" (p. 384). Large cities, Heinz and Laumann conclude, have two legal professions—one that is recruited from more privileged social origins where lawyers serve wealthy and powerful corporate clients, and the other from less prestigious backgrounds where lawyers serve individuals and small businesses. Thus, "the hierarchy of lawyers suggests a corresponding stratification of law into two systems of justice, separate and unequal" (p. 385).

GOVERNMENT

Gill observes that "[m]any lawyers are employed in government service at both the provincial and federal levels, acting as government advisors, conducting legal research, drafting legislation and serving as counsel in litigation matters involving the government" (1990:189). Spector (1972) suggests that taking positions in government agencies may be a strategy used by young lawyers for upward professional mobility. He considers employment with the government a mobility route into a more prestigious practice for the young lawyer handicapped by mediocre education or stigmatized by sex, religion, or ethnic background. It is therefore notable that a study of 100 lawyers called to the bar in British Columbia found that women are more likely to practise as government lawyers than men (Brockman, 2001).

Spector maintains that by pursuing a short-term career in a government agency, the young lawyer not able to initially break into "big league" firms gains valuable trial experience, specialized knowledge of regulatory law, and government contacts that eventually might be parlayed into a move to elite firms. Many of those entering public service are recent law school graduates who find government salaries sufficiently attractive at this stage of their careers, and seek the training that such service may offer as a prelude to private practice. Limitations on top salaries discourage some from continuing with the government, although in recent years, public service has become more attractive as a career.

The majority of lawyers serve by appointment in legal departments of a variety of federal and provincial agencies. Those who find legal research stimulating may pursue employment with either the federal or provincial law reform commissions, which conduct research into various areas of law. Various governmental departments and regulatory agencies employ lawyers. Still others are engaged as Crown attorneys, agents of either the Attorney General of Canada or the attorneys general for the provinces and territories, who respectively serve as the chief legal officers for Canada's federal, provincial, and territorial governments. Included among the most important responsibilities of Crown attorneys are preparing and conducting criminal prosecutions. The Public Prosecution Service of Canada (PPSC), which "was created on December 12, 2006, when the *Director of Public Prosecutions Act*, Part 3 of the *Federal Accountability Act*, came into force," includes 500 prosecutors among its approximately 900 full-time employees and retains over 810 private-sector lawyers as agents across Canada (Public Prosecution Service of Canada, 2016). "The PPSC is responsible for prosecuting offences under more than 40 federal statutes and for providing prosecution-related legal advice to law enforcement agencies"; among the cases it prosecutes are "those involving drugs, organized crime, terrorism, tax law, money laundering and proceeds of crime, crimes against humanity and war crimes, Criminal Code offences in the territories, and a large number of federal regulatory offences" (Public Prosecution Service of Canada, 2016). As a rule, lawyers in government are directly engaged in legal work, since law training is infrequently sought as preparation for general government service. However, a small but important minority, which is considered an exception to this rule, consists of those who have been appointed to high executive positions and those who have been elected to political office.

PRIVATE EMPLOYMENT

Lawyers are also engaged in private employment. These lawyers (often referred to as house counsels) are salaried employees of private business concerns, usually industrial corporations, insurance companies, and banks. Large corporations typically have huge legal departments with almost 500 lawyers (*Lawyer's Almanac*, 2017).

The growth of corporations, the complexity of business, and the multitude of problems posed by government regulation make it desirable, if not imperative, for some firms to have lawyers and legal departments familiar with the particular problems and conditions of the firm. In view of the increased complexity of business transactions and the growth of federal regulations, the proportion of the profession engaged in this kind of activity can be expected to increase in coming years. In addition to legal work, lawyers often serve as officers of the company and may serve on important policymaking committees, perhaps even on the board of directors. Although lawyers in legal departments are members of the bar and are entitled to appear in court, their lack of trial experience means that a firm will usually hire an outside lawyer for litigation and for court appearances. Lawyers in legal departments of business firms do not tend to move to other branches of legal work after a number of years. Many of these lawyers have been in private practice or in government service. There is some horizontal mobility between government work and private employment, but not to the same extent as between government and law firms.

JUDICIARY

A very small proportion of lawyers are members of the judiciary. The *Constitution Act, 1867* and the federal *Judges Act* govern the appointment, removal, retirement, and remuneration of federally appointed judges. The federal government appoints judges of the Supreme Court of Canada and Federal Court through the Office of the Commissioner for Federal Judicial Affairs. Under section 96 of the *Constitution Act, 1867* the federal government also appoints judges to some provincial courts: "Sometimes referred to as 'section 96 judges,' they sit in the provincial Supreme Court or Court of Appeal or in equivalent courts such as the Court of Queen's Bench, the Superior Court (in Quebec) or the General Division of the Courts of Justice (in Ontario)" (Gill, 1999:1225).

In Canada, federally appointed judges must be lawyers who have been members of a provincial bar for a minimum of ten years. According to Boyd (1998:186), Canada's federally appointed judiciary continues to be drawn "almost exclusively from the ranks of men and women who support the Conservative and Liberal parties." As well, while "efforts are being made to address the failure of the judiciary to reflect Canada's diversity," there continues to be an "overrepresentation of elderly, white Anglo males" in Canada's judiciary (Griffiths and Cunningham, 2003:174). A multi-year study by Ryerson University's Diversity Institute found that in 2012, women accounted for simply a third of federal judges (and almost a third [32 per cent] of their provincial counterparts). It also noted that visible minorities were "grossly underrepresented in Canada's judiciary, especially among federal court judges" and that "[p]eople of colour made up only 2.3 per cent of the 221 federal judges" (Keung, 2012). Its 2016 findings revealed that "while some progress has been made with female representation in the Canadian Judiciary, visible minorities and Aboriginal peoples remain under-represented particularly in Federal court appointments. Provincially appointed judges are far more representative" (Diversity Institute, 2016). Provincial appointments in most provinces occur after the applicant has been considered by a judicial advisory committee that is composed of representatives of the legal profession, the judiciary, and the public. While in some provinces prospective judges must be lawyers who have been members of the bar for five years, eligibility rules vary across the country. However, while "many so-called police magistrates are retired members of national or local police forces . . . even in provinces where judges need not be lawyers, only lawyers are now appointed" (Gill, 1999:1225). Provincial court judges who hear less serious criminal matters and civil cases involving relatively small amounts of money, are appointed and paid by the province in which they serve.

The Supreme Court of Canada, which is Canada's highest court of law, is composed of a Chief Justice and eight puisne judges. Three of the judges must be appointed from Quebec and, by convention rather than legal requirement, three judges have generally been appointed from Ontario, two from the Western provinces and one from Atlantic Canada. While law societies, legal experts, and the federal justices are typically consulted prior to a Prime Minister's appointment of a judge from a short list of qualified candidates, in comparison to their American counterparts, Canadian Supreme Court judges have traditionally been subject to far lesser degrees of public scrutiny. However, in recent years, some additional levels have been added to the appointment process.

In August 2004, the then-Liberal government added an ad hoc Committee of the House of Commons. This committee, along with a representative from the Canadian Bar Association and Canadian Judicial Council, were afforded the opportunity to question the Justice Minister about the prime minister's appointment (the proceedings were broadcast live on the Canadian Parliamentary Affairs Channel [CPAC]). With the defeat of the Liberal government, Prime Minister Harper announced further refinements to the process, maintaining that the process introduced by the Liberals "was not sufficiently open" (CBC News, 2006a). In February 2006, Harper announced that the next person he nominated to the Supreme Court would be required to appear at a televised hearing before a committee composed of 12 members of Parliament, selected from each of the four parties represented in the House of Commons in a way that ensured no party held a minority. However, he also stated that the committee would not have the power to either confirm or quash the nomination of the prospective judge, and that he would reserve that right for himself as prime minister. While the interview phase was first used in 2006, with Justice Marshall Rothstein the first justice to experience this processual stage, this phase was bypassed in 2008 when the next justice (Justice Crowell) was appointed by Prime Minister Harper; Prime Minister Harper identified "the urgency of filling the eight-month vacancy on the Supreme Court as the reason for skipping the public process" (Tibbetts, 2008). Although both of the Supreme Court justices appointed in 2011 (Justice Karakatsanis and Justice Moldaver) appeared before a multi-party committee, the committee lacked any authority to approve or deny either's appointment (MacCharles, 2011).

Supreme Court judges are appointed and paid by the federal government and may continue to hold office until they reach the age of 75. (While federally appointed judges serving on the Federal Court or a provincial superior court are also able to hold office until their mandatory retirement at age 75, provincially appointed judges are generally required to retire at age 70.) As of March 2017, there were three women among the

Supreme Court Justices of Canada. The average age of Supreme Court judges in that year was 62.3, with the youngest judge 51 years of age (the Hon. Russell Brown) and the oldest, 73 (the Rt. Hon. Madam Justice Beverley McLachlin, the first woman to be appointed Chief Justice of the Supreme Court of Canada).

Supreme Court judges earn the highest salaries among judges in Canada. As of April 1, 2015, the annual salary of Supreme Court judges was $367,300, with the base salary of the Chief Justice $396,700 (Government of Canada, 2015). In general, the average annual earnings of federally appointed judges are enviable, with an annual base salary of $308,600 and those who occupy the roles of Chief Justice and Associate Chief Justice earning $338,400 (Government of Canada, 2015). While provincial judges earn lower annual salaries ($236,950 in 2014 [up from $161,250 a decade earlier]) (Mulgrew, 2016), their salaries still greatly exceed those of justices of the peace ($139,932) and citizenship judges ($84,000–$98,800) (*Maclean's*, 2014).

While horizontal appointments from bar to bench have been common in Canada and, frequently, judges have been elevated from a lower to a high court, there is no prescribed route for the young law graduate who aspires to be a judge—no apprenticeship that he or she must serve, no service that he or she must necessarily enter (Carp, Stidham, and Manning, 2013). This is in contrast to some other countries, such as Japan and France, where there are special schools for training judges. In Scandinavian countries, judicial training is acquired during a practical internship period following law school. In the former Soviet Union, judges often lacked formal legal training and were appointed on the basis of loyalty and Communist Party affiliation (Glendon, Gordon, and Osakwe, 1994). In the United States, yet another system is employed. In that country there is no career judiciary, and in over two-thirds of American states, judges are elected, usually by popular vote and occasionally by the legislature (Streb, 2009). In a small group of states, the governor appoints judges, subject to legislative confirmation. This is also the method of selection of federal judges, who are appointed by the president, subject to confirmation by the Senate. Although some Canadians clamour for American-style judicial elections, the selection of judges in the United States has not been immune from political influence, pressure, and controversy (Davison, 2002; Shuman and Champagne, 1997). Moreover, it has not resulted in a judiciary reflective of the racial and ethnic composition of the population, and the progress of minorities on the bench has been very slow at all levels.

LAWYERS AND MONEY

The fiscal position of lawyers is often assumed to be enviable. However, contrary to conventional wisdom, the results of the 2001 Canadian census reveal that "[t]here are more sales managers and advertising executives earning at least $100,000 a year than lawyers" (Vallis, 2003:A1). Some lawyers assuredly do earn envisable amounts: in 2010, Canada's highest paid lawyer earned more than $8 million (Scallan, 2012). However, the median salary in 2016 among Canadian lawyers was simply $87,610, with wages over the last five years "almost stagnant at approximately 0.1%" (Canadian Business, 2016). In addition, the range of income among lawyers is unusually large. The incomes of a partner in a corporate law practice on Bay Street in Toronto and a solo practitioner on Selkirk Avenue in North-

End Winnipeg who battles in the legal-aid trenches are scarcely interchangeable. Several factors account for the variation in lawyers' incomes. They include the type of practice (firm or solo), the type of clientele (corporations or individuals with "minor" problems), the reputation of the law school attended, achievement in law school, age, length of practice, the degree of specialization, and the region and population of the place of practice (generally, the larger the community, the greater the average income). On the whole, lawyers in private employment do not fare as well as their corporate colleagues.

There are several ways lawyers generate income. One of these ways is encouraged by the billable hour model of assessing legal fees. Although "85% of all the legal work done in Canada is billed hourly" (Macauley, 2014b), this practice "can too easily reward inefficeincy, incompetence and even encourage duplicity" (Hutchinson, 1999:79). The economic advantages of this model for lawyers and its disadvantages for consumers was noted in *Bank of Nova Scotia v. Diemer* by both the Ontario Superior Court (2014 ONSC 365) and the Ontario Court of Appeal (2014 ONCA 851). In this case, the motions judge refused to approve the legal fees of $255,955 requested by a court-appointed receiver on behalf of its counsel and ruled that these fees were "nothing short of excessive" (at 49). In finding that a "significant reduction" of these fees was warranted and deducting $100,000 from the amount sought, Justice Goodman noted that "there appears to be excessive work done by senior counsel on routine matters. The fact work done by [senior] lawyers at higher hourly rates exacerbates the problem of the fees, as the rates claimed for senior lawyers involved in this case are as high as $750.00 and $760.00 per hour" (at 42). "In my view," he wrote, "other lawyers should have done much of this work at significantly lower rates" (at 39). He also expressed concerns about "the amount of hours expended for matters that on the face of the dockets appear to be administrative and not requiring the amount of hours docketed" (at 38). Similarly, the judgment of the Ontario Court of Appeal in this case stressed that: "A person requiring legal advice does not set out to buy time. Rather, the object of the exercise is to buy services. Moreover, there is something inherently troubling about a billing system that pits a lawyer's financial interest against that of (the) client and that has built-in incentives for inefficiency. The billable hour models has both of these undesirable features" (at 36).

Although Canadian lawyers who provide routine legal services (e.g., the preparation of a will; a residential real estate closing) may employ a flat fee structure, with the fee "determined and stipulated in the engagement letter, before the assignment even begins" (Poll, 2014), hourly billing has been the traditional norm. Moreover, while clients may press for billing alternatives, such as capped fees and flat fees, there remains a "thick fog" (Hutchinson, 1999:7) around the issues of legal fees. Unfortunately, the professional rules governing Canadian lawyers

> have little to say about the actual prices charged, other than that they be "fair and reasonable," and are more concerned with ensuring that lawyers do not engage in dubious practices, such as charging for hidden fees, splitting fees with non-lawyers, or not giving full disclosure to clients of the basis for fees charges. . . . [Moreover] [t]he incidence of discipline for charging unfair or excessive fees is extremely rare; action is taken only when there is evidence that the lawyer has actually cheated or duped the client.
> (Hutchinson, 1999: 80; see also Fleming, 1997; Wallace and Henry, 2017b)

As we noted in Chapter 6, Canadian lawyers now also take cases on a **contingency-fee** basis. This is an arrangement whereby a lawyer receives a percentage of any damages collected (Cotterman, 2016). Such fees are used primarily in medical malpractice, personal injury, and some product liability and wrongful death cases. If the plaintiff loses, there is no payment required for legal services; if the plaintiff wins, the lawyer takes his or her expenses off the top, then gets a percentage of the remainder. Nowadays, it is not unusual to hear of lawyers receiving multimillion-dollar fees, especially in large class-action suits. For example, in May 2006, a draft copy of the final resolution agreement for the settlement of claims by residential school abuse survivors indicated that the lawyers who represented the survivors would receive the largest payment ever recorded for a Canadian class action: $80 million. However, while individual survivors of residential abuse would receive, on average, $30,000, the Regina-based Merchant Law Group was expected to receive $40 million with an additional $40 million paid to a national consortium of lawyers. It was also expected that the ultimate "legal fee payout. . . [would] be higher because more than a dozen other lawyers. . . [were] involved who. . . [were] not part of the class action lawsuits" (CBC News, 2006b). Equally unsettling: A recent *Toronto Star* investigation into the practices of personal injury lawyers who work on contingency for accident victims found "two dozen examples of personal injury law firms in the province, from small outfits to well known downtown Toronto firms, using retainer agreements that state they will take, in addition to their fee, costs, or a portion of costs. That's in contravention of Ontario's *Solicitors Act*, the legislation governing the practice of law in the province" (Wallace and Henry, 2017a). It also noted that the clients of personal injury lawyers "were often in the dark about how the contingency system works, including what fees their lawyers were taking"; in protesting this situation, it pointed to the case of a woman who had hired a lawyer on contingency after being injured in a car accident "and ended up with just 25 per cent of the total settlement paid out by the insurance company" (Wallace and Henry, 2017b).

Nevertheless, the contingency-fee system does have some merits. Among them, it allows those who ordinarily could not afford legal representation to retain the services of a lawyer. However, at the same time, it has been noted that contingency fees may actually exacerbate rather than eradicate the problem of unequal access to justice. Specifically, "[t]he scope for abuse in such arrangements is great: lawyers might easily be tempted to exaggerate the difficulty of the case to boost their fees, or they might engage in unsuitable tactics to inflate the amount that a case is worth" (Hutchinson, 1999:81). It may additionally encourage lawyers to screen out weak cases because they share the risk of litigation—if they do not win, they do not collect. Although the oath taken on call to the bar in Canada customarily contains a commitment to "refuse no man's [sic] just cause," Canadian lawyers are not prohibited from refusing to represent particular clients or causes (even though some provinces have declared that lawyers must not discriminate against clients on the basis of their race, gender, or similar distinctions).

COMPETITION FOR BUSINESS

Historically, bar associations have strongly opposed advertising by lawyers (Cebula, 1998). In the common-law tradition, a lawsuit was considered an evil, albeit a necessary one. Lawmakers and judges considered litigation wasteful, expensive, time-consuming, and an invasion of privacy. It was considered acrimonious, increasing hostility and resentment among people who could otherwise find an opportunity to co-operate. It hindered productive enterprise, and society discouraged litigation where it was not absolutely imperative. Lawyers were forbidden to "stir up" litigation. Any attempt to drum up business as ordinary tradesmen did was discouraged. Lawyers were expected to wait passively for clients and to temper any entrepreneurial urge to solicit them (Olson, 1991:27).

The demise of opposition to advertising began with a simple idea. Lawsuits came to be considered an effective way to deter misconduct and to compensate wronged persons. There was also a need to increase the demand for legal services, in part because law schools kept turning out large numbers of newly minted lawyers. Many lawyers and law firms began to view law as a business that requires the use of business marketing strategies (Savell, 1994). Of course, lawsuits are not the only products of lawyers. Much of their work can be seen as preventive, non-adversarial, or defensive, such as tax planning, contract negotiation, adoption, or document drafting. But all these activities can lead to a cycle of new demands and suspicions, for much of lawyering work contains an element of adversariness and assertiveness. Thus, an uncontested divorce can turn into a contested one, and advertising can entice aggrieved parties to seek out a lawyer to help them "to drop the spouse but keep the house." Moreover, Charter decisions on the freedom of communication of other professional groups have led to a softening of earlier attitudes on advertising, and "it is now common for lawyers to use some form of advertising" (Yates, Yates, and Bain, 2000:114). Although the exact content of regulations enacted by provincial law societies vary, in the main, Canadian lawyers are allowed to advertise—provided the content of the advertising is truthful, largely informational, non-competitive, and not "in bad taste or otherwise offensive as to be prejudicial to the interests of the public or the legal profession" (Hutchinson, 1999:87). When compared to their counterparts in the United States, Canadian lawyers are far less likely to advertise their services in a serious or substantial way. In the United States, the number of lawyers advertising has risen sharply over the years and late-night American television routinely airs a steady drumbeat of messages such as "Got drunk? Got caught? Call Mike. He won't tell your mama" (Warren, 2007:A1). In Chicago, a divorce attorney placed an ad on a large billboard that showed the well-toned, barely clothed torsos of a man and a woman with the caption: "Life is short. Get a divorce." The ad overnight became controversial and was removed by the order of city officials—but not before generating a fair amount of publicity and business for the divorce attorney (*Newsweek*, 2007).

Of course, members of the legal profession in both the United States and Canada have not unanimously welcomed these developments. There is concern that lawyer advertising has contributed to the low public image of attorneys (Podgers, 1995; Randall and Johnson, 2005; Norman, 2016). Some believe that increased competition leads to a decreased quality of service. In addition, most bar associations still regard advertising as something that is vaguely unseemly. After advertising, the next step in competition for business is solicitation. While dignified and comparatively unobtrusive tactics of soliciting for business—such as schmoozing and purposeful elbow-rubbing among the elite at society functions and private clubs—have been long-accepted ways of attracting clients. Bar associations have frowned upon lawyers drumming up litigation against a particular opponent, such as the Catholic Church or Xerox. However, while

> it is accepted that activities designed to stimulate legal work where none exists, to harass or mislead potential clients, or to offer referral incentives are of ethically dubious provenance . . . the problem remains how lawyers who are driven as much by public spiritedness as commercial gain can take effective steps to ensure that the least advantaged in society are made aware of their legal rights and the means to enforce them.
>
> (Hutchinson, 1999:87)

For example, while it may appear unseemly for lawyers to send letters to solicit the business of individuals known to have legal problems, there are few actual restrictions on lawyers from making their services known. Even in-person solicitation is no longer a taboo. The scenes of airplane disasters and mine accidents may precipitate a "ravenlike descent" of tort lawyers anxious to contact the victims or their relatives.

Some large law firms are becoming more competitive by adopting modern cost-management techniques and strategic planning (Jones, 2007). Others are starting to experiment with public relations firms to handle new contacts. It is routine that major law firms have a partner for whom management has become a primary preoccupation. Many firms are also increasing the number and size of specialized departments, and there is a growth of "specialty firms," such as the type that specializes in labour law work on the side of management. The business of law in large firms, in fact, is turning out to be much like business in any field. Some even provide written service guarantees promising to resolve issues to the clients' satisfaction.

The Canadian Bar Association (2005:21) reports that "[c]hanges in supply and demand for legal services have created a number of important new trends" within the Canadian legal marketplace. For example, the demand for specific legal services has enhanced the trend toward "*commoditization* or *unbundling* of services"—a development that "demands a greater level of rigour in defining, pricing, delivering, and charging for services" and "opens the door for the potential use of paralegal suppliers for the more routine actions on some files." It also notes that Canadian lawyers are increasingly being asked to provide consumers with *alternative pricing models* that include, for example, fixed-price contracts or quantity discounts. Moreover, the CBA points out that, as firms experience continuing pressure to decrease their costs, "they may opt for mergers or alliances or, at the other end of the scale, move towards specialization or 'boutique' status. General or sole practitioners will find it increasingly difficult to survive amidst large or highly specialized competitors. Because of the changing nature of demand, firms are moving from local to regional to national to global practices." Other trends and developments that are expected to continue into the future include a "widening compensation gap, particularly between lawyers in large firms and those in sole practice or small firms; the growing trend to contract or part-time work; and, the challenges of meeting increased client expectations in a faster, interconnected world in which competitors will be prepared to offer more for less" (p. 22; see also Mercer et al., 2014).

LEGAL SERVICES FOR THE POOR AND THE NOT-SO-POOR

Canadians may require legal assistance in the preparation of wills, powers of attorney, or the purchase of real estate. They may also benefit from legal help in addressing disability-related issues, accessing social assistance, resolving employment or family-related problems or dealing with the aftermath of an incident that results in personal injury. However, utilization of lawyers varies with income, with utilization being greatest in the highest income class (Ontario Ministry of the Attorney General, 2007; Pleasence and Macourt, 2013; McMurtry et al., 2010; Flynn and Hodgson, 2017; Palmer et al., 2016.) "Education, experience, familiarity with complex systems and a steady income enable people to understand and engage more successfully with legal institutions and to devote the time and attention needed to resolve complex problems" (McEown, 2009:14). In general, low- and moderate-income families do not seek legal help for their problems (Canadian Forum on Civil Justice, 2016; Currie, 2007, 2009; McEown, 2009).

There are many reasons why people do not use a lawyer. For example, individuals may not label the difficulties they confront as "legal problems" per se or believe that legal wranglings will exacerbate, rather than quell, a conflict. As well, people may perceive that consulting a lawyer is a costly undertaking. Enforcing one's legal rights and engaging the services of lawyers are expensive and, for some, simply prohibitive. Consider: A survey conducted by *Canadian Lawyer* (2016) reported that in 2016, the national average estimated cost of a two-day trial was $56.963; the national average cost of a five-day trial was $78,737. This survey additionally reports that in 2016, the national average hourly rate for senior counsel was $448; the national average hourly rate for lawyers whose call to the bar was more recent (i.e., within the past five years) was $280 (see also McKierman, 2015). Since 1967, the main option for those Canadians who are unable to pay full legal fees has been legal aid. Legal aid plans, under which lawyers accept a significant reduction in their customary fees, are generally funded through a combination of government funds, lawyers' subsidy, and client contributions. In 1966, Ontario became the first province to enact legislation establishing a comprehensive legal aid system. By the mid-1970s, all Canadian provinces and territories had established some system of legal aid to help low-income persons obtain legal representation in criminal, family law, and other matters. Legal aid services fall within the provinces' constitutional responsibility for the administration of justice. However, since legal aid services in criminal law are a matter within federal constitutional responsibility, the federal Department of Justice became involved in legal aid programs with federal–provincial cost-sharing agreements (Mossman, 1999:1318). In 2014–15, as in previous years, governments were the major source of revenue for legal aid plans (Statistics Canada, 2016d; see also Currie, 2013).

Canada's Legal Aid Program currently "provides funding to the provinces, through its contribution agreements respecting criminal legal aid, and to the territories, through the consolidated access to justice services agreements, for the delivery of criminal legal aid services to: young persons facing proceedings under the *Youth Criminal Justice Act*, and eligible, economically disadvantaged persons charged with serious and/or complex criminal offences and facing the likelihood of incarceration; proceedings pursuant to Part XX.1 of the Criminal Code; proceedings under the *Extradition Act*; and appeals by the Crown, or in certain cases, their own appeal" (Department of Justice, 2017c). In addition, it funds:

- the delivery of immigration and refugee legal aid services in the six provinces (British Columbia, Alberta, Manitoba, Ontario, Quebec, and Newfoundland and Labrador) that currently provide legal aid services to individuals involved in the immigration and refugee determination system under the provisions of the *Immigration and Refugee Protection Act*;
- the delivery of Public Security and Anti-terrorism (PSAT) legal aid services to economically disadvantaged persons subject to terrorism prosecutions, Security Certificates issued under *Immigration and Refugee Protection Act*, and proceedings under the *Extradition Act* where the commission of a terrorist act is alleged; and,
- the management of Court-Ordered Counsel in Federal Prosecutions on behalf of the federal government, where the Attorney General of Canada is ordered by the court to provide funded defence counsel.

(Department of Justice, 2017c)

Unlike Canada's system of Medicare or universal health care, the current legal aid system does *not* provide all Canadians with basic legal services. Legal aid, we should note, is not entirely "free" to clients. All plans require the legal aid client to repay at least part of the legal fees (depending on income), and/or to give the plan a lien on any real property the client may own (the legal fees remain as a debt registered against the property, to be repaid when and if the property is sold), and/or to repay fees from any money awarded in the lawsuit (Dranoff, 2011:591). Moreover, while Canada's legal aid plans received 717,850 applications for assistance in 2014–15, only 466,923 of these applications were approved for full legal aid (Statistics Canada, 2016a, 2016b). Obtaining legal aid funding is contingent upon an individual's financial status, and it is only available to those whose household income falls within low-income eligibility limits established by provincial aid plan administrators. Canadians who are on welfare, for example, can generally expect legal aid—as long as their provincial or territorial legal aid plan covers their specific type of legal problem. In some provinces, for example, only criminal actions are covered. This situation has led some to argue that legal aid policies advantage men over women. For example, Martinson and Jackson (2017:37) observe that while "legal aid policies have advantaged the Charter rights of people accused of crimes by providing legal aid to them," this situation "primarily benefits men, including those who are charged with crimes involving violence against women." According to these scholars, the "lack of legal aid for family law" is a significant "barrier to the advancement of women's equality rights under the Charter" (p. 37). An earlier analysis of legal aid in British Columbia also found that "women are disproportionately affected by inadequate legal aid in family law," especially "in situations where a woman is attempting to leave an abusive relationship, and her life and her physical and emotional security are at risk, as is the safety of her children" (Doust, 2011:16).

In all areas of the country, legal aid officers will use their discretion in evaluating the merits of the proposed lawsuit or the validity of a defence. Although civil matters accounted for over one-half (56%) of legal aid applications in 2013/2014, criminal matters accounted for over one-half (58%) of applications approved during that period (Dupuis, 2015). However, while legal aid is designed to assist those who would be otherwise unable to afford legal representation, the current system falls short in many ways. First, it is notable that many provincial governments began slashing their legal aid budgets in the 1990s. Reductions in transfer payments to the provinces for social assistance have also adversely affected the funding available for legal aid. For example, Dranoff (2011:591–592) points out that, in response to the federal government's promise of subsidies, immigration and refugee law was initially paid for by some provincial plans. However, these subsidies have been cut back "and left the provinces to cope with the expectation that provincial plans will pay for legal aid in these areas." She grimly notes that these expectations are not always met. Second, while the Canadian Bar Association's Code of Professional Conduct exhorts lawyers "to reduce or waive a fee in cases of hardship or poverty," this does not create an enforceable obligation that obliges lawyers to serve all sectors of society equally. Rather, it merely states that lawyers "may assist in making legal services available by participating in legal aid plans and referral services." Hutchinson (1999:84) charges: "If the profession is to have any real chance of matching its rhetoric of service to the reality of social need, lawyers must begin to take seriously the obligation to provide their services at reduced rates. This obligation must be built into the basic ethical fabric of professional responsibility." In 2014–15, approximately 10,500 lawyers from both the private sector and legal aid plans provided Canadians with legal aid assistance, with the vast majority (84.2 percent) private lawyers and the remainder legal aid plan staff lawyers (Statistics Canada, 2016c).

Intini (2007) observes that "most Canadians are stuck in a kind of legal no man's land: too poor to afford a lawyer but not poor enough to qualify for legal aid." As a result, Intini reports, an "increasing number of Canadians aren't hiring anyone" when they experience legal problems and are either "turning away from the system altogether (having decided . . . that 'justice is doled out based on the size of your wallet rather than the merits of your claim') or are attempting to represent themselves with little more than a Law & Order education." Similarly, Lunau (2009a:52) maintains "[a]s the cost of hiring a lawyer soars out of reach" in Canada, "unrepresented litigants are flooding the courts in unprecedented numbers. While no definitive numbers exist, some judges, especially in family law, say it's over 60 percent in their courtrooms." Legal self-help centres, which began in Canada in 2005 in Vancouver, may allow some Canadians to obtain legal advice and provide them with guidance in the filing of documents. Unfortunately, these centres are not available across the country. Moreover, while the Department of Justice currently funds one designated "public legal education" organization in each province or territory (e.g., Community Legal Education Ontario; Legal Information Society of Nova Scotia), it should be noted that these organizations do not provide those who contact them with "legal advice" per se; rather, they furnish access to basic information about various aspects of the law (e.g., divorce, child support, family violence) in assorted pamphlets and online materials. For some, the information provided may suffice; for others, it assuredly will not (see Box 8.1).

BOX 8.1 LIFE AND LAW: THE ABORIGINAL
EDUCATION NEEDS SURVEY

Findings of the 2006–07 Aboriginal Legal Needs Survey (Native Counselling Services of Alberta et al., 2007) indicate that Aboriginal peoples confront numerous difficulties in Canadian courts. First, they note that as a legacy of colonialism, Aboriginal peoples commonly feel estranged from Canada's court system and these feelings are often coupled with a lack of knowledge of how the system works. These twinned factors may discourage Aboriginal peoples from asserting their legal rights. As a result, an Aboriginal defendant may plead guilty to a criminal charge in an attempt to bring legal proceedings to a quick end and do so without full awareness of the impact that a criminal record will have on future career opportunities and life chances. In like fashion, feelings of apathy and estrangement may result in a lack of compliance with sentencing conditions and, in turn, result in individuals facing additional charges for offences against the administration of justice (e.g., parole violations, breaches of bail conditions). Second, if "legal jargon is difficult to understand on its own . . . when translating and interpreting legal terms and rules into Aboriginal languages where those terms and laws are not commonly used, the difficulty is compounded" (p. 10). Third, the survey reports a "lack of knowledge about specific aspects of the system." For example, it notes that Status Indians who were living on reserves could believe themselves exempt from the provisions of federal statutes that regulate firearms or the provincial statutes that outline traffic and hunting/wildlife violations. However, this lack of knowledge may be at least partially attributable to the unique status of Aboriginal people within Canadian law. For example, while the *Highway Traffic Act* and the majority of provincial laws do apply to Aboriginal people both on and off-reserve, other provincial laws do not, because their contents infringe upon Aboriginal or Treaty rights and/or the provisions of the *Indian Act*. Fourth, the report notes that in relation to family court, "the most pressing legal needs issues for Aboriginal clients" derive from "a lack of understanding about the system and not knowing where to go to access resources" (pp. 14–15). This problem was especially acute in relation to the issue of child welfare and guardianship. It reports that following the apprehension of a child by the state, for example, Aboriginal parents could lack awareness of what they must do in order to have the child returned or be unable to access the necessity skills-training (e.g., parenting classes) that they needed to accomplish this goal. As a result, they faced "an increased risk of having their children put into permanent guardianship . . . by agreeing to terms in case-plans that are unattainable or not in their best interests" (p. 15). Fifth, navigating through the civil court system, with its "very defined and often inflexible procedures, language, forms, roles and processes" (p. 15), could be extraordinarily difficult for Aboriginal peoples without legal representation. Unfortunately, the findings of this survey report that there were "very few services. . . [which] aim to assist the Aboriginal population in understanding this process in a meaningful manner" (p. 15).

In the years that have passed, some improvements have occurred. For example, the avowed purpose of Legal Aid Ontario's "Aboriginal Justice Strategy" is "to improve legal aid service to Aboriginal people including First Nation people, Métis people and Inuit people, regardless of whether they live on or off-reserve, are status or non-status or live in rural or urban contexts" (Legal Aid Ontario, 2008). Towards this same end, the Legal Services Society of British Columbia, which provides legal aid in that province, operates a website that is entitled Aboriginal Legal Aid in BC (http://aboriginal.legalaid. bc.ca/are_you_Aboriginal/index); identifies its target audience as being "anyone who identifies as Aboriginal"; and emphasizes its commitment to "increasing awareness of Aboriginal legal rights and supporting the strengths of Aboriginal cultures and communities."

Canada's Criminal Code contains provisions empowering judges to appoint counsel for an accused who is not represented by a lawyer *if* the accused person is mentally unfit or is an appellant before an appeal court or the Supreme Court of Canada. As well, since persons accused of committing a sexual offence are prohibited from personally cross-examining witnesses under the age of 18, judges must appoint legal counsel in such cases to cross-examine any child witness. The *Youth Criminal Justice Act* also provides for appointment of counsel to represent a young person at any stage of proceedings if the young person is unable to retain counsel. However, this Act permits the provinces and territories to require youth or their parents to pay for their legal costs if they are fully capable of paying. In addition, in the case of *British Columbia v. Okanagan Indian Band*, the Supreme Court of Canada ruled in 2004 that trial judges could award costs before a trial is held and identified three criteria that would justify such an award: "the litigation could not proceed otherwise; the claim must obviously have merit; the issues raised transcend the individual litigant's interests, are of public importance, and have not been resolved in previous cases" (Dranoff, 2011:595). Nevertheless, in its 2007 decision in *Christie v. British Columbia (Attorney General)*, the Supreme Court ruled that "there is no general constitutional right to state-paid legal counsel in proceedings before courts and tribunals" and that "provinces can impose some limits on how and when people have a right to access the courts" (Dranoff, 2011:596).

The legal profession has almost always taken an adversarial stance to initiatives that would make legal services less costly (Podgers, 1994). At times, lawyers do provide legal services *pro bono publico* (for the public good) for indigents. However, *pro bono* work is often seen by the legal profession "as a virtuous act of *noblesse oblige* rather than [as] a basic responsibility that comes with being a lawyer" (Hutchinson, 1999:85). In consequence, organizations such as Pro Bono Law Ontario and Pro Bono Law of British Columbia are attempting to encourage law firms to make *pro bono* work a part of their firm's culture (Canadian Bar Association, 2004).

A second way of providing low-cost legal services is through prepaid legal plans (Cotterman, 2004). In some countries, the idea of legal insurance has already caught on. In Germany, for example, prepaid legal plans are widely accepted, and about 40 percent of households carry legal-expense insurance. In recent years, unions have been the prime movers in organizing prepaid plans in Canada and elsewhere. In addition, Lunau (2009a:53) reports that in some Canadian provinces, courts have responded to the growing influx of "lawyerless litigants" with, for example, Nova Scotia and Ontario recently announcing changes that will "help the unrepresented, because it will make the system work more quickly, and at lower cost." She notes, for example, that in 2010, "Ontario's small claims court (where lawyers aren't generally necessary)" began to accept cases of up to $25,000 (up from $10,000).

LAW SCHOOLS

Similar to the United States and unlike the situation in England, students entering Canadian law schools do not enter directly from high school. In both Canada and the United States, the usual minimum requirement for entrance into law school is three years of university education, although the majority of successful applicants in both countries possess an undergraduate degree upon admission. However, as demand for admission has increased, it is not surprising that the standards for admission have become more exacting. For example, almost one-quarter of the successful applicants to the University of Toronto's law school in 2008 possessed a graduate degree, and the median average grade for entrants was 85 percent (Lunau, 2009b). Moreover, while in 2007 the United States had 195 (American Bar Association–accredited) law schools and the United Kingdom 75 law schools, Canada had simply 16 common law schools, "the lowest number of law schools per capita of any Commonwealth country" and "the same number it had three decades ago, when the population was smaller by a third" (Lunau, 2009b).

Admission to law school is determined to a great extent by the combined scores of grade averages at university and Law School Admission Test (LSAT) scores. The LSAT is an American-designed, standardized test taken by all law school applicants in both Canada and the United States and has been used in various forms since 1948. The current version was administered for the first time in June 1991. The LSAT is a one half-day standardized test. It consists of five 35-minute sections of multiple-choice questions designed to measure the ability to read with understanding and insight, the ability to structure relationships and to make deductions from them, the ability to evaluate reading, the ability to apply reasoning to rules and facts, and the ability to think analytically. There is also a 30-minute writing sample that is sent directly to the applicant's law school. The score is reported on a scale of 120 to 180, with 180 as the highest possible score (LSAC, 2017).

The use of the LSAT has repeatedly drawn criticism, and questions have been raised concerning the extent to which the LSAT can predict success in law school (Liu and Holland, 2008; Panter et al., 2008; Sackett, Borneman, and Connelly, 2008). Performance criteria of success in law school have traditionally been, and continue to be, grades obtained in formal course work. More and more studies conclude that the LSAT, or a combination of LSAT and grade average, does not predict law school grades for practical purposes of selection, placement, or advisement for candidates seeking entrance into law school. There have also been accusations that its content is biased against women and non-whites and favours those who have middle-class or higher-class backgrounds (Austin, 2006; Clydesdale, 2004; Pashley, Thornton, and Duffy, 2005; Stake, 2006). For example, a task force report of the Canadian Bar Association (1993:27) reported that "Aboriginal students suggested that LSAT questions were not geared for Aboriginal understanding and were not culturally relevant." Even though there are questions about the validity and reliability of the LSAT to predict success in law school, all law schools require it as part of the admission process even though individual universities may assign lesser weight to LSAT scores than to grades achieved in previous university work.

In order to reduce barriers to entry for groups that have traditionally been marginalized, some law schools have developed admission policies with special criteria for under-represented groups. For example, some law faculties have also developed pre-law admission programs for groups targeted by equity programs (e.g., the indigenous Black and Micmac program at Dalhousie Law School). Several Canadian law schools have also attempted to employ more "holistic" criteria in selecting among applicants. For example, since 1978, the University of Windsor has employed an admission policy that aims "not only to select from among the many applicants those students who would excel in the study of law, but also to select those students who, while doing well in the study of law, would have the potential to contribute creatively and meaningfully to the law school and to the community" (Canadian Bar Association, 1993:26).

In Canada, law schools have a monopoly on the training of lawyers and are the gatekeepers for the legal profession. Entry into law schools is intensely competitive and continues to be conditioned by socioeconomic status and academic standing. Students in general come from better-educated and richer families than the general population.

In addition, obtaining a law school education has become progressively more expensive in recent years. For example, tuition at York University's Osgoode Hall increased from $3,900 in 1998 to $4,650 in 1999, $8,000 in 2000, $15,115 in 2008, and $ 24,995.98 (plus $977.42 ancillary fees) for incoming domestic students in the 2016–17 academic year (Osgoode Hall Law School, 2017). While at some Canadian universities, the tuition hikes have been relatively modest, at the University of Toronto, tuition fees rose 380 percent between 1995 and 2001, with the increases particularly steep since 1998 when the Ontario government deregulated tuition fees for professional and graduate programs and allowed institutions to establish tuition fee levels. While in 1997–98, law school tuition at the University of Toronto was $3,808, for the 2016–17 academic year, tuition fees for first-year domestic students were $34,734.82 (excluding incidental ancillary fees) (University of Toronto, 2017). In 2016–17, the average tuition fee confronted by a Canadian undergraduate student in law was $11,385 (Statistics Canada, 2016c).

Observing that "[b]etween 1997 and 2004 law school tuition fees have more than doubled at four of the five schools and more than tripled at the other" (Queen's News Centre, 2004), the 2004 Study of Accessibility to Ontario Law Schools noted that only one-fifth of current students anticipated that they would graduate from law school with no debt, 27 percent expected to have debt of $40,000 to $70,000, and 13 percent believed that they would have debt in excess of $70,000 by the time they graduated. In addition, the researchers observed a change in who is attending law school based on family income (King, Warren, and Miklas, 2004). Specifically, it found "an increase of 4.7 percent in the proportion of students' parents who earn incomes in the top 40 percent of the average Canadian family income distribution, and a decrease in the proportion of students whose parents earn incomes in the middle 20 percent of the distribution." As Jamie Cassels, then-Dean of law at the University of Victoria Law School, noted grimly more than a decade ago, the rising cost of law school tuition is likely to "affect the socio-economic diversity of the student body, and threatens to make law schools a preserve for the rich" (cited in Eggleston, 2000:8; see also Girard, 2013).

SOCIALIZATION INTO THE PROFESSION

The purpose of law school is to change people: to turn them into novice lawyers, and to instill "in them a nascent self-concept as a professional, a commitment to the value of the calling, and a claim to that elusive and esoteric style of reasoning called 'thinking like a lawyer'" (Bonsignore et al., 1989:271; Bankowski and MacLean, 2007; Schauer, 2009).

The key to an understanding of the socialization of law students is best found through an examination of the case or Socratic method (see, for example, Gee, 2010; Sullivan et al., 2007). This method of education "generally involves an intensive interrogation by the teacher of individual students concerning the facts and principles presumed to be operative" in a particular case. The method is intended to accomplish two objectives. The first is informational: instruction in the substantive rules of law. The second

> is to develop in the student a cognitive restructuring for the style analysis generally called "thinking like a lawyer." In that analysis, a student is trained to account for the factual "details" as well as legal issues determined by the court to be at the core of the dispute which may allow an intelligent prediction of what another court would do with a similar set of facts. The technique is learner-centred: students are closely questioned and their responses are often taken to direct the dialogue.
>
> (Bonsignore et al., 1989:275)

This method of learning the law through court decisions, appellate opinions, and attempts to justify those opinions still predominates, despite growing criticism, at virtually every law school in the country during at least the first year of law school. Historically, as well as today, the first year of legal education is the most dramatic of the law school's three years. It is during the first year that law students learn to read a case, frame a legal argument, and distinguish between seemingly indistinguishable ideas; then they start absorbing the mysterious language of the law, full of words like *estoppel* and *replevin*. It is during the first year that a law student learns "to think like a lawyer," to develop the habits and perspectives that will stay with him or her throughout a legal career (Turow, 1977:60).

Many students deplore the Socratic method's inconclusiveness, its failure to encourage creativity, and its lack of intellectual stimulation (Tushnet, 2008). The class atmosphere is considered to be a hostile one, with the hostility directed from the icily distant law professor toward the student on the spot. Law professors often ignore the emotional level of communication. The impersonal nature of education and mistrustful relations between faculty and students culminate in an intense emotional climate in the classroom, which can pose a threat to the students' self-esteem, self-respect, and identity. Elevated levels of depression and anxiety are ubiquitous among law students (Patrice, 2015). Many complain of a high level of stress, which will stay with them during their professional careers (Pritchard and McIntosh, 2003).

These unintended results of the Socratic method of teaching are generally rationalized by explaining that the method is meant to acclimate the students to "real life," "legal reasoning," or "thinking like a lawyer." But it is difficult to see the relationship between the psychic damage and those stated goals, "and one often gets the feeling that the recitation of 'thinking like a lawyer' has become more a talismanic justification for what is going on than an articulated educational program" (Packer and Ehrlich, 1972:30; see also Bankowski and MacLean, 2007; Sullivan et al., 2007).

In addition to the tendency of the Socratic method to provoke anxiety, hostility, and aggression in the classroom, the domination by the law professor as an authority figure suggests that another aspect of law school training is to enforce a respect for authoritative power (Bonsignore et al., 1989:277). It has also been argued that although law schools may teach students how to "think like a lawyer," they do not really teach them how to be a lawyer (Stracher, 2007). Thus, a study conducted by the Berkman Center for Internet and Society at Harvard Law School (Koo, 2007), in partnership with LexisNexis, reported that more than 75 percent of the lawyers they surveyed said that they lacked critical practice skills after completing their law school education. For example, while almost 80 percent belonged to one or more work teams, with 19 percent participating in more than five teams, only 12 percent reported that, as law students, they had worked in groups on class projects. This study also suggested that new computer technologies, such as computer simulation and networking, were seriously underused by legal educators, even within such settings as clinical education, which are the most practice-oriented.

Essentially, the objective of law school education is to indoctrinate students into the legal profession. Questions that challenge the basis of the system are seldom raised, and law students define the problems presented to them within the framework of the existing system. "Thinking like a lawyer" has traditionally meant ignoring experiences of marginalization and exclusion and failing to consider the influence of social locations and social identities. For example, the Canadian Bar Association (1993:31–32) observes that

> [while] Aboriginal students begin from a different legal perspective, little or no effort is made in most law schools to incorporate Aboriginal law or Aboriginal perceptions of law into the school curricula. For example, tax law is taught with no concern for Aboriginal tax law in Canada. However, the problem is also more fundamental. Law professors need to recognize that everything learned by Natives presents them with new perspectives. In particular, property law is foreign to the Aboriginal concept of land and land ownership. From the Aboriginal perspective, there is a false premise to property law because it is based on private ownership.

The socialization of law students tends to make them intellectually independent, but at the same time it restrains them from looking for radical solutions, "for throughout their law school education they are taught to define problems in the way they have always been defined" (Chambliss and Seidman, 1971:99). During law school, students often change their political orientation in a conservative direction (Erlanger and Klegon, 1978). For example, Fine (1997) has suggested how professional socialization of law students impacts their critical awareness of race and gender. Fine observes that women law students who enter their first year of legal studies with concerns about social justice (e.g., the need for inclusive language, an intolerance for sexist or racist remarks, and awareness of the differential participation by race and gender) have patterned their political attitudes on those of white men by the third year of their schooling. She remarks, "Social critique by race/gender does not age very well within educational institutions" (p. 61). By graduation, she writes, "the vast difference in visions for the future by race and gender" had disappeared. In addition, it is not, perhaps, surprising that "legal education seems to socialize students toward an entrepreneurial value position in which the law is presumed to be primarily a conflict-resolving mechanism and the lawyer a facilitator of client interests. The experience seems to move students away from the social welfarist value in which the law is seen as a social change mechanism, and the lawyer a facilitator of group or societal interests" (Kay, 1978:347).

Political values are often fused with the learning of law, and "students are conditioned to react to questions and issues which they have no role in forming or stimulating. Such teaching *forms* have been crucial in perpetuating the status quo in teaching *content*. For decades, the law school curriculum reflected with remarkable fidelity the commercial demands of law firm practice" (Nader, 1969:21). Students anticipate and law professors reinforce the notion that successful lawyers tend to be conservative and use conservative solutions. A financially successful lawyer needs clients who are able to pay fees. Business people and rich people in general pay larger fees than wage earners and poor people. Successful lawyers represent successful clients, and such a lawyer, "if not already attuned to the value-sets of his [sic] client, tends to adopt them" (Chambliss and Seidman, 1971:99).

In response to the escalating criticism of the socialization process of law students, there is a growing emphasis on interdisciplinary work in law schools, and on joint degrees such as law and psychology and law and business. Since the patriation of the Constitution, Canadian law schools have placed increasing emphasis on cases interpreting the *Charter of Rights and Freedoms* and how Charter cases have impacted upon such areas as administrative, constitutional, and criminal law. In response to criticism that the curriculum has failed to address pressing social needs, courses in poverty law, women and the law, and civil liberties have emerged along with those that expose students to alternative methods of resolving disputes. Feminism and critical legal studies have also served to invigorate debates within law schools, although their introduction has been marred, on occasion, by belligerence and hostility on the part of some students and faculty (McIntyre, 1995; Boyd, 2011; Bakht et al., 2007). There are also calls for the globalization of legal education (Arthurs, 1996, 1997; Collier, 2005) and increased emphasis on "clinical" training (e.g., drafting documents, writing opinions, preparing for trial and cross-examination, interviewing, and negotiating) (Schrag and Meltsner, 1998). However, some universities look with disdain on innovations that seek to provide courses that are snobbishly referred to as "vocational training."

BAR ADMISSION

The legal profession has defined the perimeters of the practice of law and carefully excluded all who cannot utter the password of bar membership. In Canada, the possession of a law degree (J.D. or LL.B.) does not entitle one to practise law. The system of articles, which aims at providing "practical" training, has endured. After the completion of a law degree, there remains a period of articling or apprenticeship with a lawyer and some combination of course work and examination. All provinces require a period of articles, although the exact length demanded of students varies. However, the rising numbers of law school graduates have made obtaining good articles difficult and forced provincial law societies to re-evaluate their post-LL.B. entrance requirements.

In addition to establishing educational qualifications of would-be lawyers, bar associations restrict admission procedures to those who are morally fit to become lawyers. Applicants for admission to the legal profession must be certified as being of "good moral character" and must swear on oath that they will uphold the highest standards of moral integrity. But this phrase is notably vague, and the first recorded case in which an applicant in Ontario was denied admission to the bar for lack of good character did not occur until 1989 (Hutchinson, 1999:61). It has also been argued that the inquiry into moral character arises too soon in the overall professional process—and before the ethical and moral sensibilities of applicants have really been put to the test.

BAR ASSOCIATIONS AS INTEREST GROUPS

In addition to restricting entry into the profession and seeking to control the activity of their members, bar associations are interest groups actively engaged in the promotion of activities that the bar considers vital to its interests, such as taking a leading part in shaping laws (especially on criminal and regulatory matters), structuring the legal system, and making recommendations for judicial positions.

More than a decade ago, the Canadian Bar Association (2005:19) acknowledged that lawyers increasingly face competition for a host of new service providers: "Accounting firms, management consultants, paralegals, service bureaus, infomediaries and dispute resolution consultants are providing new choices of service providers to the public." In a remarkably blunt admission of the threat that these new service providers pose to the legal profession, the CBA warned that "If uncontested and unregulated, these alternative choices could provide significant competition to traditional legal suppliers," and expressed chagrin over "the increased sophistication of the legal services consumer, especially in accessing information, simple forms or regulations directly online or through intermediaries. This trend will continue to have an impact on certain areas of practice (e.g., wills, real estate, insurance, traffic offences, and small claims disputes)." In addition, it predicted that some traditional areas of legal practice would become "'de-legalized' as simple language and simple process alternatives become available (especially online)" (p. 121) and that the increasing use of Alternative Dispute Resolution procedures (see Chapter 6) would impact the legal marketplace.

Of course, the bar associations, like all professional associations (and unions), have as one of their primary functions the promotion of the social, political, and economic interests of their members. Indeed, some charge that the most discernible common cause of bar associations is to represent the needs of their lawyers and those clients whose interests they regularly attend. Although bar associations have been rather successful in preserving lawyers' monopoly on legal practice and the profession's lucrative role in society, the spread of legal self-help materials and the growth of the legal self-help industry have alarmed some. Such materials dispense step-by-step guidance for solving common legal problems and translate legalese into plain English. Not surprisingly, publishers of self-help legal books and software are reporting brisk sales (Benjamin, 2001). These popular legal resources are useful for some matters such as simple wills, no-fault divorces, landlord–tenant disputes, bankruptcies, and other bread-and-butter issues that were previously the exclusive domain of lawyers. Even though many lawyers invoke the old maxim that a person who represents him- or herself "has a fool for a client," Nolo Press, one of the more successful publishers of legal self-help material, produces hundreds of titles annually and sells thousands of books. Self-Counsel Press, which advertises itself as "Canada's original and leading publisher for the layperson since 1971," offers an assortment of titles such as *The Living Together Contract* (complete with an accompanying CD).

PROFESSIONAL DISCIPLINE

One of the characteristics of a profession is a code of ethics. A profession involves, among other things, a sense of service and responsibility to the community, and the conduct required of a professional is delineated in a code of ethics for that profession. A lawyer's code of ethics deals with his or her relations with clients, other lawyers, the court, and the public (Carle, 2005; Kauffman, 2009; Rhode and Hazard, 2007). In Canada, the first attempt to establish legal ethics occurred in 1915. In 1921, the Canadian Bar Association's Canons of Legal Ethics were accepted as a template for professional discipline by CBA members and largely adopted by provincial law societies. A review of the original canons launched in 1969 by a committee of the Canadian Bar Association resulted in the introduction of a new Code of Professional Conduct in 1974 and its adoption by the provincial law societies. In 1984, another committee of the CBA was struck to review and reform the Code. The 1987 Code made only modest changes to its 1974 counterpart and continues to serve as the basis of almost all the provincial rules of professional conduct for lawyers (Hutchinson, 1999:13). In 2001, the CBA Standing Committee on Ethics and Professional Issues identified further possible changes to the CBA's Code of Professional Conduct and, in 2004, unanimously adopted an amended CBA Code. Further amendments were made at the mid-winter 2006 meeting of the CBA and incorporated into a new consolidation that was published in July 2006 (Canadian Bar Association, 2009). These rules of conduct set out the duties, obligations, and responsibilities that a lawyer has as (i) a representative of clients; (ii) an officer of the legal system; and (iii) a public citizen. It also contains a series of guidelines on matters such as fees, confidentiality of information, certain types of conflict of interest, safekeeping property, unauthorized practice of law, advertising, and reporting professional misconduct (Canadian Bar Association, 2017a). Although the CBA's *Code of Professional Conduct* "has played an integral role in the Canadian legal profession," "[m]ost Canadian law societies have now adopted the Federation of Law Societies (FLSC) of Canada's *Model Code of Professional Conduct* or plan to do so" (Canadian Bar Association, 2017b).

Nevertheless, some have charged that codes developed by lawyers function as little more than "ethical window-dressing." For example, Hutchinson (1999:12) argues that codes represent, "at best, a stylized form of professional regulation and, at worst, a self-serving paean to professional prestige" (see also Slayton, 2007:114). Others argue that the social networks in which lawyers reside and the social capital that accrues from such relationships actually encourage rule violation while buffering lawyers from being detected or sanctioned by the disciplinary boards of law societies (Kay and Hagan, 1995; Arnold and Hagan, 1992; Dinovitzer, 2006; Gunz and Gunz, 2007, 2008). Although lawyers have an obligation to report known or suspected ethical violations by other lawyers according to the ethics rules and standards of the governing bodies, most complaints against lawyers are filed by disgruntled clients or initiated by the bar council; it is rare that lawyers or judges report lawyer or judicial misconduct (Rhode and Hazard, 2007; Abel, 2010). They fail to do so for one of more of several reasons: They feel that nothing will happen if they do report an ethical violation; they do not want to ruin someone's career; they fear it would take too much time to testify in a disciplinary proceeding; they do not know where to report the misconduct; they are afraid of being sued if they do report misconduct. Although lawyers claim that ethical conduct is important and the majority is willing to report violation of professional norms; in reality, they are reluctant to do it—which raises serious concerns about the efficacy of the profession's internal modes of control.

In general, disciplinary sanctions, such as reprimands, suspensions, or disbarments, are imposed only for serious instances of misconduct, such as criminal acts, mishandling of a client's property, and flagrant violation of certain rules of professional conduct, such as breach of confidentiality. Some of these sanctions are in addition to possible criminal proceedings, which are handled separately by law-enforcement authorities, and they may be publicized as a form of "risk prevention." Of course, unhappy clients can always sue their lawyers—and, indeed, if "four out of every five Ontario lawyers—that is 80 per cent—will be sued for malpractice at least once in their career," the risk of being sued for malpractice is not limited to lawyers in Ontario but nationwide—which is why "every law society/ Chambres or Barreau program in Canada requires private practice members to carry at least $1 million in professional liability insurance" (Careless, 2016). However, research suggests that not all lawyers are equally vulnerable to disciplinary action. For example, Arnold and Hagan (1992:774) report that it is inexperienced solo practitioners who face a "heightened risk of sanctioning during a recessionary period. . . [and] it is regulatory attention more than pre-existing behavioural differences that structures these deviant careers" (see also Arnold and Hagan, 1994). Similarly, Hutchinson (1999:15) notes that while, on occasion, headlines direct attention to the wrongdoings of elite lawyers, "the (small) bulk of disciplinary activity occurs at the margins of the profession, even though there is no evidence that lawyers who work for wealthy clients are any more (or less) ethical than those who have disadvantaged clients."

How serious are lawyers about professional responsibility? It has been suggested that lawyers "have been collectively long on righteous celebration of the importance of maintaining ethical standards, but short on any action and debate" (p. 39). Evidence of this is suggested (Arthurs, 1998; 2001) by the lack of institutional vigour in disciplining lawyers for breaches of ethical rules, the reactive stance taken by law societies, and the fact that at the beginning of the new millennium only four Canadian law schools had compulsory courses on legal ethics and professional responsibility. There are, however, some hopeful signs. At the cusp of the new millennium, Arthurs (1999:xiv) observed:

> The rapidly changing demographics, market conditions, sources of intellectual capital, and professional ideologies among Canadian lawyers have created crises of professional governance, which to some extent manifest themselves in a critique of the whole apparatus of professional discipline. And, of course, changes in Canada's political economy, and in public attitudes towards elites and regulatory institutions, are bound to generate pressures for a change in how lawyers behave both individually and collectively. It would be surprising indeed if these and other important developments did not soon lead to a top-to-bottom rethinking of the style, content, and practice of professional ethics in Canada.

Slayton (2007:238) points out that the 2004 Clementi Report in Britain paved the way for a "revolution" in the regulation of lawyers by recommending that the legal profession "be overseen by a new legal services board with a lay majority chaired by a non–lawyer and accountable to Parliament" and "lose its powers to investigate complaints against lawyers," with the establishment of a new independent office specifically created for that purpose. According to Slayton (2007:238–239), "[i]t is time for very similar reforms in Canada. . . . Disciplinary action should be in the hands of an independent body; for a law society to investigate, prosecute and judge violates elementary principles of justice. Above all, it is time to put the interests of the consumer at the centre of the system."

SUMMARY

- The origins of the legal profession can be traced back to Rome. Lawyers, in the sense of a regulated group of practitioners, emerged in the late 1200s. By that time, the body of legal knowledge, including procedure, had become too much for the ordinary person to handle alone.
- Legal education in Canada was initially modelled after the British system. University-based law schools are a fairly recent method of obtaining a legal education in Canada. It was not until 1960 that a law degree was required for admission to the bar of each province.
- Lawyers have established a monopoly on legal business, and the profession of law has become the fastest-growing of all professions in Canada.
- The legal profession is highly stratified. There is substantial variation in income by types of lawyers. Income is related to such factors as the type of practice, the type of clientele, the degree of specialization, the size of the firm, age, length of practice, and the size and location of the place of practice.
- The cost of legal services is still beyond the reach of many people. Law and lawyers are expensive, and legal aid is not available to all Canadians facing all types of legal difficulties.
- In addition to setting standards for admission and practice, law societies are also responsible for disciplining those among their members who fail to meet professional

standards. Although violation of legal ethics may be punished by reprimand, suspension from the bar, or disbarment, only a very small proportion of lawyers who violate the ethical standards are ever subjected to disciplinary action.

CRITICAL THINKING QUESTIONS

1. The Canadian Bar Association's Futures Committee (2005) identified the following factors as likely to provide the "greatest challenges, risks and opportunities" to both the Canadian legal profession and to the CBA itself: the changing demographics of the profession, especially the greater presence of women; inter-generational variance in the expectations, attitudes, work habits, and career intention of lawyers; the desire among lawyers for an improved work and family balance; the growing fragmentation of the profession; new forms of marketplace competition; the proliferation of sub-groups that define the mission of their profession differently (e.g., a calling, a business, a job); the negative image of lawyers and its impact upon societal respect, consumer demand, and career satisfaction; globalization; technology; the commercialization of the profession and the introduction of business concepts into legal practice; and shifts in the volume and nature of legal work. From this list, select the one factor that you feel will pose the greatest challenge to the legal profession and/or the CBA and suggest strategies to address it.
2. An Ipsos Reid survey reported that the most common motivations among current Canadian law students for entering into the profession were, in order, "the desire to help society (35 percent), the range and flexibility of professional opportunities that a legal career provides (32 percent), and the intellectual stimulation and challenge of the law (29 percent). Far down the list was the motivation of income potential or financial stability (21 percent)" (Canadian Bar Association, 2006:17). Yet it has been noted that professional experience has an impact upon the attitudes, expectations, and intentions of lawyers. Identify factors within the practice of law that you feel might result in altered opinions of the mission of this profession.
3. Should Canada alter its method of selecting judges? What would be the advantages or disadvantages of establishing a career judiciary in this country?
4. What factors should law schools assign priority to in selecting among applicants?

ADDITIONAL RESOURCES

1. The Model Code of Professional Conduct of the Federation of Law Societies (FLSC) of Canada is accessible online at http://flsc.ca/wp-content/uploads/2014/12/Model-Code-as-amended-march-2016-FINAL.pdf.
2. Michael Ornstein's 2010 report on the "Racialization and Gender of Lawyers in Ontario" may be examined in its entirety at http://www.lsuc.on.ca/with.aspx?id=658.
3. Detailed resource and caseload statistics on legal aid in Canada may be obtained at http://www.statcan.gc.ca/pub/85f0015x/85f0015x2011000-eng.pdf.
4. To find out more about Public Legal Education and Information (PLEI) in Canada, visit the Department of Justice's website at http://www.justice.gc.ca/eng/fl-df/parent/plei-eij.html.

9

CHAPTER 9
RESEARCHING LAW IN SOCIETY

Empirical studies provide the background for many of the generalizations and conclusions reached about law and society in previous chapters. The purpose of this chapter is to show how sociologists carry out such studies by describing some of the ways they research law and the methods they use to arrive at their findings. The chapter also demonstrates the significance and applicability of sociological research to the formulation, instrumentation, and evaluation of social policy.

Figure 9.1 Sociological methods contribute to the study of law and society.
Credit: Shutterstock

LEARNING OBJECTIVES

After reading this chapter, you should be able to:

1. Identity the four major methods that sociologists use in researching law in society.

2. Describe the strengths and weaknesses of each of these four methods.

3. Provide examples of how each of the four methods have been employed in sociological investigations of law and society.

4. Explain why sociology is both a *pure* and an *applied* science.

5. Define "action research" and illustrate its use in examinations of law and society.

6. Identify three ways in which sociology has contributed to social policy and social policymaking.

7. Distinguish evaluation research from other types of research.

8. Describe why measuring the impact of any law is a complex task.

METHODS OF INQUIRY

There are four commonly used methods of data collection in sociology: the historical, observational, experimental, and survey methods.

All research is essentially a process in which choices are made at many stages. Methodological decisions are made on such diverse matters as the kind of research design to be used, the type of research population and sample, the sources of data collection, the techniques of gathering data, and the methods of analyzing the research findings (Bynner and Stribley, 2010). The differences among the four methods are more a matter of emphasis on a particular data-collection strategy for a particular research purpose than a clear-cut "either-or" distinction. For example, in the observational method, although the emphasis is on the researchers' ability to observe and record social activities as they occur, researchers may interview the participants—a technique associated with the survey and experimental methods. At all stages of sociological research, there is interplay between theory and method (Schutt, 2015). In fact, the theory chosen by researchers often determines which methods will be used in the research. The selection of the method is, to a great extent, dependent on the type of information desired.

To study a sequence of events and explanations of their meanings by participants and other observers before, during, and after their occurrence, **observation** (especially participant observation) is the best method of data collection. Researchers directly observe and participate in study systems with which they have established meaningful and durable relationships. Although observers may or may not play an active role in the events, they observe them firsthand and can record the events and the participants' experiences as they unfold. No other data-collection method can provide such a detailed description of social events. Thus, observation is best suited for studies of particular groups and certain social processes within those groups. When events are not available for observation (for example, if they occurred in the past), the **historical approach** is the logical choice of method for collecting data.

If investigators wish to study norms, rules, and status in a particular group, **intensive interviewing** of "key" persons and informants inside or outside the group is the best method of data collection. Those who set and enforce norms, rules, and status, because of their position in the group or relations with persons in the group, are the most knowledgeable about the information researchers wish to obtain. Intensive interviews (especially with open-ended questioning) allow researchers to probe for such information.

When investigators wish to determine the numbers, the proportions, the ratios, and other quantitative information about the subjects in their studies possessing certain characteristics, opinions, beliefs, and other variables, then the best method of data collection is the **survey**. The survey relies on a representative sample of the population, to which a standardized instrument can be administered.

Finally, the **experiment** is the best method of data collection when researchers want to measure the effect of certain independent variables on some dependent variables. The experimental situation provides control over the responses and the variables and gives researchers the opportunity to manipulate the independent variables. In the following pages, we will examine and illustrate these methods in greater detail.

HISTORICAL METHODS

Sociologists generally are accustomed to studying social phenomena at one time—the present. But social phenomena do not appear spontaneously and autonomously. Historical analysis can indicate the possibility that certain consequences can issue from events that are comparable to other events of the past. History is something more than a simple compilation of facts—it can generate an understanding of the processes of social change and document how a multitude of factors have served to shape the present (Cramer, 2005).

Historical research carried out by sociologists is a critical investigation of events, developments, and experiences of the past; a careful weighing of evidence to determine the validity of the sources of information regarding the past; and the interpretation of the evidence. As a substitute for direct data from the participants, contents from documents and historical materials are used as a method of data collection. These documents and materials can range from census data, archives of various types, and official files such as court records, records of property transactions, tax records, and business accounts, to personal diaries, witness accounts, judicial rhetoric in appellate court opinions, propaganda literature, and numerous other personal accounts and letters. Researchers use these sources to carry out what is generally referred to as **secondary analysis**—that is, the data were not generated or collected for the specific purpose of the study formulated by the researcher. For example, Welsh, Dawson, and Nierobisz (2002) examined 267 sexual harassment complaints against corporate respondents or employing organizations that were dealt with by the Canadian Human Rights Commission between 1978 and 1993 in an attempt to discover what types of factors (legal, extra-legal, and case-processing) resulted in a complaint being dismissed or settled. Of course, the usefulness of the historical method depends to a large extent on the accuracy and thoroughness of the documents and materials. With accurate and thorough data, researchers may be able to gain insights, generate hypotheses, and even test hypotheses (Boyle and Preves, 2000; Petrunik, 2003).

Official records and public documents have provided the data for sociological analyses attempting to establish long-term legal trends. For example, Hall (1952) has shown, on the basis of historical records, how changing social conditions and emerging social interests brought about the formulation of trespass laws in 15th-century England. More recent investigations include Banner's (2000) analysis of how British colonizers in colonial New Zealand modified the structure of the land market in that country over the course of the 19th century in order to transfer wealth from the Maori to themselves, and Asbridge's (2004) examination of the antecedents of the enactment of municipal smoking bylaws in Canada between 1970 and 1995.

The historical method is also used to test theories. For example, Baumgartner (1978) was interested in the relationship between the social statuses of the defendant and the litigant and the verdicts and sanctions awarded them. She analyzed data based on 389 cases (148 civil and 241 criminal) heard in the colony of New Haven (in what is now Connecticut) between 1639 and 1665. She found, not unexpectedly, that in both the civil and the criminal cases, individuals who enjoyed high status were more likely to receive favourable treatment by the court than their lower-status counterparts.

In addition to relying on official documents, the historical method may also be based on narrations of personal experiences, generally known as the **life-histories method**. This technique requires that researchers rely solely on persons' reporting of life experiences relevant to the research interest, with minimal commentary. Life histories are often part of ethnographic reports. In such instances, they are referred to as *memory cases* (Nader and Todd, 1978:7). This method is useful to learn about events such as conflicts or disputes that occurred in the past, particularly when there are no written records available. Obviously, this method has certain pitfalls, for life histories tend to be tainted by selective recall; that is, subjects tend to remember events that have impressed them in some way and tend to forget others. Although the life-history method has been little used in recent years, it serves several functions. First, it provides insights into a world usually overlooked by the objective methods of data collection. Second, life histories can serve as the basis for making assumptions necessary for more systematic data collection. Third, life histories, because of their details, provide insights into new or different perspectives for research. When an area has been studied extensively and has grown "sterile," life histories may break new ground for research studies. Finally, they offer an opportunity to view and study the dynamic process of social interactions and events not available with many other kinds of data.

A notable difficulty of the historical method lies in the limited accuracy and thoroughness of the documents and materials involved. Because the data are "compiled" by others with no supervision or control by researchers, researchers are, in fact, at the mercy of those who record the information. The recorders use their own definitions of situations, define and select events as important for recording, and introduce subjective perceptions, interpretations, and insights into their recordings. Therefore, researchers must ascertain the reliability and validity of documents. They should be verified for *internal consistency* (consistency between each portion of the document and other portions) and *external consistency* (consistency with empirical evidence, other documents, or both). Although the historical method provides details, and in certain cases presents a processual view of events often unmatched by other methods of data collection, it is desirable (when possible, of course) to combine this method with other data-collection methods.

OBSERVATIONAL METHODS

Observational methods can be divided into two types: those utilizing either human observers (participant observers or judges) or mechanical observers (cameras, digital recorders, and the like) and those directly eliciting responses from subjects by questioning (questionnaires, schedules, and interview guides). Observational methods can be carried out both in laboratory or controlled situations and in field or natural settings.

Participant observation has a long history of use in anthropological research. Thus, there is justification if the term conjures up the image of a social scientist living with some preliterate tribe, perhaps for several years. Indeed, much of our knowledge of primitive law comes from anthropologists who have lived in traditional societies. Of course, for anthropologists, the opportunity to observe ongoing legal phenomena (outside of an institutional setting such as a court) depends on a combination of circumstances and luck. The anthropologists have to be in the right place at the right time. Anthropological (and sociological) field researchers generally proceed by way of a kind of methodological eclecticism, choosing the method that suits the purpose and circumstances at any given time: "unobtrusive measurement, life history studies, documentary and historical analysis, statistical enumeration, in-depth interviewing, imaginative role-taking, and personal introspection are all important complements of direct observation in the field worker's repertoire" (Williamson, Karp, and Dalphin, 1982:200).

Many of the observational techniques are used in laboratory or controlled situations. For example, comparatively little empirical research has been performed with actual juries because of the legal requirements of private deliberations. Consequently, **mock trials** in which jurors or juries respond to simulated case materials have become a primary research vehicle. The mock trial permits both manipulation of important variables and replication of cases (Hillmer, 2015). Many of the laboratory jury studies deal with the deliberation processes preceding the verdict and with how the verdict is reached by juries of diverse composition deliberating under various conditions. One method of analyzing deliberations is to audiotape or videotape the deliberations and then analyze their content.

Observational methods have been used by sociologists extensively in field settings that involve direct contact with subjects and take place in relatively natural social situations. They are often part of what is called **action research**, a way to integrate knowledge with action (Reason and Bradbury, 2013). For example, Fairman and Yapp's (2005) recent examination of the ways that small and medium-sized enterprises made compliance decisions when confronted with self-regulatory and prescriptive demands also suggests the importance of tending to social processes. They report that compliance is best conceptualized as a "negotiated outcome" of the regulatory encounter. Similarly, Rousseau et al.'s (2002) analysis of the decision-making process of the Canadian Immigration and Refugee Board, as well as Hagan and Levi's (2005) investigation of prosecutorial and court practices at The Hague Tribunal for the former Yugoslavia, also suggest the utility and potential richness of observational research methods. A central finding of these studies concerns the role of discretion in the application or nonapplication of the law in legal proceedings (Westmarland, 2011).

There are both advantages and limitations to observational methods. The advantages include the opportunity to record information as the event unfolds or shortly thereafter. Thus, the validity of the recorded information can be high. Often observations are made and information is recorded independent of observed persons' abilities to record events. At times, when verbal or written communication between researchers and subjects is difficult—for example, in studying traditional societies—observation is the only method by which researchers can obtain information. Finally, observers need not rely on the willingness of the observed persons to report events.

There are also several limitations to observational research. The method is not applicable to the investigation of large social settings. The context investigated must be small enough to be dealt with exhaustively by one or a few researchers. In the case of fieldwork, there is the omnipresent possibility that the researchers' selective perception and selective memory will bias the results of the study (Khan, 2005). There is also the problem of selectivity in data collection. In any social situation, there are literally thousands of possible pieces of data. No one researcher, in other words, can account for every aspect of a situation. Researchers inevitably pull out only a segment of the data that exist, and the question inevitably arises as to whether the selected data are really representative of the situation. There is also no way to easily assess the reliability and validity of the interpretations made by researchers. As long as data are collected and presented by one or a few researchers with their own distinctive talents, faults, and idiosyncrasies, suspicion will arise about the validity of their rendering of the phenomena studied. Researchers often respond to these criticisms by suggesting that the cost of imprecision is more than compensated for by the in-depth quality of the data produced.

EXPERIMENTAL METHODS

The prevailing method for testing causal relations by social scientists, especially psychologists, is the **experiment**. Experiments may be carried out in laboratory or field settings, and they ideally begin with two or more equivalent groups, with an experimental variable introduced into only the experimental group. Researchers measure the phenomenon under study before and after the introduction of the experimental variable, thus getting a measure of the change presumably caused by the variable.

There are two common ways of setting up experimental and control groups. One is the **matched-pair technique**. For each person in the experimental group, another person similar in all important variables (age, religion, education, occupation, or anything important to the research) is found and placed in the control group. Another technique is the **random-assignment technique**, in which statistically random assignments of persons to experimental and control groups are made—such as assigning the first person to the experimental group and the next to the control group, and so on.

Experiments in sociology face certain difficulties (Schutt, 2009). An experiment involving thousands of people may be prohibitively expensive. It may take years to complete a study. Ethical and legal considerations prohibit the use of people in any experiments that may injure them. Moreover, there would be legal as well as ethical questions involved in the use of experimental methods in the study of legal services, welfare payments, or incarcerations. These types of experiments would necessarily raise a series of difficult questions. Among them: Do researchers have the right to withhold public services from some individuals simply to provide a control for experimentation? What can be said to control groups who are chosen to be similar to experimental groups but are denied benefits so that they may serve as a basis for comparison?

Many experiments, such as those dealing with juror and jury behaviour or with violence, are conducted in laboratory situations. However, laboratory experiments achieve rigorous and controlled observation at the price of unreality. The subjects are isolated from the outside and from their normal environment. In consequence, the laboratory experiment has been criticized for its unnaturalness and questioned as to its generalizability. By contrast, experimental methods that are used in non-laboratory settings increase the generalizability of results and lend greater credence to the findings, but concomitantly increase the difficulty of controlling relevant variables.

SURVEY METHODS

Survey research aims for a systematic and comprehensive collection of information about the attitudes, beliefs, and behaviours of people. The most common means of data collection are face-to-face interviews, self-administered questionnaires (for example, mail questionnaires), and telephone interviews. Typically, questionnaire or interview schedules are set up so that the same questions are asked of each respondent in the same order with exactly the same wording, and the validity of surveys is dependent on the design of the questions asked (Fink, 2009; Groves, 2009). Surveys deal with representative samples of populations. Probabilistic sampling is essential to survey studies. Survey studies tend to be larger than is typically the case in observational or experimental studies. Usually, data are collected at one time, although a survey approach can be used to study trends in opinion and behaviour over time. Because of its ability to cover large areas and many respondents, the survey method has become the dominant method of data collection in sociology.

Survey methods, like other research methods, have their pitfalls. Probably foremost among them is the response rate or the non-response rate. Because one of the important reasons for conducting a survey is that it deals with a large representative sample from a population and thus permits inference from the sampled data to the population, it is essential that the sample maintain its representativeness, which may be affected severely when a substantial number of the respondents fail to participate in the study. The return rate for mail questionnaires is generally low; a 60 percent or higher return rate is considered rather good (see, for example, Mangione, 1995; Nulty, 2008). Of course, for the interview survey, the expected response rate is higher than that of the questionnaire survey. In both cases, in addition to the subject's refusal to participate, other factors affect the response rate. They include the inability of subjects to understand the questions, the possibility that subjects may have moved or died, and the physical or mental incapacitation of the participants. Although questionnaire and interview studies have a margin of error, they are still useful. For example, public officials seldom take a position on a public issue without first reviewing public opinion polls, and legislators may delay casting a vote on an important bill until they receive the latest survey of voter opinion.

As Box 9.1 suggests, surveys also allow us to better understand why certain laws, such as Canada's hate laws, are necessary.

BOX 9.1 LIFE AND LAW: SURVEYING HATE CRIMES

The Canadian Criminal Code includes four specific offences that are recognized as hate crimes: advocating genocide; public incitement of hatred; willful promotion of hatred; and mischief in relation to religious property. In addition, other criminal offences that are motivated by hatred toward an "identifiable group" (i.e., a group that is distinguishable on the basis of, for example, "race," national or ethnic origin, or sexual orientation) may also be classified as hate crimes and subject to enhanced sentencing penalties.

Various countries worldwide have recognized the importance of monitoring the nature and prevalence of hate crimes. Indeed, 50 of the 56 nations that are members of the Organization for Security and Co-operation in Europe (OSCE) compiled statistics on these issues in 2010. Canada numbers among these nations, with statistics on police-reported hate crimes collected as part of its Uniform Crime Reporting (UCR2) Survey. In 2014, 1,295 hate crimes were reported to Canadian police services, with the majority of these crimes motivated by hatred on the basis of "race" or ethnicity (N=611); this finding is consistent with research conducted in other countries, including the United States, Scotland, Finland, Germany, and Sweden, as well as the United Kingdom (Dowden and Brennan, 2012:11). In Canada, the next most common motivation for these types of crimes were, in order, hatred on the basis of religion (N=429) and sexual orientation (N=155). The most commonly targeted "racial" group in Canada in 2014 was blacks, while religiously motivated hate crimes most often targeted adherents of Judaism. Compared to hate crimes that were racially or religiously motivated, hate crimes that were targeted at sexual orientation minorities were more likely to be violent. While just under two-thirds (65 percent) of hate crimes that targeted non-heterosexuals were violent, this was true of approximately one-third (34%) of racially motivated hate crimes and one in six religiously motivated hate crimes. "Hate crimes motivated by sexual orientation were also more likely than other types to result in physical injury to victims. More specifically, injuries were reported in 59% of violent incidents motivated by sexual orientation, compared to 40% of racially motivated violent incidents and 14% of religiously motivated violent incidents" (Dowden and Brennan, 2012:13).

Youth and young adults were both the most common perpetrators and victims of hate crimes. However, as disheartening as these statistics may be, they likely understate the scope of the problem in Canada. Criminologists generally believe that officially recorded crime statistics are a far better indicator of police activity than they are of criminal activity (Barkan, 2018; Truman and Morgan, 2016). The 2009 General Social Survey (GSS) on victimization noted that only about a third (34 percent) of Canadians who perceived themselves to have been a victim of a hate crime reported their experience(s) to police (Dauvergne and Brennan, 2011).

Survey methods have also been widely used in a variety of studies dealing with knowledge and opinions about law, evaluation of the effectiveness of the law, prestige of the law, and legal attitudes and knowledge. For example, several surveys have also found that public knowledge in a number of European countries on legal topics is considerably less than assumed by the legal authorities and by many scholars. Roberts (2000) points out that Canadians tend to underestimate the severity of sentencing practices, the harshness of prison life, and the costs of incarceration, and are generally ill-informed on the functioning of the parole system and the success and failure rates of offenders released on parole. He additionally observes that almost a decade after the *Young Offenders Act* became law, almost half the sample in a nationwide survey "admitted that they were 'not at all' or 'not very' familiar with the Act" (p. 10). Consider as well the results of an Environics poll, commissioned by the Canadian Safety Council, which found that 65 percent of Canadians—56 percent of men and 74 percent of women—think Canada's impaired driving laws are not strict enough. However, only one in ten respondents realized that a first-time impaired driving conviction at that time carried a minimum $600 fine (increased as of July 2, 2008, to a mandatory $1000) and a one-year driving prohibition. Only two in ten correctly believed that life in prison is the maximum penalty for impaired driving causing death. As Canadian Safety Council president Émile Thérien observed, "We doubt Canadians want the death penalty for impaired driving. A lot of people don't realize the law is already very strict" (Canadian Safety Council, 2000). According to this survey, better-educated individuals were less likely to know the penalties than those with lower levels of education.

THE IMPACT OF SOCIOLOGY ON SOCIAL POLICY

In every scientific field there is a distinction between pure and applied science. **Pure science** is a search for knowledge, without primary concern for its practical use. **Applied science** is the search for ways of using scientific knowledge to solve practical problems.

Sociology is both a pure and an applied science. Contemporary sociologists are attempting to contribute to improving conditions of life in society by providing policymakers with the information that is needed to make informed decisions (Belknap, 2015; Trevino and McCormack, 2016). Other fields, such as economics, are already playing a significant role in policy matters. There are attempts to reformulate legal concepts in the language and equations of the marketplace. Many law schools now employ at least one economist, and policy reforms in fields as diverse as antitrust law, environmental regulation, and criminal sentencing bear the distinctive imprint of economic analysis (see, for example, Posner, 2007).

Theoretical knowledge can and should be translated into practical applications, and the purpose of this section is to demonstrate how sociological knowledge and expertise can have an impact on social policy (Anderson, 2015). But what is **social policy**?

Although there is no consensus in the sociological literature on the term (Cochran and Malone, 2010; Lavalette and Pratt, 2006), it generally refers to purposive legal measures that are adopted and pursued by representatives of government who are responsible for dealing with particular social conditions in society. The term *policymaking* refers to the process of identifying alternative courses of action that may be followed and choosing among them.

CONTRIBUTIONS OF SOCIOLOGY TO POLICY RECOMMENDATIONS

The proposition that law should be seen in a broad social context is now almost a truism. Monahan and Walker observe that "[w]idespread acceptance of the view that law is at least in part concerned with policy making, coupled with realistic enthusiasm for empiricism has resulted in increasing use of social science materials in resolving many legal problems" (cited in Freeman and Roesch, 1992:571). Over the years, there have been many instances in which sociological knowledge, perspectives, concepts, theories, and methods have been useful in connection with the development of policy recommendations (Jimenez et al., 2016; Dean, 2006; Jordan, 2007). Canadian sociologists contributed to research that resulted in the social security and medicare systems, as well as to *La Commission d'enquête sur l'enseignement au Québec* (1963–66), which resulted in massive changes to the educational system in the province of Quebec. Sociological research also informed the recommendations of the Royal Commission on Health Services (1964–65), the Royal Commission on Bilingualism and Biculturalism (1963–69), the Royal Commission on the Status of Women in Canada (1967–70), and the Royal Commission on New Reproductive Technologies (1993).

Sociologists have also provided sensitizing concepts and theories that oriented the search for solutions of the crime problem. For example, studies of the correctional system and the operation of law enforcement in the courts have raised doubts about the effectiveness of existing criminal justice policies and of rehabilitation and treatment efforts. On the basis of sociological data, attention has been directed to such issues as accessibility of justice, alternative systems of social control, child custody in the context of parental violence, racial profiling, the need for specialized courts to deal with criminal charges of domestic violence and drug addiction, and a reconsideration of consensual crimes, or "crimes without victims" (Bazemore and Schiff, 2001; Greenwood and Boissery, 2000; Jaffe and Crooks, 2004; Murdocca, 2004; Wortley and Tanner, 2005). Sociologists have examined subjects as diverse as the relative effectiveness of promotions, anonymity, and rewards in Canadian Crime Stoppers programs (Lippert, 2002) and the extent to which the Canadian media have complied with a relatively new law (passed shortly before the 2000 Canadian electoral campaign) that seeks to regulate the publication of polls during electoral campaigns (Durand, 2002).

Feminist legal theorizing, which defines *obscenity* as that which subordinates or degrades women rather than that which offends some notion of sexuality, clearly influenced the Supreme Court's decision in the 1992 case of *R. v. Butler*. This case was a constitutional challenge that alleged that Canada's obscenity laws violated freedom-of-expression guarantees in the *Canadian Charter of Rights and Freedoms*. The ruling of the Supreme Court emphasized that the purpose of obscenity provisions, which prohibit "the undue exploitation of sex or of sex and one or more of the following subjects: namely, crime, horror, cruelty and violence" were to avoid harm rather than to express moral opprobrium. Determining whether "undue" exploitation occurred "must be made on the basis of the degree of harm that may flow from such exposure, harm of the type which predisposes persons to act in an anti-social manner." This decision, which explicitly found the obscenity provisions necessary in order to avoid harm—specifically, women's rights to equality, their sense of self-worth, and their physical safety—was lauded by the Women's Legal Education and Action Fund (LEAF), which had been granted intervener status in this case, and had argued that pornographic representations of sex combined with violence are discriminatory to women (Busby, 1999; see also Lo and Wei, 2002). However, the relationship between pornography and anti-social behaviour continues to inspire investigation and debate (see, for example, Bang et al., 2013; Struthers, 2009; Weitzer, 2013; Peters, Lederer, and Kelly, 2012; McNair, 2014; Johnson, 2015; Shelton et al., 2016).

The findings of social science research are not always viewed as compelling. For example, Erickson's (1998:263) examination of the passage of the *Controlled Drugs and Substances Act* into law in Canada in May 1997 pointedly notes that policymakers opted to reject the advice that was proffered to them by Canadian scholars from sociology and other disciplines and "[d]espite a rich legacy of empirical research pointing drug policy in a new direction, away from aggressive criminalization, the new law reaffirms both the seriously deviant status of illicit drug users and the primacy of the criminal justice model over public health and social justice alternatives." The use of mandatory minimum sentencing in Canada would also assuredly suggest a rejection of the recommendations made by experts (see, for example, Engen, 2009; Warner, 2007; Lamb, 2015).

Nevertheless, Scott and Shore (1979:20) conclude that sociology has made a contribution to recommendations for policy in three ways:

> The first is through the use of sociological concepts that are said to provide new or unique perspectives on social conditions—perspectives that are based upon more than common sense and that may in fact be inconsistent with basic notions upon which existing policies are based. . . . Second, prescriptions for policy are sometimes

suggested by the findings of sociological research undertaken primarily to advance scientific understanding of society. . . . The third is the use of sociological methods and techniques of research to obtain information about specific questions.

Of these three uses of sociology, the third is by far the most common (see, for example, Deutscher, 1999; Howard-Hassman, 2000). However, it should be noted that there is no way of precisely determining the extent to which sociology can or does contribute to policy recommendations (Kraft and Furlong, 2015). For example, in many instances the methods of empirical research, not the knowledge and concepts of sociology, have been directly responsible for policy prescriptions. Obviously, conducting research is not a skill possessed exclusively by sociologists. Moreover, there is no way of distinguishing between the contributions of intelligent and insightful individuals who happen to be trained as sociologists and the contributions of sociological knowledge and perspectives as such. Consequently, care needs to be exercised in crediting the discipline's knowledge in all cases in which sociology has had an impact on policy. Despite these qualifications, it is fair to state that sociological knowledge can, and at times does, have an impact on developing recommendations for social policy.

EVALUATION RESEARCH AND IMPACT STUDIES

Policymakers have always made judgments regarding the benefits, costs, or effects of particular policies, programs, and projects (Royse and Thyer, 2016; Fitzpatrick, Christie, and Mark, 2009; Mathison, 2005; Taylor and Balloch, 2005). Many of these judgments have been impressionistic, often influenced by ideological, partisan self-interest, and evaluational criteria. For example, a tax cut may be considered necessary and desirable because it enhances the electoral chances of the evaluator's political party, or employment insurance may be deemed "bad" because the evaluator "knows a lot of people" who improperly receive benefits. Undoubtedly, much conflict may result from this sort of evaluation because different evaluators, employing different value criteria, reach different conclusions concerning the merits of the same policy (Betcherman, 2000; Wiber, 2000).

Another type of evaluation has centred on the operation of specific policies or programs, such as the Intensive Rehabilitative Custody and Supervision program for youth who commit the most serious of violent crimes (Caputo and Valee, 2008), a "john school" designed to change the attitudes of men arrested for soliciting sex (Kennedy, Klein, and Gorzalka, 2004), or police programs (Kerley, 2005). Questions asked may include: Is the program honestly run? What are its financial costs? Who receives benefits (payments or services) and in what amounts? Is there any overlap or duplication with other programs? What is the level of community reintegration of participants? What is the degree of staff commitment? Were legal standards and procedures followed? This kind of evaluation may provide information about the honesty or efficiency in the conduct of a program but, like the impressionistic kind of evaluation, it will probably yield little, if anything, in the way of hard information on its societal effects.

Since the late 1960s, a third type of policy evaluation has been receiving increasing attention among policymakers. It is the systematic objective evaluation of programs to measure their societal impact and the extent to which they are achieving stated objectives. Consider, for example, the introduction of "no fault" compensation schemes for harm done in auto accidents. The no-fault system was originally established to ensure that accident victims were compensated for their injuries without delay. Quebec was the first jurisdiction to adopt a no-fault system in 1978. It allows no separate lawsuits for compensation, apart from the compensation provided by the government. Since that time, the Saskatchewan and Manitoba systems have been modelled on the Quebec plan, and many other jurisdictions have some version of no-fault coverage. However, while the no-fault system has been shown to provide more victims with compensation more quickly than the tort system (Bogart, 2002:106), it has also been subject to criticisms for its inadequacy in addressing the claims of those individuals who have serious and permanent injuries and unusual pain and suffering. In addition, research conducted in Australia, New Zealand, and Quebec has discerned "some troubling, unexpected implications regarding the loss of deterrence effects on dangerous driving when tort actions are abolished and no-fault schemes are substituted" (p. 106). For example, in an early assessment of the Quebec scheme, Gaudry (1988) found that the number of bodily injuries grew by 26.3 percent a year and fatalities by 6.8 percent after the introduction of the no-fault system. He suggested that these increases stemmed, at least in part, from two factors: "first, compulsory insurance requirements that cause previously uninsured motorists to drive less carefully and, second, flat premiums that significantly decrease insurance for high-risk drivers, resulting in more accidents, when before the differential rates would have priced them off the highway" (Bogart, 2002:106). Findings that indicate that no-fault schemes are associated with elevated rates of automobile accidents, injuries, and fatalities "are clearly at odds with the avowed purposes of such regimes" (Bogart, 2002:107).

For many, evaluation research has become a proper use of sociology in policy-related work (Babbie, 2017; Knutsson and Tilley, 2009). This use of social research in policy analysis has become widespread, and an entire field of specialization has developed about methods and procedures for conducting evaluation research. Technically speaking, however, there are no formal methodological differences between evaluation and non-evaluation research. They have in common the same techniques and the same basic steps that must be followed in the research process. The difference lies in the following: (1) Evaluation research uses deliberately planned intervention of some independent variable; (2) the programs it assesses assume some objective or goal as desirable; and (3) it attempts to determine the extent to which this desired goal has been reached. As Suchman (1967:15) puts it, evaluation research "asks about the *kind* of change the program views as desirable, the *means* by which this change is to be brought about, and the *signs* according to which such change can be recognized." Thus, the greatest distinction between evaluation and non-evaluation research is one of objectives. Weiss (1998:6) proposes several additional criteria that distinguish evaluation research from other types of research:

1. Evaluation research is generally conducted for a client who intends to use the research as a basis for decision-making.
2. The investigator deals with his or her client's questions as to whether the client's program is accomplishing what the client wishes it to accomplish.
3. The objective of evaluation research is to ascertain whether the program goals are being reached.

4. The investigator works in a situation where priority goes to the program as opposed to the evaluation.
5. There is always a possibility of conflicts between the researcher and the program staff because of the divergences of loyalties and objectives.
6. In evaluation research, there is an emphasis on results that are useful for policy decisions.

Social policy evaluation is essentially concerned with attempts to determine the impact of policy on real-life conditions. At a minimum, policy evaluation requires a specification of policy objectives (what we want to accomplish with a given policy), the means of realizing it (programs), and what has been accomplished toward the attainment of the objectives (impacts or outcomes). In measuring objectives, there is a need to determine not only that some change in real-life conditions has occurred, such as a reduction in the unemployment rate, but also that it was due to policy actions and not to other factors, such as private economic decisions.

DIMENSIONS OF POLICY IMPACT

Dye (2008) suggests that the impact of a policy has several dimensions, all of which must be taken into account in the course of evaluation. These include the impact on the social problem at which a policy is directed and on the people involved. Those whom the policy is intended to affect must be clearly defined—the poor, the disadvantaged, schoolchildren, or single mothers. The intended effect of the policy must then be determined. If, for example, it is an anti-poverty program, is its purpose to raise the income of the poor, to increase their opportunities for employment, or to change their attitudes and behaviour? If some combination of such objectives is intended, the evaluation of impact becomes more complicated, since priorities must be assigned to the various intended effects.

At times, it is difficult to determine the purpose of a law or a program of regulation. The determination of intent is complicated because many individuals with diverse purposes participate in the policymaking. Will consideration be given to the intention or intentions of the persons who drafted the statute or the judge who wrote the opinion creating the rule? To that of the majority of the legislature or court who voted for it? To that of the lobbyists who worked for the bill? To that purpose openly discussed or to the purpose that is implicit but never mentioned? At times, one can only conclude that a law has multiple and perhaps even conflicting purposes.

It should also be noted that a law may have intended or unintended consequences or even both. A guaranteed-income program, for example, may improve the income situation of the benefited groups, as intended. But what impact does it also have on their initiative to seek employment? Does it decrease this, as some have contended? Similarly, an agricultural price support program intended to improve farmers' incomes may lead to overproduction of the supported commodities.

The difficulties of measuring impact are most acute for those areas of conduct where the behaviour in question is hard to quantify and where it is hard to tell what the behaviour *would* have been without the intervention of the law. The laws against murder illustrate the difficulties here. There is a fairly good idea about the murder rate in most countries, but no information at all exists about the contribution that the *law* makes to this rate. In other words, there is no way of determining how high the murder rate would be if there were, for example, no punishment assigned for murder.

Knowledge of a new law by members of the legal profession also plays a role in the study of impact. To the degree that lawyers fail to keep abreast of new laws intended to protect consumers, the effectiveness of such laws will obviously be impaired. For example, a survey of 564 Alberta lawyers and 141 psychiatrists investigated their knowledge of, attitudes toward, and experiences with the Criminal Code provisions regarding mentally disordered offenders (Crisanti, Arboleda-Florez, and Stuart, 2000). It found that psychiatrists had significantly more correct responses to the survey items assessing knowledge than lawyers. However, while the; highest possible knowledge score was 27, the average score for psychiatrists was 16 and, for lawyers, merely 13. The lack of knowledge demonstrated by both lawyers and psychiatrists is troubling for many in both professions were ignorant of key Criminal Code provisions governing mentally disordered offenders. Similarly, a study conducted in the wake of the Supreme Court of Canada decision (in *Reibl v. Hughes* [1980]) on informed consent to medical treatment found that 70 percent of Canadian surgeons were unaware of what the decision was and that "a majority of those who were aware expressed views inconsistent with it" (Bogart, 2002:119). Moreover, while the General Counsel to the Canadian Medical Protective Association confidently opined that "No legal event in the last fifty years has so disturbed the practice of medicine as did the decision of the Supreme Court of Canada in *Reibl v. Hughes*" (cited in Bogart, 2002:350), a second follow-up study conducted a decade after the decision by the Supreme Court concluded that, in actuality, the decision "had had small significance for the severity and frequency of malpractice claims. . . [and] little impact on developments in other areas of health law or in jurisdictions outside Canada" (pp. 119, 350).

The study of impact is further complicated by the fact that policies may have effects on groups or situations other than those at which they are directed. These are called **spillover effects** (Wade, 1972). These spillover effects may be positive or negative. An illustration of the negative effects is the testing of nuclear devices, which may provide data for the design of nuclear power plants but may also generate hazards for the population. An illustration of a positive spillover effect is that when tariffs are lowered at the request of Canadian exporters to increase their sales abroad, consumers in Canada may benefit from lower prices caused by increased imports that lower tariffs stimulate. Obviously, in the evaluation of impact, attention must also be paid to the spillover effects.

A given legislation may also have impact on future as well as current conditions. Is a particular policy designed to improve an immediate short-term situation, or is it intended to have effects over a longer time period? The determination of long-term effects stemming from a policy is much more difficult than the assessment of short-term impacts (see, for example, Beare, 2002).

MEASURING LAW'S IMPACT

A fairly rich literature of evaluation of actual and proposed programs of law has developed using criteria derived from economics as its standard. This literature takes certain economic goals as its basic values and assesses legal programs as good or bad depending upon whether they most efficiently or rationally achieve the economic goals or make use of theoretically correct economic means. Of course, it is fairly easy to calculate the dollar costs of a particular policy when it is stated as the actual number of dollars spent on a program, its share of total government expenditures, how efficiently the funds are allocated, and so on. Other economic costs are, however, difficult to measure. For example, it is difficult to discover the expenditures by the private sector for pollution-control devices that are necessitated by air pollution control policy. Moreover, economic standards are hardly applicable to the measurement of social costs of inconvenience, dislocation, and social disruption resulting from, for instance, an urban renewal project (see, for example, Clairmont and Magill, 1999).

In addition to the difficulties inherent in the measurement of indirect costs and benefits, other complexities arise because the effects of a particular law may be symbolic (intangible) as well as material (tangible). Intended symbolic effects capitalize on popular beliefs, attitudes, and aspirations for their effectiveness. For example, taken at face value, Canada's hate laws are a symbol of equality and progressiveness in combating racism and combating the promotion of genocide. These laws define the willful promotion of hatred against any "identifiable group" as a crime. However, their discernible impact may be substantially lower than many believe. Box 9.1 noted that many hate crime incidents go unreported. In addition, while the public incitement of hatred toward an identifiable group is a criminal offence in Canada, along with advocating or promoting genocide and making public statements that "wilfully promote hatred" against any identifiable group, few are charged under Canada's propaganda laws and even fewer are convicted. For example, between 2010 and 2015, there were 26 court cases in Canada that involved hate propaganda offences or mischief relating to religious property; 14 resulted in a guilty verdict (Yang, 2017). Other laws also appear to promise more symbolically than their instrumentation actually yields in material benefits. They include antitrust activity, regulation of public utility rates, and various anti-poverty efforts. These endeavours attempt to assure people that policymakers are concerned with their welfare, although the tangible benefits are often limited.

These are some of the difficulties that need to be taken into consideration in measuring the impact of a particular law. There are several possible research approaches that can be used for measuring impact. One approach is the study of a group of individuals from the target population after it has been exposed to a program developed to cause change. This approach is referred to as the **one-shot study**. Another possible approach is to study a group of individuals both before and after exposure to a particular program (called a before-and-after study). Still another possibility would be the use of some kind of controlled experiment. But as we noted earlier in this chapter, in measuring the impact of law, one serious problem is the absence of control groups. As a result, one is rarely able to say with confidence what behaviour would have been had a law not been passed or had a different law been passed. Outside of a laboratory setting, it is difficult to apply an experimental treatment to a group that one has matched in all significant respects to another group that does not receive the treatment, so as to control for all possible sources of distortion or error. This difficulty is further accentuated by ethical problems that often arise from such research methods as the random assignment of persons to different legal remedies. One should also be aware of some of the murky statistics that seem to proliferate in the context of policy effectiveness in combating particular problems such as the drug trade, sex trafficking, or terrorist financing (Andreas and Greenhill, 2010; Limoncelli, 2010).

The final consideration of evaluation research involves the utilization of results. As Coleman (1972:6) states, "The ultimate product is not a 'contribution to existing knowledge' in the literature, but a social policy modified by the research result." In many instances, however, those who mandate and request evaluation research fail to utilize the results of that research. These people may feel committed to particular ways of doing things despite evidence that a program is ineffective. This is particularly true in instances where programs were instigated by political pressures such as the various endeavours in relation to urban renewal, corrections, and drug and alcohol rehabilitation. There are, of course, a number of other ways initiators of evaluation research can respond to the results. They include the manipulation of research outcomes for their own interests, rationalization of negative results, and, in some instances where the findings are negative, dismissal of results. The title of a recent book, *Evaluation: Seeking Truth or Power?* (Eliadis, Furubo, and Jacob, 2010) succinctly telegraphs these possibilities. Nevertheless, sociology undoubtedly has a good potential to play an active, creative, and practical role in the formulation, instrumentation, and evaluation of social policy.

SUMMARY

- Several methods can be applied in studying law in society, and more than a single method is usually involved in an investigation. The methods of sociological research include the historical, observational, experimental, and survey studies.
- Sociology, like all sciences, may be either pure or applied. Pure sociology searches for new knowledge, whereas applied sociology tries to apply sociological knowledge to practical problems.
- There is an increasing involvement of sociologists in evaluation research and impact studies. The object of evaluation research is to determine how successful a particular change effort is in achieving its goals. Impact studies are concerned with the intent of those who formulated a legal rule or policy, whether or not a legal rule was responsible for the change, knowledge of a law by its interpreters, and spillover effects.

CRITICAL THINKING QUESTIONS

1. Chapter 1 noted that sociologists interested in the law are frequently asked, "What are you doing studying law?", and differences in the professional cultures of lawyers and sociologists may discourage collaborative work. After reading this chapter, can you identify any additional factors that might complicate or frustrate the attempts of lawyers and sociologists to work together as they research law in society?
2. For decades, the topic of gender bias in the law, courts, and the legal profession has attracted significant discussion in both Canada and the United States. Design a study to investigate gender bias in an area of law that is of particular interest to you. What method(s) would you employ? What difficulties might you anticipate? How could

these problems be redressed?

3. Identify ways in which sociological surveys can impact the development of Canadian laws and social policies.

4. With reference to a law that commands your interest, what methods would you use in evaluating its impact? How would the methods that you selected allow you to answer the questions you'd like to pose?

ADDITIONAL RESOURCES

1. The Law Society of Upper Canada furnishes access to a variety of legal research tools. Visit its website at http://www.lsuc.on.ca/legal-resources/.

2. The University of British Columbia created a web-based guide for beginning law and society students. This guide, which features an enormity of useful links, may be accessed at http://guides.library.ubc.ca/lawsociety.

3. The Law and Society Association hosts Collaborative Research Networks on a wide number of issues and welcomes the creation of additional networks. Visit the Association's site at http://www.lawandsociety.org. From the list that appears on the left-hand side of the screen, select "Collaborative Research Networks."

4. The Best Guide to Canadian Legal Research, at http://legalresearch.org, is a British Columbia—based site that offers detailed instructions for searching electronic databases and conducting research on federal and provincial legislation. It also provides links to other useful sites and a forum on which those conducting research on the law can discuss their use of various research strategies.

GLOSSARY

Action research: A way to integrate knowledge with action.

Adjudication: A public and formal method of conflict resolution, best exemplified by courts. Courts have the authority to intervene in disputes whether or not the parties desire it and to render a decision and enforce compliance with that decision. In adjudication, the emphasis is on the legal rights and duties of disputants, rather than on compromises or on the mutual satisfaction of the parties.

Administrative adjudication: The process by which an administrative agency issues an order. Adjudication is the administrative equivalent of a judicial trial.

Administrative law: A body of law created by administrative agencies in the form of regulations, orders, and decisions.

Applied science: The search for ways of using scientific knowledge to solve practical problems.

Arbitration: Unlike mediation, in which a third party assists the disputants to reach their own solution, arbitration requires a final and binding decision to be made for the disputants by a third party. Disputants agree beforehand both to the intervention of a neutral third party and on the finality of the third party's decision.

Avoidance: This method of dispute resolution refers to limiting the relationship with other disputants sufficiently so that the dispute no longer remains salient (Felstiner, 1974:70). Hirschman (1970) calls this kind of behaviour "exit," which entails withdrawing from a situation or terminating or curtailing a relationship.

Before-and-after study: The study of a group of individuals both before and after exposure to a particular program.

Brutalization effect: Some theorists propose that executions cause a *brutalization effect* and increase violent crime, rather than deter it.

Case law: Law that is enacted by judges in cases that are decided in the appellate courts.

Challenge for cause: In the jury selection process, a challenge for cause can be made on the grounds that, for example, a prospective juror fails to meet the requirements of the provincial statute that governs juries (e.g., the person's occupation places him or her within an exempted category).

Charismatic authority: According to Max Weber, charismatic authority bases its claim to legitimacy on devotion to the specific and unusual sanctity, heroism, or exemplary character of an individual and the normative patterns that are revealed or ordained.

Illustrations of individuals with charismatic authority include Moses, Christ, Mohammed, and Gandhi.

Civil law: A form of private law that consists of a body of rules and procedures intended to govern the conduct of individuals in their relationships with others.

Civil liberties: Fundamental freedoms such as freedom of religion, expression, assembly, and association.

Code: A body of law (statutes) enacted by national parliaments that arrange entire fields of law in an orderly, comprehensive, cumulative, and logical way. Codes are based on the Romano-Germanic system.

Collaborative mediation: Mediation in which lawyers and clients must all agree in advance not to go to court, reducing the incentive for lawyers to recommend litigation.

Community-based mediation: Form of mediation that began in Canada as a grassroots response to such crimes as vandalism.

Compensatory style of social control: According to legal theorist Donald Black, in this form of social control a person who has broken the law is considered to have a contractual obligation and, therefore, owes the victim restitution (for example, a debtor failing to pay a creditor).

Conciliatory style of social control: In this form of social control, deviant behaviour represents one side of a social conflict in need of resolution, without consideration as to who is right or who is wrong (for example, marital disputes).

Conflict perspective: This sociological perspective considers society as consisting of individuals and groups characterized by conflict and dissension and held together by coercion. Order is temporary and unstable because all individuals and groups strive to maximize their own interests in a world of limited resources and goods. This theory cites value diversity, unequal access to economic goods, and the resulting structural cleavages of a society as the basic determinant of laws. Specifically, the origin of law is traced to the emergence of an elite class.

Conflict stage: If a grievance is not resolved, it enters into the conflict stage, in which the aggrieved party confronts the offending party and communicates his or her resentment or feelings of injustice to the person or group. The conflict phase is dyadic; that is, it involves only two parties. If it is not de-escalated or resolved at this stage, it enters into the final, *dispute stage.*

Consciousness-raising: An opportunity to test the validity of legal principles through the personal experiences of those who have been affected by those principles.

Consensus perspective: This sociological perspective describes society as a functionally integrated, relatively stable system held together by a basic consensus of values. Social order is considered as more or less permanent, and individuals can best achieve their interests through co-operation.

Contingency fee: When a lawyer agrees to be paid for his or her services only if he or she wins an award or settlement in the case, any money the lawyer gets is called a *contingency fee*.

Corporate crime: Corporate crime is distinguished from ordinary crime in two respects: the nature of the violation and the fact that administrative and civil law are more likely to be used as punishment than criminal law.

Crime: A *crime* is a public wrong, an offence that has been committed against the public.

Criminal law: Wrongs against the state, the community, and the public or "the people." A crime is a public, as opposed to an individual or private, wrong.

Culture: According to Black, culture can be measured by the volume, complexity, and diversity of ideas in a society, and by the degree of conformity to the mainstream of culture.

Customs and conventions: Weber contends that customs and conventions can be distinguished from law. *Customs* are rules of conduct in defined situations that are of relatively long duration and are generally observed without deliberation and "without thinking." *Conventions* are rules for conduct that involve a sense of duty and obligation.

Denunciation: The attempt to censure an individual for culpable criminal conduct. The court imposes a sentence to denounce the crime of which the offender has been convicted.

Deterrence: The concept of deterrence is often used to designate punishment in the form of threats directed at offenders or potential offenders so as to frighten them into law-abiding conduct. The effectiveness of these threats is conditioned by the operation of three variables: (1) the severity of the punishment for an offence; (2) the certainty that it would be applied; and (3) the speed with which it would be applied.

Deterrent effect: See *individual or specific deterrence* and *general deterrence*.

Dialectical materialism: According to this doctrine, the political, social, religious, and cultural order of any given epoch is determined by the existing system of production and forms a *superstructure* on top of this economic basis.

Dialectical perspective: Sociologists who claim to be dialectical and critical in their orientation do not seek merely to describe and explain social events. They, as scientists, also assert their right to criticize.

Direct influence: Constituent pressures that offer rewards or sanctions to lawmakers. Rewards for compliance and sanctions for noncompliance may be votes in an election or re-election campaign or financial contributions, for example.

Dispute: A dispute is a conflict of claims or rights—an assertion of right, claim, or demand on one side, met by contrary claims on the other. When courts hear disputes, they attempt to decide (*adjudicate*) between or among those who have some disagreement, misunderstanding, or competing claims.

Dispute stage: If an issue is not de-escalated or resolved at the *conflict stage*, it enters into the final, dispute stage when the conflict is made public. The dispute stage is characterized by the involvement of a third party in the disagreement.

Doctrine of paramountcy: The doctrine that when laws conflict, the national laws hold sway.

Domestic Violence Courts: Courts that specifically address domestic violence cases, and are designed to decrease court processing time, increase conviction rates, provide a focal point for victim services, and enable specialization within law enforcement and investigation (Department of Justice, 2005).

Drug Treatment Court (DTC): First introduced into this country in 1998, DTCs attempt to address the needs of non-violent individuals who are charged with criminal offences that are motivated by their addictions.

Economic determinism: The Marxian idea that economic organization, especially the ownership of property, determines the organization of the rest of society.

Empirical justice: The deciding of cases by referring to analogies and by relying on and interpreting precedents.

Environmental injustice: The tendency for socially and politically marginalized groups to bear the brunt of environmental ills from polluting industries, industrial and waste facilities, and transportation arteries (which generate vehicle emissions pollution). Also called *environmental racism.*

Environmental racism: See *environmental injustice.*

Ethnocentrism: Judging other cultures by the standards of one's own.

Experiment: Experiments are the prevailing method for testing causal relations by social scientists, especially psychologists. An experiment may be carried out in a laboratory or a field setting, and it ideally begins with two or more equivalent groups, with an experimental variable introduced into only the experimental group. The researcher measures the phenomenon under study before the introduction of the experimental variable and after, thus getting a measure of the change presumably caused by the variable.

Expressive offences: Acts in which the behaviour is an end in itself, such as murder, assault, and sex offences.

Fatalism: Feelings of resignation or powerlessness. People who are fatalistic perceive themselves to lack control over their lives and, for example, believe that everything that happens to them is caused by God or evil spirits.

Feminist practical reasoning: A method of analysis that assumes women approach the reasoning process differently than men, are more sensitive to situation and context, and tend to resist universal generalizations and principles.

Feuding: A state of recurring hostilities between families or groups, instigated by a desire to avenge an offence (insult, injury, death, or deprivation of some sort) against a member of the other group.

Folkways: Established norms of common practices such as those that specify modes of dress, etiquette, and language use.

Functionalistic model: This view of lawmaking, as formulated by Paul Bohannan (1973), argues that lawmaking is the restatement of some customs (for example, those dealing with economic transactions and contractual relations, property rights in marriage, or deviant behaviour) so that they can be enforced by legal institutions.

Garnishment: A court order directing someone who owes or possesses money due to the debtor (such as an employer) to pay all or some of that money to the court, which then turns it over to the creditor.

General deterrence: This form of crime deterrence results from the warning offered to potential criminals by the example of punishment directed at a specific wrongdoer. It aims to discourage others from criminal behaviour by making an example of the offender being punished.

Generic prejudice: Beliefs about certain groups of people or certain types of crime (e.g., judging a person as guilty or innocent based on his or her race, sex, or sexual orientation rather than on the facts of the case).

Golden rule: This premise for interpreting statutes specifies that in cases where the literal interpretation of a statute would lead to a "logical absurdity, an inconsistency or a repugnancy," the court can move from the literal interpretation—but "only so far as is necessary to remove the conflicting construction" (Olivo, 2004:71).

Grievance or preconflict stage: The grievance or preconflict stage in the dispute process is when an individual or a group perceives a situation to be unjust and considers grounds for resentment or complaint. If it is not resolved, it enters into the *conflict stage.* The grievance stage is monadic; it involves only one party.

Group influence: The influence of organized interest groups representing a special constituency. Political parties, interest groups, and citizen action groups are continually influencing the lawmaking process.

Historical research: This research, carried out by sociologists, involves the critical investigation of events, developments, and experiences of the past; a careful weighing of evidence to determine the validity of the sources of information regarding the past; and the interpretation of the evidence.

Human rights: Encompassing more than the idea of *civil liberties*, human rights also include such rights as the right to education, accommodation, and employment.

Impetus: A fundamental prerequisite for setting the mechanism of lawmaking in motion.

Incapacitation: A frequent element of judicial punishment that involves, for example, a prison term, which prevents a violator from misbehaving during the time he or she is being punished.

Indeterminacy: The law's inability to cover all situations.

Indirect influence: The form of influence that impacts the lawmaking process indirectly. Here, a lawmaker acts in the capacity of an "instructed delegate." Decisions are made on behalf of the desires of a particular constituency, for example, residents living around an airport who oppose expansion of the facilities.

Individual or specific deterrence: This form of crime deterrence may be achieved by intimidation of the person, frightening him or her against further deviance, or it may be effected through reformation, in that the lawbreaker changes his or her deviant behaviour.

Institutionalization of behaviour: Institution-alization of a pattern of behaviour refers to the establishment of a norm with provisions for its enforcement (such as nondiscrimination in employment).

Instrumental offences: Burglary, tax evasion, embezzlement, motor vehicle theft, identity theft, and other illegal activities directed toward some material end.

Interest group thesis: This idea contends that laws are created because of the special interests of certain groups in the population (Mahood, 2000). The image of society reflected by this view stresses cultural differences, value clashes, inequities, and social conflict (Hajnal and Clark, 1998).

Interest prejudice: Biases that jurors may hold due to a direct interest in the case (e.g., a relationship to the accused or a witness).

Internalization of behaviour: Internalization of a pattern of behaviour means the incorporation of the value or values implicit in a law (for example, discrimination is "wrong").

Intersectionalism: A term used in critical legal studies to "capture some of the unique dimensions and circumstances of being both a woman and a person of colour" (Friedrichs, 2006:108).

Irrational procedures: Legal procedures that rely on ethical or mystical considerations such as magic or faith in the supernatural.

Justiciability: This term is used to indicate that a conflict is viable to trial and courts. The court must be mandated to provide a remedy. In Canada, most disputes are justiciable in one court or another, although the jurisdiction of particular courts varies.

Kahdi *justice:* The justice that is dispensed by the judge of the Islamic *Shari'a* court (see Chapter 1).

Latent functions: Functions that are unintentional, unanticipated consequences of a social system that has been set up to achieve other ends (in contrast to *manifest functions*).

Law in literature school: A school of thought in which scholars explore the implications of law as it is depicted in literary classics (Scallen, 1995:705).

Legal culture: Those attributes of behaviour and attitudes that make the law of one society different from that of another.

Legal literacy: The process of acquiring critical awareness about rights and law, the ability to assert rights, and the capacity to mobilize for change (Schuler and Kadirgamar-Rajasingham, 1992).

Legal literary/rhetorical criticism school: A school of thought that employs the methods and theories of literary and rhetorical criticism to study various types of actual legal discourse (e.g., constitutional provisions, judicial opinions).

Legal positivism: Historical and evolutionary interpretations of law that consider the legal and the moral to constitute two quite separate realms (as opposed to natural law).

Legal realism: The contention that judges make law, rather than find it.

Legal storytelling: A school of thought that blends the law-in-literature and legal literary/rhetorical schools and uses personal narratives as evidence in scholarship.

Legalistic style of policing: As opposed to the *watchman style*, agencies characterized by this style tend to treat all situations, even commonplace problems of maintaining order, as if they were serious infractions of the law. Members of such agencies issue a high rate of traffic tickets and arrest a high proportion of young offenders.

Legalization: The process by which norms are moved from the social to the legal level. Not all social norms become laws; in fact, only certain norms are translated into legal norms.

Lien: A lien establishes a creditor's claim on property (such as a house or a car).

Life-histories method: A research technique that requires that the researcher rely solely on a person's reporting of life experiences relevant to the research interest with minimal commentary. Life histories are often part of ethnographic reports. In such instances, they are referred to as *memory cases* (Nader and Todd, 1978:7).

Literal rule: Sometimes called the *plain meaning rule*, this rule for interpreting statutes sets out that the statute should be applied literally, regardless of whether or not the judge approves or disapproves of its result.

Lumping it: This method of dispute resolution refers simply to inaction, to not making a claim or a complaint. Galanter says: "This is done all the time by 'claimants' who lack information or access or who knowingly decide gain is too low, cost too high (including psychic cost of litigating where such activity is repugnant)" (1974:124).

Mala in se: Behaviours that are evils in themselves with public agreement on the dangers they pose (e.g., sexual assault, homicide).

Mala prohibita: Behaviours made criminal by statute, but with no consensus as to whether the acts are criminal in themselves (e.g., prostitution, suicide).

Mandatory mediation: A non-voluntary process that creates significant pressures to settle, and is incorporated within the physical and ideological confines of the formal justice system (Sargent, 2002: 211).

Manifest functions: Functions that are built into a social system by design and are well understood by group members.

Mechanical solidarity: According to Durkheim, this form of solidarity prevails in relatively simple and homogeneous societies where unity is ensured by close interpersonal ties and similarity of habits, ideas, and attitudes.

Med-arb: A hybrid method of dispute resolution in which the issues that were not solved by mediation are submitted to arbitration, with the same person serving first as mediator, then as arbitrator.

Mediation: A dispute resolution method that interposes a disinterested and non-coercive third party, the mediator, between the disputants.

Medicalization: The process of defining behaviour as a medical problem or illness and mandating the medical profession to provide treatment for it.

Mini-trial: A hybrid dispute-resolution method in which lawyers for each disputant are given a short time (not more than a day) in which to present the basic elements of their case to senior executives of both parties. After the presentation, the senior executives try to negotiate a settlement of the case, usually with the aid of a neutral adviser. If there is no settlement, the adviser gives the parties his or her opinion of the likely outcome if the dispute were litigated.

Mischief rule: This rule for interpreting statutes addresses ambiguous legislation. It addresses the problem the statute was created to solve or "what mischief . . . the statute [was] designed to suppress, or what remedy is being advanced by it" (Yates, Yates, and Bain, 2000:39).

Mock trials: Trials in which jurors or juries respond to simulated case materials.

Moral entrepreneur theory: This theory attributes the precipitation of key events to the presence of an enterprising individual or group.

Mores: Societal norms associated with intense feelings of right or wrong and definite rules of conduct that are simply not to be violated (for example, incest).

Morphology: Those aspects of social life that can be measured by social differentiation or the degree of interdependence (for example, the extent of division of labour).

Natural law: Law based on the assumption that through reason the nature of human beings can be known, and that this knowledge can provide the basis for the social and legal ordering of human existence. Natural law is considered superior to enacted law.

Negligence: Actions that cause an unintentional harm because a person or organization failed to take reasonable precautions to ensure that their actions did not endanger others.

Negotiations: Negotiations take place when disputants seek to resolve their disagreements without the help of neutral third parties.

Normative prejudice: "Biases that occur when a juror perceives that there is such strong community interest in a particular outcome of a trial that he or she is influenced in reaching a verdict that is consistent with community sentiment rather than one based on an impartial evaluation of the trial evidence" (Vidmar and Schuller, 2001:134).

Observation: This research method, especially participant observation, seems to be the best data collection method for studying a sequence of events and their meaning as interpreted by the participants and other observers before, during, and after the events. In participant observation, the researcher directly observes and participates in the study system with which he or she has established a meaningful and durable relationship.

Observational methods: Observational methods can be divided into two types: those utilizing either human observers (participant observers or judges) or mechanical observers (cameras, audio recorders, and the like) and those directly eliciting responses from subjects by questioning (questionnaires, schedules, and interview guides). Observational methods can be carried out both in laboratory or controlled situations and in field or natural settings.

Ombudsman process: Related to mediation, this process combines mediatory and investigatory functions in dispute resolution. In a traditional sense, ombudsmen are independent agents of the legislature and they can criticize, publicize, and make recommendations, but they cannot reverse administrative actions.

One-shot study: The study of a group of individuals from the target population after it has been exposed to a program developed to cause change.

One-shotter: A type of litigant who use the courts only occasionally. Illustrations of one-shotters include an author suing his or her publisher for breach of contract, and a professor filing charges against a university for sexual or racial discrimination in promotion (Galanter, 1974).

Organic solidarity: According to Durkheim, this form of solidarity is characteristic of modern societies that are heterogeneous and differentiated by a complex division of labour.

Organization: According to Black, *organization* can be measured by the degree to which the administration of collective action in political and economic spheres is centralized.

Penal law: See *repressive and penal law.*

Penal style of social control: According to Black, in this form of social control the deviant is viewed as a violator of a prohibition and as an offender who is to be subjected to condemnation and punishment (for example, a drug pusher).

Peremptory challenge: Allows either the defense of prosecution to eliminate a potential juror without reference to a specific cause.

Plea bargaining: A form of negotiation that can be traced back to the earliest days of common law. The term *plea bargain* has been defined by the Law Reform Commission of Canada as "an agreement by the accused to plead guilty in return for the prosecutor's agreeing to take or refrain from taking a particular course of action" (Verdun-Jones and Tijerino, 2002:3).

Positive policymaking: Law that aims to create new types of relationships between groups or individuals. It often involves negative sanctions as well as positive rewards.

Praxis: The wedding of theory and action.

Preconflict stage: See *grievance or preconflict stage.*

Prerogative powers: See *royal prerogative.*

Private dispute: This kind of dispute before the courts is characterized by the absence of any initial participation by public authorities. For example, when a husband and wife quarrel, when two business persons debate the terms of a contract, or when two automobiles collide, these events are likely to give rise to private disputes (Goldman and Sarat, 1989).

Private law: This form of law is concerned with both substantive and procedural rules governing relationships between individuals.

Procedural laws: Rules regarding how substantive law is to be administered, enforced, changed, and used in the mediation of disputes.

Professionalization: As a modicum, the possession of (1) a specialized technique supported by a body of theory, (2) a career supported by an association of colleagues, and (3) a status supported by community recognition" (Foote, 1953:371).

Proscriptive policymaking: Law that aims to prevent individuals from doing things that others in society oppose as being harmful or immoral. It usually involves only negative sanctions.

Public defendant dispute: In this type of dispute, the government participates as a defendant. Such disputes involve challenges to the authority of some government agency or questions about the propriety of some government action that may be initiated by an individual or by an organization (Goldman and Sarat, 1989).

Public-initiated dispute: This type of dispute occurs when the government seeks to enforce norms of conduct or to punish individuals who breach such norms. These kinds of public disputes emerge when society attempts to control and channel social behaviour through the promulgation of binding legal norms (Goldman and Sarat, 1989).

Public-interest law: This the term is frequently used to describe the activities of law firms that represent environmentalists, consumers, and like groups, as well as test-case litigation in civil rights and poverty controversies. It is generally oriented toward causes and interests of groups, classes, or organizations, rather than individuals.

Public law: This form of law is concerned with the structure of government, the duties and powers of officials, and the relationship between the individual and the state: "It includes such subjects as constitutional law, administrative law, regulation of public utilities, criminal law and procedure, and law relating to the proprietary powers of the state and its political subdivisions" (Davis, 1962:51).

Punitive damages: An extra amount over and above the victim's proven losses in a civil case, intended to punish defendants when their conduct has been outrageous, grossly negligent, and close to criminal.

Pure science: The search for knowledge, without primary concern for its practical use.

Rational justice: Weber argues that rational justice is based on bureaucratic principles. Rationality can be further based on adherence to "eternal characteristics" (observable, concrete features) of the facts of the case.

Rational-legal authority: According to Weber, rational-legal authority bases its claims to legitimacy on a belief in the legality of normative rules and in the right of those elevated to authority to issue commands under such rules. In such authority, obedience is owed to a legally established impersonal order.

Rational procedures: Legal procedures that involve the use of logic and scientific methods to attain specific objectives.

Rationalistic model: A theory of the sociology of law that proposes that laws (in particular, criminal laws) are created as a rational means of protecting the members of society from social harm. In this perspective, crimes are considered socially injurious.

Regulatory disputes: These disputes frequently involve difficult technical questions, whereas social-policy disputes raise difficult political and value questions.

Rehabilitation: The attempt to change an individual by promoting law-abiding behaviour. This usually involves sentencing the offender to some alternative to custody, such as probation with conditions.

Reintegrative shaming: In reintegrative shaming, disapproval is expressed toward the rule-violating act, but the essential value of the offender him- or herself is reaffirmed, along with the prospect of reacceptance.

Rent-a-judge: A hybrid dispute-resolution method in which the disputants, in an attempt to avoid the use of a regular court, select a retired judge to hear and decide a pending case as an arbitrator would. The same procedure is used as in court, and the decision of the judge is legally binding.

Reparation: The court may order an offender to make reparations to individual victims or the community.

Repeat players: Litigants who engage in many similar litigations over a period of time. Whereas *one-shotters* are usually individuals, repeat players are organizations, such as finance companies, moving companies, or insurance companies (Galanter, 1974).

Repressive and penal law: In a homogeneous, undifferentiated society, a criminal act offends the collective conscience (i.e., the "totality of social likenesses," as Durkheim wrote [1912:80]), and punishment is meant to protect and preserve social solidarity.

Responsible government: A system of government that abides by the principle of parliamentary accountability.

Restitutive law: In modern heterogeneous societies, repressive law tends to give way to restitutive law, whereby restitution (sometimes called *damages*) is awarded based on a lawbreaker's wrongs committed.

Retribution: Social retaliation against an offender. Punishment of the offender for the crime that has been committed and, to an extent, punishment that (in principle) matches the impact of the crime upon its victim (for instance, a person or an organization).

Rights-based mediation: Sometimes referred to as "early neutral evaluation" or "evaluative mediation," it involves a mediator's evaluation of the case in the context of formal rules (e.g., the law or accepted principles of accounting).

Royal prerogative or prerogative powers: The residue of discretionary authority that is legally left in the hands of the Crown.

Rule of law: Dicey's doctrine that (1) no one is punishable except for a distinct breach of law, (2) all classes must be subject to the law of the land, and (3) individual rights derive from court precedents rather than from constitutional codes.

Sanctions: Related to legal efficacy, sanctions are provided to guarantee the observance and execution of legal mandates—to enforce behaviour. Among the means of coercive law enforcement are punishment by fine or imprisonment and the imposition of damage awards.

Scientific jury selection: This method consists of three steps. First, a random sample is drawn from the population and the demographic profile of this sample is compared with that of the prospective jurors. If the jurors were randomly selected, the profiles should match. If there is substantial over- or under-representation of particular characteristics (ethnic groups, age, occupation, and so forth), the jury pool can be challenged. Second, after it is established that the prospective jurors represent the population at large, a random sample is drawn from the jury pool to determine the demographic, personal, and attitudinal characteristics considered to be favourable to one's own side. Third, after establishing the psychological and demographic profile of a "favourable" juror, the social scientist can make recommendations for selection of individual jurors.

Segregation: The separation of groups in residence, workplace, and social functions.

Sentencing circles: In circle sentencing, the court typically invites "interested members of the community to join the judge, prosecutor, defence counsel, police, social service providers, community elders, along with the offender, the victim and their families and supporters" (Spiteri, 2002:2) to meet and, within a circle, discuss the crime, factors that may have impacted upon its commission, sentencing options, and strategies through which the offender may be reintegrated into the community. In Canada, sentencing circles seldom hear cases that carry a minimum punishment of over two years' imprisonment.

Service style of policing: This style combines law enforcement and maintenance of order. An emphasis is placed on community relations, the police on patrol work out of specialized units, and command is decentralized.

Shadow jury: Simulated or *shadow* juries are used to gain feedback for lawyers on how to try their cases. Most of these mock trials are conducted by jury consulting or market research firms.

Shaming: In some societies, shaming is used as a form of public reprimand in the disapproval of disputing behaviour. Ridicule directed at those guilty of antisocial conduct is also used to reduce conflict. See also *reintegrative shaming.*

Shari'a: Islamic religion states what Muslims must believe and includes the *Shari'a* ("the way to follow"), which specifies the rules for believers based on divine command and revelation.

Social change: Modifications in the way people work, rear a family, educate their children, govern themselves, and seek ultimate meaning in life; in addition, it refers to a restructuring of the basic ways people in a society relate to each other with regard to government, economies, education, religion, family life, recreation, language, and other activities.

Social control: The amount of nonlegal control to which people are subjected is a measure of their respectability, and differences between people indicate normative distance from each other.

Social movement: A type of collective behaviour whereby a group of individuals organize to promote certain changes or alterations in certain types of behaviour or procedures.

Social policy: Purposive legal measures that are adopted and pursued by representatives of government who are responsible for dealing with particular social conditions in society.

Social-policy disputes: These disputes develop when the government pursues broad national objectives that may involve or impinge upon many interests and groups, such as equality and economic opportunity, environmental protection, income security, and public health and safety (Mink and Solinger, 2004).

Sociological jurisprudence: The study of law and legal philosophy, and the use of its ideas in law to regulate conduct.

Specific deterrence: The goal of state-administered punishment is to deter the specific offender from committing further crimes.

Specific prejudice: Attitudes or beliefs about a particular case that may affect one's ability to decide the case in a way that is fair.

Spillover effects: The *spillover effect* occurs when a policy affects groups or situations other than those at which they are directed (Wade, 1972).

Standing: The traditional view of standing was that individuals should be able to bring lawsuits only if their personal legal rights had been violated.

Stare decisis: "Stand by what has been decided." The principle in common-law systems that judges should build on precedents established in past decisions.

Statutory law: Legislation passed by elected officials in legislative assemblies.

Stratification: Inequality of wealth.

Substantive laws: The rights, duties, and prohibitions administered by courts concerning what is right, wrong, permissible, and impermissible—which behaviours are to be allowed and which are prohibited (such as prohibitions against murder or the sale of narcotics).

Superstition: Uncritical acceptance of a belief that is not substantiated by facts.

Survey research: This form of research aims for a systematic and comprehensive collection of information about the attitudes, beliefs, and behaviours of people. The most common means of data collection are face-to-face interviews, self-administered questionnaires (for example, mail questionnaires), and telephone interviews.

Therapeutic style of social control: According to Black, in this form of social control the deviant's conduct is defined as abnormal; the person needs help, such as treatment by a psychiatrist.

Torts: Private wrongs of parties against each other rather than against the state or the public. The injured individual may seek redress in the courts for the harm he or she has experienced. In most cases, some form of payment is required from the offender to compensate for the injury he or she has caused.

Traditional authority: Max Weber defines *traditional authority* as that which bases its claims to legitimacy on an established belief in the sanctity of traditions and the legitimacy of the status of those exercising authority. The obligation of obedience is not a matter of acceptance of the legality of an impersonal order but, rather, a matter of personal loyalty. The "rule of elders" is illustrative of traditional authority.

Voir dire: A trial within a trial to decide upon the admissibility of evidence.

Watchman style of policing: This style emphasizes the responsibility for maintaining public order, as contrasted with traditional law enforcement. The police officer in such an agency is viewed as a peace officer, ignoring or handling informally many violations of the law and paying much greater attention to local variations in maintaining order.

Woman question: An overarching question designed to probe into the gender implications of a social practice or rule (see, for example, Lamarche, 2000). Asking the *woman question* compensates for law's failure to take into account experiences and values that are more typical of women than of men.

Writ of seizure and sale: This order results in a forced sale involving the seizure and sale at an auction of the debtor's property. The proceeds are then turned over to the creditor to satisfy the judgment.

Youth Courts: Courts that specifically address cases in which a young person, aged 12 to 17, is charged with an offence under federal youth justice laws.

REFERENCES AND FURTHER READINGS

Abadinsky, Howard. 2008. *Law and Justice: An Introduction to the American Legal System.* 6th ed. Upper Saddle River, NJ: Prentice Hall.

Abass, Ademola. 2011. *Complete International Law.* New York: Oxford University Press.

Abel, Richard L. 1973. "A Comparative Theory of Dispute Institutions in Society." *Law and Society Review* 8 (2) (Winter): 217–347.

———. 1986. "The Transformation of the American Legal Profession." *Law and Society Review* 20 (1): 7–17.

———. 1995. "What We Talk About When We Talk About Law," in Richard L. Abel (ed.), *The Law and Society Reader*, pp. 1–10. New York: New York University Press.

——— (ed.). 2003. *English Lawyers Between Market and State: The Politics of Professionalism.* Oxford, UK: Oxford University Press.

———. 2010. Lawyers in the Dock: Learning From Attorney Disciplinary Proceedings. New York: Oxford University Press.

Aboriginal Justice Inquiry of Manitoba. 1991. *The Justice System and Aboriginal People.* Vol. 1. Winnipeg: Queen's Printer.

Abramson, Jeffrey. 2000. *We, the Jury: The Jury System and the Ideal of Democracy.* Cambridge, MA: Harvard University Press.

Abrol, Manpreet. 2014. The Criminalization of Prostitution: Putting Women's Lives at Risk." *Prandium: The Journal of Historical Studies* 3(1):1–10.

Acker, James R., and Rose Bellandi. 2012. "Firmament or Folly? Protecting the Innocent, Promoting Capital Punishment, and the Paradoxes of Reconciliation." *Justice Quarterly* 29(2): 287–307.

Act Respecting Communistic Propaganda, RSQ 1941, c. 52.

Addy, George, Lori A. Cornwall, and Elisa K. Kearney. 2005. "Canada: Competition Law Compliance Strategies: The Increasingly Complex and Challenging Mandate Facing Compliance Managers." July 15. Retrieved from www.mondaq.com/i_article.asp_Q_ articleid _E_33729.

Adinkrah, Mensah. 2005. "Vigilante Homicides in Contemporary Ghana." *Journal of Criminal Justice* 33 (5) (September–October): 413–427. *Agribrands Purina Canada Inc. v. Kasamekas*, 2011 ONCA 460.

Agyeman, Julian, and Yelna Ogneva-Himmelberg. 2009. *Environmental Justice and Sustainability in the Former Soviet Union.* Cambridge, MA: MIT Press.

Ahmed v. Dalhousie University, 2014 NSSC 330.

Akers, Ronald L. 1965. "Toward a Comparative Definition of Law." *Journal of Criminal Law, Criminology, and Police Science* 56 (September): 301–306.

Akwesasne Tekaia'torehthà:ke Kaianerénhsera (Akwesasne Court Law), MCR 332 2016, Alberta Human Rights Act Chapter A-25.5

Alberta Health Services. 2017. "PChAD Info For Parents." Retrieved from www.albertahealthservices.ca/amh/Page2547.aspx.

Albisetti, James C. 2000. "Portia Ante Portas: Women and the Legal Profession in Europe, ca. 1870–1925." *Journal of Social History* 33 (4) (Summer): 825–857.

Alexander, Klinton W. and Kern Alexander. 2017. *Higher Education Law: Policy and Perspectives.* New York: Routledge.

Alexander, Rudolph, Jr. 2006. "Restorative Justice: Misunderstood and Misapplied." *Journal of Policy Practice* 5 (1): 67–81.

Allard et al. v Canada (2016) FC 236.

Allen, Mary. 2016. "Police-Reported Crime Statistics in Canada, 2015." *Juristat* 36 (1). Retrieved from www.statcan.gc.ca/pub/85-002-x/2016001/article/14642-eng.htm.

Allyn, David. 2004. *I Can't Believe I Just Did That: How Seemingly Small Embarrassments Can Wreak Havoc in Your Life—and What You Can Do to Put a Stop to Them.* New York: Jeremy P. Tarcher/Penguin.

Alther, Lis. 2012. *Blood Feud: The Hatfields and the McCoys: The Epic Story of Murder and Vengeance.* Guilford, CT: Lyons Press.

Ambrose, David. 1998. *Superstition.* New York: Warner.

American Bar Association (ABA). 2005. "Miles to Go: Progress of Minorities in the Legal Profession." Retrieved from http://74.125.95.132/search?q= cache:eUUMXeuSlIkJ:www.law.harvard.edu/ programs/plp/pdf/Projects_MilesToGo.pdf+

American Bar Association (ABA). 2007. *Dispute Resolution Directory*. Washington, DC: ABA.

American Bar Association (ABA). 2017. "Statistics." Retrieved from www.americanbar.org/groups/ legal_education/resources/statistics.html.

Amnesty International. 2008. "Secrecy Surrounds Death Penalty." April 15. Retrieved from www. amnesty.rg/en/news-and-updates/ report/secrecy-surrounds-death-penalty-20080415

———. 2016a. "Death Penality." Retrieved from www.amnesty.org/en/what-we-do/death-penalty/.

———. 2016b. *Amnesty International Global Report: Death Sentences and Executions 2015*. London: Amnesty International. Retrieved from www.amnesty.org/en/documents/act50/3487/2016/en/.

Amrane v. York University, 2016 ONSC 395.

Anderson, Helen A. 2014. "Frenemies of the Court: The Many Faces of Amicus Curiae." *University of Richmond Law Review* 49: 361–416.

Anderson, James E. 2015. *Public Policymaking*. 8th ed. Belmont, CA: Wadsworth.

Anderson, Lisa. 2003. *Pursuing Truth, Exercising Power: Social Science and Public Policy in the Twenty-First Century*. New York: Columbia University Press.

Anderson, Mark C. and Carmen L. Robertson. 2011. *Seeing Red: A History of Natives in Canadian Newspapers*. Winnipeg, MB: University of Manitoba Press.

Andreas, Peter and Kelly M. Greenhill (eds.). 2010. *Sex, Drugs, and Body Counts: The Politics of Numbers in Global Crime and Conflict*. Ithaca, NY: Cornell University Press.

Andrews v. Grand & Toy Alberta Ltd., [1978] 2 S.C.R. 229 (SCC).

Anleu, Sharyn I. Roach. 2009. *Law and Social Change*. 2nd ed. Thousand Oaks, CA: Sage.

An-Na'im, Abudullahi and Mashood Baderin. 2010. *Islam and Human Rights*. Burlington, VT: Ashgate.

Anti-Terrorism Act, SC 2001, c. 41.

Appelrouth, Scott, and Laura Desfor Edles. 2016. *Classical and Contemporary Sociological Theory: Text and Readings*. Thousand Oaks, CA: Sage Publications.

Appleton, Josie. 2016. *Officious: Rise of the Busybody State*. Winchester, UKL: Zero Books.

Arnold v. Teno, [1978] 2 S.C.R. 287 (SCC).

Arnold, Bruce L. and John Hagan. 1992. "Careers of Misconduct: The Structure of Prosecuted Professional Deviance Among Lawyers." *American Sociological Review* 57(6): 771–779.

———. 1994. "Self-Regulatory Responses to Professional Misconduct Within the Legal Profession." *Canadian Review of Sociology and Anthropology* 31(2): 168–183.

Arnold, Bruce L. and Fiona M. Kay. 1995. "Social Capital, Violations of Trust and the Vulnerability of Isolates: The Social Organization of Law Practice and Professional Self-Regulation." *International Journal of the Sociology of Law* 23(4): 321–346.

Arnold, Thurman. 1935. *The Symbols of Government*. New Haven, CT: Yale University Press.

Arrigo, Bruce A. (ed.). 1999. *Social Justice/ Criminal Justice: The Maturation of Critical Theory in Law, Crime, and Deviance*. Belmont, CA: West/Wadsworth.

———. 2002. *Punishing the Mentally Ill: A Critical Analysis of Law and Psychiatry*. Albany: State University of New York Press.

Arrigo, Bruce A. and Dragan Milovanovic (eds.). 2010. *Postmodernist and Post-Structuralist Theories of Crime*. Burlington, VT: Ashgate.

Arthur, Jennifer. 2012. "The Relationship Between Legal Gambling and Crime in Alberta." Masters of Science Thesis, University of Lethbridge.

Arthur, Jennifer N., Robert J. Williams, and Yale Belanger. 2014. "The Relationship between Legal Gambling and Crime in Alberta." *Canadian Journal of Criminology and Criminal Justice* 56(1): 49–84.

Arthurs, Harry W. 1980. "Jonah and the Whale: The Appearance, Disappearance and Reappearance of Administrative Law." *University of Toronto Law Journal* 30: 225–239.

———. 1996. "Lawyering in Canada in the 21st Century." *Windsor Yearbook of Access to Justice* 12: 202–225.

———. 1997. "Globalization of the Mind: Canadian Elites and the Restructuring of Legal Fields." *Canadian Journal of Law and Society* 12(2): 219–246.

———. 1998. "Why Canadian Law Schools Do Not Teach Legal Ethics," in K. Economides (ed.), *Ethical Challenges to Legal Education and Conduct*, pp. 105–118. Oxford: Hart.

———. 1999. "Introduction," in Allan C. Hutchinson, *Legal Ethics and Professional Ethics*, pp. x–xiv. Toronto: Irwin Law.

———. 2001. "Poor Canadian Legal Education: So Near to Wall Street, So Far from God." *Osgoode Hall Law Journal* 38(3): 381–408.

Asante, Molefi Kete. 2003. *Afrocentricity: The Theory of Social Change*. Rev. ed. Chicago, IL: African American Images.

Asbridge, Mark. 2004. "Public Place Restrictions on Smoking in Canada: Assessing the Role of the State, Media, Science and Public Health Advocacy." *Social Science and Medicine* 58(1): 13–24.

Aubert, Vilhelm. 1963. "Competition and Dissensus: Two Types of Conflict and Conflict Resolution." *Journal of Conflict Resolution* 7(1): 26–42.

———. 1969a. "Law as a Way of Resolving Conflicts: The Case of a Small Industrialized Society," in Laura Nader (ed.), *Law in Culture and Society*, pp. 282–303. Chicago: Aldine.

———. 1969b. (ed.). *Sociology of Law*. Harmondsworth, UK: Penguin.

———. 1973. "Researches in the Sociology of Law," in Michael Barkun (ed.), *Law and the Social System*, pp. 48–62. New York: Lieber-Atherton.

Auditor General of Canada. 2001. "Report of the Auditor General of Canada, 2001." Retrieved from www.oag-bvg.gc.ca/domino/reports.nsf/ html/0111xe06.html. 2002.

———. 2002. "April Report of the Auditor General of Canada." Retrieved from www.oag-bvg.gc.ca/ internet/English/ parl_oag_ 200204_e_1133.html.

Auerhahn, Kathleen. 2008. "Using Simulation Modeling to Evaluate Sentencing Reform in California: Choosing the Future." *Journal of Experimental Criminology* 4: 241–266.

Austin, Janice L. 2006. "Panel: LSAT, U.S. News and Minority Admissions." *St. John's Law Review* 80 (1): 289–299.

Axelrod, Regina S., Stacy D. Vandeveer, and David Leonnard Downie (eds.). 2010. *The Global Environment: Institutions, Law, and Policy*. 3rd ed. Washington, DC: CQ Press.

Azmier, Jason J. 2005. "Gambling in Canada 2005: Statistics and Context." Canada West Foundation, June. Retrieved from www.cwf.ca/abca/cwfl.doc.nsf/ (Publications)/6C89CD3AB8C28DD78725027004652791/$file/GamblingInCanada.pdf.

B. (R.) v. Children's Aid Society of Metropolitan Toronto (1995) 1 S.C.R. 315, 176 N.R. 161, 26 C.R.R. (2d) 202, 78 O.A.C. 1, 122 D.L.R. (4th) 1.

Baars, Grietje. 2011. "Reform of Revolution-Polanyian versus Marxism Perspectives on the Regulation of the Economic." *Northern Ireland Legal Quaterly* 62(4): 415–431.

Babbie, Earl. 2017. *The Practice of Social Research*. 7th ed. Belmont, CA: Wadsworth.

Babcock, Barbara. 2016. *Fish Raincoats: A Woman Lawyer's Life*. New Orleans: Quid Pro Books.

Backhouse, Constance. 1991. *Petticoats and Prejudice: Women and Law in Nineteenth-Century Canada*. Toronto: Women's Press.

———. 1999a. *Colour-Coded: A Legal History of Racism in Canada, 1900–1950*. Toronto: University of Toronto Press.

———. 1999b. "White Female Help and Chinese Canadian Employers: Race, Class, Gender, and Law in the Case of Yee Chun, 1924," in Nick Larsen and Brian Burtch (eds.), *Law in Society: Canadian Readings*, pp. 3–22. Toronto: Harcourt.

———. 2004. "The Doctrine of Corroboration in Sexual Assault Trials in Early 20th Century Canada and Australia," in Pierre Boyer, Linda Cardinal, and David Headon (eds.), *From Subjects to Citizens: A Hundred Years of Citizenship in Australia and Canada*, pp. 123–159. Ottawa, ON: University of Ottawa Press.

———. 2008. *Carnal Crimes: Sexual Assault Law in Canada 1900–1975*. Toronto: The Osgoode Society and Irwin Law,

Baier, Lowell E. 2016. *Inside the Equal Access to Justice Act: Environmental Litigation and the Crippling Battle over America's Lands, Endangered Species, and Critical Habitats*. Lanham, MD: Rowman & Littlefield.

Bailey, Martha. 1999. "Marriage and Marriage-Like Relationships." Ottawa: Law Commission of Canada.

———. 2000. *Marriage and Marriage-Like Relationships*. Law Commission of Canada Research Report. Retrieved from www.lcc.gc.ca/themes/pr/ cpra/bailey/bailey_main.asp.

Baker, G. Blaine. 1983. "Legal Education in Upper Canada 1895–1889: The Law Society as Educator," in David H. Flaherty (ed.), *Essays in the History of Canadian Law*, vol. 2, pp. 49–142. Toronto: University of Toronto Press.

Baker, Wayne. 2005. *America's Crisis of Values: Reality and Perception.* Princeton, NJ: Princeton University Press.

Bakht, Natasha. 2007. "Religious Arbitration in Canada: Protecting Women by Protecting Them from Religion." *Canadian Journal of Women and the Law* 19 (1): 119–144.

Bakht, Natasha, Kim Brooks, Gillian Calder, Jennifer Koshan, Sonia Lawrence, Carissima Mathen, and Debra Parkes. 2007. "Counting Outsiders: A Critical Exploration of Outsider Course Enrollment in Canadian Legal Education." *Osgoode Hall Law Journal* 45(4): 667–732.

Bala, Nicholas, Peter J. Carrington, and Julian V. Roberts. 2009. "Evaluating the Youth Criminal Justice Act After Five Years: A Qualified Success." *Canadian Journal of Criminology and Criminal Justice* 51 (2): 131–167.

Ball, Howard. 2004. *The Supreme Court in the Intimate Lives of Americans: Birth, Sex, Marriage, Childbearing, and Death.* New York: New York University Press.

Banakar, Reza. 2003. *Merging Law and Sociology: Beyond the Dichotomies in Socio-Legal Research.* Madison, WI: Galda Wilch Verlag.

Bang, Brandy, Paige L. Baker, Alexis Carpinteri, and Vincent B. Van Hasselt. 2013. *Commercial Sexual Exploitation of Children.* New York: Springer Science & Business Media.

Bank of Nova Scotia v. Diemer, 2014 ONCA 851.

Bank of Nova Scotia v. Diemer, 2014 ONSC 365.

Bankowski, Zenon and James MacLean. 2007. *The Universal and the Particular in Legal Reasoning.* Burlington, VT: Ashgate.

Banks, Cindy. 1998. "Custom in the Courts." *British Journal of Criminology* 38 (2): 299–316.

Banks, James. 2017. *Gambling, Crime and Society.* New York: Palgrave MacMillan.

Banner, Stuart. 2000. "Conquest by Contract: Wealth Transfer and Land Market Structure in Colonial New Zealand." *Law and Society Review* 34 (1): 47–96.

Bano, Masooda. 2018. *Modern Islamic Authority and Social Change: Evolving Debates in Muslim Majority Countries.* New York: Oxford University Press.

Barclay, Scott, Mary Bernstein, and Anna-Maria Marshall. 2009. *Queer Mobilizations: LGBT Activists Confront the Law.* New York: New York University Press.

Barkan, Steven E. 2018. *Criminology: A Sociological Understanding.* Upper Saddle River, NJ: Pearson.

Barkan, Steven E. and George J. Bryjak. 2011. *Fundamentals of Criminal Justice: A Sociological View.* 2nd ed. Sadbury, MA: Jones & Bartlett Learning.

Barkun, Michael. 2002. "Defending Against the Global Apocalypse: The Limits of Homeland Security." *Policy Options* 23 (6) (September): 27–32.

Barnett, Larry D. 2010. *Legal Construct, Social Concept: A Macrosociological Perspective on Law.* Piscataway, NJ: Transaction Publishers.

Barrett, Jerome T. and Joseph P. Barrett. 2004. *A History of Alternative Dispute Resolution: From the Wisdom of Solomon to U.S. v. Microsoft and Beyond.* San Francisco: Jossey-Bass.

Bartlett, Katharine T. 1991. "Feminist Legal Methods," in Katharine T. Bartlett and Rosanne Kennedy (eds.), *Feminist Legal Theory: Readings in Law and Gender,* pp. 370–403. Boulder, CO: Westview.

Bartlett, Katharine T., Angela P. Harris, and Deborah L. Rhode. 2006. *Gender and Law: Theory, Doctrine, Commentary.* 4th ed. New York: Aspen Law and Business.

Bartol, Curt R. and Anne M. Bartol. 2011. *Criminal Behavior: A Psychological Approach,* 9th ed. Boston, MA: Prentice Hall.

Bau, Lawrence. 2014. "The History and Treatment of Damages in Canada." Lindsay LLP. Retrieved from www.lindsayllp.ca/articles/the-history-and-treatment-of-damages-in-canada/.

Baughman, Galen. 2015. "Questionable Commitments." *Cato Unbound: A Journal of Debates* (June 1). Retrieved from www.cato-unbound.org/2015/06/01/galen-baughman/questionable-commitments.

Bauman, Richard W. 2002. *Ideology and Community in the First Wave of Critical Legal Studies.* Toronto: University of Toronto Press.

Baumgartner, Frank R., Jeffrey M. Berry, Marie Hojnacki, David C. Kimball, and Beth L. Lesch. 2009. *Lobbying and Policy Change: Who Wins, Who Loses, and Why.* Chicago, IL: University of Chicago Press.

Baumgartner, Mary P. 1978. "Law and Social Status in Colonial New Haven, 1639–1665," in Rita J. Simon (ed.), *Research in Law and Sociology,* vol. 1, pp. 153–174. Greenwich, CT: Jai Press.

———. 1999. *The Social Organization of Law.* 2nd ed. San Diego, CA: Academic Press.

Bazemore, Gordon and Mara Schiff (eds.). 2001. *Restorative and Community Justice.* Cincinnati, OH: Anderson.

BC Civil Liberties Association v. University of Victoria, 2016 BCCA 162.

Bean, Phillip. 2010. *Legalizing Drugs: Debates and Dilemmas*. Bristol, UK: Policy Press.

Beare, Margaret E. 1996. *Criminal Conspiracies: Organized Crime in Canada*. Toronto: ITP Nelson.

———. 2002. "Organized Corporate Criminality: Tobacco Smuggling Between Canada and the US." *Crime, Law and Social Change* 37 (3) (April): 225–243.

Beaudoin, Gerald A. 1999. "Pamajewon Case," in James H. Marsh (ed.), *The Canadian Encyclopedia: Year 2000 Edition*, p. 1753. Toronto: McClelland and Stewart.

Becker, Howard S. 1963. *Outsiders*. New York: Free Press.

Beckman v. Little Salmon/Carmacks First Nation, 2010 SCC 53 (CanLII), [2010] 3 S.C.R. 103.

Bedau, Hugo Adam and Paul G. Cassell (eds.). 2004. *Debating the Death Penalty: Should America Have Capital Punishment? The Experts on Both Sides Make Their Best Case*. New York: Oxford University Press.

Bedford v Attorney General of Canada, [2013] SCJ No.72.

Bednasek, C. Drew. 2009. *Aboriginal and Colonial Geographies of the File Hill Farm Colony*. PhD Dissertation, Queen's University, Department of History.

Beeby, Dean. 2006. "Health Canada Going After Medical Pot Users." *Canoe Network: The CNews* (February 6). Retrieved from www. cnews.canoe.ca/CNEWS/LAW/Marijuana/2006/02/05/1427232-cp.html.

———. 2015. "Court Program for Drug Addicts Helping Mostly White Males, Report Finds." *CBCNews* (December 23). Retrieved from www.cbc.ca/news/politics/drug-court-treatment-diversion-program-1.3376569.

Beeghley, Leonard. 2007. *The Structure of Social Stratification in the United States*. 5th ed. Boston, MA: Pearson/Allyn and Bacon.

Beermann, Jack M. 2006. *Administrative Law*. 2nd ed. New York: Aspen.

Beggs, John and Hugh Davies. 2009. *Police Misconduct, Complaints and Public Regulation*. New York: Oxford University Press.

Behn v. Moulton Contracting Ltd., 2013 SCC 26, [2013] 2 S.C.R. 227.

Belanger, Yale D. (ed.). 2008. *Aboriginal Self-Government in Canada: Current Trends and Issues*. 3rd ed. Saskatoon, SK: Purich Publishing.

———. 2010. "First Nations Gaming as a Self-Government Imperative: Ensuring the Health of First Nations Problem Gamblers." *International Journal of Canadian Studies* 41: 13–36.

Belknap, Joanne. 2015. "Activist Criminology: Criminologists' Responsibility to Advocate for Social and Legal Justice." *Criminology* 53 (1): 1–22.

Bell, Catherine and Michael Asch. 1997. "Challenging Assumptions: The Impact of Precedent in Aboriginal Rights Litigation," in M. Asch (ed.), *Aboriginal and Treaty Rights in Canada: Essays on Law, Equality, and Respect for Difference*, pp. 38–74. Vancouver: UBC Press.

Bella v. Young, 2006 SCC 3, [2006] 1 SCR. 108.

Belliotti, Raymond A. 1992. *Justifying Law: The Debate over Foundations, Goals, and Methods*. Philadelphia: Temple University Press.

Belton, Rachel Kleinfeld. 2005. "Competing Definitions and the Rules of Law: Implications for Practitioners." *Democracy and Rule of Law Project*. Number 55 (January), Carnegie Endowment for International Peace. Retrieved from carnegieendowment.org/files/CP55.Belton.FINAL.pdf

Benda-Beckman, Franz von, Keebet von Benda-Beckman, and Julie Eckert (eds.). 2009. *Rules of Law and Laws of Ruling*. Burlington, VT: Ashgate.

Bennion, Francis A. R. 2009. *Understanding Common Law Legislation*. New York: Oxford University Press.

Bender, Leslie. 2003. "A Lawyer's Primer on Feminist Theory and Tort," in T. Brettel Dawson (ed.), *Women, Law and Social Change: Core Readings and Current Issues*, pp. 186–187. Concord, ON: Captus.

Benjamin, Matthew. 2001. "Legal Self-Help: Cheap Counsel for Simple Cases." *U.S. News and World Report* (February 12): 54–56.

Bennett, Belinda (ed.). 2004. *Abortion*. Burlington, VT: Ashgate.

Bennis, Warren G. 1966. *Changing Organizations*. New York: McGraw-Hill.

Benoit, Cecilia, Mikael Jansson, Michaela Smith and Jackson Flagg. 2017. "'Well, It Should Be Changed for One, Because It's Our Bodies': Sex Workers' Views on Canada's Punitive Approach towards Sex Work." *Social Sciences* 6(52). Retrieved from http://www.understandingsexwork.com/sites/default/files/uploads/socsci-06-00052.pdf

Benson, Michael L. and Sally S. Simpson. 2015. *Understanding White-Collar Crime: An Opportunity Perspective*. New York: Routledge.

Berg, Axel van den and Hudson Meadwell (eds.). 2004. *The Social Sciences and Rationality: Promise, Limits and Problems*. New Brunswick, NJ: Transaction.

Berger, Benjamin. 2014. "Belonging to Law: Religious Difference,Secularism, and the Conditions of Civic Inclusion." Working Paper, Osgoode Hall Law School, Legal Studies Research Paper Series, Research Paper No. 16, 10(5). Retrieved from digitalcommons.osgoode.yorku.ca/cgi/viewcontent.cgi?article=1057&context=olsrps

Berger, Benjamin L. and Richard Moon (eds.). 2016. *Religion and the Exercise of Public Authority*. Oxford: Hart Publishing.

Berger, Morroe. 1952. *Equality by Statute*. New York: Columbia University Press.

Bergner, Keith B. and Michelle S. Jones. 2015. "Mapping the Territory: Aboriginal Title and the Decision in Tsilhqot'in Nation v British Columbia." Originally published by the Rocky Mountain Mineral Law Foundation in the Proceedings of the 61st Annual Rocky Mountain Mineral Law Institute (2015). Retrieved from www.lawsonlundell.com/media/news/511_Mapping%20the%20Territory%20RMMLF%20article.pdf.

Bériault, Yves and Oliver Borgers. 2004. "Overview of Canadian Antitrust Law." *The Antitrust Review of the Americas: A Global Competition Review Special Report*. Retrieved from www.globalcompetitionreview.com/ara/ara.cfm.

Berlow, Alan. 2001. "The Broken Machinery of Death." *American Prospect* (July 30): 16–17.

Berman, Harold J., William R. Greiner, and Samir N. Saliba. 2004. *The Nature and Functions of Law*. 6th ed. Westbury, NY: Foundation.

Bernard, Thomas J. and Megan C. Kurlychek. 2010. *The Cycle of Juvenile Justice*. 2nd ed. New York: Oxford University Press.

Betcherman, Gordon. 2000. "Structural Unemployment: How Important Are Labour Market Policies and Institutions?" *Canadian Public Policy* 26 (supplement) (July): S131–S140.

Bhonde, Pranjale. 2016. "It's 2016 But the Practice of Witch-Hunting and Killing in the Name of Superstition Still Persists in Assam." *India Times*, May 30. Retrieved from www.indiatimes.com/news/india/it-s-2016-but-the-practice-of-witch-hunting-killing-in-the-name-of-superstition-persists-in-assam-255657.html

Bill C-68, Firearms Act, Ist sess., 35th Part., 1995.

Binde, Per. 2016. "Gambling-Related Embezzlement in the Workplace: A Qualitative Study." *International Gambling Studies* 16(3): 391–407.

Binder, David A., Paul Bergman, Paul R. Tremblay, and Ian S. Weinstein. 2011. *Lawyers as Counselors: A Client-Centred Approach*. 3rd ed. St. Paul, MN: West/Thomson Reuters.

Bissonette, Aimee M. 2009. *Cyber Law*. Thousand Oaks, CA: Sage.

Bittle, Steven and Laureen Snider. 2014. "The Breakdown of Canada's Corporate Crime Laws," in Elizabeth Comack (ed.), *Locating Law*, pp. 178–197. Halifax: Fernwood.

Bittner, Egon. 1970. *The Functions of the Police in Modern Society*. Chevy Chase, MD: National Institute of Mental Health.

Black, Donald. 1973. "The Mobilization of Law." *Journal of Legal Studies* 2 (1) (January): 125–149.

———. 1976. *The Behavior of Law*. New York: Academic Press.

———. 1980. *The Manners and Customs of Police*. New York: Academic Press.

———. 1989. *Sociological Justice*. New York: Oxford University Press.

———. 1998. *The Social Structure of Right and Wrong*. Rev. ed. San Diego, CA: Academic Press.

———. 2002. "The Geometry of Law: An Interview with Donald Black." *International Review of the Sociology of Law* 30 (2): 101–130.

Black, Debra. 2015. "Court Challenge Slams New Citizenship Act as 'Anti-Canadian.'" *The Star.Com* (August 20). Retrieved from www.thestar.com/news/immigration/2015/08/20/court-challenge-slams-new-citizenship-act-as-anti-canadian.html.

Blackburn, Carole. 2009. "Differentiating Indigenous Citizenship: Seeking Multiplicity in Rights, Identity, and Sovereignty in Canada." *American Ethnologist* 36 (1): 66–78.

Blackstock, Cindy. 2011. "The Canadian Human Rights Tribunal on First Nations Child Welfare: Why If Canada Wins, Equality and Justice Lose." *Children and Youth Services Review* 33 (1): 187–194.

Blake, Sara. 2017. *Administrative Law in Canada*, 6th ed. Toronto, ON: LexisNexis

Blasser v. Royal Institution for the Advancement of Learning (1985) 1985 CanLII 3061 (QC CA), 24 D.L.R. (4th) 507.

Bloss, William P. 2010. *Under a Watchful Eye: Private Rights and Criminal Justice*. Santa Barbara, CA: Praeger.

Blumberg, Abraham S. 1979. *Criminal Justice: Issues and Ironies*. 2nd ed. New York: New Viewpoints.

Bodansky, Daniel. 2010. *The Art and Craft of International Environmental Law*. Cambridge, MA: Harvard University Press.

Bodenheimer, Edgar. 1974. *Jurisprudence: The Philosophy and Method of the Law*. Rev. ed. Cambridge, MA: Harvard University Press.

Bogart, William A. 1994. *Courts and Country: The Limits of Litigation and the Social and Political Life of Canada*. Toronto: Oxford University Press.

———. 2002. *Consequences: The Impact of Law and Its Complexity*. Toronto: University of Toronto Press.

Boggs, Sarah L. 1971. "Formal and Informal Crime Control: An Exploratory Study of Urban, Suburban, and Rural Orientations." *Sociological Quarterly* 12 (1) (Summer): 319–327.

Bogus, Carl T. 2001. *Why Law Suits Are Good for America: Disciplined Democracy, Big Business, and the Common Law*. New York: New York University Press.

———. 2004a. "Fear-Mongering Torts and the Exaggerated Death of Diving." *Harvard Journal of Law and Public Policy* 28 (1): 17–37.

———. 2004b. "Research Counters Furor over Malpractice Lawsuits." *USA Today* (March 24): 13A.

Bohaker, Heidi and Franca Iacovetta. 2009. "Making Aboriginal People 'Immigrants Too': A Comparison of Citizenship Programs for Newcomers and Indigenous Peoples in Postwar Canada, 1940s–1960s." *Canadian Historical Review* 90 (3): 427–462.

Bohannan, Paul. 1973. "The Differing Realms of the Law," in Donald Black and Maureen Mileski (eds.), *The Social Organization of the Law*, pp. 306–317. New York: Seminar.

Bohm, Robert M. 2015. *Deathquest: An Introduction to the Theory and Practice of Capital Punishment in the United States*. New York: Routledge.

Boivin, Rémi, and Gilbert Cordeau. 2011. "Measuring the Impact of Police Discretion on Official Crime Statistics: A Research Note." *Police Quarterly* 14(2): 186–203.

Bonnycastle, Kevin. 2000. "Rape Uncodified: Reconsidering Bill C-49 Amendments to Canadian Sexual Assault Laws," in Dorothy E. Chunn and Dany Lacombe (eds.), *Law as a Gendering Practice*, pp. 60–78. Don Mills, ON: Oxford University Press.

Bonsignore, John J., Ethan Katsh, Peter d'Errico, Ronald M. Pipkin, Stephen Arons, and Janet Rifkin. 1989. *Before the Law: An Introduction to the Legal Process*. 4th ed. Boston: Houghton Mifflin.

Borg, Marian J. and Karen F. Parker. 2001. "Mobilizing Law in Urban Areas: The Social Structure of Homicide Clearance Rates." *Law and Society Review* 35 (2) (June): 435–466.

Borovoy, A. Alan. 1999. *The New Anti-Liberals*. Toronto: Canadian Scholars' Press.

———. 2002. "Protest Movements and Democracy." *Policy Options* 23 (6) (September): 54–56.

Borrows, John. 2002. *Recovering Canada: The Resurgence of Indigenous Law*. Toronto: University of Toronto Press.

Bosworth, Mary. 2010. *Explaining U.S. Imprisonment*. Thousand Oaks, CA: Sage.

Bowal, Peter and Irene Wanke. 1998. "Lay Knowledge of Business Law in Canada." *Canadian Business Law Journal* 29 (3): 396–416.

Bowal, Peter and Irene Wanke. 2001. "Lay Knowledge of Courts in Canada." International *Journal of the Sociology of Law* 29(2): 173–194.

Box, Richard C. 2005. "Dialogue and Administrative Theory & Praxis: Twenty-Five Years of Public Administrative Theory." *Administrative Theory & Praxis* 27 (3): 4380466.

———. 2009. *Public Administration and Society*. 2nd ed. Armonk, NY: M. E. Sharpe.

Boyd, Neil. 1998. *Canadian Law: An Introduction*. 2nd ed. Toronto: Harcourt.

———. 2002. *Canadian Law: An Introduction*. 3rd ed. Toronto: Nelson Thomson Learning.

Boyd, Susan B. 2000. "Custody, Access, and Relocation in a Mobile Society: (En)Gendering the Best Interests Principle," in Dorothy E. Chunn and Dany Lacombe (eds.), *Law as a Gendering Practice*, pp. 158–180. Don Mills, ON: Oxford University Press.

Boyd, Susan B. 2011. "Spaces and Challenges: Feminism in Legal Academia." *UBC Law Review* 44(1): 205–220.

Boyd-Caine, Tessa. 2009. *Protecting the Public? Executive Discretion and the Release of Mentally Disordered Offenders*. Devon, UK: Willan Publishing.

Boykoff, Jules. 2012. *The Suppression of Dissent: How the State and Mass Media Squelch USAmerican Social Movements.* New York: Routledge.

Boyle, Elizabeth Heger and Sharon E. Preves. 2000. "National Politics as International Process: The Case of Anti-Female-Genital-Cutting Laws." *Law and Society Review* 34 (3): 703–737.

Braithwaite, John. 1989. *Crime, Shame and Reintegration.* Melbourne, Australia: Cambridge University Press.

Braitstein, Paula, Kathy Li, and Mark Tyndall. 2003. "Sexual Violence Among a Cohort of Injection Drug Users." *Social Science and Medicine* 57 (3) (August): 561–569.

Brake, Deborah L. 2010. *Getting in the Game: Title IX and the Women's Sports Revolution.* New York: New York University Press.

Brannigan, Augustine. 1984. *Crimes, Courts and Corrections: An Introduction to Crime and Social Control in Canada.* Toronto: Holt, Rinehart and Winston.

Brennan, Shannon and Jillian Boyce. 2013. "Family-Related Murder-Suicides." *Juristat*, Catalogue No. 85–002-X. Retrieved from www.statcan.gc.ca/pub/85-002-x/2013001/article/11805/11805-2-eng.htm.

Breyer, Stephen G. and Richard B. Stewart. 2006. *Administrative Law and Regulatory Policy.* 6th ed. New York: Aspen Law and Business.

Bricker, Darrell and Edward Greenspon. 2001. *Searching for Certainty: Inside the New Canadian Mindset.* Toronto: Random House.

Bricker, Darrell and John Wright. 2005. *What Canadians Think.* Toronto: Doubleday Canada.

Bridges, F. Stephen and C. Bennett Williamson. 2004. "Legalized Gambling and Crime in Canada." *Psychological Reports* 95(3): 747–753.

Brisbin, Richard A., Jr. 2004. "Book Review: Tournament of Appeals." Retrieved from www.bsos.umd.edu/gvpt/lpbr/subpages/reviews/flemming704.htm.

British Columbia Civil Liberties Association, et al. v. University of Victoria, et al., 2016 CanLII 82919 (SCC).

British Columbia Court of Appeal. 2017. "Civil and Family Matters." Retrieved from www.courtofappealbc.ca/civil-family-matters.

Brock, Deborah. 2009. *Making Work, Making Trouble: The Social Regulation of Sexual Labour.* Toronto: University of Toronto Press.

Brockman, Joan. 2000. "'A Wild Feminist at Her Raving Best': Reflections on Studying Gender Bias in the Legal Profession." *Resources for Feminist Research* 28 (1–2) (Spring/Summer): 61–79.

———. 2001. *Gender in the Legal Profession: Fitting or Breaking the Mould.* Vancouver: UBC Press.

Brockman, Joan, and Dorothy E. Chunn. 1993. "Gender Bias in Law and the Social Sciences," in Joan Brockman and Dorothy Chunn (eds.), *Investigating Gender Bias: Law, Courts, and the Legal Profession*, pp. 3–18. Toronto: Thompson.

Bronskill, Jim. 2016. "Justice Tracking Over 100 Court Challenges to Mandatory Minimum Penalties." *CBC News* (December 13). Retrieved from www.cbc.ca/news/politics/mandatory-minimums-constitutional-challenges-1.3893961.

Brooks, Thom (ed.). 2009. *The Rights to a Fair Trial.* Burlington, VT: Ashgate.

Brooks, Thom. 2010. *Punishment.* New York: Routledge.

Broshnahan, Maureen. 2016. "Women Leaving Criminal Law Practice in Alarming Numbers." *CBC News* (March 7). Retrieved from www.cbc.ca/news/canada/women-criminal-law-1.3476637.

Brown, Desmond H. 2002. "'They Punish Murderers, Thieves, Traitors and Sorcerers': Aboriginal Criminal Justice as Reported by Early French Observers." *Social History* 35 (70) (November): 363–391.

Brown, Jennifer. 2017. "Study Shows Law Firm Senior Leadership Still Largely White and Male." Retrieved from http://canadianlawyermag.com/legalfeeds/3637/study-shows-law-senior-leadership-still-largely-white-and-male.html

Bruff-Murphy v Gunawardena (2016) ONSC 7.

Brundage, James A. 2010. *The Medieval Origins of the Legal Professions: Canonists, Civilians, and Courts.* Chicago, IL: University of Chicago Press.

Bryant, Amorette Nelson. 2004. *Complete Guide to Federal and State Garnishment.* 3rd ed. New York: Aspen.

Bryden, Philip. 2014. "Experiential Learning at Canadian Law Schools." *Canadian Lawyer* (August 18). Retrieved from www.canadianlawyermag.com/5237/Experiential-learning-at-Canadian-law-schools.html.

Buckhorn, Robert F. 1972. *Nader, the People's Lawyer.* Englewood Cliffs, NJ: Prentice Hall.

Buckingham, Donald E., Jerome E. Bickenbach, Richard Bronaugh, and The Honourable Bertha Wilson. 1996. *Legal Ethics in Canada: Theory and Practice*. Toronto: Nelson Thomson Learning.

Buckley, F. H. 2013. "A Better Country (With Fewer Lawyers). *National Post* (July 19). Retrieved from news.nationalpost.com/full-comment/f-h-buckley-a-better-country-with-fewer-lawyers.

Bull, Hedley and Adam Watson. 2018. *The Expansion of International Society*. New York: Oxford University Press.

Bumstead, Michele. 2001. "Alternative Dispute Resolution," in Laurence M. Olivo (ed.), *Introduction to Law in Canada*, pp. 505–532. Toronto: Captus.

Burbick, Joan. 2006. *Gun Show Nation: Gun Culture and American Democracy*. New York: New Press/W. W. Norton.

Burczycka, Marta. 2016. "Trends in Self-Reported Spousal Violence in Canada, 2014. İn Family Violence in Canada: A Statistical Profile, 2014." *Juristat*, Catalogue no. 85–002-X. Retrieved from www.statcan. gc.ca/pub/85-002-x/2016001/article/14303-eng.pdf.

Burnett, Ann and Diane M. Badzinski. 2000. "An Exploratory Study of Argument in the Jury Decision-Making Process." *Communication Quarterly* 48 (4) (Fall): 380–396.

Busby, Karen. 1999. "LEAF and Pornography: Litigation on Equality and Sexual Representations," in Nick Larsen and Brian Burch (eds.), *Law in Society: Canadian Perspectives*, pp. 42–59. Toronto: Harcourt.

Bush, Robert A. and Joseph P. Folger. 2005. *The Promise of Mediation: The Transformative Model for Conflict Resolution*. Rev. ed. San Francisco: Jossey-Bass.

Bushnik, Tracey, Jocelynn L. Cook, A. Albert Yuzpe, Suzanne Tough, and John Collins. 2012. "Estimating the Prevalence of Infertility in Canada." *Human Reproduction* 27 (3): 738–746.

Butler, Cheryl Nelson. 2016. "A Critical Race Feminist Perspective on Prostitution & Sex Trafficking in America." *Yale Journal of Law & Feminism* 27(1), Article 3. Retrieved from digitalcommons.law.yale. edu/yjlf/vol27/iss1/3.

Buxton, Jane A., Azar Mehrabadi, Emma Preston, Andrew Tu, and the Canadian Community Epidemiology Network on Drug Use (CCENDU) Vancouver Site Committee. 2009. "Local Drug Use Epidemiology: Lessons Learned and Implications For Broader Comparisons." *Contemporary Drug Problems* 36:447–458.

Bynner, John and Keith M. Stribley (eds.). 2010. *Research Design: The Logic of Social Inquiry*. Piscataway, NJ: Transaction Publishers.

Cairns, Alan. 2011. *Citizens Plus: Aboriginal Peoples and the Canadian State*. Vancouve, BC: UBC Press,

Calavita, Kitty. 2010. *Invitation to Law and Society: An Introduction to the Study of Real Law*. Chicago, IL: University of Chicago Press.

Calder et al. v. Attorney-General of British Columbia (1973), 34 DLR (3rd) 145, [1973] SCR 313.

Canada (AG) v Bedford 2013 SCC 72, [2013] 3 SCR 1101.

Canada (AG) v PHS Community Services Society 2011 SCC 44, [2011] 3 SCR.

Canada Gazette. 2016. "Government Notices: Department of Health: Assisted Human Reproduction Act." 150 (40) (October 1). Retrieved from: www.gazette.gc.ca/rp-pr/p1/2016/2016-10-01/html/notice-avis-eng.php

Canada (Human Rights Comm.) v. Toronto Dominion Bank (1996) 25 C.H.R.R.D/373 (F.C.T.D.).

Canadian Bar Association. 1993. *Touchstones for Change: Equality, Diversity and Accountability: The Report on Gender Equality in the Legal Profession*. Ottawa: Author.

———. 1998. "Who Is Training Tomorrow's Lawyers? A Conversation with Dean Joost Blom QC and Dean David Cohen." Canadian Bar Association, British Columbia Branch. Retrieved from www.cba. org/bc/cba_ publications/ bartalk_02_98/guest.aspx.

———. 1999. *Racial Equality in the Legal Profession*. Resolution 99–04-A-Revised. 1999 Annual Meeting, Edmonton, Alberta (August 21–22).

———. 2004. "Pro Bono Rising." Retrieved from www.cba.org/cba/Nationa/augsep04/html.

———. 2005. "Crystal Clear: New Perspectives for the Canadian Bar Association; Report of the CBA Futures Committee." Retrieved from www.cba.org/CBA/futures/pdf/crystalclear.pdf.

———. 2006. "CBA Code of Professional Conduct." Retrieved from www.cba.org/CBA/activities/ code/.

———. 2009. "CBA Code of Professional Ethics." Retrieved from www.cba.org/CBA/activities/code/.

———. 2014. "Bill C-24, Strengthening Canadian Citizenship Act." April 24. Retrieved from www.cba. org/CMSPages/GetFile.aspx?guid=97a417ea-9a17-446d-be2b-5a8ec6769aaf.

————. 2016. "Defamation: Libel and Slander." Retrieved from /www.cbabc.org/For-the-Public/Dial-A-Law/Scripts/Your-RIghts/240B.

————.2017a. "Codes of Professional Conduct." Retrieved from www.cba.org/Publications-Resources/Practice-Tools/Ethics-and-Professional-Responsibility-(1)/Codes-of-Professional-Conduct,

————. 2017b. Codes of Professional Conduct. Retrieved from /www.cba.org/Publications-Resources/Practice-Tools/Ethics-and-Professional-Responsibility-(1)/Codes-of-Professional-Conduct

Canadian Business. 2016. "Canada's Best Jobs 2016: The Top 25 Jobs in Canada." (April 21). Retrieved from www.canadianbusiness.com/lists-and-rankings/best-jobs/2016-top-25-jobs-in-canada/image/9/.

Canadian Centre for Diversity and Inclusion. 2016a. *Diversity By the Numbers: The Legal Profession* (November 30). Retrieved from www.ccdi.ca/attachments/DBTN_TLP_2016.pdf.

————. 2016b. "Supplier Diversity in Canada: Research and Analysis of the Next Step in Diversity and Inclusion for Forward-Looking Organizations." (March 2016). Retrieved from ccdi.ca/wpcontent/uploads/2016/04/CCDI-Report-Supplier-Diversity-in-Canada-updated-4072016.pdf.

Canadian Civil Liberties Association. 2015. "Understanding Bill C-36, The Protection of Communities and Exploited Persons Act." May 13. Retrieved from https://ccla.org/understanding-bill-c-36-the-protection-of-communities-and-exploited-persons-act/.

Canadian Corrections Association. 1967. *Indians and the Law*. Ottawa: Canadian Corrections Association.

Canadian Defence Lawyers (CDL). 2016. *Civil Juries Under Ontario Rule 76 Simplified Procedure*. Retrieved from www.cdlawyers.org/doc/Front%20Page/CDL%20Letter%20on%20Civil%20Jury%20Trials%20Rule%2076%20Ontario%202016-final.pdf.

Canadian Environmental Law Association (CELA). 2017. "Who We Are." Retrieved from www.cela.ca/whoweare.

Canadian Forum on Civil Justice, Everyday Legal Problems: Overview Report. Toronto: Canadian Forum on Civil Justice. Retrieved from www.cfcj-fcjc.org.

Canadian Judicial Council. 2002. *Annual Report 2000–2001*. Retrieved from www.cjc-ccm.gc. ca.

————. 2007. *Access to Justice: Meeting the Challenge*. Retrieved from www.cjc-ccm.gc.ca/cmslib/general/news_pub_annualreport_2006-2007_en.pdf.

————. 2009. *Annual Report 2008–2009*. Retrieved from www.cjc-ccm.gc.ca/cmslib/ general/CJC-annual-report-2008–2009-finalE.pdf.

————. 2016. "Inquiry Committee Decisions." Retrieved from www.cjc-ccm.gc.ca/english/conduct_en.asp?selMenu=conduct_inquiry_en.asp.

————. 2017. "Inquiry Committee Decisions." Retrieved from www.cjc-ccm.gc.ca/english/conduct_en.asp?selMenu=conduct_inquiry_en.asp

Canadian Labour Congress. 2005. *Aboriginal Rights Resource Tool Kit*. Rev. ed. Retrieved from http://canadianlabour.ca/updir.pdf.

Canadian Labour Congress. 2017. "LGBTQ." Retrieved from http://canadianlabour.ca/issues-research/issues/lgbtq.

Canadian Lawyer. 2016. "June 2016 - The Going Rate." June: 51–53. Retrieved from www.canadianlawyermag.com/images/stories/pdfs/2016/CL_June_16-Survey.pdf.

Canadian Partnership for Responsible Gambling. 2015. "Canadian Gambling Digest 2013–2014." Retrieved from www.responsiblegambling.org/docs/default-source/default-document-library/cprg_canadian-gambling-digest_2013-14.pdf?sfvrsn=2.

Canadian Safety Council. 2000. "Reality Check: Knowledge and Perceptions of Canada's Impaired Driving Law." Retrieved from www.safety-council.org/info/traffic/impaired/reality.htm.

Cano, Mario V. and Cassia Spohn. 2012. "Circumventing the Penalty for Offenders Facing Mandatory Minimums." *Criminal Justice and Behavior* 39 (3), 308–322.

Cante, Richard C. 2010. *Gay Men and the Forms of Contemporary U.S. Culture*. Burlington, VT: Ashgate.

Canter, David, Maria Ioannou, and Donna Youngs (eds.). 2009. *Safer Sex in the City: The Experience and Management of Street Prostitution*. Burlington, VT: Ashgate.

Canter, David and Rita Zukauskiene. 2009. *Psychology and the Law*. New Haven, CT: Yale University Press.

Caplovitz, David. 1963. *The Poor Pay More*. New York: Free Press.

————. 1974. *Consumers in Trouble: A Study of Debtors in Default*. New York: Free Press.

Caputo, Tulio and Michel Vallée. 2008. *A Comparative Analysis of Youth Justice Approaches*. Prepared for the Roots of Youth Violence Report. Ottawa, ON: Centre for Initiatives for Children, Youth and Community.

Cardozo, Benjamin Nathan. 1924. *The Growth of the Law.* New Haven, CT: Yale University Press.

Careless, James. 2016. "Professional Liability Insurance." *CBA/ABC National* (February 12). Retrieved from www.nationalmagazine.ca/Members/jamesc.aspx.

Carle, Susan D. (ed.). 2005. *Lawyers' Ethics and the Pursuit of Social Justice: A Critical Reader.* New York: New York University Press.

Carlin, Jerome E. 1962. *Lawyers on Their Own.* New Brunswick, NJ: Rutgers University Press.

———. 1966. *Lawyers' Ethics: A Survey of the New York City Bar.* New York: Russell Sage Foundation.

Carp, Robert A. and Ronald Stidham. 2017. *Judicial Process in America.* 10th ed. Thousand Oaks, CA: CQ Press.

Carp, Robert A., Ronald Stidham and Kenneth L. Manning. 2010. *Judicial Process in America,* 8th ed. Washington, DC: CQ Press.

Carpay, John. 2012. "A Victory for Free Speech at the University of Calgary." National Post (May 11). Retrieved from news.nationalpost.com/full-comment/john-carpay-a-victory-for-free-speech-at-the-university-of-calgary.

———. 2016. "Opinion: Free speech on campus will prevail despite Charter ruling." Vancouver Sun (May 13). Retrieved from vancouversun.com/opinion/opinion-free-speech-on-campus-will-prevail-despite-charter-ruling.

Carpi, Daniela and Marett Leiboff (eds.). 2016. *Fables of the Law: Fairy Tales in a Legal Context.* Berlin: Walter de Gruyter.

Carr, Indira (ed.). 2009. *Computer Crime.* Burlington, VT: Ashgate.

Carrese, Paul O. 2003. *The Cloaking of Power: Montesquieu, Blackstone and the Rise of Judicial Activism.* Chicago, IL: University of Chicago Press.

Carrington, Paul D. 1984. "Of Law and the River." *Journal of Legal Education* 34 (2) (June): 222–236.

Carson, Rachel L. 1962. *Silent Spring.* Boston: Houghton Mifflin.

Carson, Robert B. 1999. "The Constitution and the Charter of Rights and Freedoms," in Laurence M. Olivo (ed.), *Introduction to Law in Canada,* pp. 361–383. Toronto: Captus Press.

Carstairs, Catherine. 2002. "Becoming a 'Hype': Heroin Consumption, Subcultural Formation and Resistance in Canada, 1945–1961." *Contemporary Drug Problems* 29 (1) (Spring): 91–115.

Carter, David L. 2002. *The Police and the Community.* 7th ed. Upper Saddle River, NJ: Prentice Hall.

Carter, Lief H. and Thomas F. Burke. 2005. *Reason in Law.* 7th ed. New York: Longman.

Casino Gambling. 1999. "Canadian Gambling Behaviour and Attitudes: Summary Report." Retrieved from www.casino-gambling-reports. com.

Casper, Jonathan. 1972. *Lawyers Before the Warren Court.* Urbana, IL: University of Illinois Press.

Caylor, Lincoln and Gannon G. Beaulne. 2014. *Parliamentary Restrictions on Judicial Discretion in Sentencing: A Defense of Mandatory Minimum Sentences.* MacDonald-Laurier Institute (May). Retrieved from www.macdonaldlaurier.ca/files/pdf/MLIMandatoryMinimumSentences-final.pdf

CBC. 2000. "Circle Sentencing System Criticized in Carcross." (November 15). Retrieved from www.cbc.ca/story/news/ national/2000/11/15/15circle.html. 2001. "Alleged Rat's Head in Big Mac Triggers Lawsuit." (March 27). Retrieved from overlawyered.com/archives/01/mar3.html.

———. 2004a. "Indepth: Steven Truscott; The Search for Justice." (October 28). Retrieved from www.cbc.ca/news/background/truscott/.

———. 2004b. "Aboriginal Sentencing Circle Ruling Upheld." (December 16). Retrieved from /www.cbc.ca/news/canada/aboriginal-sentencing-circle-ruling-upheld-1.468858.

———. 2005. "Vancouver Man Pleads Guilty to Overseas Sex Charges." (June 1). Retrieved from www.vancouver.cbc.ca/story/canada/ national/2005/06/01/bakker-050601.html.

———. 2006a. "MPs to Question New Supreme Court Pick." (February 20). Retrieved from www.cbc.ca/story/canada/national/2006/02/06/supreme-court0606220.html.

———. 2006b. "School Abuse Deal Includes $80M for Lawyers." (May 8). Retrieved from www.cbc.ca/story/ canada/national/2006/05/08/residential-legal-fees.html.

———. 2009. "Quebec Dad Sued by Daughter After Grounding Loses His Appeal." (April 7). Retrieved from www.cbc.ca/canada/montreal/story/2009/04/07/mt-quebecgirl-sues-dad-0407.html.

———. 2011. "Father in Disgraced Pathologist Case Acquitted." (May 4). Retrieved from www.cbc.ca/news/canada/toronto/father-in-disgraced-pathologist-case-acquitted-1.1010766.

———. 2012. "Tough Drug Laws Harm Health and Safety, Doctors Say." (March 29). Retrieved from www.cbc.ca/news/health/story/2012/03/27/marijuana-drug-laws-public-health.html

———. 2014. "Nipissing First Nation Passes First Ontario Aboriginal constitution." January 21. Retrieved from www.cbc.ca/news/canada/sudbury/nipissing-first-nation-passes-first-ontario-aboriginal-constitution-1.2505488.

———. 2016a."Prison Watchdog Says More Than a Quarter of Federal Inmates Are Aboriginal People."(January 16). Retrieved from www.cbc.ca/news/indigenous/aboriginal-inmates-1.3403647.

———. 2016b. "Ontario Approves Establishment of Indigenous People's Court in Thunder Bay." (November 9). Retrieved from www.cbc.ca/news/canada/thunder-bay/thunder-bay-indigenous-peoples-court-1.3843935.

———. 2016c. "Women Leaving Criminal Law Practice in Alarming Numbers." (March 7). Retrieved from www.cbc.ca/news/canada/women-criminal-law-1.3476637.

Cebula, Mark A. 1998. "Does Lawyer Advertising Adversely Influence the Image of Lawyers in the United States? An Alternative Perspective and New Empirical Evidence." *Journal of Legal Studies* 27 (2) (June): 503–518.

Canadian Environmental Law Association (CELA). 1999. "New Study Warns of Children's Health Risks from Pesticides and Calls for Urgent Changes to Pesticide Regulatory Systems." (December 1). Retrieved from www.web.net/-cela/mr991201.htm.

Chalfin, Aaron, Haviland, Amelia M., and Steven Raphael, S. 2013. "What Do Panel Studies Tell Us About a Deterrent Effect of Capital Punishment? A Critique of the Literature." *Journal of Quantitative Criminology* 29 (1): 5–43.

Chamallas, Martha E. 2012. *Introduction to Feminist Legal Theory.* New York: Wolters Kluwer.

Chambliss, Daniel F. and Russel K. Schutt. 2010. *Making Sense of the Social World: Methods of Investigation.* Thousand Oaks, CA: Sage Publications.

Chambliss, William J. 1964. "A Sociological Analysis of the Law of Vagrancy." *Social Problems* 12 (1) (Summer): 67–77.

———. 1975. "Types of Deviance and the Effectiveness of Legal Sanctions," in William J. Chambliss (ed.), *Criminal Law in Action,* pp. 398–407. Santa Barbara, CA: Hamilton.

———. 1976a. "Functional and Conflict Theories of Crime: The Heritage of Emile Durkheim and Karl Marx," in William J. Chambliss and Milton Mankoff (eds.), *Whose Law? What Order? A Conflict Approach to Criminology,* pp. 1–28. New York: John Wiley.

———. 1976b. "The State and Criminal Law," in William J. Chambliss and Milton Mankoff (eds.), *Whose Law, What Order? A Conflict Approach to Criminology,* pp. 66–106. New York: John Wiley.

———. 1978. *On the Take: From Petty Crooks to Presidents.* Bloomington: Indiana University Press.

Chambliss, William J. and Robert B. Seidman. 1971. *Law, Order, and Power.* Reading, MA: Addison-Wesley.

———. 1982. *Law, Order, and Power.* 2nd ed. Reading, MA: Addison-Wesley.

Chambliss, William J. and Marjorie S. Zatz (eds.). 1993. *Making Law: The State, the Law, and Structural Contradictions.* Bloomington: Indiana University Press.

Chan, Cheris Shun-Ching. 2004. "The Falun Gong in China: A Sociological Perspective." *China Quarterly* 179 (September): 665–683.

Charlcraft, David, Fanon Howell, Marisol Lopez Menendez, and Hector Vera (eds.). 2010. *Max Weber Matters: Interweaving Past and Present.* Burlington, VT: Ashgate.

Chase, Oscar G. 2007. *Law, Culture, and Ritual: Disputing Systems in Cross-Cultural Context.* New York: New York University Press.

Chesney-Lind, Meda and Lisa Pasko. 2004a. *The Female Offender: Girls, Women and Crime.* 2nd ed. Thousand Oaks, CA: Sage.

———. 2004b. *Girls, Women and Crime: Selected Readings.* Thousand Oaks, CA: Sage.

Chiam, Zhan, Sandra Duffy and Matilda González Gil. 2016. *Trans Legal Mapping Report 2016: Recognition Before the Law.* Geneva: ILGA.

Childbirth by Choice Trust. 2000. "History of Birth Control in Canada." Retrieved from www.cbctrust.com.

Chotalia, Shirish P. 2006. "Arbitration Using Sharia Law in Canada: A Constitutional and Human Rights Perspective." *Constitutional Forum* 15(2): 63–78.

Choudhary, Rohit. 2010. *Policing: Reinventing Strategies in a Marketing Framework.* Thousand Oaks, CA: Sage.

Choudhry, Sujit, Martha Jackman, Hugo Cyr, Brenda Cossman, Karen Busby, et al. 2005. "Open Letter to the Hon. Stephen Harper from Law Professors." Retrieved from www.law.utoronto.ca/ samesexletter.html.

Choudhry, Sujit. 2004. "Continuing the Conversation: A Reply to Manfredi and Kelly." *McGill Law Journal* 49(3): 765–778.

Choudhry, Sujit and Claire E. Hunter. 2003. "Measuring Judicial Activism on the Supreme Court of Canada: A Comment on Newfoundland (Treasury Board) v. NAPE." *McGill Law Journal* 48: 525–562.

Choudhry, Sujit and Kent Roach. 2003. "Racial and Ethnic Profiling: Statutory Discretion, Constitutional Remedies, and Democratic Accountability." *Osgoode Hall Law Journal* 41 (1): 1–36.

Chriss, James J. 2013. *Social Control: An Introduction.* Madlen, MA: Polity Press.

Christianson, Scott. 2004. *Innocent: Inside Wrongful Conviction Cases.* New York: New York University Press.

———. 2010. *The Last Gasp: The Rise and Fall of the American Gas Chamber.* Berkeley, CA: University of California Press.

Christie v British Columbia (Attorney General) 2007 SCC 21.

Chu, Sandra Ka Hon. 2012. "Supreme Court of Canada Orders Minister of Health to Exempt Supervised Injection Site from Criminal Prohibition on Drug Possession: Attorney General v. PHS Community Services Society, 2011 SCC 44 (Supreme Court of Canada)." *Human Rights and Drugs* 2 (1). Retrieved from www.academia.edu/4049352/Case_Summary-_Supreme_Court_of_Canada_orders_Minister_of_Health_to_exempt_supervised_injection_site_from_criminal_prohibition_on_drug_possession.

Chunn, Dorothy E., Susan B. Boyd, and Hester Lessard (eds.). 2007. *Reaction and Resistance: Feminism, Law, and Social Change.* Vancouver: UBC Press.

CIC News (Canadian Immigration Newsletter). 2016. "Bill to Change Canadian Citizenship Act Passes House of Commons, with Senate Approval Pending." (July 5). Retrieved from www.cicnews.com/2016/07/bill-change-canadian-citizenship-act-passes-house-commons-senate-approval-pending-078363.html.

City News. 2007. "A Miscarriage of Justice: Court of Appeal Clears Steven Truscott." August 28. Retrieved from www.citynews.ca/news/ news_14138.aspx.

Clairmont, Donald H. and Dennis W. Magill. 1999. *Africville: The Life and Death of a Canadian Black Community.* Toronto: Canadian Scholars' Press.

Clark, David S. 1990. "Civil Litigation Trends in Europe and Latin America Since 1945: The Advantage of Intracountry Comparisons." *Law and Society Review* 24 (2): 549–569.

——— (ed.). 2007. *Encyclopedia of Law and Society.* 3 vols. Thousand Oaks, CA: Sage.

Clark, David S. (ed.). 2007. *Encyclopedia of Law and Society.* 3 vols. Thousand Oaks, CA: Sage Publications.

Clarke, Tony. 2002. "The Recriminalization of Dissent." *Policy Options* 23 (6) (September): 49–50.

Clinard, Marshall B. and Daniel J. Abbott. 1973. *Crime in Developing Countries: A Comparative Perspective.* New York: John Wiley.

Clinard, Marshall B. and Robert F. Meier. 2016. *Sociology of Deviant Behavior.* 16th ed. Belmont, CA: Wadsworth/Thomson Learning.

Clost v. Relkie, 2012 BCSC 1393.

Clydesdale, Timothy T. 2004. "A Forked River Runs Through Law School: Toward Understanding Race, Gender, Age and Related Gaps in Law School Performance and Bar Passage." *Law and Social Inquiry* 29 (4) (Fall): 711–769.

Cochran, Charles L. and Eloise F. Malone. 2010. *Public Policy: Perspectives and Choices.* 4th ed. New York: McGraw-Hill.

Cohen, Felix. 1959. *Ethical Systems and Legal Ideals.* New York: Cornell University Press.

Cohen, Stanley A. 2001. States of Denial: Knowledge About Atrocities and Suffering. Cambridge: Cambridge University Press. 2005. *Privacy, Crime and Terror: Legal Rights and Security in a Time of Peril.* Markham, ON: LexisNexis.

Cohn, Alvin W. 1976. *Crime and Justice Administration.* Philadelphia: Lippincott.

Cole, David D., Federico Fabbrini & Stephen Schulhofer (eds.). 2017. *Surveillance, Privacy and Trans-Atlantic Relations.* Oxford: Hart Publishing.

Coleman, James W. 1972. *Policy Research in Social Science.* Morristown, NJ: General Learning.

———. 2006. *The Criminal Elite: The Sociology of White Collar Crime.* 6th ed. New York: St. Martin's.

Collier, George. 1989. "The Impact of Second Republic Labor Reforms in Spain," in June Starr and Jane F. Collier (eds.), *History and Power in the Study of Law: New Directions in Legal Anthropology,* pp. 201–222. Ithaca, NY: Cornell University Press.

Collier, Jane Fishburne. 1973. *Law and Social Change in Zinacantan*. Stanford, CA: Stanford University Press.

Collier, Richard. 1995. *Masculinity, Law and the Family*. New York: Routledge.

———. 2005. "The Law School, the Legal Academy and the 'Global Knowledge Economy': Reflections on a Growing Debate." *Social and Legal Studies* 14 (2) (June): 259–265.

Collins, Hugh. 1996. *Marxism and Law*. New York: Oxford University Press.

Coltri, Laurie S. 2004. *Conflict Diagnosis and Alternative Dispute Resolution*. Upper Saddle River, NJ: Prentice Hall.

———. 2010. *Alternative Dispute Resolution: A Conflict Diagnosis Approach*. 2nd ed. Boston, MA: Prentice Hall.

Comack, Elizabeth and Gillian Balfour. 2004. *The Power to Criminalize: Violence, Inequality and the Law*. Halifax: Fernwood.

Committee on Homosexual Offenses and Prostitution. 1963. *Report of the Committee on Homosexual Offenses and Prostitution* [Wolfenden Report]. Chair Lord Wolfenden. Briarcliff Manor, NY: Stein and Day.

Communications, Energy and Paperworkers Union of Canada, Local 30 v Irving Pulp & Paper Ltd., 2013 SCC 34.

Competition Act (R.S.C., 1985, c. C-34).

Competition Tribunal. 2017. "Welcome to the Competition Tribunal." Retrieved from www.ct-tc.gc.ca/Home.asp.

Conacher, Duff. 2016. "Before Making Any Other Changes, Make the 5-Year Ban on Federal Lobbying an Actual Ban, and Make It Fair, and Strengthen Enforcement." *Democracy Watch* (May 16). Retrieved from democracywatch.ca/20160516-make-5-year-ban-on-federal-lobbying-an-actual-ban/

Condon, Mary. 2000. "Limited by Law? Corporate Law and the Family Firm," in Dorothy E. Chunn and Dany Lacombe (eds.), *Law as a Gendering Practice*, pp. 181–198. Don Mills, ON: Oxford University Press.

Connolly, Anthony J. 2010. *Cultural Difference on Trial: The Nature and Limits of Judicial Understanding*. Burlington, VT: Ashgate.

Conrad, Peter. 1996. "The Medicalization of Deviance in American Culture," in Earl Rubington and Martin S. Weinberg (eds.), *Deviance: The Interactionist Perspective*, pp. 69–77. 6th ed. Boston: Allyn and Bacon.

Consumer Packaging and Labelling Act (R.S.C., 1985, c. C-38).

Controlled Drugs and Substances Act SC 1996, c. 19.

Cooney, Mark. 1994. "Evidence of Partisanship." *Law and Society Review* 28 (4) (October): 833–858.

———. 2003. "Missing the Mark: Reflections on Greenberg's Comment." *Criminology* 41 (4): 1419–1426.

Cooney, Mark and Scott Phillips. 2002. "Typologizing Violence: A Blackian Perspective." *International Journal of Sociology and Social Policy* 22 (7–8): 75–108.

Cooper, Merrill, Joan Brockman, and Irene Hoffart. 2004. *Final Report on Equity and Diversity in Alberta's Legal Profession*. Report prepared for the Joint Committee on Equality, Equity and Diversity of the Law Society of Alberta; Canada Bar Association, Alberta Branch; Faculty of Law, University of Calgary; and Faculty of Law, University of Alberta.

Corbiere v. Canada (Minister of Indian and Northern Affairs), [1999] 2 SCR 203, 1999 CanLII 687 (SCC).

Cormack, Bradin T, Martha C. Nussbaum and Richard Strier. 2013. *Shakespeare and the Law: A Conversation Across Disciplines and Professions*. Chicago, IL: University of Chicago Press.

Correctional Service of Canada. 2009. "Aboriginal Initiatives." Retrieved from www.csc-scc.gc.ca/text/prgrm/abinit/who-eng.shtml.

Correll, Shelley J., Stephen Benard, and In Paik. 2007. "Getting a Job: Is There a Motherhood Penalty?" *American Journal of Sociology* 112 (5): 1297–1339.

Cotterman, James D. (ed.). 2016. *Compensation Plans for Law Firms*. 6th ed. Chicago, IL: American Bar Association, Law Practice Management Section.

Cotterrell, Roger (ed.). 2006. *Law, Culture and Society: Legal Ideas in the Mirror of Social Theory*. Burlington, VA: Ashgate.

Coulthard, Glen S. 2007. "Subjects of Empire: Indigenous Peoples and the 'Politics of Recognition' in Canada." *Contemporary Political Theory* 6(4): 437–460.

Court Challenges Program. 1995. "Annual Report 1994–1995." Retrieved from www.ccppcj.ca/documents/annrep9495.html.

————. 2006. "Who We Are." Retrieved from www.ccppcj.ca/e/about/ about.shtml.

Cowan, Sharon. 2005. "'Gender Is No Substitute for Sex': A Comparative Human Rights Analysis of the Legal Resolution of Sexual Identity." *Feminist Legal Studies* 13 (1): 67–96.

Cownie, Fiona. 2010. *English Legal System in Context.* 4th ed. New York: Oxford University Press.

Cox, Noel. 2006. *Technology and Legal Systems.* Burlington, VA: Ashgate.

Cox, Stephen. 2009. *The Big House: Image and Reality of the American Prison.* New Haven, CT: Yale University Press.

Cozic, Charles P. and Paul A. Winters (eds.). 1995. *Gambling.* San Diego, CA: Greenhaven.

Cram, Ian. 2006. *Contested Words: Legal Restrictions on Freedom of Speech in Liberal Democracies.* Burlington, VT: Ashgate.

Cramer, Renee Ann. 2005. "Perceptions of the Process: Indian Gaming as It Affects Federal Tribal Acknowledgment: Law and Practices." *Law and Policy* 27 (4) (October): 578–605.

Crank, John P. 1994. "Watchman and Community: Myth and Institutionalization in Policing." *Law and Society Review* 28 (2) (May): 325–351.

————. 2015. *Understanding Police Culture,* 2nd ed. New York: Routledge.

Crenshaw, Kimberle Williams. 1998. "Demarginalizing the Intersection of Race and Sex: A Black Feminist Critique of Antidiscrimination Doctrine, Feminist Theory and Antiracist Doctrine." *University of Chicago Legal Forum* 189: 139–142.

Crespi, Irving. 1979. "Modern Marketing Techniques: They Could Work in Washington, Too." *Public Opinion* 2 (3) (June–July): 16–19, 58–59.

CRIC (Centre for Research and Information on Canada). 2004. "Facing the Future: Relations Between Aboriginal and Non-Aboriginal Canadians." (June). Retrieved from www.cric.ca/pdf/cahiers/cricpapers_june2004.pdf.

————. 2006. "Legislation, Treaties and Claims." Retrieved from www.cric.ca/en_html/guide/aboriginal/ aboriginal_treaties.htmlCRIC.

Criminal Intelligence Service Canada. 2002. "Annual Report 2002." Retrieved from www.cisc.gc.ca/AnnualReport2002/Cisc2002/exploit2002.html.

Crisanti, Annette S., Julio Arboleda-Florez, and Heather Stuart. 2000. "The Canadian Criminal Code Provisions for Mentally Disordered Offenders: A Survey of Experiences, Attitudes and Knowledge." *Canadian Journal of Psychiatry* 45 (9) (November): 816–821.

Crocker, Diane and Val Marie Johnson. 2010. *Poverty, Regulation & Social Justice: Readings on the Criminalization of Poverty.* Halifax: Fernwood Publishing.

Crutcher, Nicole. 2001. "The Legislative History of Mandatory Minimum Penalties of Imprisonment in Canada." *Osgoode Hall Law Journal* 39(2/3): 273–285.

Csillag, Ron. 2006. "Ont. Law Passed to Ban Faith-Based Arbitration." *Canadian Jewish News* (July 6). Retrieved from www.cjnews. com/view/article.asp?id+8601.

CTV. 2005. "Faith-Based Arbitration." September 12. Retrieved from www.ctv.ca/servlet/ArticleNews/story/CTVNews/1126539690860_121948890.

————. 2016. "SCC Says Two Tough-on-Crime Laws Are Unconstitutional." (April 15). Retrieved from www.ctvnews.ca/canada/scc-says-two-tough-on-crime-laws-are-unconstitutional-1.2860487.

Cukier, Wendy and Victor W. Sidel. 2006. *The Global Gun Epidemic.* Portsmouth, NH: Greenwood.

Currie, Ab. 2013. "The State of Civil Legal Aid in Canada: By the Numbers in 2011–2012." *Canadian Forum on Civil Justice Newsletter* (May 13). Retrieved from www.cfcj-fcjc.org/a2jblog/the-state-of-civil-legal-aid-in-canada-by-the-numbers-in-2011–2012.

Currie, Ab. 2009. The Legal Problems of Everyday Life: The Nature, Extent and Consequences of Justiciable Problems Experienced by Canadians. Ottawa: Department of Justice Canada. Retrieved from www.justice.gc.ca.

Currie, Ab. 2007. "National Survey of the Civil Justice Problems of Low and Moderate Income Canadians: Incidence and Patterns." Ottawa: Department of Justice Canada. Retrieved from www.justice.gc.ca.

Cusac, Anne-Marie. 2009. *Cruel and Unusual: The Culture of Punishment in America.* New Haven, CT: Yale University Press.

Cyr v. Anderson, 2014 NSCA 51.

Danelski, David J. 1974. "The Limits of Law," in J. Roland Pennock and John W. Chapman (eds.), *The Limits of Law,* pp. 8–27. New York: Lieber-Atherton.

Darwall, Stephen. 2013. *Morality, Authority, and Law: Essays in Second-Personal Ethics*. New York: Oxford University Press.

Das Gupta, Tanis. 1999. "The Politics of Multiculturalism: 'Immigrant Women' and the Canadian State," in Enakshi Dua and Angela Robertson (eds.), *Scratching the Surface: Canadian Anti-Racist Feminist Thought*, pp. 187–206. Toronto: Women's Press.

Daston, Lorraine and Michael Stolleis (eds.). 2010. *Natural Law and Laws of Nature in Early Modern Europe: Jurisprudence, Theology, Moral and Natural Philosophy*. Burlington, VT: Ashgate.

Dauvergne, Mia. 2008. "Crime Statistics in Canada, 2008." *Juristat* 28 (7). Catalogue no. 85–002-x. Ottawa: Minister of Industry. 2009. "Trends in Police-Reported Drug Offences in Canada." *Juristat: Canadian Centre for Justice Statistics* 29.2 (2009): 1C.

Dauvergne, Mia and Shannon Brennan. 2011. "Police-Reported Hate Crime in Canada, 2009." *Juristat*. Statistics Canada Catalogue no. 85–002-X. Statistics Canada, Ottawa.

Davies, Bryan. 2009. *Alternative Dispute Resolution*. Mountain View, CA: Mindsource Technologies Inc.

Davies, Libby. 2008. "Canada's Medical Marijuana Program Needs Reform." (June 19). Retrieved from www.libbydavies.ca/parliament/ openletter/2008/ob/18/canadas-medical-marijuana-program-needs-reform.

Davies, Paul and John Emshwiller. 2006. " Split Verdict on Selecting Juries Quickly." *Wall Street Journal* (February 1): B1–B2.

Davis, F. James. 1962. "Law as a Type of Social Control," in F. James Davis, Henry H. Foster Jr., C. Ray Jeffery and E. Eugene Davis (eds.), *Society and the Law: New Meanings for an Old Profession*, pp. 39–63. New York: Free Press.

Davis, Kenneth Culp. 1975a. *Administrative Law and Government*. 2nd ed. St. Paul, MN: West.
————. 1975b. *Police Discretion*. St. Paul, MN: West.

Davison, Charles. 2002. "Wheel of Fortune? Not! Choosing Judges." *LawNow* 27 (2) (October/November): 17–18.

Dawson, Myrna. 2003. "The Cost of 'Lost' Intimacy: The Effect of Relationship State on Criminal Justice Decision Making." *British Journal of Criminology* 43 (3) (Autumn): 689–709.

Dawson, T. Brettel and Jennifer Quaile. 1998. "A Collage of Firsts," in T. Brettel Dawson (ed.), *Women, Law and Social Change: Core Readings and Current Issues*, pp. 119–120. North York, ON: Captus.

Dawson, T. Brettel, Jennifer Quaile, and Grant Holly. 2002. "A Collage of Firsts," in T. Brettel Dawson (ed.), *Women, Law and Social Change: Core Readings and Current Issues*, pp. 103–105. 4th ed. A Special Prepublication Printing for Carleton University 51.301—Women and the Legal Process (Part 1). Concord, ON: Captus.

Dean, Hartley. 2012. *Social Policy*, 2nd ed. Malden, MA: Polity Press.

Death Penalty Information Center (DPIC). 2016. "Facts About the Death Penalty." (December 9). Retrieved from www.deathpenaltyinfo.org/documents/FactSheet.pdf.

Delgado, Richard and Jean Stefancic (eds.). 2012. *Critical Race Theory: An Introduction*, Second Edition. New York: New York University Press

Delgamuukw v. *British Columbia* [1997] 3 S.C.R. 1010.

Dempsey, John S. and Linda S. Forst. 2016. *An Introduction to Policing*. 6th ed. Belmont, CA: Wadsworth.

Department of Justice Canada. 2005. "Reference to the Supreme Court of Canada." Retrieved from www.justice.gc.ca/en/news/nr/2003/ doc_30946.html.
————. 2008a. "The Anti-Terrorism Act." Retrieved from canada.justice.gc/ca/eng/antiter/faq/index.html.
————. 2009. "Public Legal Education and Information." Retrieved from www.justice.gc.ca/eng/pi/pb-dgp/prog/plei-pvij.html.
————. 2011. "Backgrounder: Safe Streets & Communities Act." Retrieved from www.justice.gc.ca/eng/news-nouv/nr-cp/2012/doc_32713.html.
————. 2010. "Government Re-Introduces Legislation to Crack Down on Organized Drug Crime." May 5. Retrieved from http://news.gc.ca/web/article-en.do?nid=529889.
————. 2012. "Canada's Court System." Retrieved from www.canadajustice.gc.ca.
————. 2015a. "Drug Use and Offending." Retrieved from www.justice.gc.ca/eng/rp-pr/csj-sjc/jsp-sjp/qa02_2-qr02_2/p1.html.

————. 2015b. " Drug Treatment Court Funding Program Evaluation." Retrieved from www.justice. gc.ca/eng/rp-pr/cp-pm/eval/rep-rap/2015/dtcfp-pfttt/dtcfp-pfttt.pdf.

————. 2015c. "Technical Paper: Bill C-36, Protection of Communities and Exploited Persons Act." Retrieved from www.justice.gc.ca/eng/rp-pr/other-autre/protect/p1.html.

————. 2016a. "Current Marijuana Laws." Retrieved from www.justice.gc.ca/eng/cj-jp/marijuanalaw-loi.html.

————. 2016b. "Civil and Criminal Cases." Retrieved from www.justice.gc.ca/eng/csj-sjc/just/08.html.

————. 2017a. "Civil and Criminal Cases." Retrieved from www.justice.gc.ca/eng/csj-sjc/just/08.html.

————. 2017b. Technical Paper: Bill C-36, *Protection of Communities and Exploited Persons Act*. Retrieved from http://www.justice.gc.ca/eng/rp-pr/other-autre/protect/p1.html.

————. 2017c. "Legal Aid Program." Retrieved from www.justice.gc.ca/eng/fund-fina/gov-gouv/aid-aide.html.

Desai, Gaurav, Felipe Smith, and Supriya Nair. 2003. "Introduction: Law, Literature and Ethnic Subjects: Critical Essay." *MELUS* (Spring): 3–17.

de Soto, Hernando. 2001. *The Mystery of Capital: Why Capitalism Triumphs in the West and Fails Everywhere Else*. New York: Basic Books.

de Tocqueville, Alexis. 1835/1961. *Democracy in America*. Vol. 1. New York: Schocken.

Deutscher, Irwin. 1999. *Making a Difference: The Practice of Sociology*. Somerset, NJ: Transaction.

Devlin, Patrick. 1965. *The Enforcement of Morals*. New York: Oxford University Press.

De Vries, Laura. 2011. *Conflict in Caledonia: Aboriginal Land Rights and the Rule of Law*. Vancouver: UBC Press.

Dezhbakhsh, Hashem and Paul H. Rubin. 2011. "From the 'Econometrics of Capital Punishment'to the 'Capital Punishment'of Econometrics: On the Use and Abuse of Sensitivity Analysis." *Applied Economics* 43 (25): 3655–3670.

Di Gioacchino, Debora, Sergio Ginebri, and Laura Sabani (eds.). 2004. *The Role of Organized Interest Groups in Policy Making*. New York: Palgrave Macmillan.

Diamant, Neil J., Stanley B. Lubman, and Kevin J. O'Brien (eds.). 2005. *Engaging the Law in China: State, Society and Possibilities for Justice*. Stanford, CA: Stanford University Press.

Dicey, Albert Venn. 1905. *Lectures on the Relation Between the Law and Public Opinion in England During the Nineteenth Century*. London: Palgrave Macmillan.

Dickson, Jamie. 2015. *The Honour and Dishonour of the Crown: Making Sense of Aboriginal Law in Canada*. Saskatoon, SK: Purich Publishing Ltd.

Diesfeld, Kate and Ian Freckelton (eds.). 2003. *Involuntary Detention and Therapeutic Jurisprudence: International Perspectives on Civil Commitment*. Burlington, VT: Ashgate/Darmouth.

Dinovitzer, Ronit. 2006. "Social Capital and Constraints on Legal Careers." *Law and Society Review* 40 (2) (June): 445–479.

Dinovitzer, Ronit. 2015. "Law and Beyond: A National Study of Canadian Law Graduates", University of Toronto. Retrieved from individual.utoronto.ca/dinovitzer/images/LABReport.pdf.

Ditmore, Melissa Hope. 2011. *Prostitution and Sex Work*. Santa Barbara, CA: Greenwood.

Diversity Institute. 2016. " New Judicial Appointments Align with Diversity Institute Research and Recommendations." August 2. Retrieved from www.ryerson.ca/diversity/news/2016-08-01/.

Dixon, Jo, Aaron Kupchik, and Joachim Savelsberg (eds.). 2007. *Criminal Courts*. Burlington, VT: Ashgate.

Domnarski, William. 2003. "Law and Literature." *Legal Studies Forum* 27 (1): 109–129.

Donnelly, Bebhinn. 2007. *A Natural Law Approach to Normativity*. Burlington, VT: Ashgate.

Donovan, James M. 2008. *Legal Anthroplogy: An Introduction*. Lanham, MD: AltaMira Press.

Dorsey, Dale. 2016. *The Limits of Moral Authority*. New York: Oxford University Press.

Douglas, Kevin S. and William J. Koch. 2001. "Civil Commitment and Civil Competence," in Regina A. Schuller and James R. P. Ogloff (eds.), *Introduction to Psychology and Law: Canadian Perspectives*, pp. 353–374. Toronto, ON: University of Toronto Press.

Doust, Leonard T. 2011. Foundation for Change. British Columbia Public Commission on Legal Aid. The Law Society of British Columbia. Retrived from www.lawsocietybc.ca

Dow, David R. 2009. *America's Prophets. How Judicial Activism Makes America Great*. Santa Barbara, CA: Praeger/ABC-CLIO.

Dowbiggin, Ian. 2012. "Parsing Mental Illness." *Literary Review of Canada*, March. Retrieved from http://reviewcanada.ca/magazine/2012/03/letters/.

Dowden, Cara and Shannon Brennan. 2012. "Police-Reported Hate Crime in Canada, 2010." *Juristat*. Statistics Canada Catalogue no. 85–002-x. Statistics Canada, Ottawa.

Downes, David and Paul Rock. 2003. *Understanding Deviance: A Guide to the Sociology of Crime and Rule Breaking*. 4th ed. Oxford, UK: Oxford University Press.

Downes, Larry. 2009. *The Laws of Disruption: Harnessing the New Forces that Govern Life and Business in the Digital Age*. New York: Basic.

Dranoff, Linda Silver. 2011. *Everyone's Guide to the Law: A Handbook for Canadians*. 4th ed. Toronto: HarperCollins.

Dror, Yehezkel. 1968. "Law and Social Change," in Rita James Simon (ed.), *The Sociology of Law*, pp. 663–680. San Francisco: Chandler.

———. 1970. "Law as a Tool of Directed Social Change." *American Behavioral Scientist* 13: 553–559.

Drucker, Mitchell. 2013. "Canadian v. American Defamation Law: What Can We Learn from Hyperlinks." *Canada-U.S. Law Journal* 38(1): 141–166.

Dua, Enakshi. 1999. "Canadian Anti-Racist Feminist Thought: Scratching the Surface of Racism," in Enakshi Dua and Angela Robertson (eds.), *Scratching the Surface: Canadian Anti-Racist Feminist Thought*, pp. 7–31. Toronto: Women's Press.

du Bois-Pedain, Antje, Magnus Ulväng and Petter Asp. 2017. *Criminal Law and the Authority of the State*. Oxford: Hart Publishing.

Duff-Brown, Beth. 2005. "Jews, Muslims to Seek Tribunals in Canada." *ABC News*. Retrieved from www.abcnews.go.com/International/ print?id=1126490.

Duffy, Maureen. 2017. *Detention of Terrorism Suspects Political Discourse and Fragmented Practices*. Oxford: Hart Publishing.

Duhaime, Lloyd. 2012. "Contempt of Court: A Contemnor's Guide to the Legal Universe." Retrieved from www.duhaime.org/LegalResources/CivilLitigation/LawArticle-1263/Contempt-of-Court-A-Contemnors-Guide-to-the-Legal-Universe.aspx

Dupuis, Manon Diane. 2015. "Legal aid in Canada, 2013/2014." Statistics Canada, *Juristat*. Retrieved from www.statcan.gc.ca/pub/85-002-x/2015001/article/14159-eng.htm.

Durand, Claire. 2002. "The 2000 Canadian Election and Poll Reporting Under the New Elections Act." *Canadian Public Policy* 28 (4) (December): 539–545.

Durkheim, Emile. 1893/1964. *The Division of Labor in Society*. Trans. George Simpson. New York: Free Press.

———. 1912/1965. *The Elementary Forms of Religious Life*. New York: Free Press.

Durlauf, Steven N., Chao Fu, and Salvador Navarro. 2013. "Capital Punishment and Deterrence: Understanding Disparate Results." *Journal of Quantitative Criminology* 29 (1):103–121.

Dyck, Erika and Maureen Lux. 2016. "Population Control in the "Global North"?: Canada's Response to Indigenous Reproductive Rights and Neo-Eugenics." Canadian Historical Review 97(4): 481–512.

Dye, Thomas R. 2008. Understanding Public Policy. 12th ed. Upper Saddle River, NJ: Prentice Hall.

Easton, Susan (ed.). 2009. *Marx and Law*. Burlington, VT: Ashgate.

Eckhoff, Torstein. 1978. "The Mediator: The Judge and the Administrator in Conflict-Resolution," in Sheldon Goldman and Austin Sarat (eds.), *American Court Systems: Readings in Judicial Process and Behavior*, pp. 31–41. San Francisco: W. H. Freeman.

Ecojustice. 2017. "What We Do and Why We Do It." Retrieved from www.ecojustice.ca/approach/.

Economist. 1979. "The Odour of Solvency." 273 (7101) (October 6): 104.

———. 2002a. "A Jail by Another Name." (December 21): 52–53.

———. 2002b. "Mom's Boys." (May 11): 36.

———. 2004."London's Cops Look to New York." (February 21): 53–54.

———. 2010. "Justice in the United Arab Emirates: What a Muddle." (January 16): 48.

Eder, Klaus. 1977. "Rationalist and Normative Approaches to the Sociological Study of Law." *Law and Society Review* 12 (1) (Fall): 133–144.

Edgeworth, Brendan. 2003. *Law, Modernity, Postmodernity: Legal Change in the Contracting State*. Burlington, VT: Ashgate.

Edmonton Journal. 2005. "Action on Crystal Meth." (October 26): A18.

Egale. 2017. "About Egale Canada Human Rights Trust." Retrieved from https://egale.ca/about/.

————. 2016. *Working in Solidarity: Broadening Canada's Overseas Assistance Programs to be More Inclusive of LGBTQI2S Minorities Rights Globally*. Submission to Global Affairs Canada—LGBTQI2S International Development. (November 7). Retrieved from https://egale.ca/gac-submission-2016/.

Eggleston, David. 2000. "Raising the Bar: The Ever-Higher Cost of a Legal Education." *Canadian Lawyer* 24 (8) (August): 8–12.

Ehrlich, Eugen. 1975. *Fundamental Principles of the Sociology of Law*. Trans. Walter L. Mall. New York: Arno.

Ehrmann, Henry W. 1976. *Comparative Legal Cultures*. Englewood Cliffs, NJ: Prentice Hall.

Eicher, Sharon (ed.). 2009. *Corruption in International Business: The Challenge of Cultural and Legal Diversity*. Burlington, VT: Ashgate.

Eldridge v. British Columbia (Attorney General) [1997] 3 SCR 624.

Eliadis, Pearl, Jan-Eric Furubo, and Steven Jacob (eds.). 2010. *Evaluation: Seeking Truth or Power? Comparative Policy Evaluation*. Vol. 17. Piscataway, NJ: Transaction Publishers.

Elliott, David W. 2005. *Law and Aboriginal Peoples in Canada*. 5th ed. Concord, ON: Captus.

Embrick, David G. 2015. "Two Nations, Revisited: The Lynching of Black and Brown Bodies, Police Brutality, and Racial Control in 'Post-Racial' Amerikkka." *Critical Sociology* 41(6): 835–843.

Ende, Werner and Udo Steinbach (eds.). 2010. *Islam in the World Today: A Handbook of Politics, Religion, Culture, and Society*. Ithaca, NY: Cornell University Press.

Engel, David M. and Jaruwan S. Engel. 2011. *Tort, Custom, and Karma: Globalization and Legal Consciousness in Thailand*. Stanford, CA: Stanford University Press.

Engen, Rodney L. 2009. "Assessing Determinate and Presumptive Sentencing—Making Research Relevant." *Criminology and Public Policy* 8(2): 323–336.

Entrop v. Imperial Oil Ltd. (2000), 189 D.L.R. (4th) 14.

Eorsi, Gyula and Attila Harmathy. 1971. *Law and Economic Reform in Socialistic Countries*. Budapest: Akademiai Kiado.

Erickson, Patricia G. 1998. "Neglected and Rejected: A Case Study of the Impact of Social Research on Canadian Drug Policy." *Canadian Journal of Sociology* 23 (2/3): 263–280.

Erickson, Patricia G., Jennifer Butters, and Patti McGillicuddy. 2000. "Crack and Prostitution: Gender, Myths and Experiences." *Journal of Drug Issues* 30 (4) (Fall): 767–788.

Erikson, Kai T. 1966. *Wayward Puritans: A Study in the Sociology of Deviance*. New York: John Wiley.

Eriksson, Anna. 2009. *Justice in Transition: Community Restorative Justice in Northern Ireland*. Devon, UL: Willan Publishing.

Erlanger, Howard S. and Douglas A. Klegon. 1978. "Socialization Effects of Professional School: The Law School Experience and Student Orientations to Public Interest Concerns." *Law and Society Review* 13 (1) (Fall): 11–35.

Essex, Nathan L. 2009. *The 200 Most Frequently Asked Legal Questions for Educators*. Thousand Oaks, CA: Corwin.

Etzioni, Amitai. 1973. *The Genetic Fix*. New York: Palgrave Macmillan.

European Monitoring Centre for Drugs and Drug Addictions. 2008. "Annual Report: The State of the Drugs Problem in Europe." Retrieved from www.emcdda.europa.eu/publications/annual-report/2008.

Evan, William M. 1965. "Law as an Instrument of Social Change," in Alvin W. Gouldner and S. M. Miller (eds.), *Applied Sociology: Opportunities and Problems*, pp. 285–293. New York: Free Press.

————. 1990. *Social Structure and Law: Theoretical and Empirical Perspectives*. Newbury Park, CA: Sage.

Evans, Donald G. 2001. "Canada's First Drug Treatment Court." *Corrections Today* 63 (3) (June): 30–31.

Ewick, Patricia and Susan Silbey. 2003. "Narrating Social Structure: Stories of Resistance to Legal Authority." *American Journal of Sociology* 108 (6) (May): 1328–1375.

Fagan, Jeffrey A. 2016. "Capital Punishment: Deterrent Effects & Capital Costs." Retrieved from www.law.columbia.edu/law_school/communications/reports/summer06/capitalpunish.

Fairman, Robyn and Charlotte Yapp. 2005. "Enforced Self-Regulation, Prescription, and Conceptions of Compliance Within Small Businesses: The Impact of Enforcement." *Law and Policy* 27 (4) (October): 491–519.

Farget, Doris. 2014. "Words that Fly Back and Forth Between Two Mutually Oblivious Worlds: What is the Legal Meaning of an 'Indigenous Way of Life'?" *The Canadian Journal of Law and Jurisprudence* 27(1): 239–258.

Farney, James. 2012. *Social Conservatives and Party Politics in Canada and the United States*. Toronto: University of Toronto Press.

Farrahany, Nita (ed.). 2009. *The Impact of Behavioral Sciences on Criminal Law*. New York: Oxford University Press.

Farrand, Benjamin. 2015. "Lobbying and Lawmaking in the European Union: The Development of Copyright Law and the Rejection of the Anti-Counterfeiting Trade Agreement." *Oxford Journal of Legal Studies* 35(3): 487–514.

Fearon, Joseph. 2016. "Why We Should Reduce the Number of Civil Trials Decided By Juries." *Now*. (October 11). Retrieved from https://nowtoronto.com/news/why-we-should-reduce-the-number-of-civil-trials-decided-by-juries/.

Federation of Law Societies of Canada. 2015. "2014 Statistical Report." Retrieved from http://docs.flsc.ca/2014-Statistics.pdf.

———. 2017. "About Us." Retrieved from http://flsc.ca/about-us/

Feinberg, Joel and Jules Coleman (eds.). 2008. *Philosophy of Law*, 8th ed. Belmont, CA: Wadsworth Publishing Company.

Feld, Andrew D. 2006. "Cultural and Medical Malpractice: Lessons from Japan; Is the 'Reluctant Plaintiff' a Myth?" *American Journal of Gastroenterology* 101: 1949–1950.

Feldman, Charles. 2015. "Parliament and Supreme Court of Canada Reference Cases." Publication No. 2015–44-E (August 12). Retrieved from www.lop.parl.gc.ca/Content/LOP/ResearchPublications/2015-44-e.pdf.

Feldman, Daniel L. 2016. *Administrative Law: The Sources and Limits of Government Agency Power*. Thousand Oaks, CA: CQ Press.

Felstiner, William L. F. 1974. "Influences of Social Organization on Dispute Processing." *Law and Society Review* 9 (1) (Fall): 63–94.

Felstiner, William, Richard Abel, and Austin Sarat. 1980. "The Emergence and Transformation of Disputes: Naming, Blaming, Claiming. . . " *Law and Society Review* 15 (3/4): 631–654.

Ferguson, Christopher J. (ed.). 2010. *Violent Crime: Clinical and Social Implications*. Thousand Oaks, CA: Sage.

Fernandes v. Carleton University, 2016 ONCA 719.

Fernandez, Luis Alberto. 2008. *Policing Dissent: Social Control and the Anti-Globalization Movement*. New Brunswick, NJ: Rutgers University Press.

Feuer, Lewis S. 2010. *Ideology and the Ideologists*. With a new introduction by Irving Lous Horowitz. Piscataway, NJ: Transaction Publishers.

Filax, Gloria. 2004. "Producing Homophobia in Alberta, Canada in the 1990s." *Journal of Historical Sociology* 17 (1) (March): 87–120.

Fine, Michelle. 1997. "Witnessing Whiteness," in Michelle Fine, Lois Weis, Linda C. Powell and L. Mun Wong (eds.), *Off White: Readings on Race, Power, and Society*, pp. 57–65. London: Routledge.

Fine, Sean. 2016. "Federal Government Plans to Reduce Use of Mandatory Minimum Prison Sentences." *Globe & Mail* (November 1). Retrieved from www.theglobeandmail.com/news/national/ottawa-plans-to-reduce-use-of-mandatory-prison-sentences/article32609570/

Fineman, Martha Albertson, Jack E. Jackson, and Adam P. Romero (eds.). 2009. *Feminist and Queer Legal Theory: Intimate Encoutners and Uncomfortable Conversations*. Burlington, VT: Ashgate.

Fink, Arlene. 2009. *How to Conduct Surveys, a Step-by-Step Guide*. 4th ed. Thousand Oaks, CA: Sage.

Fisher, George. 2003. *Plea Bargaining's Triumph: A History of Plea Bargaining in America*. Stanford, CA: Stanford University Press.

Fisher, Joseph C. 1997. *Killer Among Us*. Westport, CT: Praeger/Greenwood.

Fisse, Brent and John Braithwaite. 1993. "The Impact of Publicity on Corporate Offenders: The Ford Motor Company and the Pinto Papers," in Delos H. Kelly (ed.), *Deviant Behavior: A Text-Reader in the Sociology of Deviance*, pp. 627–640. New York: St. Martin's.

Fitzgerald, Robin T. and Peter J. Carrington. 2011. "Disproportionate Minority Contact in Canada: Police and Visible Minority Youth." *Canadian Journal of Criminology and Criminal Justice* 53(4): 449–486.

Fitzpatrick, Jody, Christina Christie, and Melvin M. Mark. 2009. *Evaluation in Action: Interviews with Expert Evaluators*. Thousand Oaks, CA: Sage Publications.

Fleming, Macklin. 1997. *Lawyers, Money, and Success: The Consequences of Dollar Obsessions*. Westport, CT: Quorum.

Flemming, Roy B. 2004. *Tournament of Appeals: Granting Judicial Review in Canada*. Vancouver, BC: UBC Press.

Flemming, Roy B. and Glen S. Krutz. 2002. "Repeat Litigators and Agenda Setting on the Supreme Court of Canada." *Canadian Journal of Political Science* 35 (4) (December): 811–833.

Fleras, Augie. 2005. *Social Problems in Canada: Conditions, Constructions and Challenges.* 4th ed. Toronto: Pearson.

———. 2017a. *Unequal Relations: A Critical Introduction to Race, Ethnic and Aboriginal Dynamics in Canada,* 8th ed. Toronto: Pearson.

———. 2017b. *Inequality Matters: Diversity and Exclusion in Canada.* Toronto: Oxford University Press.

Fleury-Steiner, Benjamin and Laura Beth Nielsen (eds.). 2006. *The New Civil Rights Research: A Constitutive Approach.* Aldershot, Hants, UK: Ashgate.

Flynn, Asher and Jacqueline Hodgson (eds.). 2017. *Access to Justice and Legal Aid: Comparative Perspectives on Unmet Legal Need.* Oxford: Hart Publishing.

Focus on Law Studies. 2003. "Gun Laws and Policies: A Dialogue." 18 (2) (Spring): 1–20.

Fong, Petti. 2012. "Alberta Court Sides with Ex-students Who Criticized Prof." *Toronto Star* (May 9). Retrieved from www.thestar.com/news/canada/2012/05/09/alberta_court_sides_with_exstudents_who_criticized_prof.html.

Foote, Nelson N. 1953. "The Professionalization of Labor in Detroit." *American Journal of Sociology* 58 (4) (January): 371–380.

Forcese, Craig and Aaron Freeman. 2005. *The Laws of Government: The Legal Foundations of Canadian Democracy.* Toronto: Irwin Law.

Forester, John. 2009. *Dealing with Differences: The Drama of Mediating Public Disputes.* New York: Oxford University Press.

Forst, Martin L. 1978. *Civil Commitment and Social Control.* Lexington, MA: Heath.

Forum of Canadian Ombudsman. 2011. "What Is an Ombudsman/Ombudsperson?" Retrieved from www.ombudsmanforum.ca/en/?page_id=172/.

Foster, George M. 1973. *Traditional Societies and Technological Change.* 2nd ed. New York: Harper and Row.

Foster, Hamar, Heather Raven, and Jeremy Webber (eds.). 2011. *Let Right Be Done: Aboriginal Title, the Calder Case, and the Future of Indigenous Rights.* Vancouver, BC: UBC Press.

Foucault, Michel. 1977. *Discipline and Punish: The Birth of the Prison.* Trans. Alan Sheridan. New York: Pantheon.

Frank, Christopher. 2010. *Master and Servant Law: Chartists, Trade Unions, Radical Lawyers and the Magistracy in England, 1840–1865.* Burlington, VT: Ashgate.

Frank, Jeffrey. 1994. "Voting and Contributing: Political Participation in Canada," in *Canadian Social Trends: A Canadian Studies Reader,* vol. 2, pp. 333–337. Toronto: Thompson.

Frank, Jerome. 1930. *Law and the Modern Mind.* New York: Coward-McCann.

Franke, Katherine M. 2001. "Theorizing Yes: An Essay on Feminism, Law, and Desire." *Columbia Law Review* 101 (1) (January): 181–208.

Freeman, Michael and Oliver G. Goodenough (eds.). 2010. *Law, Mind and Brain.* Burlington, VT: Ashgate.

Freeman, Michael and Andrew Lewis (eds.). 1999. *Law and Literature.* Oxford, UK: Oxford University Press.

Freeman, Richard J. and Ronald Roesch. 1992. "Psycholegal Education: Training for Forum and Function," in Dorothy K. Kagehiro and William S. Laufer (eds.), *Handbook of Psychology and Law,* pp. 567–576. New York: Springer-Verlag.

Freund, Jennifer A. 2007. "Police Civil Liability for Negligent Investigation: An Analysis of the Supreme Court of Canada Decision in Hill v. Hamilton-Wentworth Regional Police Services Board." *Criminal Law Quarterly* 53: 469–489.

Friedland, Martin L. (ed.). 1989. *Sanctions and Rewards in the Legal System: A Multidisciplinary Approach.* Toronto: University of Toronto Press.

Friedman, Lawrence M. 1969. "Legal Culture and Social Development." *Law and Society Review* 4 (1): 29–44.

———. 1973a. "General Theory of Law and Social Change," in J. S. Ziegel (ed.), *Law and Social Change,* pp. 17–33. Toronto: Osgoode Hall Law School, York University.

———. 1973b. *A History of American Law.* New York: Simon and Schuster.

———. 1975. *The Legal System: A Social Science Perspective.* New York: Russell Sage Foundation.

———. 1977. *Law and Society: An Introduction.* Englewood Cliffs, NJ: Prentice Hall.

———. 1998. *American Law: An Introduction.* 2nd ed. New York: W. W. Norton.

————. 2002. *American Law in the Twentieth Century*. New Haven, CT: Yale University Press.

————. 2005a. *A History of American Law*. 3rd ed. New York: Simon & Schuster/Touchstone Book.

————. 2005b. "Coming of Age: Law and Society Enters an Exclusive Club." *Annual Review of Law and Social Science* 1 (December): 1–16.

————. 2016. *Impact: How the Law Affects Behavior*. Cambridge, MA: Harvard University Press.

Friedman, Robert L. 2000. *Red Mafiya: How the Russian Mob Has Invaded America*. Boston: Little, Brown.

Friedmann, Wolfgang. 1972. *Law in a Changing Society*. 2nd ed. New York: Columbia University Press.

Friedrich, Carl J. 1958. *The Philosophy of Law in Historical Perspective*. Chicago: University of Chicago Press.

Friedrichs, David O. 2006. *Law in Our Lives: An Introduction*. Los Angeles: Roxbury 2010. *Law in Our Lives: An Introduction*. 2nd ed. Los Angeles: Roxbury.

————. 2010. *Trusted Criminals: White Collar Crime in Contemporary Society*. 4th edition. Belmont, CA: Wadsworth/Thomson Learning.

Fu, Ziqiu. 2003. "Guest Editor's Introduction." *Chinese Law and Government* 36 (3) (May/June): 3–6.

Fuller, Lon. 1968. *Anatomy of the Law*. New York: Praeger.

————. 1969. *The Morality of Law*. Rev. ed. New Haven, CT: Yale University Press.

Fullick, Melonie. 2012. "It's a Legal Matter, From Now On. . . ." *University Affairs* (May 22). Retrieved from www.universityaffairs.ca/opinion/speculative-diction/its-a-legal-matter-from-now-on/.

Furniss, Elizabeth. 2001. "Aboriginal Justice, the Media, and the Symbolic Management of Aboriginal/Euro-Canadian Relations." *American Indian Culture and Research Journal* 25 (2): 1–36.

Gaillard, Emmanual. 2000. "Alternative Dispute Resolution (ADR) à la Française." *New York Law Journal* (June 1): 1–3.

Gajda, Amy. 2010. *The Trials of Academia: The New Era of Campus Litigation*. Cambridge, MA: Harvard University Press.

Galanter, Marc. 1974. "Why the 'Haves' Come Out Ahead: Speculations on the Limits of Legal Change." *Law and Society Review* 9 (1): 95–160.

————. 1975. "Afterword: Explaining Litigation." *Law and Society Review* 9 (2): 347–368.

————. 1977. "The Modernization of Law," in Lawrence M. Friedman and Stewart Macaulay (eds.), *Law and the Behavioral Sciences*, pp. 1046–1060. 2nd ed. Indianapolis, ID: Bobbs-Merrill.

————. 1988. "Beyond the Litigation Panic," in Walter Olson (ed.), *New Directions in Liability Law*, pp. 18–30. New York: Academy of Political Science.

————. 1992. "The Debased Debate on Civil Justice." Working Paper DPRP (May). Institute for Legal Studies. Madison: University of Wisconsin.

Gaming Magazine. 2001. "Winners and Losers: Millions at Stake in Native Dispute over Casino Profits." Retrieved from gamingmagazine.com/managearticle.asp?c=620anda=138.

Garcia-Lopez, Gladys. 2008. "Nunca Te Toman En Cuenta (They Never Take You into Account): The Challenges of Inclusion and Strategies for Success of Chicana Attorneys." *Gender and Society* 22 (5) (October): 590–612.

Gardam, Kevin and Audrey R. Giles. 2016. "Media Representations of Policies Concerning Education Access and Their Roles in Seven First Nations Students' Deaths in Northern Ontario." *The International Indigenous Policy Journal* 7 (1). Retrieved from http://ir.lib.uwo.ca/ iipj/vol7/iss1/1.

Garland, David. 2001. *The Culture of Control: Crime and Social Order in Contemporary Society*. Chicago: University of Chicago Press.

Garner, Bryan A. 2001. *Legal Writing in Plain English: A Text with Exercises*. Chicago: University of Chicago Press.

Garrett, Brandon L. and Peter J. Neufeld. 2009. "Invalid Forensic Science Testimony and Wrongful Convictions." *Virginia Law Review* 1: 1–97.

Garrick, Rick. 2016. "Indigenous Peoples Court in Thunder Bay Gets Approval." *Wawatay News* (December 10). Retrieved from www.wawataynews.ca/community/indigenous-peoples-court-thunder-bay-gets-approval.

Garzone, Giuliana. 2000. "Legal Translation and Functionalist Approaches: A Contradiction in Terms?" *ASTTI/ETI*, 395–414. Retrieved from www.tradulex.com/Actes2000/Garzone.pdf

Gaudreault, Arlène. 2009. "The Limits of Restorative Justice." Symposium 2009. Retrieved from www.victimsweek.gc.ca/symp-colloque/past-passe/2009/presentation/arlg_1.html.

Gaudry, M. 1988. "The Effects on Road Safety of the Compulsory Insurance, Flat Premium Rating and No-Fault Features of the 1978 Quebec Automobile Act," appendix to *Report of the Inquiry into Motor Vehicle Accident Compensation in Ontario* (Osborne Report). Toronto: Queen's Printer.

Gauthier c. Saint-Germain, 2010 ONCA 309, 264 O.A.C. 336.

Gavigan, Shelley A. M. 2000. "Mothers, Other Mothers, and Others: The Legal Challenges and Contradictions of Lesbian Parents," in Dorothy Chunn and Dany Lacombe (eds.), *Law as a Gendering Practice*, pp. 100–118. Don Mills, ON: Oxford University Press.

Gee, James Paul. 2014. *An Introduction to Discourse Analysis: Theory and Method*. 4th ed. New York: Routledge.

Geiger-Oneto, Stephanie and Scott Phillips. 2003. "Driving While Black: The Role of Race, Sex, and Social Status." *Journal of Ethnicity in Criminal Justice* 1 (2): 1–25.

Geis, Gilbert. 1978. "Deterring Corporate Crime," in M. David Ermann and Richard J. Lundman (eds.), *Corporate and Governmental Deviance: Problems of Organizational Behavior in Contemporary Society*, pp. 278–296. New York: Oxford University Press.

———. 1994. "Corporate Crime: 'Three Strikes You're Out?'" *Multinational Monitor* 15 (6) (June): 30–31.

Geist, Michael (ed.). 2015. *Law, Privacy and Surveillance in Canada in the Post-Snowden Era*. Ottawa, ON: University of Ottawa Press.

Gellhorn, Ernest and Ronald M. Levin. 1997. *Administrative Law and Process in a Nutshell*. 4th ed. St. Paul, MN: West.

Georgakopoulas, Alexia (ed.). 2017. *The Mediation Handbook: Research, Theory and Practice*. New York: Routledge.

Gerson, Stuart M. 1994. "Computers Generate Litigation Explosion." *National Law Journal* 16 (31) (April 4): A17.

Gerstein, Ralph M. and Lois Gerstein. 2007. *Education Law: A Practical Guide for Attorneys, Teachers, Administrators and Student Advocates*. 2nd ed. Tucson, AZ: Lawyers & Judges Publishing.

Ghanea, Nazila. 2004. "Human Rights of Religious Minorities and of Women in the Middle East." *Human Rights Quarterly* 26 (3) (August): 705–729.

Ghanim, David. 2010. *Gender and Violence in the Middle East*. Santa Barbara, CA: Prager.

Gibbs, John C. 2010. *Moral Development and Reality: Beyond the Theories of Kohlberg and Hoffman*. 2nd ed. Thousand Oaks, CA: Sage.

Gibson, James L. and Gregory A. Caldeira. 1996. "The Legal Cultures of Europe." *Law and Society Review* 30 (1) (February): 55–85.

Giffen, P. J., Shirley Endicott, and Sylvia Lambert. 1991. *Panic and Indifference: The Politics of Canada's Drug Laws*. Toronto: Canadian Centre on Substance Abuse.

Gill, David. 1988. *The Market for Legal Services*. Vancouver: The Fraser Institute.

Gill, Gerald L. 1990. *The Canadian Legal System*. 3rd ed. Toronto: Carswell.

———. 1999. "Judiciary," in James H. Marsh (ed.), *The Canadian Encyclopedia: Year 2000 Edition*, pp. 1224–1225. Toronto: McClelland and Stewart.

Gillespie, Alisdair. 2009. *The English Legal System*. New York: Oxford University Press.

Gilmore, G. 1977. *The Ages of American Law*. New Haven, CT: Yale University Press.

Ginsberg, Margery B. and Pablo Fiene. 2004. *Motivation Matters: A Workbook for School Change*. San Francisco, CA: Jossey-Bass.

Ginsberg, Morris. 1965. *On Justice in Society*. Ithaca, NY: Cornell University Press.

Ginsburg, Tom and Glenn Hoetker. 2005. "The Unreluctant Litigant? An Empirical Analysis of Japan's Turn to Litigation." Illinois Law and Economics Working Papers Series, Working Paper no. LE04–990. Retrieved from www.law-bepress.com.

Girard, Claude. 2001. "Fiscal Treatment of Social Allocations and Human Rights." *Canadian Journal of Law and Society* 16 (2): 119–135.

Girard, Eric C. 2013. "What I Learned At Law School: The Poor Need Not Apply." *Globe and Mail*, November 17. Retrieved from www.theglobeandmail.com/life/facts-and-arguments/what-i-learned-at-law-school-the-poor-need-not-apply/article15443887/.

Glasbeck, Amanda. 2010. *Feminized Justice: The Torotno Women's Court, 1913–34*. Vancouver, BC: UBC Press.

Glazer, Nathan. 1975. "Towards an Imperial Judiciary?" *Public Interest* 41 (Fall): 104–123.

Glendon, Mary Ann, Michael Wallace Gordon, and Christopher Osakwe. 1994. *Comparative Legal Traditions*. 2nd ed. St. Paul, MN: West.

Glenn, Patrick. 2010. *Legal Traditions of the World: Sustainable Diversity in Law*. 4th ed. New York: Oxford University Press.

Globe and Mail. 2005. "Sharia (Islamic Law) Protestors Target Canada." (August 31). Retrieved from www.freemuslims.org/news/article.php?article=876.

Gold, Susan Dudley. 2005. *Brown v. Board of Education: Separate but Equal?* New York: Benchmark Books.

Goldberg, Stephen B., Frank E. A. Sander, Nancy H. Rogers, and Sarah Rudolph Cole. 2012. *Dispute Resolution: Negotiation, Mediation, and Other Processes*. 6th ed. New York: Aspen.

Goldman, Sheldon and Austin Sarat (eds.). 1978. *American Court Systems: Readings in Judicial Process and Behavior*. San Francisco: W. H. Freeman.

———. 1989. *American Court Systems: Readings in Judicial Process and Behavior*. 2nd ed. New York: Longman.

Goldstein, Philip. 2005. *Post-Marxist Theory*. Albany, NY: State University of New York Press.

Goode, Erich. 2016. *Deviant Behavior*. 10th ed. New York: Routledge.

Goold, Benjamin J. and Daniel Neyland (eds.) 2009. *New Directions in Surveillance and Privacy*. Devon, UK: Willan Publishing.

Gorman, Elizabeth R. 2005. "Gender Stereotypes, Same-Gender Preferences, and Organizational Variation in the Hiring of Women: Evidence from Law Firms." *American Sociological Review* 70 (4) (August): 702–728.

Gossett, Jennifer L. and Sarah Byrne. 2002. "'Click Here': A Content Analysis of Internet Rape Sites." *Gender and Society* 16 (5) (October): 689–709.

Gottfredson, Denise C. 2017. "Prevention Research in Schools." *Criminology & Public Policy* 16 (1): 7–27.

Government of Canada. 2005. "Amendments of Lobbyists Registration Act to Come into Force." Retrieved from www.faa.lfi.gc.ca/fs-fi/04fs-fi_e.asp.

———. 2006. "Toughening the Lobbyists Registration Act." Retrieved from www.faa.lfi.gc.ca/fs-fi/04fs-fi_e.asp.

———. 2010a. "The Government of Canada's Approach to Implementation of the Inherent Right and the Negotiation of Aboriginal Self-Government." (September 15). Retrieved from www.aadnc-aandc.gc.ca/eng/1100100031843/1100100031844.

———. 2010b. "Nisga'a Final Agreement 2001 Annual Report." Retrieved from www.aadnc-aandc.gc.ca/eng/1100100031762/1100100031764.

———. 2014a. "Renewing the Comprehensive Land Claims Policy: Towards a Framework for Addressing Section 35 Aboriginal Rights." Retrieved from www.aadnc-aandc.gc.ca/eng/1408631807053/1408631881247.

———. 2014b. "National Anti-Drug Strategy." Retrieved from www.healthycanadians.gc.ca/anti-drug-antidrogue/about-apropos/index-eng.php.

———. 2015a. Fact Sheet: Aboriginal Self-Government." Retrieved from www.aadnc-aandc.gc.ca/eng/1100100016293/1100100016294."

———. 2015b. "Fact Sheet: Implementation of Final Agreements." Retrieved from www.aadnc-aandc.gc.ca/eng/1100100030580/1100100030581.

———. 2015c. "Renewing the Federal Comprehensive Land Claims Policy." April 2. Retrieved from www.aadnc-aandc.gc.ca/eng/1405693409911/1405693617207.

———. 2015d. "Considerations Which Apply to an Application for Appointment." April 1. Retrieved from www.fja-cmf.gc.ca/appointments-nominations/considerations-eng.html.

———. 2015e. "Competition Bureau." November 5. Retrieved from www.competitionbureau.gc.ca/eic/site/cb-bc.nsf/eng/04058.html.

———. 2016a. "News Release: Government of Canada Plans to Introduce Regulations to Support the Assisted Human Reproduction Act." September 30. Retrieved from http://news.gc.ca/web/article-en.do?nid=1131339.

———. 2016b. "Japanese Auto Parts Company Fined $13 Million for Participating in a Bid-Rigging Conspiracy." Competition Bureau Media Centre. April 1. Retrieved from Goulet, Jean-Guy A. 2010. "Legal Victories for the Dene Tha? Their Significance for Aboriginal Rights in Canada." *Anthropologica* 52(1):15–31.

Government of Manitoba. 2017. *Youth Drug Stabilization Act—Information for Parents*. Retrieved from www.gov.mb.ca/healthyliving/addictions/ydsa.html.

Government of Ontario. 2016. *Civil Cases: Suing and Being Sued in the Superior Court of Justice.* Retrieved from www.attorneygeneral.jus.gov.on.ca/english/courts/civil/suing_and_being_sued_7.php.

Grabosky, Peter. 2016. *Cybercrime.* Upper Saddle River, NJ: Pearson.

Graglia, Lino A. 1994. "Do Judges Have a Policy-making Role in the American System of Government?" *Harvard Journal of Law and Public Policy* 17 (1) (Winter): 119–130.

Gram, David. 2006. "As Part of Sentence, Man Told He Can't Go Home Again." *Seattle Times* (July 5): A4.

Grana, Sheryl. 2009. *Women and Justice.* 2nd ed. Lanham, MD: Rowman & Littlefield.

Granfield, Robert and Lynn Mather (eds.). 2009. *Private Lawyers and the Public Interest: The Evolving Role of Pro Bono in the Legal Profession.* New York: Oxford University Press.

Grassy Narrows First Nation v. Ontario (Natural Resources), [2014] 2 SCR 447, 2014 SCC 48 (CanLII).

Graves, Frank. 2014. "Rethinking the Public Interest: Evolving Trends in Values and Attitudes." #Can2020 Conference. Ottawa, Ontario. October 2. Retrieved from www.ekospolitics.com/wp-content/uploads/rethinking_the_public_interest_october_2_2014.pdf.

Graves, Frank. 2017. "Understanding the Shifting Meaning of the Middle Class." EKOS Politics. March. Retrieved from www.ekos.com/studies/MiddleClass.pdf.

Gray, David E. 2010. *Doing Research in the Real World.* Thousand Oaks, CA: Sage Publications.

Green, Melvyn. 1986. "A History of Canadian Narcotics Control: The Formative Years," in Neil Boyd (ed.), *The Social Dimensions of Law,* pp. 24–40. Scarborough, ON: Prentice Hall.

Green, Stuart P. 2006. *Lying, Cheating, and Stealing: A Moral Theory of White-Collar Crime.* New York: Oxford University Press.

Green, Traci, Catherine Hankins, and Darlene Palmer. 2003. "Ascertaining the Need for a Supervised Injecting Facility (SIF): The Burden of Public Injecting in Montreal, Canada." *Journal of Drug Issues* 33 (3) (Summer): 713–731.

Greenaway, William K. and Stephan L. Brickey (eds.). 1978. *Law and Social Control in Canada.* Scarborough, ON: Prentice Hall.

Greenberg, Judith G., Martha L. Minow, and Dorothy E. Roberts. 2008. *Women and the Law.* 4th ed. New York: Foundation Press.

Greene, Edith and Michael Johns. 2001. "Jurors Use of Instructions on Negligence." *Journal of Applied Social Psychology* 31 (5): 840–859.

Greenhouse, Carol J. 1989. "Interpreting American Litigiousness," in June Starr and Jane F. Collier (eds.), *History and Power in the Study of Law: New Directions in Legal Anthropology,* pp. 252–273. Ithaca, NY: Cornell University Press.

Greenwood, F. Murray and Beverley Boissery. 2000. *Uncertain Justice: Canadian Women and Punishment, 1754–1953.* Toronto: Dundurn.

Griffin, James. 2009. *On Human Rights.* New York: Oxford University Press.

Griffiths, Curt T. and Alison Hatch Cunningham. 2003. *Canadian Criminal Justice.* Scarborough, ON: Nelson.

Grillo, Ralph, Roger Ballard, Allesandro Ferrari, Andre Koekema, Marcel Maussen, and Prakash Shah (eds.). 2009. *Legal Practice and Cultural Diversity.* Burlington, VT: Ashgate.

Grossi, Paolo. 2010. *A History of European Law.* New York: Wiley-Blackwell.

Grossman, Joel B. and Mary H. Grossman (eds.). 1971. *Law and Social Change in Modern America.* Pacific Palisades, CA: Goodyear.

Groves, Robert M. 2009. *Survey Methodology.* 2nd ed. Hoboken, NJ: John Wiley.

Gudgeon, Chris. 2003. *The Naked Truth.* Vancouver: Greystone.

Gulliver, Philip H. 1969. "Introduction to Case Studies of Law in Non-Western Societies," in Laura Nader (ed.), *Law in Culture and Society,* pp. 11–23. Chicago: Aldine.

———. 1979. *Disputes and Negotiations: A Cross-Cultural Perspective.* New York: Academic Press.

Gunnell, Barbara. 2000. "A Tale of the Power of Ordinary Folk." *New Statesman* (February 21): 30.

Gunning, Jennifer, Soren Holm, and Ian Kenway (eds.). 2009. *Ethics, Law and Society.* Vol. IV. Burlington, VT: Ashgate.

Gunz, Hugh and Sally Gunz. 2007. "Hired Professional to Hired Gun: An Identity Approach to Understanding the Ethical Behaviour of Professionals in Non-Professional Organizations." *Human Relations* 60 (6) (June): 851–887.

Gunz, Sally and Hugh Gunz. 2008. "Ethical Decision Making and the Employed Lawyer." *Journal of Business Ethics* 81 (4) (September): 927–944.

Gupta, Dipak K. 2010. *Analyzing Public Policy: Concepts, Tools, and Techniques.* 2nd ed. Washington, DC: CQ Press.

Gürbilek, Nurdan. 2015. *Sessizin Payı.* Istanbul: Metis.

Gureyev, P. P. and P. I. Sedugin (eds.). 1977. *Legislation in the USSR.* Trans. Denis Ogden. Moscow: Progress.

Gusfield, Joseph R. 1967. "Moral Passage: The Symbolic Process in Public Designations of Deviance." *Social Problems* 15 (2) (Fall): 175–188.

Haas, Ernst B. 2008. *Beyond the Nation State: Functionalism and International Organization.* Wivenhoe Park, Colchester: ECPR Press.

Habermas, Jürgen. 2015. *The Theory of Communicative Action.* Volume 2: Lifeworld and System: The Critique of Functionalist Reason. Translated by Thomas McCarthy. Hoboken, NJ: Wiley/Polity.

Hackler, James C. 2003. *Canadian Criminology: Strategies and Perspectives.* 3rd ed. Toronto: Prentice Hall.

Hagan, John, Marie Huxter, and Patricia Parker. 1988. "Class Structure and Legal Practice: Inequality and Mobility Among Toronto Lawyers." *Law and Society Review* 22 (1): 9–55.

Hagan, John and Fiona Kay. 1995. *Gender in Practice: A Study of Lawyer's Lives.* Oxford: Oxford University Press.

———. 1999. "Cultivating Clients in the Competition for Partnership: Gender and the Organizational Restructuring of Law Firms in the 1990s." *Law and Society Review* 33 (3): 517–555.

———. 2007. "Even Lawyers Get the Blues: Gender, Depression, and Job Satisfaction in Legal Practice." *Law and Society Review* 41 (1): 51–78.

Hagan, John and Ron Levi. 2005. "Crimes of War and the Force of Law." *Social Forces* 83 (4) (June): 1499–1534.

Hagan, John and Rick Linden. 2016. "Corporate and White-Collar Crime," in Rick Linden (ed.), *Criminology: A Canadian Perspective,* 8th ed., pp. 468–499. Toronto, ON: Nelson Education.

Haida Nation v. British Columbia (Minister of Forests), 2004 SCC 73 (CanLII), [2004] 3 S.C.R. 511.

Hajnal, Zoltan L. and Terry Nichols Clark. 1998. "The Local Interest-Group System: Who Governs and Why?" *Social Science Quarterly* 79 (1) (March): 227–242.

Hall, Anthony J. 2000. "Racial Discrimination in Legislation, Litigation, Legend and Lore." *Canadian Ethnic Studies* 32 (2): 119–135.

Hall, Brian and Cookie Lazarus. 2016. "Aboriginal Gaming Challenges in Canada: First Nations Gambling Law." Retrieved from www.lazchar.com/2016/04/11/aboriginal_first_nations_gamibling-law_canada/.

Hall, Jerome. 1952. *Theft, Law and Society.* 2nd ed. Indianapolis, ID: Bobbs-Merrill.

Hallaq, Wael B. (ed.). 2004. *The Formation of Islamic Law.* Burlington, VT: Ashgate.

Hallaq, Wael B. 2009. *An Introduction to Islamic Law.* Cambridge, UK: Cambridge University Press.

Halperin, Rick. 2004. "Life on Hold." (June 19). Retrieved from venus.soci.niu.edu/~archives/ABOLISH/rick-halperin/sept04/0771.html.

Hamilton, Jennifer A. 2008. *Indigeneity in the Courtroom: Law, Culture, and the Production of Difference in North American Courts.* New York: Routledge.

Hanawalt, Barbara A. 1998. *"Of Good and Ill Repute": Gender and Social Control in Medieval England.* New York: Oxford University Press.

Handler, Joel F. 1978. *Social Movements and the Legal System: A Theory of Law Reform and Social Change.* New York: Academic Press.

Haney-Lopez, Ian F. 1997. *White by Law: The Legal Construction of Race.* New York: New York University Press.

Hans, Valerie P. (ed.). 2006. *The Jury System: Contemporary Scholarship.* Burlington, VT: Ashgate.

Harding, Robert. 2005. "The Media, Aboriginal People and Common Sense." *The Canadian Journal of Native Studies* XXV (1): 311–335.

Harding, Robert. 2006. "Historical Representations of Aboriginal People in the Canadian News Media." *Discourse & Society,* 17 (2): 205–235.

Harmon, Heather. 2016. "Illegal Gambling in Canada." *GP: Gaming Post* (March 12). Retrieved from www.gamingpost.ca/canadian-casino-news/illegal-gambling-canada/.

Harris, Kathleen. 2016. "Supreme Court Strikes Down 2 Conservative Sentencing Reforms." *CBC.* (April 15). Retrieved from www.cbc.ca/news/politics/supreme-court-sentencing-mandatory-minumums-1.3537150.

Harman, Danna. 2010. "Where Debt Collectors Use Shame as a Tactic." *The Christian Science Monitor* (February 14): 13.

Hastie, Robyn E. and Anita Kothari. 2009. "Tobacco Control Interest Groups and Their Influence on Parliamentary Committees in Canada." *Health Studies Publications.* Paper 12. http://ir.lib.uwo.ca/healthstudiespub/12.

Hatch, Alison. 1995. "Historical Legacies of Crime and Criminal Justice in Canada," in Margaret A. Jackson and Curt T. Griffiths (eds.), *Canadian Criminology: Perspectives on Crime and Criminality*, pp. 247–272. Toronto: Harcourt.

Hausegger, Lori, Matthew Hennigar, and Troy Riddell. 2009. *Canadian Courts: Law, Politics, and Process.* Toronto: Oxford University Press.

Hayden, Carol and Dennis Gough. 2010. *Implementing Restorative Justice in Children's Residential Care.* Bristol, UK: The Foundation Press.

Haynes, John Michael, Gretchen L. Haynes, and Larry Sun Fong. 2004. *Medication: Positive Conflict Management.* Albany, NY: State University of New York Press.

Hedican, Edward J. 2012. "Policing Aboriginal Protests and Confrontations: Some Policy Recommendations." *The International Indigenous Policy Journal* 3 (2). Retrieved from http://ir.lib.uwo.ca/iipj/vol3/iss2/1.

Heinrich, Erika. 2013. "Canadian Jurisprudence Regarding the Right to Legal Aid." *Lawyers' Rights Watch Canada* (September 2). Retrieved from www.lrwc.org/canadian-jurisprudence-regarding-the-right-to-legal-aid-report/.

Heinz, John P. and Edward O. Laumann. 1994. *Chicago Lawyers: The Social Structure of the Bar.* Rev. ed. Evanston, IL: Northwestern University Press.

Heinzelman, Susan Sage. 2010. *Riding the Black Ram: Law, Literature, and Gender.* Palo Alto, CA: Stanford University Press.

Helfer, Laurence R., and Graeme W. Austin. 2011. *Human Rights and Intellectual Property: Mapping the Global Interface.* Cambridge University Press.

Hellman, Hal. 2004. *Great Feuds in Technology: Ten of the Liveliest Disputes Ever.* Hoboken, NJ: John Wiley and Sons.

Hemmens, Craig, David C. Brody, and Cassia Spohn. 2017. *Criminal Courts: A Contemporary Perspective.* Thousand Oaks, CA: Sage.

Henderson, Harry. 2005. *Gun Control*, Revised ed. New York: Facts on File.

Henderson, Jennifer and Pauline Wakeham. 2009. "Colonial Reckoning, National Reconciliation? Aboriginal Peoples and the Culture of Redress in Canada." *ESC: English Studies in Canada* 35 (1): 1–26.

Henderson, William B. 2016. "Law of Indigenous People." *Historica Canada.* Retrieved from www.thecanadianencyclopedia.ca/en/article/aboriginal-people-law/.

Henry, Frances and Carol Tator, 2002. *Discourses of Domination: Racial Bias in the Canadian English-Language Press.* Toronto, ON: University of Toronto Press.

Henry, Frances, Carol Tator, Winston Mattis, and Tim Rees. 2000. *The Colour of Democracy: Racism in Canadian Society.* 2nd ed. Toronto: Harcourt.

Henry, Stuart and Scott A. Lukas (eds.). 2009. *Recent Developments in Criminological Theory.* Burlington, VT: Ashgate.

Herman, Didi. 1994. *Rights of Passage: Struggles for Lesbian and Gay Legal Equality.* Toronto: University of Toronto Press.

Hertzler, J. O. 1961. *American Social Institutions.* Boston: Allyn and Bacon.

Hesli, Vicki L. 2007. *Governments and Politics in Russia and the Post-Soviet Region.* Boston: Houghton Mifflin.

Hessick, F. Andrew. 2015. "Cases, Controversies, and Diversity." *Northwestern University Law Review* 109: 57–109.

Hier, Sean P. and Josh Greenberg (eds.) 2010. *Surveillance: Power, Problems and Politics.* Vancouver, BC: UBC Press.

Higgins, Paul and Mitchell B. Mackinem (eds.). 2010. *Problem-Solving Courts: Justice for the Twenty-First Century?* Santa Barbara, CA: Praeger.

Hill, Michael. 2006. *Social Policy in the Modern World.* Malden, MA: Blackwell.

Hill v. Church of Scientology of Toronto, [1995] 2 S.C.R. 1130.

Hillmer, Barbara. 2015. "Focus Group vs. Mock Trial: Which Is the Best for You?" Retrieved from litigationinsights.com/jury-consulting/focus-group-mock-trial-best-choice-advantage/.

Hirschman, Albert O. 1970. *Exit, Voice, and Loyalty: Responses to Decline in Firms, Organizations, and States.* Cambridge, MA: Harvard University Press.

Hirshman, Linda. 2016. *Sisters in Law: How Sandra Day O'Connor and Ruth Bader Ginsburg Went to the Supreme Court and Changed the World.* New York: Harper Perennial.

Hobbs, Robert J. 2011. *Fair Debt Collection.* 7th ed. Boston: National Consumer Law Center.

Hoebel, E. Adamson. 1954. *The Law of Primitive Man: A Study of Comparative Legal Dynamics.* Cambridge, MA: Harvard University Press.

Hoehn, Felix. 2012. *Reconciling Sovereignties: Aboriginal Nations and Canada.* Saskatoon, SK: Native Law Centre, University of Saskatchewan.

Hoffman, Jan. 2004. "Finding the Ideal Jury, Keeping Fingers Crossed." *New York Times* (March 11): B2.

Hogeveen, Bryan and Andrew Woolford. 2012. "Contemporary Critical Criminology," in Rick Linden (ed.). *Criminology: A Canadian Perspective,* pp. 377–407. Toronto: Nelson Education.

Hogg, Peter. 1997. *Constitutional Law of Canada.* 4th ed. Toronto: Carswell.

Holcomb, Jefferson E., Marian R. Williams, and Stephen Demuth. 2004. "White Female Victims and Death Penalty Disparity Research." *Justice Quarterly* 21 (4) (December): 877–902.

Holmes, Oliver Wendell, Jr. 1897. "The Path of the Law." *Harvard Law Review* 10 (March): 457–461.

———. 1881/1963. *The Common Law.* Ed. Mark D. Howe. Cambridge, MA: Harvard University Press.

———. 2004. *The Common Law: With a New Introduction by Tim Griffin.* New Brunswick, NJ: Transaction Publishers.

Holmes, Ronald M. and Stephen T. Holmes. 2010. *Serial Murder.* 3rd ed. Thousand Oaks, CA: Sage.

Holyoke, Thomas T. 2014. *Interest Groups and Lobbying: Pursuing Political Interests in Amerca.* Boulder, CO: Westview Press.

Hong, Peter Y. 1999. "Judge Cuts Award Against GM to $1.2 Billion." *Los Angeles Times* (August 27). Retrieved from rticles.latimes.com/1999/aug/27/local/me-4217.

Hood, Roger. 2002. *The Death Penalty: A Worldwide Perspective.* New York: Oxford University Press.

Horowitz, Alan V. 2002. *Creating Mental Illness.* Chicago, IL: University of Chicago Press.

Horowitz, Irwin A. and Kenneth S. Bordens. 2002. "The Effects of Jury Size, Evidence Complexity and Note Taking on Jury Process and Performance in a Civil Trial." *Journal of Applied Psychology* 87 (1) (February): 121–130.

Horvath, Miranda and Jennifer Brown (eds.). 2009. *Rape: Challenging Contemporary Thinking.* Devon, UK: Willan Publishing.

Hosseini, Behdad. 2013. "Types of Damages in Civil Litigation." Retrieved from www.hosseinilaw.com/types-of-damages-in-civil-litigation/.

Howard, Robert M. 2002. "Litigation, Courts, and Bureaucratic Policy: Equity, Efficiency and the Internal Revenue Service." *American Politics Research* 30 (6): 583–607.

Howard-Hassman, Rhoda E. 2000. "Multiculturalism, Human Rights and Cultural Relativism: Canadian Civic Leaders Discuss Women's Rights and Gay and Lesbian Rights." *Netherlands Quarterly of Human Rights* 18 (4) (December): 493–514.

Huff, C. Ronald and Martin Killias.2010. *Wrongful Conviction: International Perspectives on Miscarriages of Justice.* Philadelphia, PA: Temple University Press.

Huff, Toby E. and Wolfgang Schlucter (eds.). 1999. *Max Weber and Islam.* New Brunswick, NJ: Transaction.

Hughes, John C. 1995. *The Federal Courts, Politics, and the Rule of Law.* New York: HarperCollins.

Human Rights Act, S.N.W.T. 2002,c.18.

Human Rights Watch, 2017. *World Report 2017.* Retrieved from www.hrw.org/world-report/2017.

Hunt, Alan. 1978. *The Sociological Movement in Law.* Philadelphia: Temple University Press.

Hunter, Ian. 2006. "What Next? Anti-Harassment Training in the Crib?" *The Globe and Mail* (December 29): A15.

Husak, Douglas. 2010. *Overcriminalization: The Limits of Criminal Law.* New York: Oxford University Press.

Hutchinson, Allan C. 1999. *Legal Ethics and Professional Responsibility.* Toronto: Irwin Law.

———. 2002. "Legal Aid or Lawyers' Aid?" *Globe and Mail* (August 13): A17.

———. 2005. *Evolution and the Common Law.* New York: Cambridge University Press.

Iacobucci, Frank. 2013. "First Nations Representation on Ontario Juries." Retrieved from www.attorneygeneral.jus.gov.on.ca/english/about/pubs/iacobucci/First_Nations_Representation_Ontario_Juries.html.

Immigration and Refugee Protection Act (S.C. 2001, c. 27).

Imperial Oil Limited v. Communications, Energy & Paperworkers Union of Canada, Local 900, 2009 ONCA 420, (2009), 306 D.L.R. (4th) 385.

Intini, John. 2007. "No Justice for the Middle Class." *Maclean's* (September 10). Retrieved from ww.clp. utoronto.ca/media/no-justice-middle-class.htm.

Ireland, Nicole. 2016. "'The Impact on Society is Enormous': In Legal Profession, Depression, Addiction Hurts Clients, Too." *CBC News* (November 26). Retrieved from www.cbc.ca/news/health/lawyers-mental-health-addiction-problems-1.3865545.

Jackson, Liane. 2016. "Minority Women are Disappearing from BigLaw—and Here's Why." *Abajournal. com* (March 1). Retrieved from www.americanbar.org/groups/legal_education/resources/statistics.html.

Jacob, Herbert. 1984. *Justice in America: Courts, Lawyers, and the Judicial Process.* 4th ed. Boston: Little, Brown.

————. 1995. *Law and Politics in the United States.* 2nd ed. Ft. Washington, PA: HarperCollins.

————. 1997. "The Governance of Trial Judges." *Law and Society Review* 32 (1): 3–30.

Jacoby, Henry. 1973. *The Bureaucratization of the World.* Trans. Eveline L. Kanes. Berkeley: University of California Press.

Jaffe, Peter G. and Claire V. Crooks. 2004. "Partner Violence and Child Custody Cases: A Cross-National Comparison of Legal Reforms and Issues." *Violence Against Women* 10 (8) (August): 917–934.

Jaffer v. York University, 2010 ONCA 654.

Janisch, Hudson N. 1999. "Regulatory Process," in James H. Marsh (ed.), *The Canadian Encyclopedia: Year 2000 Edition*, p. 1994. Toronto: McClelland and Stewart.

Jarviluoma, Helmi, Pirkko Moisala, and Anni Vilkko. 2003. *Gender and Qualitative Methods.* Thousand Oaks, CA: Sage.

Jeffery, C. Ray 1962. "The Legal Profession," in F. James Davis, Henry H. Foster, Jr., C. Ray Jeffery and E. Eugene Davis (eds.), *Society and the Law: New Meanings for an Old Profession*, pp. 313–356. New York: Free Press.

Jewell, Malcolm E. and Samuel C. Patterson. 1986. *The Legislative Process in the United States*, 4th ed. New York: Random House.

Jewkes, Yvonne and Majid Yar (eds.). 2009. *Handbook of Internet Crime.* Devon, UK: Willan Publishing.

Jimenez, Jillian. 2010. *Social Policy and Social Change: Toward the Creation of Social and Economic Justice.* Thousand Oaks, CA: Sage.

Jimenez, Jillian A., Eileen Mayers Pasztor, Ruth M Chambers, and Cheryl Pearlman Fujii. 2016. *Social Policy and Social Change: Toward the Creation of Social and Economic Justice*, 2nd ed. Thousands Oak, CA: Sage Publications

Johns, Fleur (ed.). 2010. *International Legal Personality.* Burlington, VT: Ashgate.

Johnson, Holly and Myrna Dawson. 2011. *Violence Against Women: Research and Policy Perspectives.* Oxford University Press. Don Mills, ON.

Johnson, Holly and Karen Rodgers. 1993. "A Statistical Overview of Women in Crime in Canada," in Ellen Adelberg and Claudia Currie (eds.), *Women in Conflict with the Law*, pp. 95–116. Vancouver, BC: Press Gang.

Johnson, Rebecca. 2000. "If Choice Is the Answer, What Is the Question? Spelunking in *Symes* v. *Canada*," in Dorothy Chunn and Dany Lacombe (eds.), *Law as a Gendering Practice*, pp. 199–222. Don Mills, ON: Oxford University Press.

Johnson, Scott A. 2015. "The Role of Pornography in Sexual Offenses: Information for Law Enforcement & Forensic Psychologists." *International Journal of Emergency Mental Health & Human Resilience* 17(1): 239–242.

Johnson, Shelly. 2014. "Developing First Nations Courts in Canada: Elders as Foundational to Indigenous Therapeutic Jurisprudence." *Journal of Indigenous Social Development* 3(2):1–14.

Johnston, Hank (ed.). 2010. *Culture, Social Movements, and Protest.* Burlington, VT: Ashgate.

Jonakait, Randolph N. 2003. *The American Jury System.* New Haven, CT: Yale University Press.

Jones, Ashby. 2007. "More Law Firms Charge Fixed Fees for Routine Jobs."*Wall Street Journal* (May 2): B1.

Jordan, Bill. 2007. *Social Policy for the Twenty-First Century.* Malden, MA: Blackwell.

Judicial System Glossary. 2012. "Contempt of Court." Retrieved from www.ndcourts.gov/court/GLOSSARY.htm.

Justice Centre for Constitutional Freedoms. 2016. "Campus Freedom Index: More Than 25 Universities Fail Campus Free Speech Test." November 1. Retrieved from www.jccf.ca/2016-campus-freedom-index-more-than-25-universities-fail-campus-free-speech-test/

Kagan, Robert A. 1984. "The Routinization of Debt Collection: An Essay on Social Change and Conflict in Courts." *Law and Society Review* 18 (3): 323–371.

———. 1995. "What Socio-Legal Scholars Should Do When There Is Too Much Law to Study." *Journal of Law and Society* 22 (1) (March): 140–148.

Kahn, Susan Martha. 2000. *Reproducing Jews: A Cultural Account of Assisted Conception in Israel.* Durham, NC: Duke University Press.

Kahnawake Gaming Commission. 2017. "Interactive Gaming." Retrieved from www.gamingcommission.ca/. *Kahnawake Gaming Law.* MCR 26/1996–97.

Kallen, Evelyn. 2003. *Ethnicity and Human Rights in Canada.* 3rd ed. Don Mills, ON: Oxford University Press.

Kanefield, Teri. 2014. Guilty?: Crime, Punishment, and the Changing Face of Justice. Houghton Mifflin Harcourt.

Kaplin, William A., and Barbara E. Lee. 2006. *The Law of Higher Education.* 4th ed. San Francisco, CA: Jossey-Bass.

Karmen, Andrew. 2013. *Crime Victims: An Introduction to Victimology.* 8th ed. Belmont, CA: Wadsworth.

Karp, David R. 1998. "The Judicial and Judicious Use of Shame Penalties." *Crime and Delinquency* 44 (2) (April): 277–294.

Kauffman, Kent D. 2009. *Legal Ethics.* 2nd ed. Clifton Park, NY: Delmar Cengage Learning.

Kawashima, Takeyoshi. 1969. "Dispute Resolution in Japan," in Vilhelm Aubert (ed.), *Sociology of Law,* pp. 182–193. Harmondsworth, UK: Penguin.

Kay, Fiona M., Cristi Masuch, and Paula Curry. 2004. *Diversity and Change: The Contemporary Legal Profession in Ontario.* Report to the Law Society of Upper Canada (September).

Kay, Fiona M. and John Hagan. 1995. "The Persistent Glass Ceiling: Gendered Inequalities in the Earnings of Lawyers." *British Journal of Sociology* 46(2): 279–310.

Kay, Susan Ann. 1978. "Socializing the Future Elite: The Nonimpact of a Law School." *Social Science Quarterly* 59 (2) (September): 347–356.

Kearne, Joseph D. and Thomas W. Merrill. 2000. "The Influence of Amicus Curiae Briefs on the Supreme Court." *University of Pennsylvania Law Review* 148: 173–855.

Kearney, Hugh. 1970. *Scholars and Gentlemen: Universities and Society in Pre-Industrial Britain.* Ithaca, NY: Cornell University Press.

Keith, Ronald C. and Zhiqiu Lin. 2003. "The 'Falun Gong Problem': Politics and the Struggle for the Rule of Law in China." *China Quarterly* 175 (September): 623–642.

Kellar, Dan. 2011. "Presenting the Movement's Narratives: Organizing Alternative Media," in Tom Malleson and David Wachsmuth (eds.), *Whose Streets: The Toronto G20 and the Challenges of Summit Protest,* pp. 71–84. Toronto: Between the Lines.

Kelleher, Michael D. and C. L. Kelleher. 1998. *Murder Most Rare: The Female Serial Killer.* Westport, CT: Praeger/Greenwood.

Kelly, James B. 2005. *Governing with the Charter: Legislative and Judicial Activism and Framers' Intent.* Vancouver, BC: UBC Press.

Kelsen, Hans. 1967. *The Pure Theory of Law.* 2nd ed. Trans. M. Knight. Los Angeles: University of California Press.

Kennedy, Duncan. 2007. *Legal Education and the Reproduction of Hierarchy: A Polemic Against the System: A Critical Edition.* New York: New York University Press.

Kennedy, M. Alexis, Carolin Klein, and Boris B. Gorzalka. 2004. "Attitude Change Following a Diversion Program for Men Who Solicit Sex." *Journal of Offender Rehabilitation* 40: 41–60.

Kerley, Kent R. (ed.). 2005. *Policing and Program Evaluation.* Upper Saddle River, NJ: Prentice Hall.

Kerr, Dana, Yu-Luen Ma, and Joan T. Schmit. 2006. "Do Extensive Government Social Programs Reduce Liability Costs?" Proposal to the American Risk and Insurance Association Annual Meeting, Washington DC. (August). Retrieved from www.terry.uga.edu/insurance/docs/schmit_liability_costs.pdf.

Kerwin, Cornelius M. 2003. *Rulemaking: How Government Agencies Write Law and Make Policies.* 3rd ed. Washington, DC: CQ Press.

Kerwin, Cornelius M. and Scott R. Furlong. 2010. *Rulemaking: How Government Agencies Write Law and Make Policy*. 4th ed. Washington, DC: CQ Press.

Keung, Nicholas. 2012. "Very Few Visible Minorities Among Canadian Judges, Study Finds." *Toronto Star*, June 27. Retrieved from www.thestar.com/news/gta/2012/06/27/few_visible_minorities_among_canadian_judges_study_finds.html

Khan, Shahnaz. 2005. "Reconfiguring the Native Informant: Positionality in the Global Age." *Signs* 30 (4) (Summer): 2017–2035.

Khenti, Akwatu. 2014. "The Canadian War on Drugs: Structural Violence and Unequal Treatment of Black Canadians." *International Journal of Drug Policy* 25 (2): 190–195.

Kilgour, David and David Matas. 2008. "Press Release." August 22. Retrieved from http://organharvestinvestigation.net/release/pr-2008-08-22.htm.

Kilgour, David, David Matas, and Ethan Gutmann. 2016. *Bloody Harvest: The Slaughter: An Update* (June 22). Retrieved from ndorganpillaging.org/wp-content/uploads/2016/06/Bloody_Harvest-The_Slaughter-June-23-V2.pdf.

Kilty, Jennifer M. (ed.). 2014. *Within the Confines: Women and the Law in Canada*. Toronto: Canadian Scholar's Press.

King, Alan J. C., Wendy K. Warren, and Sharon R. Miklas. 2004. "Study of Accessibility to Ontario Law Schools: Executive Summary." Retrieved from www.lsuc.on.ca/media/convjan05accessibilitystudy.pdf.

Kinsman, Gary. 1996. The *Regulation of Desire: Homo and Hetero Sexualities*. Rev. ed. Montreal: Black Rose.

———. 2001. *Whose National Security? Canadian State Surveillance and the Creation of Enemies*. Toronto: Between the Lines.

Kinsman, Gary and Patrizia Gentile. 2010. *The Canadian War on Queers: National Security as Sexual Regulation*. Vancouver, BC: UBC Press.

Kirchgässner, Gebhard. 2011. "Econometric Estimates of Deterrence of the Death Penalty: Facts or Ideology?" *Kyklos* 64 (3): 448–478.

Kirchmeier, Jeffrey L. 2015. *Imprisoned by the Past: Warren McCleskey and the American Death Penalty*. New York: Oxford University Press.

Klein, Mitchell S. G. 1984. *Law, Courts, and Policy*. Englewood Cliffs, NJ: Prentice Hall.

Kleining, John and James P. Levine. 2005. *Jury Ethics: Jury Conduct and Jury Dynamics*. Boudler, CO: Paradigm.

Kleinman, Sherryl. 2007. *Feminist Fieldwork Analysis*. Thousand Oaks, CA: Sage.

Klockars, Carl B., Sanja Kutnjak Ivkovic, and M. R. Haberfeld (eds.). 2004. *The Contours of Police Integrity*. Thousand Oaks, CA: Sage.

Klosek, Jacqueline. 2010. *The Right to Know: Your Guide to Using and Defending Freedom of Information Law in the United States*. Santa Barbara, CA: Praeger.

Knowles, Valerie. 2016. *Strangers At Our Gates: Canadian Immigration and Immigration Policy, 1540–2015*, 4th edition. Toronto: Dundurn.

Koenig, Thomas and Michael Rustad. 2004. *In Defense of Tort Law*. New York: New York University Press.

Kohlberg, Lawrence. 1964. "Development of Moral Character and Ideology," in L. Hoffman and M. Hoffman (eds.), *Review of Child Development Research*, Vol. 1, pp. 383–431. New York: Russell Sage Foundation.

———. 1967. "Moral Education, Religious Education, and the Public Schools: A Developmental Approach," in T. Sizer (ed.), *Religion and Public Education*, pp. 164–183. Boston: Houghton Mifflin.

Kong, Rebecca and Kathy AuCoin. 2008. "Female Offenders in Canada." *Juristat* 28 (1). Statistics Canada Catalogue 85-002-X. Retrieved from www.statcan.gc.ca/pub/85-002-x/2008001/article/10509-eng.htm.

Koo, Gene. 2007. *New Skills, New Learning: Legal Education and the Promise of New Technology*. Berkman Center Research Publication no. 2007–4 (March 26). Retrieved from http://ssrn.com/abstract=976646.

Koshan, Jennifer (ed.). 2017. *The Right to Say No Marital Rape and Law Reform in Canada, Kenya, Ghana and Malaw*. Oxford: Hart Publishing.

Kotecha, Krupa M. 2016. "Charter Application in the University Context: An Inquiry of Necessity." *Educational Law Journal* 26 (1): 21–52.

Kozlowski, Marh. 2003. *The Myth of the Imperial Judiciary: Why the Right Is Wrong About the Courts*. New York: New York University Press.

Kraft, Michael E. and Scott R. Furlong. 2015. *Public Policy: Politics, Analysis and Alternatives*. 5th ed. Washington, DC: CQ Press.

Krane, Joshua A. 2011. "Property, Proportionality and Instruments of Crime." *National Journal of Constitutional Law* 29 (2): 159–187.

Krauss, Clifford. 2004. "Canadian Police Image Taking Hit Thanks to Scandals." *Seattle Times* (January 25): A13.

Kriesberg, Louis. 2007. *Constructive Conflicts: From Escalation to Resolution.* 3rd ed. Lanham, MD: Rowman and Littlefield.

Kritzer, Herbert M. 1990. *The Justice Broker: Lawyers and Ordinary Litigation.* New York: Oxford University Press.

———. 2002. *Legal Systems of the World: A Political, Social and Cultural Encyclopedia.* Santa Barbara, CA: ABC-CLIO.

Kuokkanen, Rauna. 2015. "Gendered Violence and Politics in Indigenous Communities: The Cases of Aboriginal People in Canada and the Sami in Scandinavia." *International Feminist Journal of Politics* 17 (2): 271–288.

Kurlantzick, Joshua. 2003. "The Dragon Still Has Teeth: How the West Winks at Chinese Repression." *World Policy Journal* 20 (1) (Spring): 49–58.

Lace, Suzanne (ed.). 2005. *The Glass Consumer: Life in a Surveillance Society.* Bristol, UK: Polity Press.

Ladd, Everett C., Jr. and Seymour Martin Lipset. 1973. *Professors, Unions and American Higher Education.* Washington, DC: American Enterprise Institute for Public Policy Research.

Lahey, Kathleen. 2003. "On Silences, Screams and Scholarship: An Introduction to Feminist Legal Theory," in T. Brettel Dawson (ed.), *Women, Law and Social Change: Core Readings and Current Issues*, pp. 191–192. Concord, ON: Captus.

Lamarche, Lucie. 2000. "Quebec Feminism, The Crisis of Rights and Research in the Law: Some Reasons to Worry . . . and Some Reasons to Hope." *Cahiers de recherche sociologique* 34: 99–126.

Lamb, Matthew C. 2015. "A Return To Rehabilitation: Mandatory Minimum Sentencing in an Era Of Mass Incaraceration." *Journal of Legislation* 41(1):126–150.

Lambert, Ronald D. and James E. Curtis. 1993. "Perceived Party Choice and Class Voting." *Canadian Journal of Political Science* 26: 273–286.

Lambertus, Sandra. 2004. *Wartime Images, Peacetime Wounds: The Media and the Standoff at Gustafsen Lake Standoff.* Toronto, ON: University of Toronto Press.

Lange, Marc. 2009. *Laws and Law Makers: Science, Metaphysics, and the Laws of Nature.* New York: Oxford University Press.

Langer, Amin and Graham K. Brown, eds. 2016. *Building Sustainable Peace: Timing and Sequence of Post-Conflict Reconstruction and Peace-Building.* Oxford: Oxford University Press.

Larocque, Sylvain, Robert Chodos, Benjamin Waterhouse, and Louisa Blair. 2006. *Gay Marriage: The Story of a Canadian Social Revolution.* Toronto: James Lorimer.

Larson, Magali Sarfatti. 1977. *The Rise of Professionalism: A Sociological Analysis.* Berkeley: University of California Press.

Lassman, Peter (ed.). 2006. *Max Weber.* Burlington, VT: Ashgate.

Lauderdale, Pat. 1997. "Indigenous North American Jurisprudence." *International Journal of Comparative Sociology* 38 (1–2) (June): 131–149.

Lauks, Rebeka. 2012. "The Alberta Court of Appeal Finds Universities Are Subject to Charter Scrutiny in *Pridgen v. University of Calgary*, 2012." *ABCA* 139. Retrieved from www.aspercentre. ca/Assets/Asper+Digital+Assets/David+Asper+Centre/Asper+Digital+Assets/Rebeka+Lauks+-+Summaries+$!26+Documents/Summary+-+Pridgen+v+University+of+Calgary$!2c+2012+AB CA+139.pdf.

Lavallee, Lynn F. and Jennifer M. Poole. 2010. "Beyond Recovery: Colonization, Health and Healing for Indigenous People in Canada." *International Journal of Mental Health and Addiction* 8 (2): 271–281.

Lavalette, Michael and Alan Pratt (eds.). 2006. *Social Policy: Theories, Concepts and Issues.* 3rd ed. Thousand Oaks, CA: Sage.

Law Society of British Columbia. 2012. "Towards a More Representative Legal Profession: Better Practices, Better Workplaces, Better Results." Retrieved from www.lawsociety.bc.ca/docs/publications/reports/Diversity_2012.pdf.

———. 2009. "Final Report—Aboriginal Bar Consultation." (January 29). Retrieved from http://rc.lsuc.on.ca/pdf/equity/aboriginalBarConsultation.pdf.

Law Society of Upper Canada. 2006. "The Changing Face of the Legal Profession." Retrieved from www.lsuc.on.ca/news/a/fact/changing/.

———. 2013. "Fact Sheet: Statistical Snapshot of Lawyers in Ontario." Retrieved from www.lsuc.on.ca/uploadedFiles/Equity_and_Diversity/Members2/2013_Snapshot_Lawyers.pdf.

———. 2016. Challenges Faced by Racialized Licensees Working Group, Report to Convocation. "Working Together for Change: Strategies to Address Issues of Systemic Racism in the Legal Professions." (September 22).

Lawyer's Almanac. 2017. New York: Wolters Kluwer.

Laycock, David and Lynda Erickson, eds. 2015. *Reviving Social Democracy: The Near Death and Surprising Rise of the Federal NDP.* Vancouver: UBC Press.

Lazarus, Richard J. 2004. *The Making of Environmental Law.* Chicago, IL: University of Chicago Press.

LeBourdais, Isabel. 1966. *The Trial of Steven Truscott.* Toronto: McClelland and Stewart.

Legal Aid Ontario. 2008. "The Development of Legal Aid Ontario's Aboriginal Strategy." June 20. Retrieved from www.legalaid.on.ca/en/publications/downloads/0807-29_DiscussionPaper_public.pdf.

Leigh-Bell, Timothy. 2016. "Should Civil Jury Trials Be Abolished in Ontario?" (February 15). Retrieved from www.linkedin.com/pulse/should-civil-jury-trials-abolished-ontario-timothy-leigh-bell.

Leiper, Jean MacKenzie. 2006. *Bar Codes: Women in the Legal Profession.* Vancouver: UBC Press.

Leishman, Rory. 2006. *Against Judicial Activism: The Decline of Freedom and Democracy in Canada.* Kingston/Montreal: McGill-Queen's University Press.

Leiter, Brian. 2014. "Marx, Law, Ideology, Legal Positivism," University of Chicago Public Law & Legal Theory Working Paper, No. 482. Retrieved from http://chicagounbound.uchicago.edu/cgi/viewcontent.cgi?article=1924&context=public_law_and_legal_theory.

Lempert, Richard O. 1978. "More Tales of Two Courts: Exploring Changes in the 'Dispute Settlement Function' of Trial Courts." *Law and Society Review* 13 (1) (Fall): 91–138.

———. 2001. "Activist Scholarship." *Law and Society Review* 35 (1): 25–32.

Lempert, Richard and Joseph Sanders. 1986. *An Invitation to Law and Social Science.* New York: Longman.

Levine, Bertram J. 2009. *The Art of Lobbying: Building Trust and Selling Policy.* Washington, DC: CQ Press.

Levine, James P. 1970. "Methodological Concerns in Studying Supreme Court Efficacy." *Law and Society Review* 4 (1) (May): 583–592.

Levine, Martin Lyon (ed.). 2009. *Mental Illness, Medicine and Law.* Burlington, VT: Ashgate.

Levit, Nancy, and Robert R.M. Verchick. 2016. *Feminist Legal Theory: A Primer.* New York: NYU Press.

Levitz, Jennifer. 2009. "Volunteer 5–0: Civilian Patrols Grow as Recession Puts Citizens on Guard." *Wall Street Journal* (September 8): A1.

Lewans, Matthew. 2016. *Administrative Law and Judicial Deference.* Oxford: Hart Publishing

Lewicki, Roy J., Bruce Barry, and David M. Saunders. 2011. *Essentials of Negotiation.* 5th ed. Boston: McGraw-Hill/Irwin.

Leyton, Marco. 2016. "Legalizing Marijuana." *Journal of Psychiatry & Neuroscience* 41 (2): 75–76.

Libin, Kevin. 2009. "Sentencing Circles for Aboriginals: Good Justice?" *National Post* (February 27). Retrieved from www.nationalpost.com/news/story.html?id=1337495.

Lieberman, Joel D. and Daniel A. Krauss (eds.). 2010a. *Jury Psychology: Social Aspects of Trial Process: Psychology in the Courtroom.* Vol. 1. Burlington, VT: Ashgate.

———. 2010b. *Psychological Expertise in Court: Psychology in the Courtroom.* Vol. 2. Burlington, VT: Ashgate.

Limoncelli, Stephanie A. 2010. *The Politics of Trafficking: The First International Movement to Combat the Sexual Exploitation of Women.* Palo Alto, CA: Stanford University Press.

Lindal v. Lindal ([1981] S.C.J. No. 108 (SCC).

Lindquist, Stefanie and Frank Cross. 2009. *Measuring Judicial Activism.* New York: Oxford University Press

Lindsey, Tim and Pip Nicholson. 2016. *Drugs Law and Legal Practice in Southeast Asia Indonesia, Singapore and Vietnam.* Oxford: Hart Publishing.

Ling, Justin. 2017. "Key Parts of Citizenship Revocation Process Struck Down." *National Magazine*, http://www.nationalmagazine.ca/Articles/May-2017/Key-parts-of-citizenship-revocation-process-struck.aspx.

Lippert, Randy. 2002. "Policing Property and Moral Risk Through Promotions, Anonymization and Rewards: Crime Stoppers Revisited." *Social and Legal Studies* 11 (4): 475–402.

Lipschutz, Ronnie D. (ed.). 2006. *Civil Societies and Social Movements*. Burlington, VT: Ashgate.

Liu, Mei and Paul W. Holland. 2008. "Exploring Population Sensitivity of Linking Functions Across Three Law School Admission Test Administrations." *Applied Psychological Measurement* 32 (1) (January): 27–44.

Llewellyn, Karl N. 1930/1960. *The Bramble Bush*. Dobbs Ferry, NY: Oceana.

Llewellyn, Karl N. and E. Adamson Hoebel. 1941. *The Cheyenne Way: Conflict and Case Law in Primitive Jurisprudence*. Norman, OK: University of Oklahoma Press.

Lloyd, Sally A., April L. Few, and Katherine R. Allen. 2010. *Handbook of Family Studies*. Thousand Oaks, CA: Sage.

Lo, Ven-hwei and Ran Wei. 2002. "Third-Person Effect, Gender Pornography on the Internet." *Journal of Broadcasting and Electronic Media* 46 (1) (March): 13–33.

Lobbying Act RSC., 1985, c. 44 (4th Supp.).

Loewenberg, Gerhard, Peverill Squire, and D. Roderick Kiewiet (eds.). 2002. *Legislatures: Comparative Perspectives on Representative Assemblies*. Ann Arbor: University of Michigan Press.

Loh, Wallace D. 1984. *Social Research in the Judicial Process: Cases, Readings, and Text*. New York: Russell Sage Foundation.

Long, John S. and Jennifer S. H. Brown (eds.). 2016. *Together We Survive: Ethnographic Intuitions, Friendships, and Conversations*. Montreal/Kingston: McGill-Queen's University Press.

Lorber, Judith. 2009. *Gender Inequality: Feminist Theories and Politics*. 4th ed. New York: Oxford University Press.

Lothian, Tamara and Roberto Mangabeira Unger. 2012. "Crisis, Slump, Superstition and Recovery: Thinking and Acting Beyond Vulgar Keynesianism." Columbia University Center for Law & Economic Studies, Working Paper No. 394, December 22. Retrieved from https://papers.ssrn.com/sol3/papers.cfm?abstract_id=1780454.

Lott, John. 2003. *The Bias Against Guns: Why Almost Everything You've Heard About Gun Control Is Wrong*. Washington, DC: Regnery.

———. 2006. (ed.). *Straight Shooting: Guns, Economics, and Public Policy*. Bellevue, WA: Merril Press.

———. 2010. *More Guns, Less Crime: Understanding Crime and Gun Control Laws*. 3rd ed. Chicago, IL: University of Chicago Press.

Lovelace v. Canada, 1983 Can. Hum. Rts. Y.B. 305 (1983).

Lovell, Jarret S. 2009. *Crimes of Dissent: Civil Disobedience, Criminal Justice, and the Politics of Conscience*. New York: New York University Press.

LSAC. 2017, "About the LSAT." Retrieved from www.lsac.org/jd/lsat/about-the-lsat.

Lunau, Kate. 2009a. "When Lawyers Are Only for the Rich." *Maclean's* (January 19): 52–53.

———. 2009b. "Where's a Lawyer When You Need One." *Maclean's* (February 2). Retrieved from www2.macleans.ca/2009/02/02/where%e2%80%99s-a-lawyer-when-you-need-one/.

Luo, Shuze. 2000. "Some Hot Issues in Our Work on Religion." *Chinese Law and Government* 33 (2) (March/April): 101–106.

Luyster, Deborah. 1997. "Crossing the Bar-Lawyering Skills in Law and Literature." The Column of the Legal Education Committee, *Michigan Bar Association Journal*. Retrieved from www.michbar.org/journal/article.cfm?articleID=376andvolumeID=27.

Lyman, Michael D. 2010. *The Police: An Introduction*. 4th ed. Upper Saddle River, NJ: Prentice Hall.

MacArthur, Cecilia. 2016. "Kahnawake Mohawk Council Chief Calls For Banishment of Known Drug Dealers." CBC News (October 14). Retrieved from www.cbc.ca/news/canada/montreal/kahnawake-mohawk-chief-drugs-banishment-1.3803559.

Macaulay, Ann. 2014a. "How to Retain Top Female Talent, and What Women Should Look for in a Law Firm." *The Canadian Bar Association* (October 10). Retrieved from www.cba.org/Publications-Resources/CBA-Practice-Link/Young-Lawyers/2014/How-to-Retain-Top-Female-Talent,-and-What-Women-Sh.

Macaulay, Ann. 2014b. "The Billable Hour – Here to Stay?" March 12. *Canadian Bar Association*. Retrieved from www.cba.org/Publications-Resources/CBA-Practice-Link/solo/2014/The-Billable-Hour%E2%80%94Here-to-Stay.

Macaulay, Stewart. 1969. "Non-Contractual Relations in Business," in Vilhelm Aubert (ed.), *Sociology of Law*, pp. 194–209. Harmondsworth, UK: Penguin.

MacCharles, Tonda. 2011. "Supreme Court Appointments Highlight a Secret Process." *The Toronto Star* (October 17). Retrieved from www.thestar.com/news/canada/2011/10/17/supreme_court_appointments_highlight_a_secret_process.html.

MacDonald, Ian. 2016. "Competition & Antitrust Law." *Gowling LWG*. Retrieved from gowlingwlg.com/en/canada/insights-resources/guide-to-doing-business-in-canada-competition-and-antitrust-law?utm_source=Mondaq&utm_medium=syndication&utm_campaign=View-Original.

Macdonald, Keith M. 1995. *The Sociology of Professions*. Thousand Oaks, CA: Sage.

Macdonald, Nancy. 2016. "Canada's Prisons are the 'New Residential Schools.'" *Maclean's* (February 18). Retrieved from www.macleans.ca/news/canada/canadas-prisons-are-the-new-residential-schools/.

Macfarlane, Emmett. 2010. "Consensus and Unanimity at the Supreme Court of Canada." *Supreme Court Law Review* 52 SCLR (2d) 379–410.

MacFarlane, Julie. 2008. *The New Lawyer: How Settlement Is Transforming the Practice of Law*. Vancouver: UBC Press.

Macfarlane, Julie, John Manwaring, Ellen Zweibel, Gemma Smyth, and Arthur Pearlstein. 2011. *Dispute Resolution: Readings and Case Studies*. 3rd ed. Toronto: Emond Montgomery Publications.

Macklin, A. 1992. "*Symes* v. *M. N. R.*: Where Sex Meets Class." *Canadian Journal of Women and the Law* 5: 498–517.

Maclean's. 2006. "Avoiding the Evil Eye." (March 6): 11.

———. 2014. "Steps of the Court: What Judges Earn in Canada." (September 27). Retrieved from www.macleans.ca/economy/money-economy/steps-of-the-court/.

Mac Neil, Michael. 2002. "Governing Employment," in Michael Mac Neil, Neil Sargent, and Peter Swan (eds.), *Law, Regulation, and Governance*, pp. 171–187. Don Mills, ON: Oxford University Press.

Madon, Natasha S. 2016. "The Retention of Women in the Private Practice of Criminal Law: Research Report." Criminal Lawyers' Association (March). Retrieved from www.criminallawyers.ca/wp-content/uploads/2016/03/CLA-Womens-StudyMarch-2016.pdf.

Mahood, H. R. 2000. *Interest Group Politics in America: A New Intensity*. Englewood Cliffs, NJ: Prentice Hall.

Mai, Joseph and Andrey Stoyanov. 2014. "Home Country Bias in the Legal System: Empirical Evidence from the Intellectual Property Rights Protection in Canada." Retrieved from www.yorku.ca/andreyst/files/Stoyanov_Mai_IPR.pdf.

Maine, Sir Henry Sumner. 1861. *Ancient Law*. London: J. Murray.

———. 2003. *Ancient Law: Its Connection with the Early History of Society, and Its Relation to Modern Ideas*. Holmes Beach, FL: Gaunt.

Malleson, Tom and David Wachsmuth (ed.). 2011. *Whose Streets? The Toronto G20 and the Challenges of Summit Protest*. Toronto: Between the Lines.

Mandel v Fakhim, 2016 ONSC 6538 (CanLII). Retrieved December 26 from http://canlii.ca/t/gv6pd.

Mangione, Thomas W. 1995. *Mail Surveys*. Thousand Oaks, CA: Sage.

Manitoba Public Inquiry into the Administration of Justice and Aboriginal People. 1991. *Report of the Aboriginal Justice Inquiry of Manitoba*. Winnipeg: The Inquiry.

Manson, Allan, and James Turk. 2007. *Free Speech in Fearful Times: After 9/11 in Canada, the U.S., Australia & Europe*. Toronto: Lorimer.

Manwaring, John. 2011. "Negotiation," in Julie Macfarlane, John Manwaring, Ellen Zweibel, Gemma Smyth and Arthur Pearlstein (eds.), *Dispute Resolution: Readings and Case Studies*, 3rd ed., pp. 99–260. Toronto: Emond Montgomery Publications.

Marcus, Paul and Vicki C. Waye. 2010. "Australia and the United States: Two Common Criminal Justice Systems Uncommonly at Odds Part 2." *Tulane Journal of International & Comparative Law* 18 (2): 9–78.

Marez, Curtis. 2004. *Drug Wars: The Political Economy of Narcotics*. Minneapolis, MN: University of Minnesota Press.

Marin, Michael. 2015. Should the Charter Apply to Universities? (February 4, 2016). *National Journal of Constitutional Law* 35 (1): 2015. Retrieved from SSRN: https://ssrn.com/abstract=2728115.

Marinucci, Mimi. 2016. *Feminism is Queer: The Intimate Connection Between Queer and Feminist Theory*. London: Zed Books Ltd.

Marlin, Marguerite. 2016. "Interest Groups and Parliamentary Committees: Leveling the Playing Field." *Canadian Parliamentary Review* (Spring): 24–28.

Marshall, Katherine. 2011. "Gambling." *Perspectives on Labour and Income*. Statistics Canada Catalogue no. 75–001-X. Retrieved from www.statcan.gc.ca/pub/75-001-x/topics-sujets/pdf/topics-sujets/gambling-jeuxdehasard-2009-eng.pdf.

Martinson, Donna and Margaret Jackson. 2017. "Family Violence and Evolving Judicial Roles: Judges as Equality Guardians in Family Law Case." *Canadian Journal of Family Law* 30(1): 11–70.

Marx, Karl. 1959. "A Contribution to the Critique of Political Economy," in L. S. Feuer (ed.), *Marx and Engels: Basic Writing on Politics and Philosophy*, pp. 42–46. Garden City, NY: Doubleday.

Marx, Karl and Friedrich Engels. 1848/1955. *The Communist Manifesto*. New York: Appleton-Century-Crofts.

Mas, Susana. 2016. "Transgender Canadians Should 'Feel free and Safe' to be Themselves Under New Liberal bill." *CBC News* (May 17). Retrieved from www.cbc.ca/news/politics/transgender-bill-trudeau-government-1.3585522.

Matamanadzo, Sarudzayi M., Francisco Valdes and Sheila Velez. 2016a. "Kindling the Programmatic Production of Critical and Outsider Legal Scholarship, 1996–2016)." *Whittier Law Review* 37(3): 439–510.

Matamanadzo, Sarudzayi M., Francisco Valdes, and Sheila I. Velez-Martinez. 2016. "Latcrit Theory at XX: Kindling the Programmatic Production of Critical and Outsider Legal Scholarship, 1996–2016." Charleston Law Review 10(2): 297–377.

Mathison, Sandra (ed.). 2005. *Encyclopedia of Education*. Thousand Oaks, CA: Sage.

Matsushita, Mitsuo. 2015. "Reflections on the Function of the Appellate Body," in G. Marceau (ed.), *A History of Law and Lawyers in the GATT/WTO: The Development of the Rule of Law in the Multilateral Trading System*, pp. 547–558. Cambridge: Cambridge University Press.

Matza, David. 2010. *Becoming Delinquent*. Piscataway, NJ: Transaction Publishers.

May-Chahal, Corinne, Leslie Humphreys, Alison Clifton, Brian Francis, and Gerda Reith. 2017. "Gambling Harm and Crime Careers." *Journal of Gambling Studies* 33(1): 65–84.

Mayhew, Leon H. 1971. "Stability and Change in Legal Systems," in Bernard Barber and Alex Inkeles (eds.), *Stability and Social Change*, pp. 187–210. Boston: Little, Brown.

Mays, Larry G. and Peter R. Gregware (eds.). 2009. *Courts and Justice: A Reader*. 4th ed. Prospect Heights, IL: Waveland.

Maxwell, Ashley. 2015. "Adult Criminal Court Statistics in Canada, 2013–2014." *Juristat*. Retrieved from www.statcan.gc.ca/pub/85-002-x/2015001/article/14226-eng.htm.

Mazer, Brian M. 1989. "Access to Legal Education and the Profession in Canada," in Rajeev Dhavan, Neil Kibble, and William Twining (eds.), *Access to Legal Education and the Legal Profession*, pp. 114–131. London: Butterworths.

McAdam, Doug and David A. Snow (eds.) 2010. *Readings on Social Movements: Origins, Dynamics, Outcomes*. 2nd ed. New York: Oxford University Press.

McAlinden, Anne-Marie. 2005. "The Use of 'Shame' with Sexual Offenders." *British Journal of Criminology* 45 (3) (May): 373–394.

McAllister, Kelli. 2016. "When is a Settlement Agreement Reached? Federal Court of Appeal Provides Guidance in Apotex Inc v Allergan Inc, 2016 FCA 155." *Canadian Appeals Monitor* (July 5). Retrieved from www.canadianappeals.com/2016/07/05/when-is-a-settlement-agreement-reached-federal-court-of-appeal-provides-guidance-in-apotex-inc-v-allergan-inc-2016-fca-155/

McCann, Charles R. 2004. *Individualism and the Social Order: The Social Element in Liberal Thought*. New York: Routledge.

McCann, Michael (ed.). 2006. *Law and Social Movements*. Burlington, VT: Ashgate.

McCartney, Scott. 2010. "Forcing Airlines to Play Nice with Fliers." *Wall Street Journal* (March 4): D1, D2.

McCarthy, John F. 2005. "Between Adat and State: Institutional Arrangements on Sumatra's Forest Frontier." *Human Ecology* 33 (1) (February): 57–82.

McCloskey, Robert G. 2016. *The American Supreme Court*. 6th ed. Chicago, IL: University of Chicago Press.

McCorkle, Suzanne and Melanie Reese. 2010. *Personal Conflict Management: Theory and Practice*. Boston, MA: Allyn and Bacon.

McCormick, Peter. 1994. *Canada's Courts*. Toronto: James Lorimer.

———. 2006. "Where Does the Supreme Court Caseload Come From? Appeals from the Atlantic Courts of Appeal, 2000–2005." Retrieved from www.cpsa-acsp.ca/papers-2006/McCormick.pdf.

McCormick, Peter. 2000. *Supreme at Last: The Evolution of the Supreme Court of Canada.* Toronto, ON: James Lorimer & Company Ltd.

———. 2005. "Selecting the Supremes: The Appointment of Judges to the Supreme Court of Canada." *The Journal of Appellate. Pracice & Process* 7(1). Retrieved from http://lawrepository.ualr.edu/appellatepracticeprocess/vol7/iss1/2.

———. 2010. *Selecting Trial Court Judges: A Comparison of Contemporary Practices. Study commissioned by the Commission of Inquiry into the Appointment Process for Judges in Quebec.* Retrieved from file:///C:/Users/Adie/Downloads/McCormick__1er_septembre_2010%20(2).pdf.

McCormick, Peter and Ian Greene. 1990. *Judges and Judging: Inside the Canadian Judicial System.* Toronto: James Lorimer.

McCullagh, Declan. 2002. "Report: Anti-Terror Efforts Pinch Privacy." *CNET News.com* (September 3). Retrieved from news.cnet.com/2102–1023–956286.html.

McElroy, Justin. 2016. "Transgender rights supported by most Canadians, poll finds." *CBC News* (September 7). Retrieved from www.cbc.ca/news/canada/british-columbia/canada-transgender-rights-1.3750829.

McEown, Carol. 2009. "Civil Legal Need Research Report, 2nd ed." Law Foundation of British Columbia. Retrieved from www.lawfoundationbc.org/wp-content/uploads/Civil-Legal-Needs-Research-FINAL.pdf

McGirr, Lisa. 2016. *The War on Alcohol: Prohibition and the Rise of the American State.* New York: W.W. Norton.

McGuire, Kevin T. 1994. "Amici Curiae and Strategies for Gaining Access to the Supreme Court." *Political Research Quarterly* 47 (4) (December): 821–838.

McIlroy, Anne. 2005. "One Law to Rule Them All." *Guardian Unlimited.* (September 14). Retrieved from www.guardian.co.uk/elsewhere/journalist/story/0,7792,1569677,00.html.

McIntyre, Lisa J. 1994. *Law in the Sociological Enterprise: A Reconstruction.* Boulder, CO: Westview Press.

McIntyre, Sheila. 1995. "Gender Bias Within the Law School: 'The Memo' and Its Impact," in The Chilly Collective (eds.), *Breaking Anonymity: The Chilly Climate for Women Faculty*, pp. 211–264. Waterloo, ON: Wilfred Laurier University Press.

McIvor v. Canada (Registrar of Indian and Northern Affairs), 2009 BCCA 153 (CanLII).

McKay-Panos, Linda. 2014. "The Increasing Importance of Reference Decisions in Canadian Law." *LawNow* 38(6). Retrieved from www.lawnow.org/increasing-importance-reference-decisions-canadian-law/.

———. 2015. "Does the Charter Apply to Universities? *Pridgen* Distinguished in U Vic Case." Retrieved from http://ablawg.ca/2015/02/06/5332/.

McKay-Panos, Linda. 2016. "BCCA Unfortunately Chooses Not to Follow Alberta's Lead on the Issue of Whether the *Charter* Applies to Universities." Retrieved from http://ablawg.ca/2016/05/25/bcca-unfortunately-chooses-not-to-follow-albertas-lead-on-the-issue-of-whether-the-charter-applies-to-universities/.

McKee, Phoenix Anne. 2011. "Sex Work Is Real Work." *Shameless* 19: 28–29.

McKiernan, Michael. 2015. "The Going Rate." *Canadian Lawyer Magazine* (June). Retrieved from www.canadianlawyermag.com/images/stories/pdfs/Surveys/2015/CL_June_15_GoingRate.pdf.

McLachlin, Beverley, The Honourable Madam Justice. 1992. "Rules and Discretion in the Governance of Canada." *Saskatchewan Law Review* 56: 168–179.

———. 2002. "Coming of Age: Canadian Nationhood and the Charter of Rights." Retrieved from www.Scc-csc.gc.ca/court-cour/ju/spe-dis/bm02–04–17-eng.asp.

McLellan, Anne. 2016. *A Framework for the Legalization and Regulation of Cannabis in Canada: The Final Report of the Task Force on Cannabis Legalization and Regulation.* Retrieved from http://healthycanadians.gc.ca/task-force-marijuana-groupe-etude/framework-cadre/index-eng.php.

McLeod, Julie and Rachel Thompson. 2010. *Researching Social Change: Qualitative Approaches.* Thousand Oaks, CA: Sage.

McLeod-Kilmurray, Heather and Linda Collins. 2014. *The Canadian Law of Toxic Torts.* Toronto: Carswell.

McMichael, Philip. 2017. *Development and Social Change.* 6th ed. Thousand Oaks, CA: Sage.

McMillan LLP. 2011a. *Competition and Anti-Trust in Canada.* Retrieved from www.mcmillan.ca/files/Competition_and_Antitrust_in_Canada.pdf.

———. 2011b. *Litigating in Canada: A Brief Guide For U.S. Clients.* Retrieved from www.mcmillan.ca/files/Litigating%20in%20Canada%20-%20A%20brief%20guide%20for%20U.S.%20Clients.pdf.

McMurtry, R. Roy Marion Boyd, John McCamus, and Lorne Sossin. 2010. *Listening to Ontarians: Report of the Ontario Civil Legal Needs Project.* Toronto: The Ontario Civil Legal Needs Project Steering Committee. Retrieved from www.lsuc.on.ca/media/may3110_oclnreport_final.pdf.

McNair, Brian. 2014. "Rethinking the Effects Paradigm in Porn Studies." *Porn Studies* 1(1–2): 161–171.

McOrmond-Plummer, Leslie, Jennifer Y. Levy-Peck, Patricia Easteal (eds.). 2014. *Intimate Partner Sexual Violence: A Multidisiciplinary Guide to Improving Services and Support for Survivors of Rape and Abuse.* London: Jessica Kingsley Publishers.

McSheffrey, Kevin. 2016. "Mississauga First Nation ratifies its constitution." *Eliotlakestandard.ca.* (April 22). Retrieved from www.elliotlakestandard.ca/2015/04/23/mississauga-first-nation-ratifies-its-constitution.

Mears, T. Lambert. 2004. *The Institutes of Gaius and Justinian: The Twelve Tables, and the CXVIIIth and CXVIIth Novels, with Introduction and Translation.* Clark, NJ: Lawbook Exchange.

Meier, Robert F. and Gilbert Geis. 2006. *Criminal Justice and Moral Issues.* New York: Oxford University Press.

Meine, Manfred F. and Thomas P. Dunn. 2012. "Policing the Police: Using Ethics Education and Training to Combat Official Deviance." *Journal of US-China Public Administration* 9 (9): 1069–1075.

Melchers, Ron. 2003. "Do Toronto Police Engage in Racial Profiling?" *Canadian Journal of Criminology and Criminal Justice* 45 (3): 347–366.

Melling, Tom. 1994. "Dispute Resolution Within Legislative Institutions." *Stanford Law Review* 46 (6) (July): 1677–1715.

Melzer, Scott. 2009. *Gun Crusaders: The NRA's Culture War.* New York: New York University Press.

Meng, Yunliang, Sulaimon Giwa, and Uzo Anucha. 2015. "Is There Racial Discrimination in Police Stop-and-Searches of Black Youth? A Toronto Case Study." *Canadian Journal of Family and Youth* 7 (1): 115–148.

Menkel-Meadow, Carrie (ed.). 2003. *Dispute Processing and Conflict Resolution: Theory, Practice and Policy.* Burlington, VT: Ashgate.

Mercer, Malcolm, Susan McGrath, Constance Backhouse, Marion Boyd, Ross Earnshaw, Susan Elliott, Carol Hartman, Jacqueline Horvat, Brian Lawrie, Jeffrey Lem, Jan Richardson, James Scarfone, Alan Silverstein, and Peter Wardle. 2014. "Alternative Business Structures and the Legal Profession in Ontario: A Discussion Paper," Toronto: The Law Society of Upper Canada,

Merritt, Nancy, Terry Fain, and Susan Turner. 2006. "Oregon's Get Tough Sentencing Reform: A Lesson in Justice System Adaptation." *Criminology and Public Policy* 5 (1): 5–36.

Mikisew Cree Free Nation v. Canada (Minister of Canadian Heritage) 2005 SCC 69.

Milgram, Stanley. 1975. *Obedience to Authority.* New York: Harper Colophon.

Milkman, Ruth, Joshua Bloom, and Victor Narro (eds.). 2010. *Working for Justice: The L.A. Model of Organizing and Advocacy.* Ithaca, NY: Cornell University Press.

Millar, Paul, and Akwasi Owusu-Bempah. 2011. "Whitewashing Criminal Justice in Canada: Preventing Research through Data Suppression." *Canadian Journal of Law and Society* 26(3): 653–661.

Miller, Adam. 2013. "Medical Fraud North of the 49th." *CMAJ* 185(1): E31–E33.

Miller, Arthur Selwyn. 1979. *Social Change and Fundamental Law: America's Evolving Constitution.* Westport, CT: Greenwood.

Miller, Robert J., Jacinta Ruru, Larissa Behrendt and Traey Lindberg. 2012. *Discovering Indigenous Lands: The Doctrine of Discovery in the English Colonies.* New York: Oxford University Press.

Miller, Seumas. 2010. "Integrity Systems and Professional Reporting in Police Organizations." *Criminal Justice Ethics* 29 (3): 241–257.

Millman, Brock. 2016. *Polarity, Patriotism and Dissent in Great-War Canada, 1914–1919.* Toronto: University of Toronto Press.

Mills, C. Wright. 1957. *The Power Elite.* New York: Oxford University Press.

Milovanovic, Dragan. 2003. *A Primer in the Sociology of Law.* 3rd ed. New York: Criminal Justice Press.

Minda, Gary. 1997. "Law and Literature at Century's End." *Cardozo Studies in Law and Literature* 9 (2): 245–258.

Mink, Gwendolyn, and Rickie Solinger (eds.) 2004. *Welfare: A Documentary History of U.S. Policy and Politics.* New York: New York University Press.

Moghtaderi, Hossein and Anna Du Vent. 2013. "Application for Leave to Appeal to the Supreme Court of Canada: A Practical Guide." Retrieved from www.geramilaw.com/wpcontent/uploads/2015/03/ApplicationForLeaveAtTheSCCGuide.pdf.

Mohawk Council of Akwesasne. 2016. Akwesasne Tekaia'torehthà:ke Kaianerénhsera (Akwesasne Court Law) Kaiahnehronshera iehiontakwa Number: 2016-01. Retrieved from www.akwesasne.ca/sites/default/files/mcr-atk-acl2016.pdf.

Monaghan, Jeffrey and Kevin Walby. 2012a. "' . . . They Attacked the City': Security Intelligence, the Sociology of Protest Policing, and the Anarchist Threat at the 2010 Toronto G20 Summit." Current Sociology 60 (5): 653–671.

Monaghan, Jeffrey and Kevin Walby. 2012b. "Making Up 'Terror Identities': Security Intelligence, Canada's Integrated Threat Assessment Centre and Social Movement Suppression." Policing and Society 60 (5): 653–671.

Monahan, John and Laurens Walker. 1991. "Judicial Use of Social Science Research." Law and Human Behavior 15 (6) (December): 571–584.

Monahan, John and Laurens Walker. 2010. Social Science in Law: Cases and Materials. 7th ed. New York: Thomson Reuters/Foundation Press Inc.

Montesquieu, Baron de. 1748/1989. The Spirit of the Laws. Trans. and ed. Anne M. Cohler, Basia Carolyn Miller, and Harold Samuel Stone. Cambridge: Cambridge University Press.

Moore, Christopher. 1997. The Law Society of Upper Canada and Ontario Lawyers, 1797–1997. Toronto: University of Toronto Press.

Moore, Elizabeth and Michael Mills. 1990. "The Neglected Victims and Unexamined Costs of White Collar Crime." Crime and Delinquency 36: 408–418.

Moore, Matthew D. and Nicholas L. Recker. 2016. "Social Capital, Types of Crime, and Social Control." Crime & Delinquency 62 (6): 728–747.

Moore v. British Columbia (Education), [2012] 3 SCR 360, 2012 SCC 61.

Morales, Alfonso (ed.). 2003. Renascent Pragmatism: Studies in Law and Social Sciences. Burlington, VT: Ashgate.

Moran, Leslie J. (ed.). 2006. Sexuality and Identity. Burlington, VA: Ashgate.

Morawetz, Thomas. 1993. "Ethics and Style: The Lessons of Literature for Law." Stanford Law Review 45: 497–521.

Morellato, Maria and Mandell Pinder. 2009. "Aboriginal Title and Rights: Foundational Principles and Recent Developments." 2009 Constitutional & Human Rights Conference, The McLachlin Court's First Decade: Reflections on the Past and Projections for the Future. June 19, Ottawa, Ontario.

Morgan, Neil. 2000. Mandatory Sentences in Australia: Where Have We Been and Where Are We Going?" Criminal Law Journal 24: 164–184.

Morgan, Vanessa Sloan and Heather Castleden. 2014. "Framing Indigenous—Settler Relations within British Columbia's Modern Treaty Context: A Discourse Analysis of the Maa-nulth Treaty in Mainstream Media." International Indigenous Policy Journal 5 (3): 1–19.

Morgenthau, Hans. 1993. Politics Among Nations. New York: McGraw-Hill. Revised by Kenneth W. Thompson.

Morriss, Andrew P., Bruce Yandle, and Andrew Dorchak. 2009. Regulation by Litigation. New Haven, CT: Yale University Press.

Morton, Desmond. 2007. Working People: An Illustrated History of the Canadian Labour Movement. 5th ed. Montreal and Kingston: McGill-Queen's University Press.

Morton, Desmond and Morton Weinfeld (eds.). 1998. Who Speaks for Canada? Words That Shape a Country. Toronto: McClelland and Stewart.

Morton, Frederick Lee. 2002. Law, Politics and the Judicial Process in Canada. 3rd ed. Calgary, Alta: University of Calgary Press.

Mossman, Mary Jane. 1994. "Gender Equality, Family Law, and Access to Justice." International Journal of Law and the Family 8 (3) (December): 357–373.

———. 1998. "The Paradox of Feminist Engagement with Law," in Nancy Mandell (ed.), Feminist Issues: Race, Class, and Sexuality, pp. 180–207. 2nd ed. Scarborough, ON: Allyn and Bacon.

———. 1999. "Legal Aid," in James H. Marsh (ed.), The Canadian Encyclopedia, pp. 1318–1319. Toronto: McClelland and Stewart.

Mousourakis, George. 2007. A Legal History of Rome. New York: Routledge.

Moynihan, Daniel Patrick. 1969. *Maximum Feasible Misunderstanding*. New York: Free Press.

———. 1979. "Social Science and the Courts." *Public Interest* 54 (Winter): 12–31.

Mugford, Rebecca, and John Weekes. 2006. "Mandatory and Coerced Treatment." *Canadian Centre on Substance Abuse*. Retrieved from www.ccsa.ca/2006%20CCSA%20Documents/ccsa-003648-2006.pdf.

Muhlhahn, Klaus. 2009. *Criminal Justice in China: A History*. Cambridge, MA: Harvard University Press.

Mulgrew, Ian. 2016. "Provincial Court Judges' Salary Demands Are Out of Step with Reality." *Vancouver Sun* (February 16). Retrieved from www.vancouversun.com/business/mulgrew+provincial+court+judges+salary+demands+step+with+reality/11723835/story.html.

Mullan, David. 2001. *Administrative Law*. Toronto: Irwin.

Mullis, Jeffrey. 1995. "Medical Malpractice, Social Structure and Social Control." *Sociological Forum* 10 (1) (March): 135–163.

Mundy, Martha (ed.). 2002. *Law and Anthropology*. Aldershot, UK: Ashgate/Dartmouth.

Munger, Frank. 2001. "Inquiry and Activism in Law and Society." *Law and Society Review* 35 (1): 7–20.

Munro, Vanessa E. and Marina della Giusta (eds.). 2008. *Demanding Sx: Critical Reflections on the Regulation of Prostitution*. Burlington, VT: Ashgate.

Muravyeva, Marianna. 2017. *The Foundations of Russian Law*. Oxford: Hart Publishing.

Murdocca, Carmela. 2004. "The Racial Profile: Governing Race Through Knowledge Production." *Canadian Journal of Law and Society* 19 (2): 153–167.

Nadelmann, Ethan A. 2017. "An End to Marijuana Prohibition: The Drive to Legalize Pick Ups," in Thomas Hickey (ed.), *Taking Sides: Clashing Views in Crime and Criminology*, 12th ed., pp. 320–324. Dubuque, IA: McGraw-Hill.

Nader, Laura and Harry F. Todd, Jr. 1978. "Introduction: The Disputing Process," in Laura Nader and Harry F. Todd, Jr. (eds.), *The Disputing Process: Law in Ten Societies*, pp. 1–40. New York: Columbia University Press.

Nader, Ralph. 1965. *Unsafe at Any Speed: The Designed-in Dangers of the American Automobile*. New York: Grossman.

———. 1969. "Law Schools and Law Firms." *New Republic* (October 11): 21–23.

Nagel, Stuart S. 1975. *Improving the Legal Process*. Lexington, MA: Heath.

Nagin, Daniel S., Robert M. Solow, and Cynthia Lum. 2015. "Deterrence, Criminal Opportunities, and Police." *Criminology* 53 (1): 74–100.

Nasheri, Hedie. 1998. *Betrayal of Due Process: A Comparative Assessment of Plea Bargaining in the United States and Canada*. Lanham, MD: University Press of America.

Native Counseling Services of Alberta, Patti LaBoucane—Benson, Nadine Callihoo, Racquel Fraser, and Kristin Raworth. 2007. "Aboriginal Legal Education Needs Survey 2006–2007." Retrieved from www.ncsa.ca/documents/LENS2007_FINAL.pdf.

National Council on Problem Gambling. 2017. "Advocacy." Retrieved from www.ncpgambling.org/programs-resources/advocacy/.

Naudie, Christopher and Shuli Rodal. 2017. "Competition Criminal Enforcement in Canada: The Year in Review 2016." *Osler, Hoskin & Harcourt LLP*. Retrieved from www.osler.com/osler/media/Osler/reports/competition/Competition-Criminal-Enforcement-in-Canada-Year-in-review-2016.pdf.

Naudie, Christopher, Michelle Lally, and Lawrence Ritchie. 2015. "Competition Criminal Enforcement in Canada: 2014 Year in Review." *Osler, Hoskin & Harcourt LLP*. Retrieved from www.osler.com/osler/media/Osler/reports/competition/Competition-Criminal-Enforcement-in-Canada-2014-Year-in-Review.pdf.

Negley, Glen. 1965. *Political Authority and Moral Judgement*. Durham, NC: Duke University Press.

Nelken, David (ed.). 2009. *Beyond Law in Contex: Developing a Sociological Understanding of Law*. Burlington, VT: Ashgate.

Nelson, Adie and Augie Fleras. 1995. *Social Problems in Canada*. Toronto: Pearson Education.

Nelson, Cary. 2010. *No University Is an Island: Saving Academic Freedom*. New York: New York University press.

Nelson, Robert L. 2001. "Law, Democracy, and Domination: Law and Society Research as Critical." *Law and Society Review* 35 (1): 33–37.

Nelson, Todd D. (ed.). 2009. *Handbook of Prejudice, Stereotyping and Discrimination*. New York: Psychology Press.

Neufeld, Roxanne L. 2013. "Contempt of Court." Retrieved from www.westlawnextcanada.com/blog/insider/ced-an-overview-of-the-law-contempt-of-court-77/.

New Brunswick (Minister of Health and Community Services) v. G.(J.) [1999] 3 SCR. 46.

Newman, Dwight G. 2014. *Revisiting the Duty to Consult Aboriginal Peoples*. Saskatoon, SK: Purich Publishing Ltd.

Nicholson, Katie, Vera-Lynn Kubinec, and Katie Pedersen. 2017. "10 Manitoba Lawyers Misappropriated Nearly $2M But Face No Criminal Charges." *CBC News* (February 16). Retrieved from cbc.ca/news/canada/manitoba/10-manitoba-lawyers-misappropriated-nearly-2m-but-face-no-criminal-charges-1.3982660.

Nickels, Ernest L., and Arvind Verma. 2008. "Dimensions of Police Culture: A study in Canada, India, and Japan." *Policing: An International Journal of Police Strategies & Management* 31(2): 186–209.

Nielsen, Jorgen S. and Lisbet Christoffersen (eds.). 2010. *Shari'a as Discourse: Legal Traditions and the Encounter with Europe*. Burlington, VT: Ashgate.

Nikolaev v. Fakhredinov, 2015 ONSC 6267.

Nimkoff, Meyer F. 1957. "Obstacles to Innovation," in Francis R. Allen, Hornell Hart, Delbert C. Miller, William F. Ogburn, and Meyer F. Nimkoff, *Technology and Social Change*, pp. 56–71. New York: Appleton-Century-Crofts.

Nisbet, Robert A. 1969. *Social Change and History*. New York: Oxford University Press.

———. 2000. *Twilight of Authority*. Indianapolis, IN: Liberty Fund.

Nisga'a Final Agreement (1999). Retrieved from www.nnkn.ca/files/u28/nis-eng.pdf.

Nissenbaum, Helen. 2009. *Privacy in Context: Technology, Policy, and the Integrity of Social Life*. Palo Alto, CA: Stanford University Press.

Nonet, Philippe. 1976. "For Jurisprudential Sociology." *Law and Society Review* 10 (4) (Summer): 525–545.

Nonet, Philippe and Philip Selznick. 2001. *Law and Society in Transition: Toward Responsive Law*. New Brunswick, NJ: Transaction.

Norman, Jim. 2016. "Americans Rate Healthcare Providers High on Honesty, Ethics." Retrieved from www.gallup.com/poll/200057/americans-rate-healthcare-providers-high-honesty-ethics.aspx.

Norrander, Barbara and Clyde Wilcox (eds.). 2009. *Understanding Public Opinion*. 3rd ed. Washington, DC: CQ Press.

Noskova, Polina. 2016. "Volkswagen Brand's U.S. Sales Fall 22% in Eighth Straight Drop." *Bloomberg Business* (July 1). Retrieved from www.bloomberg.com/news/articles/2016-07-01/volkswagen-brand-s-u-s-sales-fall-22-in-eighth-stright-drop.

Nova Scotia Barristers' Society. 2016. "Administrative Law." Retrieved from https://nsbs.org/sites/default/files/ftp/BarReviewMaterials/AdministrativeLaw2015.pdf.

Nuijten, Monique and Gerhard Anders (eds.). 2009. *Corruption and the Secret of Law: A Legal Anthropological Perspective*. Burlington, VT: Ashgate.

Nulty, Duncan D. 2008. "The Adequacy of Response Rates to Online and Paper Surveys: What Can Be Done?" *Assessment & Evaluation in High Education* 33 (3): 301–314.

Nunavut Act (S.C. 1993, c. 28).

Nunavut Land Claims Agreement Act (S.C. 1993, c. 29).

Nunavut Tunngavik Incorporated. (2004). "Kangikhiteagumaven: A Plain Language Guide to the Nunavut Land Claims Agreement." Retrieved from www.tunngavik.com/documents/publications/2004-00-00-A-Plain-Language-Guide-to-the-Nunavut-Land-Claims-Agreement-English.pdf.

Nussbaum, Martha C. 2010. *From Disgust to Humanity: Sexual Orientation and Constitutional Law*. New York: Oxford University Press.

Oberschall, Anthony. 1973. *Social Conflict and Social Movements*. Englewood Cliffs, NJ: Prentice Hall.

O'Brien, Connie. 2017. "Can Pre-Employment Tests Identify White-Collar Criminals and Reduce Fraud Risk in Your Organization?" *Journal of Forensic & Investigative Accounting* 9 (1): 621–636.

O'Brien, Timothy L. 1998. "Gambling: Married to the Action, for Better or Worse." *New York Times* (November 8): WK3.

O'Callaghan, Kevin. 2014. "Two Landmark Aboriginal Cases From Canada's Highest Court." *Mining Law Committee Newsletter* 6 (2): 6–8.

Oda, Hiroshi. 2009. *Japanese Law*. 3rd ed. New York: Oxford University Press.

Office of the Commissioner of Lobbying of Canada. 2012. "The Lobbying Act." February 15. Retrieved from https://lobbycanada.gc.ca/eic/site/012.nsf/eng/h_00008.html.

———. 2014. "Frequently Asked Questions." Retrieved from https://lobbycanada.gc.ca/eic/site/012.nsf/eng/00884.html.

Office of the Registrar of Lobbyists. 2005. "Message from the Registrar of Lobbyists." Retrieved from http://strategis.ic.gc.ca/epic/internet/inlobbyist-lobbyiste.nsf/en/Home.

Ogletree, Charles J. and Austin Sarat (eds.). 2006. *From Lynch Mobs to the Killing State: Race and Death Peanlty in America.* New York: New York University Press.

Ogrodnik, Marysia, Pierre Kopp, Xavier Bongaerts, and Juan M. Tecco. 2015. "An Economic Analysis of Different Cannabis Decriminalization Scenarios." *Psychiatr Danub* 27 (Supplement 1): S309–S314.

fOleinik, Anton N. 2003. *Organized Crime, Prison and Post-Soviet Societies.* Burlington, VT: Ashgate.

Oliver, Rachel. 2015. "Issues Affecting Women in the Legal Profession." Retrieved from ms-jd.org/blog/article/issues-affecting-women-in-the-legal-profession.

Olivo, Laurence M. 2001a. "Introduction to Legal Studies: Law as a Concept and System," in Laurence Olivo (ed.), *Introduction to Law in Canada,* pp. 1–19. Concord, ON: Captus.

———. 2001b. "Types of Law," in Laurence Olivo (ed.), *Introduction to Law in Canada,* pp. 83–92. Concord, ON: Captus.

———. 2004. "Sources of Law," in Laurence M. Olivo (ed.), *Introduction to Law in Canada,* pp. 63–82. Concord, ON: Captus.

Olson, Walter K. 1991. "The Selling of the Law." *American Enterprise* (January–February): 27–35.

O'Mahoney, David, and Jonathan Doak. 2017. *Reimagining Restorative Justice: Agency and Accountability in the Criminal Process.* Oxford: Hart Publishing.

Omond, Geordon. 2016. "B.C. Strikes Down Two of Stephen Harper's Mandatory-Minimum Drug Laws." *The Star.com* (April 25). Retrieved from www.thestar.com/news/canada/2016/04/25/BC-strikes-down-two-of-stephen-harpers-mandatory-minimum-drug-laws.htm.

Ong, Larry. 2016. "Some Places in China Waver on Persecution of Falun Gong." *Epoch Times* (December 20). Retrieved from www.theepochtimes.com/n3/2200993-some-places-in-china-waver-on-persecution-of-falun-gong/.

Ontario Ministry of the Attorney General. 2007. "Access to Justice: Represented Litigants." Retrieved from www.attorneygeneral.jus.gov.on.ca/english/about/oubs/cjrp/080_unrepresented.asp.

———. 2008. "Ontario Compensates Steven Truscott: News Release." July 7. Retrieved from www.attorney.general.jus.gov.on.ca/english/news/2008/20080707-truscott-nr.asp.

Oppenheimer, Mark. 2006. "College Goes to Court." *Wall Street Journal* (July 14): W9.

Oriola, Temitope, Nicole Neverson, and Charles T. Adeyanju. 2012. "'They Should Have Just Taken a Gun and Shot My Son': Taser Deployment and the Downtrodden in Canada." *Social Identities* 18(1): 65–83.

Orkin, Andrew J. 2003. "When the Law Breaks Down: Aboriginal Peoples in Canada and Governmental Defiance of the Rule of Law." *Osgoode Hall Law Journal* 41 (2/3): 445–463.

Ornstein, Michael. 2010. *Racialization and Gender of Lawyers in Ontario. A Report for the Law Society of Upper Canada* (April). Retrieved from www.lsuc.on.ca/media/convapril10_ornstein.pdf .

Osborne, Coulter A. 2007. "Civil Justice Reform Project." Retrieved from www.attorneygeneral.jus.gov.on.ca/english/about/pubs/cjrp/.

Osborne, Philip H. 2003. *The Law of Torts.* 2nd ed. Toronto: Irwin Law.

Oscapella, Eugene. 2012. *Changing the Frame: A New Approach to Drug Policy in Canada.* Vancouver, BC: Canadian Drug Policy Coalition

Osgoode Hall Law School. 2017. "Tuition and Fees: 2016–2017 JD Program Fee." Retrieved from www.osgoode.yorku.ca/resources-and-services/financial-services/tuition-fees/.

Osoyoos Indian Band v. Oliver (Town), [2001] 3 SCR 746, 2001 SCC 85 (CanLII).

Ost, Francois. 2006. "The Law as Mirrored in Literature." *SubStance* 35 (1): 3–19.

Packer, Herbert L. and Thomas Ehrlich. 1972. *New Directions in Legal Education.* New York: McGraw-Hill.

Pagnattaro, Marisa Anne, Daniel R. Cahoy, Julie Manning, O. Lee Reed, and Peter J. Shedd. 2016. *The Legal and Regulatory Environment of Business.* 16th ed. New York: McGraw-Hill.

Palermo, George B., Maxine Aldridge White, Lew A. Wasserman, and William Hanrahan. 1998. "Plea Bargaining: Injustice for All?" *International Journal of Offender Therapy and Comparative Criminology* 42 (2) (June): 111–123.

Palmer, Michael and Simon Roberts. 1998. *Dispute Processes: ADR and the Primary Forms of Decision Making*. London: Butterworths.

Palmer, Ellie, Tom Cornford, Yseult Marique and Audrey Guinchard (eds.). 2016. *Access to Justice: Beyond the Policies and Politics of Austerity*. Oxford: Hart Publishing.

Panter, A. T., Charles E. Daye, Walter R. Allen, Linda F. Wightman, and Meera Deo. 2008. "Everyday Discrimination in a National Sample of Law Students." *Journal of Diversity in Higher Education* 1 (2) (June): 67–79.

Parisi, Francesco. 2004. "Rent-Seeking Through Litigation: Adversarial and Inquisitorial Systems Compared." *International Review of Law and Economics* 22 (2): 193–216.

———. 2008. *The Economics of Law Making*. New York: Oxford University Press.

Parkin, Tom. 2016. "It's Raining Lobbyists in Ottawa." *Toronto Sun* (July 17). Retrieved from www.torontosun.com/2016/07/17/its-raining-lobbyists-in-ottawa.

Parliament of Canada. 2009. Bill C-26 *Home Page*. Retrieved from www.parl.gc.ca/legisinfo/index.asp?Language=E&query=5330&List=toc&session=15.

Parsons, Talcott. 1962. "The Law and Social Control," in William M. Evan (ed.), *Law and Sociology: Exploratory Essays*, pp. 56–62. New York: Free Press.

———. 1964. "Evolutionary Universals in Society." *American Sociological Review* 29 (3) (June): 339–357.

Partridge, Mark V. B. 2009. *Alternative Dispute Resolution: An Essential Competency for Lawyers*. New York: Oxford University Press.

Pashley, Peter J., Andrea E. Thornton, and Jennifer R. Duffy. 2005. "Access and Diversity in Law School Admissions," in Wayne J. Camara and Ernest W. Kimmel (eds.), *Choosing Students: Higher Education Admissions Tools for the 21st Century*, pp. 231–249. Mahwah, NJ: Lawrence Erlbaum Associates.

Patrice, Joe. 2015. "If You're In Law School, You're Probably Depressed." *Above the Law* (January 15). Retrieved from http://abovethelaw.com/2015/01/if-youre-in-law-school-youre-probably-depressed/.

Patry, Marc W. 2008. "Civil Liability for Negligent Police Investigation: Canadian Developments." *The Open Law Journal* 1: 23–2.

Patterson, Dennis (ed.). 2010. *A Companion to Philosophy of Law and Legal Theory*. 2nd ed. Hoboken, NJ: Wiley-Blackwell.

Payne, Brian J. 2017. *White-Collar Crime: The Essentials*. Thousand Oaks, CA: Sage Publications.

Peach, Lucinda. 2002. *Legislating Morality: Pluralism and Religious Identity in Lawmaking*. New York: Oxford University Press.

Peay, Jill. 2005. *Seminal Issues in Mental Health Law*. Burlington, VT: Ashgate.

Peel, Michael. 2006. "Reach Versus Risk: Why Big Law Firms Are Split on the Merits of Going Global." *Financial Times* (December 14): 13.

Penalver, Eduardo Moises and Sonia K. Katyal. 2010. *Property Outlaws*. New Haven, CT: Yale University Press.

Peppers, Todd C. and Laura Trevvett Anderson. 2009. *Anatomy of an Execution: The Life and Death of Douglas Christopher Thomas*. Hanover, NH: University Press of New England.

Perelman, Michael. 2003. "The Political Economy of Intellectual Property." *Monthly Review* 54 (8) (January): 29–37.

Perry, Barbara and Ryan Scrivens. 2015. "Uneasy Alliances: A Look at the Right-Wing Extremist Movement in Canada." *Studies in Conflict & Terrorism* 39 (3): 819–841.

Peters, Julie Stone. 2005. "Law, Literature and the Vanishing Real: On the Future of an Interdisciplinary Illusion." *PMLA* 120 (2): 442–453.

Peters, Anne and Isabelle Ley (eds.). 2016. *The Freedom of Peaceful Assembly in Europe*. Oxford: Hart Publishing.

Peters, Robert W., Laura J. Lederer, and Shane Kelly. 2012. "The Slave and the Porn Star: Sexual Trafficking and Pornography." *Journal of Human Rights and Civil Society* 5:1–22.

Petrunik, Michael. 2003. "The Hare and the Tortoise: Dangerousness and Sex Offender Policy in the United States and Canada." *Canadian Journal of Criminology and Criminal Justice* 45 (1) (January): 43–72.

Phillips, Scott. 2003. "The Social Structure of Vengeance: A Test of Black's Model." *Criminology* 41 (3) (August): 673–708.

Phillips, Scott and Mark Cooney. 2005. "Aiding Peace, Abetting Violence: Third Parties and the Management of Conflict." *American Sociological Review* 70 (2) (April): 334–354.

Philpott, Amelia. 2016. "A Few Words on the Tekaia'torehthà: ke Kaianerenhsera (Akwesasne Court Law) to Commemorate the 'Birthday' of the Akwesasne Mohawk Court." McGill University Human Rights Interns (Blog) August 25. Retrieved from blogs.mcgill.ca/humanrightsinterns/tag/akwesasne/

Piana, Daniela. 2010. *Judicial Accountabilities in New Europe: From Rules of Law to Quality of Justice.* Burlington, VT: Ashgate.

Picard, Cheryl A. and R. P. Saunders. 2002. "The Regulation of Mediation," in Michael Mac Neil, Neil Sargent, and Peter Swann (eds.), *Law, Regulation, and Governance,* pp. 223–238. Don Mills, ON: Oxford University Press.

Piccinato, Milica. 2009. *Plea Bargaining.* Department of Justice Canada. Retrieved from www.justice. gc.ca/eng/pi/icg-gci/toc-tdm.html.

Piven, Frances Fox and Richard A. Cloward. 1993. *Regulating the Poor: The Functions of Public Welfare.* Rev. ed. New York: Vintage.

Pleasence, Pascoe and Deborah Macourt. 2013. "What Price Justice? Income and the Use of Lawyers." *Updating Justice* 31: 1–5. Retrieved from www.lawfoundation.net.au/ljf/site/templates/UpdatingJustice/$file/UJ_31_Lawyer_use_and_income_FINAL.pdf

Plessis, Paul du. 2010. *Borkowski's Textbook on Roman Law.* 4th ed. New York: Oxford University Press.

Podgers, James. 1994. "Chasing the Ideal: As More Americans Find Themselves Priced Out of the System, the Struggle Goes on to Fulfill the Promise of Equal Justice for All." *ABA Journal* 80 (August): 56–61.

———. 1995. "Sorting Out Image, Ads, Ethics." *ABA Journal* 81 (March): 94–95.

Poell, Thomas and Eric Borra. 2012. "Twitter, YouTube, and Flickr as Platforms of Alternative Journalism: The Social Media Account of the 2010 Toronto G20 Protests." *Journalism* 13 (6): 695–713.

Polinsky, Mitchell and Daniel L. Rubinfeld. 1998. "Does the English Rule Discourage Low-Probability-of-Prevailing Plaintiffs?" *Journal of Legal Studies* 27 (January): 141–160.

Poll, Edward. 2014. "Is Flat Fee Billing a Viable Alternative?" *Canadian Bar Association,* October 21. Retrieved from www.cba.org/Publications-Resources/CBA-Practice-Link/solo/2014/Is-Flat-Fee-Billing-a-Viable-Alternative.

Porter, John. 1965. *The Vertical Mosaic: An Analysis of Social Class and Power in Canada.* Toronto: University of Toronto Press.

Posner, Richard A. 1995. "The Sociology of the Sociology of Law: A View From Economics." *European Journal of Law and Economics* 2(4), 263–284.

———. 1996. *The Federal Courts: Challenge and Reform.* Cambridge, MA: Harvard University Press.

———. 2005. *Law and Literature: A Misunderstoood Relation: A Revised and Enlarged Edition.* Cambridge, MA: Harvard University Press.

———. 2007. *Economic Analysis of Law.* 7th ed. New York: Aspen.

Pospisil, Leopold. 1971. *Anthropology of Law: A Comparative Theory.* New York: Harper and Row.

Pottage, Alain and Martha Mundy (eds.). 2004. *Law, Anthropology and the Constitution of the Social: Making Persons and Things.* New York: Cambridge University Press.

Pound, Roscoe. 1941a. *In My Philosophy of Law.* St. Paul, MN: West.

———. 1941b. "Justice According to Law." *Columbia Law Review* 14 (1): 1–26.

———. 1943. "A Survey of Social Interests." *Harvard Law Review* 57 (October): 1–39.

———. 1959. *Jurisprudence.* Vols. 1 and 2. St. Paul, MN: West.

Pozadski, Alexandra. 2016. "Businesses Look Forward to Canada's Legal-Pot Push in 2017." *The Globe and Mail* (December 26). Retrieved from www.theglobeandmail.com/report-on-business/businesses-look-forward-to-canadas-push-for-legal-marijuana-in-2017/article33433291/.

Pratt, Anna and Sara K. Thompson. 2008. "Chivalry,'Race'and Discretion at the Canadian Border." *British Journal of Criminology* 48(5): 620–640.

Prentice, Robert A. and Jonathan J. Koehler. 2003. "A Normality Bias in Legal Decision Making." *Cornell Law Review* 88 (3) (March): 583–651.

Priban, Jiri, Pauline Roberts, and James Young (eds.). 2003. *Systems of Justice in Transition: Central European Experiences since 1989.* Burlington, VT: Ashgate.

Price, David E. 1972. *Who Makes the Law? Creativity and Power in Senate Committees.* Cambridge, MA: Schenkman.

Pridgen v. University of Calgary 2010 ABQB 644 (CanLii), aff'd in part by 2012 ABCA 139 (CanLII).

Pridgen v. University of Calgary, 2012 ABCA 139, 350 DLR (4th) 1; [2012] 11 WWR 477; 524 AR 251; [2012] CarswellAlta 797; 545 WAC 251.

Pritchard, Mary E. and Daniel N. McIntosh. 2003. "What Predicts Adjustment Among Law Students? A Longitudinal Panel Study." *Journal of Social Psychology* 143 (6) (December): 727–745.

Proceeds of Crime (Money Laundering) and Terrorist Financing Act (S.C. 2000, c. 17),

Pross, A. Paul and Zach Parrott. 2017. "Lobbying in Canada." *Historica Canada.* Retrieved from www.thecanadianencyclopedia.ca/en/article/lobbying/.

Prosterman, Roy L., Robert Mitchell, and Tim Handstad (eds.). 2010. *One Billing Rising: Law, Land and the Alleviation of Global Poverty.* Chicago, IL: University of Chicago Press.

Protection of Children Abusing Drugs Act. SA 2005, c P-27.5.

Protection Of Children Abusing Drugs Act. Alberta Regulation 138/2006.

Protection of Communities and Exploited Persons Act (SC 2014, c. 25).

Ptacek, James (ed.). 2009. *Restorative Justice and Violence Against Women.* New York: Oxford University Press.

Public Prosecution Service of Canada. 2014. 3.7: *Resolution Discussions.* Retrieved from www.ppsc-sppc.gc.ca/eng/pub/fpsd-sfpg/fps-sfp/tpd/d-g-eng.pdf.

Public Prosecution Service of Canada. 2016. "About The Public Prosecution Service of Canada." Retrieved from www.ppsc-sppc.gc.ca/eng/bas/index.html#intro

Public Safety Act, 2002 (S.C. 2004, c. 15).

Public Safety Canada. 2011. "Illicit Drugs." Retrieved from www.publicsafety.gc.ca/prg/le/dr-eng.aspxm

———. 2015. "Substance Abuse." Retrieved from www.publicsafety.gc.ca/cnt/cntrng-crm/crrctns/sbstnc-bs-en.aspx.

Pue, W. Wesley. 2009. "Development: A Short History of the Canadian Law and Society Association." August 3. Retrieved from www.acds-clsa.org/en/development.cfm.

———. 2016. *Lawyers' Empire: Legal Professions and Cultural Authority, 1780–1950.* Vancouver, BC: UBC Press.

Pue, W. Wesley and David Sugarman (eds.). 2003. *Lawyers and Vampires: Cultural Histories of Legal Professions.* Portland, OR: Hart.

Quade, Vicki. 1995. "There Is No Sisterhood: Non-White Women Lawyers Say They're Still at the Bottom of the Heap." *Human Rights* 22 (1) (Winter): 8–13.

Quaile, Jennifer. 2002. "'At the Mercy' of Patriarchy: Women and the Struggle over Child Support," in T. Brettel Dawson (ed.), *Women, Law and Social Change: Core Readings and Current Issues,* pp. 238–257. 4th ed. Toronto: Captus.

Quan, Douglas. 2016. "Right-Wing Extremist Groups 'prevalent' Across Canada, Study Warns." *National Post* (February 12). Retrieved from http://news.nationalpost.com/news/canada/right-wing-extremist-groups-prevalent-across-canada-study-warns.

Queen's News Centre. 2004. "Ontario Law Schools Attract a Great Diversity of Students." (November 9). Retrieved from www.qnc.queensu.ca/story_loader.php?id=4191238807603.

Quinney, Richard. 1970. *The Social Reality of Crime.* Boston: Little, Brown.

———. 1974. *The Critique of Legal Order: Crime Control in Capitalist Society.* Boston: Little, Brown.

———. 1975. *Criminology: Analysis and Critique of Crime in America.* Boston: Little, Brown.

———. 2002. *Critique of Legal Order: Crime Control in Capitalist Society.* New Brunswick, NJ: Transaction Books.

Quong-Wing v. R. (Supreme Court of Canada) [1913-14] 49 SCR 44.

Rabinovitch, Jannit and Susan Strega. 2004. "The PEERS Story: Effective Services Sidestep the Controversies." *Violence Against Women* 10 (2) (February): 140–159.

Rabson, Mia. 2005. "Manitoba Lobbying Ottawa for Drug-Treatment Court." *Winnipeg Free Press* (April 11): A3.

Raiswell, James. 2014. "A New Lawyer's Guide to Networking." *Canadian Bar Association.* Retrieved from www.cba.org/PublicationsResources/CBA-Practice-Link/Young-Lawyers/2014/A-new-lawyer-s-guide-to-networking.

Ramazanoglu, Caroline and Janet Holland. 2002. *Feminist Methodology: Challenges and Choices.* Thousand Oaks, CA: Sage.

Ramos, Howard. 2006. "What Causes Canadian Aboriginal Protest? Examining Resources, Opportunities and Identity, 1951–2000." *Canadian Journal of Sociology* 31: 211–235.

Ramseyer, J. Mark and Eric B. Rasmusen. 2010. *Comparative Litigation Rates.* Discussion Paper No. 681, Harvard Law School. Retrieved from www.law.harvard.edu/programs/olin_center/papers/pdf/Ramseyer_681.pdf.

Randall, Kerry and Andru J. Johnson. 2005. *The Lawyer's Guide to Effective Yellow Pages Advertising*. Chicago, IL: American Bar Association.

Ransome, Paul. 2010. *Social Theory for Beginners*. Bristol, UK: The Policy Press.

Rapping, Elayne. 2004. *Law and Justice as Seen on TV*. New York: New York University Press.

Rawls, John. 2001. *Justice as Fairness: A Restatement*. Ed. Erin Kelly. Cambridge, MA: Belknap/Harvard University Press.

Raymond, Janice G. 2003. "10 Reasons for Not Legalizing Prostitution." Retrieved from www.rapereliefshelter.bc.ca/learn/resources/10-reasons-not-legalizing-prostitution.

Ratych v. Bloomer, [1990] 1 S.C.R. 940.

Ray, Arthur J. 2016. *Aboriginal Rights Claims and the Making and Remaking of History*. Montreal/Kingston: McGill-Queen's University Press.

Raz, Joseph. 2009. *The Authority of Law: Essays on Law and Morality*. 2nd ed. New York: Oxford University Press.

Razack, Sherene. 1998. *Looking White People in the Eye: Gender, Race and Culture in the Courtrooms and Classroom*. Toronto: University of Toronto Press.

RCMP. 2006. "Integrated Proceeds of Crime." (February 3). Retrieved from www.rcmp-grc.gc.ca/un/prog_serv/fed_serv/ipoc_e.htm.

———. 2012. "Proceeds of Crime." (January 13). Retrieved from www.rcmp-grc.gc.ca/poc-pdc/index-eng.htm.

———. 2016. "CFSEU Dismantles Illegal Video Gaming Operation." (January 14). Retrieved from www.rcmp-grc.gc.ca/en/news/2016/14/cfseu-dismantles-illegal-video-gaming-operation.

Re Mechanical Contractors Association Sarnia v UA Local 663, 2014 ONSC 6909.

Real Women of Canada. 2017. "About." Retrieved from www.realwomenofcanada.ca/about-us/.

Reason, Peter and Hilary Bradbury (eds.). 2013. *Handbook of Action Research, Participative Inquiry and Practice, 2nd edition*. Thousand Oaks, CA: Sage.

Reasons, Charles E. and Robert M. Rich (eds.). 1978. *The Sociology of Law: A Conflict Perspective*. Toronto: Butterworths.

Reed, O. Lee. 2010. *The Legal and Regulatory Environment of Business*, 15th ed. Boston, MA: McGraw-Hill/Irwin.

Reid, Daniel. 2013. " Reputation Matters: How Canadian Courts are Balancing Protection of Reputation and Freedom of Expression." *Harper Grey LLP*. Retrieved from www.harpergrey.com/~ASSETS/DOCUMENT/PAPER___DANIEL_REID___REPUTATION_MATTERS(1).pdf

Reference re Assisted Human Reproduction Act, 2010 SCC 61, [2010] 3 SCR 457.

Reference re Same-Sex Marriage, [2004] 3 SCR 698.

Reference re Secession of Quebec, [1998] 2 SCR 217

Reference re Senate Reform, 2014 SCC 32

Reference re Supreme Court Act, ss. 5 and 6, 2014 SCC 21, [2014] 1 S.C.R. 433.

Régimbald, Guy. 2015. *Canadian Administrative Law*, 2nd ed. Toronto, ON: LexisNexis.

Reilly, J. Nolan. 1999. "Winnipeg General Strike," in James H. Marsh (ed.), *The Canadian Encyclopedia: Year 2000 Edition*, p. 2525. Toronto: McClelland and Stewart.

Reiss, Albert J., Jr. 1971. *The Police and the Public*. New Haven, CT: Yale University Press.

Reiss, Albert J., Jr. and David J. Bordua. 1967. "Environment and Organization: A Perspective on the Police," in David J. Bordua (ed.), *The Police: Six Sociological Essays*, pp. 25–55. New York: John Wiley.

Religious Tolerance.org. 2001. "Extraditing Accused Murderers to the U.S." Retrieved from www.religioustolerance.org/execut5.htm.

———. 2005. "Executing Innocent People: Studies of the Reliability of the Legal System in Capital Cases." Retrieved from www.religioustolerance.org/executg2.htm.

Relis, Tamara. 2002. "Civil Litigation from Litigants' Perspectives: What We Know and What We Don't Know About the Litigation Experience of Individual Litigants." *Studies in Law, Politics and Society* 25 (1): 151–212.

Reske, Henry J. 1994b. "Ralph Nader's New Project: Law Centers to Help the Small Group Instead of the Little Guy." *ABA Journal* 80 (May): 32–33.

Resnick, Judith. 1990. "Constructing the Canon." *Yale Journal of Law and the Humanities* 2 (1): 221–230.

Reutter, Mark. 2005. "Waning Economy, Increasing Numbers of Lawyers Fuel Litigation in
   Japan." *University of Illinois News Bulletin* (July 21). Retrieved from http://news.illinois.edu/
   NEWS/06/0721japan.html.
Rhode, Deborah L. and Geoffrey C. Hazard, Jr. 2007. *Professional Responsibility and Regulation.* 2nd ed.
   New York: Foundation.
Rhode, Deborah L. and David Luban (eds.). 2005. *Legal Ethics: Law Stories.* Eagan, MN: Foundation Press.
Rice, Stephen K. and Michael D. White, eds. 2010. *Race, Ethnicity and Policing: New and Essential Readings.*
   New York: New York University Press.
Richards, David A. J. 2016. "Literature and Resisting Injustice: Melville and Hawthorne on Patriarchal
   Manhood and Homophobia." *Law & Literature* 29(1): 109–122.
Richardson, Diane and Steven Seidman (eds.). 2002. *Handbook of Lesbian and Gay Studies.* Thousand Oaks,
   CA: Sage.
Richland, Justin B. and Sarah Deer. 2010. *Introduction to Tribal Legal Studies.* 2nd ed. Lanham, MD:
   AltaMira Press.
Ripley, Randall B. 1988. *Congress: Process and Policy.* 4th ed. New York: W. W. Norton.
Roach, Kent. 2005. "Common Law Bills of Rights as Dialogue between Courts and Legislatures."
   University of Toronto Law Journal 55 (3): 733–766.
Roach, Kent and David Schneiderman. 2013. "Freedom of Expression in Canada." 61 S.C.L.R. (2d):
   429–525.
Roach, Steven C. 2005. "Arab States and the Role of Islam in the International Criminal Court." *Political
   Studies* 53 (1) (March): 143–161.
Roberts, Julian V. 2000. "Introduction to Criminal Justice in Canada," in Julian V. Roberts (ed.),
   Criminal Justice in Canada: A Reader, pp. 3–15. Toronto: Harcourt.
———. 2001. "Sentencing, Parole, and Psychology," in Regina A. Schuller and James R. P. Ogloff (eds.),
   Introduction to Psychology and Law, pp. 188–213. Toronto: University of Toronto Press.
Roberts, Simon. 1979. *Order and Dispute: An Introduction to Legal Anthropology.* New York: St. Martin's.
Robertson, Grant and Beppi Grosariol. 2006. "Litigation: Grammarians Take Heed of Telecomma Dispute:
   Legal and Business Scholars Are Riveted by Rogers, Aliant Punctuation Debate." *Globe and Mail*
   (December 29): B4.
Robertson, Neil. 2012. "Policing: Fundamental Principles in a Canadian Context." *Canadian Public
   Administration* 55 (3): 343–363.
Roesch, Ronald, Stephen L. Golding, Valerie P. Hans, and N. Dickon Reppucci. 1991. "Social Science and
   the Courts: The Role of Amicus Curiae Briefs." *Law and Human Behavior* 15 (1) (February): 1–11.
Rosati, Massimo. 2009. *Ritual and the Sacred: A Neo-Durkheimian Analysis of Politics, Religion and Self.*
   Burlington, VT: Ashgate.
Rosen, Jeffrey. 2001. "In Lieu of Manners." *New York Times Magazine* (February 4): 49–51.
Rosenberg, Gerald N. 2008. *The Hollow Hope: Can Courts Bring About Social Change.* Chicago: University
   of Chicago Press.
Rosenbloom, David H. and Robert S. Kravchuck. 2005. *Public Administration: Understanding Management,
   Politics, and Law in the Public Sector.* 6th ed. New York: McGraw-Hill.
Ross, E. Adamson. 1901/1922. *Social Control.* New York: MacMillan.
Ross, Laurence H. 1980. *Settled Out of Court.* 2nd ed. Chicago: Aldine.
Ross, Rupert. 1992. *Dancing with a Ghost: Exploring Indian Reality.* Markham, ON: Octopus.
Ross, William H. and Donald E. Conlon. 2000. "Hybrid Forms of Third-Party Dispute Resolution:
   Theoretical Implications of Combining Mediation and Arbitration." *Academy of Management Review* 25
   (2) (April): 416–427.
Rothwell, Gary R. and J. Norman Baldwin. 2007. "Whistle-Blowing and the Code of Conduct in Police
   Agencies." *Crime and Delinquency* 53 (4): 8–10.
Rouland, Norbert. 1994. *Legal Anthropology.* Trans. Philippe G. Planel. Stanford, CA: Stanford University
   Press.
Rousseau, Cécile, François Crépeau, Patricia Foxen, and France Houle. 2002. "The Complexity of
   Determining Refugeehood: A Multidisciplinary Analysis of the Decision-Making Process of the
   Canadian Immigration and Refugee Board." *Journal of Refugee Studies* 15 (1) (March): 43–70.

Royse, David and Bruce A. Thyer. 2016. *Program Evaluation: An Introduction to an Evidence-Based Approach.* Boston, MA: Cengage.

Rozell, Mark J. and Clyde Wilcox. 2006. *Interest Groups in American Campaigns: The New Face of Electioneering.* 2nd ed. Washington, DC: CQ Press.

Rozell, Mark J., Clyde Wilcox, and David Madland. 2006. *Interest Groups in American Campaigns.* 2nd ed. Washington, DC: CQ Press.

Rule, James B. 2009. *Privacy in Peril: How We Are Sacrificing a Fundamental Right in Exchange for Security and Convenience.* New York: Oxford University Press.

Rusche, Georg and Otto Kurchheimer. 2003. *Punishment and Social Control.* New Brunswick, NJ: Transaction.

R. v. Anthony-Cook, 2016 SCC 43.

R. v. Born with A Tooth, [1993] 7066 (AB QB).

R. v. Brant, 2011 CarswellOnt 3005, 2011 ONCA 362, [2011] O.J. No. 2062, 94 W.C.B. (2d) 412.*R. v.* Butler (1992), 70 CCC (3d) 129 (SCC); reconsideration refused (1993), [1993] 2 WWR lxi (SCC).

R. v. Dickey, 2016 BCCA 177, 2016 CarswellBC 1107, 2016 BCCA 177, [2016] B.C.W.L.D. 3316, [2016] B.C.W.L.D. 3323, [2016] B.C.W.L.D. 3430, [2016] B.C.J. No. 815, 129 W.C.B. (2d) 626, 335 C.C.C. (3d) 478, 353 C.R.R. (2d) 278, 386 B.C.A.C. 121, 667 W.A.C. 121.

R. v. Edgar, 2010 ONCA 529 (CanLII), 101 OR (3d) 161.

R. v. Gladstone, [1996] 2 SCR 723, 1996 CanLII 160 (SCC).

R. v. Gladue, [1999] 1 S.C.R. 688.

R. v. Ipeelee, 2012 SCC 13.

R. v. Kokopenace, 2015 SCC 28, [2015] 2 S.C.R. 398.

R. v. Lloyd, 2016 SCC 13, [2016] 1 S.C.R. 130.

R. v. Marshall, [1999] 3 SCR 456, 1999 CanLII 665 (SCC).

R. v. Marshall; R. v. Bernard, [2005] 2 SCR 220, 2005 SCC 43 (CanLII).

R. v. Morin, 1995 CanLII 3999 (SK CA).

R. v. Munson, 2001 SKQB 530 (CanLII), [2002] 3 W.W.R. 105, affirmed 2003 SKCA 28 (CanLII), 172 C.C.C. (3d) 515.

R. v. Nepoose, (1991) 5867 (AB QB).

R, v, Nixon, 2011 SCC 45 (CanLII), [2011] 2 SCR 566.

R v Nur, 2015 SCC 15.

R. v. P. (J.A.). 1991. 6 C.R. (4th) 126. R. v. P. (J.A.). NWTR [1991].

R. v. Parker, (2000), 49 O.R. (3d) 48.

R. v. Pamajewon, [1996] 2 SCR 821.

R v Safarzadeh-Markhali, 2016 SCC 14.

R. v. Sappier; R. v. Gray, [2006] 2 SCR 686, 2006 SCC 54 (CanLII).

R, v, Smith, 2015 SCC 34, [2015] 2 SCR 602.

R. v. Sparrow, [1990] 1 S.C.R. 1075.

R. v. Williams, [1998] 1 SCR 1128.

Sable Offshore Energy v. Ameron International Corp., 2013 SCC 37.

Sackett, Paul R., Matthew J. Borneman, and Brian S. Connelly. 2008. "High Stakes Testing in Higher Education and Employment: Appraising the Evidence for Validity and Fairness." *American Psychologist* 63 (4) (May): 215–227.

Saeed, Abdullah. 2004. *Freedom of Religion, Apostasy and Islam.* Burlington, VT: Ashgate.

Sajo, Andras. 2003. "From Corruption to Extortion: Conceptualization of Post-Communist Corruption." *Crime, Law and Social Change* 40 (2/3) (October): 171–195.

Sákéj, James and Youngblood Henderson. 2002. "Sui Generis and Treaty Citizenship." *Citizenship Studies* 6(4): 415–440.

Salinger, Lawrence M. 2005. *The Encyclopedia of White Collar and Corporate Crime.* Thousand Oaks, CA: Sage.

Samborn, Hope V. 2000. "Higher Hurdles for Women." *American Bar Association Journal* 86: 30–34.

Samuels, Suzanne. 2006. *Law, Politics and Society: An Introduction to American Law.* Boston: Houghton Mifflin.

Sandberg, Sveinung and Willy Pederson. 2009. *Street Capital: Black Cannabis Dealers in a White Welfare State.* Bristol, UK: Policy Press.

Sangster, Joan. 2002. *Girl Trouble: Female Delinquency in English Canada.* Toronto: Between the Lines.

Sarat, Austin. 1989. "Alternatives to Formal Adjudication," in Sheldon Goldman and Austin Sarat (eds.), *American Court Systems: Readings in Judicial Process and Behavior*, pp. 33–40. 2nd ed. New York: Longman.

———. 2004. *Social Organization of Law.* Los Angeles: Roxbury.

———. 2005, *Dissent in Dangerous Times.* Ann Arbor, MI: University of Michigan Press.

———. 2011. *Sovereignty, Emergency, Legality.* New York: Cambridge University Press.

Sarat, Austin and William L. F. Felstiner. 1995. *Divorce Lawyers and Their Clients: Power and Meaning in the Legal Process.* New York: Oxford University Press.

Sarat, Austin and Stuart Scheingold (eds.). 1998. *Cause Lawyering: Political Commitments and Professional Responsibilities.* New York: Oxford University Press.

Sargent, Neil C. 2002. "Is There Any Justice in Alternative Justice?" in Michael Mac Neil, Neil Sargent, and Peter Swan (eds.), *Law, Regulation and Governance*, pp. 204–222. Don Mills, ON: Oxford University Press.

Sarver Jr, Vernon Thomas. 2014. "Abolishing the Death Penalty: An Untested Legal Argument." *American Journal of Criminal Justice* 39(4): 808-817.

Sataline, Suzanne. 2007. "Who's Wrong When Rights Collide? Transgender Professor Claims Job Discrimination in Firising; School Cites Religious Freedom." *Wall Street Journal* (March 6): B1, B12.

Sauvageau, Florian, David Schneiderman, and David Taras. 2006. *The Last Word: Media Coverage of the Supreme Court of Canada.* Vancouver: UBC Press.

Savell, Lawrence. 1994. "I'm Bill Low: File With Me and Win, Win, Win!" *National Law Journal* 17 (3) (September 19): A23.

Savona, Ernesto, Francesco Calderoni, and Alessia Maria Remmerswaal. 2011. *Understudied Areas of Organized Crime Offending: A Discussion of the Canadian Situation in the International Context.* Ottawa, ON: Public Safety Canada.

Scallen, Eileen A. 1995. "American Legal Argumentation: The Law and Literature/Rhetoric Movement." *Argumentation* 9: 705–717.

Scallan, Niamh. 2012. "The Verdict: Lawyer Well Paid at $8 Million." *Toronto Star*, March 30. Retrieved from www.thestar.com/news/canada/2012/03/30/the_verdict_lawyer_well_paid_at_8_million.html.

Schauer, Frederick. 2009. *Thinking Like a Lawyer: A New Introduction to Legal Reasoning.* Cambridge, MA: Harvard University Press.

Scheingold, Stuart A. and Austin Sarat. 2004. *Something to Believe In: Politics, Professionalism and Cause Lawyering.* Stanford, CA: Stanford University Press.

Scherrer, Amandine. 2010. *G8 Against Transational Organized Crime.* Burlington, VT: Ashgate.

Schmaus, Warren. 2004. *Rethinking Durkheim and His Tradition.* New York: Cambridge University Press.

Schmidt, Steve. 2001. "Canadian Courts Restrict Drug Tests." *National Post* (December 19): A1, A8.

Scholes, Laurie Lamoureux. 2002. "The Canadian Council of Muslim Women: A Profile of the First 18 Years." *Journal of Muslim Minority Affairs* 22 (2) (October): 413–425.

Schrag, Philip G. and Michael Meltsner. 1998. *Reflections on Clinical Legal Education.* Boston: Northeastern University Press.

Schram, Sanford E. 2002. *Praxis for the Poor: Piven and Cloward and the Future of Social Science in Social Welfare.* New York: New York University Press.

Schuler, Margaret and Sakuntala Kadirgamar-Rajasingham (eds.). 1992. *Legal Literacy: A Tool for Women's Empowerment.* New York: UNIFEM.

Schuller, Regina A. and Meagan Yarmey. 2001. "The Jury: Deciding Guilt and Innocence," in Regina A. Schuller and James R. P. Ogloff (eds.), *Introduction to Psychology and Law: Canadian Perspectives*, pp. 157–187. Toronto: University of Toronto Press.

Schur, Edward M. 1968. *Law and Society.* New York: Random House.

Schutt, Russell K. 2015. *Investigating the Social World, the Process and Practice of Research.* 8th ed. Thousand Oaks, CA: Pine Forge Press.

Schwartz, Richard D. and James C. Miller. 1975. "Legal Evolution and Societal Complexity," in Ronald L. Akers and Richard Hawkins (eds.), *Law and Control in Society*, pp. 52–62. Englewood Cliffs, NJ: Prentice Hall.

Scott, Robert A. and Arnold R. Shore. 1979. *Why Sociology Does Not Apply: A Study of the Use of Sociology in Public Policy*. New York: Elsevier.

Scott, Steffanie. 2003. "Gender, Household Headship and Entitlements to Land: New Vulnerabilities in Vietnam's Decollectivization." *Gender, Technology and Development* 7 (2) (May–August): 233–263.

Scoular, Jane and Teela Sanders (eds.). 2010. *Regulating Sex/Work: From Crime Control to Neo-Liberalism*. New York: Wiley-Blackwell.

Scully, Alexa. 2012. "Decolonization, Reinhabitation and Reconciliation: Aboriginal and PlaceBased Education." *Canadian Journal of Environmental Education* 17: 148–58.

Sechzer, Jeri Altneu. 2004. "'Islam and Woman: Where Tradition Meets Modernity': History and Interpretations of Islamic Women's Status." *Sex Roles* 51 (5/6) (September): 263–272.

Segura, Denise A. and Patricia Zavella. 2008. "Introduction: Gendered Borderlands." *Gender and Society* 22 (5) (October): 537–544.

Seidman, Robert B. 1978. *The State, Law and Development*. New York: St. Martin's.

Selznick, Philip. 1961. "Sociology and Natural Law." *Natural Law Forum* 6: 84–108.

———. 1969. *Law, Society and Industrial Justice*. New York: Russell Sage Foundation.

Sen, Amartya. 2009. *The Idea of Justice*. Cambridge, MA: Harvard University Press.

Sevigny, Eric L. 2009. "Excessive Uniformity in Federal Drug Sentencing." *Journal of Quantitative Criminology*, 25: 155–180.

Shaffer, Martha. 2003. "The Battered Woman Syndrome Revisited: Some Complicating Thoughts Five Years After *R. v. Lavallee*," in T. Brettel Dawson (ed.), *Women, Law and Social Change: Core Readings and Current Issues*, pp. 207–213. Concord, ON: Captus.

Shaham, Ron. 2010. *The Expert Witness in Islamic Courts: Medicine and Crafts in the Service of Law*. Chicago, IL: University of Chicago Press.

Sharp, Cassandra and Marett Leiboff (eds). 2016. *Cultural Legal Studies: Law's Popular Cultures and the Metamorphosis of Law*. New York: Routledge.

Shaver, Frances M. 1993. "Prostitution: A Female Crime?" in Ellen Adelberg and Claudia Currie (eds.), *In Conflict with the Law: Women and the Canadian Justice System*, pp. 153–173. Vancouver: Press Gang.

Shdaimah, Corey S. 2009. *Negotiating Justice. Progressive Lawyering, Low-Income Clients, and the Quest for Social Change*. New York: New York University Press.

Sheehy, Elizabeth, ed. 2012. *Sexual Assault in Canada: Law, Legal Practice and Women's Activism*. Ottawa: University of Ottawa Press.

Shelton, Joy, Jennifer Eakin, Tia Hoffer, Yvonne Muirhead, and Jessica Owens. 2016. "Online Child Sexual Exploitation: An Investigative Analysis of Offender Characteristics and Offending Behavior." *Aggression and Violent Behavior* 30:15–23.

Sheppard, R. Ronald and Garry J. Smith. 2013. "Gambling," in James H. Marsh (ed.), *The Canadian Encyclopedia*. Retrieved from www.thecanadianencyclopedia.ca/en/article/gambling/.

Sher, Julian. 1983. *White Hoods: Canada's Ku Klux Klan*. Vancouver: New Star.

Shibutani, Tamotsu. 1961. *Society and Personality: An Interactionist Approach to Social Psychology*. Englewood Cliffs, NJ: Prentice Hall.

Shuman, Daniel W. and Anthony Champagne. 1997. "Removing the People from the Legal Process: The Rhetoric and Research on Judicial Selection and Juries." *Psychology, Public Policy, and Law* 3 (2–3) (June–September): 242–258.

Shuy, Roger W. 2010. *The Language of Defamation Cases*. New York: Oxford University Press.

Siegel, Larry J. 1998. *Criminology: Theories, Patterns, and Typologies*. 6th ed. Belmont, CA: Wadsworth.

Silletta, Franco. 2015. "Revisiting Charter Application to Universities." *Appeal: Review of Current Law & Legal Reform* 20: 79–97.

Simon, Jonathan. 2009. *Governing Through Crime: How the War on Crime Transformed American Democracy and Created a Culture of Fear*. New York: Oxford University Press.

Simon, Leonore, Bruce Sales, and Lee Sechrest. 1992. "Licensure of Functions," in Dorothy K. Kagehiro and William S. Laufer (eds.), *Handbook of Psychology and Law*, pp. 542–563. New York: Springer-Verlag.

Simon v. the Queen [1985] 2 SCR 387.

Simonsen, Karen-Margrete and Ditlev Tamm. 2017. "Law and Literature - the Danish Way on a Danish Crime Story." *Law & Literature* 29(1): 123–141.

Simpson, A. W. B. 1988. *Invitation to Law.* Oxford, UK: Basil Blackwell.

Simpson, Sally and Carole Gibbs (eds.) 2007. *Corporate Crime.* Burlington, VT: Ashgate.

Sinha, Maire. 2013. "Family Violence in Canada: A Statistical Profile, 2011." *Juristat.* Catalogue no. 85–002-X. Retrieved from www.statcan.gc.ca/pub/85-002-x/2013001/article/11805-eng.pdf.

Skolnick, Jerome H. 1994. *Justice Without Trial: Law Enforcement in Democratic Society.* 3rd ed. New York: Palgrave Macmillan.

Slayton, Philip. 2007. *Lawyers Gone Bad: Money, Sex and Madness in Canada's Legal Profession.* Toronto: Viking Canada.

———. 2015. "Is the SCC Out of Control?" *Canadian Lawyer* 39 (5): 16–17.

Slee, Tom. 2012. "Click to Judge." *LRC: Literary Review of Canada* 20 (3): 13–15.

Smit, Anneke and Marcia Valiante (eds.). 2015. *Public Interest, Private Property: Law and Planning Policy in Canada.* Vancouver, BC: UBC Press.

Smith, Beverley. 1989. *Professional Conduct for Canadian Lawyers.* Toronto: Butterworths.

Smith, Clay J., Jr. (ed.). 2000. *Rebels in Law: Voices in History of Black Women Lawyers.* Ann Arbor, MI: University of Michigan Press.

Smith, Charles C. 2008. "Who is Afraid of the Big Bad Social Constructionists? Or Shedding Light on the Unpardonable Whiteness of the Canadian Legal Profession." (June 2008). Retrieved from www.lsuc.on.ca/media/fourthcolloquiumsmith.pdf.

Smith, Jim. 1999. "Inmates: Prison Chow's Bad, Videos Are Old." *Philadelphia Daily News* (October 8). Retrieved from http://overlawyered.com/archives/99oct2.html.

Smith, Marion. 2009. *A Civil Society?* Toronto, ON: University of Toronto Press.

Smith, Stephen and Ronan Deazley, eds. 2010. *The Legal, Medical and Cultural Regulation of the Body: Transformation and Transgression.* Burlington, VT: Ashgate.

Smyth, Gemma. "Mediation," in Macfarlane, Julie, John Manwaring, Ellen Zweibel, Gemma Smyth, Arthur Pearlstein, 2011. *Dispute Resolution: Readings and Case Studies*, 3rd ed., pp. 261–418. Toronto: Emond Montgomery Publications.

Snider, Laureen. 1999. "White-collar Crime," in James H. Marsh (ed.), *The Canadian Encyclopedia: Year 2000 Edition*, p. 2504. Toronto: McClelland and Stewart.

———. 2003. "Constituting the Punishable Woman: Atavistic Man Incarcerates Postmodern Woman." *British Journal of Criminology* 43 (2): 354–378.

Snow, David A., Sarah A. Soule, and Hanspeter Kriesi (eds.). 2004. *The Blackwell Companion to Social Movements.* Malden, MA: Blackwell.

Snyder, Emily. 2014. "Indigenous Feminist Legal Theory." *Canadian Journal of Women and the Law* 26(2): 365–401.

Soeharno, Jonathan. 2016. *The Integrity of the Judge: A Philosophical Inquiry.* New York: Routledge.

Sollors, Werner. 2000. *Interracialism: Black-White Intermarriage in American History, Literature and Law.* New York: Oxford University Press.

Solovo, Daniel D. 2009. *Understanding Privacy.* Cambridge, MA: Harvard University Press.

Somer, Kristin L., Irwin A Horowitz, and Martin J. Bourgeois. 2001. "When Juries Fail to Grasp the Law: Biased Evidence Processing in Individual and Group Decision Making." *Personality and Social Psychology Bulletin* 27 (3) (March): 309–320.

Songer, Donald R. 2008. *The Transformation of the Supreme Court of Canada: An Empirical Examination.* Toronto, ON: University of Toronto Press.

Spector, Malcolm. 1972. "The Rise and Fall of a Mobility Route." *Social Problems* 20 (2) (Fall): 173–185.

Spector, Malcolm and John I. Kitsuse. 1973. "Social Problems: A Reformulation." *Social Problems* 21 (2) (Fall): 145–159.

Spencer, Herbert. 1899. *The Principles of Sociology (II).* New York: D. Appleton.

Spiteri, Melani. 2002. "Sentencing Circles for Aboriginal Offenders in Canada: Furthering the Idea of Aboriginal Justice Within a Western Framework." Paper presented at the Third International Conference on Confedercing, Circles and Other Restorative Practices, August 8–10, Minneapolis, Minnesota. Retrieved from www.iirp.org/library/mn02/mn02_spiteri.html.

Spohn, Cassia. 2009, *How Do Judges Decide? The Search for Fairness and Justice in Punishment.* 2nd ed. Thousand Oaks, CA: Sage.

Spratt, Michael. 2017. "Why Plea Bargains Can Be A Deal with the Devil." (January 31). Retrieved from www.michaelspratt.com/law-blog/plea-bargaining-a-deal-with-the-devil.

Staggenborg, Suzanne. 2016. *Social Movements*, 2nd ed. New York: Oxford University Press.

Stake, Jeffrey Evans. 2006. "Minority Admissions to Law School: More Trouble Ahead and Two Solutions." *St. John's Law Review* 80 (1): 301–321.

Stark, Barbara (ed.). 2015. *International Law and Its Discontents: Confronting Crises*. Cambridge: Cambridge University Press.

Starr, Katherine. 2016. "Changes Coming Soon to Citizenship Act, John McCallum Says." CBC News (February 18). Retrieved from www.cbc.ca/news/politics/mccallum-immigrants-citizenship-act-language-requirement-1.3453658.

Statistics Canada. 1998. *Canada Yearbook 1999*. Ottawa: Minister of Industry.

———. 2002. "Fact-Sheet on Gambling." *Perspectives on Labour and Income* 3 (7) (July): 1–5. Catalogue No. 75–001-XIE. Retrieved from www.statcan/english/indepth/indepth/freepub/82_221_XIE/00502/tables/htm/22142.htm.

———. 2015. "Homicide in Canada, 2014." *The Daily*, 25 November. Retrieved from www.statcan.gc.ca/daily-quotidien/151125/dq151125a-eng.htm.

———. 2016a. "Legal Aid Statistics (Approved Applications)."April 20. Retrieved from www.statcan.gc.ca/tables-tableaux/sum-som/l01/cst01/legal18d-eng.htm.

———. 2016b. "Legal Aid Statistics (Applications). April 20. Retrieved from www.statcan.gc.ca/tables-tableaux/sum-som/l01/cst01/legal18c-eng.htm.

———. 2016c. "Tuition Fees For Degree Programs, 2016/2017." The Daily, 9 July. Retrieved from http://www.statcan.gc.ca/daily-quotidien/160907/dq160907a-eng.htm.

———. 2017. "Police Resources in Canada, 2016." The Daily, March 29. Retrieved from www.statcan.gc.ca/daily-quotidien/170329/dq170329c-eng.htm

Steckley, John L. 2016. *Indian Agents: Rulers of the Reserves*. New York: Peter Lang.

Sterba, James P. (ed.). 2004. *Morality in Practice*. 7th ed. Belmont, CA: Thomson/Wadsworth.

Stevens, Robert. 1973. "Law Schools and Law Students." *Virginia Law Review* 59 (4) (April): 551–707.

———. 1983. *Law School: Legal Education in America from the 1850s to the 1980s*. Chapel Hill, NC: University of North Carolina Press.

Stewart, Pamela J. and Andrew Strathern (eds.). 2010. *Ritual*. Burlington, VT: Ashgate.

Stobbs, Nigel and Geraldine Mackenzie. 2009. "Evaluating the Performance of Indigenous Sentencing Courts." *AILR* 13(2): 90–105.

Stone, Christopher D. 1978. "Social Control of Corporate Behavior," in M. David Ermann and Richard J. Lundman (eds.), *Corporate and Governmental Deviants: Problems of Organizational Behavior in Contemporary Society*, pp. 241–258. New York: Oxford University Press.

———. 2010. *Should Trees Have Standing? Law, Morality and the Environment*, 3rd ed. New York: Oxford University Press.

Stone, Julius. 1964. *Legal System and Lawyers' Reasonings*. Stanford: Stanford University Press.

———. 1966. *Law and the Social Sciences in the Second Half Century*. Minneapolis, MN: University of Minnesota Press.

Stracher, Cameron. 2001. "How to Bill 25 Hours in One Day." *New York Times Magazine* (April 8): 74.

———. 2007. "Meet the Clients." *Wall Street Journal* (January 26): W11.

Strashin, Jamie. 2016a. "Why Canadian Sports Gamblers Bet Billions Offshore." *CBC* (May 3). Retrieved from www.cbc.ca/sports/sports-gambling-canada-bettors-go-offshore-1.3562500

———. 2016b. "Online Sports Gambling Thrives in Canada's Legal 'Grey Zone.'" *CBC* (May 2). Retrieved from www.cbc.ca/sports/sports-gambling-canada-1.3559733.

Strathern, Marilyn. 2005. "Experiments in Interdisciplinarity." *Social Anthropology* 13 (1) (February): 75–90.

Strauss, Marina and Simon Tuck. 2005. "Tribunal Rules Sears Broke Law by Inflating Tire Savings." *Globe and Mail* (January 25): B1, B8.

Streb, Matthew J. ed. 2009. *Running for Judge: The Rising Political, Financial, and Legal Stakes of Judicial Elections*. New York: New York University Press.

Strengthening Canadian Citizenship Act (An Act to Amend the Citizenship Act and to Make Consequential Amendments to other Acts) S.C. 2014, c. 22.

Strickland, Ruth Ann. 2004. *Restorative Justice*. New York: Peter Lang.

Struthers, William M. 2009. *Wired for Intimacy: How Pornography Hijacks the Male Brain*. Downers Grove, IL: IVP.

Stuart v The University of Western Ontario, 2015 ONSC 5168.

Suchman, Edward A. 1967. *Evaluative Research: Principles and Practice in Public Service and Social Action Programs*. New York: Russell Sage.

Suk, Jeannie. 2009. *At Home in the Law: How the Domestic Violence Revolution Transforms Privacy*. New Haven, CT: Yale University Press.

Sullivan, Eileen. 2009. "Police Support Citizen's Terrorism Watch: Program Opens in Lose Angeles." *Bellingham Herald* (October 4): A1, A2.

Sullivan, William M., Anne Colby, Judith Welch Wegner, Lloyd Bond, and Lee S. Shulman. 2007. *Educating Lawyers: Preparation for the Profession of Law*. San Francisco, CA: Jossey-Bass.

Sullum, Jacob. 2003. *Saying Yes: In Defense of Drug Use*. New York: J. P. Tarcher/Putnam.

Summers, Robert S. and George G. Howard. 1972. *Law: Its Nature, Functions and Limits*. 2nd ed. Englewood Cliffs, NJ: Prentice Hall.

Sumner, William Graham. 1906. *Folkways*. Boston: Ginn.

———. 1886/1940. "The Challenge of Facts," in Maurice R. Davie (ed.), *Sumner Today*, pp. 67–93. New Haven, CT: Yale University Press.

Suncor Energy Inc. v. Unifor Local 707A, 2016 ABQB 269.

Sun-Rype Products Ltd. v. Archer Daniels Midland Company, 2013 SCC 58.

Sunstein, Cass R. 2003. *Why Societies Need Dissent*. Cambridge, MA: Harvard University Press.

Supreme Court of Canada. 2016. "Category 2: Applications for Leave Submitted." Retrieved from www.scc-csc.ca/case-dossier/stat/cat2-eng.aspx#cat2a.

Susskind, Richard. 2008. *The End of Lawyers? Rethinking the Nature of Legal Services*. New York: Oxford University Press.

Sutherland, Edwin H. 1949. *White Collar Crime*. New York: Dryden.

Sutherland, Edwin H. and Donald C. Cressey. 1974. *Criminology*. 9th ed. Philadelphia: Lippincott.

Swartz, Joel. 1978. "Silent Killers at Work," in M. David Ermann and Richard Landmann (eds.), *Corporate and Governmental Deviance*, pp. 114–128. New York: Oxford University Press.

Sylvestre, Marie-Eve. 2010. "Disorder and Public Spaces in Montreal: Repression (and Resistance) Through Law, Politics, and Police Discretion." *Urban Geography* 31(6): 803–824.

Switzman v. Elbing [1957] S.C.R. 285.

Taku River Tlingit First Nation v. British Columbia (Project Assessment Director), [2004] 3 SCR 550, 2004 SCC 74 (CanLII).

Tanovich, David M. 2006. *The Colour of Justice: Policing Race in Canada*. Toronto: Irwin Law.

Tashbrook, Linda. 2004. *Survey on Licensing*. Buffalo, NY: W. S. Hein.

Task Force on Aboriginal Peoples in Federal Corrections. 1989. *Final Report*. Ottawa: Minister of Supply and Services.

Task Force on the Criminal Justice System and Its Impact on the Indian and Metis People of Alberta. 1991. *Report of the Task Force on the Criminal Justice System and Its Impact on the Indian and Metis*. Edmonton: The Task Force.

Taylor, David and Susan Balloch (eds.). 2005. *The Politics of Evaluation: Participation and Policy Implementation*. Bristol, UK: Policy Press.

Terrill, Richard J. 2009. *World Criminal Justice Systems: A Survey*. 7th ed. Cincinnati, OH: Anderson.

———. 2015. *World Criminal Justice Systems: A Survey*. 9th ed. Cincinnati, OH: Anderson.

Tepperman, Lorne and Kristy Wanner. 2009. *Problem Gambling in Canada*. Toronto, ON: Oxford University Press.

Terrill, William, Eugene A. Paoline, and Peter K. Manning. "Police Culture and Coercion." *Criminology* 41.4 (2003): 1003–1034

Textile Labelling Act (R.S.C., 1985, c. T-10).

Thompson, Duncan C. 1979. *How to Become a Lawyer in Canada*. Edmonton, AB: Acorn.

Thompson, Martin J. and Thomas Slade. 2011, "Gauthier v. Saint-Germain: A Forthcoming Lesson from the Supreme Court of Canada on Educational Malpractice?" Retrieved from www.mcmillan.ca/Files/118912_Gauthier_v_Saint-Germain.pdf.

Thornton v. School District No. 57 (Prince George) et al., [1978] 2 S.C.R. 267 (SCC).

Thornton, Patricia M. 2002. "Framing Dissent in Contemporary China: Irony, Ambiquity and Metonymy." *China Quarterly* 171 (September): 661–681.

Thurman, Quint C. and J. D. Jamieson. 2005. *Police Problem Solving*. Florence, KY: LexisNexis-Anderson.

Thurman, Quint C. and Jihong Zhao. 2004. *Contemporary Policing: Controversies, Challenges, and Solutions: An Anthology*. Los Angeles: Roxbury.

Thurman, Quint, Jihong Zhao, and Andrew Giacomazzi. 2001. *Community Policing in a Community Area: An Introduction and Exploration*. Los Angeles: Roxbury.

Tibbetts, Janice. 2008a. "Critics of Sentencing Circles Says Aboriginal Tradition Too Lenient." *Edmonton Journal* (November 4). Retrieved from www.pressreader.com/canada/edmonton-journ al/20081104/281595236367208.

Tibbets, Janice. 2008b. "PM Names Thomas Cromwell to Supreme Court." *National Post*, 22 December. Retrieved from archive.is/20081224205429/http://www.nationalpost.com/news/story. html#selection-1029.133-1029.262.

Tiersma, Peter. 2010. *Parchment, Paper, Pixels: Law and the Technologies of Communication*. Chicago, IL: University of Chicago Press.

Tigar, Michael E. 2000. *Law and the Rise of Capitalism*. New York: Monthly Review Press.

Tilly, Charles and Sidney Tarrow. 2007. *Contentious Politics*. Boulder, CO: Paradigm.

Times of India. 2016. "More Than 150 Women Across India Were Killed in 2014 Because They Were Thought To Be Witches." March 17. Retrieved from www.indiatimes.com/news/india/more-than-150-woman-were-killed-across-india-in-2014-because-they-were-thought-to-be-witches-252138.html

Tomasic, Roman. 1985. *The Sociology of Law*. London, UK: Sage.

Tonry, Michael. 2016. *Sentencing Fragments*. New York: Oxford University Press.

———. 2009. "The Mostly Unintended Effects of Mandatory Peanlties: Two Centuries of Consistent Findings." In Michael Tonry (ed.), *Crime and Justice: A Review of Research*, vol. 38. Chicago, IL: University of Chicago Press.

———. 2010. *Thinking About Punishment: Penal Policy Across Space, Time and Discipline*. Burlington, VT: Ashgate.

Towers, Chris. 2011. *Experiencing Social Policy: An Introductory Guide*. Bristol, UK: The Policy Press.

Towers, Perrin. 2006a. "U.S. Tort Costs and Cross-Border Perspectives: 2005 Update." Retrieved from www.towersperrin.com/tillinghast.

———. 2006b. "U.S. Tort Costs Reach a Record $260 Billion." (March). Retrieved from www. towersperrin.com/tp/jsp/masterbrand_webcache_html.

Transparency International. 2017. "Corruption Perceptions Index 2016.". Retrieved from www. transparency.org/news/feature/corruption_perceptions_index_2016.

Trebilcock, Bob. 2006. "Child Molesters on the Internet: Are They in Your Home?" in Thomas Hickey (ed.), *Taking Sides: Clashing Views in Crime and Criminology*, pp. 192–198. Dubuque, IA: McGraw-Hill.

Tremblay, Luci. 2002. "Quebec City and the Summits of 2001: Priority on People, Concerns for Freedom." *Policy Options* 23 (6) (September): 51–53.

Trevino, A. Javier (ed.). 2007. *The Classic Writings in Law and Society: Contemporary Comments and Criticisms*. New Brunswick, NJ: Transaction.

Trevino, A. Javier. 2008. *The Sociology of Law: Classical and Contemporary Perspectives*. New Brunswick, NJ: Transaction Publishers.

Trevino, A. Javier and Karen M. McCormack (eds.). 2016. *Service Sociology and Academic Engagement in Social Problems*. New York: Routledge.

Trial Lawyers Association of British Columbia v. British Columbia (Attorney General), 2016 BCSC 1391.

Truman, Jennifer L. and Rachel E. Morgan. 2016. *Criminal Victimization 2015*. Washington, DC: Bureau of Justice Statistics, U.S. Department of Justice.

Truth in Sentencing Act (SC 2009, c. 29).

Tsilhqot'in Nation v. British Columbia, 2014 SCC 44, [2014] 2 S.C.R. 256.

Tsilhqot'in National Government, 2014, Summary of the Tsilhqot'in Aboriginal Title Case (William Case) Decision. Retrieved from www.tsilhqotin.ca/PDFs/2014_07_03_Summary_SCC_Decision. pdf.

Tunney, Catharine. 2016. "Marijuana Legalization in Canada: What We Know and Don't Know." *CBC.ca* (July 2). Retrieved from www.cbc.ca/news/politics/marijuana-legislation-knowns-unknowns-1,3660258.

Turk, Austin T. 1972. *Legal Sanctioning and Social Control*. Rockville, MD: National Institute of Mental Health.

———. 1978. "Law as a Weapon in Social Conflict," in Charles E. Reasons and Robert M. Rich (eds.), *The Sociology of Law: A Conflict Perspective*, pp. 213–232. Toronto: Butterworths.

———. 2004. "Sociology of Terrorism." *Annual Review of Sociology* 30: 271–286.

Turner, Dale Antony. 2006. *This Is Not A Peace Pipe: Towards a Critical Indigenous Philosophy*. Toronto: University of Toronto Press.

Turner, Jonathan H. 1972. *Patterns of Social Organization: A Survey of Social Institutions*. New York: McGraw-Hill.

———. 2003. *The Structure of Sociological Theory*. 7th ed. Belmont, CA: Wadsworth.

Turner, Jonathan H., Leonard Beeghley, and Charles H. Powers. 2007. *The Emergence of Sociological Theory*. 6th ed. Belmont, CA: Thomson Higher Education.

Turner, Jonathan H. and Alexandra R. Maryanski. 1979. *Functionalism*. Menlo Park, CA: Benjamin/ Cummings.

———. 1995. "Is 'Neofunctionalism' Really Functional?" in Donald McQuarie (ed.), *Readings in Contemporary Sociological Theory: From Modernity to Post-Modernity*, pp. 49–62. Upper Saddle River, NJ: Prentice Hall.

Turner, Nigel E., Denise L. Preston, Crystal Saunders, Steven McAvoy, and Umesh Jain. 2009. "The Relationship of Problem Gambling to Criminal Behavior in a Sample of Canadian Male Federal Offenders." *Journal of Gambling Studies* 25: 153–169.

Turner, Nigel E., Randy Stinchfield, John McCready, Steven McAvoy, and Peter Ferentzy. 2016. "Endorsement of Criminal Behavior Amongst Offenders: Implications for DSM-5 Gambling Disorder." *Journal of Gambling Studies* 32(1): 35–45.

Turner, Ralph and Lewis M. Killian. 1987. *Collective Behavior*. 3rd ed. Englewood Cliffs, NJ: Prentice Hall.

Turow, Scott. 1977. "The Trouble with Law School." *Harvard Magazine* 80 (1) (September–October): 60–64.

Tushnet, Mark. 2005. "Critical Legal Theory (Without Modifiers) in the United States." *Journal of Political Philosophy* 13 (99): 99–112.

———. 2008. *Legal Scholarship and Education*. Burlington, VT: Ashgate.

Twersky-Glasner, Aviva. 2005. "Police Personality: What is it and Why are They Like That?." Journal of Police and Criminal Psychology 20(1): 56–67.

Tyler, Tom R. 2006. *Why People Obey the Law*. New Haven, CT: Yale University Press.

Ulmer, Jeffrey, Megan C. Kurlychek, and John H. Kramer. 2007. "Prosecutorial Discretion and the Imposition of Mandatory Minimum Sentences." *Journal of Research in Crime and Delinquency* 44 (4): 427–458.

Umphrey, Marta Merrill (ed.). 2009. *Trial*. Burlington, VT: Ashgate.

Unger, Roberto Mangabeira. 1976. *Law in Modern Society: Toward a Criticism of Social Theory*. New York: Free Press.

———. 1986. *The Critical Legal Studies Movement*. Cambridge, MA: Harvard University Press.

———. 1998. *Democracy Realized: The Progressive Alternative*. New York: Verso.

———. 2004. *Politics: A Work in Constructive Social Theory*. New York: Verso.

———. 2009. *The Left Alternative*. New York: Verso.

———. 2015. *The Critical Legal Studies Movement: Another Time, A Greater Task*. London: Verso.

Unger, Roberto Mangabeira and Cornel West. 1998. *The Future of American Progressivism: An Initiative for Political and Economic Reform*. Boston: Beacon.

University of Ottawa v Association of Professors of The University of Ottawa, 2014 CanLII 100735 (ON LA).

University of Toronto, Faculty of Law. 2017. "JD Program Fees." Retrieved from www.law.utoronto.ca/ academic-programs/jd-program/financial-aid-and-fees/student-fees-jd-program#jd_fees.

University of Waterloo. 2006. "Prof Leads Worldwide Tobacco Project." *Daily Bulletin* (February 7). Retrieved from www.adm.waterloo.ca/bulletin/2006/feb/07tu.html.

Ursel, Jane, Leslie Tutty, and Janice LeMaistre. 2008. *What's Law Got To do With It: The Law, Specialized Courts and Domestic Violence in Canada*. Toronto: Cormorant Press.

Usman, Elizabeth. 2016. "Nurturing the Law Student's Soul: Why Law Schools Are Still Struggling to Teach Professionalism and How to Do Better in an Age of Consumerism." *Marquette Law Review* 99 (4): 1021–1072.

Vago, Steven. 2004. *Social Change.* 5th ed. Upper Saddle River, NJ: Prentice Hall.

Valdes, Francisco. 2016. "Sexual Minorities in Legal Academia: A Retrospection on Community, Action, Remembrance, and Liberation." *Journal of Legal Education* 66(3): 510–530.

Valiante, Giuseppe. 2016. "Akwesasne Creates First Court in Canada For and By Indigenous People." *CBC News* (October 2). Retrieved from www.cbc.ca/news/canada/montreal/akwesasne-indigenous-court-canada-1.3787969.

Vallis, Mary. 2003. "More Wealthy Sales, Ad Execs than Lawyers: Census Surprise." *National Post* (March 12): A1, A10.

Valverde, Mariana. 2012. *Everyday Law on the Street: City Governance in an Age of Diversity.* Chicago: University of Chicago Press.

Vancouver Sun. 1999. "Global Capitalism Update: A Eunuch Approach to Collecting Bad Debts." (May 29): E3.

van den Berghe, Pierre L. 1967. "Dialectic and Functionalism: Toward a Synthesis," in Nicholas Demerath and Richard A. Peterson (eds.), *System Change and Conflict: A Reader on Contemporary Sociological Theory and the Debate over Functionalism*, pp. 294–310. New York: Free Press.

Vandor, Les. 2001. *Legal Counsel.* Toronto: ECW Press.

VanDuzer, John A., Penelope Simons, and Graham Mayeda. 2013. *Integrating Sustainable Development into International Investment Agreements.* London: Commonwealth Secretariat.

van Geel, Tyll R. 2016. *Understanding Supreme Court Opinions.* 6th ed. New York: Longman.

Vanhala, Lisa. 2011. "Social Movements Lashing Back: Law, Social Change and Intra-Social Movement Backlash in Canada." *Studies in Law, Politics and Society* 54: 113–140.

van Heugten, Kate, and Anita Gibbs (Eds.). 2015. *Social Work for Sociologists: Theory and Practice.* New York: Palgrave Macmillan.

van Kleef, Gerben A. 2016. *The Interpersonal Dynamics of Emotion.* Cambridge: Cambridge University Press.

Van Wagner, Estair. 2016. "Law's Ecological Relations - The Legal Structure of People-Place Relations in Ontario's Aggregate Extraction Conflicts." *Projections 12: The MIT Journal of Planning* (spring): 35–66.

Vatz, Richard. 1980. "Rhetoric and the Law," in Lee S. Weinberg and Judith W. Weinberg (eds.), *Law and Society: An Interdisciplinary Introduction*, pp. 160–163. Washington, DC: University Press of America.

Vaughan, Diane. 1998. "Rational Choice, Situated Action, and the Social Control of Organizations." *Law and Society Review* 32 (1): 23–57.

Venton, Margot and Kaithlyn Mitchell. 2015. "A Dark Day for Environmental Justice in Canada." *Huffington Post* (March 31). Retrieved from www.huffingtonpost.ca/ecojustice/environmental-justice-canada_b_6547682.html.

Verdun-Jones, Simon. 2016. "Criminal Law." in Rick Linden (ed.), *Criminology: A Canadian Perspective.* 8th ed., 55–89. Toronto: Nelson Education.

Verdun-Jones, Simon N. and Adamira A. Tijerino. 2002. "Victim Participating in the Plea Negotiation Process in Canada." Department of Justice Canada, Policy Centre for Victim Issues. Retrieved from www.justice.gc.ca/en/ps/rs/rep/2002/vppnpc/vppnpc.html.

————. 2004. "Four Models of Victim Involvement During Plea Negotiations: Bridging the Gap Between Legal Reforms and Current Legal Practice." *Canadian Journal of Criminology and Criminal Justice* 46 (4) (July): 471–500.

Vidmar, Neil (ed.). 2002. "Case Studies of Pre- and Mid-trial Prejudice in Criminal and Civil Litigation." *Law and Human Behavior* 26 (1): 73–105.

Vidmar, Neil and Valerie P. Hans. 2007. *American Juries: The Verdict.* Amherst, NY: Prometheus Books.

Vidmar, Neil and Regina A. Schuller. 2001. "The Jury: Selecting Twelve Impartial Peers," in Regina A. Schuller and James R. P. Ogloff (eds.), *Introduction to Psychology and Law: Canadian Perspectives*, pp. 126–156. Toronto: University of Toronto Press.

Volti, Rudi. 2010. *Society and Technological Change.* 6th ed. New York: St. Martin's.

Voren, Robert van. 2009. *On Dissidents and Madness: From the Soviet Union of Leonid Brezhnev to the "Soviet Union" of Vladimir Putin.* New York: Rodopi Publishers.

————. 2013. *Psychiatry as a Tool for Coercion in Post-Soviet Countries.* Brussels, Belgium: European Parliament Directorate-General for External Policies.

———. 2016. "Ending Political Abuse of Psychiatry: Where We Are at and What Needs to Be Done." *BJPsych Bulletin* 40(1):30–33.

Wacks, Raymond. 2009. *Understanding Jurisprudence: An Introduction to Legal Theory*. 2nd ed. New York: Oxford University Press.

Wade, Larry L. 1972. *The Elements of Public Policy*. Columbus, OH: Merrill.

Wagner, Anne, and Sophie Cacciaguidi-Fahy (eds.). 2008. *Obscurity and Clarity in the Law: Prospects and Challenges*. Burlington, VT: Ashgate.

Wal-Mart Litigation Project. 2017. "What You Should Know About Suing Wal-Mart." Retrieved from www.wal-martlitigation.com/index.php?p=su

Walker, Samuel. 2015. *Sense and Nonsense About Crime, Drugs, and Communities*. Stanford, CT: Cengage Learning.

Wall Street Journal. 2016. "Political Psychiatry: How China Uses 'Ankang' Hospitals to Silence Dissent." (April 19). Retrieved from blogs.wsj.com/chinarealtime/2016/04/19/political-psychiatry-how-china-uses-ankang-hospitals-to-silence-dissent/.

Wallace, Kenyon. 2009. "Problem Gambler Suing OLC for $3.5 Billion." *Toronto Star* (April 8). Retrieved from www.thestar.com/printArticle/615431.

Wallace, Kenyon and Michele Henry. 2017a. "Double-Dipping Lawyers Taking Big Slice of Injury Settlements." *Toronto Star*, January 28. Retrieved from www.thestar.com/news/investigations/2017/01/28/double-dipping-lawyers-taking-big-slice-of-injury-settlements.html.

———. 2017b. "Contigency Fees By Personal Injury Lawyers Should Be Limited, Report Says." Toronto Star, April 23. Retrieved from www.thestar.com/news/queenspark/2017/04/23/contingency-fees-by-ontario-personal-injury-lawyers-should-be-limited-report-says.html.

Wallace, Kenyon, Rachel Mendleson, and Dale Brazao. 2017. "Broken Trust." *The Star.com*. Retrieved from projects.thestar.com/broken-trust/.

Walter, Nicholas. 2012. "Religious Arbitration in the United States and Canada." *Santa Clara Law Review* 52 (4): 501–569.

Ward, Lester F. 1906. *Applied Sociology*. Boston: Ginn.

Warden, Rob. 2009. "Reflections on Capital Punishment." *Northwestern Journal of Law and Social Policy* 4 (2). Retrieved from scholarlycommons.law.northwestern.edu/cgi/viewcontent.cgi?article=1040&context=njlsp.

Warner, Kate. 2007. "Mandatory Sentencing and the Role of the Academic." *Criminal Law Forum* 18(3–4), 321–347.

Warner, Tom. 2002. *Never Going Back: A History of Queer Activism in Canada*. Toronto: University of Toronto Press.

Warren, Kenneth F. 2010. Administrative Law in the Political System. 5th ed. Boulder, CO: Westview Press.

Warren, Susan. 2007. "Spring Break Is a Legal Speciality for Ben Bollinger: Florida Lawyer Enjoys a Spike in His Business; Defendants in Flip-Flops." *Wall Street Journal* (March 17): A1, A10.

Warskett, Rosemary. 2002. "Law, Regulation, and Becoming 'Uncivil': Contestation and Reconstruction Within the Federal Administrative State," in Michael Mac Neil, Neil Sargent, and Peter Swan (eds.), *Law, Regulation, and Governance*, pp. 188–202. Don Mills, ON: Oxford University Press.

Wass, Victoria and Robert McNabb. 2006. "Pay, Promotion and Parenthood Among Women Solicitors." *Work, Employment and Society* 20 (2): 289–308.

Werb, Dan, Bohdan Nosyk, Thomas Kerr, Benedikt Fischer, Julio Montaner, and Evan Wood. 2012. "Estimating the Economic Value of British Columbia's Domestic Cannabis Market: Implications for Provincial Cannabis Policy." *International Journal of Drug Policy* 23(6): 436–441.

Weber, Max. 1921/1968. *Economy and Society*. 3 vols. Trans. Guenther Roth and Claus Wittich. New York: Badminster.

———. 1947. *The Theory of Social Economic Organizations*. Ed. Talcott Parsons. Glencoe, IL: Free Press.

———. 1954. *Law in Economy and Society*. Ed. Max Rheinstein. Trans. Edward Shils and Max Rheinstein. Cambridge, MA: Harvard University Press.

Webster, Cheryl Marie, Anthony N. Doob, and Franklin E. Zimring. 2006. "Proposition 8 and Crime Rates in California: The Case of the Disappearing Deterrent." *Criminology and Public Policy* 5 (3): 417–447.

Weeks, Carly. 2015. "We Need to Talk About Assisted Reproduction in Canada." *The Globe and Mail* (February 15). www.theglobeandmail.com/life/health-and-fitness/health/we-need-to-talk-about-assisted-reproduction-in-canada/article22988791/.

Weibust, Inger. 2010. *Great Leviathans: The Case for a Federal Role in Environmental Policy*. Burlington, VT: Ashgate.

Weinrib, Ernest J. 2012. *The Idea of Private Law*. New York: Oxford University Press.

Weisberg, Richard. 2005. "Two Recent Assessments of Law and Literature." (September 1). Retrieved from http://lawlit.blogspot.com/2005/90/two-recent-assessments-of-law-and.html.

Weiss, Carol. 1998. *Evaluation Research: Methods for Studying Programs and Policies*. 2nd ed. Upper Saddle River, NJ: Prentice Hall.

Weitzer, Ronald. 2011. *Legalizing Prostitution: From Illicit Vice to Lawful Business*. New York: NYU Press.
———. 2013. "Sex Trafficking and the Sex Industry: The Need for Evidence-Based Theory and Legislation." *Journal of Criminal Law & Criminology* 101(4): 1337–1370.

Welsh, Brandon C. and David P. Farrington. 2009. *Making Public Places Safer: Surveillance and Crime Prevention*. New York: Oxford University Press.

Welsh, Sandy, Myrna Dawson, and Annette Nierobisz. 2002. "Legal Factors, Extra-Legal Factors, or Changes in the Law? Using Criminal Justice Research to Understand the Resolution of Sexual Harassment Complaints." *Social Problems* 49 (4) (November): 605–623.

Westervelt, Saundra D. and Kimberly J. Cook.2010. "Framing Innocents: The Wrongly Convicted as Victims of State Harm." *Crime, Law and Social Change* 53 (3): 259–275.

Westmarland, Louise. 2011. *Researching Crime and Justice*. Devon, UK: Willan Publishing.

Wherry, Aaron. 2016. "Justin Trudeau Promises 'full protection' with Transgender Rights Bill." *CBC News* (May 16). Retrieved from www.cbc.ca/news/politics/trudeau-transgender-rights-1.3584482.

Whitaker, Reg. 2012. "Citizen Khadr: Either Omar Khadr Has Certain Basic Rights Or No Canadian Does. Which Is It?" Literary Review of Canada. April. Retrieved from http://reviewcanada.ca/magazine/2012/04/citizen-khadr/

Whitaker, Reg, Gregory S. Kealey, and Andrew Parnaby. 2012. *Secret Service: Political Policing in Canada: From the Fenians to Fortress America*. Toronto, ON: University of Toronto Press.

White, G. Edward. 2006. *Oliver Wendell Holmes, Sage of the Supreme Court*. New York: Oxford University Press.

White, James Boyd. 1973. *The Legal Imagination: Studies in the Nature of Legal Thought and Expression*. Boston: Little, Brown.

White, Michael. 1999. "GM Ordered to Pay Accident Victims $49 B." *National Post* (July 10): A1.

Whiten v. Pilot Insurance Co., [2002] 1 S.C.R. 595, 2002 SCC 18.

Whitla, William. 1995. "A Chronology of Women in Canada," in Nancy Mandell (ed.), *Feminist Issues: Race, Class and Sexuality*, pp. 315–53. Scarborough, ON: Prentice Hall.

Whyte, Martin King. 2011. *Myth of the Social Volcano: Perceptions of Inequality and Distributive Injustice in Contemporary China*. Stanford, CA: Stanford University Press.

Wiber, Melanie G. 2000. "Fishing Rights as an Example of the Economic Rhetoric of Privatization: Calling for an Implicated Economics." *Canadian Review of Sociology and Anthropology* 37 (3) (August): 267–288.

Wigmore, John H. 1913. "Introduction," in John Marshall Gest, in *The Lawyer in Literature*, pp. ix–xii. Boston: Boston Book.

Wilensky, Harold L. 1964. "The Professionalization of Everyone?" *American Journal of Sociology* 70 (2) (September): 137–158.

Williams Robert J., Jurgen Rehm, and Rhys M. G. Stevens. 2011. *The Social and Economic Impacts of Gambling*. Final report prepared for the Canadian Consortium for Gambling Research (March 11). Retrieved from www.uleth.ca/dspace/bitstream/handle/10133/1286/SEIG_FINAL_REPORT_2011.pdf

Williams, Robert J., Jennifer Royston, and Brad F. Hagen. 2005. "Gambling and Problem Gambling Within Forensic Populations: A Review of the Literature." *Criminal Justice and Behavior* 32(6): 665–689.

Williams Robert J., Beverly L. West, and Robert I. Simpson. 2012. *Prevention of Problem Gambling: A Comprehensive Review of the Evidence, and Identified Best Practices*. Report prepared for the Ontario Problem Gambling Research Centre and the Ontario Ministry of Health & Long Term Care (October 1). Retrieved from www.uleth.ca/dspace/bitstream/handle/10133/3121/2012-PREVENTION-OPGRC.pdf?sequence=3.

Williams, Susan H. 2004. *Truth, Autonomy and Speech: Feminist Theory and the First Amendment*. New York: New York University Press.

————. 1991. "The Equality Crisis: Some Reflections on Culture, Courts, and Feminism," in Katharine T. Bartlett and Rosanne Kennedy (eds.), *Feminist Legal Theory: Readings in Law and Gender*, pp. 15–34. Boulder, CO: Westview.

Williamson, John B., David A. Karp, and John R. Dalphin. 1982. *The Research Craft: An Introduction to Social Science Methods*. 2nd ed. Boston: Little, Brown.

Willis, James J., and Stephen D. Mastrofski. 2017. "Understanding the Culture of Craft: Lessons From Two Police Agencies." *Journal of Crime and Justice* 40(1): 84–100.

Willock, I. D. 1974. "Getting on with Sociologists." *British Journal of Law and Society* 1 (1): 3–12.

Wilson, H. T. 2002. "Rationality and Capitalism in Max Weber's Analysis of Western Modernity." *Journal of Classical Sociology* 2 (1) (March): 93–106.

Wilson, James Q. 1968a. "The Police and the Delinquent in Two Cities," in Stanton Wheeler (ed.), *Controlling Delinquents*, pp. 9–30. New York: John Wiley.

————. 1968b. *Varieties of Police Behavior*. Cambridge, MA: Harvard University Press.

Wing, Adrien Katherine (ed.). 2003. *Critical Race Feminism: A Reader*. 2nd ed. New York: New York University Press.

Winnipeg Child and Family Services (Northwest Area) v. G. (D.F.), [1997] 3 S.C.R. 925.

Wolfe, Alan and Erik C. Owens, eds. 2009. *Gambling: Mapping the American Moral Landscape*. Waco, TX: Baylor University Press.

Wolfendon Report. 1963. *Report of the Committee on Homosexual Offenses and Prostitution*. Briarcliff Manor, NY: Stein & Day.

Wong, Kam K. 1998. "Black's Theory on the Behavior of Law Revisited II: A Restatement of Black's Concept of Law." *International Journal of Sociology* 26 (1) (March): 75–120.

Wood, Philip R. 2016. *The Fall of the Priests and the Rise of the Lawyers*. Oxford: Hart Publishing.

Woods, Michael, Jon Anderson, Steven Guilbert, and Suzie Watkin. 2012. "'The Country (side) Is Angry': Emotion and Explanation in Protest Mobilization." *Social & Cultural Geography* 6: 567–85.

Woolford, Andrew. 2009. "Ontological Destruction: Genocide and Canadian Aboriginal Peoples 1." *Genocide Studies and Prevention* 4 (1): 81–97.

World Prison Brief. 2016. "World Prison Brief Data." Retrieved from www.prisonstudies.org/world-prison-brief-data.

Wortley, Scot, and Akwasi Owusu-Bempah. 2011. "The Usual Suspects: Police Stop and Search Practices in Canada." *Policing and Society* 21(4): 395–407.

Wortley, Scot and Julian Tanner. 2005. "Inflammatory Rhetoric? Baseless Accusations? A Response to Gabor's Critique of Racial Profiling Research in Canada." *Canadian Journal of Criminology and Criminal Justice* 47 (3) (July): 581–609.

Wright, Barry. 2010. "Civilianising the 'Blue Code'? An Examination of Attitudes to Misconduct in the Police Extended Family." *International Journal of Police Science and Management* 12 (3): 339–356.

Wrightsman, Lawrence S., Michael T. Nietzel, and Milliam H. Fortune. 1998. *Psychology and the Legal System*. 4th ed. Pacific Grove, CA: Brooks/Cole.

Wynn, Joan Ransohoff and Clifford Goldman. 1974. "Gambling in New York City: The Case for Legalization," in Lee Rainwater (ed.), *Social Problems and Public Policy, Deviance and Liberty*, pp. 66–75. Chicago: Aldine.

Yalden, Maxwell. 2009. *Transforming Rights: Reflections from the Front Lines*. Toronto: University of Toronto.

Yang, Jennifer. 2017. "Why Hate Crimes are Hard to Prosecute." *Toronto Star*, February 27. <www.thestar.com/news/gta/2017/02/27/why-hate-crimes-are-hard-to-prosecute.html>

Yao, Deborah. 2006. "With New Device, Late Car Payment Like a Dead Battery: Draconian Tool?" *Seattle Times* (June 13): A2.

Yates, Richard A., Ruth Whidden Yates, and Penny Bain. 2000. *Introduction to Law in Canada*. 2nd ed. Scarborough, ON: Allyn and Bacon.

Yen v Alberta (Ministry of Advanced Education and Technology), 2010 ABQB 380 (CanLII), 495 AR 292

Yogis, John A., Randall R. Duplak, and J. Royden Trainor. 1996. *Sexual Orientation and Canadian Law*. Toronto: Emond Montgomery.

Yorke, Jon (ed.). 2009. *Against the Death Penalty: International Initiatives and Implications*. Burlington, VT: Ashgate.

Young, Karen. 2005. "Does the Australian Competition and Consumer Commission Engage in 'Trial by Media'?" *Law and Policy* 27 (4) (October): 549–577.

Young, Simon, ed. 2009. *Civil Forfeiture of Criminal Property: Legal Measures for Targeting the Proceeds of Crime*. Northampton, MA: Edward Elgar Publishing Inc.

Youth Drug Detoxification and Stabilization Act, C.C.S.M. c. Y50.

Youth Drug Stabilization (Support for Parents) Act. (S.M. 2006, c. 22).

Yukon Government. 2017. "Legislative Amendments Will Protect the Rights of Transgender Yukoners." (March 13). Retrieved from www.gov.yk.ca/news/17-044.html#.WNkZtNIrKUl.

Zaibert, Leo. 2006. *Punishment and Retribution*. Burlington, VT: Ashgate.

Zamir, Eyal and Barak Medina. 2010. *Law, Economics, and Morality*. New York: Oxford University Press.

Zeni, John-Paul. 2016. "Chronic Pain Cases—Beware of the Civil Jury: A Review of Mandel V. Fakhim." *Accident Benefit Reporter* 34. Retrieved from www.thomsonrogers.com/resources/accident-benefit-reporter/articles/chronic-pain-cases-beware-civil-jury-review-mandel-v-fakhim/

Zernova, Margarita. 2008, *Restorative Justice: Ideals and Realities*. Burlington, VT: Ashgate.

Zero Tolerance for Barbaric Cultural Practices Act (S.C. 2015, c. 29).

Zifcak, Spencer (ed.). 2005. *Globalisation and the Rule of Law*. New York: Routledge.

Zimmerman, Ann. 2006. "Creative Crooks, as Shoplifters Use High-Tech Scams, Retail Losses Rise." *Wall Street Journal* (October 25): A1, A12.

Zimring, Franklin, and Gordon Hawkins. 1975. "The Legal Threat as an Instrument of Social Change," in Ronald L. Akers and Richard Hawkins (eds.), *Law and Control in Society*, pp. 329–339. Englewood Cliffs, NJ: Prentice Hall.

———. 1997. *Crime Is Not the Problem: Lethal Violence in America*. New York: Oxford University Press.

INDEX